A-Z HERTFORDSHIRE

G000310739

CONTENTS

REFERENCE

Motorway	**M1**
Primary Route	**A10**
A Road	A1000
B Road	B1368
Dual Carriageway	
One-way Street Traffic flow on A Roads is also indicated by a heavy line on the driver's left.	→
Under Construction Road Opening dates are correct at the time of publication.	
Proposed Road	
Junction Name (London Area)	APEX CORNER
Restricted Access	
Pedestrianized Road	
Track & Footpath	
Residential Walkway	
London Low Emission Zone For information contact Transport for London (www.tfl.gov.uk/roadusers/lez)	
Railway Stations:	Tunnel Level Crossing
National Rail Network	
Overground Station	
Underground	●
Heritage Station	
Built-up Area	CHURCH STREET
Local Authority Boundary	— ∙ — ∙ —
Posttown Boundary	
Postcode Boundary (within Posttown)	
Map Continuation	90
Large Scale Centres	166

Airport	✈
Car Park (selected)	**P**
Church or Chapel	†
Cycleway (selected)	
Fire Station	■
Hospital	**H**
House Numbers (A & B Roads only)	13 8
Information Centre	**i**
National Grid Reference	525
Park and Ride	**P+R**
Police Station	▲
Post Office	★
Safety Camera with Speed Limit Fixed cameras and long term road works cameras. Symbols do not indicate camera direction.	(30)
Toilet: without facilities for the Disabled with facilities for the Disabled Disabled use only	▽ ▽ ▽
Viewpoint	❋ ❋
Educational Establishment	▭
Hospital or Healthcare Building	▭
Industrial Building	▭
Leisure or Recreational Facility	▭
Place of Interest	▭
Public Building	▭
Shopping Centre or Market	▭
Other Selected Buildings	▭

SCALE

Map Pages 4-165
1:19,000 3⅓ inches (8.47cm) to 1 mile 5.26cm to 1km

0   ¼   ½   ¾ Mile

0   250   500   750 Metres   1 Kilometre

Map Page 166
1:9,500 6⅔ inches (16.94cm) to 1 mile 10.53cm to 1km

0   ⅛   ¼   ⅜ Mile

0   100   200   300   400   500 Metres

Copyright of Geographers' A-Z Map Company Limited

Telephone: 01732 781000 (Enquiries & Trade Sales)
             01732 783422 (Retail Sales)

www.az.co.uk
Copyright © Geographers' A-Z Map Co. Ltd.
Edition 5 2013

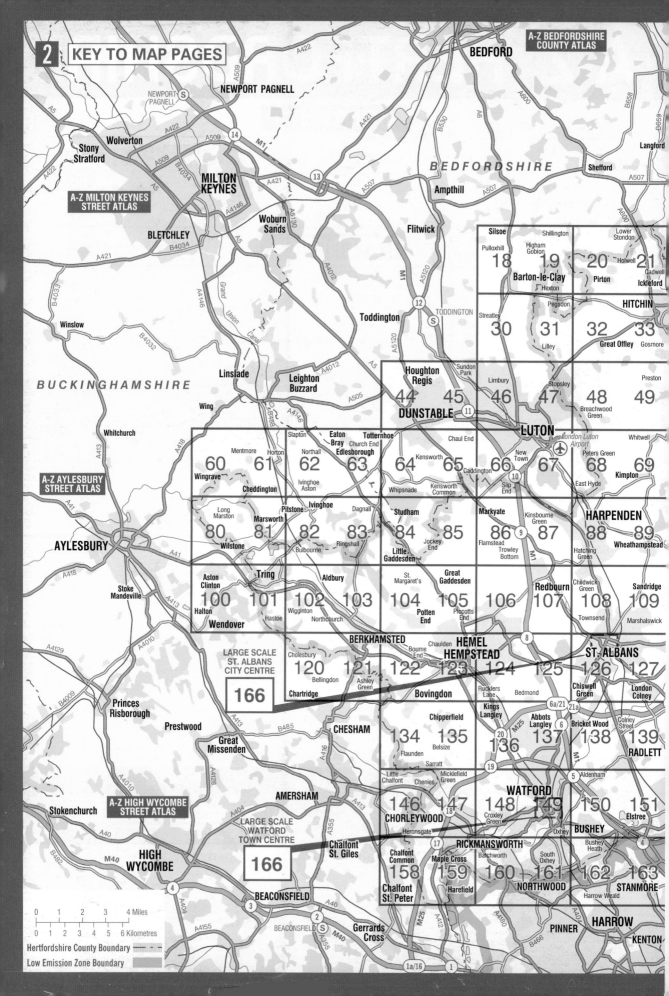

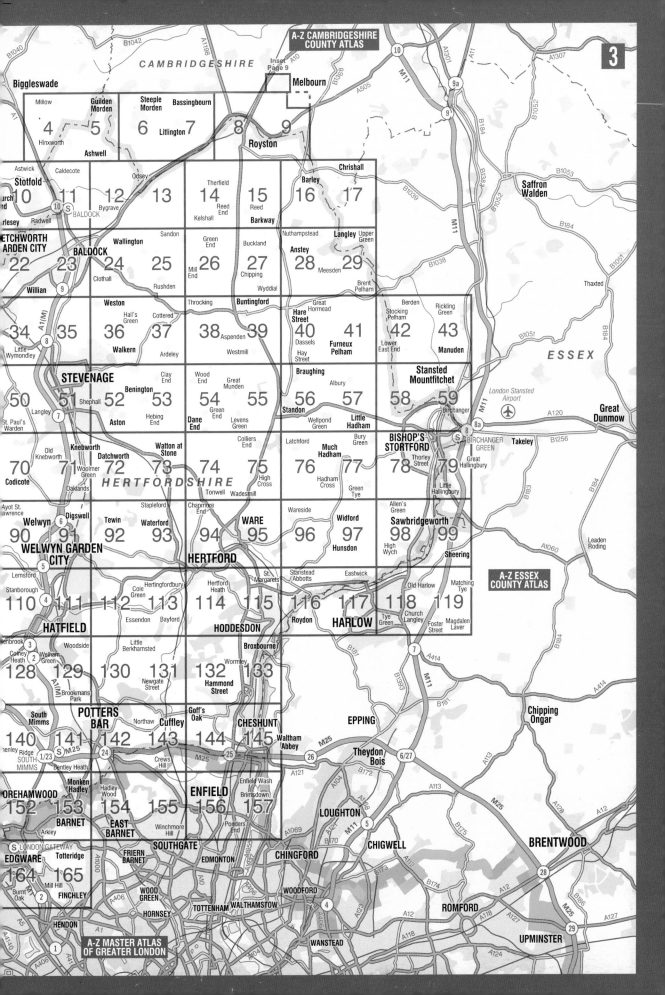

4

STRATTON
PARK
MANOR
CT.

A Park Corner Farm

B

LANE **C** BIGGLESWADE **D**

Newton

ROAD **23**

HALLSIDE
SPRINGFIELD HIGH
Sch
LA
CHAPEL ST.
TREE
HIGH
F
Church
Farm

G

1

DUNTON LANE

Nursery

Nursery

DUNTON

Millow Hall
Farm

Millow Lodge
Farm

Millow

2

STRATTON BUS. PK.

43

Millow Hill
Farm

Millow Bury

3

Works

Stratton Farm

Stratton Farm
Cottages

Millowbury Farm

Pla

G-R-E-E-N L-A-N-E

GREEN

4

42

LONDON

A1

Newspring Farm

Ash
Plantation

5

Pumping
Station

**Biggleswade
SG18**

Bleak Hall
Smallholding

6

41

Bleak Hall
Cottages

Lower Farm
Cottages

The Old
Rectory

Lower
Farm

THE
BARNS

Manor
Farm

Bleak Hall

7

EDWORTH

Bleak Hall
Farm

Manor Farm

†

Tall
Trees

Orchard
Lodge

STREET
ARNOLDS

Hillside
Cottage

LA.
Hill
Cottage

Hinxworth

Middle
Farm

8

Topler's Hill

Reservoir
(Covered)

Water
Tower

RoO

Tower
Close

ROAD

GREAT

CENTRAL BEDFORDSHIRE
NORTH HERTFORDSHIRE

Playing
Field

HIGH
FRANCIS RD.
CHRIST'S
CHAPEL
War
Mem.
ST.
BONNETTS
ASHWELL

Sewage
Works

Thorns
Farm

PARKERS
LA.

Bury End
Farm

Dewmead
Farm

40

EDWORTH

9

A1

NORTH

Glebe
Farm

Jack's
House

Place
Farm

NEW
INN
HINXWORTH RD.
ROAD

Pulter's
Farm

Hinxworth
Place

A

10 ▽

B

ROAD **22**

C

D

11 ▽

E

F

23

24

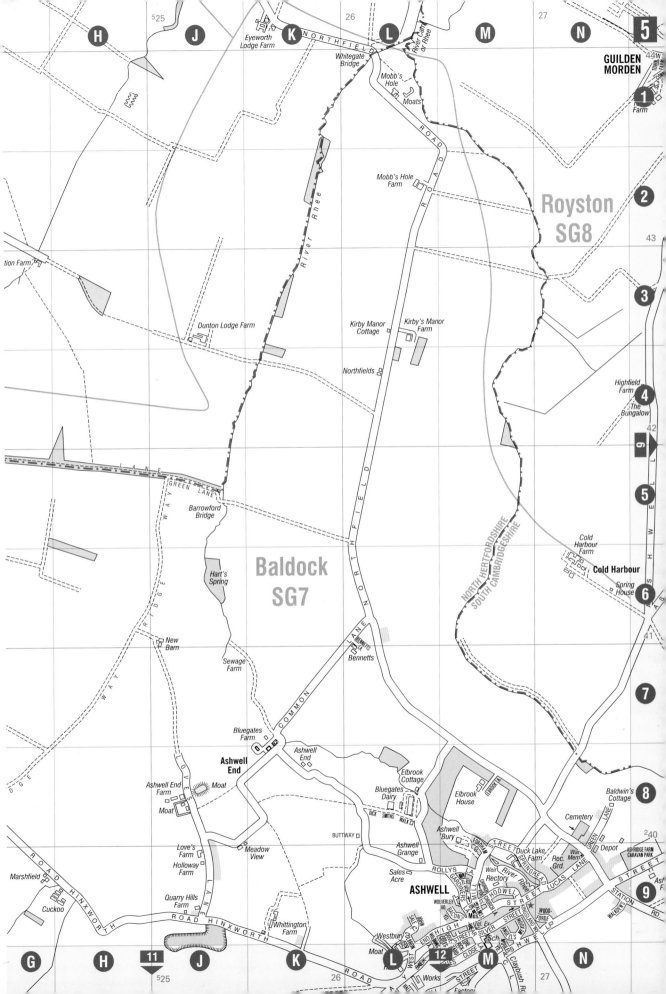

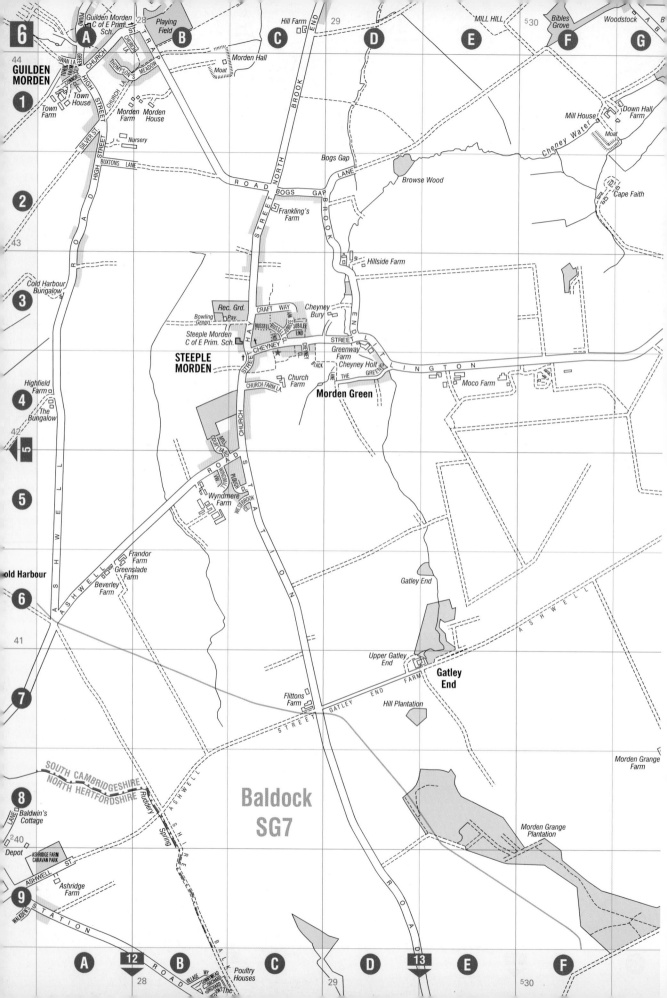

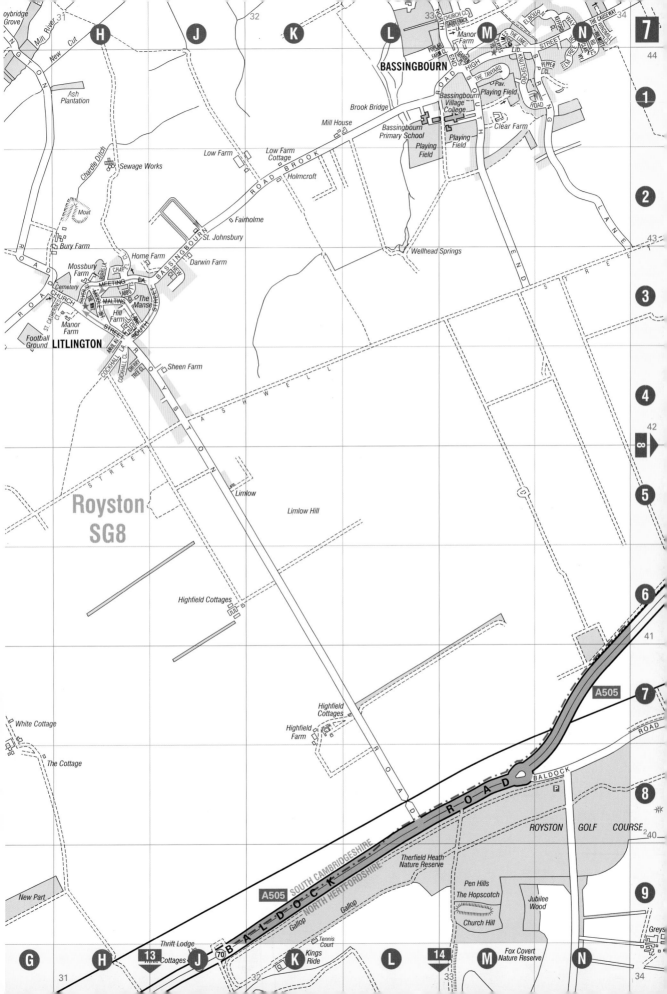

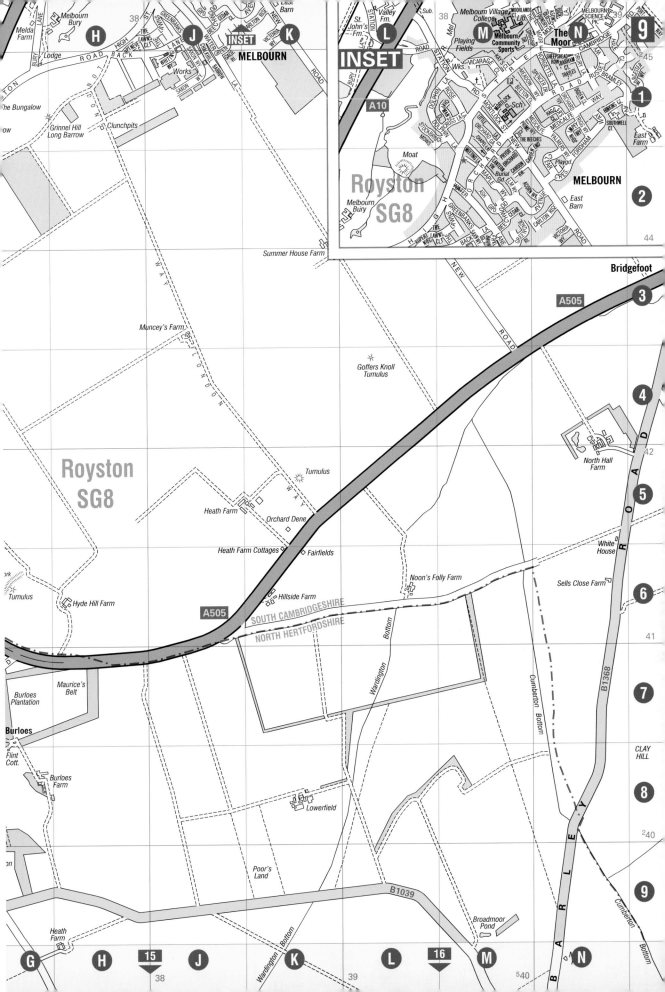

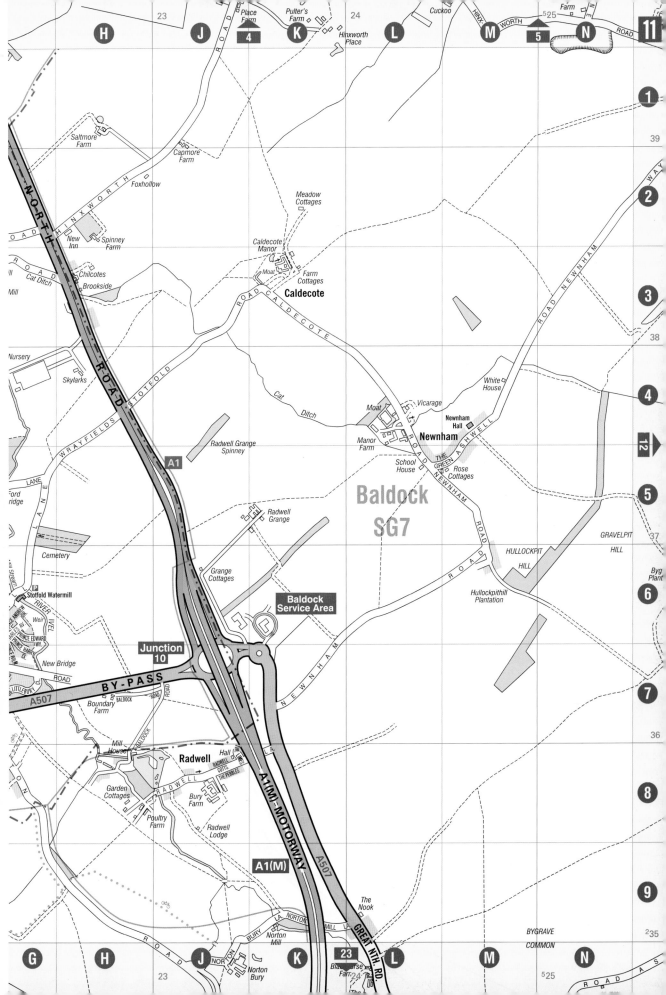

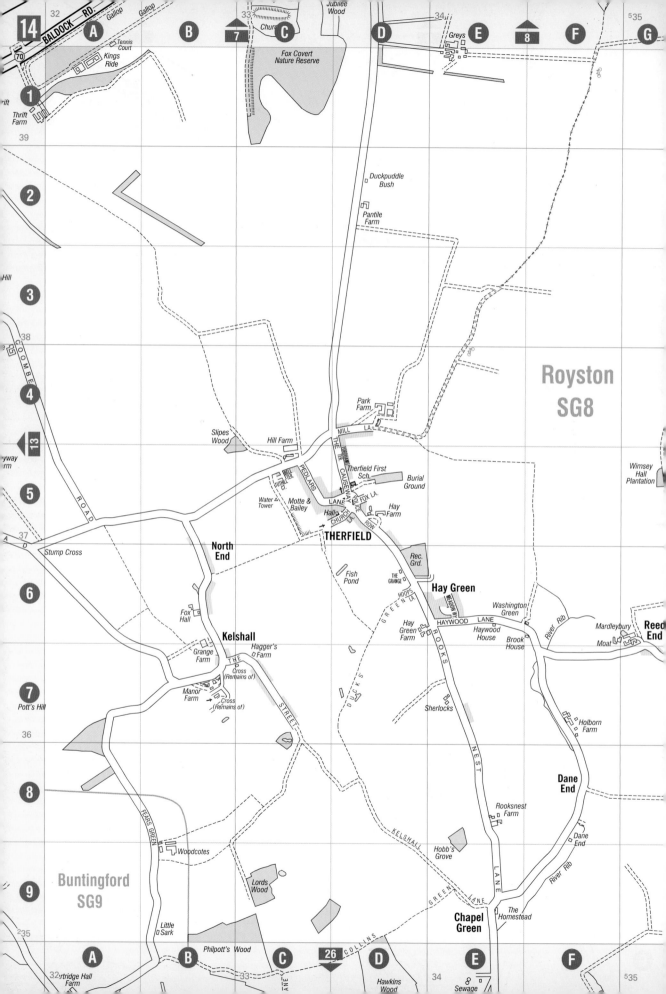

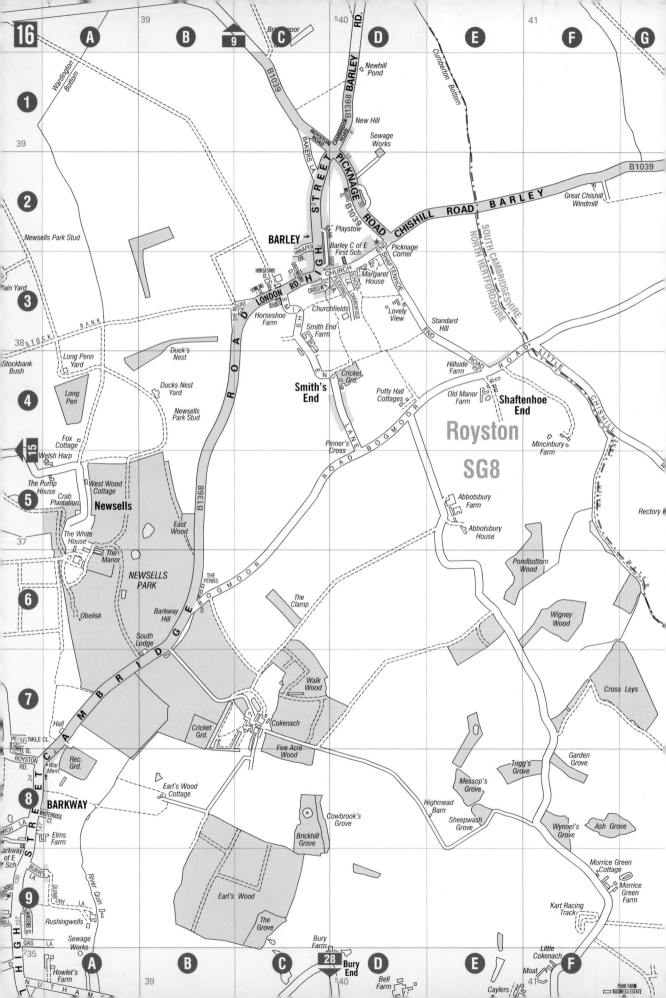

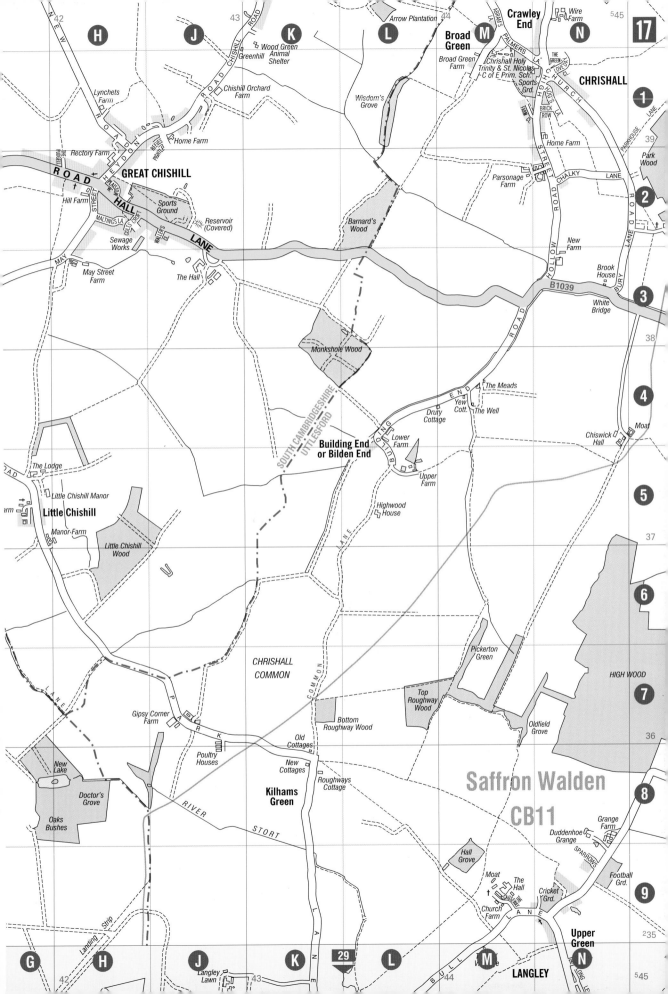

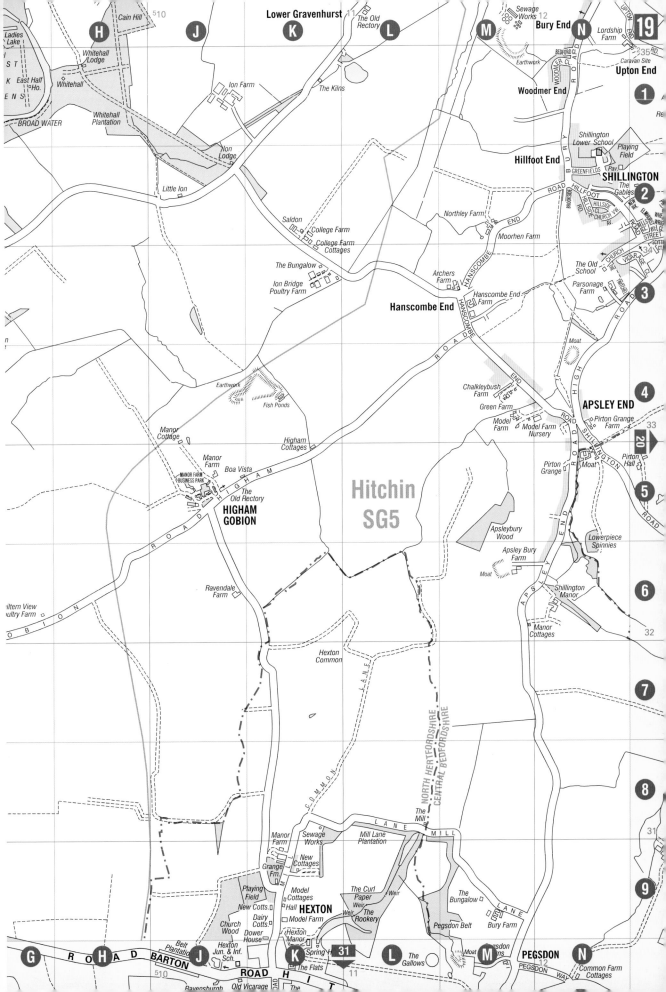

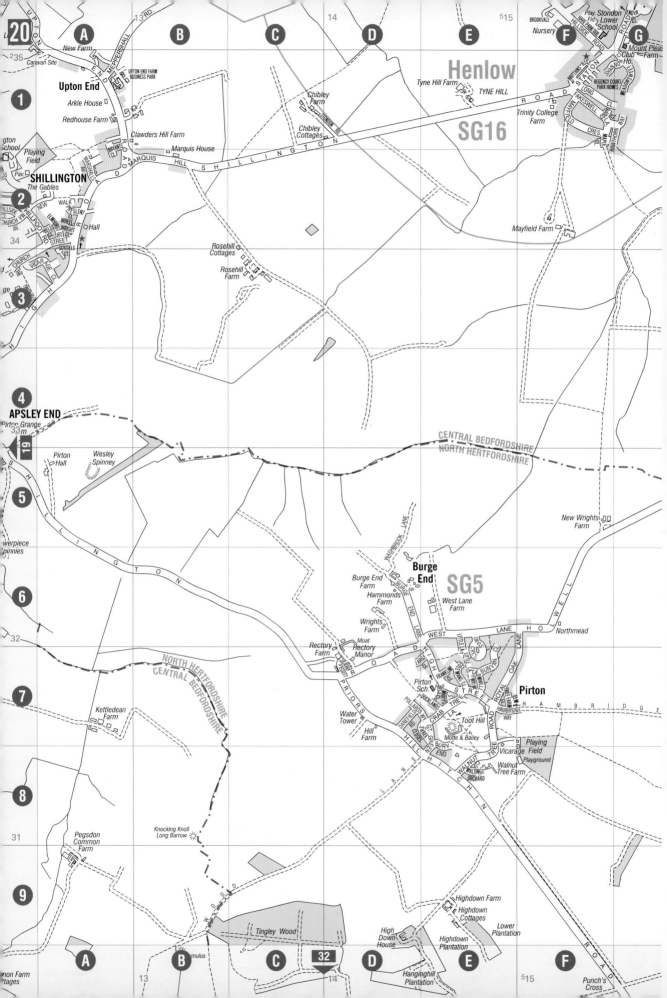

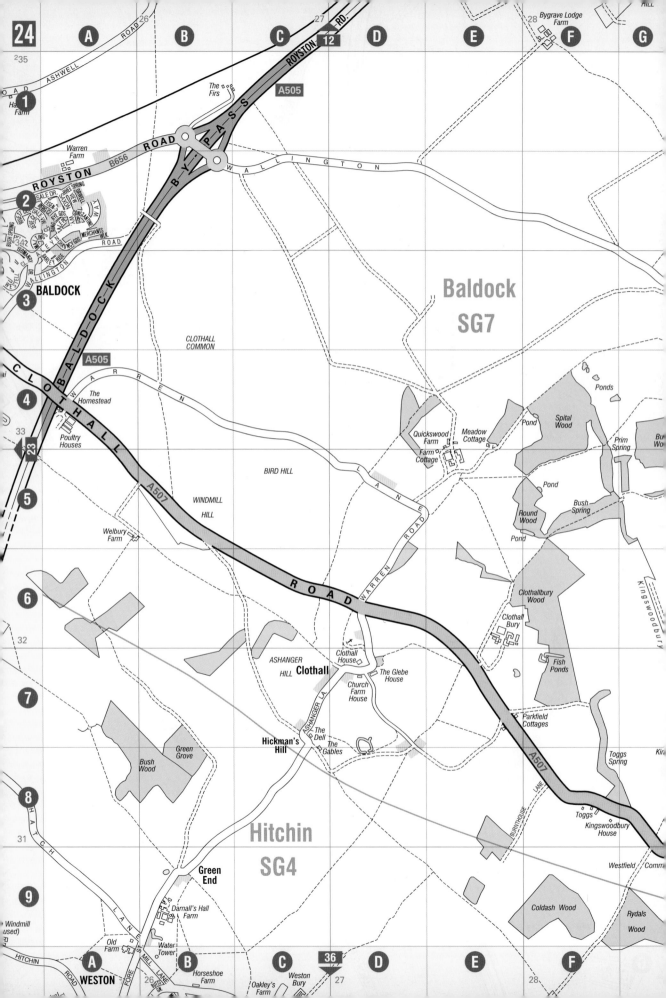

A **B** **C** **D** **E** **F** **G**

235

1

A505

The Firs

ROYSTON   ROAD   BY-PASS   ROYSTON   RD.

12

ASHWELL   ROAD   26   27

Warren
Farm

Baldock
SG7

ROYSTON   B656   ROAD

WALLINGTON

2

Hall
Farm

342

SALE DR.
THREE SPRING
SAXON
CONSTANTINE
KING'S
CHAUNCY GDS
MERCHANTS WLK
BARLEY RISE
YEOMANRY CL.
BUSH SPRING
WALLINGTON   ROAD

BALDOCK

3

Baldock

CLOTHALL
COMMON

A505

4

CLOTHALL   BALDOCK   WARREN   LANE

The Homestead

Quickswood
Farm

Meadow
Cottage

Pond

Spital
Wood

Ponds

Prim
Spring

Bur
Wo

33

23

Poultry
Houses

Farm
Cottage

Pond

5

WINDMILL
HILL

BIRD HILL

A507

Welbury
Farm

WARREN   LANE   ROAD   A507   ROAD

Pond

Round
Wood

Bush
Spring

Pond

Clothallbury
Wood

Kingswoodbury

6

Clothall
Bury

Fish
Ponds

32

ASHANGER

HILL   Clothall

Clothall
House

The Glebe
House

7

ASHANGER LA.

Church
Farm
House

Parkfield
Cottages

Bush
Wood

Green
Grove

Hickman's
Hill

The
Dell

The
Gables

Toggs
Spring

Kira

8

31

HATCH

BURYHOUSE LANE

Toggs

Kingswoodbury
House

Hitchin
SG4

Green
End

Westfield   Comm

9

Windmill
(used)

LANES

Darnall's Hall
Farm

Water
Tower

Old Farm

Coldash Wood

Rydals
Wood

HITCHIN

A **B** **C** **D** **E** **F**

WESTON

FORE   MILL LANE   26   27   28

Horseshoe
Farm

Oakley's
Farm

Weston
Bury

36

A 32 B 33 C 34 D E 535 F G

1 Partridge Hall Farm · Little Sark · Philpott's Wood · COLLINS LANE · Hawkins Wood · Chapel Green · The Homestead · Brandish Wood

Smallholding · Vicarage Hall · Sandon Bury · Park Lane · The Mount · Sewage Works

2 Sandon · Sandon Junior Mixed & Infant Sch. · PAYNE END RD. · DARK LA · RUSHDEN · Moat · Cock's Lodge · Notley Green · NOTLEY LANE · Slate Hall Farm · RIVER RIB

Sayfield Cottages · 34

3 Poultry Houses · Tichney Wood · Rockells Jersey Farm · Walnut Farm · Five House Farm · Moat · Short Lane · Slate Hall Farm · SANDON ROAD

4 Green End · Green End Farm · Nursery · BECKFIELD LANE · Chain Walk · Beckfield Farm · West Wood · Hodenhoe Manor · WHITELEY

33 · 25 · Friars Grange · Moat · Doebridge Farm · Ash Stub · Fish Pond

5 Friars Wood · FRIARS LANE · Bird's Nest Farm · Mill End · Hyde Hall Cottages · Hyde Hall Farm · Buckland Bottom

The Colt House · Wood Farm · Mill End Farm · Berrymeads · EAST HERTFORDSHIRE · NORTH HERTFORDSHIRE

6 Bush Wood · Burhill Wood · The Tryst

32

7 Lye-End Farm · Little Manor Farm · Whitehall · BURGESS LANE · SANDON LANE · Brookside · LANE · MILL HILL

Broadfield Lodge Farm

8 Lodge Farm · Chapel Wood · Middle Wood · Great Wood · Bush Wood · Park Wood · Ellen Green · Steward's Ley · Four Acre Wood

31 · Hall Farm · Blunt's Wood

9 Broadfield Hall · Foxholes Wood · Needle Spring · Boldero's Wood · Middle Farm · Middle Farm Cottages · Lower Farm · Lower Farm Cottages

Southfields Farm · Pond · THROCKING

HORNEYPOOL LANE · 32 · A · B · 33 · C · 38 · Little Wood · D · 34 · E · Thistley · F · 535

Old

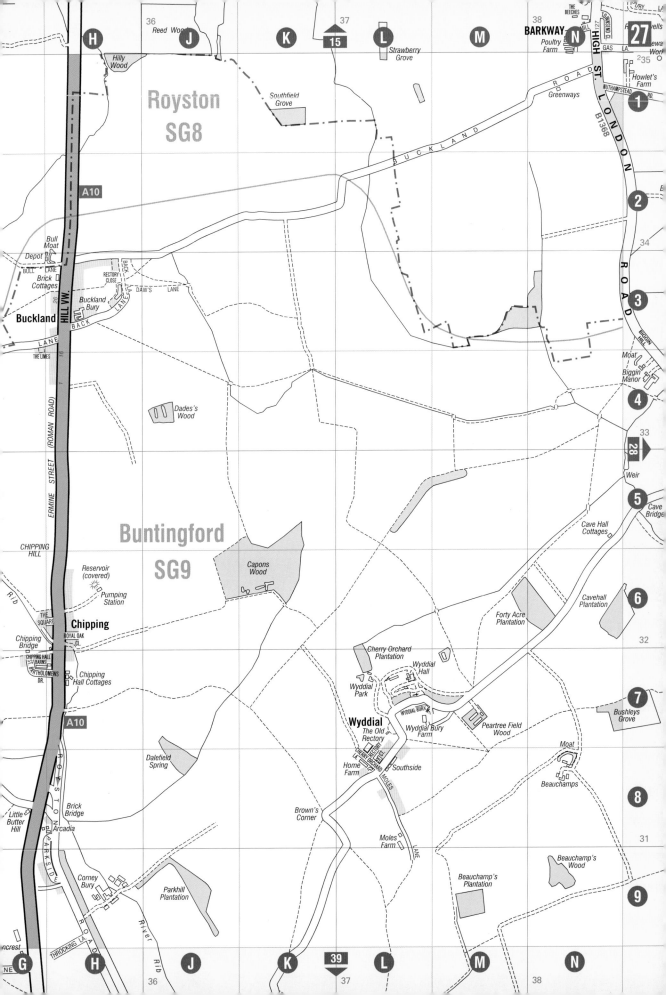

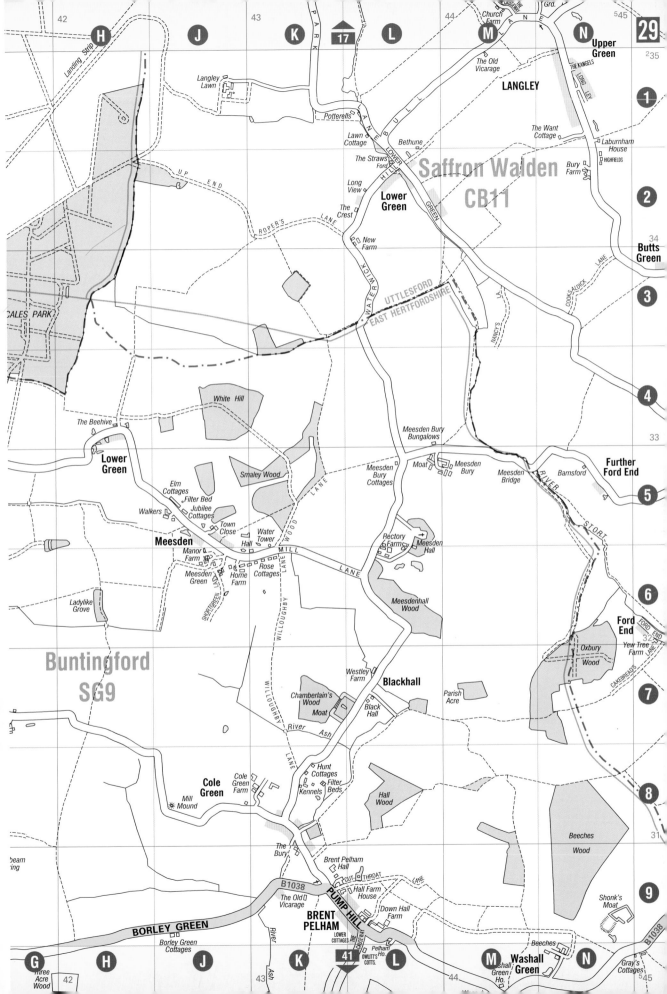

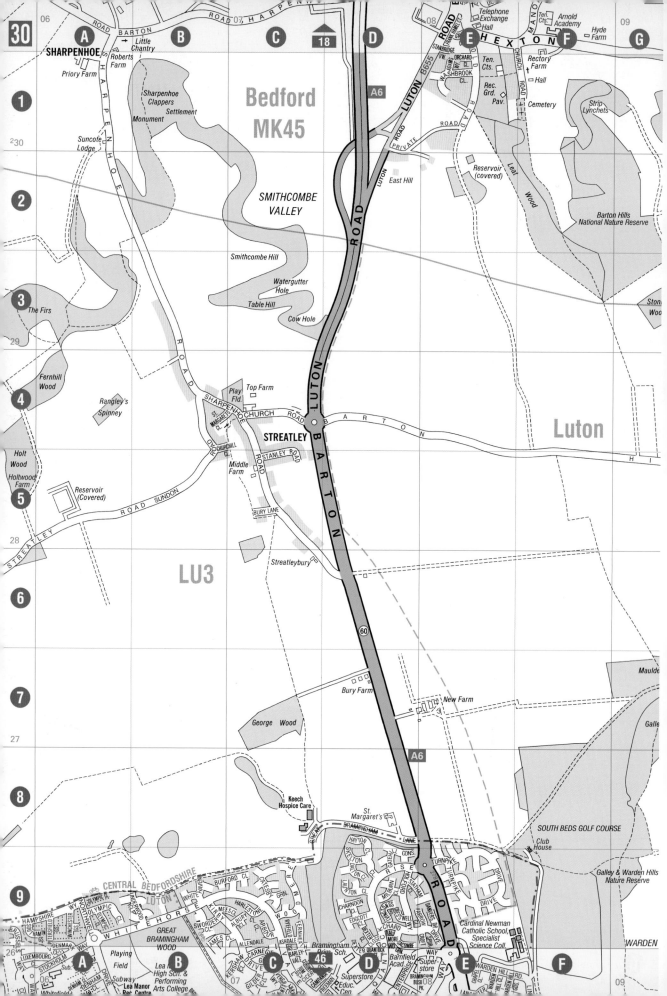

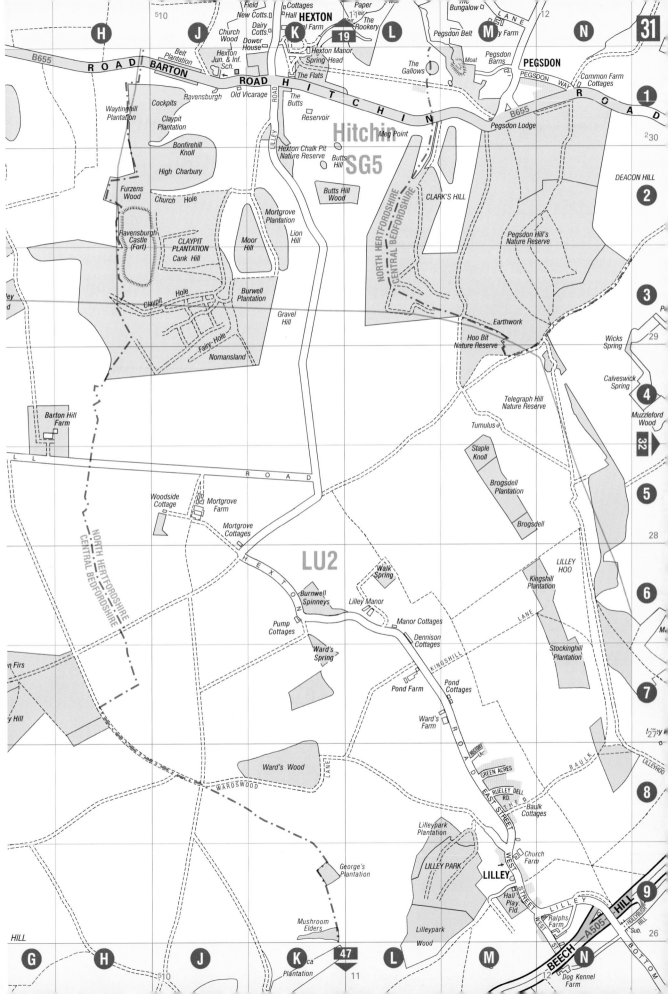

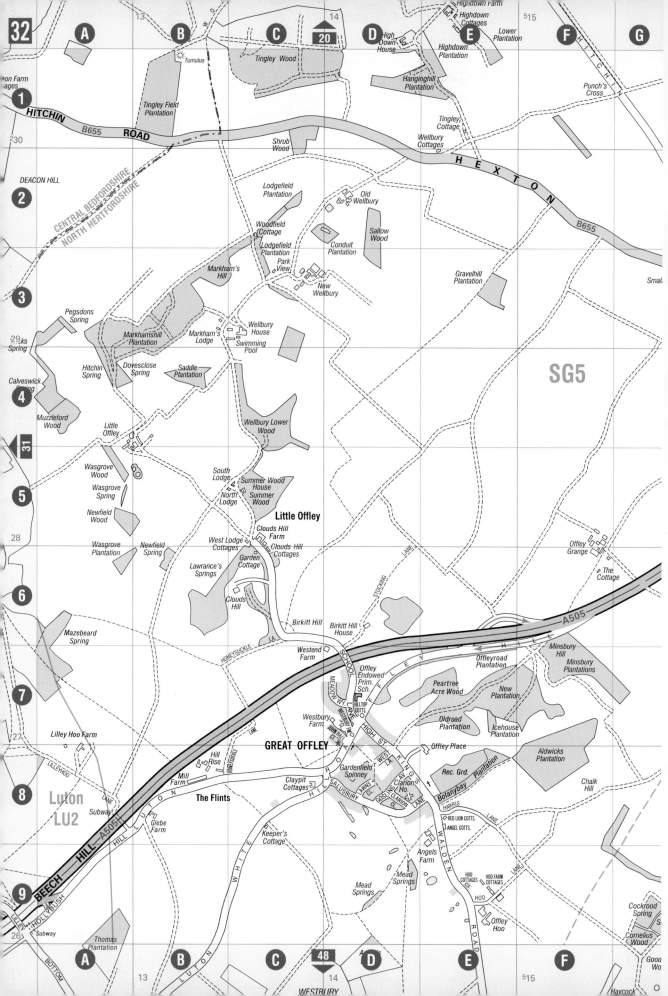

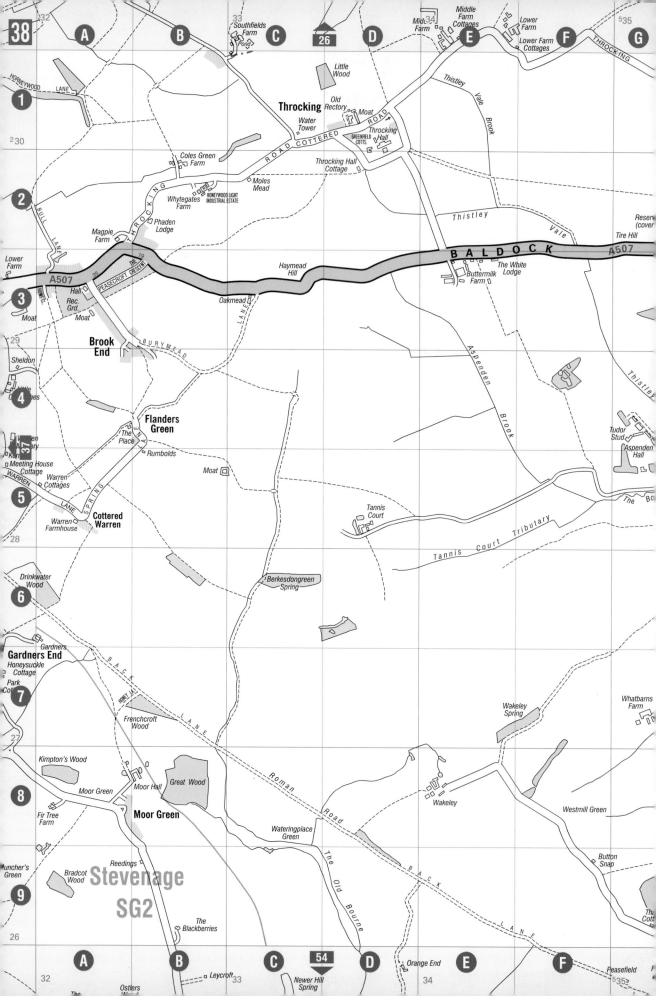

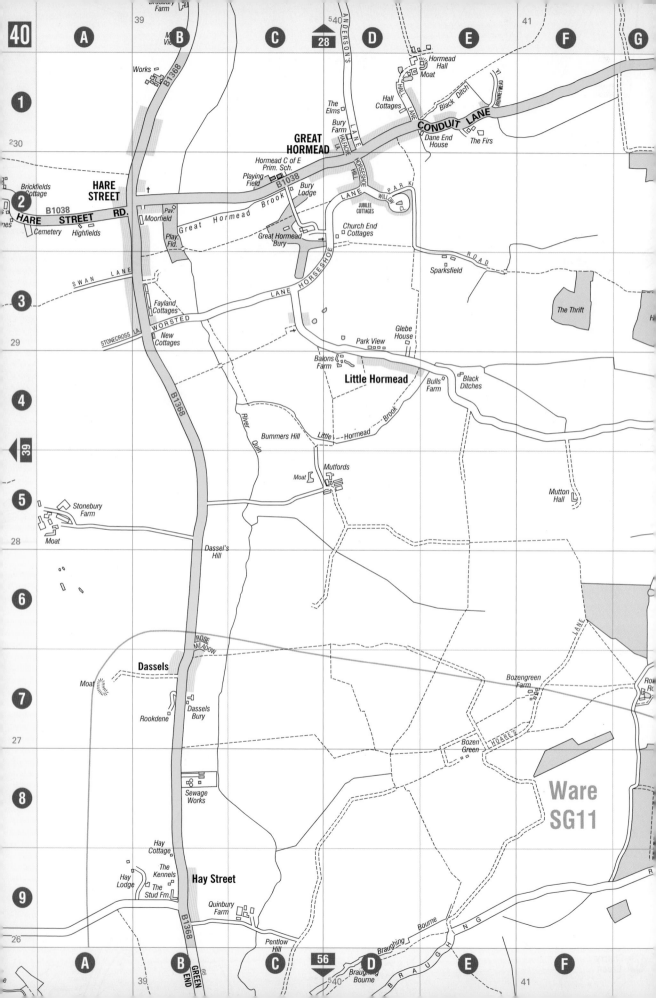

A 39 B C 28 D E F 41 G

1

²30

HARE STREET

HARE STREET RD.

2 B1038

GREAT HORMEAD

Works

Brickfields Cottage

Cemetery Highfields

Moorfield

Pav.

Play. Fld.

SWAN LANE

3

29

Fayland Cottages

STONECROSS LA.

WORSTED

New Cottages

4

◄ **39**

B1368

River Quin

LANE HORSESHOE

Great Hormead Brook

Hormead C of E Prim. Sch.

Playing Field

B1038

Bury Lodge

Great Hormead Bury

JUBILEE COTTAGES

Church End Cottages

Sparksfield

ROAD

Glebe House

Park View

Balons Farm

Little Hormead

Bulls Farm

Black Ditches

The Elms

Bury Farm

Hall Cottages

CONDUIT LANE

Dane End House

The Firs

Hormead Hall

Moat

Black Ditch

HALL LANE

ANDERSON'S

HORSESHOE HILL

WILLOW CL.

PARK

BRONNIEMEAD

The Thrift

5

28

Stonebury Farm

Moat

Bummers Hill

Little Hormead Brook

Moat

Mutfords

Mutton Hall

6

Dassel's Hill

7

27

Moat

ROSE MEADOW

Dassels

Rookdene

Dassels Bury

Bozengreen Farm

Bozen Green

HOARES

LANE

8

Sewage Works

Ware SG11

9

26

Hay Cottage

Hay Lodge

The Kennels

The Stud Fm.

Hay Street

B1368

Quinbury Farm

Pentlow Hill

Braughing Bourne

Braughing Bourne

BRAUGHING

BOURNE

28

56

540

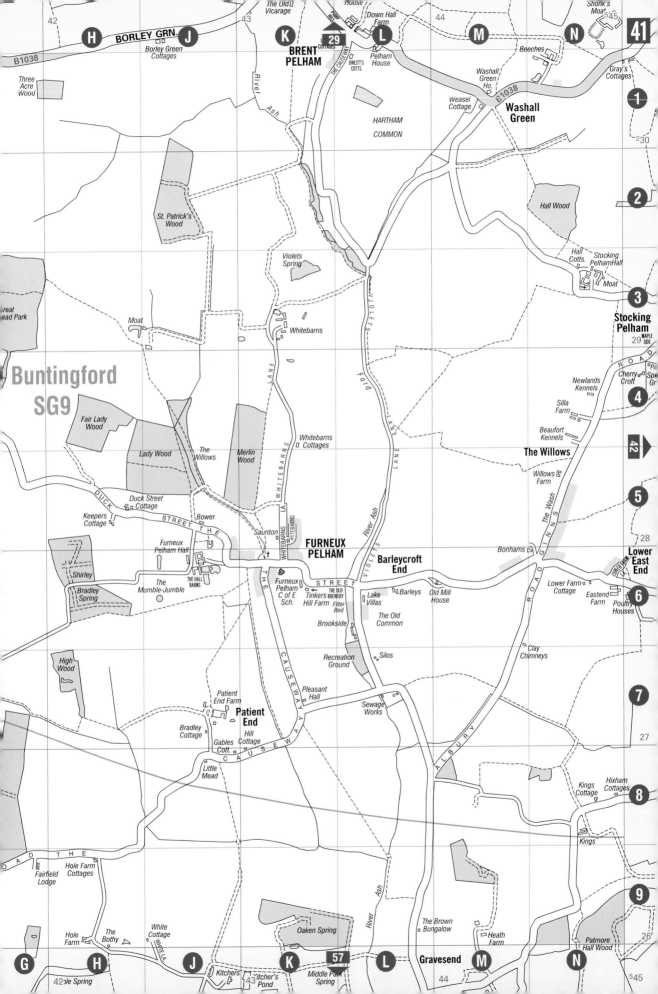

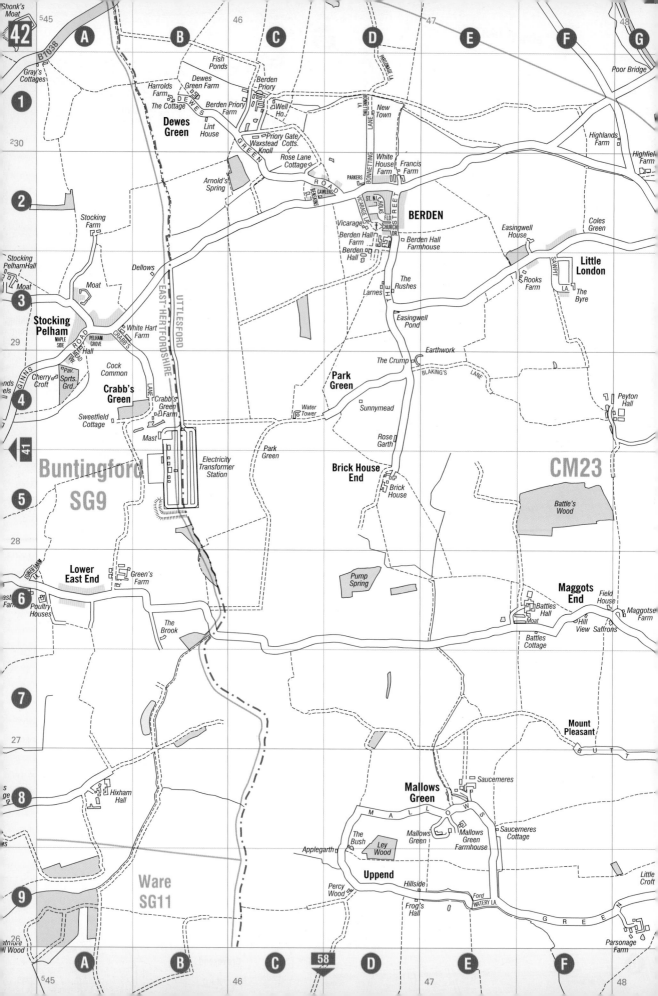

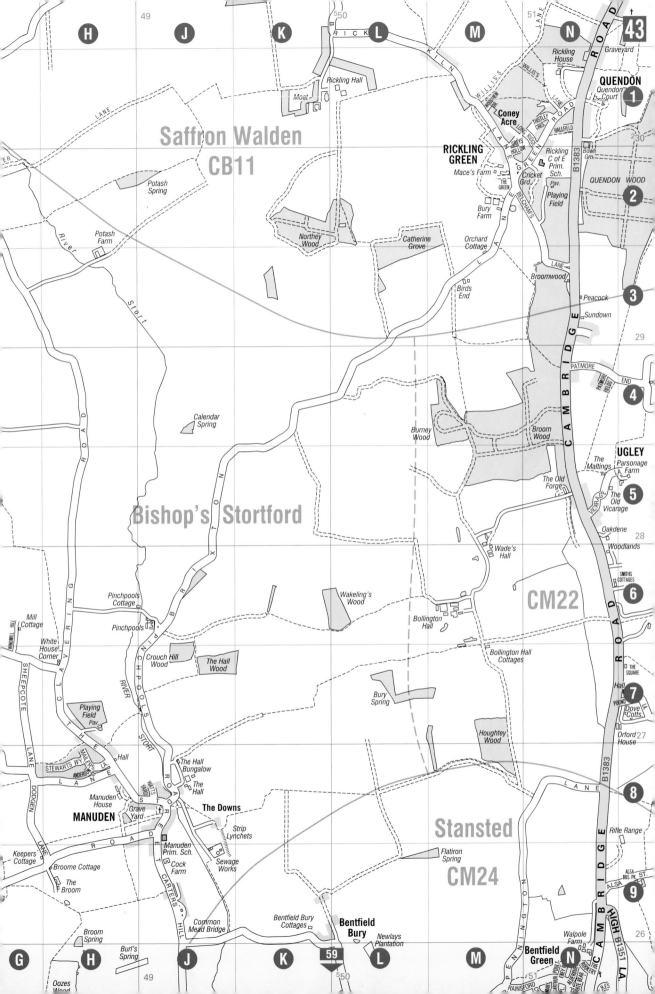

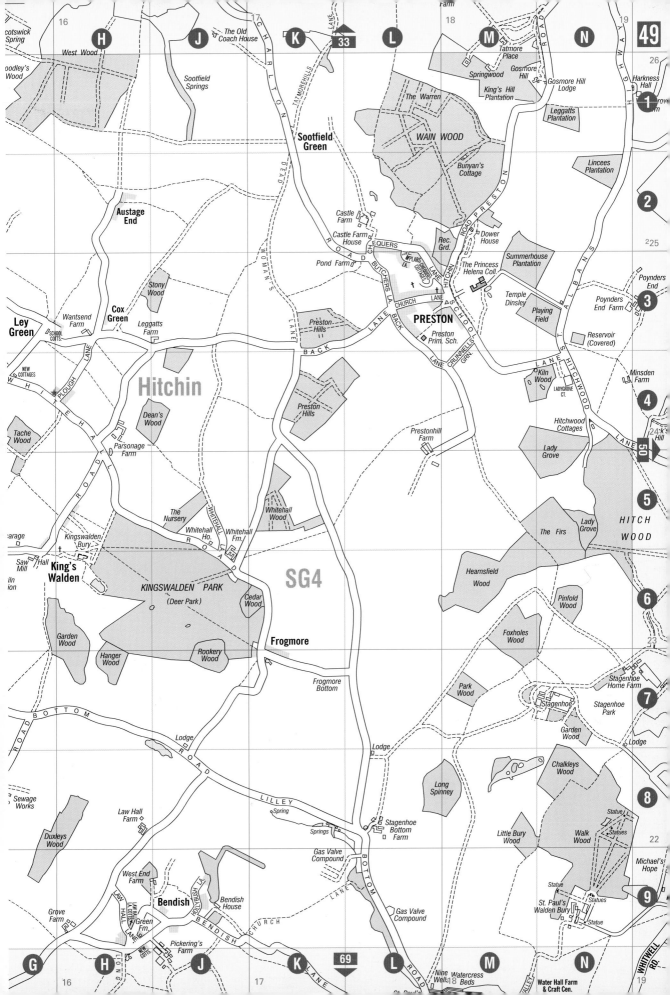

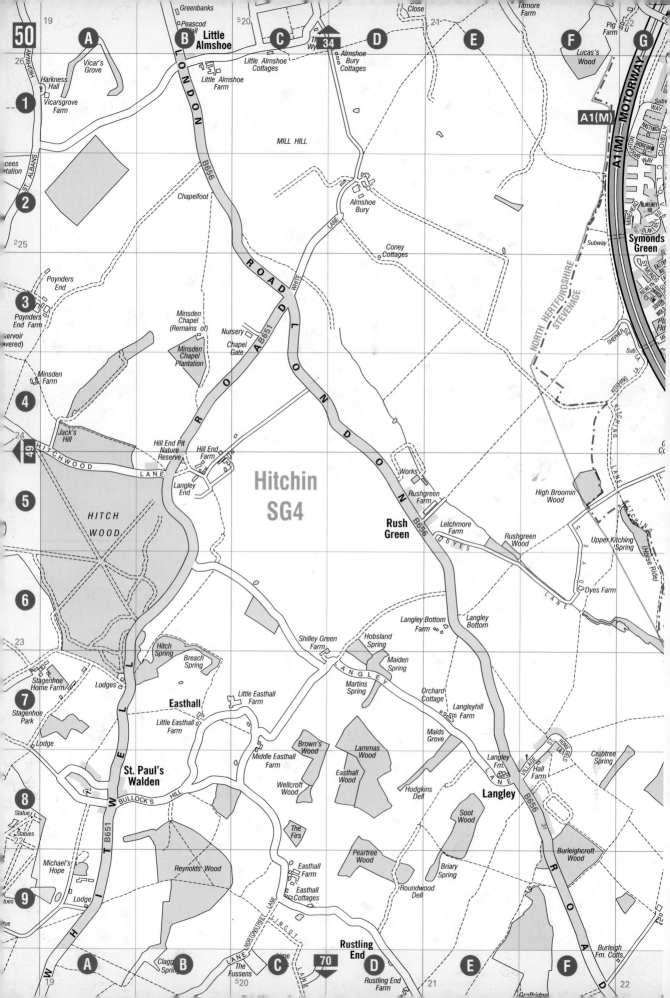

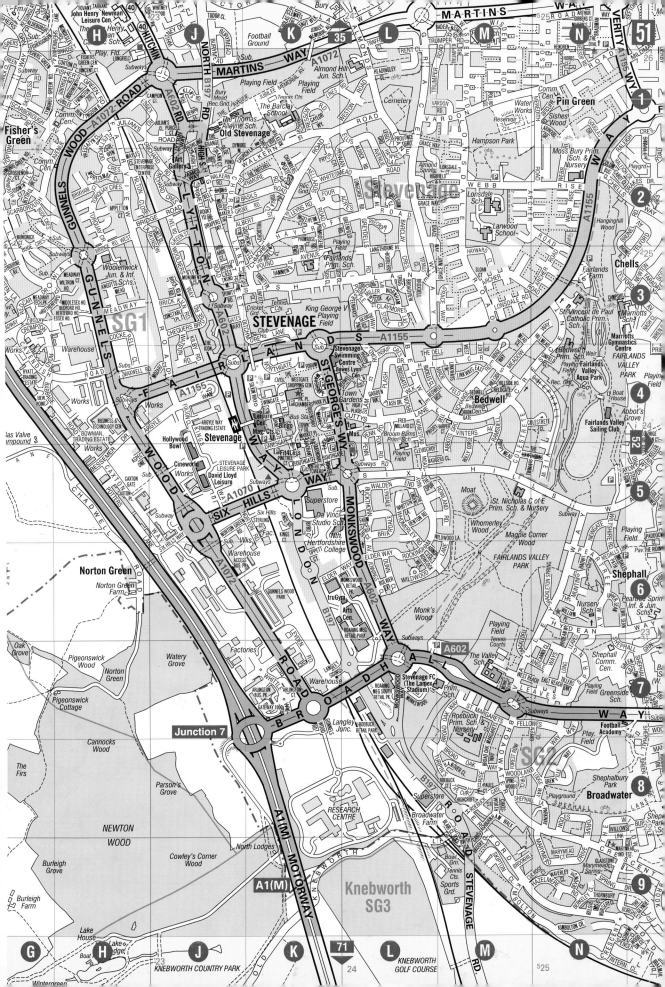

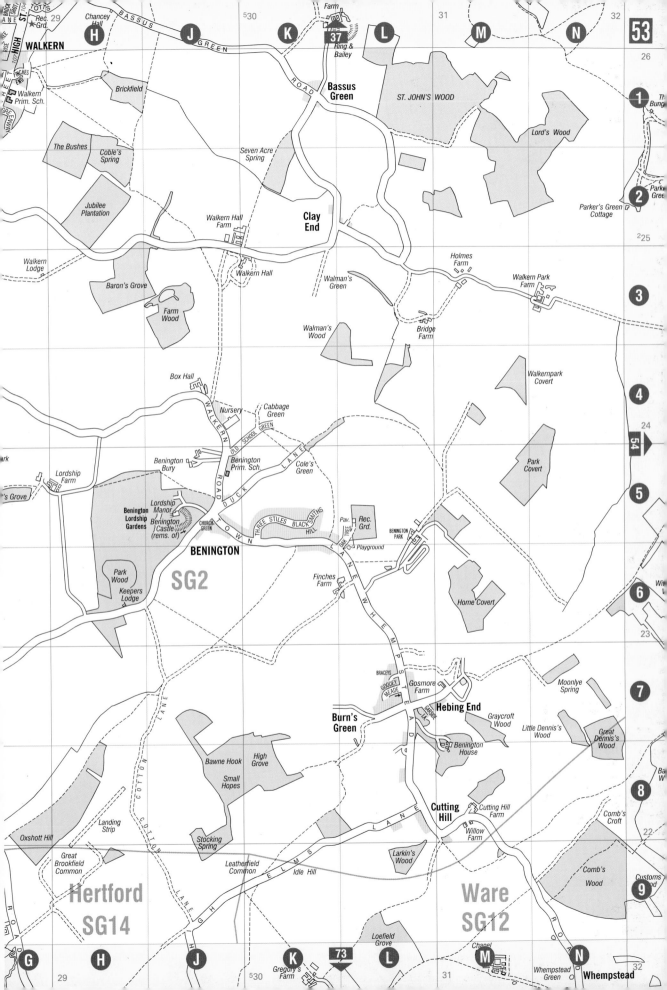

32   33   33   34   535

A   B   C   D   E   F   G

38

The Blackberries

Leycroft

Newer Hill Spring

Orange End

Peasefield

The Cott

1   The Bungalow
Ostlers Wood
Lite's Farm   **Wood End**
Hightree Farm
Coates Manor Farm

Cowley Spring

2   Parker's Green Cottage
Cherry Farm
Greenlands
Parker's Green
Highbury Farm
Badger's Green

The Old Bourne

Rush Green Cottages

Mill Farm

Thrift Wood

Rush Green

Stevenage SG2

3   Little Lye Grove

Sander's Green

4   Stag Hall Farm

24   Moat

53   Bugby's Farm

Ware

5   Baxter's Spring

Shout's Wood

6   Witnesses Wood

Great Munden Farm

Libury Hall

Haultwick

FROGS HALL LA.

Woolston Farm

GIFFORD'S STREET

WENTWORTH COTTS.

Hornbeam Common

Gifford's Wood

Dane End Tributary

Goldsell Common

7   Great Dennis's Wood

Graves Wood

Pav. Cricket Ground

Green End Farm

Green End

King's Hill

Bandy Common

SG12

Banfield Wood

The Wilderness

Radio Receiving Station

Fellowsfield Common

8   Comb's Croft

Three Corner Wood

Kings Wood

Lordship's Farm

22   Apsley Common

Little Munden C of E Prim. Sch.

Short Whiteley Common

Fullars Common

Moorfield Common

Comb's Wood

9   Customs Wood

Easington Common

CHURCH LANE

Trenchen Hill

Long Spring

The Old Bourne

WINDMILL RD.

KINGSFIELD RD.

GLADSTONE

KENNEDY RD.

PAGET

DOUNCELEY AV.

Echo Wood

Crabcroft Spring

DANE END

Dane End Farm

74

MUNDEN ROAD

Whitehill Farm

White Hill

The Hollow

A   B   C   D   E   F

32   33   33 Football Grd.   34   535

Hemnstead

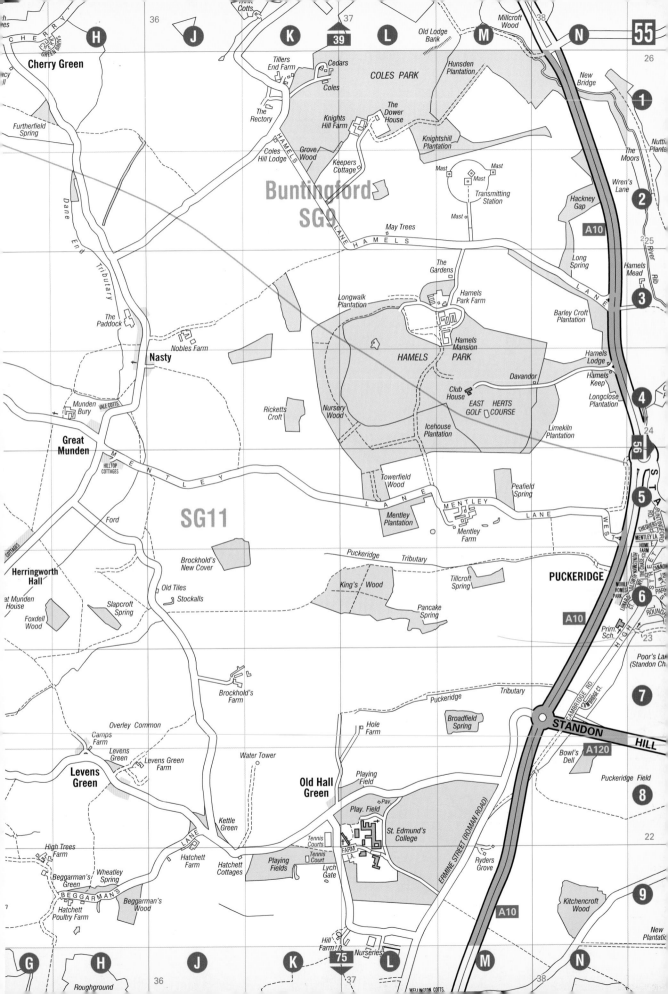

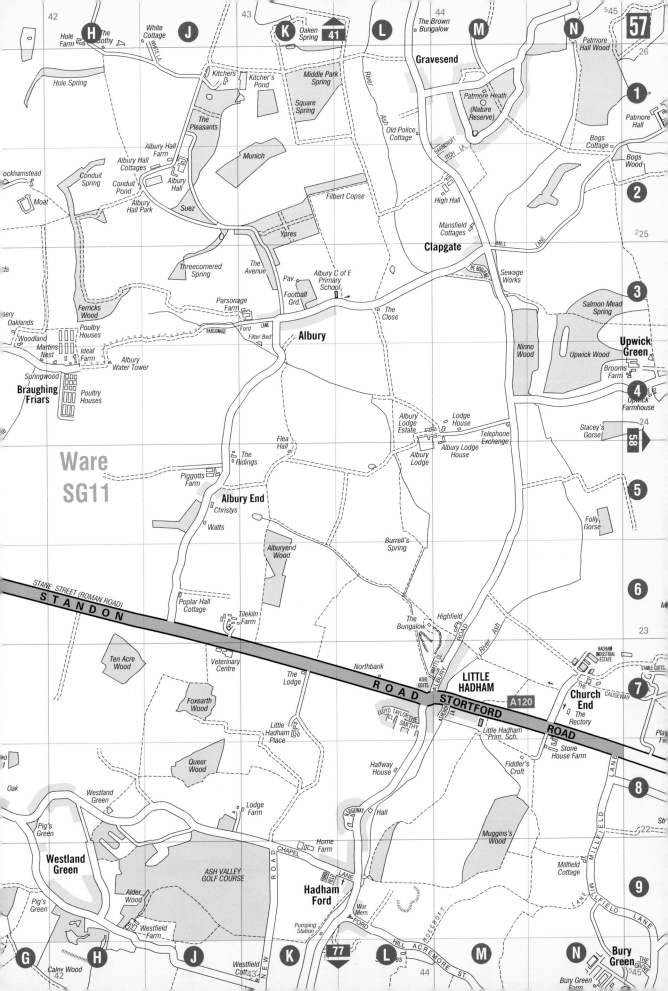

60

A   B   C   D   E   F   G

1

2

3

4

5

6

7

8

9

87   88   89

A   B   C   D   E   F

21

²20

19

18

17

A418

Westpark Farm

AYLESBURY   ROAD

Ladymead

Lower Wingbury Farm

Windmill Hill Buildings

Windmill Hill

Mentmore Cross Roads

Upper Wingbury Farm

WINGBURY COURTYARD BUSINESS VILLAGE

ROAD

LODGE ROAD

The E

Wing Lodge

CRAFTON LODGE ROAD

Little Chapel Farm

Crafton Farm

Crafton

Reddings

New Spinney

Crafton Lodge

Crafton Stud

Sewage Works

ABBOTTS WAY

WINSLOW

Sch.

MINES

Nup End

Manor Farm

BALDWIN

BELL LEYS

WINGRAVE

HIGHTON

Helsthorpe Farm

THE TEAM

PARSONAGE FARM

CASTLE

CHURCH ST.

DARK LANE

Macintyre Sch.

COMM. REC! GRD.

GREEN

Cen. Grd.

REC. GROUND

ESSEX YD.

JENKINS CT.

MILL LANE

Maltby's Farm

Sewage Works

STRAWS HADLEY CT.

Straws Hadley Farm

MOAT

GREENACRES

LOWER END

Windmill Hill Farm

RINGTON ROAD

Mitchell Leys Farm

Aylesbury

HP22

Lower Windmill Hill Farm

Aylesbury Vale

Dacorum

Broadmead Farm

Thistlebrook Farm

ROAD

Alnwick Farm

DRIVE

Boarscroft Farm

BRANDON CT.

ALNWICK

Tring

HP23

Thistle Brook

80

Whitwell Farm

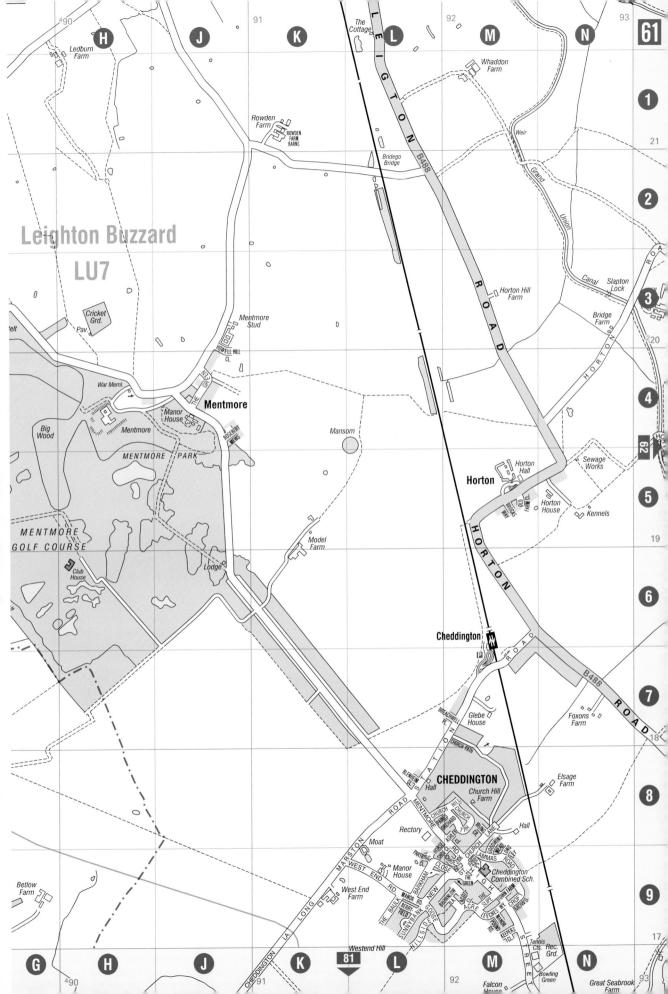

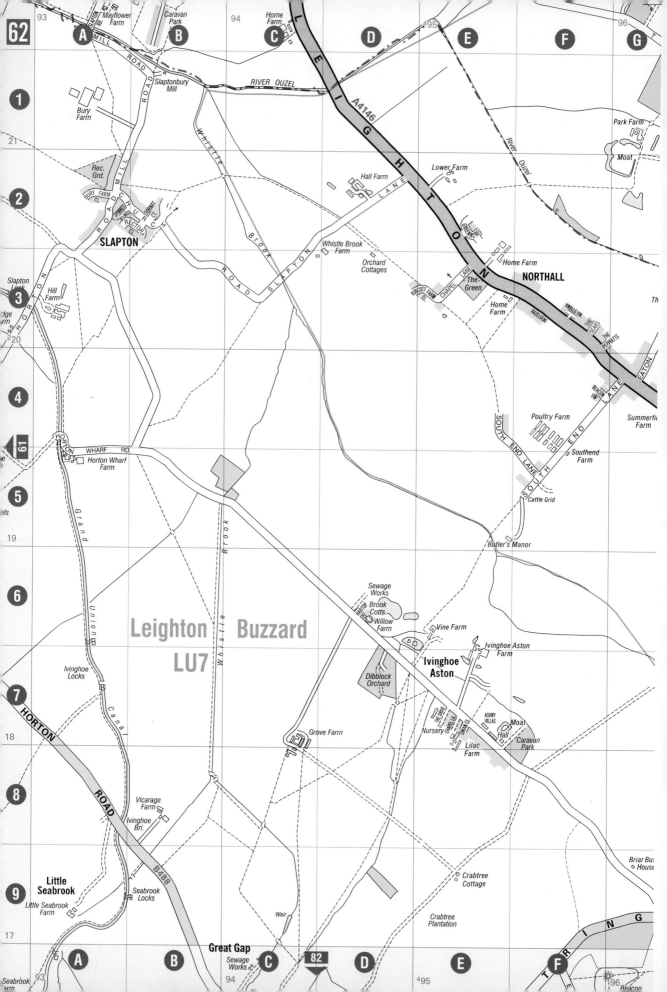

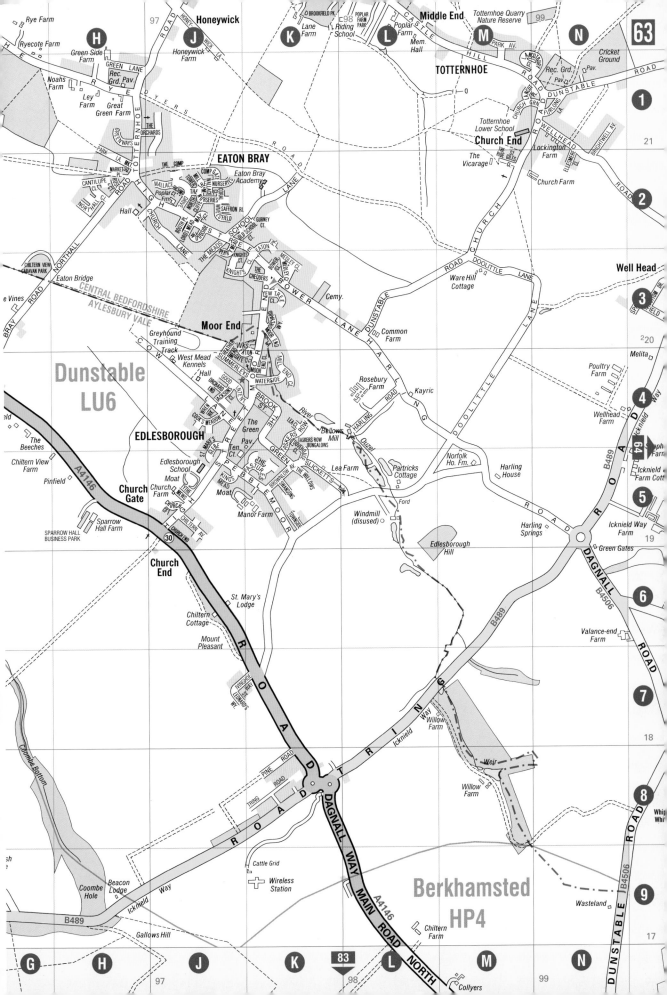

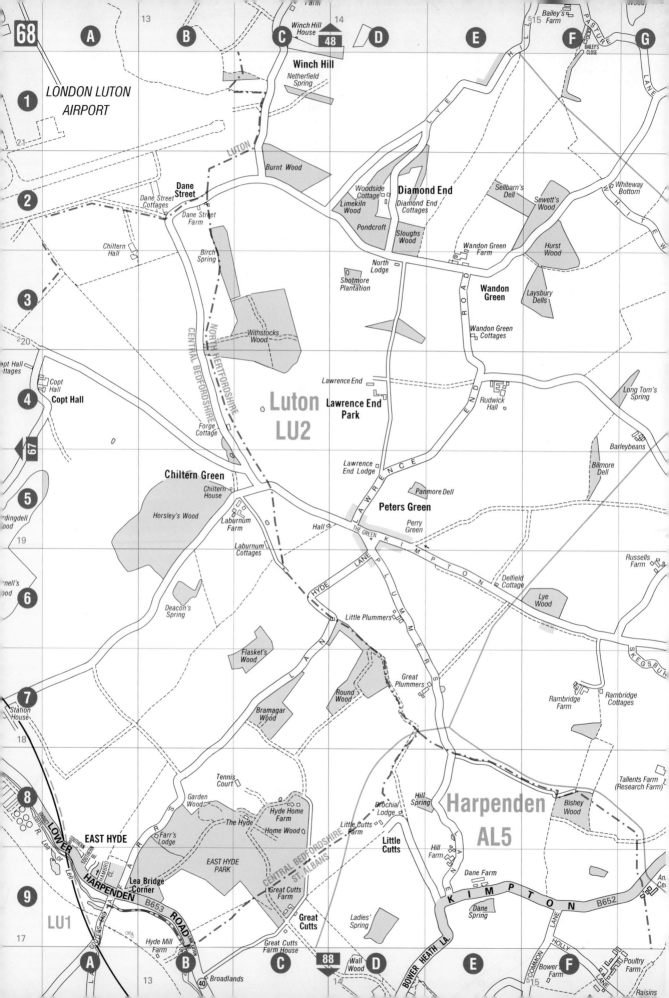

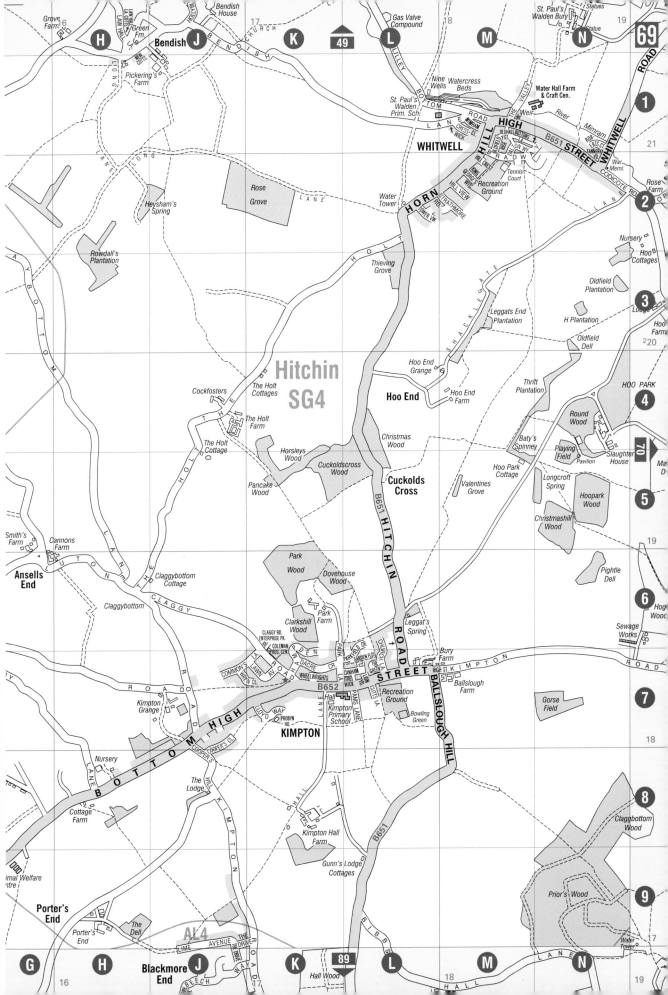

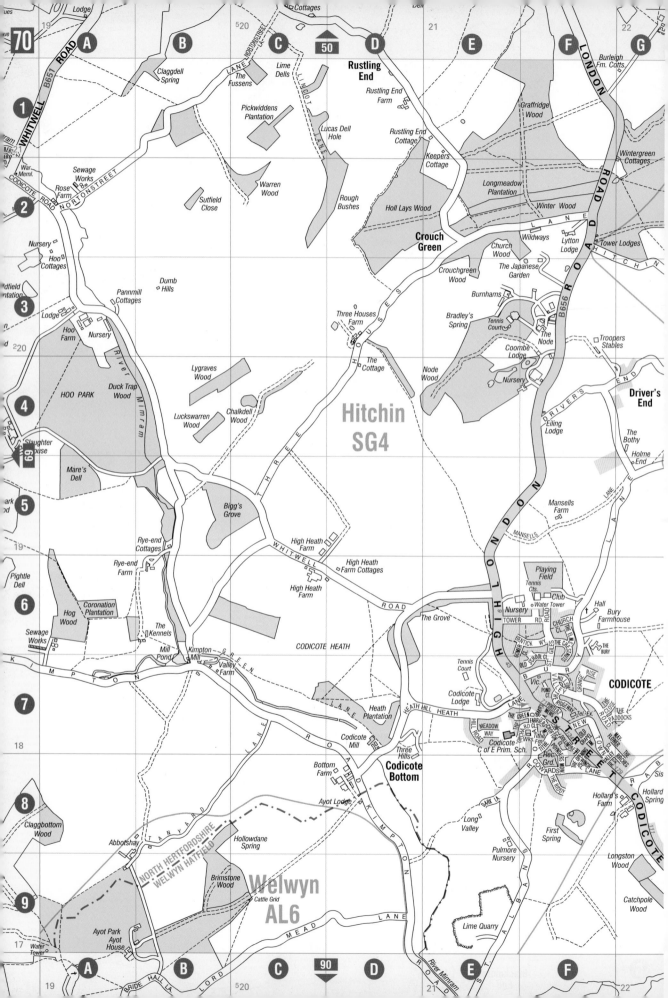

A B C D E F G

1

2

3

4

5

6

7

8

9

Lodge
Cottages
WHITWELL ROAD B651
Claggdell Spring
The Fussens
Lime Dells
Cottages
50
Rustling End
London Road
Burleigh Fm. Cotts.

Pickwiddens Plantation
Lucas Dell Hole
Rustling End Farm
Rustling End Cottage
Keepers Cottage
Graffridge Wood
Wintergreen Cottages

War Meml.
Sewage Works
Rose Farm
CODICOTE ROAD
NORTONSTREET
Warren Wood
Sutfield Close
Rough Bushes
Holl Lays Wood
Longmeadow Plantation
Winter Wood
Wildways
Lytton Lodge
Tower Lodges
HITCHIN

Nursery
Hoo Cottages
Dumb Hills
Pannmill Cottages
Crouch Green
Church Wood
Crouchgreen Wood
Burnhams
The Japanese Garden
B656 ROAD
The Node
Troopers Stables

dfield ntation
Lodge
Hoo Farm
Nursery
River Mimram
Lygraves Wood
Three Houses Farm
The Cottage
Bradley's Spring
Tennis Court
Coombe Lodge
Nursery
Driver's End

220
HOO PARK
Duck Trap Wood
Luckswarren Wood
Chalkdell Wood
Hitchin SG4
Node Wood
DRIVER'S
Eiling Lodge
The Bothy
Holme End

Slaughter House
69
Mare's Dell
Bigg's Grove
THREE
Mansells Farm
LANE

rk d
Pightle Dell
Rye-end Cottages
Rye-end Farm
WHITWELL
High Heath Farm Cottages
High Heath Farm
ROAD
MANSELLS
LONDON
Playing Field
Tennis Cts.
Club
Hall
Bury Farmhouse

Hog Wood
Coronation Plantation
The Kennels
Mill Pond
Kimpton Mill
Valley Farm
High Heath
CODICOTE HEATH
The Grove
Water Tower
TOWER RD.
Nursery
CHURCH
The Bury

Sewage Works
KIMPTON
GREEN
LANE
Heath Plantation
Codicote Mill
HEATH HILL HEATH
Tennis Court
Codicote Lodge
CODICOTE

18
ROAD
Three Hills
Codicote C of E Prim. Sch.
MEADOW WAY
S T R E E T
The Paddocks

Claggbottom Wood
Abbotshay
TANYARD
Hollowdane Spring
Bottom Farm
Ayot Lodge
Codicote Bottom
Long Valley
First Spring
Hollard's Farm
Hollard Spring

NORTH HERTFORDSHIRE
WELWYN HATFIELD
Brimstone Wood
Cattle Grid
Welwyn AL6
Pulmore Nursery
Longston Wood

Water Tower
Ayot Park
Ayot House
BRIDE HALL LA.
LORD
MEAD
KIMPTON
LANE
River Mimram
ST ALBAN
Lime Quarry
Catchpole Wood

A B C D **90** E F

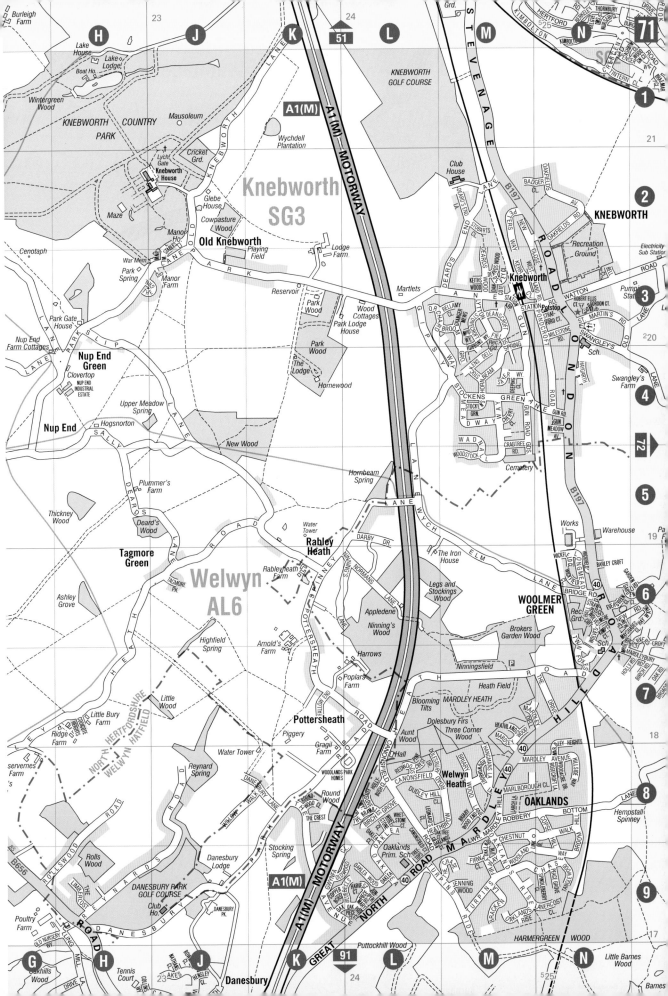

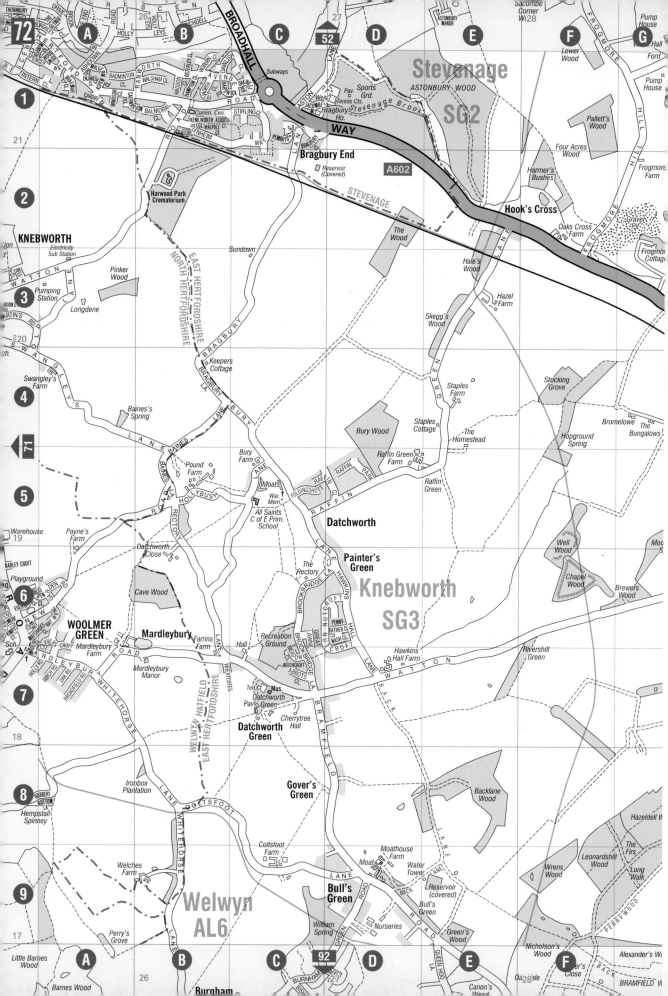

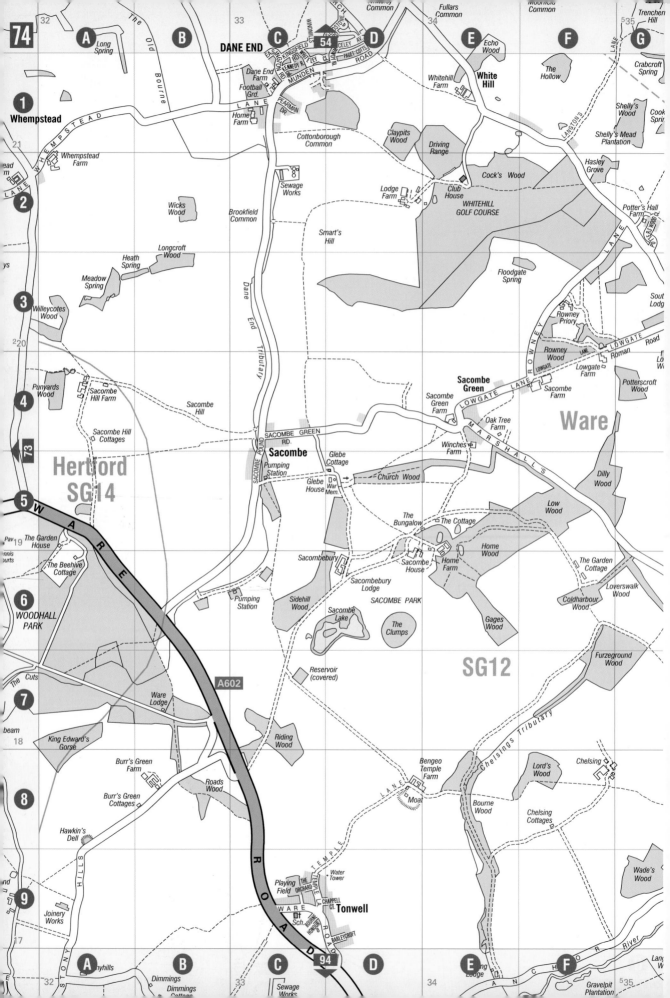

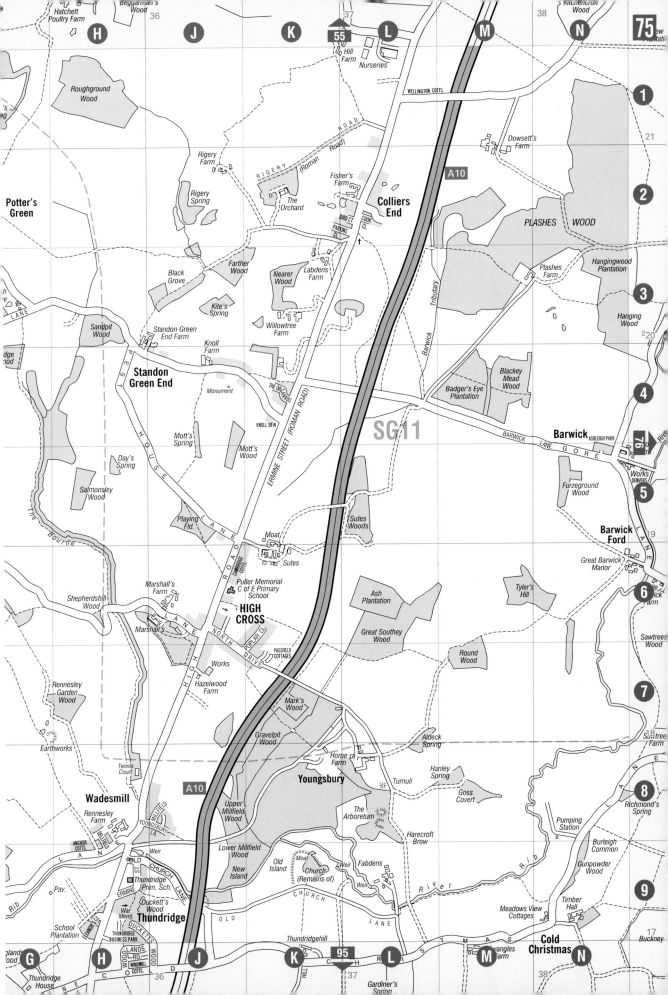

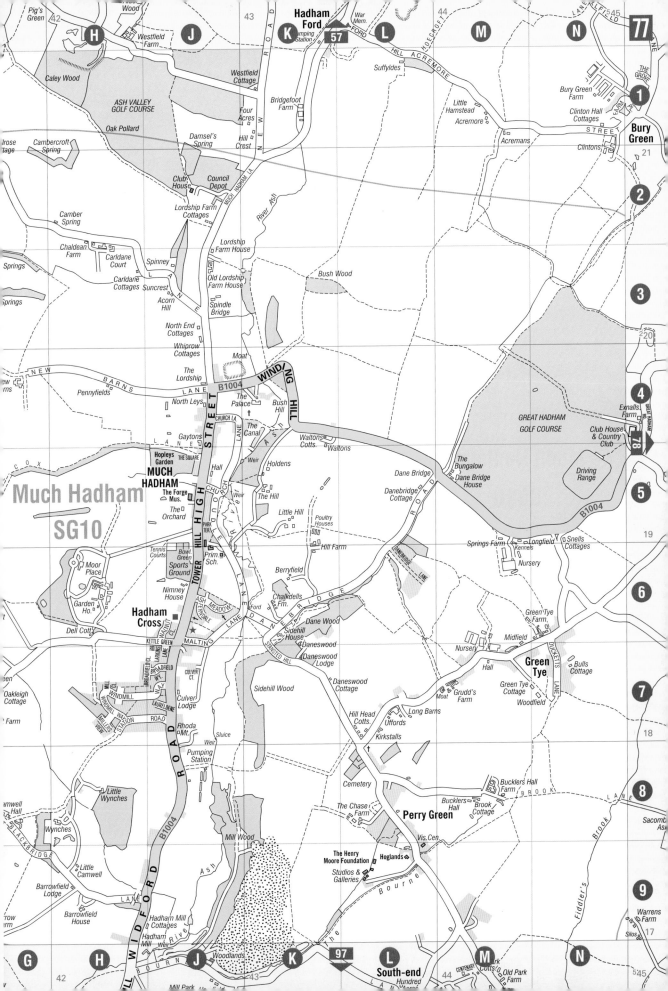

A   87   B   Thistle Brook   C   88   D   E   89   F   G

17

1   Wind Pump (Disused)   Whitwell Farm

Marstongate Langdale Cottages
Marstongate Station

2   Long Leys Farm
The Paddock   POTASH LANE   Old Toms Farm
16   Folly Farm   Red House Farm   Central Farm

3   DACORUM   AYLESBURY VALE   Fox Covert   All Saints' Church (Remains of)   Old Church Farm   STATION   CHAPEL LA.   ALDERPARK MDW.   Moat   Church Farm   Loxley   Sch   Church Farm   BROMLEY WK.

4   Millfield
Astrope
215   ASTROPE   Astrope Folly   Astrop Farm

Aylesbury
HP22   Manor Farm   Potash Farm   PUTTENHAM CT.   Dover Castle

5   Grange Farm   CHURCH RD.   Potash Bungalows
The Old Rectory   Puttenham
Draytonmead Farm   Rectory Farm

COLLEGE BUSINESS PARK   COLLEGE   Works

6   Merrymead Farm   Grand Union Canal (Aylesbur
Monks Court   PUTTENHAM
14   Grand Union Canal (Aylesbury Arm)   Weir   Red House   M   AI   N

7   COLLEGE ROAD   ROAD

College Farm

Aston Clinton Household Waste Recycling Centre   Subway

8   Dropshot Farm   A41   Cherry Farm
13   Works   NORTH   A   S   T   O   N   C   L   I   N   T   O   N   ICKNIELD

Lower Farm   B489   LOWER
9   Moat   Model Row   Buckland   BY   PASS   A41
TURNERS MDW.   Sunny Brook Farm   Moat   Sunningdale Farm
NORMILL TER.   AKEMAN STREET   AYLESBURY   ROAD   Moat Farm   Church Farm   Manor Cottage   Inglands
A   B   The Lawn   C   100   D   Buckland Ho.   E   F   Bannock
(Roman Road)   87   Brook Farm   Aston Clinton   88   89

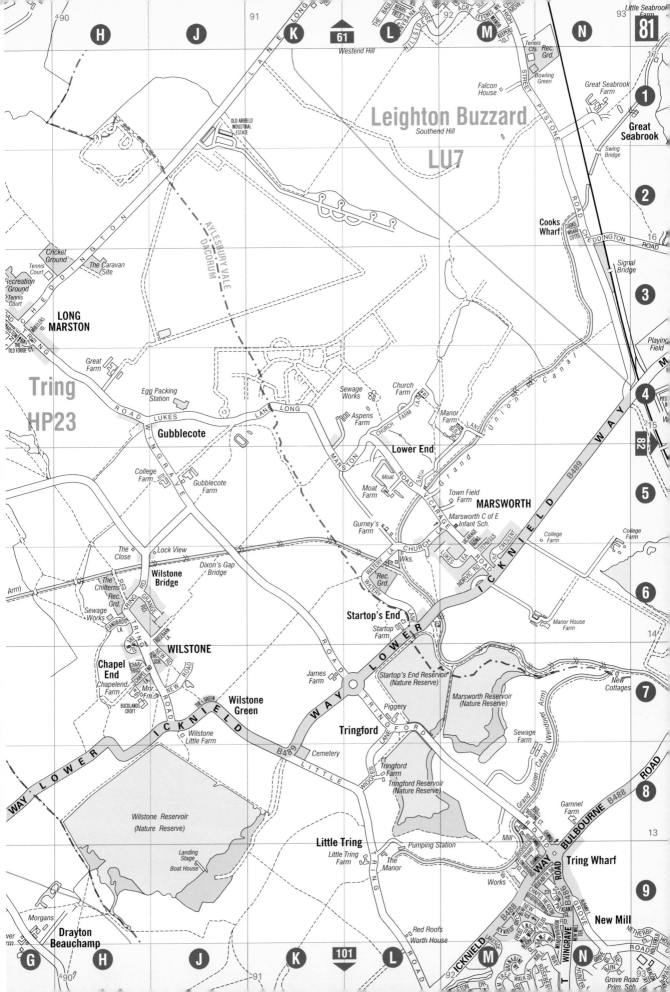

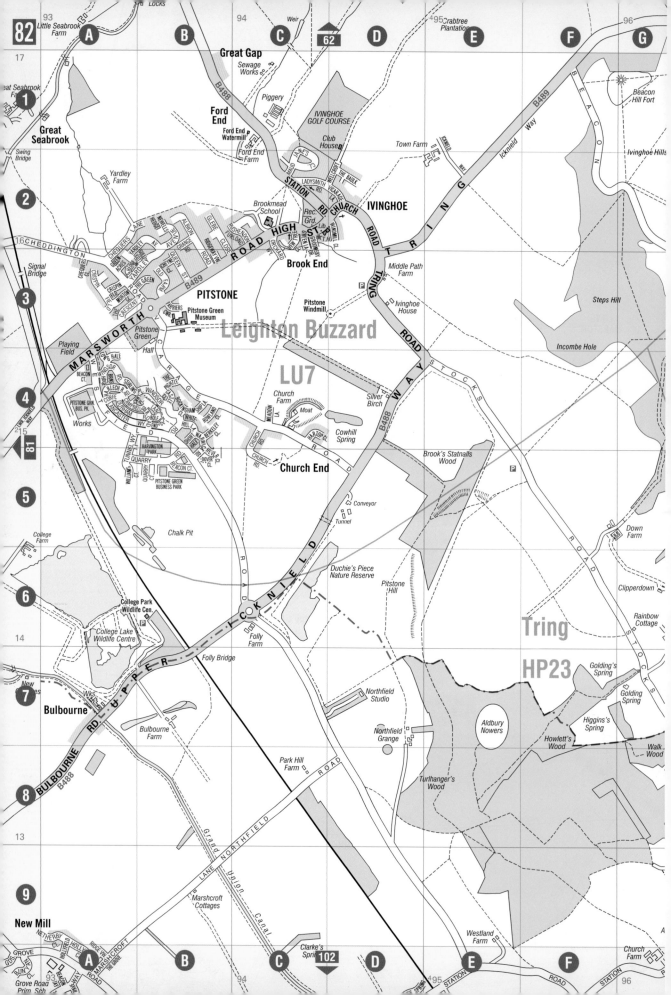

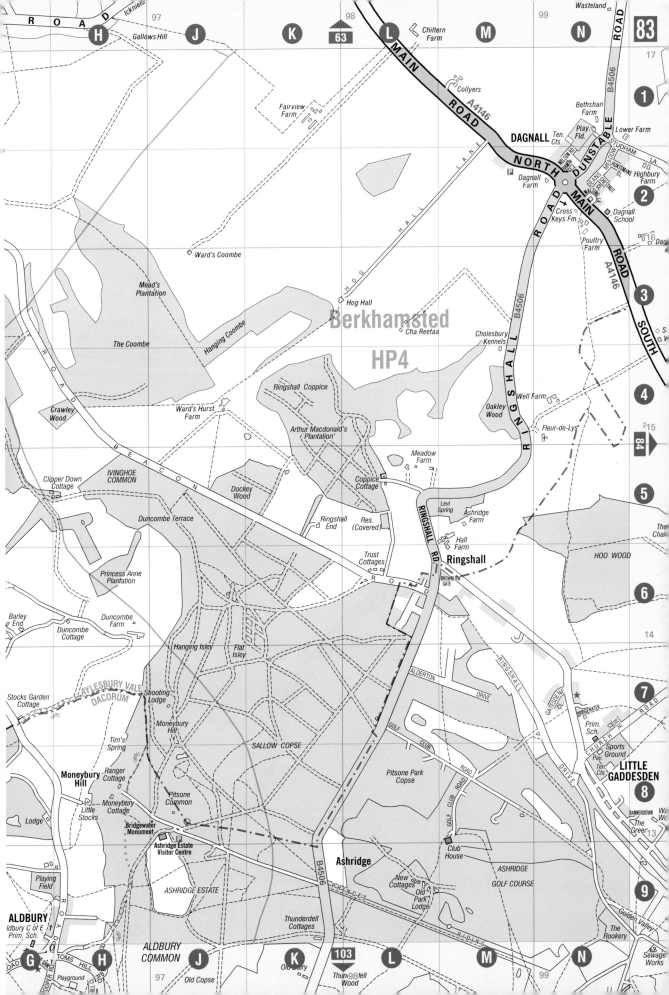

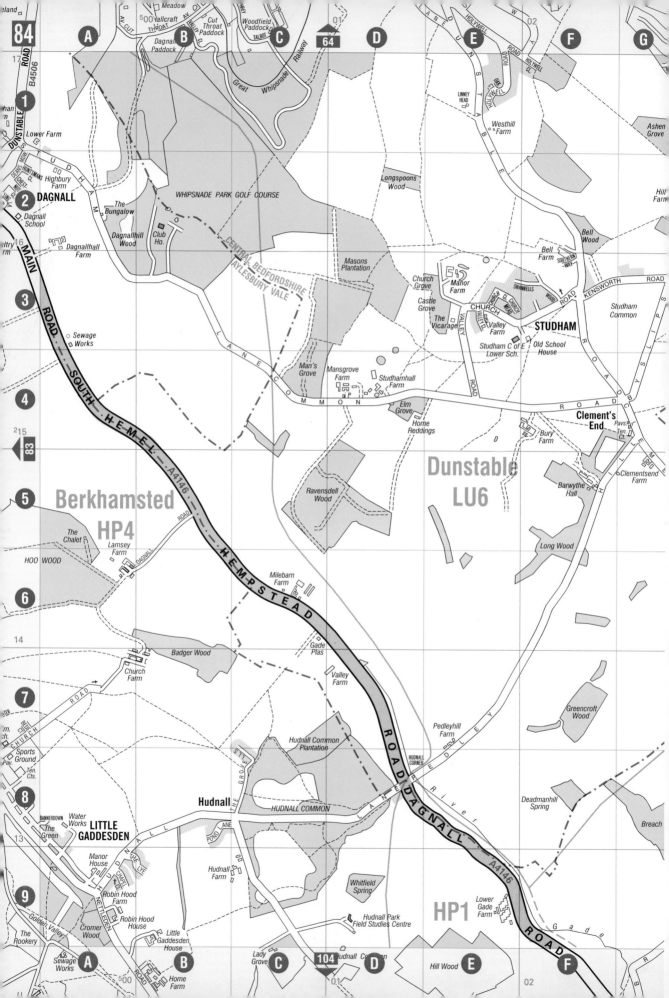

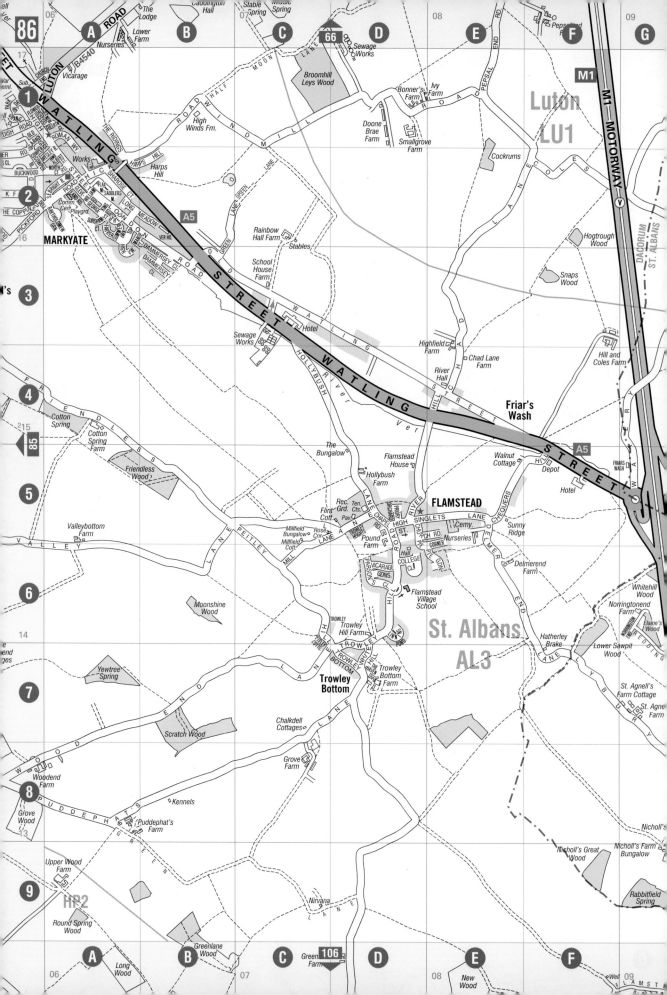

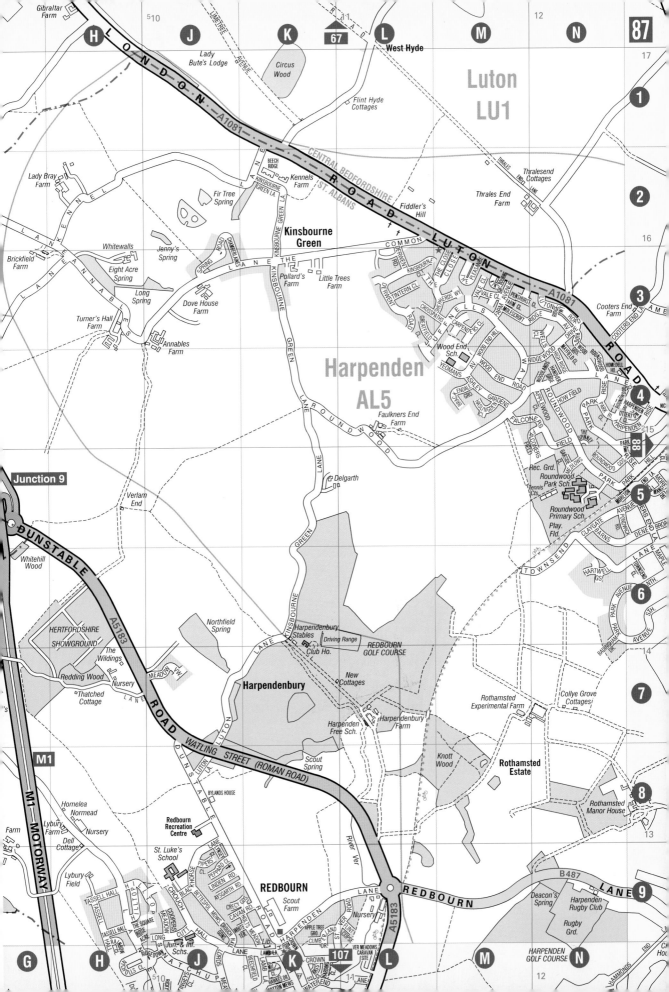

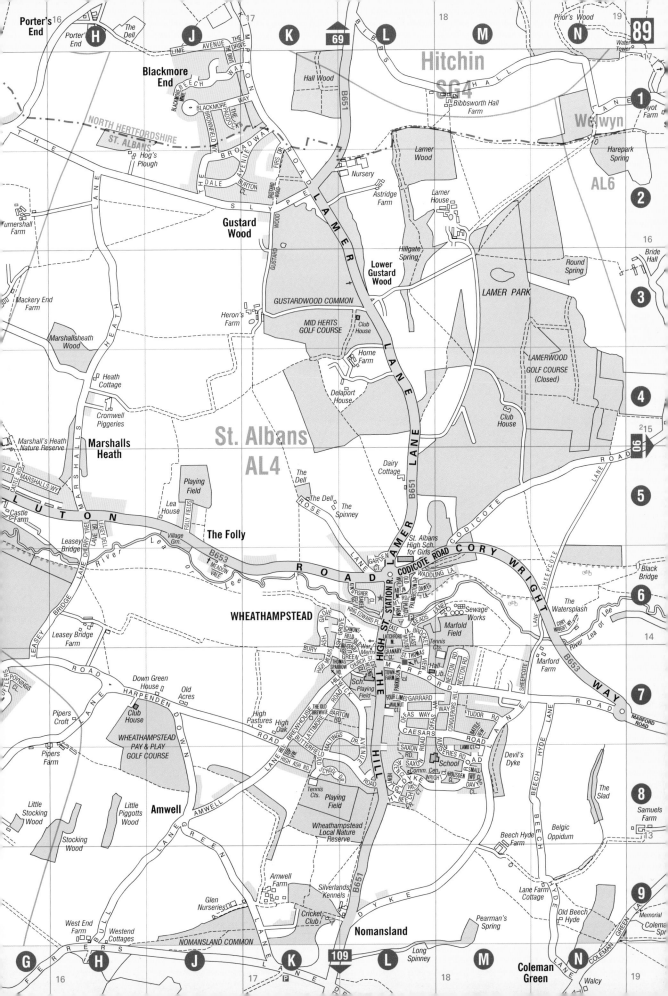

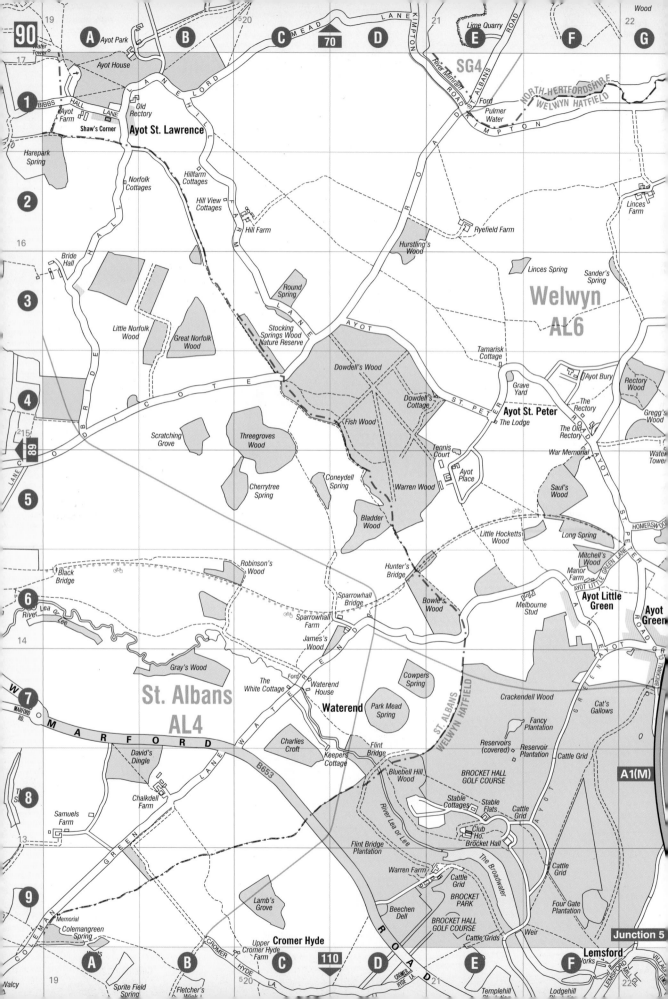

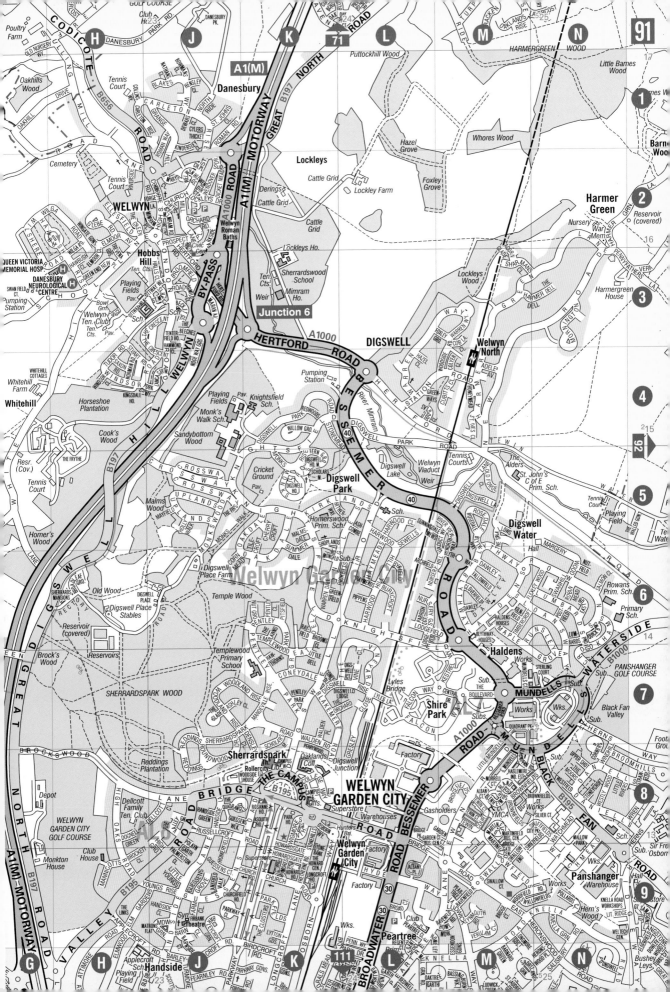

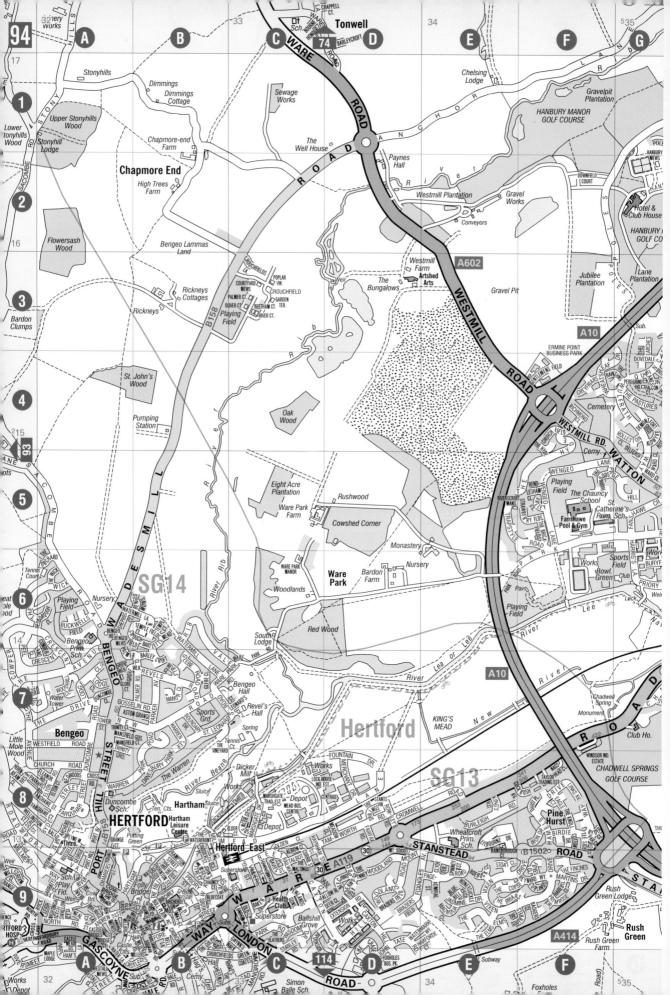

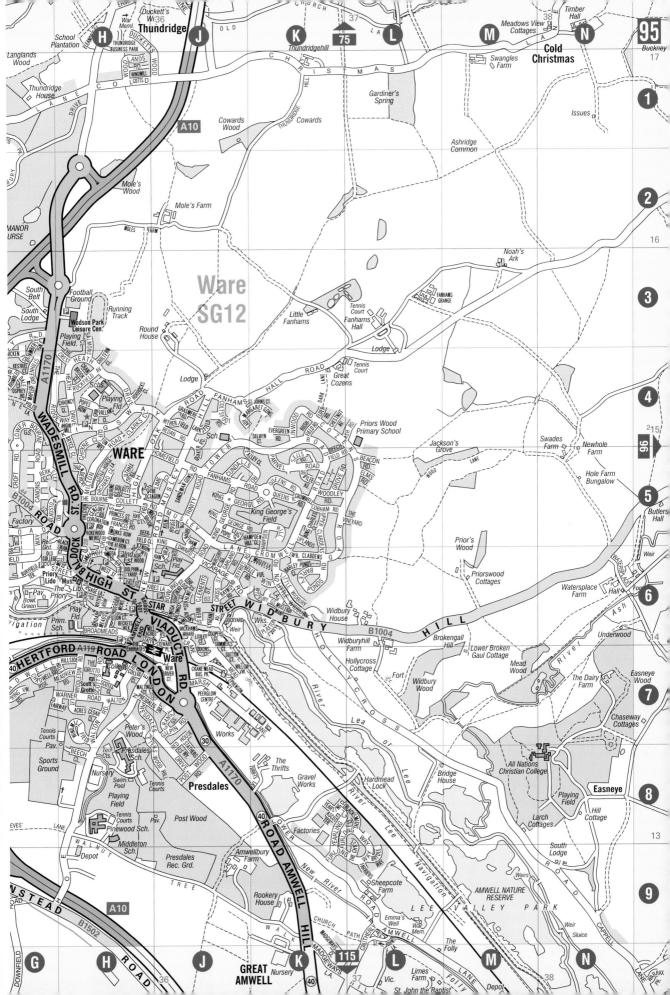

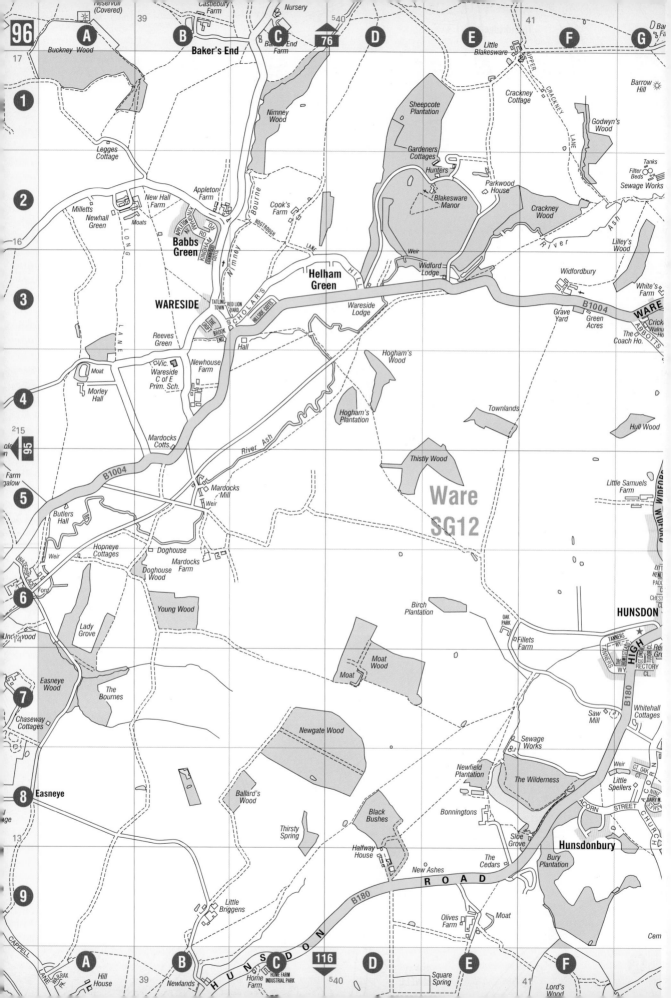

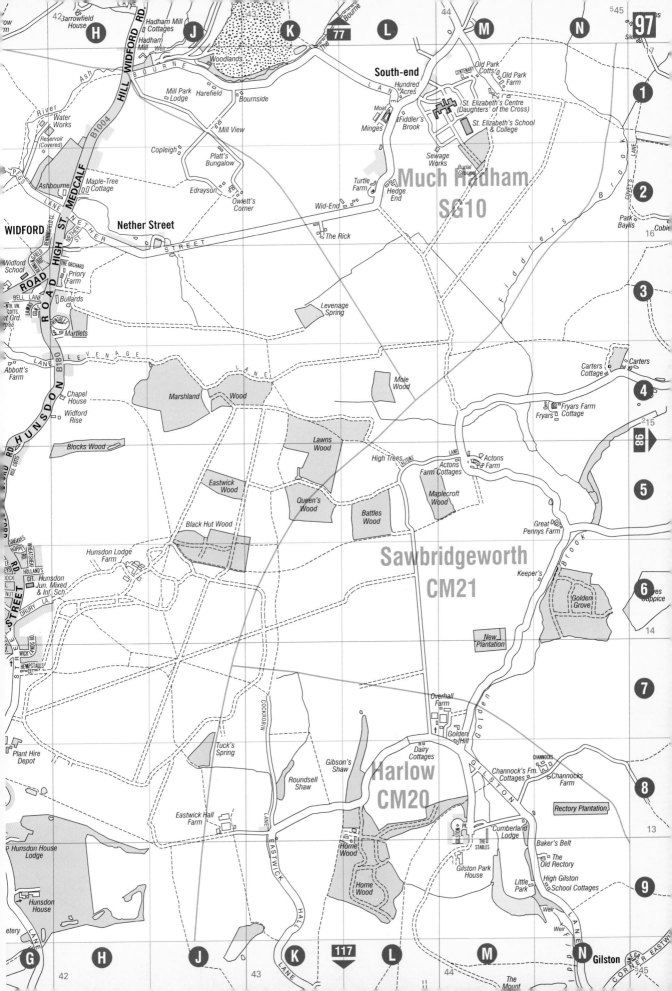

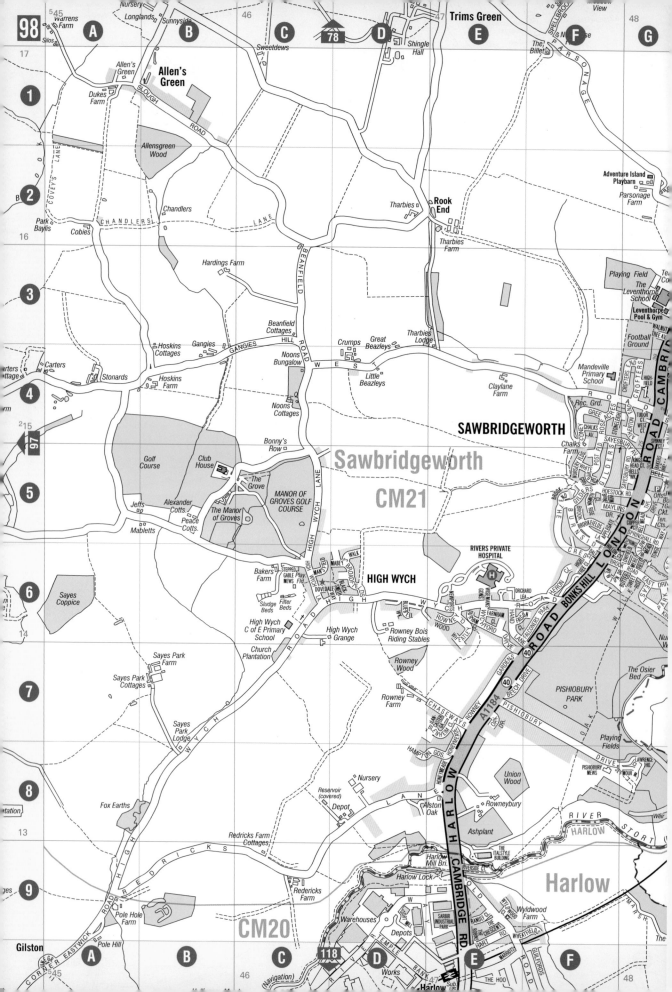

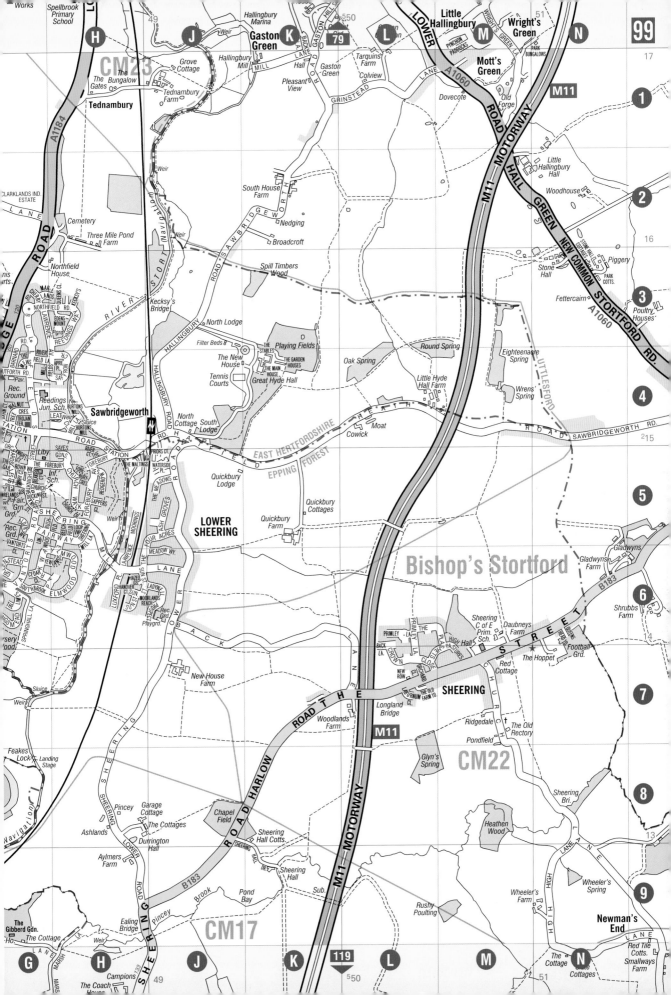

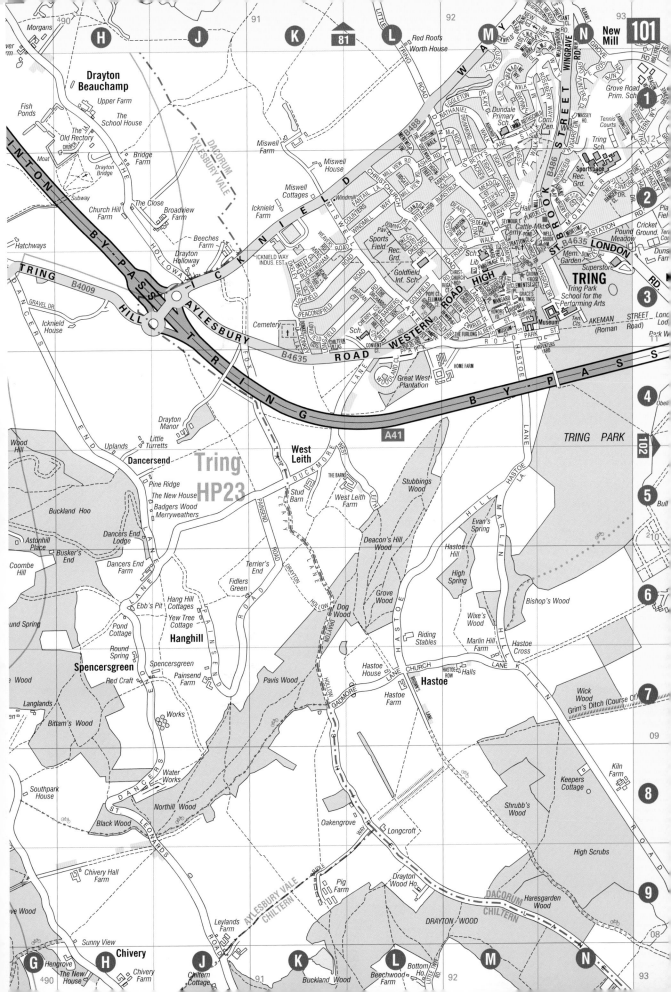

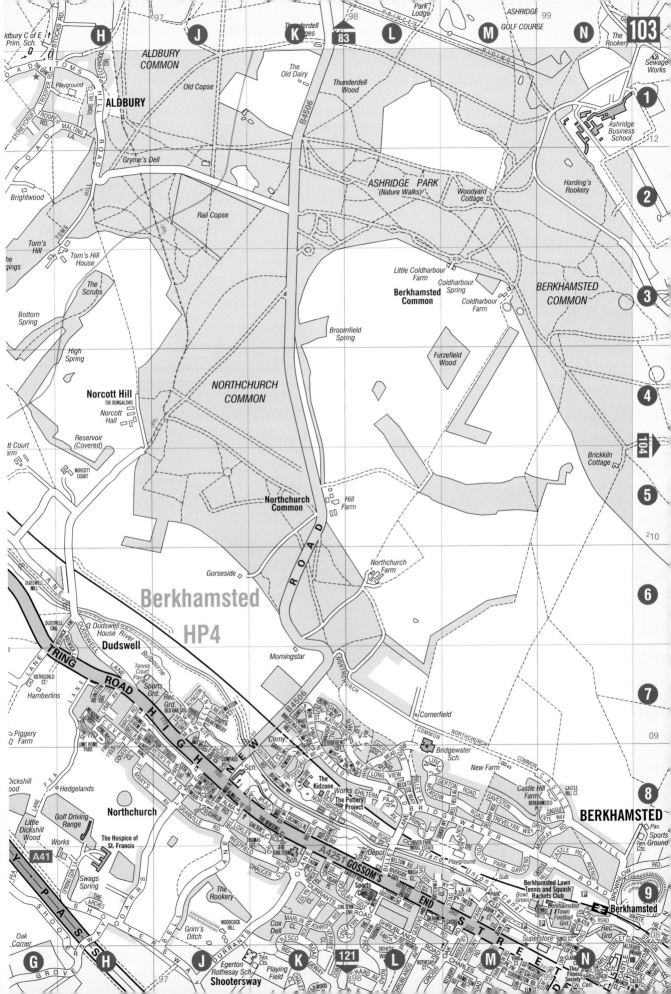

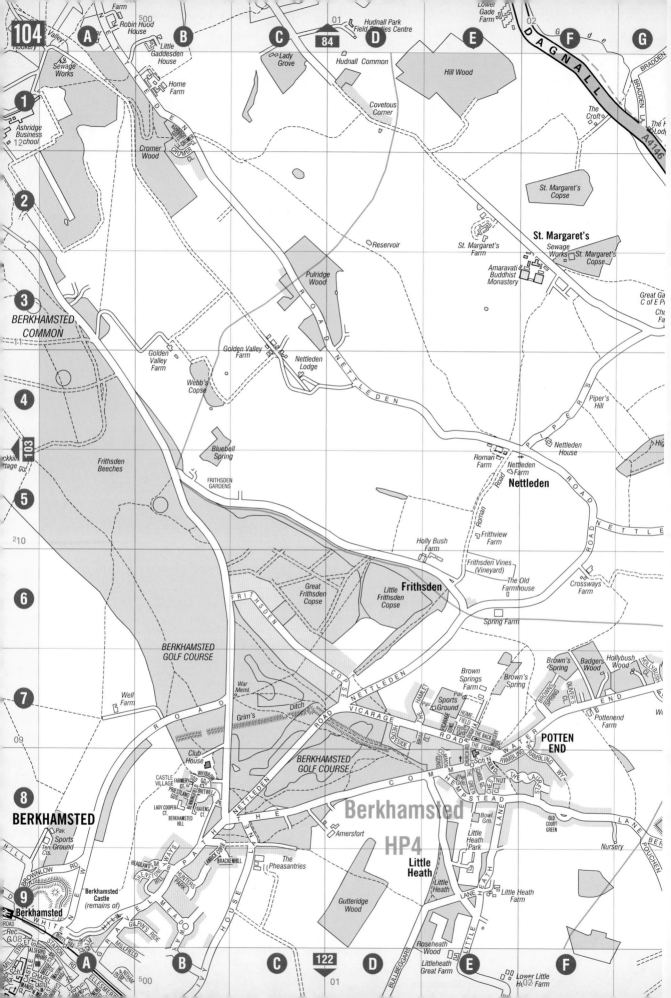

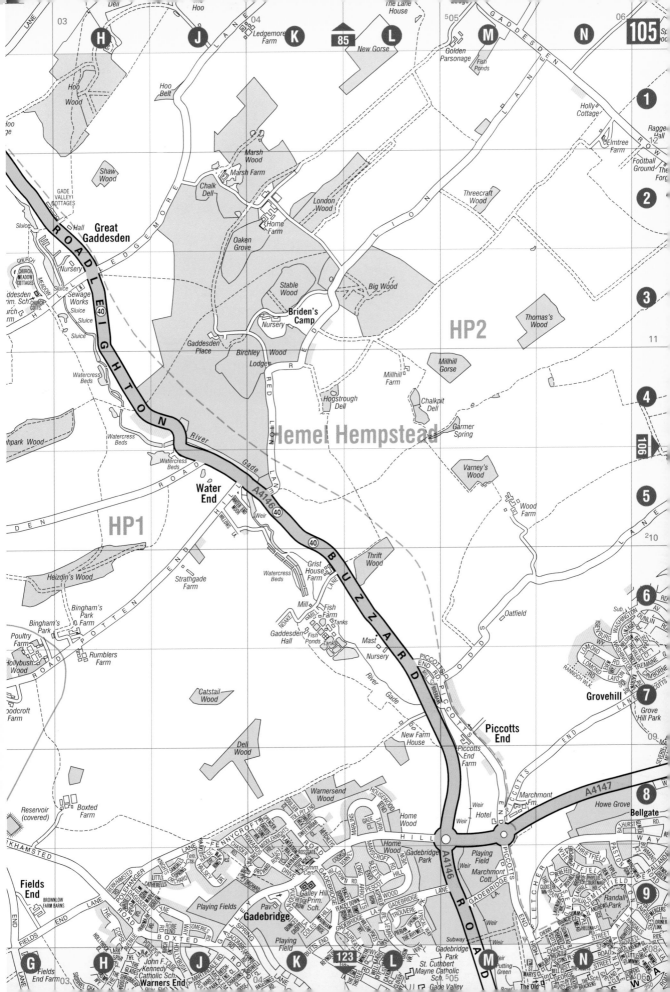

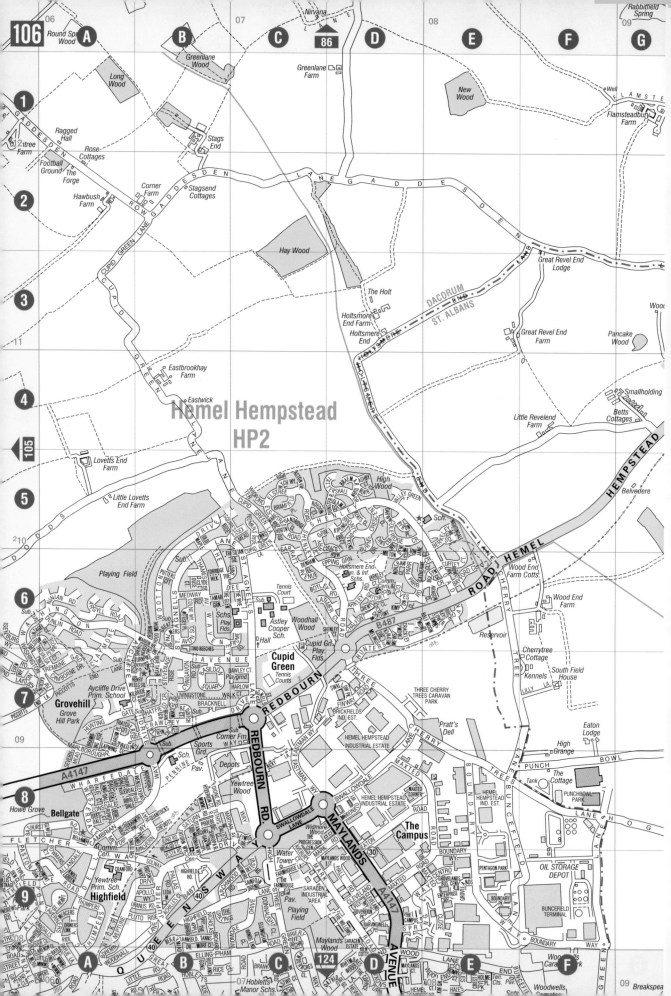

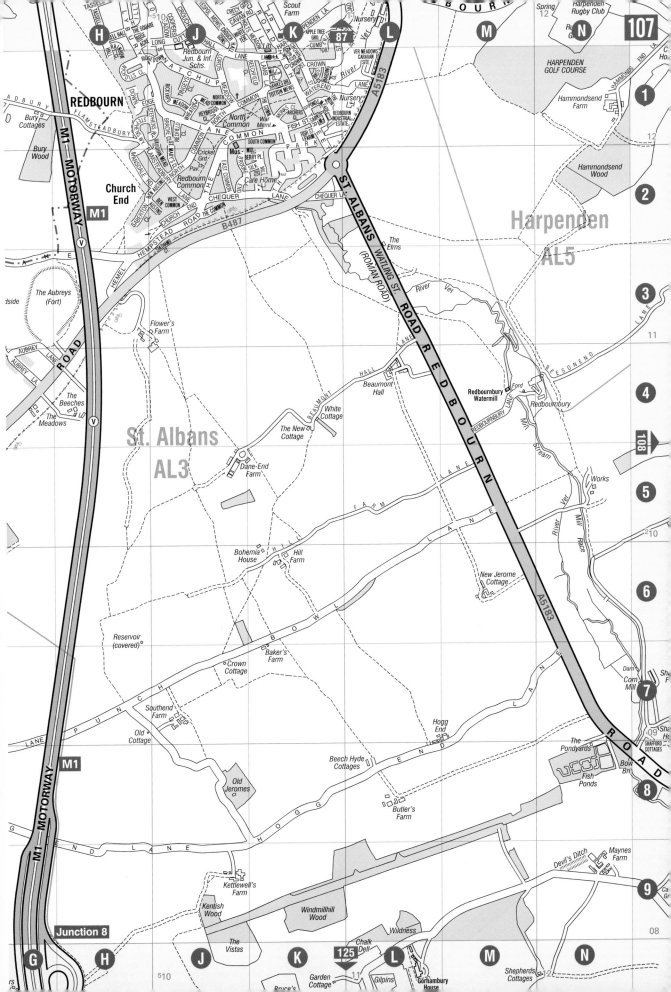

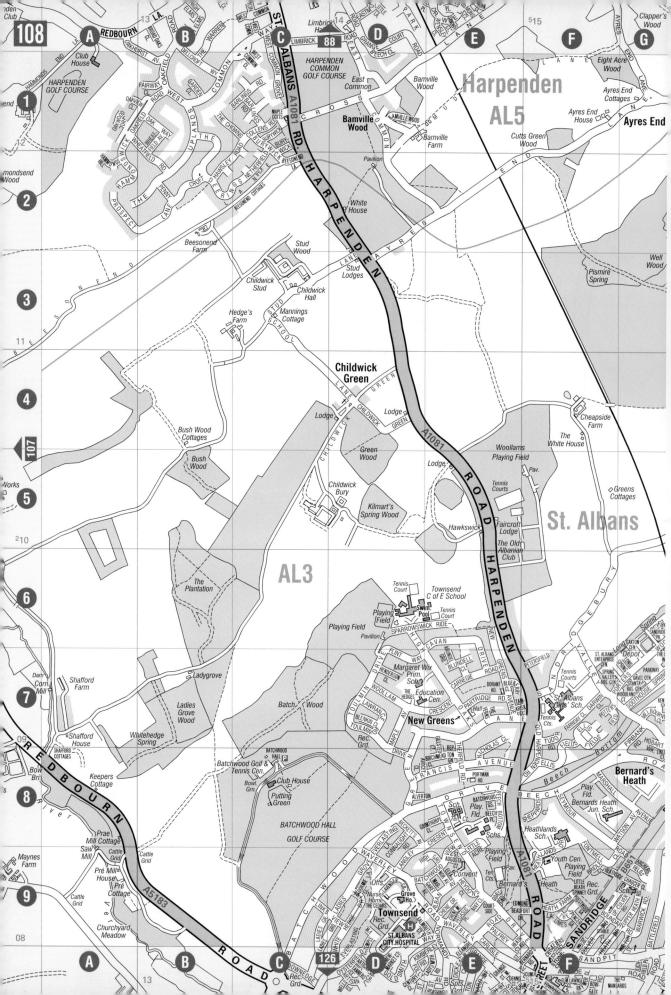

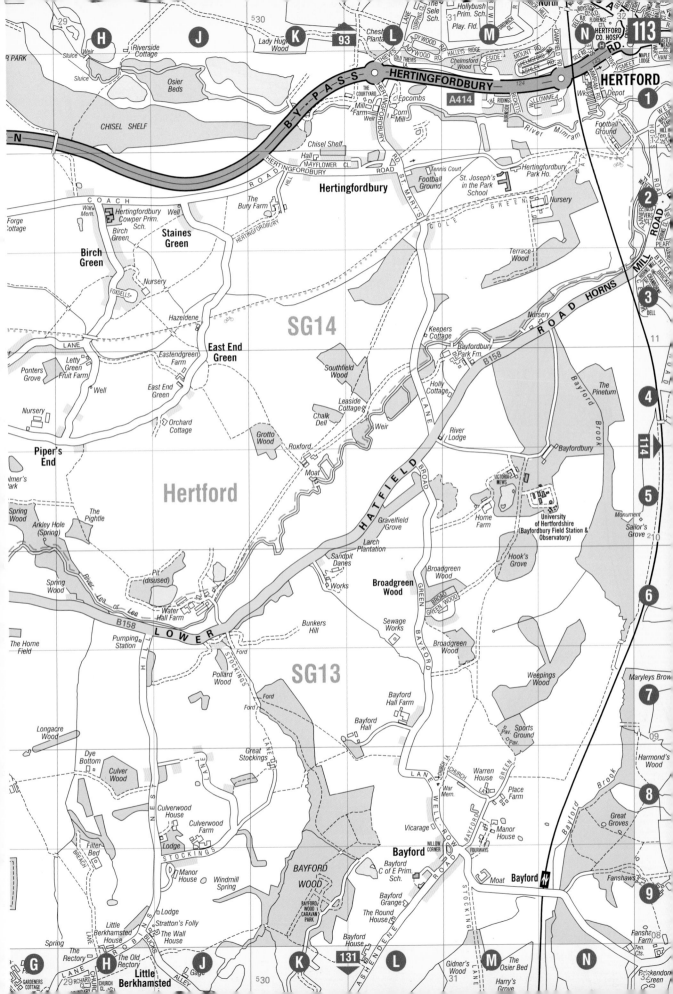

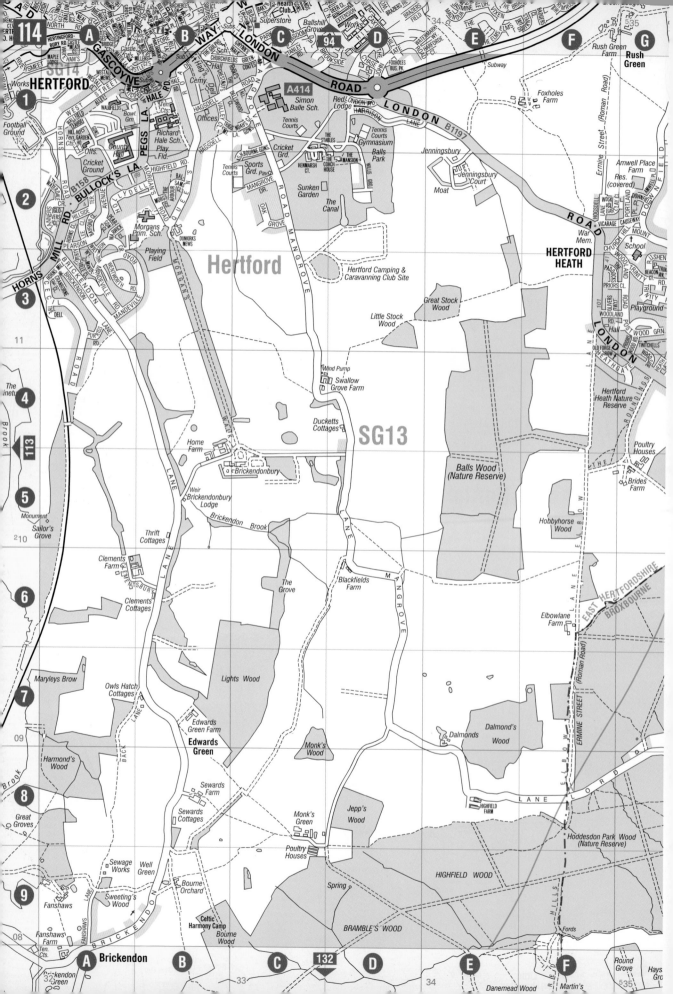

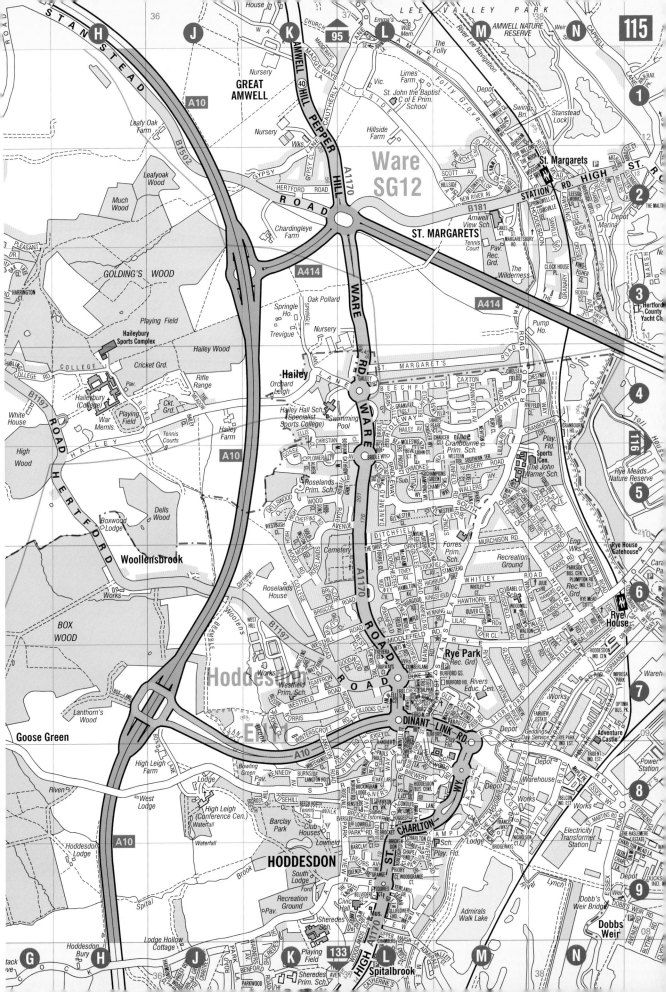

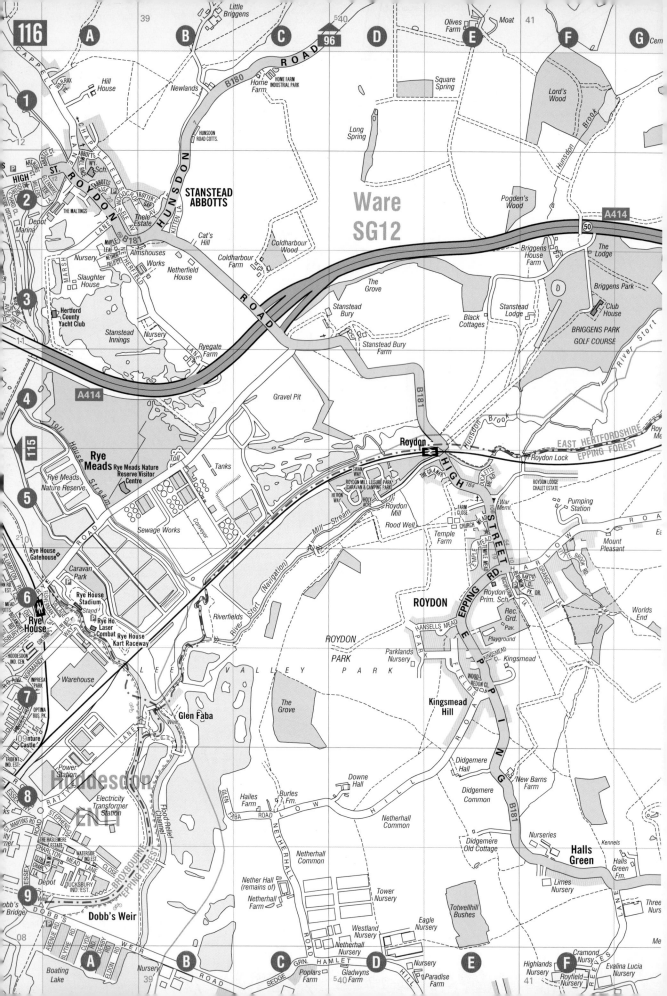

A B C 96 D E F G

Little Briggens
540
Olives Farm
Moat
Cem

1
39
41
WAR.RAX
Hill House
Newlands
B180
Home Farm
Home Farm Industrial Park
Square Spring
Lord's Wood
Hunsdon Brook
12

HIGH ST.
HUNSDON ROAD COTTS.
Long Spring

2
ROYDON
The Maltings
STANSTEAD ABBOTTS
Pogden's Wood
A414
50

Depot Marina
Thele Estate
Cat's Hill
Coldharbour Wood
The Lodge

3
Nursery
Almshouses
Works
Netherfield House
Coldharbour Farm
The Grove
Stanstead Lodge
Briggens House Farm
Briggens Park
Club House

Slaughter House
Hertford County Yacht Club
Stanstead Innings
Nursery
Stanstead Bury
Black Cottages
BRIGGENS PARK GOLF COURSE

11
Ryegate Farm
Stanstead Bury Farm
River Stort

4
A414
Gravel Pit
B181
Hunsdon Brook
EAST HERTFORDSHIRE
EPPING FOREST

115
Rye Meads
Rye Meads Nature Reserve Visitor Centre
Toll
Tanks
SWAN WAY
Roydon
Roydon Lock
Roydon Lodge Chalet Estate

5
Rye Meads Nature Reserve
Conveyor
Sewage Works
ROYDON MILL LEISURE PARK (CARAVAN & CAMPING PARK)
HERON WAY
HOLY ACRE
Roydon Mill
Rood Well
THE GRANARY
DUCKETTS MEAD
FARM CLOSE
CHURCH
Pumping Station
Mount Pleasant

210
Rye House Gatehouse
Mill Stream
Temple Farm
War Meml.
TEMPLE MEAD
HIGH STREET

6
Caravan Park
Rye House Stadium
Stand
Rye Ho. Laser Combat
Rye House Kart Raceway
Riverfields
River Stort (Navigation)
ROYDON PARK PARK
HANSELLS MEAD
ROYDON
Roydon Prim. Sch.
Rec. Grd.
Pav.
Worlds End

Rye House
Warehouse
ROYDON PARK
Parklands Nursery
Kingsmead
Kingsmead Hill

7
IMPRESA PARK
OPTIMA BUS. PK.
TRIDENT IND. EST.
Glen Faba
Weir
LEE VALLEY PARK
The Grove
Kingsmead Hill
EPPING ROAD

109 nture Castle
Power Station
Didgemere Hall
New Barns Farm

8
Hoddesdon
EN11
Electricity Transformer Station
GLEN FABA ROAD
Hailes Farm
Burles Fm.
Downe Hall
Netherhall Common
Didgemere Common
B181
Nurseries
Kennels

The Haslemere Estate
WATERSIDE IND. EST.
Depot
DUCKSBURY IND. EST.
BROXBOURNE EPPING FOREST
Nether Hall (remains of)
Netherhall Farm
Halls Green
Halls Green Fm.

9
08
Weir
Dobb's Bridge
Dobb's Weir
AVENUE RD.
CLYDE RD.
BLYTHE RD.
ELDON RD.
DERBY RD.
WEIR ROAD
Nursery
SEDGE GRN.
Poplars Farm
540
Gladwyns Farm
NETHERHALL HAMLET
HILL
Westland Nursery
Netherhall Nursery
Eagle Nursery
Paradise Farm
Totwellhill Bushes
Limes Nursery
Cramond Nursy.
Highlands Nursery
Royfield Nursery
Evalina Lucia Nursery

Boating Lake
A
39
B
C
D
41
E
F

Ware SG12

39 540 41

A B C D E F

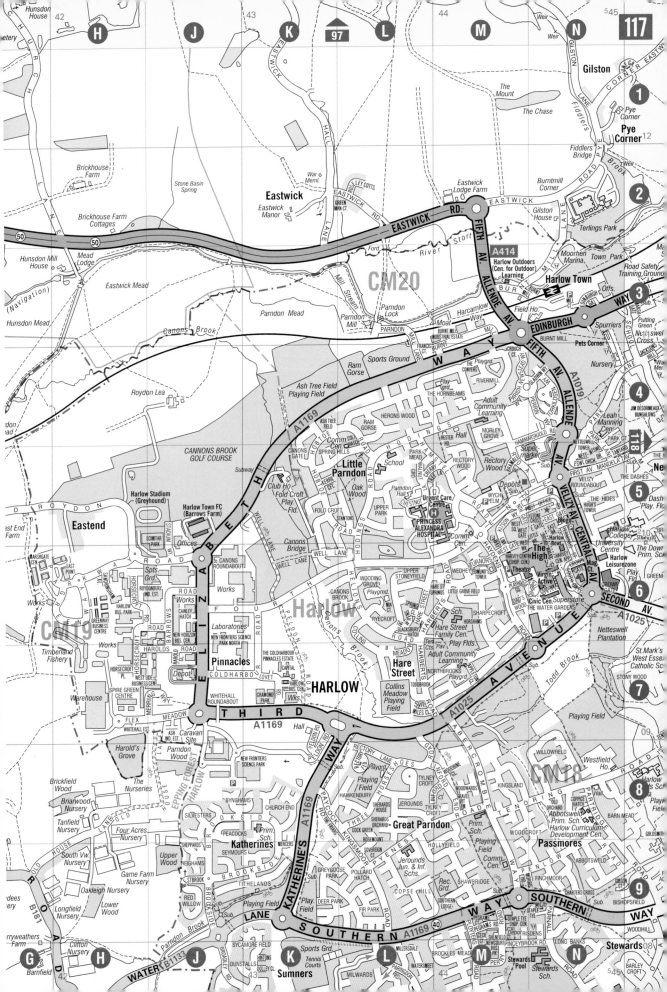

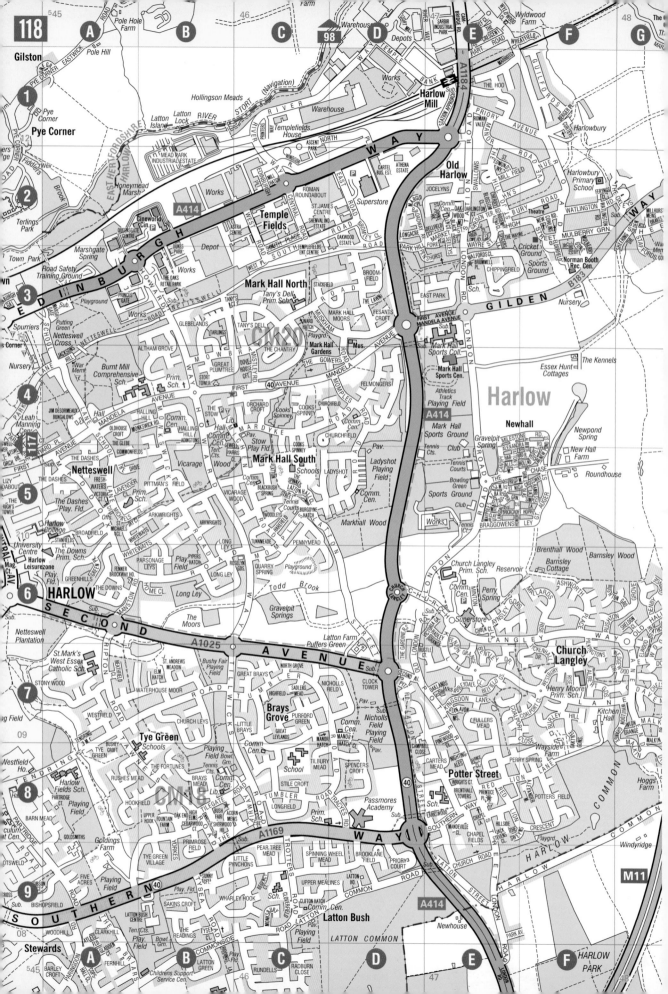

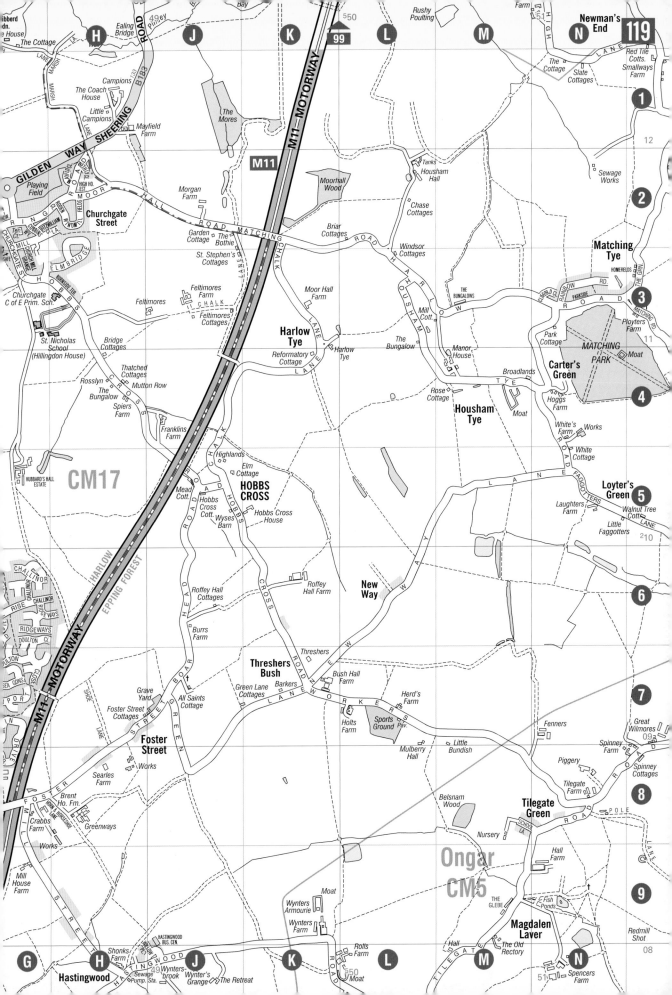

Newman's End

H J K L M N

Ealing Bridge

Rushy Poulting

The Cottage

Red Tile Cotts.
Smallways
Farm

Slate Cottages
The Cottage

Sewage Works

Campions

The Coach House

Little Campions

Mayfield Farm

Morgan Farm

The Mores

Moorhall Wood

Tanks
Housham Hall

Chase Cottages

Matching Tye

Churchgate Street

Garden Cottage
The Bothie
St. Stephen's Cottages

Briar Cottages

Windsor Cottages

The Bungalows

Homefields
The Grn.

Playing Field

Feltimores Farm
Feltimores
Feltimores Cottages

Moor Hall Farm

Mill Cott.

Parkside

Ployters Farm

Churchgate C of E Prim. Sch.

Bridge Cottages

Harlow Tye

Reformatory Cottage

Harlow Tye

The Bungalow

Manor House

Park Cottage

MATCHING PARK

Carter's Green

Moat

St. Nicholas School (Hillingdon House)

Thatched Cottages
Mutton Row

Rosslyn
The Bungalow
Spiers Farm

Broadlands

Hoggs Farm

Rose Cottage

Housham Tye

Moat

White's Farm
Works

White Cottage

HUBBARD'S HALL ESTATE

Franklins Farm

Highlands

Elm Cottage

HOBBS CROSS

Loyter's Green

Laughters Farm

Walnut Tree Cotts

CM17

Mead Cott.

Hobbs Cross Cott.

Wyses Barn

Hobbs Cross House

Little Faggotters

Roffey Hall Cottages

Roffey Hall Farm

New Way

HARLOW

EPPING FOREST

M11 MOTORWAY

Burrs Farm

Threshers

Threshers Bush

Bush Hall Farm

Herd's Farm

Fenners

Great Wilmores

Grave Yard

All Saints Cottage

Green Lane Cottages
Barkers

Holts Farm

Sports Ground Pav.

Spinney Farm

Foster Street Cottages

Foster Street

Mulberry Hall

Little Bundish

Piggery

Tilegate Farm

Spinney Cottages

Searles Farm

Works

Belsnam Wood

Tilegate Green

Hall Farm

Brent Ho. Fm.

Greenways

Nursery

SCHOOL LA.

Crabbs Farm

Works

Mill House Farm

Ongar CM5

THE GLEBE

Fish Ponds

Redmill Shot

Wynters Armourie

Wynters Farm

Magdalen Laver

The Old Rectory

G H J K L M N

Hastingwood

Shonks Farm

HASTINGWOOD BUS. CEN.

Sewage Pump. Sta.

Wynter's Grange

The Retreat

Rolls Farm

Moat

Hall

Spencers Farm

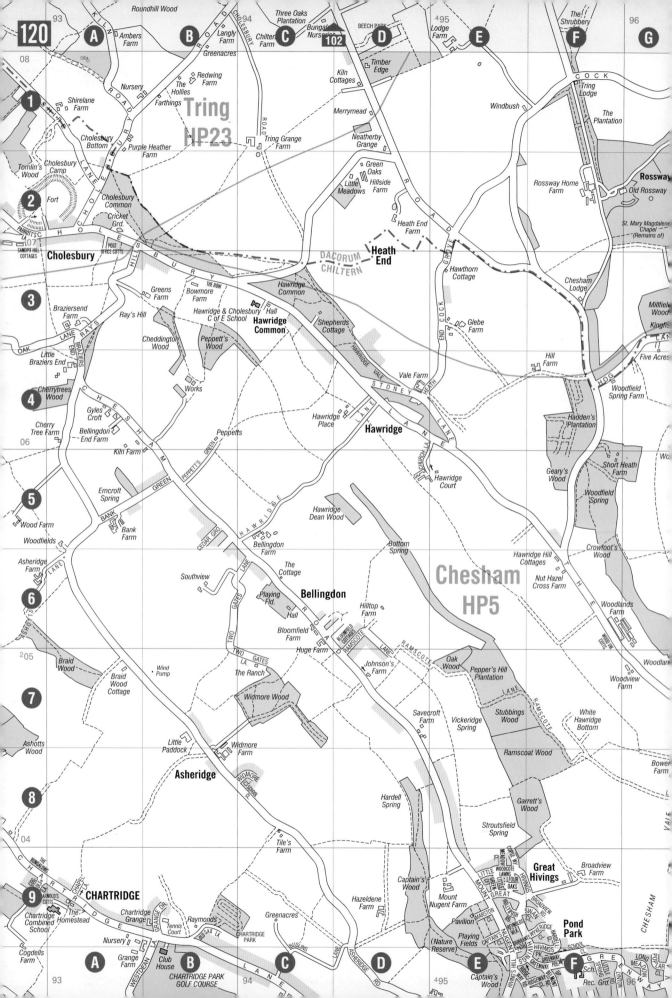

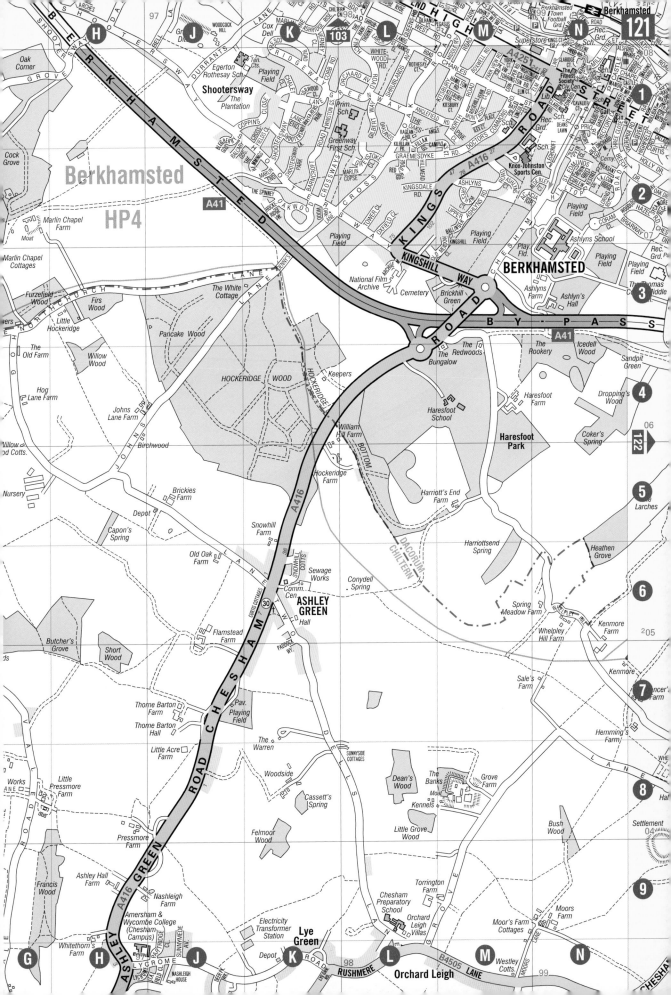

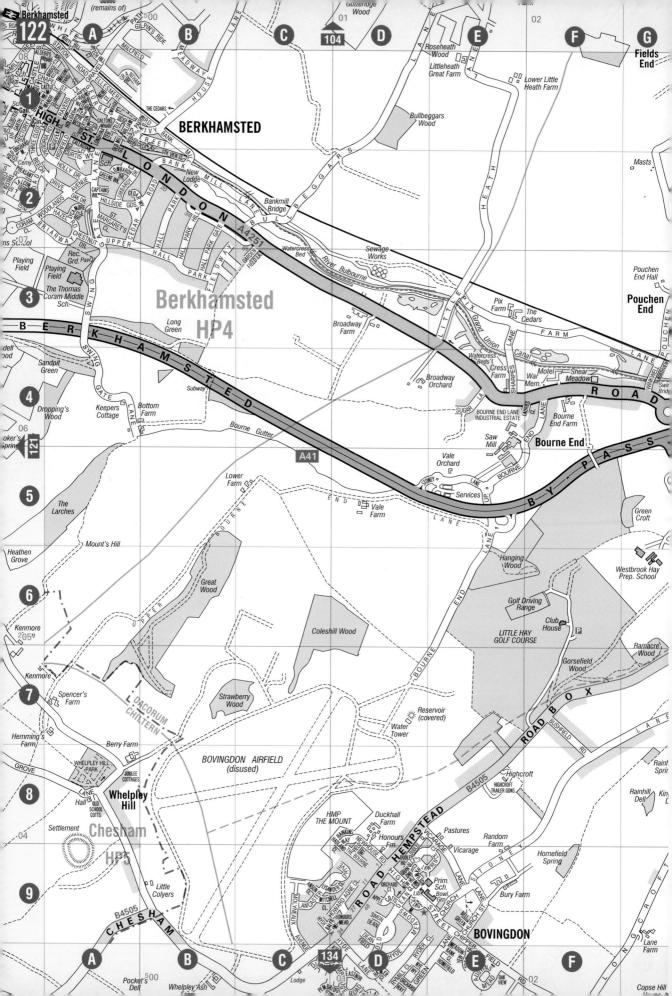

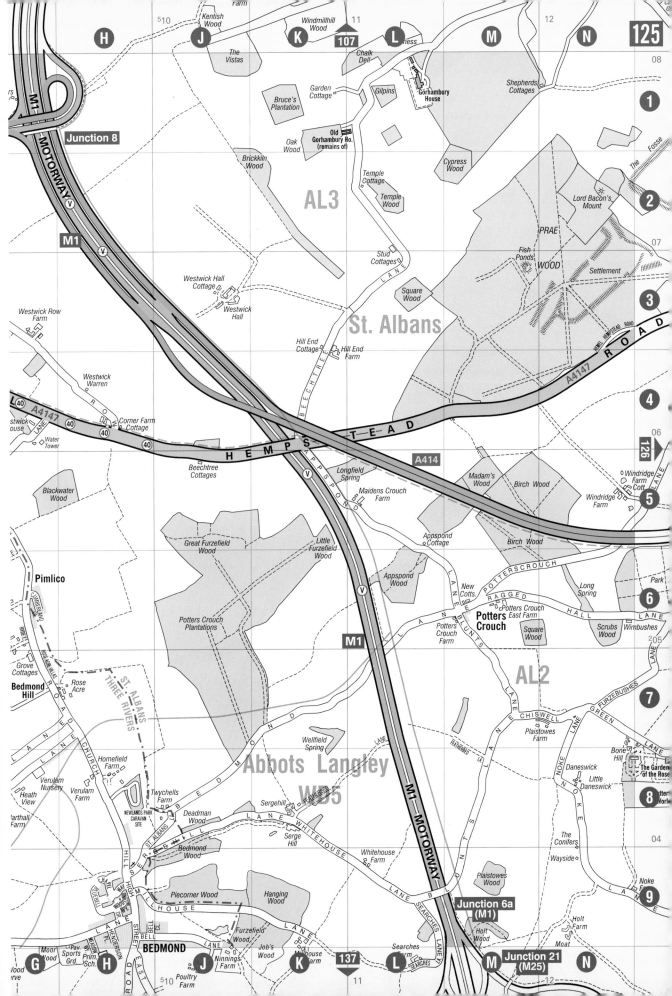

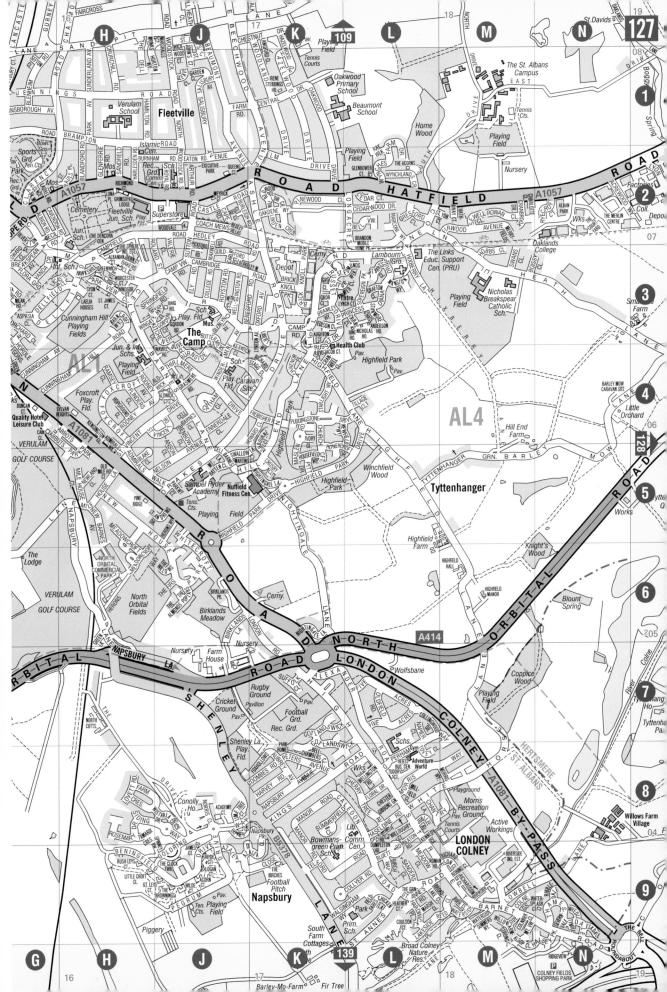

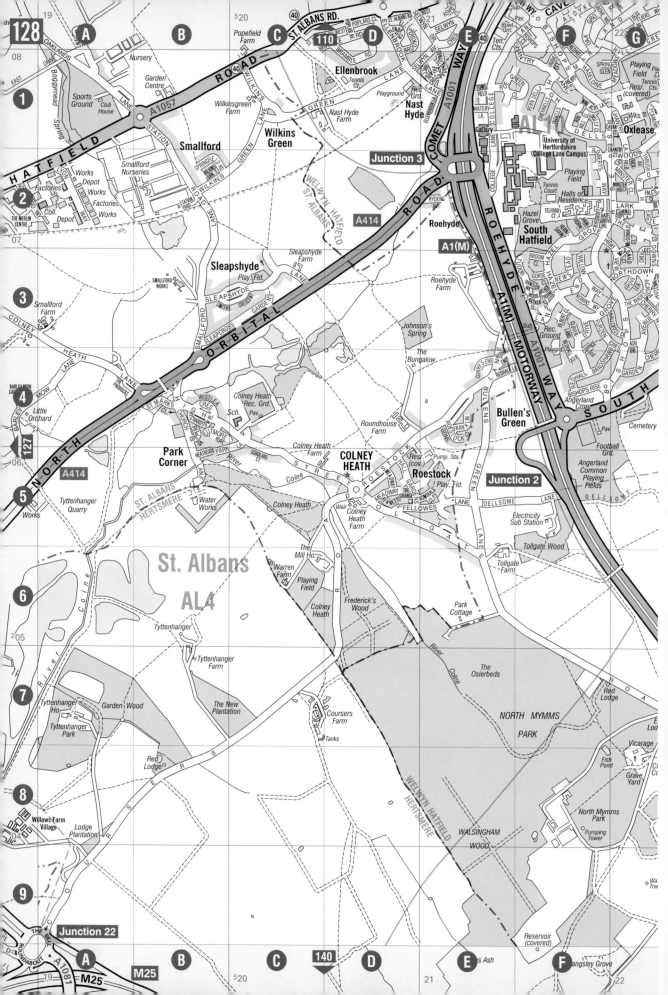

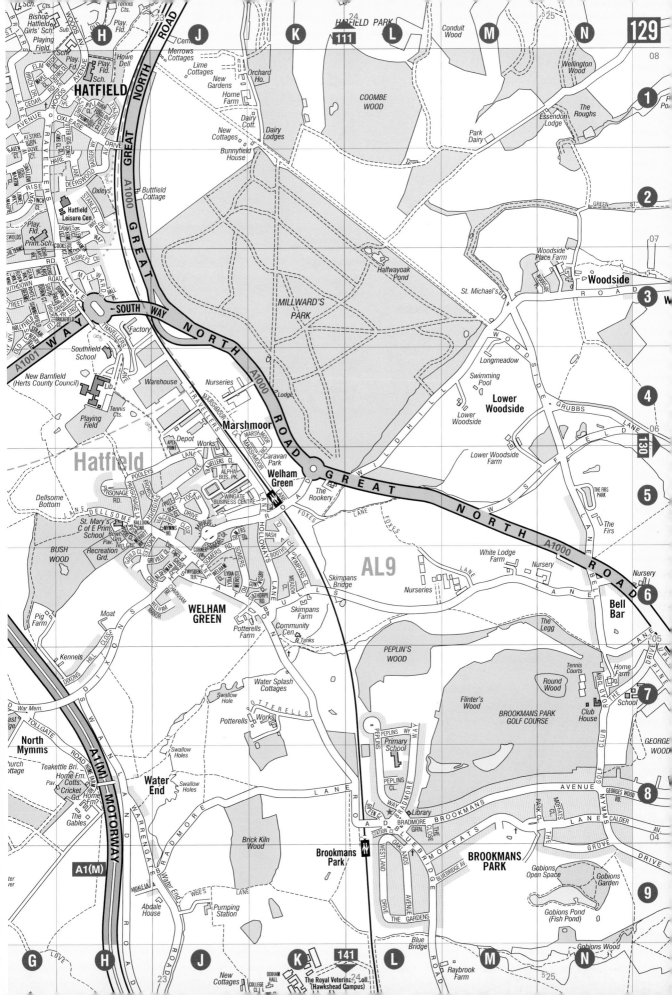

A B C D E F G

112

08

26

27

28

Sandpit Grove

1 Pope's Pondholes

Deeve Wood

Pope's Farm

Harefield Wood

Long Wood

ESSENDON PLACE

ESSENDON GOLF & COUNTRY CLUB

THE COURTYARD

BEDWELL HALL

BEDWELL PARK

Berkhamsted Lane Plantation

Essendon Place Farm

2 GREEN STREET

07

Bath Wood

Home Wood

Wildhill Brook

Poultry House

Belvedere Farm

Panther's Wood

Tennis Cts.

Bedwell Lodge Farm

Cucumber Hall Farm

WELWYN HATFIELD
EAST HERTFORDSHIRE

Woodside

WILDHILL

Brewhouse Farm

Waterfalls

CAMFIELD PLACE

Camfield Farm

Duncan's Wood

Little Elephant

Hoppett's Wood

Whitbury Wood

3 Woodside Green

Wildhill

Nursery

Riding School

WARRENWOOD MEWS

Warren Wood

Meadow Cottage

Nine Acre Wood

Birch Wood

Hatfield AL9

The Lodge

Warren Wood

4 GRUBBS

06

Westfield Lodge

Woodhill

Chestnut Farm

Birchwood Cotts.

129

Woodhill House

Woodhill Farm

THE FIRS PARK

5 Westfield Ho.

Woodhill Farm

WOODFIELD

Woodfield Farm

Coldharbour Farm

The Firs

Kentish Lane Farm

Barbers Lodge Farm

Nursery

6 Mast

Water Tower

Reservoir (covered)

Hell Wood

Bell Bar

Mast

205

Bell

Mast

Brookmans Park Transmitting Station

Edge House

Coldharbour Plantation

Home Farm

Mast

Mymfield

Broombarns Wood

7 Chancellor's School

ROWBOURNE HILL

GEORGE'S WOOD

8 GEORGES WOOD ROAD

CALDER

SHRUBLANDS

AVENUE

CALDER AV.

WOODLANDS

GREAT WOOD COUNTRY PARK

Great Wood Visitors Centre

04

MYMMS

Monkswell

Grimes Brook

Gobions Garden

SHEPHERDS

The Cottages

Mymwood Ho.

B157

9 Woodside Cottages

Tennis Courts

Sheepwell Cotts.

Pavs.

CHAPEL

Playing Field

Woodlands

WELL WOOD

Potters Bar

142

Queen School

Vine Cottage

STABLE MEWS

26

A B C D E F

28

133

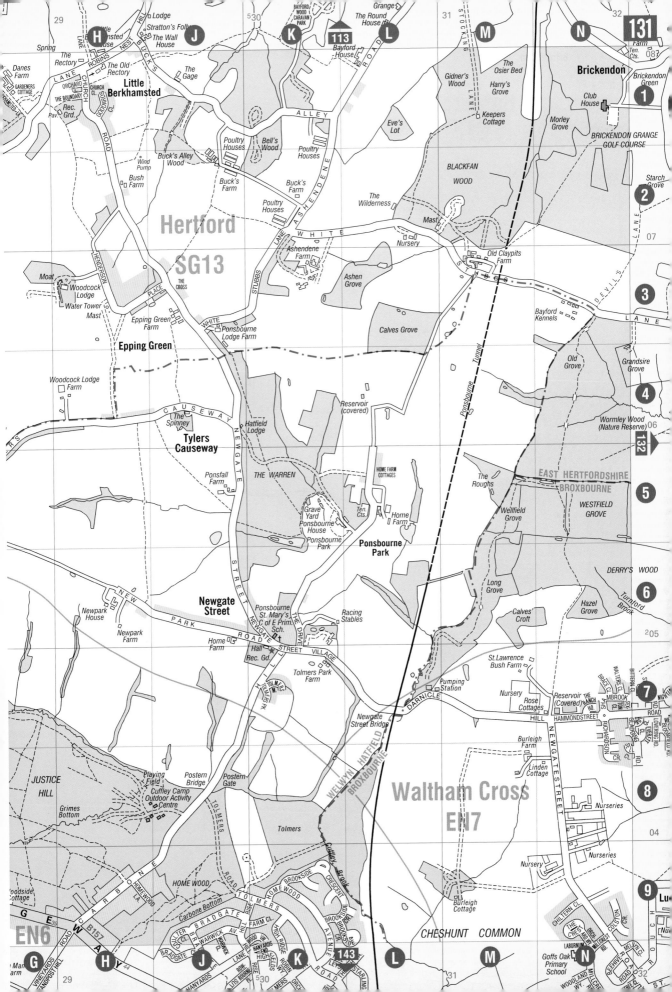

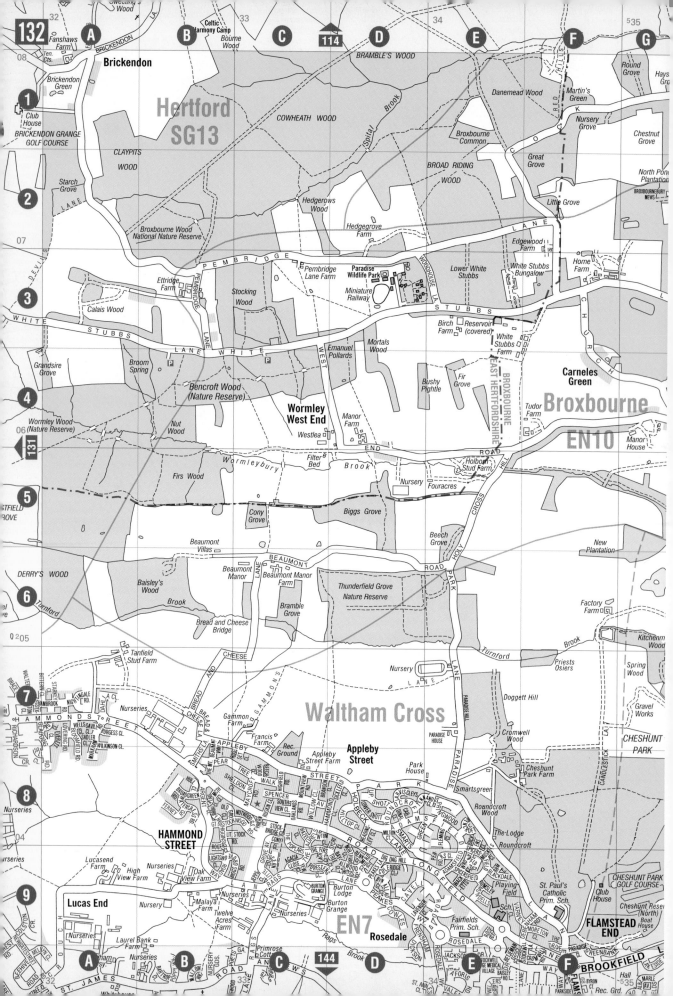

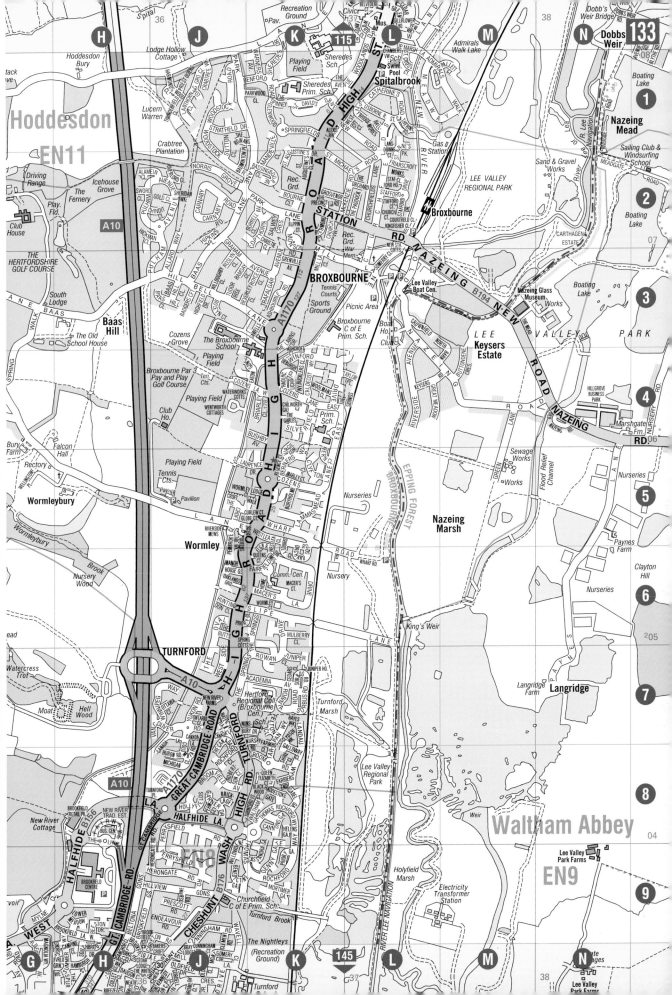

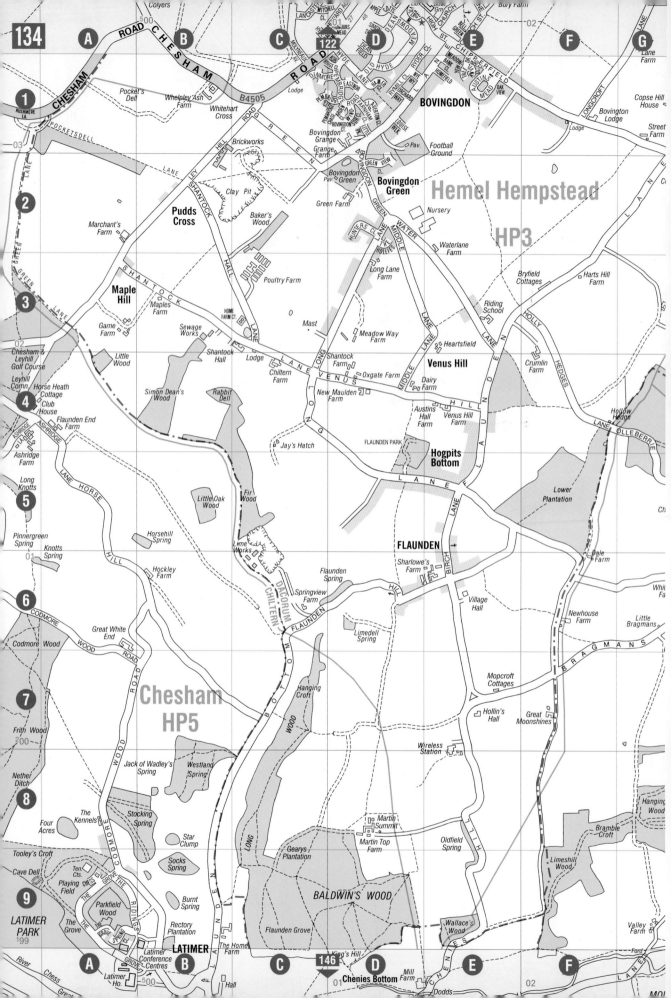

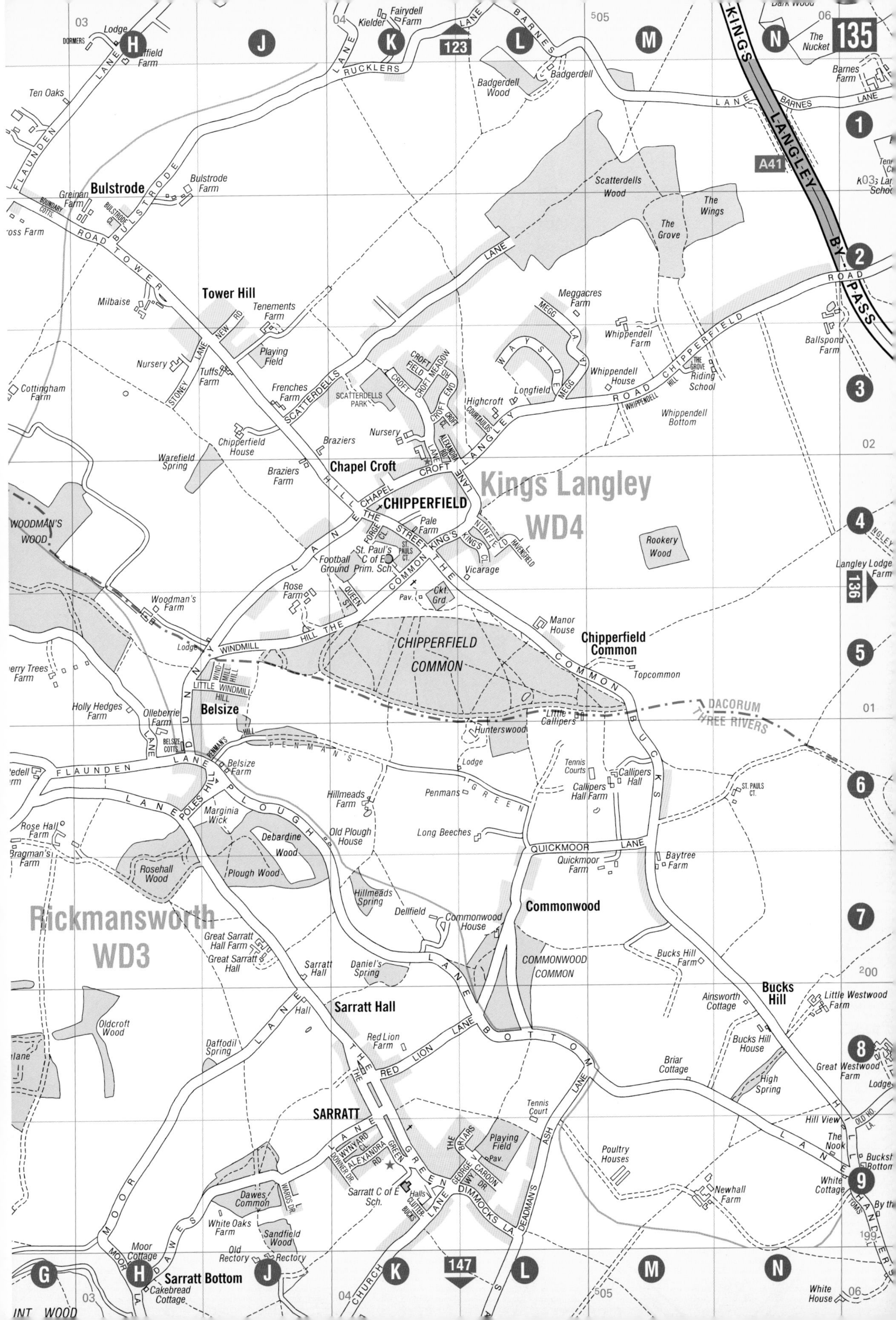

Fairydell Farm
Kielder
Lodge
DORMERS
Duffield Farm
RUCKLERS LANE
BARNES LANE
123
Badgerdell Wood
Badgerdell
The Nucket
Barnes Farm
KINGS LANGLEY BY-PASS
A41
Ten Oaks
FLAUNDEN LANE
Bulstrode
Bulstrode Farm
Greinan Farm
BOUNDARY COTTS.
BULSTRODE CL.
BULSTRODE LANE
TOWER ROAD
Scatterdells Wood
The Wings
The Grove
Tower Hill
Milbaise
Tenements Farm
NEW RD
Playing Field
Meggacres Farm
MEGG LA.
WAYSIDE
Whippendell Farm
Ballspond Farm
CHIPPERFIELD ROAD
THE GROVE Riding School
Nursery
Tuffs Farm
STONEY LANE
Cottingham Farm
Frenches Farm
SCATTERDELLS LANE
SCATTERDELLS PARK
CROFT FIELD
CROFT MEADOW
CROFT END
Whippendell House
Longfield
Highcroft
COURTAULDS
WHIPPENDELL HILL
Whippendell Bottom
Chipperfield House
Braziers
Nursery
ALEXANDRA RD
Warefield Spring
Braziers Farm
Chapel Croft
CHAPEL CROFT
LANGLEY LANE
Kings Langley
WD4
CHIPPERFIELD
WOODMAN'S WOOD
Pale Farm
FORGE CL.
THE STREET
ST. PAULS CT.
St. Paul's C of E Prim. Sch.
KING'S LANE
KING'S CL.
NUNFIELD
HAVENSFIELD
Rookery Wood
Langley Lodge Farm
136
Football Ground
QUEEN ST
THE COMMON
Vicarage
Rose Farm
Ckt. Grd.
Pav.
Woodman's Farm
Manor House
THE HILL
CHIPPERFIELD COMMON
Chipperfield Common
Lodge
WINDMILL HILL
Topcommon
Herry Trees Farm
WINDMILL HILL
LITTLE WINDMILL HILL
DUNNY LANE
COMMON
DACORUM
THREE RIVERS
Holly Hedges Farm
Olleberrie Farm
Belsize
Little Callipers
Hunterswood
BELSIZE COTTS.
PENMAN'S HILL
PENMANS GREEN
Belsize Farm
FLAUNDEN LANE
Lodge
Tennis Courts
Callipers Hall
BUCKS HILL
ST. PAULS CT.
Hillmeads Farm
Penmans
Callipers Hall Farm
POLES HILL
PLOUGH LANE
Marginia Wick
Rose Hall Farm
Debardine Wood
Old Plough House
Long Beeches
QUICKMOOR LANE
Baytree Farm
Quickmoor Farm
Bragman's Farm
Rosehall Wood
Plough Wood
Hillmeads Spring
Commonwood
Rickmansworth
WD3
Dellfield
Commonwood House
Great Sarratt Hall Farm
Great Sarratt Hall
Sarratt Hall
Daniel's Spring
COMMONWOOD COMMON
Bucks Hill Farm
Oldcroft Wood
Hall
Sarratt Hall
Ainsworth Cottage
Bucks Hill
Little Westwood Farm
Daffodil Spring
Red Lion Farm
BOTTOM LANE
Bucks Hill House
RED LION LANE
THE GREEN
Briar Cottage
Great Westwood Farm
High Spring
Lodge
SARRATT
Tennis Court
THE BRIARS
Playing Field
Pav.
Hill View
OLD NO. LA.
The Nook
Poultry Houses
ASH LANE
MOOR LANE
WYNYARD CL.
DOWNER DR.
ALEXANDRA RD
GREEN
GEORGE V WAY
CARDON DR.
Bucks Bottom
Sarratt C of E Sch.
Halls
CLUTTERBUCKS
DIMMOCKS LA.
DEADMAN'S ASH LANE
Newhall Farm
White Cottage
CHANDLER'S LANE
Dawes Common
WARDS DR.
By the
DAWES LANE
White Oaks Farm
Sandfield Wood
Moor Cottage
Old Rectory
Rectory
147
Sarratt Bottom
Cakebread Cottage
CHURCH LANE
White House
03
04
505
06
02
01
200
199
1
2
3
4
5
6
7
8
9
G
H
J
K
L
M
N

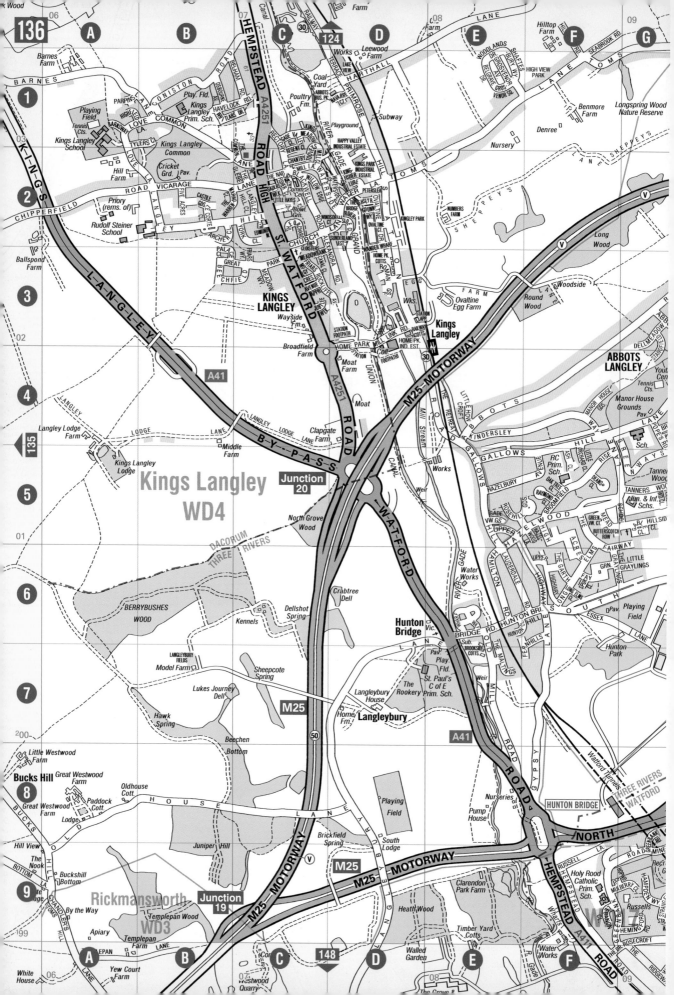

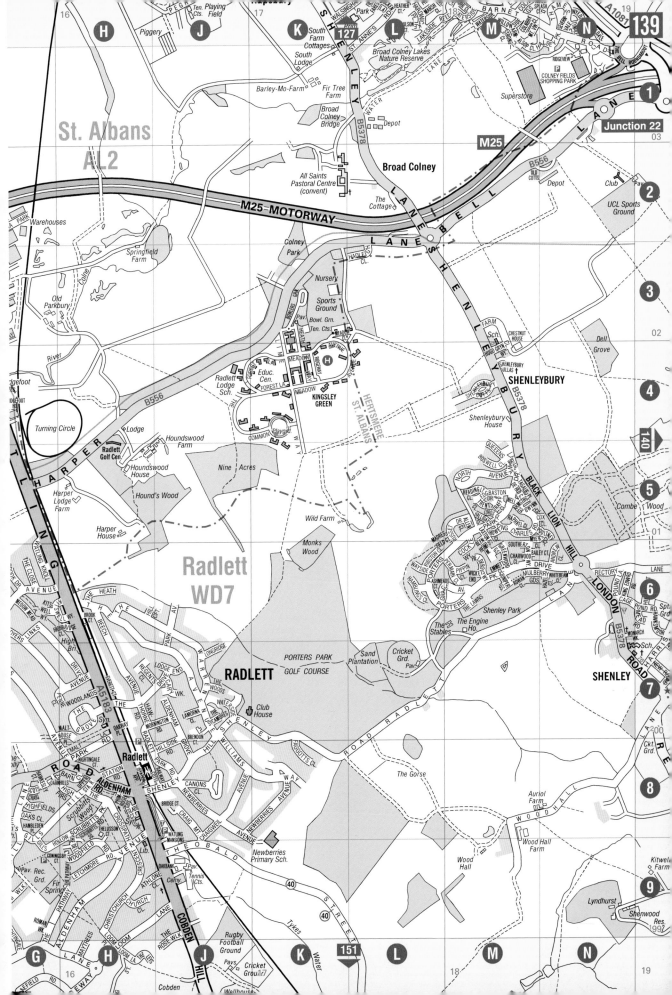

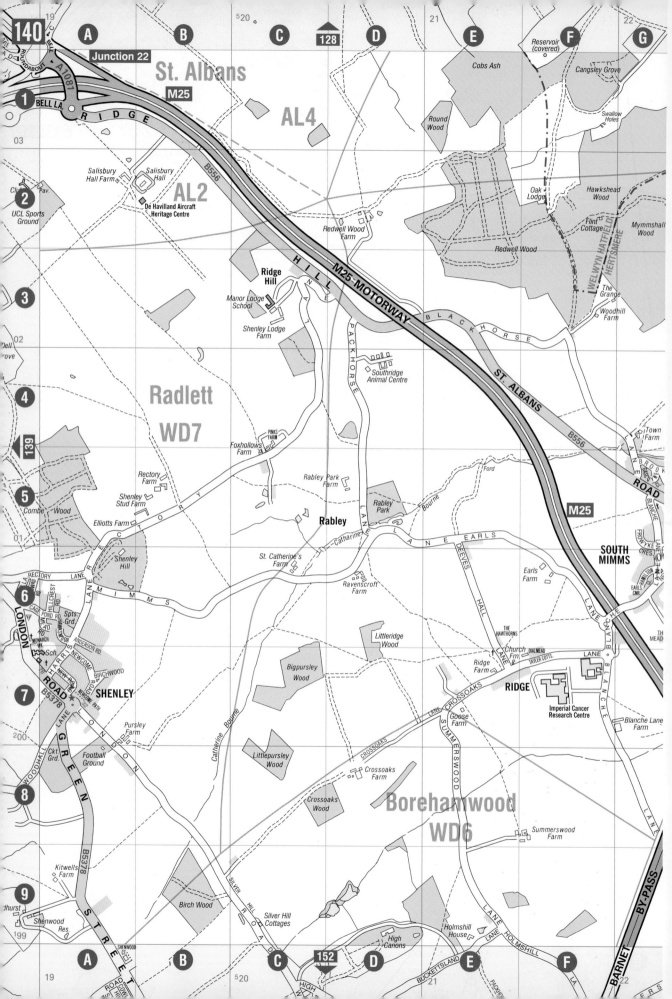

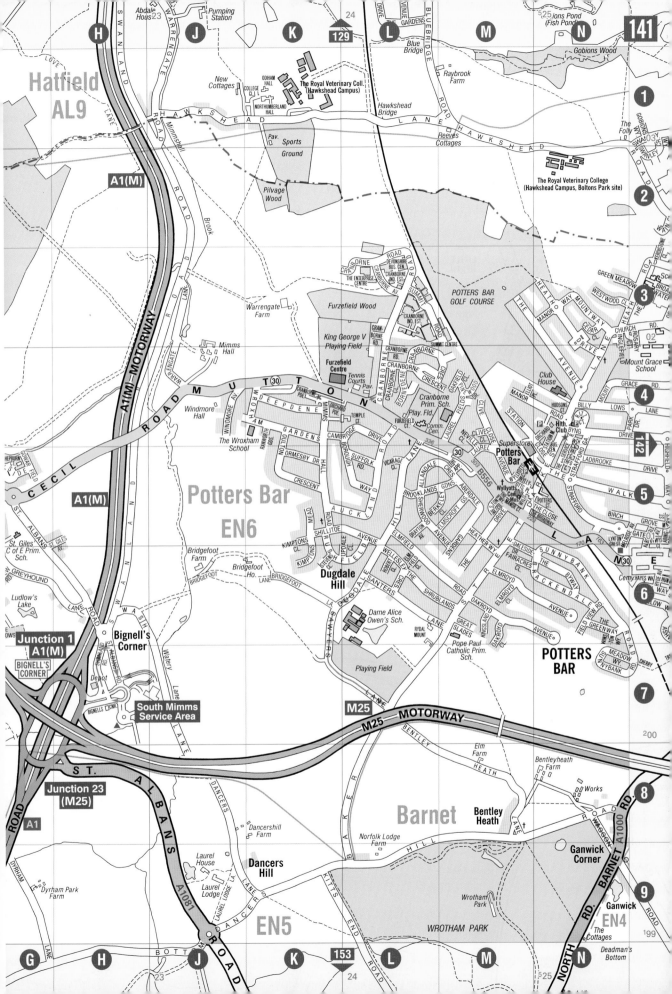

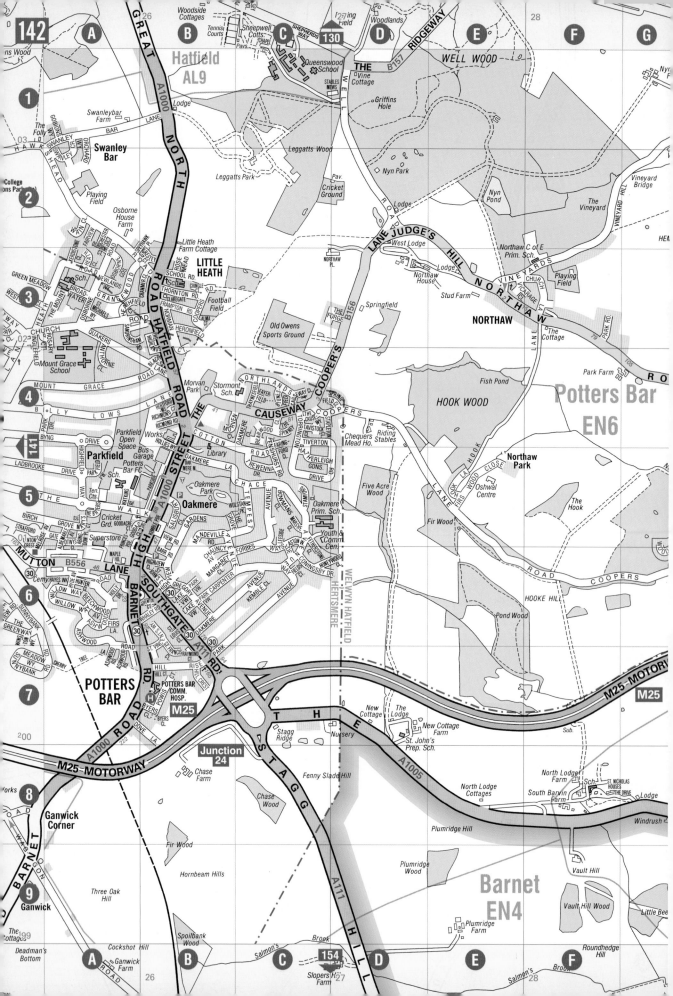

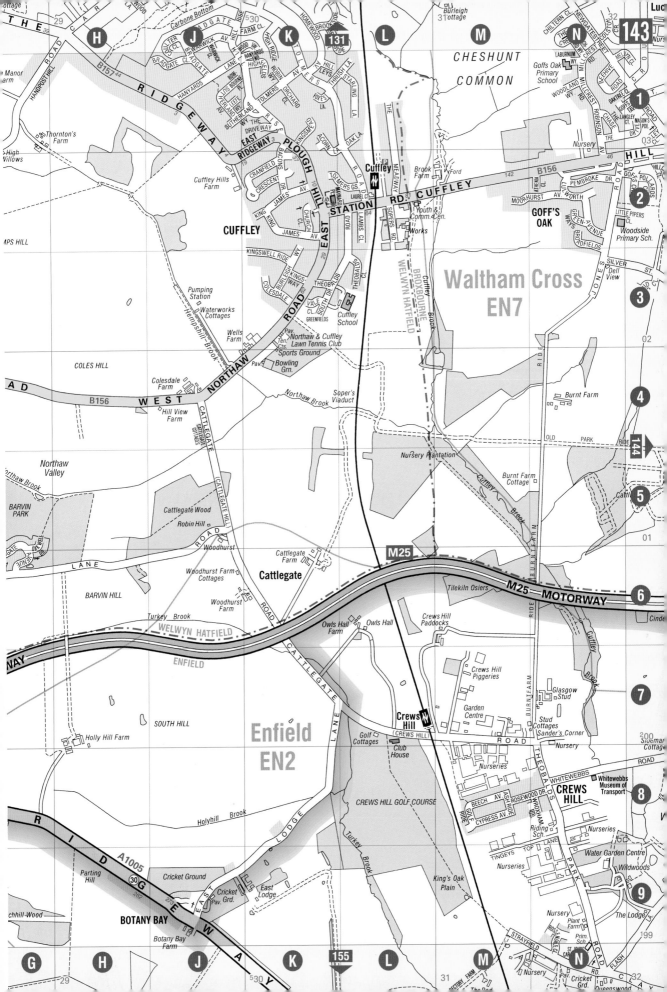

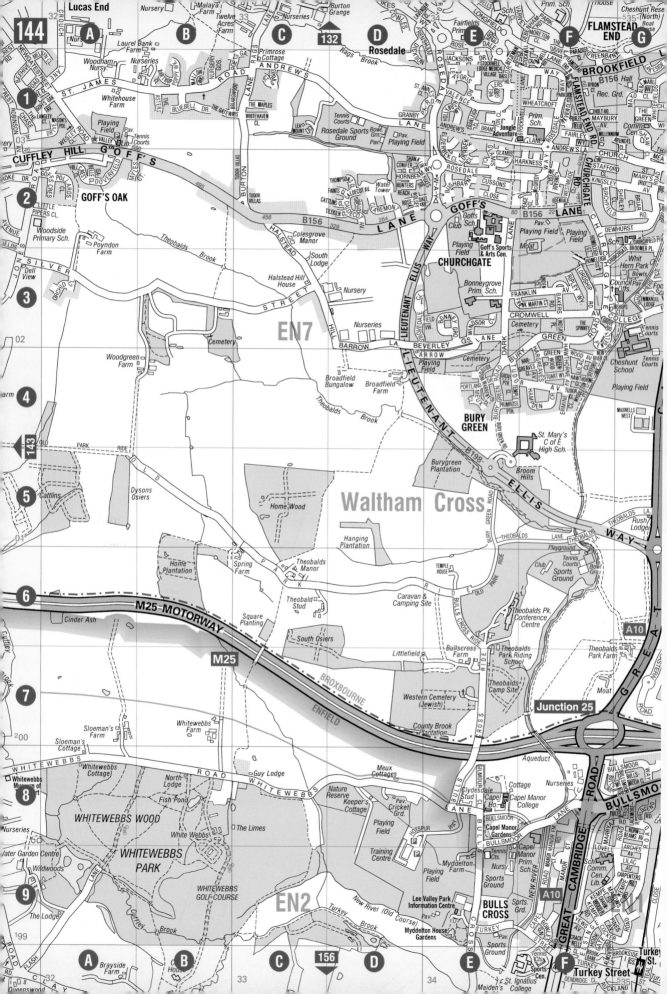

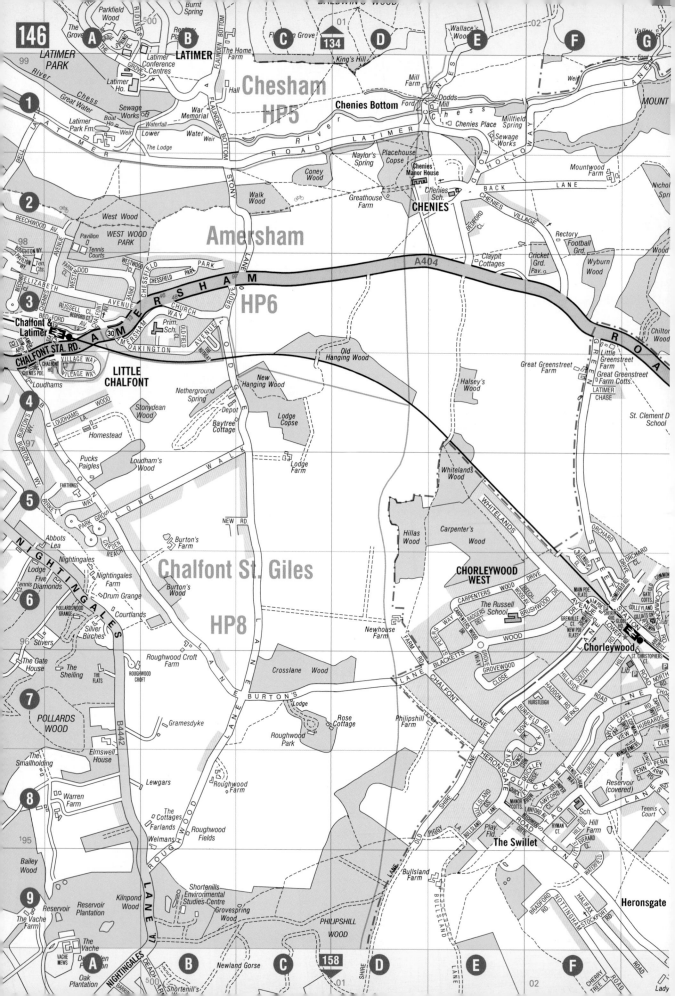

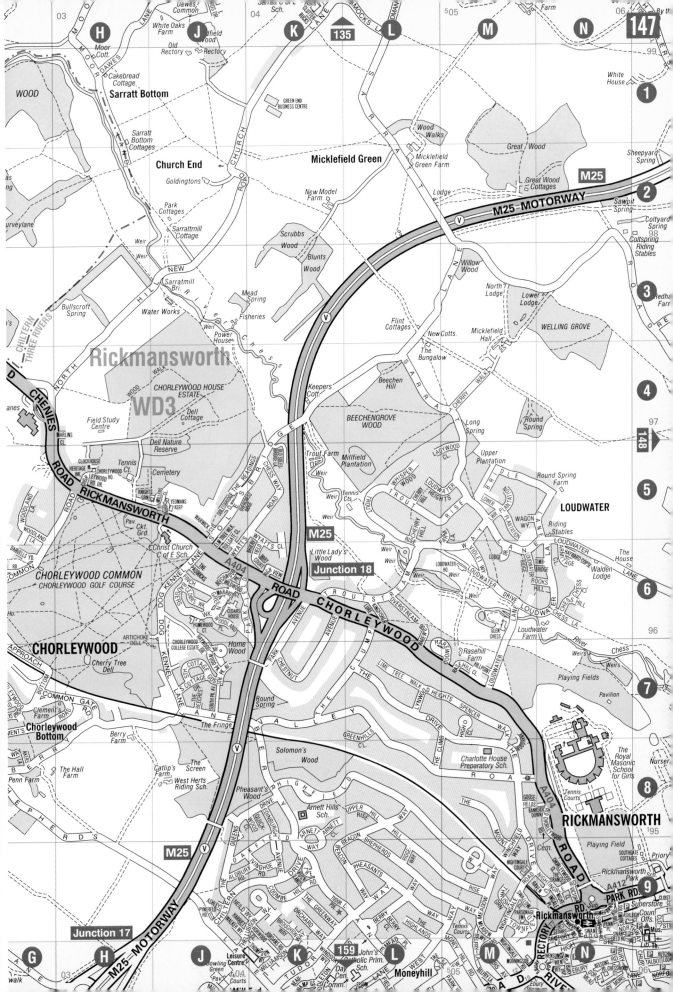

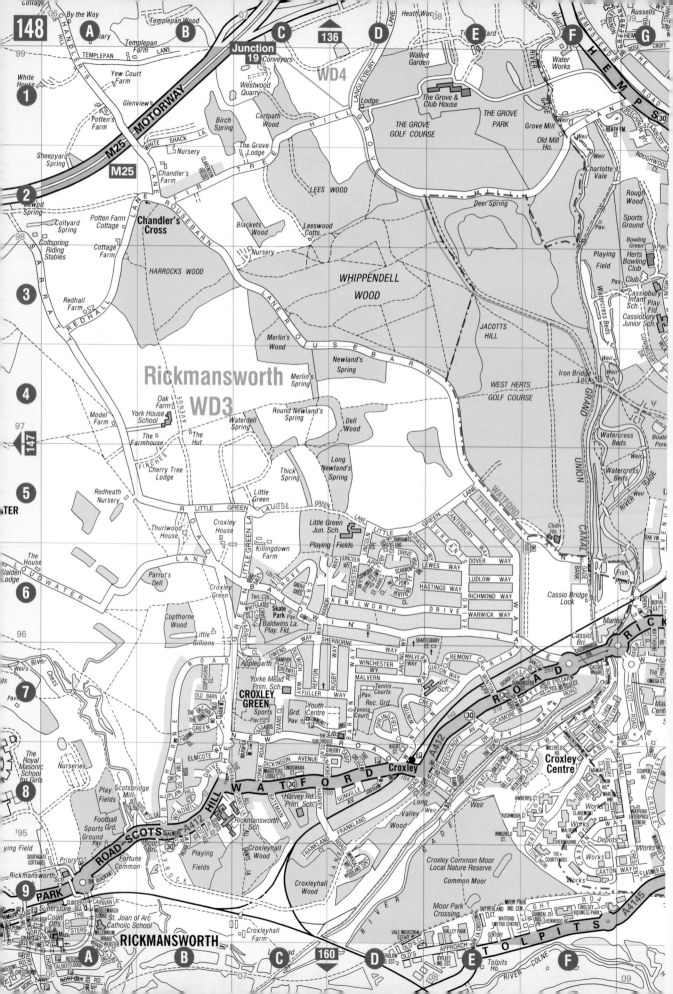

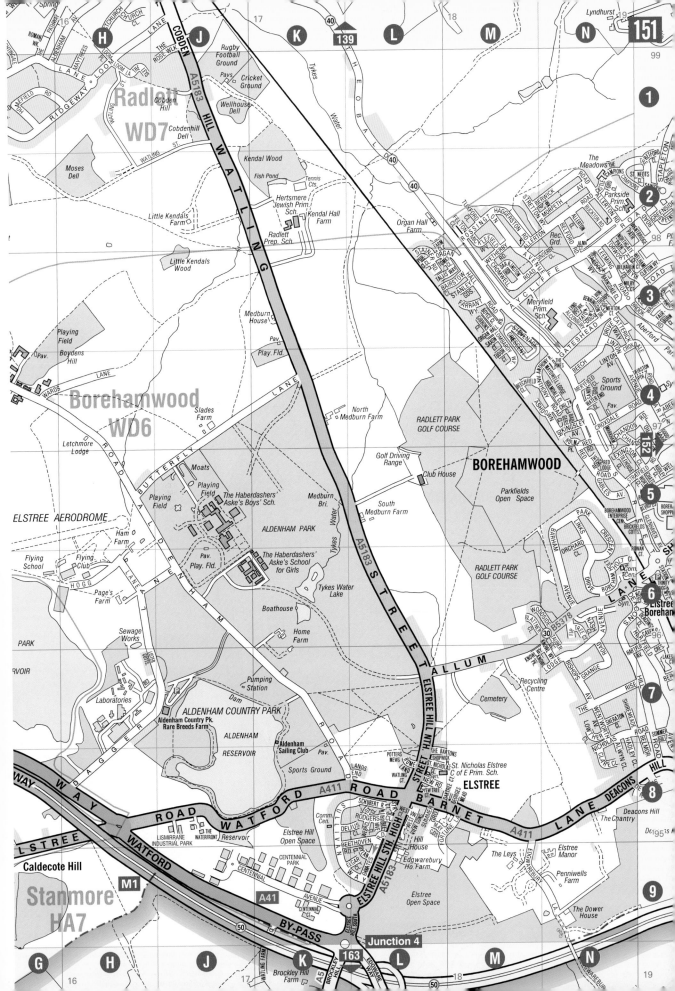

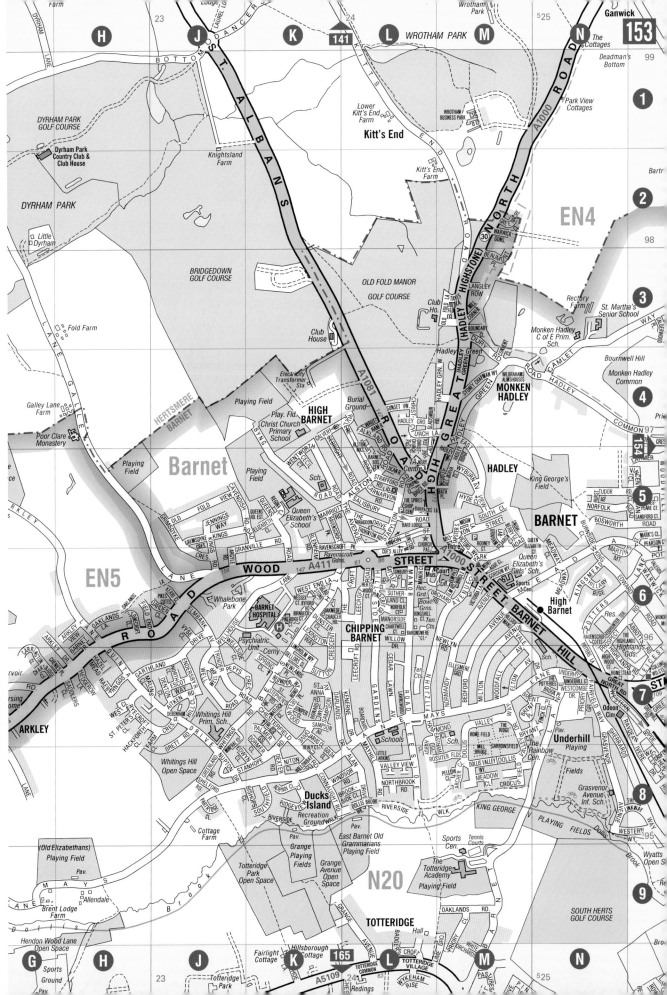

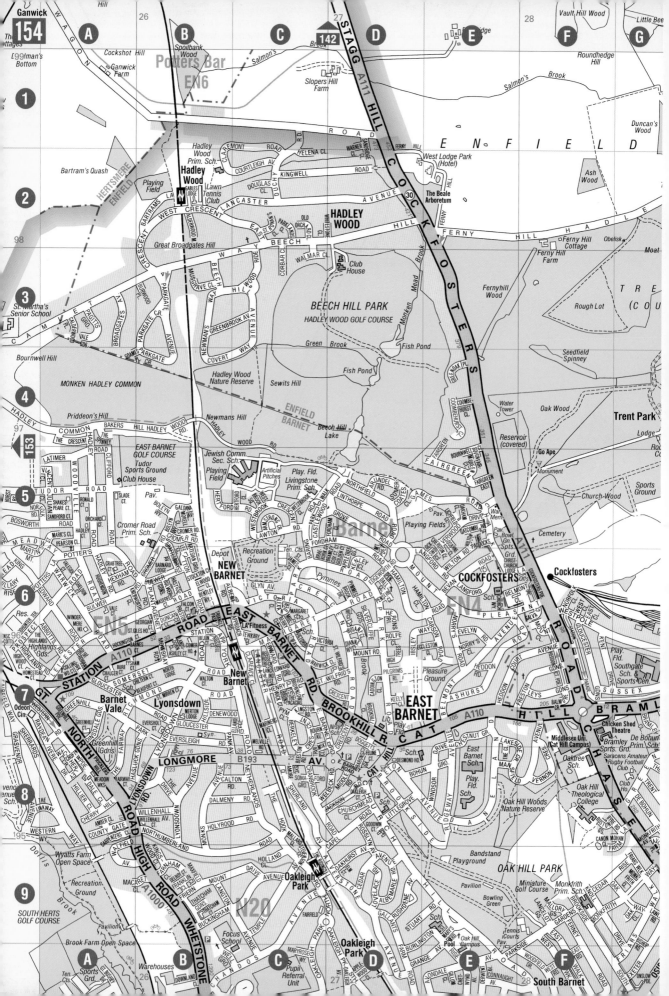

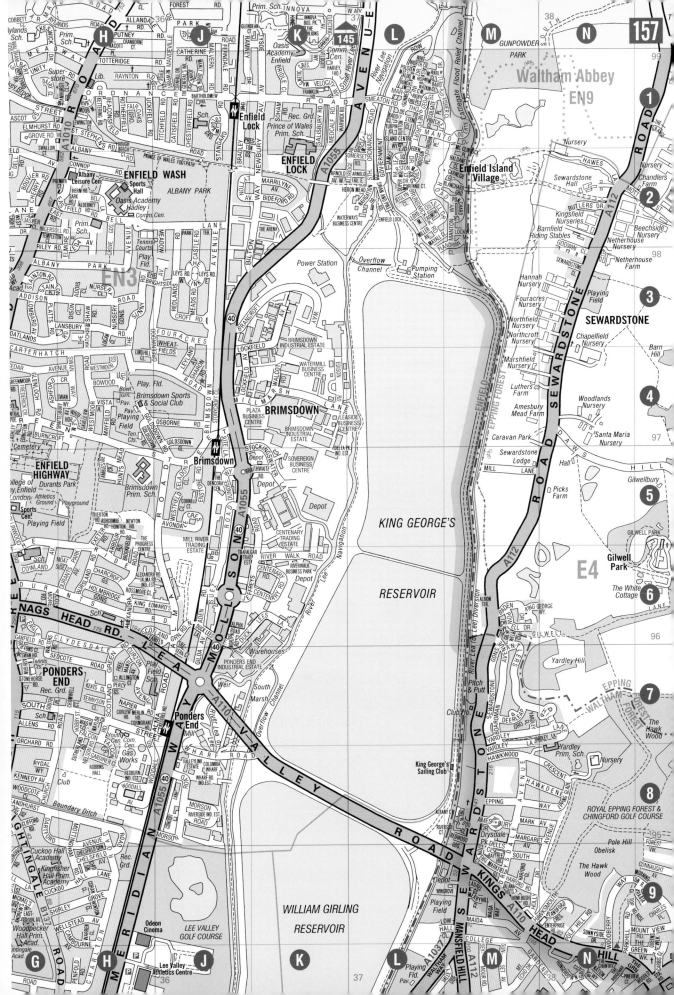

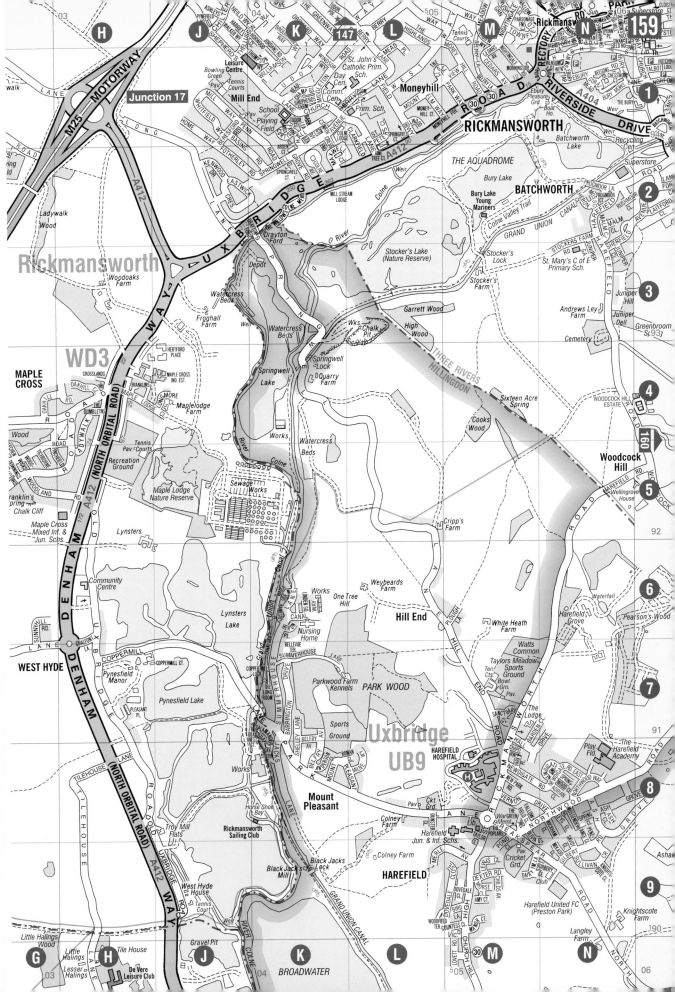

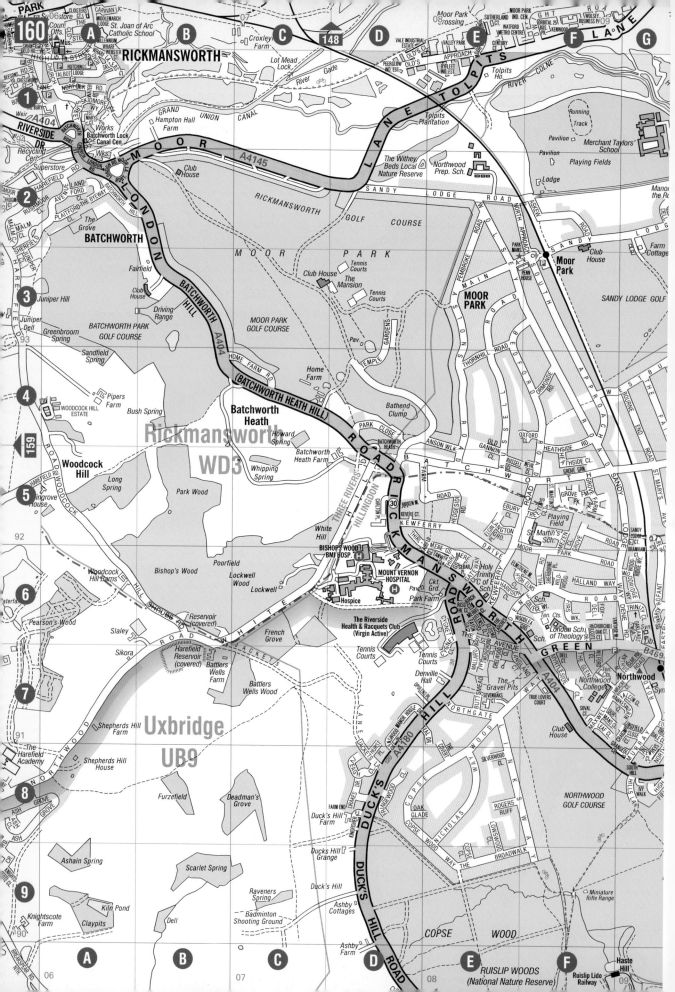

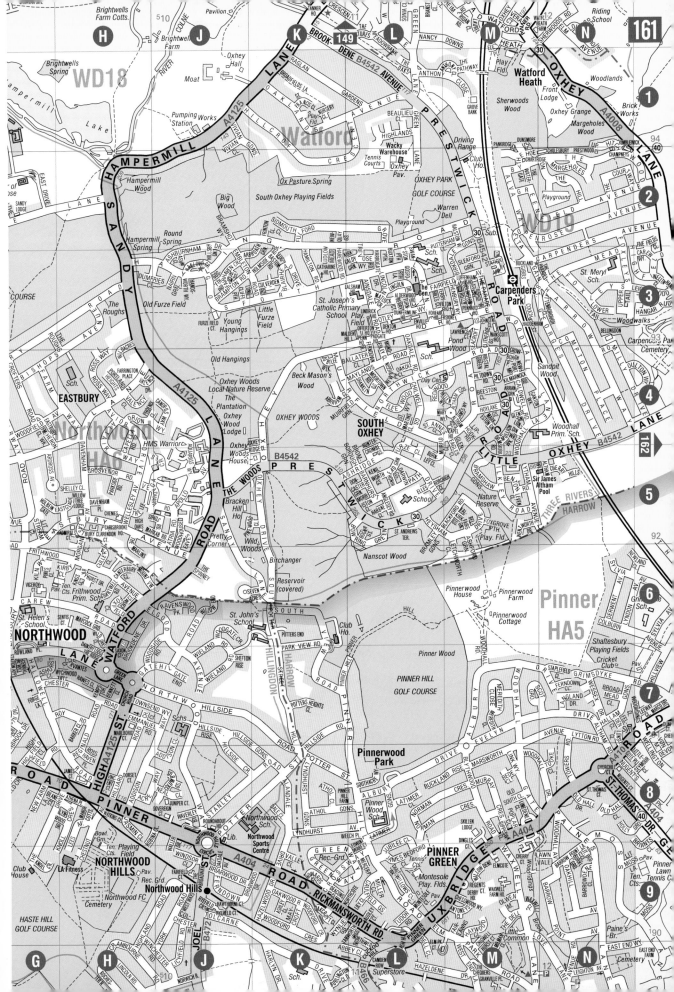

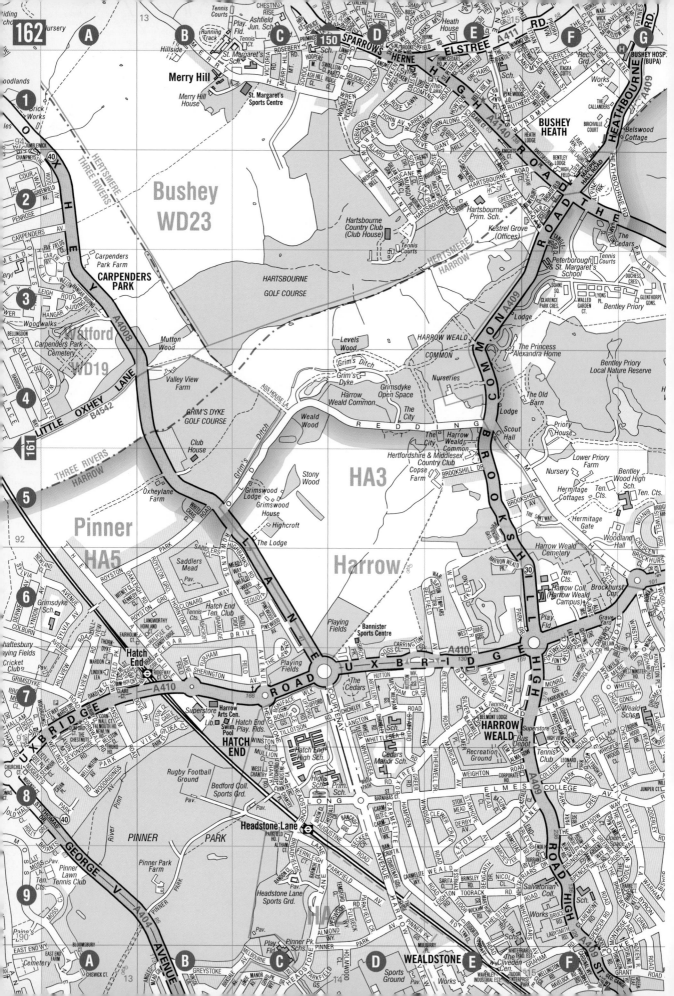

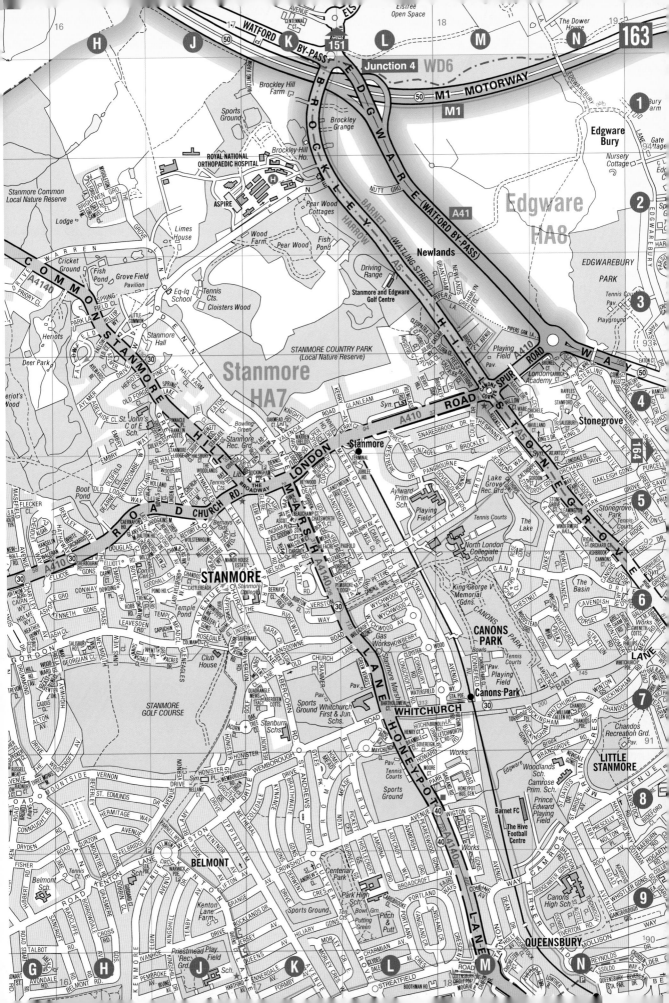

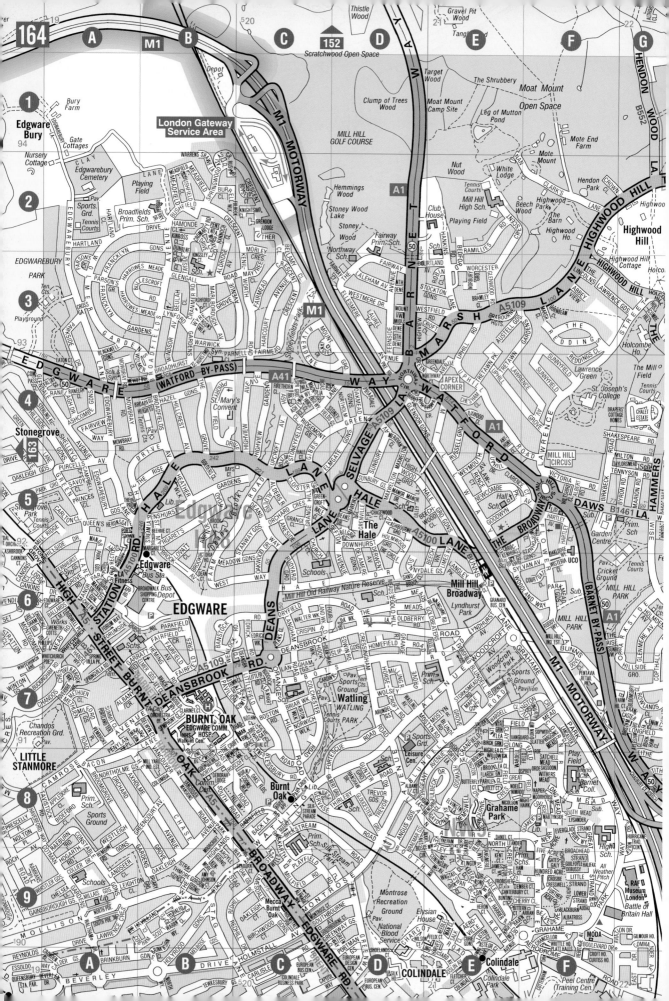

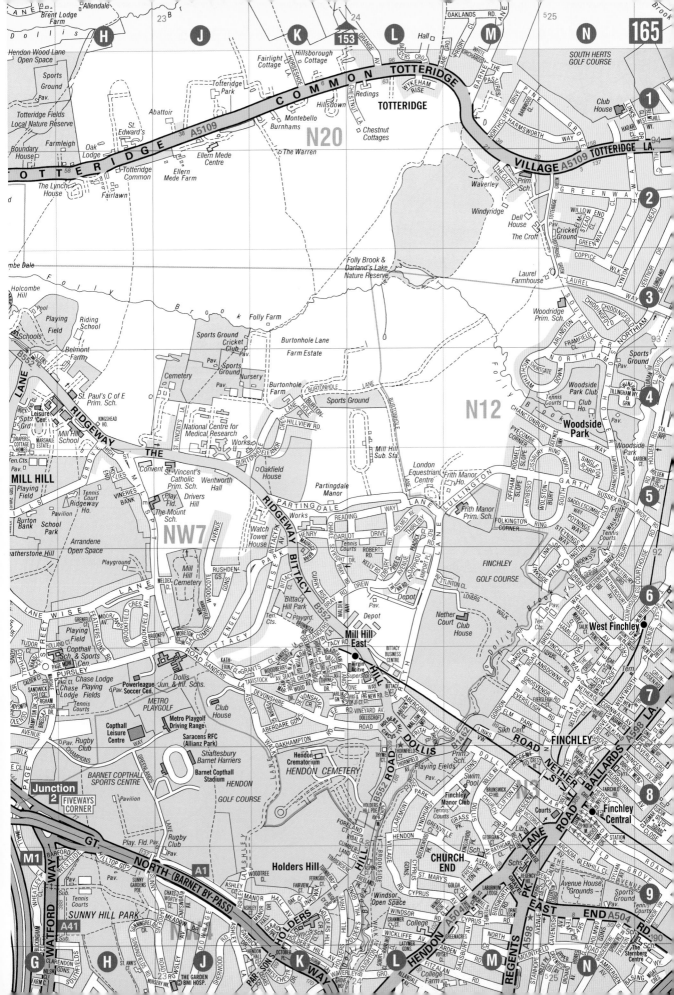

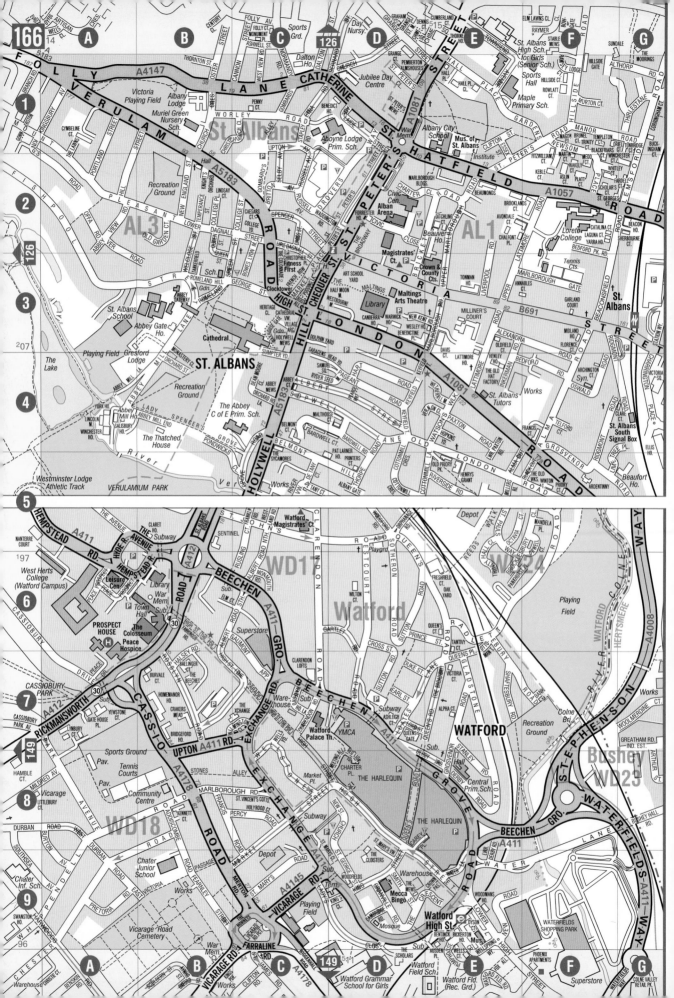

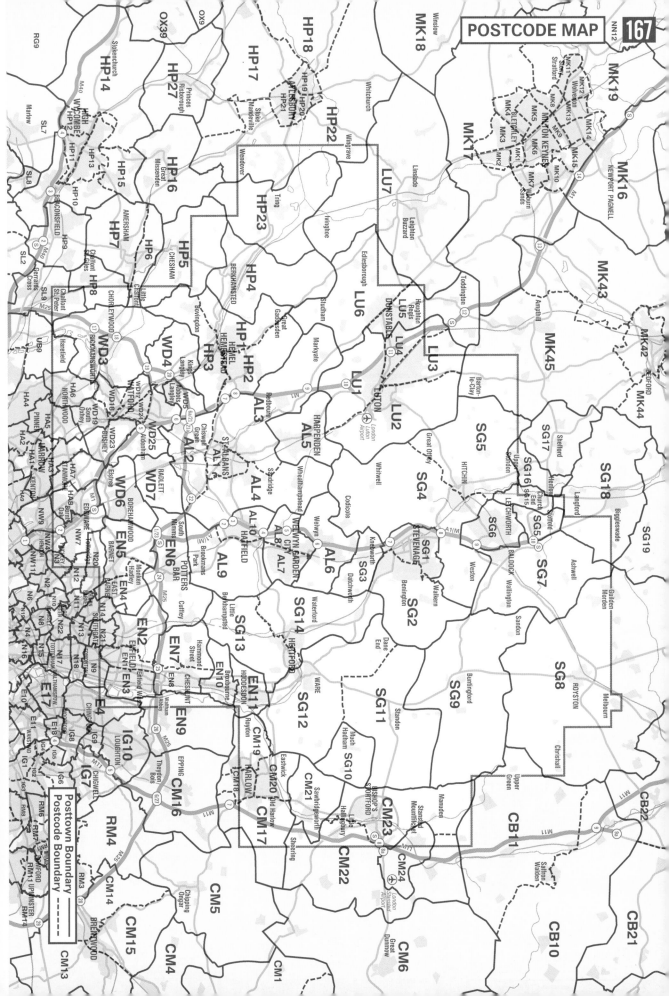

NN12

HP18
MK18
Winslow
MK19
NN12

Stokenchurch
Wycombe
HP14
HP27
Princes Risborough
HP17
LONGSTON
HP19 HP20
HP21
HP22
Whitchurch
MK17
Milton Keynes
MK12
Stony Stratford
MK11
Wolverton
MK13
MK8
MK9
MK19
MK5
MK6
MK14
MK4
MK3
MK1
MK15
MK2
MK7 Woburn Sands
MK10
Newport Pagnell
MK16

Marlow
RG9
SL7
High Wycombe
HP12
HP11
HP13
HP10
Great Missenden
HP16
Tring
HP23
Wendover
Ivinghoe
Edlesborough
Linslade
Leighton Buzzard
LU7
Toddington
Ampthill
MK43
MK42
BEDFORD
MK44

SL8
Beaconsfield
Amersham
HP7
HP6
Chesham
HP5
HP4
BERKHAMSTED
Studham
Markyate
LU6
Houghton Regis
DUNSTABLE
LU5
LU4
LU3
Barton-le-Clay
MK45

Gerrards Cross
SL9
SL2
Chalfont St Peter
HP8
HP9
Chalfont St Giles
Little Chalfont
CHORLEYWOOD
Bovingdon
HEMEL HEMPSTEAD
HP1 HP2
HP3
Kings Langley
Abbots Langley
Redbourn
AL3
HARPENDEN
AL5
Wheathampstead
Whitwell
Codicote
LU1
LUTON
London Luton Airport
LU2
Great Offley
HITCHIN
SG5
SG4
SG17
Shefford
Langford
SG16
Henlow
SG15
SG5
SG18
Biggleswade
SG19

UB9
Harefield
NORTHWOOD
WD3
RICKMANSWORTH
WD4
WATFORD
WD17 WD24
WD19
WD18
WD25
Aldenham
St ALBANS
AL1
AL4
AL2
Sandridge
WELWYN GARDEN CITY
AL8 AL7
AL6
Welwyn
Knebworth
SG3
Datchworth
STEVENAGE
SG1
SG2
Benington
Walkern
Weston
SG6
LETCHWORTH
Upper Caldecote
SG14
SG7
BALDOCK
Wallington
Ashwell
Sandon
SG8
Guilden Morden
Melbourn
Steeple Morden
ROYSTON

HA6
South Oxhey
PINNER
HA5
HA4
HA2
HA3
HARROW
HA1
STANMORE
HA7
HA8
EDGWARE
BOREHAMWOOD
WD6
Elstree
WD7
RADLETT
AL10
HATFIELD
AL9
Brookmans Park
POTTERS BAR
EN6
Cuffley
Little Berkhamsted
SG13
HERTFORD
SG12
Waterford
Bramfield
Dane End
SG11
Standon
Much Hadham
SG10
SG9
Buntingford
Chrishall
CB11
CB22

NW9
Burnt Oak
Mill Hill
NW7
N20
Totteridge
N12
Whetstone
EAST BARNET
New Barnet
EN4
EN5
Hadley
Monken Hadley
BARNET
EN2
ENFIELD
EN1 EN2
EN3
Enfield Wash
CHESHUNT
EN8
Waltham Abbey
EN9
WARE
Wareside
Eastwick
Sawbridgeworth
CM21
BISHOP'S STORTFORD
CM23
Stansted Mountfitchet
Upper Green
CB10
Saffron Walden
CB21

NW11
N2
N3
HORNSEY
N8
N10
N6
N4
N15
N22
N11
WOOD GREEN
N13
N14
SOUTHGATE
N21
N9
N18
N17
TOTTENHAM
N7
N16
WALTHAMSTOW
E17
CHINGFORD
E4
LOUGHTON
IG10
Theydon Bois
EPPING
CM16
CM17
Old Harlow
HARLOW
CM20
Little Hallingbury
Manuden
London Stansted Airport
CM24
CM6
Great Dunmow

E10
E11
WANSTEAD
E18
IG8
WOODFORD
IG9
BUCKHURST HILL
CHIGWELL
IG7
RM4
CHIPPING ONGAR
CM5
CM15
BRENTWOOD
CM14
CM13
RM3
ROMFORD
RM1
RM7
RM5
RM6
RM8
RM9
RM11
UPMINSTER
RM14
DARTFORD
RM13
CM22
Sheering
CM18
CM19
Roydon
HODDESDON
EN11
Broxbourne
EN10
Hammond Street
Waltham Cross
EN7
EN8

Posttown Boundary
Postcode Boundary ──────

HP15
SL8
AMERSHAM

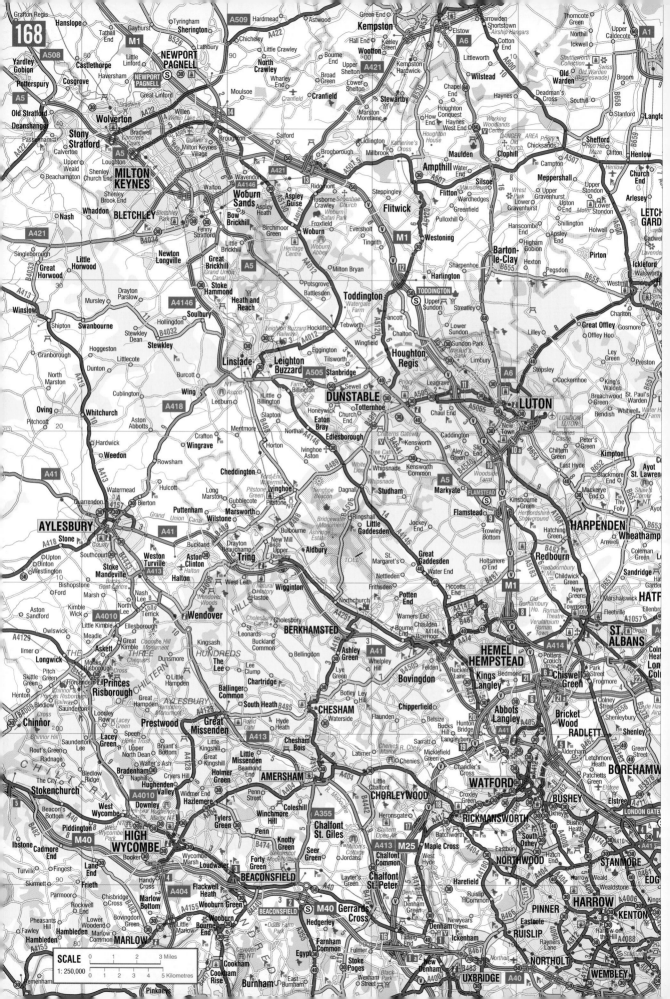

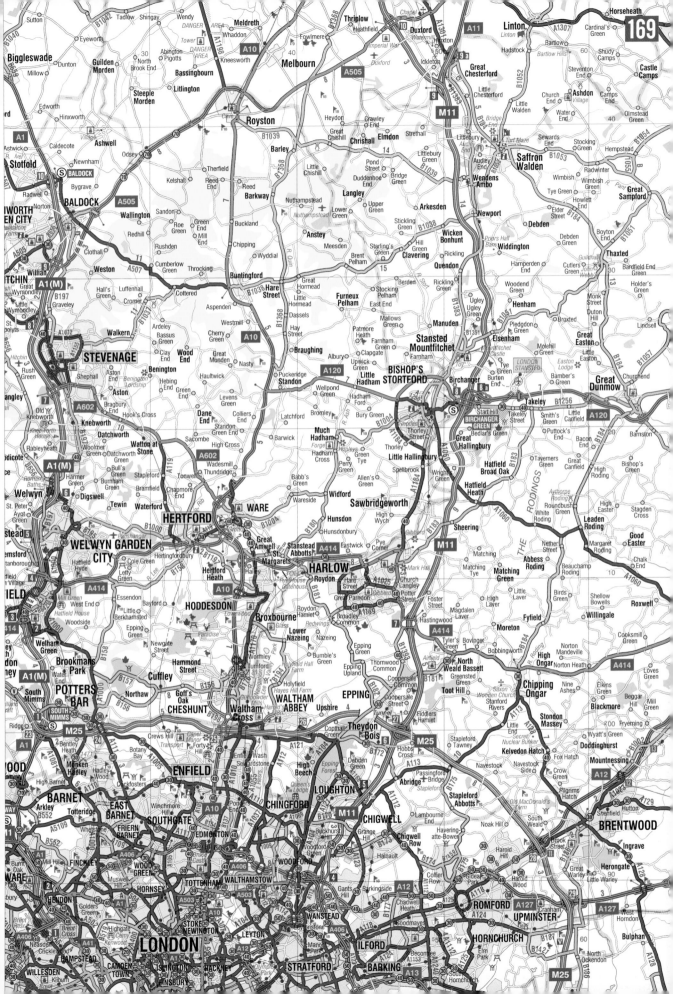

INDEX

Including Streets, Places & Areas, Industrial Estates, Selected Flats & Walkways,
Junction Names & Service Areas, Stations and Selected Places of Interest.

HOW TO USE THIS INDEX

1. Each street name is followed by its Postcode District (or, if outside the London Postcodes, by its Locality Abbreviation(s)) and then by its map reference;
e.g. **Abbey Av.** AL3: St Alb . . . .5B **126** is in the AL3 Postcode District and the St Albans Locality and is to be found in square 5B on page **126**. The page number is shown in bold type.

2. A strict alphabetical order is followed in which Av., Rd., St., etc. (though abbreviated) are read in full and as part of the street name; e.g. **Apple Tree Gro.** appears after **Appletree Gdns.** but before **Appletrees**

3. Streets and a selection of flats and walkways that cannot be shown on the mapping, appear in the index with the thoroughfare to which they are connected shown in brackets;
e.g. **Abingdon Ct.** EN8: Wal C . . . 6J **145** (off High St.)

4. Addresses that are in more than one part are referred to as not continuous.

5. Places and areas are shown in the index in BLUE TYPE and the map reference is to the actual map square in which the town centre or area is located and not to the place name shown on the map;
e.g. ABBOTS LANGLEY . . . 4G 137

6. An example of a selected place of interest is Ashwell Village Mus. . . . 9M 5

7. An example of a station is Apsley Station (Rail) . . . .7A 124. Included are Rail (Rail), Underground (Underground) and Overground (Overground) Stations.

8. Junction names and Service Areas are shown in the index in **BOLD CAPITAL TYPE**; e.g. **APEX CORNER** 4E **164**

9. Map references for entries that appear on large scale page **166** are shown first, with small scale map references shown in brackets;
e.g. **Abbey Mill La.** AL3: St Alb 4A **166** (3D **126**)

GENERAL ABBREVIATIONS

All. : Alley	**Cotts.** : Cottages	**Ind.** : Industrial	**Res.** : Residential
App. : Approach	**Ct.** : Court	**Info.** : Information	**Ri.** : Rise
Arc. : Arcade	**Cres.** : Crescent	**La.** : Lane	**Rd.** : Road
Av. : Avenue	**Cft.** : Croft	**Lit.** : Little	**Rdbt.** : Roundabout
Blvd. : Boulevard	**Dr.** : Drive	**Lwr.** : Lower	**Shop.** : Shopping
Bri. : Bridge	**E.** : East	**Mnr.** : Manor	**Sth.** : South
B'way. : Broadway	**Ent.** : Enterprise	**Mans.** : Mansions	**Sq.** : Square
Bldgs. : Buildings	**Est.** : Estate	**Mkt.** : Market	**Sta.** : Station
Bungs. : Bungalows	**Fld.** : Field	**Mdw.** : Meadow	**St.** : Street
Bus. : Business	**Flds.** : Fields	**Mdws.** : Meadows	**Ter.** : Terrace
C'way. : Causeway	**Gdn.** : Garden	**M.** : Mews	**Twr.** : Tower
Cen. : Centre	**Gdns.** : Gardens	**Mt.** : Mount	**Trad.** : Trading
Chu. : Church	**Gth.** : Garth	**Mus.** : Museum	**Up.** : Upper
Circ. : Circle	**Ga.** : Gate	**Nth.** : North	**Va.** : Vale
Cir. : Circus	**Gt.** : Great	**Pde.** : Parade	**Vw.** : View
Cl. : Close	**Grn.** : Green	**Pk.** : Park	**Vs.** : Villas
Coll. : College	**Gro.** : Grove	**Pas.** : Passage	**Vis.** : Visitors
Comn. : Common	**Hgts.** : Heights	**Pl.** : Place	**Wlk.** : Walk
Cnr. : Corner	**Ho.** : House	**Pct.** : Precinct	**W.** : West
Cott. : Cottage	**Ho's.** : Houses	**Quad.** : Quadrant	**Yd.** : Yard

LOCALITY ABBREVIATIONS

Abb L : **Abbots Langley**	C End : **Chapmore End**	Gt Hal : **Great Hallingbury**	Lill : **Lilley**
Ab P : **Abington Pigotts**	C'ton : **Charlton**	Gt Hor : **Great Hormead**	Lit : **Litlington**
Alb : **Albury**	C'dge : **Chartridge**	Gt Mun : **Great Munden**	Lit B : **Little Berkhamsted**
Aldb : **Aldbury**	Ched : **Cheddington**	Gt Off : **Great Offley**	L Bill : **Little Billington**
A'ham : **Aldenham**	Chen : **Chenies**	Gt Wym : **Great Wymondsley**	L Chal : **Little Chalfont**
Aley G : **Aley Green**	C'ham : **Chesham**	Gub : **Gubblecote**	L Chis : **Little Chishill**
All G : **Allen's Green**	C'hunt : **Cheshunt**	G Mor : **Guilden Morden**	Lit G : **Little Gaddesden**
Ans : **Anstey**	Chippf : **Chipperfield**	Had W : **Hadley Wood**	L Had : **Little Hadham**
Ard : **Ardeley**	Chippg : **Chipping**	Hail : **Hailey**	L Hal : **Little Hallingbury**
Ark : **Arkley**	Chis G : **Chiswell Green**	Halt : **Halton**	L Wym : **Little Wymondley**
Arl : **Arlesey**	Chiv : **Chivery**	Hare : **Harefield**	Lon C : **London Colney**
Ashe : **Asheridge**	Chol : **Cholesbury**	H St : **Hare Street**	Lon M : **Long Marston**
Ash G : **Ashley Green**	Chor : **Chorleywood**	Harl : **Harlow**	Loud : **Loudwater**
Ashw : **Ashwell**	Chris : **Chrishall**	Harp : **Harpenden**	L Ston : **Lower Stondon**
Asp : **Aspenden**	Clav : **Clavering**	Harr : **Harrow**	L Sun : **Lower Sundon**
A'ton : **Aston**	Clo : **Clothall**	Har W : **Harrow Weald**	Luff : **Luffenhall**
Ast C : **Aston Clinton**	C'hoe : **Cockernhoe**	Hast : **Hastoe**	Lut : **Luton**
Ast E : **Aston End**	C'ters : **Cockfosters**	Hat E : **Hatch End**	Lye G : **Lye Green**
Astw : **Astwick**	Cod : **Codicote**	Hat : **Hatfield**	M Lav : **Magdalen Laver**
Ayot L : **Ayot St Lawrence**	Col G : **Cole Green**	Hat H : **Hatfield Heath**	Man : **Manuden**
Ayot P : **Ayot St Peter**	Col E : **Colliers End**	Hau : **Haultwick**	Map C : **Maple Cross**
Bald : **Baldock**	Col H : **Colney Heath**	Haw : **Hawridge**	Mark : **Markyate**
Bark : **Barkway**	Col S : **Colney Street**	Hem H : **Hemel Hempstead**	Mars : **Marsworth**
Barl : **Barley**	Cot : **Cottered**	Henl : **Henlow**	M Tye : **Matching Tye**
Barn : **Barnet**	Cow R : **Cow Roast**	Hero : **Heronsgate**	Mee : **Meesden**
Bar C : **Barton-le-Clay**	Craf : **Crafton**	H'ford : **Hertford**	Melb : **Melbourn**
Barw : **Barwick**	Crew H : **Crews Hill**	Hert H : **Hertford Heath**	Meld : **Meldreth**
Bass : **Bassingbourn**	Crom : **Cromer**	H'bury : **Hertingfordbury**	Ment : **Mentmore**
Bay : **Bayford**	Crox G : **Croxley Green**	Hex : **Hexton**	M Had : **Much Hadham**
B'bury : **Bayfordbury**	Cuff : **Cuffley**	Hey : **Heydon**	Naz : **Nazeing**
Bed : **Bedmond**	Dag : **Dagnall**	H Gob : **Higham Gobion**	Net : **Nettleden**
Bell : **Bellingdon**	Dan E : **Dane End**	H Cro : **High Cross**	N Bar : **New Barnet**
Ben : **Bendish**	Dat : **Datchworth**	H Lav : **High Laver**	New S : **Newgate Street**
B'ton : **Benington**	Den : **Denham**	H Wyc : **High Wych**	N Gnd : **New Ground**
Ber : **Berden**	Dray B : **Drayton Beauchamp**	Hinx : **Hinxworth**	New : **Newnham**
Berk : **Berkhamsted**	Duns : **Dunstable**	Hit : **Hitchin**	N'all : **Northall**
Bid : **Bidwell**	Dunt : **Dunton**	Hod : **Hoddesdon**	N'haw : **Northaw**
Big : **Biggleswade**	E Bar : **East Barnet**	Hol : **Holwell**	N Mym : **North Mymms**
Bill : **Billington**	E Hyd : **East Hyde**	Hort : **Horton**	North : **Northwood**
Birc : **Birchanger**	E'cote : **Eastcote**	Hou R : **Houghton Regis**	Nort : **Norton**
Bir G : **Birch Green**	East : **Eastwick**	How G : **Howe Green**	Nuth : **Nuthampstead**
Bis S : **Bishop's Stortford**	Eat B : **Eaton Bray**	Huns : **Hunsdon**	Ods : **Odsey**
Bore : **Borehamwood**	Edg : **Edgware**	Hun C : **Hunton Cross**	Old G : **Old Hall Green**
Bov : **Bovingdon**	Edle : **Edlesborough**	Ick : **Ickleford**	Old K : **Old Knebworth**
Bram : **Bramfield**	Edw : **Edworth**	I'hoe : **Ivinghoe**	Orch L : **Orchard Leigh**
B'ing : **Braughing**	Elst : **Elstree**	I Ast : **Ivinghoe Aston**	Pans : **Panshanger**
Bre G : **Breachwood Green**	Enf : **Enfield**	Kel : **Kelshall**	Par S : **Park Street**
B Pel : **Brent Pelham**	Enf H : **Enfield Highway**	Kens : **Kensworth**	Pegs : **Pegsdon**
B'don : **Brickendon**	Enf L : **Enfield Lock**	Ken : **Kenton**	Pep : **Pepperstock**
Bri W : **Bricket Wood**	Enf W : **Enfield Wash**	Kimp : **Kimpton**	P Grn : **Peters Green**
Brim : **Brimsdown**	Epp G : **Epping Green**	Kin L : **Kings Langley**	Pin : **Pinner**
B Pk : **Brookmans Park**	Ess : **Essendon**	K Wal : **King's Walden**	Pirt : **Pirton**
Brox : **Broxbourne**	Farn : **Farnham**	Kneb : **Knebworth**	Pits : **Pitstone**
Buck : **Buckland**	Flam : **Flamstead**	Knee : **Kneesworth**	Pon E : **Ponders End**
Buc C : **Buckland Common**	Flau : **Flaunden**	L'ford : **Langford**	Pot E : **Potten End**
Buc H : **Bucks Hill**	Flit : **Flitton**	Lang : **Langley**	Pot B : **Potters Bar**
Bulb : **Bulbourne**	Frog : **Frogmore**	L'bury : **Langleybury**	Pot C : **Potters Crouch**
Bunt : **Buntingford**	Fur P : **Furneux Pelham**	L Lwr : **Langley Lower Green**	Pres : **Preston**
Bush : **Bushey**	Gad R : **Gaddesden Row**	L Upp : **Langley Upper Green**	Puck : **Puckeridge**
B Hea : **Bushy Heath**	Ger C : **Gerrards Cross**	Latch : **Latchford**	Pull : **Pulloxhill**
Byg : **Bygrave**	Gil : **Gilston**	Lati : **Latimer**	Putt : **Puttenham**
Cad : **Caddington**	Gof O : **Goff's Oak**	Led : **Ledburn**	Que : **Quendon**
Cald : **Caldecote**	Gos : **Gosmore**	Lem : **Lemsford**	Rab H : **Rabley Heath**
Chal G : **Chalfont St Giles**	G'ley : **Graveley**	Let H : **Letchmore Heath**	Rad : **Radlett**
Chal P : **Chalfont St Peter**	G'urst : **Gravenhurst**	L Gar : **Letchworth Garden City**	R'well : **Radwell**
Chalg : **Chalgrave**	Gt A : **Great Amwell**	Let G : **Letty Green**	Red : **Redbourn**
Chalt : **Chalton**	Gt Chi : **Great Chishill**	Ley H : **Ley Hill**	Reed : **Reed**
Chan C : **Chandler's Cross**	Gt Gad : **Great Gaddesden**		Rick : **Rickling**

1st Bowl—Alexander M.

Rick G : **Rickling Green**
R'orth : **Rickmansworth**
Rid : **Ridge**
Ring : **Ringshall**
Royd : **Roydon**
Roys : **Royston**
Rush : **Rushden**
R Grn : **Rush Green**
Sac : **Sacombe**
St Alb : **St Albans**
St Ipo : **St Ipollitts**
St Leo : **St Leonards**
St Wal : **St Pauls Walden**
S'don : **Sandon**
San : **Sandridge**
Sar : **Sarratt**
Saw : **Sawbridgeworth**
Sew : **Sewell**
Shar : **Sharpenhoe**
She : **Sheering**
Shen : **Shenley**
Shil : **Shillington**
Sil : **Silsoe**
Slapt : **Slapton**
S End : **Slip End**
Smal : **Smallford**
S Mim : **South Mimms**
Spel : **Spellbrook**
S Grn : **Staines Green**
Stand : **Standon**
Stanm : **Stanmore**
Stan A : **Stanstead Abbotts**
Stans : **Stansted**
Stap : **Stapleford**
S Mor : **Steeple Morden**
Stev : **Stevenage**
S Pel : **Stocking Pelham**
Stot : **Stotfold**
Stre : **Streatley**
Stud : **Studham**
Tea G : **Tea Green**
Tew : **Tewin**
Ther : **Therfield**
Thorl : **Thorley**
Thorn : **Thorn**
Throck : **Throcking**
Thun : **Thundridge**
Tonw : **Tonwell**
Tot : **Totternhoe**
Tring : **Tring**
T'ford : **Tringford**
Turn : **Turnford**
Ugl : **Ugley**
U Sto : **Upper Stondon**
U Sun : **Upper Sundon**
Wad : **Wadesmill**
Walk : **Walkern**
Wall : **Wallington**
Wal A : **Waltham Abbey**
Wal C : **Waltham Cross**
Wan E : **Wandon End**
Wan G : **Wandon Green**
Ware : **Ware**
W'side : **Wareside**
Water : **Waterford**
Watf : **Watford**
Watt S : **Watton at Stone**
Weal : **Wealdstone**
Welh G : **Welham Green**
Wel : **Welwyn**
Welw G : **Welwyn Garden City**
Wen : **Wendover**
W Hyd : **West Hyde**
W'mill : **Westmill**
W'ton : **Weston**
West T : **Weston Turville**
Wheat : **Wheathampstead**
Whel H : **Whelpley Hill**
Whem : **Whempstead**
Whip : **Whipsnade**
Whit : **Whitwell**
Widd : **Widdial**
Widf : **Widford**
Wigg : **Wigginton**
Will : **Willan**
Wils : **Wilstone**
Wing : **Wing**
W'field : **Wingfield**
W'rave : **Wingrave**
W End : **Wood End**
Wood : **Woodside**
Worm : **Wormley**

1st Bowl
Bishop's Stortford 2H 79
(within Anchor Street Leisure Pk.)

A

A1 Golf Driving Range 5E 152
Aashiana Ct. WD18: Watf 8J 149
Abbey Av. AL3: St Alb 5B 126
Abbey Cl. HA5: Pin .9K 161
Abbey Ct. AL1: St Alb 4C 166
EN9: Wal A 7M 145
Abbeydale Cl. CM17: Harl 7E 118
Abbey Dr. LU2: Lut 8J 47
WD5: Abb L 5J 137
Abbeygate Bus. Centre, The *LU2: Lut* *9H 47*
(off Hitchin Rd.)
Abbey Gateway AL3: St Alb 3B 166 (2D 126)
Abbey Mead Ind. Est. EN9: Wal A 8N 145
Abbey Mead Ind. Pk. EN9: Wal A 7M 145
Abbey M. AL1: St Alb 4C 166
LU6: Duns 2F 64
Abbey Mill End AL3: St Alb 4B 166 (3D 126)
Abbey Mill La. AL3: St Alb 4A 166 (3D 126)
Abbey Mills EN9: Wal A 6M 145
Abbey Rd. EN1: Enf .7C 156
EN8: Wal C 7J 145
Abbey Theatre 4D 126
Abbey Vw. AL1: St Alb 4E 126
EN9: Wal A 6M 145
NW7 . . . . .3F 164
WD7: Rad 8G 138
WD25: Watf 9M 137
Abbey View Golf Course 4D 126
Abbey Vw. Rd. AL3: St Alb 2A 166 (2D 126)
Abbey Wlk. LU5: Hou R 3H 45
Abbis Orchard SG5: Ick 6M 21
Abbots Av. AL1: St Alb 5F 126
Abbots Av. W. AL1: St Alb 5E 126
Abbotsbury Ct. WD25: Watf 5K 137
Abbots Bus. Pk. WD4: Kin L 1C 136
Abbots Cl. SG3: Dat .7C 72
Abbots Ct. LU2: Lut .8J 47
Abbots Gro. SG1: Stev 5M 51
Abbots Hill HP3: Hem H 7C 124
ABBOTS LANGLEY .4G 137
Abbots Pk. AL1: St Alb 4H 127
Abbots Pl. WD6: Bore 1B 152
Abbots Ri. WD4: Kin L 8B 124
Abbots Rd. HA8: Edg 7C 164
WD5: Abb L 4E 136
Abbots Vw. WD4: Kin L 9B 124
Abbotsweld CM18: Harl 9N 117
Abbots Wood Pde. LU2: Lut 8J 47
Abbots Wood Rd. LU2: Lut 8J 47
Abbots Yd. SG8: Roys 7D 8
Abbott John M. AL4: Wheat 6L 89
Abbotts Cl. SG8: Lit .3H 7
Abbotts Ct. SG12: Stan A 2A 116
Abbotts Cres. EN2: Enf 4N 155
Abbotts La. SG12: Widf 3G 96
Abbotts Ri. SG12: Stan A 2A 116
Abbotts Rd. EN5: N Bar 6A 154
SG6: L Gar 5D 22
Abbotts Way CM23: Bis S 5G 78
HP22: W'rave 4A 60
SG12: Stan A 2A 116
Abdale La. AL9: N Mym 9H 129
Abel Cl. HP2: Hem H 2C 124
Abercorn Cl. NW7 . . . . .7L 165
Abercorn Dell WD23: B Hea 2D 162
Abercorn Rd. HA7: Stanm 7K 163
LU4: Lut 6J 45
NW7 . . . . .7L 165
Abercrombie Dr. EN1: Enf 3E 156
Abercrombie Way CM18: Harl 7M 117
Aberdale Gdns. EN6: Pot B 5M 141
Aberdare Gdns. NW7 . . . . .7K 165
Aberdare Rd. EN3: Pon E 6G 156
Aberdeen Cotts. HA7: Stanm 7K 163
Aberdeen Rd. HA3: Weal 9G 162
Aberford Rd. WD6: Bore 4A 152
Abigail Cl. LU3: Lut .6F 46
Abigail Ct. LU3: Lut .6F 46
Abingdon Ct. *EN8: Wal C* *6J 145*
(off High St.)
Abingdon Pl. EN6: Pot B 5A 142
Abingdon Rd. LU4: Lut 6M 45
Abinger Cl. SG1: Stev 6L 51
Abington Rd. SG8: Ab P, Lit 1G 6
Abraham Cl. WD19: Watf 4K 161
Abrams La. SG8: Chris 1M 17
Abridge Cl. EN8: Wal C 8H 145
Abstacle Hill HP23: Tring 3L 101
Acacia Cl. EN7: C'hunt 9C 132
HA7: Stanm 6F 162
Acacia Gro. HP4: Berk 2M 121
Acacia Ho. SL9: Chal P 8B 158
Acacia Rd. EN2: Enf .3B 156
Acacias, The EN4: E Bar 7C 154
Acacias Ct. *EN11: Hod* *8L 115*
(off Brocket Rd.)
Acacia St. AL10: Hat 3G 128
Acacia Vs. *LU6: Duns* *9E 44*
(off Icknield St.)
Acacia Wlk. AL5: Harp 9E 88
HP23: Tring 3K 101
Academia Av. EN10: Turn 7K 133
Academy, The *LU1: Lut* *2G 66*
(off Holly St.)
Academy Ct. AL2: Lon C 8J 127
WD6: Bore 6A 152
Academy Ho. *WD6: Bore* *6A 152*
(off Academy Ct.)
Access Bus. Pk. SG1: Stev 6J 51
Acer Ct. *EN3: Enf H* *5J 157*
(off Enstone Rd.)
Acers AL2: Par S 1D 138
Achilles Cl. HP2: Hem H 9B 106
Acklington Dr. NW9 .8E 164
Ackroyd Rd. SG8: Roys 5E 8
Acme Rd. WD24: Watf 2J 149
Acorn Cl. EN2: Enf 3N 155
HA7: Stanm 7J 163
LU2: Lut 6H 47
Acorn Ct. AL2: Lon C .9J 127
EN8: Wal C 6H 145
Acorn Glade AL6: Wel 3M 91
Acorn La. EN6: Cuff .1K 143
Acorn M. CM18: Harl .8B 118
Acorn Pl. WD24: Watf 1J 149
Acorn Rd. HP3: Hem H 3C 124
Acorns, The AL4: St Alb 2L 127
LU2: Lut *8F 46*
(off Bedford Rd.)
Acorn St. SG12: Huns 8F 96
Acremore St. SG11: L Had 1L 77
Acre Piece SG4: Hit .4A 34
Acre Way HA6: North 8H 161
Acrewood HP2: Hem H 3A 124
Acrewood Way AL4: St Alb 2N 127
Acton Cl. EN8: C'hunt 4J 145
Actons La. CM21: H Wyc 5L 97
Acworth Cl. N9 . . . . .9G 156
Acworth Ct. *LU4: Lut* *4M 45*
(off Acworth Cres.)
Acworth Cres. LU4: Lut 4M 45
Adams Cl. N3 . . . . .7N 165
Adams Ct. WD25: Watf 9M 137
Adamsfield EN7: C'hunt 8D 132
Adams Ho. *CM20: Harl* *5N 117*
(off Post Office Rd.)
Adamsrill Cl. EN1: Enf 8B 156
Adams Way HP23: Tring 1N 101
Adam's Yd. SG14: H'ford 9B 94
Adderley Rd. CM23: Bis S 1H 79
HA3: Weal 8G 162
Addington Cotts. HP22: Wen 9A 100
Addington Way LU4: Lut 6N 45
Addis Cl. EN3: Enf H 3H 157
Addiscombe Rd. WD18: Watf 8B 166 (6K 149)
Addison Av. N14 . . . . .8G 155
Addison Cl. HA6: North 8J 161
Addison Rd. EN3: Enf H 3G 157
Addison Way HA6: North 8H 161
Adelaide Cl. EN1: Enf 2C 156
HA7: Stanm 4H 163
Adelaide St. AL3: St Alb 1D 166 (1E 126)
LU1: Lut 1F 66
Adele Av. AL6: Wel 4M 91
Aden Rd. EN3: Brim .6J 157
ADEYFIELD 2C 124
Adeyfield Gdns. HP2: Hem H 1B 124
Adeyfield Rd. HP2: Hem H 2A 124
Adhara Rd. HA6: North 5J 161
Adingtons CM20: Harl 4B 118
Adlington Ct. LU4: Lut 4M 45
Admiral Dr. SG1: Stev 9B 36
Admiral Hood Ho. SL9: Chal P 4B 158
Admirals Cl. AL4: Col H 5E 128
Admirals Ct. HA6: North 5H 161
Admiral St. SG13: H'ford 9E 94
Admirals Wlk. AL1: St Alb 4H 127
EN11: Hod 1L 133
Admiral Way HP4: Berk 8K 103
Adrian Cl. EN5: Barn 8K 153
HP1: Hem H 3L 123
UB9: Hare 8N 159
Adrian Rd. WD5: Abb L 4G 137
Adstock M. SL9: Chal P 8A 158
Adstone Rd. LU1: Cad 5B 66
Adventure Castle 7N 115
Adventure Island Playbarn 2F 98
Adventure World 8L 127
Aerodrome Rd. NW9 .9F 164
Aerodrome Way WD25: Watf 7H 137
Aeroville NW9 . . . . .9E 164
Agricola Pl. EN1: Enf 7D 156
Aidans Cl. LU6: Duns 8B 44
Ailantus Ct. HA8: Edg 5N 163
Ailsworth Rd. LU3: Lut 3B 46
Ainsdale Cres. HA5: Pin 9B 162
Ainsdale Rd. WD19: Watf 3L 161
Ainsland Ct. LU4: Lut 7L 45
Ainsley Cl. N9 . . . . .9C 156
Aintree Rd. SG8: Roys 7F 8
Aintree Way SG1: Stev 1B 52
Airedale HP2: Hem H 8A 106
LU4: Lut 5M 45
Airport App. Rd. LU2: Lut 9M 47
Airport Executive Pk. LU2: Lut 9L 47
Airport Way LU1: Lut 5G 67
LU2: Lut 2L 67
Aitken Rd. EN5: Barn 7J 153
Akeman Cl. AL3: St Alb 4A 126
Akeman St. HP23: N Gnd 4E 102
HP23: Tring 3M 101
Akers Ct. EN8: Wal C 5J 145
Akers La. WD3: Chor 8G 147
Alamein Cl. EN10: Brox 2H 133
Alana Hgts. E4 . . . . .9M 157
Alandale Dr. HA5: Pin 8K 161
Alan Dr. EN5: Barn .8L 153
Alban Arena (Theatre & Cinema)
. . . . .2D 166 (2E 126)
Alban Av. AL3: St Alb 9E 108
Alban Ct. *AL1: St Alb* *2J 127*
(off Burleigh Rd.)
AL7: Welw G 8M 91
Alban Cres. WD6: Bore 3B 152
Alban Ho. WD6: Bore 3B 152
Albanian Ct. AL1: St Alb 3H 127
Alban Pk. AL4: St Alb 2N 127
Alban Rd. SG6: L Gar .8J 23
Albans Vw. WD25: Watf 6K 137
Alban Way AL10: Hat 9F 110
Albanwood WD25: Watf 6K 137
Albany Cl. WD23: Bush 8E 150
Albany Ct. AL5: Harp 7D 88
E4 . . . . .8L 157
HA8: Edg 8D 164
LU1: Lut 9D 46
Albany Cres. HA8: Edg 7A 164
Albany Ga. AL1: St Alb 5D 166 (3E 126)
Albany Leisure Cen. .2H 157
Albany M. *AL2: Chis G* *9B 126*
(off Nth. Orbital Rd.)
SG12: Ware 6J 95
Albany Pk. Av. EN3: Enf W 3G 157
Albany Pl. AL7: Welw G 9L 91
Albany Rd. EN3: Enf W 1H 157
Albany Ter. HP23: Tring 9N 81
Alba Rd. CM17: Harl .5E 118
Albaster Av. LU5: Hou R 6D 44
Albatross NW9 . . . . .9F 164
Albatross Ct. SG13: H'ford 8F 94
Albatross Way AL10: Hat 8D 110
Albemarle Av. EN6: Pot B 6A 142
EN8: C'hunt 1G 144
Albemarle Pk. HA7: Stanm 5K 163
Albemarle Rd. EN4: E Bar 9D 154
Albermarle Cl. LU4: Lut 6J 45
Alberta Rd. EN1: Enf 8D 156
Albert Ct. *EN8: Wal C* *7K 145*
(off Holdbrook Sth.)
LU6: Duns 1F 64
Albert Gdns. CM17: Harl 7F 118
LU1: Lut 2G 67
Albertine St. CM17: Harl 4F 118
Albert Pl. N3 . . . . .8N 165
Albert Rd. EN4: E Bar 6B 154
LU1: Lut 2G 67
NW7 . . . . .5F 164
SG15: Arl 8A 10
Albert Rd. Nth. WD17: Watf 6C 166 (5K 149)
Albert Rd. Sth. WD17: Watf 6B 166 (5K 149)
Albert St. AL1: St Alb 4C 166 (3E 126)
AL3: Mark 2A 86
HP23: Tring 3M 101
SG1: Stev 2J 51
Albion, The SG12: Ware 5H 95
Albion Cl. SG13: H'ford 9C 94
Albion Ct. LU2: Lut .9G 46
LU6: Duns 9E 44
Albion Hill HP2: Hem H 3N 123
Albion M. LU6: Duns .9E 44
Albion Path *LU2: Lut* *9G 46*
(off Dudley St.)
Albion Pl. *HP23: Tring* *3M 101*
(off Akeman St.)
Albion Rd. AL1: St Alb 2G 127
LU2: Lut 9G 46
LU7: Pits 2B 82
Albion St. LU6: Duns .9E 44
Albion Ter. E4 . . . . .6M 157
Albuhera Cl. EN2: Enf 3M 155
ALBURY 3K 57
Albury Cl. LU3: Lut 9C 30
Albury Dr. HA5: Pin .8L 161
ALBURY END 5J 57
Albury Gro. Rd. EN8: C'hunt 3H 145
Albury Ride EN8: C'hunt 4H 145
Albury Rd. SG9: Fur P 8M 41
SG11: L Had 7M 57
Albury Wlk. EN8: C'hunt 3G 145
(not continuous)
Albyn Ho. HP2: Hem H 2N 123
Alconbury AL7: Welw G 9D 92
CM23: Bis S 8K 59
Alconbury Cl. WD6: Bore 3N 151
Alcorns, The CM24: Stans 1N 59
Alcuin Ct. HA7: Stanm 7K 163
Aldbanks LU6: Duns .8C 44
ALDBURY 1G 103
Aldbury Cl. AL4: St Alb 6K 109
WD25: Watf 9M 137
Aldbury Gdns. *HP23: Tring* *9N 81*
(off Morefields)
Aldbury Gro. AL7: Welw G 9A 92
Aldbury M. N9 . . . . .9B 156
Aldbury Rd. WD3: R'orth 9J 147
Aldeburgh Cl. SG1: Stev 9G 35
ALDENHAM 2C 150
Aldenham Av. WD7: Rad 9H 139
Aldenham Cl. LU4: Lut 6J 45
Aldenham Country Park 7J 151
Aldenham Country Park Rare Breeds Farm
. . . . .7J 151
Aldenham Golf Course 2C 150
Aldenham Gro. WD7: Rad 7J 139
Aldenham Hall *AL10: Hat* *8E 110*
(off Mosquito Way)
Aldenham Rd. WD6: Elst 5H 151
WD7: Rad 8H 139
WD19: Watf 8N 149
WD23: Bush 8N 149
WD25: Let H 3F 150
Aldenham Sailing Club 7K 151
Alden Mead *HA5: Hat E* *6B 162*
(off The Avenue)
Alderbury Rd. CM24: Stans 1N 59
Alder Cl. AL2: Par S .1C 138
CM23: Bis S 4F 78
EN11: Hod 6M 115
SG7: Bald 4L 23
Alder Ct. LU3: Lut 6D 46
Alder Cres. LU3: Lut .5C 46
Alderley Ct. HP4: Berk 2N 121
Alderman Cl. AL9: Welh G 6J 129
Aldermere Av. EN8: C'hunt 1G 145
Alderney Ho. EN3: Enf W 2H 157
WD18: Watf 8H 149
Alderpark Mdw.
HP23: Lon M 3G 80
Alders, The N21 . . . . .8M 155
Aldersbrook Av. EN1: Enf 4C 156
Alders Cl. HA8: Edg .5C 164
Alders End La. AL5: Harp 5A 88
Alders Rd. HA8: Edg .5C 164
Alders Wlk. CM21: Saw 5G 99
Alderton Cl. LU2: Lut 8M 47
Alderton Dr. HP4: Lit G 7L 83
Alder Wlk. WD25: Watf 8K 137
Alderwood Ho. WD19: Watf 3L 161
Alderwood M. EN4: Had W 2B 154
Aldhous Cl. LU3: Lut .4D 46
Aldis M. EN3: Enf L .1L 157
Aldock AL7: Welw G .3N 111
Aldock Rd. SG1: Stev .2L 51
Aldridge Av. EN3: Enf L 2L 157
HA7: Stanm 8M 163
HA8: Edg 3B 164
Aldridge Ct. SG7: Bald 2L 23
Aldridge Wlk. N14 . . . . .9K 155
Aldwick AL1: St Alb .4J 127
Aldwickbury Cres. AL5: Harp 6E 88
Aldwickbury Park Golf Course 7F 88
Aldwick Ct. AL1: St Alb 4J 127
Aldwick Rd. AL5: Harp 7F 88
Aldwyck Ct. HP1: Hem H 1M 123
Aldwyck Ho. LU5: Duns 7D 44
Aldwyke Ri. SG12: Ware 4G 94
Aldykes AL10: Hat 9F 110
Alesia Rd. LU3: Lut .3A 46
Alexander Cl. EN4: E Bar 6C 154
Alexander Ct. EN8: C'hunt 3H 145
Alexander Ga. SG1: Stev 1B 52
Alexander M. CM17: Harl 8F 118

Alexander Rd.—Artesian Gro.

Alexander Rd. AL2: Lon C 7K 127
SG5: Stot 6F 10
SG14: H'ford 9M 93
Alexandra Av. LU3: Lut 6E 46
Alexandra Ct. N14 . . . . . 7H 155
WD24: Watf 4L 149
Alexandra M. WD17: Watf 4J 149
Alexandra Rd. AL1: St Alb 3E 166 (2F 126)
(not continuous)
CM17: Harl 5E 118
EN3: Pon E 6H 157
HP2: Hem H 1N 123
N9 . . . . . 9F 156
SG5: Hit 1N 33
WD3: Sar 9K 135
WD4: Chippf 3K 135
WD4: Kin L 2C 136
WD6: Bore 2D 152
WD17: Watf 4J 149
Alexandra Rd. Ind. Est. EN3: Pon E 6H 157
Alexandra Way EN8: Wal C 7K 145
Alex Ct. HP2: Hem H 1N 123
Alexis Row EN10: Brox 1K 133
ALEY GREEN 6B 66
Aleyn Way SG7: Bald 2A 24
Alfred St. LU5: Duns 9F 44
Alfriston Cl. LU2: Lut 6L 47
Algar Cl. HA7: Stanm 5G 163
Alice Cl. *EN5: N Bar* *6B 154*
(off Station App.)
Alington La. SG6: L Gar 8F 22
Alison Ct. HP2: Hem H 1E 124
Allandale AL3: St Alb 5C 126
HP2: Hem H 9N 105
Allandale Av. N3 . . . . . 9L 165
Allandale Cres. EN6: Pot B 5L 141
Allandale Rd. EN3: Enf W 9H 145
Allard Cl. EN7: C'hunt 9D 132
Allard Cres. WD23: B Hea 1D 162
Allard Ho. *NW9* *9F 164*
(off Boulevard Dr.)
Allard Way EN10: Brox 3J 133
Alldicks Rd. HP3: Hem H 4B 124
Allenby Av. LU5: Duns 8K 45
Allen Cl. AL4: Wheat 8L 89
LU5: Duns 9G 44
WD7: Shen 5M 139
Allen Ct. AL10: Hat 2H 129
Allendale LU3: Lut 9C 30
Allende Av. / Fifth Av. CM20: Harl 3M 117
(not continuous)
ALLEN'S GREEN 1B 98
Allens Rd. EN3: Pon E 7G 157
Allerton Cl. WD6: Bore 2N 151
Allerton Rd. WD6: Bore 2M 151
Alleyns Rd. SG1: Stev 2K 51
Alleys, The HP2: Hem H 1N 123
Allianz Park 7J 165
Allied Bus. Cen. AL5: Harp 3D 88
Allington Ct. EN3: Pon E 7H 157
Allis M. CM17: Harl 5E 118
Allison SG6: L Gar 6J 23
All Saints Cl. CM23: Bis S 9J 59
All Saints Cres. WD25: Watf 6M 137
All Saints La. WD3: Crox G 8C 148
All Saints M. HA3: Har W 6F 162
All Saints Rd. LU5: Hou R 4E 44
Allum La. WD6: Elst 7L 151
Allwood Rd. EN7: C'hunt 9D 132
Alma Ct. EN6: Pot B 3B 142
HP4: Berk 8J 103
WD6: Bore 2N 151
Alma Cut AL1: St Alb 5E 166 (3F 126)
Alma Link LU1: Lut 1F 66
Alma Pl. WD25: Watf 9N 137
Alma Rd. AL1: St Alb 4F 166 (3F 126)
EN3: Enf H, Pon E 7J 157
HP4: Berk 8J 103
Alma Rd. Ind. Est. EN3: Pon E 6H 157
Alma Row HA3: Har W 8E 162
Alma St. LU1: Lut 1F 66
Alma St. Pas. *LU1: Lut* *1F 66*
(off Alma St.)
Almond Cl. LU3: Lut 5D 46
(Carolyn Ct.)
LU3: Lut 4C 46
(Lonsdale Cl.)
Almonds, The AL1: St Alb 6J 127
Almonds La. SG1: Stev 9L 35
Almond Wlk. AL10: Hat 3G 129
Almond Way HA2: Harr 9C 162
WD6: Bore 6B 152
Almshouse La. EN1: Enf 1F 156
Almshouses *CM17: Harl* *2G 118*
(off Sheering Rd.)
Almshouses, The *EN8: C'hunt* *3H 145*
(off Turner's Hill)
Alms La. SG7: Ashw 9M 5
Alnwick Dr. HP23: Lon M 9D 60
Alpha Bus. Pk. AL9: Welh G 5J 129
Alpha Ct. EN11: Hod 7L 115
WD17: Watf 7E 166
Alpha Pl. CM23: Bis S 9H 59
Alpha Rd. EN3: Pon E 6J 157
Alpine Cl. SG4: Hit 5A 34
Alpine Ter. *LU1: Lut* *2F 66*
(off Stockwood Cres.)
Alpine Wlk. HA7: Stanm 2F 162
Alpine Way LU3: Lut 1N 45
Alsa Bus. Pk. CM24: Stans 9N 43
Alsa St. CM24: Stans 9N 43
Alsford Wharf HP4: Berk 1N 121
Alsop Cl. AL2: Lon C 9M 127
LU5: Hou R 4E 44
Alston Rd. EN5: Barn 5L 153
HP1: Hem H 3K 123
Alston Works EN5: Barn 4L 153
Altair Way HA6: North 4H 161
Altham Ct. HA2: Harr 8C 162
Altham Gdns. WD19: Watf 4M 161
Altham Gro. CM20: Harl 4B 118
Altham Rd. HA5: Pin 7N 161
Altham Way WD19: Watf 5N 161
Althorp Cl. EN5: Ark 9G 152
Althorp Rd. AL1: St Alb 1F 166 (1G 126)
LU3: Lut 8E 46
Alton Av. HA7: Stanm 7G 163
Alton Gdns. LU1: Lut 3H 67
Alton Rd. LU1: Lut 3H 67
Altwood AL5: Harp 6E 88
Alva Way WD19: Watf 2M 161
Alverstone Av. EN4: E Bar 9D 154
Alverton AL3: St Alb 8D 108
Alwin Pl. WD18: Watf 6G 149
Alwyn Cl. LU2: Lut 7G 46
WD6: Elst 8N 151
Alyngton HP4: Berk 7J 103
Alzey Gdns. AL5: Harp 7E 88
Amber Cl. EN5: N Bar 8A 154
Amberden Av. N3 . . . . . 9N 165
Amberley Cl. AL5: Harp 5C 88
LU2: Lut 5M 47
Amberley Gdns. EN1: Enf 9C 156
Amberley Grn. SG12: Ware 3G 95
Amberley Rd. EN1: Enf 9D 156
Amberley Ter. *WD19: Watf* *8N 149*
(off Villiers Rd.)
Amberry Ct. *CM20: Harl* *5N 117*
(off Netteswell Dr.)
Amberside Ct. HP3: Hem H 5L 123
Ambleside *AL5: Harp* *5E 88*
(off Langdale Av.)
LU3: Lut 4B 46
Ambleside Cres. EN3: Enf H 5H 157
Ambrose La. AL5: Harp 3A 88
Amelia Ho. *NW9* *9F 164*
(off Boulevard Dr.)
Amenbury Ct. AL5: Harp 6B 88
Amenbury La. AL5: Harp 6A 88
Amersham Ho. *WD18: Watf* *9G 149*
(off Chenies Way)
Amersham Pl. HP7: L Chal 3A 146
Amersham Rd. HP6: L Chal 3A 146
SL9: Chal P 4A 158
WD3: Chen 3A 146
Amersham Way HP6: L Chal 3A 146
Amesbury Ct. EN2: Enf 4M 155
Amesbury Dr. E4 . . . . . 8M 157
Ames Cl. LU3: Lut 9B 30
Amethyst Ct. *EN3: Enf H* *5J 157*
(off Enstone Rd.)
Amethyst Wlk. AL8: Welw G 2H 111
Amhurst Cl. EN3: Enf W 1H 157
Amhurst Rd. LU4: Lut 6J 45
Amias Dr. HA8: Edg 4M 163
Amiot Ho. *NW9* *9F 164*
(off Heritage Av.)
Amor Way SG6: L Gar 5H 23
Amport Pl. NW7 . . . . . 6L 165
AMWELL 8J 89
Amwell Cl. EN2: Enf 7B 156
WD25: Watf 8N 137
Amwell Comn. AL7: Welw G 1A 112
Amwell Ct. EN11: Hod 7L 115
Amwell End SG12: Ware 6H 95
Amwell Hill SG12: Gt A 9K 95
Amwell La. AL4: Wheat 8J 89
SG12: Gt A, Stan A 9L 95
Amwell Nature Reserve 9M 95
Amwell Pl. SG13: Hert H 2G 114
Amwell St. EN11: Hod 7L 115
(not continuous)
Amy Johnson Ct. HA8: Edg 9B 164
Anchor Cl. EN8: C'hunt 1H 145
Anchor Cotts. SG12: Wad 9H 75
Anchor Ct. EN1: Enf 7C 156
Anchor La. HP1: Hem H 4L 123
(not continuous)
SG12: Tonw, Wad 1D 94
Anchor Rd. SG7: Bald 4M 23
Anchor St. CM23: Bis S 2J 79
Anchor Street Leisure Pk. 2H 79
Ancient Almshouses *EN8: C'hunt* *3H 145*
(off Turner's Hill)
ANDELLS END 6G 69
Anderson Cl. CM23: Man 8H 43
N21 . . . . . 7L 155
UB9: Hare 8K 159
Anderson Ho. AL4: St Alb 3L 127
Anderson Rd. SG2: Stev 3C 52
WD7: Shen 6A 140
Andersons Ho. SG5: Hit 2N 33
Anderson's La. SG9: Gt Hor 9D 28
Anderson Wlk. SG5: Stot 1C 22
Andover Cl. LU4: Lut 3M 45
Andrew Cl. WD7: Shen 6N 139
Andrew Reed Ct. *WD24: Watf* *4L 149*
(off Keele Cl.)
Andrews Cl. HP2: Hem H 9N 105
Andrewsfield AL7: Welw G 9B 92
Andrew's La. EN7: C'hunt, Gof O 1C 144
Anelle Ri. HP3: Hem H 6B 124
Anershall HP22: W'rave 5A 60
Angel Cl. LU4: Lut 6N 45
Angel Cotts. SG5: Gt Off 8E 32
Angelica Av. SG5: Stot 7F 10
Angell's Mdw. SG7: Ashw 9M 5
Angel Pavement *SG8: Roys* *7D 8*
(off Market Hill)
Angels La. LU5: Hou R 4E 44
Anglefield Rd. HP4: Berk 1L 121
Angle Pl. HP4: Berk 1L 121
(not continuous)
Anglesey Cl. CM23: Bis S 1E 78
Anglesey Rd. EN3: Pon E 6F 156
WD19: Watf 5L 161
Anglesmede Cres. HA5: Pin 9B 162
Angle Ways SG2: Stev 7N 51
Anglian Bus. Pk. SG8: Roys 6B 8
Anglian Cl. WD24: Watf 4L 149
Angotts Mead SG1: Stev 3H 51
Angus Cl. LU4: Lut 6K 45
Angus Gdns. NW9 . . . . . 8D 164
Anise Ct. *SG1: Stev* *8B 36*
(off Admiral Dr.)
Anmer Gdns. LU4: Lut 5L 45
Anmersh Gro. HA7: Stanm 8L 163
Annables Ct. AL1: St Alb 3E 166
Annables La. AL5: Harp 3H 87
Annette Cl. HA3: Weal 9F 162
Anns Cl. HP23: Tring 3K 101
Ansell Ct. SG1: Stev 9H 35
Anselm Rd. HA5: Hat E 7A 162
Anson Cl. AL1: St Alb 4J 127
AL4: San 5K 109
HP3: Bov 9C 122
Anson Wlk. HA6: North 4E 160
Anstee Rd. LU4: Lut 3L 45
ANSTEY 5D 28
Anston Ct. HP3: Hem H 6N 123
Anthony Cl. NW7 . . . . . 4E 164
WD19: Watf 1L 161
Anthony Gdns. LU1: Lut 3F 66
Anthony Rd. WD6: Bore 4N 151
Anthorne Cl. EN6: Pot B 4A 142
Anthus M. HA6: North 7G 160
Antlers Hill E4 . . . . . 7M 157
Antoinette Ct. WD5: Abb L 2H 137
Antoneys Cl. HA5: Pin 9M 161
Antonine Ga. AL3: St Alb 3B 126
Anvil Av. SG8: Lit 3H 7
Anvil Cl. HP3: Bov 1E 134
Anvil Ct. LU3: Lut 4A 46
SG9: Bunt 2J 39
Anvil Ho. AL5: Harp 5B 88
Anvil Pl. AL2: Chis G 8B 126
Apex Bus. Cen. LU5: Duns 7F 44
APEX CORNER 4E 164
Apex Pde. *NW7* *4D 164*
(off Selvage La.)
Apex Point AL9: Welh G 4J 129
Aplins Cl. AL5: Harp 5A 88
Apollo Av. HA6: North 5J 161
Apollo Cl. LU5: Duns 1G 65
Apollo Ct. AL10: Hat 9E 110
SG1: Stev *8B 36*
(off Admiral Dr.)
Apollo Way HP2: Hem H 9B 106
SG2: Stev 1B 52
Appleby Dr. WD3: Crox G 6D 148
Appleby Gdns. LU6: Duns 1E 64
APPLEBY STREET 8D 132
Appleby St. EN7: C'hunt 7B 132
Apple Cotts. HP3: Bov 9D 122
Applecroft AL2: Par S 1C 138
HP4: Berk 8J 103
SG16: L Ston 1J 21
Applecroft Rd. AL8: Welw G 9H 91
LU2: Lut 5L 47
Appledore Cl. HA8: Edg 8A 164
Appledore Way NW7 . . . . . 7K 165
Applefield HP7: L Chal 3A 146
Appleford Cl. EN11: Hod 6K 115
Applegate CM21: Saw 5F 98
Apple Glebe MK45: Bar C 9E 18
Apple Gro. EN1: Enf 5C 156
LU4: Lut 5J 45
Apple Orchard, The HP2: Hem H 9B 106
Appleton Av. SG12: W'side 2B 96
Appleton Cl. CM19: Harl 7M 117
Appleton Ct. SG1: Stev 2H 51
Appleton Flds. CM23: Bis S 4G 79
Appletree Gdns. EN4: E Bar 6D 154
Apple Tree Gro. AL3: Red 9K 87
Appletrees *SG5: Hit* *4M 33*
(off Wratten Rd. W.)
Appletree Wlk. WD25: Watf 7K 137
Applewood Cl. AL5: Harp 4N 87
N20 . . . . . 9D 154
Appleyard Ter. EN3: Enf W 1G 157
Approach, The EN1: Enf 4F 156
EN6: Pot B 5M 141
Approach Rd. AL1: St Alb 3F 126
EN4: E Bar 6C 154
HA8: Edg 6A 164
Appspond La. AL2: Pot C 5K 125
HP3: Hem H 5K 125
April Pl. CM21: Saw 4H 99
APSLEY 6A 124
Apsley Cl. CM23: Bis S 4H 79
APSLEY END 4N 19
Apsley End Rd. SG5: Shil 6M 19
Apsley Grange HP3: Hem H 7A 124
Apsley Ind. Est. HP3: Hem H 6N 123
Apsley Lock HP3: Hem H 7A 124
Apsley Mills Retail Pk. HP3: Hem H 6A 124
Apsley Station (Rail) 7A 124
Apton Ct. CM23: Bis S 1H 79
Apton Flds. CM23: Bis S 2H 79
Apton Rd. CM23: Bis S 2H 79
Aquadrome, The 2M 159
Aquarius Way HA6: North 5J 161
Aquasplash 3B 124
Arabia Cl. E4 . . . . . 9N 157
Arado Ho. *NW9* *9F 164*
(off Boulevard Dr.)
Aragon Cl. EN2: Enf 2L 155
HP2: Hem H 6E 106
Aragon Pk. LU5: Hou R 6E 44
Aran Cl. AL5: Harp 9E 88
Aran Dr. HA7: Stanm 4K 163
Arbon Ct. SG14: H'ford 9A 94
Arbour, The SG13: H'ford 2B 114
Arbour Cl. LU3: Lut 9C 30
Arbour Rd. EN3: Pon E 5H 157
Arbroath Grn. WD19: Watf 3J 161
Arbroath Rd. LU3: Lut 1D 46
Arcade, The *AL10: Hat* *8H 111*
(off Robin Hood La.)
LU4: Lut 8E 46
SG5: Hit 3M 33
SG6: L Gar 5F 22
Arcade Wlk. SG5: Hit 3M 33
Arcadia Av. N3 . . . . . 9N 165
Arcadian Ct. AL5: Harp 5B 88
Archer Cl. EN5: Barn 8M 153
WD4: Kin L 2B 136
Archer Pl. CM23: Bis S 2H 79
Archer Rd. SG1: Stev 3M 51
Archers SG9: Bunt 2K 39
Archers Cl. AL3: Red 1K 107
SG14: H'ford 8A 94
Archers Ct. SG5: Hit 3M 33
Archers Dr. EN3: Enf H 4G 156
Archers Flds. AL1: St Alb 9G 108
Archers Grn. SG14: Pans 7D 92
Archers Grn. La. AL6: Tew 6C 92
Archers Ride AL7: Welw G 2A 112
Archers Way SG6: L Gar 5D 22
Archery Cl. HA3: Weal 9G 163
Arches, The SG6: L Gar 4G 23
Archfield AL7: Welw G 6L 91
Archibald Cl. EN3: Enf W 9H 145
Archington Ct. AL1: St Alb 4F 166
Archive Cl. HP22: Ast C 1C 100
Archive M. HP4: Berk 3L 121
Arch Rd. SG4: Gt Wym 6D 34
Archway Ct. *HP1: Hem H* *1N 123*
(off Chapel St.)
Archway Ho. AL9: Hat 8J 111
Archway Pde. LU3: Lut 5B 46
Archway Rd. LU3: Lut 5A 46
Arcon Ter. N9 . . . . . 9E 156
Arctic Ho. *NW9* *9F 164*
(off Heritage Av.)
ARDELEY 7L 37
Arden Cl. HP3: Bov 1D 134
WD23: B Hea 9G 150
Arden Ct. WD3: R'orth 2K 159
WD17: Watf *3J 149*
(off Lockhart Rd.)
Arden Gro. AL5: Harp 6C 88
Arden Pl. LU2: Lut 8G 47
Arden Press Way SG6: L Gar 5H 23
Arden Press Way Ind. Est. SG6: L Gar 5H 23
Arden Rd. N3 . . . . . 9M 165
Ardens Marsh AL4: St Alb 8M 109
Ardens Way AL4: St Alb 8L 109
Ardentinny AL1: St Alb 5F 166
Ardleigh Grn. LU2: Lut 8M 47
Ardley Cl. LU6: Duns 3F 64
Ardross Av. HA6: North 5G 161
Arena, The EN3: Enf L 2K 157
Arena Pde. SG6: L Gar 5F 22
Arenson Way LU5: Duns 7E 44
Argan Cl. EN5: Barn 5M 153
Argent Ct. *EN5: N Bar* *6B 154*
(off Leicester Rd.)
Argent Way EN7: C'hunt, Gof O 8B 132
Argyle Ct. WD18: Watf 6H 149
Argyle Rd. EN5: Barn 6J 153
N12 . . . . . 5N 165
Argyle Way SG1: Stev 4J 51
Argyle Way Trad. Est. SG1: Stev 4J 51
Argyll Av. LU3: Lut 7E 46
Argyll Gdns. HA8: Edg 9B 164
Argyll Rd. HP2: Hem H 6A 106
Arianne Bus. Cen. LU5: Hou R 6E 44
ARKLEY 7G 153
Arkley Ct. HP2: Hem H 6D 106
Arkley Dr. EN5: Ark 6G 153
Arkley Golf Course 7F 152
Arkley La. EN5: Ark 2F 152
Arkley Pk. EN5: Ark 9D 152
Arkley Rd. HP2: Hem H 6D 106
Arkley Vw. EN5: Ark 6H 153
Arklow Ct. WD3: Chor 6G 146
Arkwrights CM20: Harl 5B 118
(not continuous)
ARLESEY 8A 10
Arlesey Ho. *SG15: Arl* *4A 10*
(off Church End)
Arlesey Old Moat Nature Reserve 5A 10
Arlesey Rd. SG5: Ick 8M 21
SG5: Stot 5D 10
SG6: L Gar 4A 22
SG15: Arl 5N 21
SG16: Henl 4A 10
(not continuous)
Arlesey Station (Rail) 4A 10
Arlesey-Stotfold By-Pass SG5: Stot 8E 10
SG15: Arl 4A 10
Arlingham M. *EN9: Wal A* *6N 145*
(off Sun St.)
Arlington N12 . . . . . 3N 165
Arlington Bus. Pk. SG1: Stev 7K 51
Arlington Ct. SG1: Stev 7K 51
Arlington Cres. EN8: Wal C 7J 145
Arlington Grn. NW7 . . . . . 7K 165
Armand Cl. WD17: Watf 2H 149
Armfield Rd. EN2: Enf 3B 156
Armitage Cl. WD3: Loud 6N 147
Armitage Gdns. LU4: Lut 8N 45
Armourers Cl. CM23: Bis S 4D 78
Armour Ri. SG4: Hit 9B 22
Armstrong Cl. AL2: Lon C 9M 127
WD6: Bore 5C 152
Armstrong Cres. EN4: C'ters 5C 154
Armstrong Gdns. WD7: Shen 5M 139
Armstrong Pl. *HP1: Hem H* *1N 123*
(off High St.)
Arnald Way LU5: Hou R 5D 44
Arncliffe Cres. LU2: Lut 8G 46
Arndale Ri. *LU2: Lut* *9H 47*
(off Moulton Ri.)
Arnett Cl. WD3: R'orth 8K 147
Arnett Way WD3: R'orth 8K 147
Arnold Av. E. EN3: Enf L 2L 157
Arnold Av. W. EN3: Enf L 2K 157
Arnold Cl. LU2: Lut 6J 47
MK45: Bar C 9E 18
SG1: Stev 8K 35
SG4: Hit 2B 34
Arnold Rd. EN9: Wal A 8N 145
Arnold's Cotts. HP5: C'dge 9A 120
Arnolds La. SG7: Hinx 7F 4
Arnold Ter. HA7: Stanm 5G 162
Arran Cl. HP3: Hem H 4E 124
Arran Ct. LU1: Lut 1F 66
NW9 . . . . . 9F 164
Arran Grn. WD19: Watf 4M 161
Arran Ho. WD18: Watf 8J 149
Arranmore Ct. WD23: Bush 6N 149
Arretine Cl. AL3: St Alb 4A 126
Arrow Cl. LU3: Lut 3A 46
Artesian Gro. EN5: N Bar 6B 154

Arthur Gibbens Ct.—Baddeley Cl.

Arthur Gibbens Ct. SG1: Stev 9N 35
Arthur Rd. AL1: St Alb 2J 127
Arthurs Ct. SG12: Stan A 2N 115
Arthur St. LU1: Lut 2G 66
WD23: Bush 8G 166 (6M 149)
Artichoke Dell WD3: Chor 6H 147
Artillery Pl. HA3: Har W 7D 162
Artisan Ct. *CM23: Bis S* 3J 79
(off Tanners Wharf)
Artisan Cres. AL3: St Alb 1A 166 (1D 126)
(not continuous)
Art School Yd. AL1: St Alb 3D 166
Artshed Arts 3E 94
Arundel Cl. EN8: C'hunt 1G 144
HP2: Hem H 1D 124
SG2: A'ton 6D 52
Arundel Dr. WD6: Bore 6C 152
Arundel Gdns. HA8: Edg 7D 164
Arundel Gro. AL3: St Alb 7E 108
Arundel Ho. *WD6: Bore* 6C 152
(off Arundel Dr.)
Arundel Rd. EN4: C'ters 5D 154
LU4: Lut 6C 46
WD5: Abb L 5J 137
Arwood M. SG7: Bald 3M 23
Asbury Ct. *N21* 7K 155
(off Pennington Dr.)
Ascent Ho. *NW9* 9F 164
(off Boulevard Dr.)
Ascent Pk. CM20: Harl 1C 118
Ascot Cl. CM23: Bis S 9L 59
WD6: Elst 7A 152
Ascot Ct. WD3: Crox G 8D 148
Ascot Cres. SG1: Stev 9A 36
(not continuous)
Ascot Dr. SG6: L Gar 5H 23
Ascot Gdns. EN3: Enf W 1G 157
Ascot Ind. Est. SG6: L Gar 7H 23
Ascot Pl. HA7: Stanm 5K 163
Ascot Rd. LU3: Lut 7D 46
SG8: Roys 7F 8
WD18: Watf 7G 148
Ascots La. AL7: Welw G 5L 111
AL9: Hat 5L 111
Ascot Ter. SG12: Gt A 8K 95
Ashanger La. SG7: Clo 7C 24
Ashbottom Cl. SG2: Stev 1N 71
Ashbourne AL2: Bri W 4A 138
Ashbourne Cl. SG6: L Gar 8H 23
Ashbourne Ct. AL4: St Alb 5K 127
Ashbourne Gdns.
SG13: H'ford 2C 114
Ashbourne Gro. NW7 5D 164
Ashbourne Rd. EN10: Brox 3K 133
Ashbourne Sq. HA6: North 6G 160
ASHBROOK 6C 34
Ashbrook HA8: Edg 6N 163
Ashbrook La. SG4: St Ipo 7B 34
Ashburnham Cl. WD19: Watf 3J 161
Ashburnham Dr. WD19: Watf 3J 161
Ashburnham Rd. LU1: Lut 1D 66
Ashburnham Wlk. SG2: Stev 8M 51
Ashbury Cl. AL10: Hat 9E 110
Ashby Ct. HP2: Hem H 5D 106
Ashby Dr. MK45: Bar C 8E 18
Ashby Gdns. AL1: St Alb 6E 126
Ashby Ri. CM23: Bis S 8K 59
Ashby Rd. HP4: Berk 7H 103
WD24: Watf 2J 149
Ashby Vs. LU7: I Ast 7E 62
Ash Cl. AL9: B Pk 7N 129
HA7: Stanm 6H 163
HA8: Edg 4C 164
UB9: Hare 8N 159
WD5: Abb L 5F 136
WD25: Watf 8K 137
Ashcombe AL8: Welw G 5L 91
Ashcombe Gdns. HA8: Edg 4A 164
Ashcombe Ho. EN3: Pon E 5H 157
Ash Copse AL2: Bri W 4A 138
Ashcroft HA5: Hat E 6B 162
LU6: Duns 8C 44
Ashcroft Cl. AL5: Harp 7F 88
Ashcroft Ct. EN10: Brox 3K 133
Ashcroft La. SG11: L Had 7M 57
Ashcroft Rd. LU2: Lut 5K 47
Ashcroft Ter. HP23: Tring 1M 101
Ashdale CM23: Bis S 4F 78
Ashdale Gdns. LU3: Lut 9C 30
Ashdale Gro. HA7: Stanm 6G 163
Ashdales AL1: St Alb 6E 126
Ashdon Rd. WD23: Bush 5M 149
Ashdown SG6: L Gar 2E 22
Ashdown Cres. EN8: C'hunt 1J 145
Ashdown Dr. WD6: Bore 4N 151
Ashdown Rd. EN3: Enf H 4G 156
SG2: Stev 1A 72
Ash Dr. AL10: Hat 3G 128
SG4: St Ipo 6A 34
Ashe Cotts. SG11: L Had 7L 57
Ashendene Rd. SG13: Bay 2K 131
ASHERIDGE 8B 120
Asheridge Rd. HP5: C'ham 9D 120
Ashfield Av. WD23: Bush 8C 150
Ashfields WD25: Watf 8H 137
Ashfield Way LU3: Lut 3C 46
Ashford Ct. HA8: Edg 3B 164
Ashford Cres. EN3: Enf H 4G 157
Ashford Grn. WD19: Watf 5M 161
Ashfords *SG9: Bunt* 2J 39
(off Paddock Rd.)
Ash Gro. AL4: Wheat 6K 89
EN1: Enf 9C 156
HP3: Hem H 6B 124
LU5: Duns 9G 44
SG8: Melb 2M 9
UB9: Hare 8N 159
Ashgrove M. SG8: Bark 9N 15
Ash Groves CM21: Saw 5J 99
Ash Hill Cl. WD23: Bush 1C 162
Ash Hill Dr. HA5: Pin 9L 161
Ash Ind. Est. CM19: Harl 7J 117
Ashlea Rd. SL9: Chal P 9A 158
Ashleigh SG2: Stev 5A 52
Ashleigh Ct. EN11: Hod 9L 115
N14 9H 155
WD3: R'orth 9N 147
WD17: Watf 7D 166
Ashleigh Pk. SG11: Barw 4N 75
Ashley Cl. AL8: Welw G 7J 91
HA5: Pin 9K 161
HP3: Hem H 4B 124
LU7: Ched 8M 61
NW4 9J 165
Ashley Ct. AL10: Hat 8G 111
EN5: N Bar 7B 154
NW4 9J 165
Ashley Dr. WD6: Bore 7C 152
Ashley Gdns. AL5: Harp 4M 87
ASHLEY GREEN 6K 121
Ashley Grn. Rd. HP5: C'ham 9H 121
Ashley La. NW4 9J 165
Ashley Rd. AL1: St Alb 2K 127
EN3: Enf H 4G 157
SG14: H'ford 1M 113
Ashleys WD3: R'orth 9J 147
Ashley Wlk. NW7 7J 165
Ashlyn Cl. WD23: Bush 6N 149
Ashlyn Ct. WD23: Bush 6N 149
Ashlyns Ct. HP4: Berk 2M 121
Ashlyns Rd. HP4: Berk 2M 121
Ashmead N14 7H 155
Ash Mdw. SG10: M Had 6J 77
Ashmeads Ct. WD7: Shen 6L 139
Ash Mill SG8: Bark 9N 15
Ashmore Gdns. HP3: Hem H 3D 124
Ashotts La. HP5: Ashe, C'dge 6A 120
Ash Ride EN2: Crew H 8M 143
ASHRIDGE 9L 83
Ashridge Cl. HP3: Bov 1C 134
Ashridge Cotts. HP4: Lit G 1B 104
Ashridge Ct. N14 7H 155
Ashridge Dr. AL2: Bri W 3N 137
WD19: Watf 5L 161
Ashridge Estate 9J 83
Ashridge Estate Vis. Cen. 9J 83
Ashridge Farm Caravan Pk. SG7: Ashw 9A 6
Ashridge Golf Course 9M 83
Ashridge Ho. *WD18: Watf* 9G 149
(off Chenies Way)
Ashridge La. HP5: Ley H 4A 134
Ashridge Park 2L 103
Ashridge Ri. HP4: Berk 9K 103
Ash Rd. HP23: Tring 2L 101
LU4: Lut 9D 46
SG12: Ware 4L 95
Ashton Rd. EN3: Enf W 9J 145
LU1: Lut 3G 66
LU6: Duns 8E 44
Ashton's La. SG7: Bald 5M 23
Ashton Sq. LU6: Duns 9E 44
Ashtree Ct. AL1: St Alb 2G 126
Ash Tree Fld. CM20: Harl 4K 117
Ash Tree Rd. LU5: Hou R 3E 44
WD24: Watf 9K 137
Ashtree Way HP1: Hem H 3K 123
Ashurst Cl. HA6: North 7G 161
Ashurst Rd. EN4: C'ters 7E 154
Ash Va. WD3: Map C 5G 158
Ash Valley Golf Course 2J 77
Ashville Trad. Est. SG7: Bald 2N 23
Ashville Way SG7: Bald 2N 23
Ash Way SG8: Roys 7F 8
ASHWELL 9M 5
Ashwell *SG1: Stev* 8J 35
(off Lister Cl.)
Ashwell Av. LU3: Lut 1M 45
Ashwell Cl. SG4: G'ley 6H 35
Ashwell Comn. SG4: G'ley 6H 35
ASHWELL END 8J 5
Ashwell Hall *AL10: Hat* 8E 110
(off Mosquito Way)
Ashwell & Morden Station (Rail) 2J 13
Ashwell Pde. *LU3: Lut* 1M 45
(off Ashwell Av.)
Ashwell Pk. AL5: Harp 6E 88
Ashwell Pl. WD24: Watf 1J 149
Ashwell Rd. SG7: Byg 1A 24
SG7: Hinx 8F 4
SG7: New 4M 11
SG8: G Mor, S Mor 6A 6
Ashwell St. AL3: St Alb 1C 166 (1E 126)
SG7: Ashw 1B 12
SG8: Bass, Lit, S Mor 6F 6
Ashwells Way HP8: Chal G 2A 158
Ashwell Village Mus. 9M 5
Ashwell Wlk. LU5: Hou R 3H 45
Ashwood SG12: Ware 6H 95
Ashwood Ho. *HA5: Hat E* 6B 162
(off The Avenue)
Ashwood M. AL1: St Alb 4E 126
Ashwood Rd. EN6: Pot B 6A 142
Ashworth Pl. CM17: Harl 6F 118
Askew Rd. HA6: North 2F 160
Aslin Ct. AL1: St Alb 2F 166
Aspasia Cl. AL1: St Alb 3G 127
Aspect One SG1: Stev 5H 51
Aspen Cl. AL2: Bri W 3N 137
SG2: Stev 1A 72
Aspen Ct. NW4 9L 165
ASPENDEN 5H 39
Aspenden Rd. SG9: Asp, Bunt 5J 39
(not continuous)
Aspen Pk. Dr. WD25: Watf 8K 137
Aspens, The CM23: Bis S 6K 59
SG4: Hit 4A 34
Aspens Pl. HP1: Hem H 5J 123
Aspen Way AL7: Welw G 1B 112
EN3: Enf W 8H 145
Aspfield Row HP1: Hem H 9L 105
ASPIRE National Training Cen. 2J 163
Aspley Cl. LU4: Lut 6H 45
Asquith Ct. SG2: Stev 1B 72
Asquith Ho. AL8: Welw G 8K 91
AL10: Hat 8G 111
Ass Ho. La. HA3: Har W 4C 162
Astall Cl. HA3: Har W 8F 162
Aster Cl. CM23: Bis S 2F 78
Asters, The EN7: Gof O 1B 144
Astley Grn. LU2: Lut 7M 47
Astley Rd. HP1: Hem H 2M 123
ASTON 7D 52
Astonbury Mnr. SG2: A'ton 9E 52
ASTON CLINTON 1D 100
Aston Clinton By-Pass HP22: Ast C, Buck 9A 80
Aston Cl. *SG1: Stev* 8J 35
(off Lister Cl.)
WD23: Bush 8D 150
WD24: Watf 4L 149
Aston Ct. *LU3: Lut* 5B 46
(off Sarum Rd.)
ASTON END 4D 52
Aston End Rd. SG2: A'ton 7D 52
Aston Grange SG14: H'ford 7A 94
ASTON HILL 5F 100
Aston Hill HP22: Halt 4E 100
Astonia Ho. *SG7: Bald* 4M 23
(off High St.)
Aston La. SG2: A'ton 7D 52
SG2: A'ton, Stev 1C 72
Aston Ri. SG4: Hit 4B 34
Aston Rd. SG11: Stand 7A 56
Astons Rd. HA6: North 3E 160
Aston Vw. HP2: Hem H 5C 106
Aston Way EN6: Pot B 5C 142
Astoria Ho. *NW9* 9F 164
(off Boulevard Dr.)
Astra Cen. CM20: Harl 2C 118
Astra Ct. LU2: Lut 7H 47
WD18: Watf 7H 149
ASTROPE 4F 80
Astrope La. HP23: Lon M 4F 80
ASTWICK 2E 10
Astwick Av. AL10: Hat 6F 110
Astwick Mnr. AL10: Hat 6C 110
Astwick Rd. SG5: Astw, Stot 2E 10
Athelstan Rd. HP3: Hem H 5B 124
Athelstan Wlk. Nth. AL7: Welw G 1L 111
Athelstan Wlk. Sth. AL7: Welw G 1K 111
Athelstone Rd. HA3: Weal 9E 162
Athena Est. CM20: Harl 2D 118
Athena Pl. HA6: North 8H 161
Athenia Cl. EN7: Gof O 2N 143
Atherstone Rd. LU4: Lut 8N 45
Atherton End CM21: Saw 4G 98
Athlone Cl. WD7: Rad 9H 139
Athol Cl. HA5: Pin 8K 161
Athole Gdns. EN1: Enf 7C 156
Athol Gdns. HA5: Pin 8K 161
Atholl Cl. LU3: Lut 1N 45
Atkinson Cl. WD23: Bush 9F 150
Atlas Cres. HA8: Edg 2B 164
Atria Rd. HA6: North 5J 161
Attenborough Cl. WD19: Watf 3N 161
Attimore Cl. AL8: Welw G 1H 111
Attimore Rd. AL8: Welw G 1H 111
Auber Cl. EN11: Hod 5K 115
Aubretia Ho. AL7: Welw G 1A 112
Aubrey Av. AL2: Lon C 8K 127
Aubrey Gdns. LU4: Lut 3L 45
Aubrey La. AL3: Red 4G 107
Aubreys SG6: L Gar 9F 22
Aubrey's Rd. HP1: Hem H 3H 123
Aubries SG2: Walk 9G 36
Auckland Cl. EN1: Enf 1F 156
Auckland Rd. EN6: Pot B 5L 141
Auction Ho. Courtyard *LU1: Lut* 1G 67
(off John St.)
Audax NW9 9F 164
Auden Dr. WD6: Bore 7A 152
Audley Cl. WD6: Bore 5A 152
Audley Ct. HA5: Pin 9L 161
Audley Gdns. EN9: Wal A 7N 145
Audley Pl. LU2: Lut 8J 47
Audley Rd. EN2: Enf 4N 155
Audrey Gdns. CM23: Bis S 4H 79
Audwick Cl. EN8: C'hunt 1J 145
Augustine Ct. EN9: Wal A 6M 145
Augustine Rd. HA3: Har W 8C 162
Augustus Cl. AL3: St Alb 4B 126
HA7: Stanm 3L 163
Augustus Ga. SG2: Stev 1C 52
Ausden Pl. WD17: Watf 9E 166
AUSTAGE END 2H 49
Austell Gdns. NW7 3E 164
Austell Hgts. *NW7* 3E 164
(off Austell Gdns.)
Austen Paths SG2: Stev 3B 52
Austenway SL9: Chal P 9B 158
AUSTENWOOD 9A 158
Austenwood Cl. SL9: Chal P 9A 158
Austenwood La. SL9: Chal P 9A 158
Austin Ct. EN1: Enf 7C 156
Austin Rd. LU3: Lut 5D 46
LU6: Duns 7C 44
Austins Mead HP3: Bov 1E 134
Austins Pl. HP2: Hem H 1N 123
Austin Vs. WD25: Watf 4K 137
Autumn Cl. EN1: Enf 3E 156
Autumn Glades HP3: Hem H 4E 124
Autumn Gro. AL7: Welw G 2A 112
Avalon Cl. EN2: Enf 4M 155
WD25: Watf 5N 137
Avalon Ct. WD25: A'ham 3B 150
Avebury Av. LU2: Lut 5F 46
Avebury Ct. HP2: Hem H 9C 106
Aventine Ct. *AL1: St Alb* 3E 126
(off Holywell Hill)
Avenue, The AL6: Wel 8K 71
EN5: Barn 5L 153
EN6: Pot B 3M 141
EN11: Hod 1K 133
HA3: Har W 8G 162
HA5: Hat E 6A 162
HA6: North 6E 160
HP1: Hem H 1H 123
LU4: Lut 4N 45
LU6: Duns 1B 64
N3 9N 165
SG1: Stev 1J 51
SG4: Hit 3A 34
SG5: Stot 6F 10
Avenue, The SG14: H'ford 7N 93
WD7: Rad 6H 139
WD17: Watf 5A 166 (4J 149)
WD23: Bush 6A 150
Avenue App. WD4: Kin L 3C 136
Avenue Cl. N14 8H 155
Avenue Ct. *AL6: Wel* 9L 71
(off The Avenue)
N14 8H 155
Avenue Grimaldi LU3: Lut 6C 46
Avenue One SG6: L Gar 4J 23
Avenue Pde. N21 9B 156
Avenue Pl. CM23: Bis S 2J 79
Avenue Ri. WD23: Bush 7B 150
Avenue Rd. AL1: St Alb 1F 126
CM23: Bis S 2J 79
EN11: Hod 9A 116
HA5: Pin 9N 161
N14 9H 155
Avenue St Nicholas AL5: Harp 6B 88
Avenue Ter. WD19: Watf 8N 149
Avia Cl. HP3: Hem H 6N 123
Avian Av. AL2: Frog 1F 138
Aviation Av. AL10: Hat 8E 110
Aviation Dr. NW9 9G 164
Avion Cres. NW9 8G 164
Avior Dr. HA6: North 4H 161
Avocet SG6: L Gar 2E 22
Avocet Cl. AL3: St Alb 8D 108
Avon Cl. WD25: Watf 7L 137
Avon Ct. AL5: Harp 6C 88
HA5: Hat E 7B 162
(off The Avenue)
LU1: Lut 9E 46
(off Avondale Rd.)
Avondale Av. EN4: E Bar 9E 154
Avondale Ct. AL1: St Alb 2E 166 (2F 126)
Avondale Cres. EN3: Enf H 5J 157
Avondale Rd. HA3: Weal 9G 163
LU1: Lut 9E 46
Avon Dr. SG1: Stev 7M 35
Avon M. HA5: Hat E 7A 162
Avon Sq. HP2: Hem H 6B 106
Avro Ho. *NW9* 9F 164
(off Boulevard Dr.)
Awberry Ct. WD18: Watf 8F 148
Axe Cl. LU3: Lut 3A 46
Axholme Av. HA8: Edg 8A 164
Aycliffe Dr. HP2: Hem H 7A 106
Aycliffe Rd. WD6: Bore 3M 151
Aydon Rd. LU3: Lut 3D 46
Aylands Rd. EN3: Enf W 9G 145
Aylesbury Rd. HP22: Ast C 9A 80
HP22: Wen 8A 100
HP23: Tring 3J 101
LU7: Wing 2A 60
Aylesford Ct. SG6: L Gar 4J 23
Aylesham Cl. NW7 7G 164
Aylets Fld. CM18: Harl 9A 118
Ayley Cft. EN1: Enf 7E 156
Aylmer Cl. HA7: Stanm 4H 163
Aylmer Dr. HA7: Stanm 4H 163
Aylott Ct. SG14: Watt S 4J 73
Aylotts Cl. SG9: Bunt 2H 39
Aylsham Rd. EN11: Hod 7N 115
Aylward Dr. SG2: Stev 5A 52
Aylwards Ri. HA7: Stanm 4H 163
Aynho St. WD18: Watf 9B 166 (7K 149)
Aynscombe Cl. LU6: Duns 9C 44
Aynsley Gdns. CM17: Harl 6E 118
Aynsworth Av. CM23: Bis S 7J 59
AYOT GREEN 6G 90
Ayot Grn. AL6: Ayot P, Wel 7F 90
AL8: Lem 8F 90
AYOT LITTLE GREEN 6F 90
Ayot Lit. Green La. AL6: Ayot P 6F 90
Ayot Path WD6: Bore 1A 152
AYOT ST LAWRENCE 1A 90
AYOT ST PETER 4E 90
Ayot St Peter Rd. AL6: Ayot P 3D 90
Ayr Cl. SG1: Stev 1B 52
AYRES END 1G 108
Ayres End La. AL3: Harp, St Alb 2D 108
AL5: Harp 8F 88
Aysgarth Cl. AL5: Harp 7C 88
Aysgarth Rd. AL3: Red 9J 87
Azalea Cl. AL2: Lon C 9J 127

B

BAAS HILL 3H 133
Baas Hill EN10: Brox 3G 133
Baas Hill Cl. EN10: Brox 3J 133
Baas La. EN10: Brox 3J 133
Babbage Rd. SG1: Stev 4G 51
BABBS GREEN 2B 96
Babington Rd. HP22: Halt 8C 100
Back, The HP4: Pot E 7E 104
Back La. AL6: Tew 5D 92
CM22: L Hal 9K 79
CM22: She 6J 99
(not continuous)
HA8: Edg 8C 164
SG3: Dat 7D 72
SG4: Pres 3K 49
SG6: L Gar 5K 23
SG7: Bald 4L 23
SG8: Melb 1H 9
SG9: Buck 3H 27
SG9: Cot, W'mill 7A 38
(not continuous)
SG13: B'don 8A 114
SG14: Bram 1F 92
WD3: Chen 2E 146
WD25: Let H 3F 150
Back St. HP22: Wen 9A 100
LU2: Lut 9G 47
SG7: Ashw 1B 12
Bacon La. HA8: Edg 8A 164
Bacons Dr. EN6: Cuff 2K 143
Bacon's Yd. SG7: Ashw 9M 5
Baddeley Cl. EN3: Enf L 1L 157
SG2: Stev 7A 52

Baden Dr.—Bearton Cl.

Baden Dr. E4 6M 157
Bader Cl. AL7: Welw G 9B 92
SG1: Stev 9M 35
Bader Ct. *NW9* 9F 164
(off Runway Cl.)
Badger Cl. SG3: Kneb 2M 71
Badgers CM23: Bis S 3G 78
Badgers Cl. EN2: Enf 5N 155
SG1: Stev 5L 51
SG13: H'ford 9F 94
WD6: Bore 4N 151
Badgers Ct. WD25: Watf 7H 137
Badgers Cft. EN10: Brox 3J 133
HP2: Hem H 3F 124
N20 9L 153
Badgers Dell WD3: Chor 6E 146
Badgers Ga. LU6: Duns 9B 44
Badgers Mdw. HP22: Halt 9B 100
Badgers Wlk. AL6: Tew 2B 92
WD3: Chor 6J 147
Badger Way AL10: Hat 2H 129
Badingham Dr. AL5: Harp 7N 87
Badminton Cl. SG2: Stev 1A 72
WD6: Bore 4A 152
Badminton Ho. *WD24: Watf* 4L 149
(off Anglian Cl.)
Badminton Pl. EN10: Brox 2J 133
Bagenal Ho. WD5: Abb L 5H 137
Bagshot Rd. EN1: Enf 9D 156
Bagwicks Cl. LU3: Lut 2A 46
Bailey Hill Ct. *LU1: Lut* 3G 67
(off Farley Hill)
Bailey's Cl. SG4: Bre G 9F 48
Baileys M. *HP1: Hem H* 9N 105
(off High St.)
Bailey St. LU1: Lut 2H 67
Baines La. SG3: Dat 5B 72
Baird Cl. WD23: Bush 8C 150
Baird Pl. HP22: Halt 8C 100
Baird Rd. EN1: Enf 5F 156
Bairstow Cl. WD6: Bore 3M 151
Baisley Ho. EN7: C'hunt 1E 144
Bakehouse Ct. *SG9: Bunt* 3J 39
(off High St.)
Baker Ct. WD6: Bore 4B 152
Bakers Cl. AL1: St Alb 3H 127
Bakers Ct. *CM23: Bis S* 1J 79
(off Hockerill St.)
Bakerscroft EN8: C'hunt 1J 145
BAKER'S END 9B 76
Bakers Gro. AL7: Welw G 8B 92
Bakers Hill EN5: N Bar 4A 154
Bakers La. LU6: Kens 8H 65
SG4: Cod 7F 70
SG8: Barl 1C 16
Bakers M. SG4: Hit 1B 34
Bakers Rd. EN7: C'hunt 3F 144
Baker St. EN1: Enf 5B 156
EN6: Pot B 8L 141
LU1: Lut 3G 66
(not continuous)
SG1: Stev 2J 51
SG13: H'ford 9C 94
Bakers Wlk. CM21: Saw 5G 98
Bakery Cl. CM19: Royd 6F 116
Bakery Ct. CM24: Stans 3M 59
Bakery Path *HA8: Edg* 6B 164
(off St Margaret's Rd.)
Bakewell Cl. LU4: Lut 8M 45
Balcary Gdns. HP4: Berk 2J 121
Balcombe Cl. LU2: Lut 5L 47
Balcon Way WD6: Bore 3C 152
BALDOCK 3M 23
Baldock By-Pass SG4: W'ton 8L 23
SG7: Bald 8L 23
Baldock Cl. LU4: Lut 6J 45
Baldock Ind. Est. SG7: Bald 4M 23
Baldock La. SG6: L Gar, Will 9H 23
SG7: Bald 8J 23
Baldock Mus. 3L 23
Baldock Rd. SG5: Stot 7G 10
(not continuous)
SG6: L Gar 8F 22
SG7: Ods, S End 5H 13
SG8: Roys 5H 13
SG9: Bunt 3E 38
BALDOCK SERVICE AREA 6K 11
Baldock Station (Rail) 2M 23
Baldock St. SG8: Roys 7C 8
SG12: Ware 6H 95
Baldock Way WD6: Bore 3N 151
Baldways Cl. HP22: W'rave 5B 60
Baldwin Rd. WD17: Watf 2J 149
Baldwins AL7: Welw G 9A 92
Baldwin's La. WD3: Crox G 6C 148
Balfour Ct. *AL5: Harp* 4D 88
(off Station Rd.)
Balfour Ho. *LU1: Lut* 9G 46
(off Guildford St.)
Balfour M. HP3: Bov 9D 122
Balfour St. SG14: H'ford 8A 94
Baliol Chambers *SG4: Hit* 3N 33
(off Hollow La.)
Baliol Rd. SG5: Hit 2N 33
Ballards La. N3 8N 165
Ballards M. HA8: Edg 6A 164
Ballards Row HP22: Ast C 9C 80
Ballater Cl. WD19: Watf 4L 161
Ball Ho. *NW9* 9F 164
(off Aerodrome Rd.)
BALLINGDON BOTTOM 7J 85
Ballinger Ct. HP4: Berk 2M 121
WD18: Watf 7B 166 (5K 149)
Balloon Cnr. AL9: Welh G 5H 129
Ballslough Hill SG4: Kimp 7L 69
Balls Wood (Nature Reserve) 5E 114
Balmoral Cl. AL2: Par S 1D 138
SG2: Stev 1B 72
Balmoral Dr. WD6: Bore 7D 152
Balmoral Rd. EN3: Enf W 9H 145
LU5: Hou R 4H 45
SG5: Hit 1M 33
WD5: Abb L 5J 137
WD24: Watf 2L 149
Balmore Cres. EN4: C'ters 7F 154
Balmore Wood LU3: Lut 9D 30
Balsams Cl. SG13: H'ford 2B 114
Bampton Ho. NW7 7G 165
Bampton Rd. LU4: Lut 8L 45
BAMVILLE WOOD 1D 108
Bamville Wood AL5: Harp 1D 108
Banbury Cl. EN2: Enf 3N 155
LU4: Lut 5B 46
Banbury St. WD18: Watf 7J 149
Bancroft SG5: Hit 3N 33
Bancroft Ct. SG5: Hit 2M 33
Bancroft Gdns. HA3: Har W 8D 162
Bancroft Rd. HA3: Har W 9D 162
LU3: Lut 4D 46
Bandley Ri. SG2: Stev 6B 52
Bank Cl. LU4: Lut 5M 45
Bank Ct. HP1: Hem H 3M 123
Bank Grn. HP5: Bell 5A 120
Bank Mill HP4: Berk 1B 122
Bank Mill La. HP4: Berk 2B 122
Bank Side SG8: Barl 2C 16
Bankside EN2: Enf 3N 155
HP22: Wen 9A 100
Bankside Cl. LU5: Bid 4D 44
UB9: Hare 6K 159
Bankside Down WD3: R'orth 8M 147
Banks La. CM24: Stans 4N 59
Banks Rd. WD6: Bore 4C 152
Bannatyne's Health Club
Luton 2G 66
(off Regent St.)
Bannerdown HP4: Lit G 8A 84
Banninster Gdns. SG8: Roys 5E 8
Bannister Sports Centre 6D 162
Banstock Rd. HA8: Edg 6B 164
Bantam Ho. *NW9* 9F 164
(off Heritage Av.)
Banting Dr. N21 7L 155
Banton Cl. EN1: Enf 4F 156
Barbaraville Camp AL9: Hat 6M 111
Barbel Cl. EN8: Wal C 7L 145
Barber Cl. N21 9M 155
Barberry Rd. HP1: Hem H 2K 123
Barbers La. *LU1: Lut* 1G 66
(off Silver St.)
Barbers Wlk. HP23: Tring 3L 101
Barchester Rd. HA3: Har W 9E 162
Barclay Cl. SG13: Hert H 2F 114
WD18: Watf 8J 149
Barclay Ct. EN11: Hod 9L 115
LU2: Lut 9H 47
Barclay Cres. SG1: Stev 2L 51
Barclay Gdns. SG1: Stev 1K 51
Barden Cl. UB9: Hare 7M 159
Bards Cnr. HP1: Hem H 1L 123
Bardwell Ct. AL1: St Alb 4C 166
Bardwell Rd. AL1: St Alb 4D 166 (3E 126)
Barfolds AL9: Welh G 5J 129
Barford Cl. NW4 9G 165
Barford Ri. LU2: Lut 8M 47
Barge Ho. HP3: Hem H 6B 124
Bargrove Av. HP1: Hem H 3K 123
Barham Av. WD6: Elst 5N 151
Barham Ct. SG8: Melb 1N 9
Barham Rd. SG2: Stev 4B 52
Baring Rd. EN4: C'ters 6C 154
Barker Cl. HA6: North 7H 161
Barkers Mead CM22: L Hal 7K 79
Barkham Cl. LU7: Ched 9L 61
Barking Cl. LU4: Lut 3L 45
Barkston Path WD6: Bore 2A 152
BARKWAY 8N 15
Barkway Park Golf Course 1B 28
Barkway Rd. SG8: Roys 8D 8
SG9: Ans 4E 28
Barkway St. SG8: Roys 8D 8
BARLEY 2D 16
Barley Brow LU6: Duns 6B 44
WD25: Watf 4K 137
Barley Cl. WD23: Bush 7C 150
Barleycorn, The *LU3: Lut* 9F 46
(off Brook St.)
Barley Cft. CM18: Harl 9A 118
HP2: Hem H 2E 124
SG14: H'ford 7B 94
Barleycroft SG2: Stev 6B 52
SG3: Dat 6N 71
SG9: Bunt 4J 39
SG12: Tonw 9D 74
SG14: Water 4M 93
BARLEYCROFT END 6L 41
Barleycroft Grn. AL8: Welw G 9J 91
Barleycroft Rd. AL8: Welw G 1J 111
Barleyfield Way LU5: Hou R 5D 44
Barley Hills CM23: Bis S 4G 78
Barley La. LU4: Lut 4M 45
Barley Mow Caravan Site AL4: St Alb 4N 127
Barley Mow La. AL4: St Alb 5M 127
Barley Ponds Cl. SG12: Ware 6K 95
Barley Ponds Rd. SG12: Ware 6K 95
Barley Ri. AL5: Harp 3D 88
SG7: Bald 3A 24
Barley Rd. SG8: Barl, Gt Chi, Hey 1D 16
SG8: Gt Chi 2E 16
Barleyvale LU3: Lut 1C 46
Barlings Rd. AL5: Harp 1C 108
Barlow Cl. AL10: Hat 7D 110
Barlow Rd. HP22: Wen 9B 100
Barmor Cl. HA2: Harr 9C 162
Barmouth Row HP2: Hem H 8A 106
Barnabas Ct. EN2: Enf 6M 155
Barnack Gro. SG8: Roys 6C 8
Barnacres Rd. HP3: Hem H 7B 124
Barnard Grn. AL7: Welw G 1M 111
Barnard Lodge EN5: N Bar 6B 154
Barnard Rd. CM21: Saw 4G 99
EN1: Enf 4F 156
LU1: Lut 1C 66
Barnard Way HP3: Hem H 3A 124
Barn Cl. AL8: Welw G 9J 91
HP3: Hem H 5B 124
WD7: Rad 8H 139
Barn Ct. CM21: Saw 4G 99
Barn Cres. HA7: Stanm 6K 163
Barncroft SG11: Alb 2M 57
Barncroft Rd. HP4: Berk 2K 121
Barncroft Way AL1: St Alb 3H 127
Barndell Cl. SG5: Stot 6F 10
Barndicott AL7: Welw G 9B 92
Barndicott Ho. AL7: Welw G 9B 92
Barnes Ct. EN5: N Bar 6A 154
Barnes La. WD4: Kin L 9L 123
Barnes Ri. WD4: Kin L 9B 124
BARNES WOOD 1A 92
BARNET 5L 153
Barnet Burnt Oak Leisure Cen. 8D 164
Barnet Bus. Cen. EN5: Barn 5L 153
Barnet By-Pass NW4 9J 165
NW7 6F 164
Barnet By-Pass Rd. EN5: Ark, Barn 5E 152
WD6: Bore 8D 152
Barnet Copthall Stadium 8J 165
Barnet FC 8M 163
BARNET GATE 8F 152
Barnet Ga. La. EN5: Ark 8F 152
Barnet Hill EN5: Barn 6M 153
Barnet La. EN5: Barn 1M 165
N20 1M 165
WD6: Bore, Elst 8L 151
(not continuous)
Barnet Mus. 6L 153
Barnet Rd. AL2: Lon C 9M 127
EN5: Ark 8D 152
EN5: Barn, Pot B 9N 141
EN6: Pot B 6A 142
BARNET VALE 7A 154
Barnet Way NW7 8D 152
Barnfield HP3: Hem H 5B 124
Barnfield Av. LU2: Lut 4F 46
Barnfield Cl. EN11: Hod 6L 115
Barnfield Ct. AL5: Harp 7D 88
Barnfield Rd. AL4: St Alb 8K 109
AL5: Harp 7D 88
AL7: Welw G 2L 111
HA8: Edg 8C 164
Barnhurst Path WD19: Watf 5L 161
Barn Lea WD3: R'orth 1K 159
Barn Mead CM18: Harl 8N 117
Barns, The HP23: Tring 5K 101
SG18: Edw 6D 4
Barnsdale Cl. WD6: Bore 3N 151
Barns Dene AL5: Harp 5N 87
Barnside Ct. AL8: Welw G 9J 91
Barnston Cl. LU2: Lut 8M 47
Barnsway WD4: Kin L 1A 136
Barn Theatre, The
Welwyn Garden City 9J 91
Barnwell SG2: Stev 6A 52
Barnwood Cl. N20 1M 165
Baron Ct. SG1: Stev 9H 35
Barons, The CM23: Bis S 3F 78
Barons Ct. *LU3: Lut* 8F 46
(off Earls Meade)
Barons Ga. EN4: E Bar 8D 154
Baronsmere Ct. EN5: Barn 6L 153
Barracks La. EN5: Barn 5L 153
Barra Cl. HP3: Hem H 5E 124
Barra Ho. *WD18: Watf* 8H 149
(off Scammell Way)
Barrass Cl. EN3: Enf L 1L 157
Barratt Ind. Pk. LU2: Lut 2L 67
Barratt Way HA3: Weal 9E 162
Barrells Down Rd. CM23: Bis S 8G 59
Barrett La. CM23: Bis S 1H 79
Barrie Av. LU6: Duns 6B 44
Barrie Ct. *EN5: N Bar* 7B 154
(off Lyonsdown Rd.)
Barrington Dr. UB9: Hare 7K 159
Barrington M. AL7: Welw G 1A 112
Barrington Pk. Gdns. HP8: Chal G 1A 158
Barrington Rd. SG6: L Gar 7F 22
(not continuous)
Barrons Row AL5: Harp 8E 88
Barrowby Cl. LU2: Lut 8M 47
Barrowdene Cl. HA5: Pin 9N 161
Barrow La. EN7: C'hunt, Gof O 3D 144
(not continuous)
Barrow Point Av. HA5: Pin 9N 161
Barrow Point La. HA5: Pin 9N 161
Barrows Farm 5J 117
Barrows Rd. CM19: Harl 6J 117
Barr Rd. EN6: Pot B 6B 142
Barry Cl. AL2: Chis G 7C 126
Barry Ct. *SG1: Stev* 1H 51
(off Huntingdon Rd.)
WD18: Watf 7L 149
(off Cardiff Rd.)
Bartel Cl. HP3: Hem H 4F 124
Bartholomew Ct. HA8: Edg 7L 163
Bartholomew Grn. AL3: Mark 2A 86
Bartholomew Ho. EN3: Enf W 1J 157
Bartholomew Rd. CM23: Bis S 2H 79
Bartletts Hillside Cl. SL9: Chal P 7B 158
Bartletts Mead SG14: H'ford 6B 94
Barton Av. LU5: Duns 9G 45
Barton Cl. AL5: Harp 4D 88
Barton Hill Rd. LU2: Lill, Stre 4D 30
Barton Hills National Nature Reserve 2F 30
Barton Ind. Est. MK45: Bar C 7C 18
BARTON-LE-CLAY 9E 18
Barton Rd. AL4: Wheat 7K 89
LU3: Lut, Stre 4C 30
MK45: Pull, Sil 3B 18
MK45: Shar 9A 18
MK45: Sil 1E 18
SG5: Hex 1J 31
Bartons, The WD6: Elst 8L 151
Barton Way WD3: Crox G 7D 148
WD6: Bore 4A 152
Bartrams La. EN4: Had W 2B 154
Bartrop Cl. EN7: Gof O 1B 144
BARWICK 5N 75
BARWICK FORD 5N 75
Barwick La. SG11: Barw 4M 75
Basbow La. CM23: Bis S 1H 79
Basildon Cl. WD18: Watf 8E 148
Basildon Ct. HP3: Hem H 7B 124
Basildon Sq. HP2: Hem H 7B 106
Basil M. CM17: Harl 5E 118
Basils Rd. SG1: Stev 2J 51
Basing Rd. WD3: R'orth 1J 159
Basing Way N3 9N 165
Baslow Cl. HA3: Har W 8E 162
Bassett Cl. AL3: Red 1K 107
Bassil Rd. HP2: Hem H 3N 123
BASSINGBOURN 1M 7
Bassingbourne Cl. EN10: Brox 2K 133
Bassingbourn Rd. SG8: Lit, Bass 3J 7
Bassingburn Wlk. AL7: Welw G 1M 111
BASSUS GREEN 1K 53
Bassus Grn. Rd. SG2: Walk 9H 37
Batchelors SG11: Puck 7B 56
Batchwood Dr. AL3: St Alb 1C 126
Batchwood Gdns. AL3: St Alb 8E 108
Batchwood Hall AL3: St Alb 8C 108
Batchwood Hall Golf Course 8C 108
Batchwood Vw. AL3: St Alb 9D 108
BATCHWORTH 2A 160
BATCHWORTH HEATH 4C 160
Batchworth Heath WD3: R'orth 4D 160
Batchworth Heath Hill WD3: R'orth 4C 160
Batchworth Hill WD3: R'orth 2A 160
(not continuous)
Batchworth La. HA6: North 5E 160
Batchworth Lock Canal Cen. 1A 160
Batchworth Park Golf Course 3A 160
Batchworth Rdbt. WD3: R'orth 1A 160
Bateman Rd. WD3: Crox G 8C 148
BATFORD 4E 88
Batford Cl. AL7: Welw G 1A 112
Batford Mill Ind. Est. AL5: Harp 5E 88
Batford Rd. AL5: Harp 4E 88
Bath Pl. EN5: Barn 5M 153
Bath Rd. LU3: Lut 7F 46
Bathurst Rd. HP2: Hem H 8N 105
Batley Rd. EN2: Enf 3A 156
Batterdale AL9: Hat 8J 111
Battilion Ho. *NW9* 9F 164
(off Heritage Av.)
Battlefield Rd. AL1: St Alb 9G 108
BATTLERS GREEN 9F 138
Battlers Grn. Dr. WD7: Rad 1F 150
Battleview AL4: Wheat 7M 89
Baud Cl. SG11: L Had 7A 58
Baulk, The LU2: Lill 8M 31
LU7: Ched 9L 61
LU7: I'hoe 2D 82
Bawdsey Cl. SG1: Stev 1H 51
Baxter Rd. WD24: Watf 9J 137
Bay Cl. LU4: Lut 3L 45
Bay Ct. HP4: Berk 1M 121
BAYFORD 9L 113
Bayford Cl. HP2: Hem H 6E 106
SG13: H'ford 2A 114
Bayford Grn. SG13: Bay 8M 113
Bayford La. SG13: Bay 6L 113
Bayford Station (Rail) 9N 113
Bayford Way CM24: Stans 5M 59
Bayford Wood Caravan Pk. SG13: Bay 9K 113
Bayhurst Dr. HA6: North 6H 161
Baylam Dell LU2: Lut 8N 47
Bayley Mead HP1: Hem H 4L 123
Baylie Ct. HP2: Hem H 1A 124
Baylie La. HP2: Hem H 1A 124
Bayliss Cl. N21 7K 155
Baynes Cl. EN1: Enf 3E 156
Bays Ct. HA8: Edg 5B 164
Bay Tree Cl. AL2: Par S 1D 138
Baytree Cl. EN7: C'hunt 9D 132
Baytree Ho. E4 9M 157
Baytree Wlk. WD17: Watf 2H 149
Bayworth SG6: L Gar 6H 23
Bazile Rd. N21 8M 155
BBC Elstree 5A 152
Beacon Av. LU6: Duns 1B 64
Beacon Cl. SL9: Chal P 7B 158
Beacon Ct. LU7: Pits 5B 82
(Quarry Rd.)
LU7: Pits 4A 82
(Westfield Rd.)
SG13: Hert H 3G 114
Beacon Hill Fort 1G 82
Beacon Ho. AL1: St Alb 2G 166 (2G 126)
Beacon Rd. HP4: Ring 5H 83
LU7: I'hoe 1F 82
SG12: Ware 5L 95
Beacons, The AL10: Hat 8J 111
SG1: Stev 7A 36
Beaconsfield LU2: Lut 9K 47
Beaconsfield Cl. AL10: Hat 8J 111
Beaconsfield Ct. *AL10: Hat* 7J 111
(off Beaconsfield Rd.)
WD25: Watf 5K 137
(off Horseshoe La.)
Beaconsfield Rd. AL1: St Alb 3F 166 (2F 126)
AL10: Hat 8J 111
EN3: Enf W 1H 157
HP22: Ast C 1D 100
HP23: Tring 3K 101
Beacon Vw. LU6: N'all 4F 62
Beacon Way HP23: Tring 1A 102
WD3: R'orth 9K 147
Beadles, The CM22: L Hal 8K 79
Beadlow Rd. LU4: Lut 5J 45
Beagle Cl. WD7: Rad 1G 150
Beale Arboretum, The 2E 154
Beale Cl. SG2: Stev 3B 52
Beale St. LU6: Duns 8D 44
Beamish Dr. WD23: B Hea 1D 162
Beane Av. SG2: Stev 3C 52
Beane River Vw. SG14: H'ford 9A 94
Beane Rd. SG14: H'ford 9N 93
Beane Lodge SG14: Watt S 4J 73
Beaneside, The SG14: Watt S 4J 73
Beane Wlk. SG2: Stev 3C 52
Beanfield Rd. CM21: H Wyc, Saw 3C 98
Beanley Cl. LU2: Lut 7N 47
Beardow Gro. N14 8H 155
Bear La. SG7: Ashw 9M 5
Bearton Av. SG5: Hit 2M 33
Bearton Cl. SG5: Hit 1M 33

Bearton Ct.—Berry Way

Bearton Ct. SG5: Hit ... 1M **33**
Bearton Grn. SG5: Hit ... 1L **33**
Bearton Rd. SG5: Hit ... 1L **33**
Bearwood Cl. EN6: Pot B ... 4C **142**
Beatrice Rd. N9 ... 9G **156**
Beatty Rd. EN8: Wal C ... 7K **145**
HA7: Stanm ... 6K **163**
Beauchamp Ct. *EN5: Barn ... 6M 153*
(off Victors Way)
HA7: Stanm ... 5K **163**
Beauchamp Gdns. WD3: R'orth ... 1K **159**
Beauchamps AL7: Welw G ... 1A **112**
Beau Ct. *HA7: Stanm ... 7L 163*
(off Hitchin La.)
Beaufort Ct. EN5: N Bar ... 7B **154**
Beaulieu Cl. WD19: Watf ... 1L **161**
Beaulieu Dr. EN9: Wal A ... 6M **145**
Beaulieu Gdns. N21 ... 9A **156**
Beaumayes Cl. HP1: Hem H ... 3L **123**
Beaumonds AL1: St Alb ... 2E **166** (2F **126**)
Beaumont Av. AL1: St Alb ... 9J **109**
Beaumont Cen. EN8: C'hunt ... 3H **145**
Beaumont Cl. SG5: Hit ... 2L **33**
Beaumont Ct. AL5: Harp ... 6C **88**
NW9 ... 9F 164
(off Cherry Cl.)
Beaumont Ga. *WD7: Rad ... 8H 139*
(off Shenley Hill)
Beaumont Hall La. AL3: St Alb ... 4K **107**
Beaumont Pk. Dr. CM19: Royd ... 6E **116**
Beaumont Pl. EN5: Barn ... 3M **153**
Beaumont Rd. EN10: Brox ... 6C **132**
LU3: Lut ... 7D **46**
Beaumont Vw. EN7: C'hunt ... 8B **132**
Beaumont Works *AL1: St Alb ... 2J 127*
(off Hedley Rd.)
Beazley Cl. SG12: Ware ... 5J **95**
Beckbury Cl. LU2: Lut ... 7N **47**
Becket Gdns. AL6: Wel ... 3J **91**
Beckets Sq. HP4: Berk ... 8L **103**
Beckets Wlk. SG12: Ware ... 6H **95**
Becketts SG14: H'ford ... 1M **113**
Beckett's Av. AL3: St Alb ... 8D **108**
Beckfield La. SG9: S'don ... 4A **26**
Beckham Cl. LU2: Lut ... 2F **46**
Becks Cl. AL3: Mark ... 2N **85**
Bedale Rd. EN2: Enf ... 2A **156**
Bede Cl. HA5: Pin ... 8M **161**
Bede Ct. HP4: Lit G ... 7N **83**
Bedford Av. EN5: Barn ... 7M **153**
HP6: L Chal ... 3A **146**
Bedford Cl. SG5: Shil ... 1N **19**
WD3: Chen ... 2E **146**
Bedford Ct. HP6: L Chal ... 3A **146**
LU5: Hou R ... 5E **44**
Bedford Cres. EN3: Enf W ... 8J **145**
Bedford Gdns. LU3: Lut ... 9F **46**
Bedford Ho. SG1: Stev ... 3H **51**
Bedford Pk. Rd.
AL1: St Alb ... 2F **166** (2F **126**)
Bedford Rd. AL1: St Alb ... 4E **166** (3F **126**)
HA6: North ... 3E **160**
LU5: Bid, Hou R, Thorn ... 1D **44**
N9 ... 9F **156**
NW7 ... 2E **164**
SG5: Hit, Hol, Ick ... 1J **21**
SG6: L Gar ... 4D **22**
SG16: Henl, L Ston ... 1J **21**
Bedford Sq. LU5: Hou R ... 5E **44**
Bedford St. HP4: Berk ... 1A **122**
SG5: Hit ... 3L **33**
WD24: Watf ... 3K **149**
BEDMOND ... 9H **125**
BEDMOND HILL ... 7G **125**
Bedmond La. AL2: Pot C ... 8J **125**
AL3: St Alb ... 4A **126**
WD5: Bed ... 8J **125**
Bedmond Rd. HP3: Hem H ... 3E **124**
WD5: Abb L, Bed ... 2H **137**
BEDWELL ... 4M **51**
Bedwell Av. AL9: How G, Lit B ... 6F **112**
Bedwell Cl. AL7: Welw G ... 1L **111**
Bedwell Cres. SG1: Stev ... 4L **51**
Bedwell Hall AL9: Ess ... 1E **130**
Bedwell La. SG1: Stev ... 4L **51**
Bedwell Park ... 1E **130**
Bedwell Pk. SG1: Stev ... 4M **51**
Bedwell Ri. SG1: Stev ... 4L **51**
Beech Av. EN2: Crew H ... 8M **143**
WD7: Rad ... 6H **139**
Beech Bottom AL3: St Alb ... 8E **108**
Beech Cl. AL5: Harp ... 1D **108**
AL10: Hat ... 1G **129**
LU6: Duns ... 3H **65**
N9 ... 8E **156**
SG12: Ware ... 8H **95**
Beech Ct. AL5: Harp ... 4A **88**
Beech Cres. AL4: Wheat ... 8L **89**
Beechcroft HP4: Berk ... 2N **121**
SG3: Dat ... 7C **72**
Beechcroft Av. WD3: Crox G ... 8E **148**
Beechcroft Pl. *HA6: North ... 5H 161*
(off Eastbury Av.)
Beechcroft Rd. WD23: Bush ... 7N **149**
Beech Dr. CM21: Saw ... 7E **98**
HP4: Berk ... 2N **121**
SG2: Stev ... 6A **52**
WD6: Bore ... 4N **151**
Beechen Gro. WD17: Watf ... 6B **166** (5K **149**)
Beechen Wood WD3: Map C ... 5G **159**
Beeches, The AL2: Par S ... 9E **126**
AL6: Wel ... 3J **91**
HP22: Wen ... 9B **100**
HP23: Tring ... 2A **102**
SG4: Hit ... 4A **34**
SG8: Bark ... 9N **15**
SG8: Melb ... 1M **9**
SG8: Roys ... 7D **8**
WD3: Chor ... 7J **147**
WD18: Watf ... 7B **166**
Beech Farm Dr. AL4: St Alb ... 7N **109**
Beechfield CM21: Saw ... 5H **99**
EN11: Hod ... 4L **115**
WD4: Kin L ... 3B **136**
Beechfield Cl. AL3: Red ... 1K **107**
WD6: Bore ... 4M **151**
Beechfield Ct. WD17: Watf ... 3J **149**
Beechfield Rd. AL7: Welw G ... 2L **111**
HP1: Hem H ... 3L **123**
SG12: Ware ... 5K **95**
Beech Grn. LU6: Duns ... 8C **44**
Beech Gro. HP23: Tring ... 2A **102**
Beech Hill EN4: Had W ... 2C **154**
LU2: Lill, Lut ... 2L **47**
SG6: L Gar ... 4D **22**
Beech Hill Av. EN4: Had W ... 3B **154**
Beech Hill Ct. HP4: Berk ... 9A **104**
Beech Hill Path LU4: Lut ... 8D **46**
Beech Ho. EN11: Hod ... 8K **115**
Beech Hyde La. AL4: Wheat ... 8N **89**
Beeching Cl. AL5: Harp ... 3C **88**
Beechlands CM23: Bis S ... 3H **79**
Beecholm M. *EN8: C'hunt ... 1J 145*
(off The Colonade)
Beech Pk. HP23: Wigg ... 9D **102**
Beechpark Way WD17: Watf ... 1G **148**
Beech Pl. AL3: St Alb ... 8E **108**
Beech Ridge AL5: Harp ... 2K **87**
Beechridge Way SG7: Bald ... 5M **23**
Beech Rd. AL3: St Alb ... 8F **108**
LU1: Lut ... 9E **46**
LU6: Duns, Kens ... 3H **65**
WD24: Watf ... 1J **149**
Beech Tree Cl. HA7: Stanm ... 5K **163**
Beechtree La. AL3: St Alb ... 4K **125**
Beech Tree Way LU5: Hou R ... 4E **44**
Beech Wlk. EN11: Hod ... 8K **115**
HP23: Tring ... 2A 102
(off Mortimer Hill)
NW7 ... 6E **164**
Beech Way AL4: Wheat ... 1J **89**
Beechwood Av. AL1: St Alb ... 9J **109**
EN6: Pot B ... 6A **142**
HP6: L Chal ... 2A **146**
SG8: Melb ... 2M **9**
WD3: Chor ... 6E **146**
Beechwood Cl. EN7: C'hunt ... 8C **132**
HP6: L Chal ... 3A **146**
NW7 ... 5E **164**
SG5: Hit ... 9L **21**
SG7: Bald ... 6M **23**
SG13: H'ford ... 9D **94**
Beechwood Cotts. WD3: Chor ... 8F **146**
Beechwood Ct. LU6: Duns ... 1C **64**
Beechwood Dr. HP23: Aldb ... 1H **103**
Beechwood Ho. *HP22: Ast C ... 1E 100*
(off Beechwood Way)
Beechwood La. HP22: Halt, Wen ... 9C **100**
Beechwood Pk. HP3: Hem H ... 5J **123**
LU1: Cad ... 4A **66**
WD3: Chor ... 6J **147**
Beechwood Ri. WD24: Watf ... 9K **137**
Beechwood Rd. LU4: Lut ... 5N **45**
Beechwood Way HP22: Ast C ... 1E **100**
BEECROFT ... 8C **44**
Beecroft La. SG2: Walk ... 8G **37**
Beecroft Way LU6: Duns ... 9C **44**
Beehive Cl. WD6: Elst ... 8L **151**
Beehive Ct. HA8: Edg ... 5B **164**
Beehive Grn. AL7: Welw G ... 2N **111**
Beehive La. AL7: Welw G ... 3N **111**
Beehive Rd. EN7: Gof O ... 1N **143**
Beesonend Cotts. AL5: Harp ... 2C **108**
Beesonend La. AL5: Harp ... 4N **107**
Beesons Yd. WD3: R'orth ... 1N **159**
Beeston Cl. WD19: Watf ... 4M **161**
Beeston Dr. EN8: C'hunt ... 9H **133**
Beeston Rd. EN4: E Bar ... 8C **154**
Beetham Ct. SG12: C End ... 3C **94**
Beethoven Rd. WD6: Elst ... 8K **151**
Beeton Cl. HA5: Hat E ... 7B **162**
SG8: Melb ... 1M **9**
Beeton Ct. SG5: Stot ... 1C **22**
Beggarman's La. SG11: Old G ... 9H **55**
Beggars Bush La. WD18: Watf ... 7F **148**
Beggars Hollow EN2: Enf ... 1B **156**
Beggars La.
HP23: Aldb, N Gnd, Tring ... 1D **102**
Bejun Ct. EN5: N Bar ... 6B **154**
Beken Ct. WD25: Watf ... 8L **137**
Belcham's La. CB11: Que, Rick G ... 2M **43**
Belcher Rd. EN11: Hod ... 7L **115**
Belcon Ind. Est. EN11: Hod ... 8N **115**
Beldam Av. SG8: Roys ... 8D **8**
Beldams Ga. CM23: Bis S ... 2L **79**
Beldams La. CM23: Bis S ... 3K **79**
Belfairs Grn. WD19: Watf ... 5M **161**
Belfield Gdns. CM17: Harl ... 7E **118**
Belford Rd. WD6: Bore ... 2N **151**
Belfry, The LU2: Lut ... 3G **47**
WD24: Watf ... 3L **149**
Belfry Av. UB9: Hare ... 7K **159**
Belfry La. WD3: R'orth ... 1M **159**
Belgrave Av. WD18: Watf ... 7H **149**
Belgrave Cl. AL4: St Alb ... 7K **109**
N14 ... 7H **155**
NW7 ... 5D **164**
Belgrave Dr. WD4: Kin L ... 1E **136**
Belgrave Gdns. HA7: Stanm ... 5K **163**
N14 ... 7J **155**
Belgrave Ho. CM23: Bis S ... 9K **59**
Belgrave M. SG2: Stev ... 9N **51**
Belgrave Rd. LU4: Lut ... 4N **45**
Belgravia Cl. EN5: Barn ... 5M **153**
Belham Rd. WD4: Kin L ... 1B **136**
Belhaven Ct. WD6: Bore ... 3N **151**
Bell Acre SG6: L Gar ... 7H **23**
Bell Acre Gdns. SG6: L Gar ... 7H **23**
Bellamy Cl. HA8: Edg ... 2C **164**
SG3: Kneb ... 3M **71**
WD17: Watf ... 3J **149**
Bellamy Ct. HA7: Stanm ... 8J **163**
Bellamy Dr. HA7: Stanm ... 8J **163**
Bellamy Rd. EN2: Enf ... 4B **156**
EN8: C'hunt ... 2J **145**
BELL BAR ... 6N **129**
Bell Barns SG9: Bunt ... 3J **39**
Bellchambers Cl. AL2: Lon C ... 8K **127**
Bell Cl. HA5: Pin ... 9L **161**
SG3: Kneb ... 3N **71**
SG4: Hit ... 4B **34**
WD5: Bed ... 9H **125**
Bellerby Ri. LU4: Lut ... 3L **45**
Belle Vue La. WD23: B Hea ... 1E **162**
Belle Vue Rd. SG12: Ware ... 6J **95**
Bellevue Ter. UB9: Hare ... 7K **159**
Bellfield Av. HA3: Har W ... 6E **162**
BELLGATE ... 8A **106**
Bellgate HP2: Hem H ... 8A **106**
Bell Grn. HP3: Bov ... 9E **122**
BELLINGDON ... 6D **120**
Bellingdon WD19: Watf ... 3N **161**
Bellis Ho. AL7: Welw G ... 2A **112**
Bell La. AL2: Lon C ... 2M **139**
AL9: B Pk ... 6N **129**
EN3: Enf H, Enf W ... 2H **157**
EN10: Brox ... 3J **133**
EN11: Hod ... 8L **115**
HP4: Berk ... 9J **103**
HP6: L Chal ... 2A **146**
SG1: Stev ... 2J **51**
SG8: Nuth ... 1D **28**
SG12: Widf ... 3G **97**
SG14: H'ford ... 9B **94**
WD5: Bed ... 9H **125**
Bell Leys HP22: W'rave ... 5A **60**
Bell Mead CM21: Saw ... 5G **98**
Bellmount Wood Av. WD17: Watf ... 3G **149**
Bell Rd. EN1: Enf ... 3B **156**
Bell Roundabout, The
AL2: Lon C ... 9A **128**
Bell Row SG7: Bald ... 3L **23**
Bells Cl. SG5: Shil ... 2A **20**
Bells Hill CM23: Bis S ... 1G **79**
EN5: Barn ... 7K **153**
Bell St. CM21: Saw ... 5G **98**
Bells Wlk. CM21: Saw ... 5G **98**
Bell Ter. SG8: Ther ... 5C **14**
Bell Vw. AL4: St Alb ... 2L **127**
Bell Wlk. HP22: W'rave ... 5A **60**
Belmers Rd. HP23: Wigg ... 5B **102**
BELMONT ... 9H **163**
Belmont Av. EN4: C'ters ... 7E **154**
Belmont Circ. HA3: Ken ... 8J **163**
Belmont Cl. EN4: C'ters ... 6E **154**
N20 ... 1N **165**
Belmont Ct. AL1: St Alb ... 4C **166** (3E **126**)
Belmont Hill AL1: St Alb ... 4C **166** (3E **126**)
Belmont La. HA7: Stanm ... 8K **163**
Belmont Lodge HA3: Har W ... 7E **162**
Belmont Rd. HA3: Weal ... 9H **163**
HP3: Hem H ... 5A **124**
LU1: Lut ... 1E **66**
WD23: Bush ... 7N **149**
Belmor WD6: Elst ... 8A **152**
Belper Rd. LU4: Lut ... 7N **45**
Belsham Pl. LU2: Lut ... 7N **47**
BELSIZE ... 5J **135**
Belsize Cl. AL4: St Alb ... 6K **109**
HP3: Hem H ... 3C **124**
Belsize Cotts. WD4: Chippf ... 6H **135**
Belsize Rd. HA3: Har W ... 7E **162**
HP3: Hem H ... 3C **124**
LU4: Lut ... 6H **45**
Belswains Grn. HP3: Hem H ... 5A **124**
Belswains La. HP3: Hem H ... 5A **124**
Beltona Gdns. EN8: C'hunt ... 9H **133**
Belton Rd. HP4: Berk ... 9L **103**
Belvedere Ct. EN11: Hod ... 9L **115**
WD19: Watf ... 8N **149**
Belvedere Gdns. AL2: Chis G ... 9B **126**
Belvedere Rd. LU3: Lut ... 4D **46**
Belvedere Strand NW9 ... 9F **164**
Bembridge Gdns. LU3: Lut ... 2B **46**
Bembridge Pl. WD25: Watf ... 6J **137**
Ben Austins AL3: Red ... 2J **107**
Benbow Cl. AL1: St Alb ... 4J **127**
Benbroke Pl. SG4: W'ton ... 6A **36**
Benchley Hill SG4: Hit ... 2C **34**
Benchleys Rd. HP1: Hem H ... 4J **123**
Bench Mnr. Cres. SL9: Chal P ... 9A **158**
Bencroft EN7: C'hunt ... 8E **132**
Bencroft Rd. HP2: Hem H ... 2A **124**
BENDISH ... 9H **49**
Bendish La. SG4: Ben, Whit ... 9J **49**
Bendysh Rd. WD23: Bush ... 5N **149**
Benedict Ho. AL3: St Alb ... 1C **166**
Benedictine Ga. EN8: C'hunt ... 9J **133**
Benedictine Pl. AL1: St Alb ... 3D **166**
Benford Rd. EN11: Hod ... 1K **133**
Bengarth Dr. HA3: Har W ... 9E **162**
BENGEO ... 8A **94**
Bengeo Ho. SG14: H'ford ... 6A **94**
Bengeo Mdws. SG14: H'ford ... 6B **94**
Bengeo M. SG14: H'ford ... 6A **94**
Bengeo St. SG14: H'ford ... 7A **94**
Ben Hale Cl. HA7: Stanm ... 5J **163**
Benhooks Av. CM23: Bis S ... 3G **78**
Benhooks Pl. *CM23: Bis S ... 3G 79*
(off Benhooks Av.)
Beningfield Dr. AL2: Lon C ... 9H **127**
BENINGTON ... 5J **53**
Benington Cl. LU2: Lut ... 4G **47**
Benington Lordship Gdns. ... 5H **53**
Benington Pk. SG2: B'ton ... 5L **53**
Benington Rd. SG2: A'ton ... 7D **52**
SG2: Walk ... 3F **52**
Benneck Ho. WD18: Watf ... 8G **149**
Bennets Lodge EN2: Enf ... 5N **155**
Bennett Cl. AL7: Welw G ... 4M **111**
HA6: North ... 7H **161**
Bennett Ct. SG6: L Gar ... 6G **23**
(Holmdale)
SG6: L Gar ... 5F **22**
(Station Rd.)
Bennetts Cl. AL4: Col H ... 5D **128**
LU6: Duns ... 1E **64**
BENNETTS END ... 5C **124**
Bennetts End Cl. HP3: Hem H ... 4B **124**
Bennetts End Rd. HP3: Hem H ... 3B **124**
Bennetts Fld. WD23: Bush ... 6N **149**
Bennetts Ga. HP3: Hem H ... 5C **124**
Bennetts La. SG7: Ashw ... 6L **5**
SG9: Rush ... 8K **25**
Benning Av. LU6: Duns ... 9C **44**
Benningfield Cl. SG12: Widf ... 2G **97**
Benningfield Gdns. HP4: Berk ... 8B **104**
Benningfield Rd. SG12: Widf ... 3G **97**
Benningholme Rd. HA8: Edg ... 6E **164**
Bennington Dr. WD6: Bore ... 3N **151**
Benskin Rd. WD18: Watf ... 9A **166** (7J **149**)
Benskins Cl. CM23: Ber ... 2C **42**
Benslow La. SG4: Hit ... 3A **34**
Benslow Pl. SG4: Hit ... 3A **34**
Benslow Ri. SG4: Hit ... 3A **34**
Benson Cl. LU3: Lut ... 2B **46**
Benstede SG2: Stev ... 9B **52**
Benstede Ct. EN11: Hod ... 8L **115**
Bentcroft Wood (Nature Reserve) ... 4B **132**
BENTFIELD BOWER ... 1K **59**
BENTFIELD BURY ... 1K **59**
Bentfield C'way. CM24: Stans ... 2M **59**
BENTFIELD END ... 2M **59**
Bentfield Gdns. CM24: Stans ... 2M **59**
BENTFIELD GREEN ... 1M **59**
Bentfield Grn. CM24: Stans ... 2L **59**
Bentfield Ho. *NW9 ... 9F 164*
(off Heritage Av.)
Bentfield Orchard CM24: Stans ... 2M **59**
Bentfield Pl. CM24: Stans ... 2M **59**
Bentfield Rd. CM24: Stans ... 1M **59**
Bentick Way SG4: Cod ... 6F **70**
Bentinck Ho. WD17: Watf ... 9E **166**
Bentley Cl. CM23: Bis S ... 3H **79**
Bentley Ct. *LU1: Lut ... 9E 46*
(off Moor St.)
Bentley Dr. CM17: Harl ... 7E **118**
CM24: Stans ... 5N **59**
BENTLEY HEATH ... 8M **141**
Bentley Heath La. EN5: Barn ... 7L **141**
Bentley Lodge WD23: B Hea ... 2F **162**
Bentley M. EN1: Enf ... 8B **156**
Bentley Priory Local Nature Reserve ... 4F **162**
Bentley Rd. SG14: H'ford ... 8K **93**
Bentley Way EN5: N Bar ... 6B **154**
HA7: Stanm ... 5H **163**
Benton Rd. WD19: Watf ... 5M **161**
Bentons, The HP4: Berk ... 8K **103**
Bentsley Cl. AL4: St Alb ... 7K **109**
Berberry Cl. HA8: Edg ... 4C **164**
Berceau Wlk. WD17: Watf ... 3G **149**
BERDEN ... 2D **42**
Berefeld HP2: Hem H ... 9N **105**
Beresford Gdns. EN1: Enf ... 6C **156**
Beresford Rd. AL1: St Alb ... 3J **127**
LU4: Lut ... 8C **46**
WD3: R'orth ... 1J **159**
BERICOT GREEN ... 8D **92**
Bericot Way AL7: Welw G ... 9B **92**
Berkeley SG6: L Gar ... 7G **23**
Berkeley Cl. EN6: Pot B ... 5L **141**
LU7: Pits ... 4B **82**
SG2: Stev ... 9N **51**
SG5: Hit ... 2L **33**
SG12: Ware ... 5G **95**
WD5: Abb L ... 5H **137**
WD6: Elst ... 7A **152**
Berkeley Ct. AL5: Harp ... 5B **88**
N14 ... 8H **155**
WD3: Crox G ... 7F **148**
Berkeley Cres. EN4: E Bar ... 7C **154**
Berkeley Gdns. N21 ... 9B **156**
Berkeley M. AL1: St Alb ... 3J **127**
Berkeley Path LU2: Lut ... 9G **46**
Berkeley Sq. HP2: Hem H ... 5E **106**
BERKHAMSTED ... 1N **121**
Berkhamsted By-Pass
HP1: Hem H ... 3C **102**
HP4: Berk ... 3C **102**
HP23: Wigg ... 3C **102**
Berkhamsted Castle ... 9A **104**
BERKHAMSTED COMMON ... 3M **103**
Berkhamsted Golf Course ... 8B **104**
Berkhamsted Hill HP4: Berk ... 8B **104**
Berkhamsted La. AL9: Ess ... 2E **130**
SG13: Lit B ... 2E **130**
Berkhamsted Lawn Tennis & Squash Rackets Club ... 9M **103**
Berkhamsted Pl. HP4: Berk ... 8M **103**
Berkhamsted Rd. HP1: Hem H ... 8G **104**
(not continuous)
Berkhamsted Sports Cen. ... 9L **103**
Berkhamsted Station (Rail) ... 9N **103**
Berkley Av. EN8: Wal C ... 7H **145**
Berkley Cl. AL4: St Alb ... 7K **109**
Berkley Ct. *HP4: Berk ... 1N 121*
(off Mill St.)
Berkley Pl. EN8: Wal C ... 7H **145**
Berks Hill WD3: Chor ... 7F **146**
Bermer Rd. WD24: Watf ... 3L **149**
Bernard Cl. LU5: Duns ... 8F **44**
Bernard Gro. EN9: Wal A ... 6M **145**
BERNARD'S HEATH ... 8G **108**
Bernard St. AL3: St Alb ... 1D **166** (1E **126**)
Bernays Cl. HA7: Stanm ... 6K **163**
Berners Dr. AL1: St Alb ... 5F **126**
Berners Way EN10: Worm ... 5K **133**
Bernhardt Cres. SG2: Stev ... 3B **52**
Bernhart Cl. HA8: Edg ... 7C **164**
Berridge Grn. HA8: Edg ... 7A **164**
Berries, The AL4: St Alb ... 7H **109**
Berrow Cl. LU2: Lut ... 7N **47**
Berry Av. WD24: Watf ... 9K **137**
Berry Cl. N21 ... 9N **155**
WD3: R'orth ... 9L **147**
Berryfield LU7: Ched ... 9L **61**
BERRYGROVE ... 2A **150**
Berry Gro. La. WD25: A'ham ... 2N **149**
(Otterspool La.)
WD25: A'ham ... 3B **150**
(Otterspool Way)
Berry Hill HA7: Stanm ... 4L **163**
Berry La. WD3: Chor, R'orth ... 8G **147**
Berry Leys LU3: Lut ... 2A **46**
Berrymead HP2: Hem H ... 9B **106**
Berry Way WD3: R'orth ... 9L **147**

Bert Collins Ct.—Botany Lodge

Bert Collins Ct. LU1: Lut 1E 66
(off Wolston Cl.)
Berthold M. EN9: Wal A 6M 145
Bertram Rd. EN1: Enf 6E 156
Bert Way EN1: Enf 6D 156
Berwick Cl. EN8: Wal C 7L 145
HA7: Stanm 6G 163
SG1: Stev 1G 50
Berwick Pl. AL7: Welw G 3K 111
Berwick Rd. WD6: Bore 2N 151
Besant Ho. WD24: Watf 4M 149
Besford Cl. LU2: Lut 7N 47
Bessemer Cl. SG5: Hit 9M 21
Bessemer Dr. SG1: Stev 5H 51
Bessemer Rd. AL7: Welw G 8L 91
AL8: Welw G 4L 91
Bestway Bus. Cen.
LU1: Lut 9B 46
Bethune Cl. LU1: Lut 2D 66
Bethune Ct. LU1: Lut 2D 66
Betjeman Cl. AL5: Harp 6D 88
EN7: C'hunt 1E 144
Betjeman Gdns. WD3: Chor 6G 146
Betjeman Rd. SG8: Roys 5D 8
Betjeman Way HP1: Hem H 9L 105
Betony Va. SG8: Roys 8E 8
Bettespol Mdws. AL3: Red 9J 87
Betty Dodd Ct. LU4: Lut 5N 45
Betty Entwistle Ho. AL1: St Alb 5E 126
Betty Paterson Ho.
HP1: Hem H 2M 123
(off Astley Rd.)
Betty's La. HP23: Tring 2M 101
Beulah Cl. HA8: Edg 3B 164
Bevan Cl. HP3: Hem H 4N 123
Bevan Ho. WD24: Watf 4M 149
Bevan Rd. EN4: C'ters 6E 154
Beveridge Ct. N21 7K 155
(off Pennington Dr.)
Beverley Cl. EN1: Enf 6C 156
EN10: Brox 3J 133
SG8: Roys 5B 8
Beverley Ct. N14 9H 155
Beverley Dr. HA8: Edg 9A 164
Beverley Gdns.
AL4: St Alb 7L 109
AL7: Welw G 9B 92
EN7: C'hunt 3E 144
HA7: Stanm 8H 163
Beverley Rd. LU4: Lut 8B 46
SG1: Stev 8A 36
Bevil Ct. EN11: Hod 5L 115
Bewcastle Gdns. EN2: Enf 6K 155
Bewdley Cl. AL5: Harp 9E 88
Bewley Cl. EN8: C'hunt 4H 145
Bexhill Rd. LU2: Lut 7M 47
Beyers Gdns. EN11: Hod 5L 115
Beyers Prospect EN11: Hod 4L 115
Beyers Ride EN11: Hod 5L 115
Bibbs Hall La. AL6: Ayot L 9L 69
SG4: Kimp 9L 69
Bibshall Cres. LU6: Duns 2F 64
Bibsworth Rd. N3 9M 165
Bickerton Ho. WD17: Watf 9E 166
Bicknoller Rd. EN1: Enf 3C 156
Biddenham Turn WD25: Watf 8L 137
Bideford Cl. HA8: Edg 8A 164
Bideford Gdns. EN1: Enf 9C 156
LU3: Lut 5F 46
Bideford Rd. EN3: Enf L 2K 157
BIDWELL 3D 44
Bidwell Cl. LU5: Hou R 4E 44
SG6: L Gar 6H 23
Bidwell Hill LU5: Hou R 4D 44
Bidwell Path LU5: Hou R 5E 44
Biggin, The SG5: Hit 4N 33
(off Biggin La.)
Biggin Hill SG9: Ans 3A 28
Biggin La. SG5: Hit 4N 33
Biggleswade Rd. SG18: Dunt 1C 4
Biggs Ct. NW9 9E 164
(off Harvey Cl.)
Biggs Gro. Rd. EN7: C'hunt 9C 132
BIGNELL'S CORNER 6H 141
BIGNELL'S CORNER 7G 141
Bignells Cnr. EN6: S Mim 7H 141
Big Space
Harpenden 7C 88
Bigthan Rd. LU5: Duns 9F 44
BILDEN END 4L 17
Billet La. HP4: Berk 9L 103
(not continuous)
Billy Lows La. EN6: Pot B 4N 141
Bilton Rd. SG4: Hit 9N 21
Bilton Way EN3: Enf L 3J 157
LU1: Lut 9B 46
Bilton Way Ind. Est. LU1: Lut 9B 46
Bincote Rd. EN2: Enf 5L 155
Binder Cl. LU4: Lut 5H 45
Binder Ct. LU4: Lut 5H 45
(off Binder Cl.)
Bingen Rd. SG5: Hit 1K 33
Bingham Cl. HP1: Hem H 9J 105
Bingley Rd. EN11: Hod 8N 115
Binham Cl. LU2: Lut 2F 46
Binyon Cres. HA7: Stanm 5G 162
Biopark Dr. AL7: Welw G 9K 91
Birchall La. SG14: Col G, Pans 2D 112
Birchalls CM24: Stans 1N 59
Birchall Wood AL7: Welw G 1B 112
BIRCHANGER 7M 59
BIRCHANGER GREEN SERVICE AREA 1N 79
Birchanger Ind. Est. CM23: Bis S 7K 59
Birchanger La. CM23: Birc 6L 59
Birch Copse AL2: Bri W 3N 137
Birch Ct. AL7: Welw G 3N 111
HA6: North 6E 160
Birch Dr. AL10: Hat 1G 129
WD3: Map C 5G 158
Birchen Gro. LU2: Lut 6H 47
Bircherley Ct. SG14: H'ford 9B 94
(off Priory St.)
Bircherley Grn. SG14: H'ford 9B 94
Bircherley St. SG14: H'ford 9B 94
Birches, The AL2: Lon C 9K 127
HP3: Hem H 5J 123
LU4: Lut 7L 45
N21 8L 155
SG4: Cod 8G 70
SG6: L Gar 3E 22
WD23: Bush 7D 150
Birchfield Rd. EN8: C'hunt 2F 144
BIRCH GREEN 2H 113
Birch Grn. HP1: Hem H 1J 123
NW9 7E 164
Birch Gro. AL6: Wel 8L 71
EN6: Pot B 5N 141
Birch La. HP3: Flau 6E 134
Birch Leys HP2: Hem H 6E 106
Birch Link LU4: Lut 8E 46
Birchmead WD17: Watf 2H 149
Birchmead Cl. AL3: St Alb 8E 108
Birch Pk. HA3: Har W 7D 162
Birch Rd. HP4: Berk 7H 103
SG3: Dat 7A 72
Birch Side LU6: Duns 2G 65
Birchside Path LU6: Duns 2G 65
Birch Tree Wlk. WD17: Watf 1H 149
Birchville Ct. WD23: B Hea 1F 162
Birch Wlk. WD6: Bore 3A 152
Birch Way AL2: Lon C 9L 127
AL5: Harp 7D 88
Birchway AL10: Hat 7H 111
BIRCHWOOD 6H 111
Birchwood CM23: Birc 7M 59
WD7: Shen 7A 140
Birchwood Av. AL10: Hat 7G 110
Birchwood Cl. AL10: Hat 7G 111
Birchwood Ct. HA8: Edg 9C 164
Birchwood Ho. AL7: Welw G 9A 92
Birchwood Leisure Cen. 6H 111
Birchwood Way AL2: Par S 1C 138
Bird Ct. SG11: Col E 2L 75
Birdcroft Rd. AL8: Welw G 1K 111
Birdie Way SG13: H'ford 8F 94
Bird La. UB9: Hare 9M 159
Birds Cl. AL7: Welw G 2A 112
Birdsfoot La. LU3: Lut 4D 46
Birds Hill SG6: L Gar 5G 22
Birdwing Wlk. SG1: Stev 9B 36
Birkbeck Rd. EN2: Enf 3B 156
NW7 5F 164
Birkdale Av. HA5: Pin 9B 162
Birkdale Gdns. WD19: Watf 3M 161
Birken M. HA6: North 5D 160
Birkett Way HP8: Chal G 5A 146
Birklands La. AL1: St Alb 6J 127
Birklands Pk. AL1: St Alb 6J 127
Birling Dr. LU2: Lut 4L 47
Birnbeck Ct. EN5: Barn 6K 153
Birstal Grn. WD19: Watf 4M 161
Birtchnell Cl. HP4: Berk 9L 103
Birtley Cft. LU2: Lut 8N 47
BISCOT 7E 46
Biscot Rd. LU3: Lut 6D 46
Bishop Gray Ri. CM23: Bis S 8K 59
Bishop Ken Rd. HA3: Weal 9G 162
Bishop Rd. N14 9G 154
Bishops Av. CM23: Bis S 5H 79
HA6: North 4G 161
WD6: Elst 7N 151
Bishops Cl. AL4: St Alb 7H 109
AL10: Hat 9F 110
EN1: Enf 4F 156
EN5: Barn 8K 153
Bishopscote Rd. LU3: Lut 6D 46
Bishops Ct. EN8: C'hunt 3G 144
LU2: Lut 8F 46
(off Earls Meade)
WD5: Abb L 4H 137
Bishop Seth Ward Almhouse 3J 39
(off Market Hill)
Bishops Fld. HP22: Ast C 2F 100
Bishopsfield CM18: Harl 9N 117
Bishop's Gth. AL4: St Alb 7H 109
Bishops Mead HP1: Hem H 4L 123
Bishop's Palace (remains of) 9K 111
Bishops Pk. Cen. CM23: Bis S 9E 58
Bishops Pk. Way CM23: Bis S, Thorl 2D 78
Bishops Sq. AL10: Hat 8E 110
Bishops Ri. AL10: Hat 9F 110
Bishops Rd. AL6: Tew 1C 92
BISHOP'S STORTFORD 1H 79
Bishop's Stortford Bus. Cen. CM23: Bis S 2J 79
Bishop's Stortford FC 9M 59
Bishop's Stortford Golf Course 1M 79
Bishop's Stortford Sports Hall, The 4H 79
Bishop's Stortford Station (Rail) 2J 79
Biskra WD17: Watf 3J 149
Bisley Cl. EN8: Wal C 6H 145
Bit, The HP23: Wigg 5B 102
Bittacy Bus. Cen. NW7 7L 165
Bittacy Cl. NW7 6K 165
Bittacy Ct. NW7 7L 165
Bittacy Hill NW7 6K 165
Bittacy Pk. Av. NW7 5K 165
Bittacy Ri. NW7 6J 165
Bittacy Rd. NW7 6K 165
Bittern Cl. EN7: C'hunt 7A 132
HP3: Hem H 7B 124
SG2: Stev 7C 52
Bittern Ct. NW9 9E 164
Bittern Way SG6: L Gar 2E 22
Blackberry Mead SG2: Stev 6C 52
Blackbirds La. WD25: A'ham 7D 138
Black Boy Wood AL2: Bri W 3B 138
Blackbridge La. SG10: M Had 8G 77
Blackburn NW9 9F 164
Blackburn Rd. LU5: Hou R 6E 44
Blackbury Cl. EN6: Pot B 4B 142
Blackbushe CM23: Bis S 8K 59
Blackbush Spring CM20: Harl 5C 118
Black Cut AL1: St Alb 5F 166 (3F 126)
Blackdale EN7: C'hunt 9E 132
Blackdown Cl. SG1: Stev 7A 36
Blackett-Ord Ct. SG8: Roys 6D 8
Blacketts Wood Dr. WD3: Chor 7E 146
Black Fan Cl. EN2: Enf 3A 156
Black Fan Rd. AL7: Welw G 8M 91
(not continuous)
Blackford Rd. WD19: Watf 5M 161
Blackfriars Ct. AL1: St Alb 1F 166
Black Grn. Wood Cl. AL2: Par S 2C 138
BLACKHALL 7L 29
Blackhill La. MK45: Pull 3A 18
Blackhorse Cl. SG4: Hit 5A 34
(off Blackhorse La.)
Blackhorse La. AL3: Red 9J 87
EN6: S Mim 3E 140
SG4: Hit 6N 33
Blackhorse Rd. SG6: L Gar 3J 23
Black La. SG8: S Mor 4C 6
Blackley Cl. WD17: Watf 1H 149
Black Lion Ct. CM17: Harl 2E 118
Black Lion Hill WD7: Shen 5M 139
Black Lion St. CM17: Harl 2E 118
(off Market St.)
Blackmoor La. WD18: Watf 7F 148
Blackmore SG6: L Gar 8H 23
BLACKMORE END 1J 89
Blackmore Ga. HP22: Buck 2F 100
Blackmore Mnr. AL4: Wheat 1J 89
Blackmore Way AL4: Wheat 1J 89
Blacksmith Cl. CM23: Bis S 3D 78
Blacksmith Row HP3: Hem H 3E 124
Blacksmiths Cl. SG5: Stot 5F 10
SG12: Gt A 8L 95
Blacksmiths Ct. LU6: Duns 9E 44
(off Matthew St.)
Blacksmiths Hill SG2: B'ton 5K 53
Blacksmiths La. AL3: St Alb 2C 126
SG8: Reed 7H 15
Blacksmiths Row AL3: Mark 2A 86
(off High St.)
Blacksmith Way CM21: H Wyc 6D 98
Black Swan Ct. SG12: Ware 5H 95
Black Swan La. LU3: Lut 4C 46
Blackthorn Cl. AL4: St Alb 8K 109
WD25: Watf 5K 137
Blackthorn Dr. LU2: Lut 5L 47
Blackthorne Cl. AL10: Hat 3F 128
Black Thorn Rd. LU5: Hou R 3F 44
Blackthorn Rd. AL7: Welw G 1N 111
Blackwater La. HP3: Hem H 5G 124
Blackwell Cl. HA3: Har W 7E 162
N21 7K 155
Blackwell Dr. WD19: Watf 8L 149
Blackwell Gdns. HA8: Edg 4A 164
Blackwell Rd. WD4: Kin L 2C 136
Blackwood Ct. EN10: Turn 8K 133
Bladon Cl. SG4: L Wym 7F 34
Blaine Cl. HP23: Tring 9M 81
Blair Cl. CM23: Bis S 1E 78
HP2: Hem H 5D 106
SG2: Stev 8M 51
Blairhead Dr. WD19: Watf 3K 161
Blake Cl. AL1: St Alb 5H 127
SG8: Roys 4D 8
Blake Ct. N21 7L 155
Blakedown LU2: Lut 8G 46
Blakelands MK45: Bar C 9F 18
Blakemere Rd. AL8: Welw G 7K 91
Blake M. CM24: Stans 5M 59
Blakemore End Rd.
SG4: L Wym 8D 34
Blakeney Dr. LU2: Lut 2E 46
Blakeney Ho. SG1: Stev 2G 50
Blakeney Rd. SG1: Stev 2G 50
Blakes Ct. CM21: Saw 5G 99
Blakesware Gdns. N9 9B 156
Blakes Way AL6: Wel 1J 91
Blaking's La. CM23: Ber 4E 42
Blanchard Dr. WD18: Watf 6G 149
Blanchard Gro. EN3: Enf L 2M 157
Blanche La. EN6: S Mim 5G 140
Blandford Av. LU2: Lut 3F 46
Blandford Cres. E4 9N 157
Blandford Rd. AL1: St Alb 2H 127
Blanes, The SG12: Ware 4G 94
Blattner Cl. WD6: Elst 6M 151
Blaxland Ter. EN8: C'hunt 1H 145
(off Davison Dr.)
Blaydon Rd. LU2: Lut 9J 47
Blegberry Gdns. HP4: Berk 1J 121
Blenheim Cl. CM21: Saw 7E 98
LU7: Ched 8L 61
N21 9A 156
WD19: Watf 9L 149
Blenheim Ct. AL7: Welw G 8M 91
CM23: Bis S 1E 78
Blenheim Cres. LU3: Lut 7E 46
Blenheim M. WD7: Shen 6M 139
Blenheim Rd. AL1: St Alb 1G 127
EN5: Barn 5K 153
WD5: Abb L 5J 137
Blenheim Way SG2: Stev 1B 72
Blenkin Cl. AL3: St Alb 7D 108
Bleriot NW9 9F 164
(off Belvedere Strand)
Blessbury Rd. HA8: Edg 8C 164
Bletchley Ct. HA7: Stanm 7M 163
(off Hitchin Way)
Blind La. SG9: Cot 5L 37
Blindman's La. EN8: C'hunt 3H 145
Blind Tom's La. CM23: Farn 3J 59
Bliss Ho. EN1: Enf 2E 156
Bloomfield Av. LU2: Lut 8J 47
Bloomfield Cotts. HP5: Bell 6D 120
Bloomfield Rd. AL5: Harp 4A 88
EN7: C'hunt 7A 132
Bloomsbury Cl. NW7 7G 164
Bloomsbury Ct. HA5: Pin 9A 162
Bloomsbury Gdns.
LU5: Hou R 4G 44
Blossom La. EN2: Enf 3A 156
Blow's Downs 9H 45
Blows Rd. LU5: Duns 1G 64
Bluebell Cl. AL2: Par S 9D 126
HP1: Hem H 3H 123
SG13: H'ford 9E 94
Bluebell Ct. NW9 8E 164
(off Heybourne Cres.)
Bluebell Dr. EN7: Gof O 1B 144
SG16: L Ston 1H 21
WD5: Bed 9H 125
Bluebells AL6: Wel 9L 71
Bluebell Wlk. CM21: Saw 6D 98
Bluebell Way AL10: Hat 5F 110
Bluebell Wood Cl. LU1: Lut 1B 66
Blueberry Cl. AL3: St Alb 7E 108
WD19: Watf 9L 149
Bluebird Way AL2: Bri W 3A 138
Bluebridge Av. AL9: B Pk 9L 129
Bluebridge Rd. AL9: B Pk 8L 129
Bluecoat Ct. SG14: H'ford 9B 94
Bluecoats Av. SG14: H'ford 9B 94
Bluecoat Yd. SG12: Ware 6H 95
(off East St.)
BLUE HILL 2H 73
Bluehouse Hill AL3: St Alb 3B 126
Blundell Rd. AL2: Lon C 9L 127
Blundell Cl. AL3: St Alb 7E 108
Blundell Rd. HA8: Edg 8D 164
LU3: Lut 6C 46
Blunesfield EN6: Pot B 4C 142
Blunts La. AL2: Pot C 6M 125
WD5: Bed 9M 125
Blydon Ct. N21 7L 155
(off Chaseville Pk. Rd.)
Blyth Cl. SG1: Stev 2G 51
WD6: Bore 3N 151
Blythe Pl. LU1: Lut 2F 66
(off Russell St.)
Blythe Rd. EN11: Hod 9A 116
Blyth Path LU1: Lut 2F 66
(off Russell Ri.)
Blythway AL7: Welw G 5M 91
Blythway Ho's. AL7: Welw G 6M 91
Blythwood Gdns. CM24: Stans 3M 59
Blythwood Rd. HA5: Pin 8M 161
Boardman Av. E4 7M 157
Boardman Cl. EN5: Barn 7L 153
Boar Head Rd. CM17: Harl 7J 119
Boarhound NW9 9F 164
(off Further Acre)
Bockings SG2: Walk 9H 37
Boddington Rd. HP22: Wen 9B 100
Bodiam Cl. EN1: Enf 4C 156
Bodiam Path LU7: Pits 4A 82
(off Durham Rd.)
Bodmin NW9 9F 164
(off Further Acre)
Bodmin Rd. LU4: Lut 5B 46
Bodnor Ga. SG7: Bald 3M 23
Bodwell Cl. HP1: Hem H 1K 123
Bogmoor Rd. SG8: Bark, Barl 6B 16
Bognor Gdns. WD19: Watf 5L 161
Bogs Gap La. SG8: S Mor 2C 6
Bohemia HP2: Hem H 1A 124
Bohun Gro. EN4: E Bar 8D 154
Boissy Cl. AL4: St Alb 3M 127
Bolebec End LU7: Pits 4B 82
Boleyn Av. EN1: Enf 3F 156
Boleyn Cl. HP2: Hem H 6E 106
Boleyn Ct. EN10: Brox 3J 133
Boleyn Dr. AL1: St Alb 4E 126
Boleyn Way EN5: N Bar 5B 154
Bolingbroke Rd. LU1: Lut 2D 66
Boling Brook AL4: St Alb 7H 109
Bolney Grn. LU2: Lut 6M 47
Bolton Rd. LU1: Lut 1H 67
Bond Ct. AL5: Harp 4A 88
Bondor Bus. Cen. SG7: Bald 4M 23
Bonham Carter Rd. HP22: Halt 7C 100
Bonham Ct. HP22: Ast C 1C 100
Boniface Gdns. HA3: Har W 7C 162
Boniface Wlk. HA3: Har W 7C 162
Bonington Ho. EN1: Enf 7E 156
Bonks Hill CM21: Saw 6F 98
Bonner Ct. EN8: C'hunt 1H 145
(off Coopers Wlk.)
Bonnetting La. CM23: Ber 1D 42
Bonney Gro. EN7: C'hunt 3E 144
Bonnick Cl. LU1: Lut 2E 66
Boot All. AL3: St Alb 3C 166
Boothman Ho. HA3: Ken 9L 163
Booth Pl. LU6: Eat B 2J 63
Booth Rd. NW9 9D 164
Booths Cl. AL9: Welh G 6K 129
Boot Pde. HA8: Edg 6A 164
(off High St.)
Borden Av. EN1: Enf 8B 156
Borders Way LU5: Hou R 3F 44
(off Black Thorn Rd.)
Boreham Holt WD6: Elst 6N 151
BOREHAMWOOD 5A 152
Borehamwood Ent. Cen. WD6: Bore 5N 151
Borehamwood Ind. Pk. WD6: Bore 4D 152
Borehamwood Shop. Pk. WD6: Bore 5A 152
Borham M. EN11: Hod 5L 115
Borley Grn. SG9: B Pel 9H 29
Bornedene EN6: Pot B 4L 141
Borodale AL5: Harp 6B 88
Borough Rd. LU5: Duns 1G 64
Borough Way EN6: Pot B 5L 141
Borrell Cl. EN10: Brox 2K 133
Borrowdale Av. HA3: Weal 9H 163
LU6: Duns 2F 64
Borrowdale Ct. EN2: Enf 3A 156
HP2: Hem H 8A 106
Bosanquet Rd. EN11: Hod 6N 115
Boscombe Cir. NW9 8D 164
Boscombe Ct. SG6: L Gar 5H 23
Boscombe Rd. LU5: Duns 7F 44
Bose Cl. N3 8L 165
Bosmore Rd. LU3: Lut 3B 46
Boston Rd. HA8: Edg 7C 164
Boswell Cl. WD7: Shen 5M 139
Boswell Dr. SG5: Ick 7M 21
Boswell Gdns. SG1: Stev 9K 35
Boswick La. HP4: Berk 6H 103
Bosworth Rd. EN5: N Bar 5N 153
BOTANY BAY 9J 143
Botany Bay La. SG1: Stev 7N 35
Botany Cl. EN4: E Bar 6D 154
Botany Lodge SG1: Stev 7A 36

176 A-Z Hertfordshire

Botham Cl.—Bridleway Sth.

Botham Cl. HA8: Edg 7C 164
Botley Rd. HP2: Hem H 6C 106
Bottom Dr. LU6: Eat B 3A 64
Bottom Ho. La. HP23: N Gnd, Wigg 6E 102
Bottom La. WD3: Buc H 8L 135
WD4: Buc H 8L 135
Bough Beech Ct. EN3: Enf W 1H 157
Boughton Way HP6: L Chal 2A 146
Boulevard, The AL7: Welw G 7M 91
WD18: Watf 7F 148
Boulevard 25 WD6: Bore 5A 152
Boulevard Dr. NW9 9F 164
Boulton Rd. SG1: Stev 8B 36
Bounce, The HP2: Hem H 9N 105
Boundary, The SG13: Lit B 1H 131
Boundary Cl. CM23: Bis S 3J 79
EN5: Barn 3M 153
SG16: Henl 1J 21
Boundary Cotts. HP3: Bov 2G 135
Boundary Ct. AL7: Welw G 4M 111
Boundary Dr. SG14: H'ford 7B 94
Boundary Ho. AL7: Welw G 3K 111
EN8: C'hunt 5H 145
Boundary La. AL7: Welw G 3L 111
Boundary Pk. HP2: Hem H 9E 106
Boundary Rd. AL1: St Alb 9F 108
CM23: Bis S 3J 79
N9 8G 157
SL9: Chal P 7A 158
Boundary Way HP2: Hem H 8E 106
WD25: Watf 5K 137
Bounds Fld. SG11: L Had 9B 58
Bourn Av. EN4: E Bar 7C 154
Bourne, The AL5: Harp 5A 88
(not continuous)
CM23: Bis S 9K 59
HP3: Bov 9D 122
SG9: Asp 5J 39
SG11: Alb 3M 57
SG12: Ware 5H 95
Bourne Cl. EN10: Brox 2K 133
SG12: Ware 5H 95
BOURNE END 4F 122
Bourne End La. HP1: Hem H 7D 122
Bourne End La. Ind. Est. HP1: Hem H 4E 122
Bourne End Rd. HA6: North 4G 160
Bournehall WD23: Bush 8B 150
Bournehall Av. WD23: Bush 7B 150
Bournehall La. WD23: Bush 8B 150
Bournehall Rd. WD23: Bush 8B 150
Bourne Honour SG12: Tonw 9C 74
Bourne La. SG10: M Had 1J 97
Bournemead WD23: Bush 8C 150
Bournemouth Rd. SG1: Stev 1H 51
Bourne Rd. HP4: Berk 9K 103
WD23: Bush 7B 150
Bournwell Cl. EN4: C'ters 5E 154
Bouvier Rd. EN3: Enf W 2G 157
BOVINGDON 9D 122
Bovingdon Ct. HP3: Bov 1D 134
WD23: Bush 7C 150
(off Farrington Av.)
Bovingdon Cres. WD25: Watf 7M 137
BOVINGDON GREEN 2D 134
Bovingdon Grn. HP3: Bov 2D 134
Bovingdon La. NW9 8E 164
Bowbrookvale LU2: Lut 8A 48
Bowcock Wlk. SG1: Stev 6L 51
Bower Cl. LU6: Eat B 3K 63
Bower Ct. *E4 9N 157*
(off The Ridgeway)
BOWER HEATH 1D 88
Bower Heath La. AL5: Harp 2D 88
Bower La. LU6: Eat B 3K 63
Bowershott SG6: L Gar 7G 23
Bower's Pde. AL5: Harp 6B 88
Bowers Way AL5: Harp 5B 88
Bowes Lyon Cen. 4L 51
Bowes Lyon M. AL3: St Alb 3C 166 (2E 126)
Bowgate AL1: St Alb 1F 166 (1F 126)
Bowland Cres. LU6: Duns 2D 64
Bowlers Grn. WD7: Shen 3K 139
Bowlers Mead SG9: Bunt 2H 39
Bowles Grn. EN1: Enf 9F 144
Bowles Way LU6: Duns 3G 65
Bowling Cl. AL5: Harp 8C 88
CM23: Bis S 2H 79
Bowling Ct. WD18: Watf 6J 149
Bowling Grn. SG1: Stev 1J 51
Bowling Grn. La. LU2: Lut 7G 46
SG9: Bunt 2H 39
Bowling Ho. *CM23: Bis S 1J 79*
(off Heron Ct.)
Bowling La. CM23: Bis S 3L 79
Bowling Rd. SG12: Ware 6J 95
Bowls Cl. HA7: Stanm 5J 163
Bowmans Av. SG4: Hit 3B 34
Bowmans Cl. AL6: Wel 1J 91
EN6: Pot B 5C 142
LU6: Duns 1F 64
Bowmans Ct. HP2: Hem H 9A 106
Bowmans Grn. WD25: Watf 9N 137
Bowmans Way LU6: Duns 1F 64
Bowman Trad. Est. SG1: Stev 4H 51
Bowood Rd. EN3: Enf H 4H 157
Bowring Grn. WD19: Watf 5L 161
Bowsher Ct. SG12: Ware 6J 95
Bowstridge La. HP8: Chal G 5A 158
Bowyer Ct. EN8: Wal C 6K 145
Bowyer Dr. SG6: L Gar 5H 23
Bowyers HP2: Hem H 9N 105
Bowyer's Cl. SG5: Hit 1L 33
Boxberry Cl. SG1: Stev 3L 51
Boxelder Cl. HA8: Edg 5C 164
Boxfield AL7: Welw G 3A 112
Boxfield Gallery, The *4K 51*
(within Stevenage Arts & Leisure Cen.)
Boxfield Grn. SG2: Stev 1C 52
Boxgrove Cl. LU2: Lut 4L 47
Boxhill HP2: Hem H 9N 105
Box La. EN11: Hod 7H 115
(not continuous)
HP3: Hem H 7F 122
BOXMOOR 4L 123
Boxmoor Playhouse Theatre 4M 123
Boxted Cl. LU4: Lut 4M 45
Boxted Rd. HP1: Hem H 9J 105
Boxtree La. HA3: Har W 8D 162
Boxtree Rd. HA3: Har W 7E 162
Boxwell Rd. HP4: Berk 1M 121
Boyce Cl. WD6: Bore 3M 151
Boyce Ct. *WD17: Watf 3J 149*
(off Lockhart Rd.)
Boyd Carpenter Ho. SL9: Chal P 5C 158
Boyd Cl. CM23: Bis S 9K 59
Boyd Ho. AL7: Welw G 9B 92
Boyes Cres. AL2: Lon C 8J 127
Boyle Av. HA7: Stanm 6H 163
Boyle Cl. LU2: Lut 9G 46
Boyseland Ct. HA8: Edg 2C 164
Brabourne Hgts. NW7 3E 164
Braceby Cl. LU3: Lut 3B 46
Brace Cl. EN7: C'hunt 7N 131
Braceys SG2: B'ton 7L 53
Brache Cl. AL3: Red 1J 107
Brache Ct. LU1: Lut 2H 67
Bracken Cl. WD6: Bore 3B 152
Bracken Ct. AL10: Hat 5F 110
Brackendale EN6: Pot B 6N 141
Brackendale Gro. AL5: Harp 4M 87
LU3: Lut 4C 46
Brackendene AL2: Bri W 3A 138
Brackenhill HP4: Berk 9B 104
Bracken La. AL6: Wel 9M 71
Brackens, The EN1: Enf 9C 156
HP2: Hem H 1N 123
Brackenwood Lodge *EN5: N Bar 6N 153*
(off Prospect Rd.)
Bracklesham Gdns. LU2: Lut 6M 47
Brackley Cl. HA8: Edg 7B 164
Bracknell Cl. LU4: Lut 6J 45
Bracknell Pl. HP2: Hem H 7B 106
Bradbery WD3: Map C 5G 158
Bradbury Cl. WD6: Bore 3B 152
Bradden Cotts. HP2: Gad R 7J 85
Bradden La. HP2: Gad R 1G 104
Bradden Mdw. HP2: Gad R 7J 85
Braddon Ct. EN5: Barn 5L 153
Bradford Rd. WD3: Hero 9F 146
Bradgate EN6: Cuff 9J 131
Bradgate Cl. EN6: Cuff 1J 143
Bradgers Hill Rd. LU2: Lut 5G 46
Bradley Comn. CM23: Birc 6L 59
Bradley Ct. *EN3: Enf L 2J 157*
(off Bradley Rd.)
Bradley Rd. EN3: Enf L 2J 157
EN9: Wal A 8N 145
LU4: Lut 8M 45
Bradleys Cnr. SG4: Hit 1C 34
Bradman Row HA8: Edg 7C 164
Bradman Way SG1: Stev 9N 35
Bradmore Ct. *EN3: Enf H 5J 157*
(off Enstone Rd.)
Bradmore Grn. AL9: B Pk 8L 129
Bradmore La. AL9: N Mym 9J 129
Bradmore Way AL9: B Pk 8L 129
Bradon *NW9 9F 164*
(off Further Acre)
Brad Rd. NW7 6K 165
Bradshaw Cl. SG2: Stev 6A 52
Bradshaw Dr. NW7 7K 165
Bradshaw Rd. WD24: Watf 3L 149
Bradshaws AL10: Hat 4F 128
Bradshaws Cl. MK45: Bar C 8E 18
Bradway SG4: Whit 2M 69
Braeburn Ct. EN4: E Bar 6C 154
Braeburn Wlk. SG8: Roys 6C 8
Braemar Cl. SG2: Stev 1A 72
Braemar Ct. WD23: Bush 8B 150
Braemar Gdns. NW9 8D 164
Braemar Turn HP2: Hem H 5D 106
Braeside Cl. HA5: Hat E 7B 162
Bragbury Cl. SG2: Stev 1C 72
BRAGBURY END 1C 72
Bragbury La. SG2: Stev 4B 72
SG3: Dat 4B 72
Braggowens Ley CM17: Harl 5E 118
Bragmans La. WD3: Sar 7F 134
Braham Ct. *SG5: Hit 3M 33*
(off Nun's Cl.)
Brain Cl. AL10: Hat 8H 111
Braintree Cl. LU4: Lut 6J 45
Braithwaite Ct. LU3: Lut 8F 46
WD17: Watf 2J 149
Braithwaite Gdns. HA7: Stanm 8K 163
Braithwaite Rd. EN3: Brim 5K 157
Brakynbery HP4: Berk 7J 103
Bramble Cl. AL5: Harp 4A 88
HA7: Stanm 7L 163
LU4: Lut 5M 45
SL9: Chal P 6B 158
WD25: Watf 7J 137
Bramble La. EN11: Hod 6J 115
Bramble Ri. CM20: Harl 5M 117
Bramble Rd. AL10: Hat 9D 110
LU4: Lut 5M 45
Brambles, The AL1: St Alb 4E 126
AL6: Wel 8L 71
CM23: Bis S 2E 78
EN8: C'hunt 4H 145
SG1: Stev 8K 35
SG8: Roys 8E 8
SG12: Ware 4G 94
Brambling Cl. WD23: Bush 6N 149
Brambling Ri. HP2: Hem H 7A 106
BRAMFIELD 3H 93
Bramfield SG4: Hit 4B 34
WD25: Watf 7N 137
Bramfield Ct. SG14: H'ford 8M 93
Bramfield La. SG14: Bram, Water 5K 93
Bramfield Pl. HP2: Hem H 5C 106
Bramfield Rd. SG3: Dat 7C 72
SG14: H'ford 6K 93
Bramham Ct. HA6: North 5G 160
Bramhanger Acre LU3: Lut 2N 45
Bramingham Bus. Pk. LU3: Lut 1D 46
Bramingham Rd. LU3: Lut 4A 46
Bramleas WD18: Watf 7H 149
Bramley Av. SG8: Melb 1N 9
Bramley Cl. N14 7G 154
NW7 3E 164
SG7: Bald 2M 23
Bramley Ct. EN4: E Bar 6D 154
LU5: Duns 8G 45
WD25: Watf 5K 137
Bramley Gdns. WD19: Watf 6L 161
Bramley Ho. Ct. EN2: Enf 1B 156
Bramley Pde. N14 6J 155
Bramley Rd. N14 7G 154
Bramley Sports Ground 7F 154
Bramley Way AL4: St Alb 3K 127
Brampton Cl. AL5: Harp 6E 88
EN7: C'hunt 1E 144
Brampton Pk. Rd. SG5: Hit 1M 33
Brampton Ri. LU6: Duns 2F 64
Brampton Rd. AL1: St Alb 1H 127
SG8: Roys 7F 8
WD19: Watf 3J 161
Brampton Ter. *WD6: Bore 2A 152*
(off Stapleton Rd.)
Bramshaw Gdns. WD19: Watf 5M 161
Bramshott Cl. SG4: Hit 6N 33
Bramshot Way WD19: Watf 2J 161
Brancaster Dr. NW7 7G 164
Branch Cl. AL10: Hat 7J 111
Branch Rd. AL2: Par S 9E 126
AL3: St Alb 1A 166 (1C 126)
Brancroft Way EN3: Brim 3J 157
Brandles Rd. SG6: L Gar 8G 23
Brandon Cl. EN7: C'hunt 8C 132
Brandon Ct. HP23: Lon M 9C 60
Brandon Mobile Home Pk.
AL4: St Alb 2L 127
Brandreth Av. LU5: Duns 8H 45
Brand St. SG5: Hit 3M 33
Branksome Cl. HP2: Hem H 1C 124
Branscombe Gdns. N21 9M 155
Branscombe Ho. WD24: Watf 1J 149
Bransgrove Rd. HA8: Edg 8N 163
Branston Cl. WD19: Watf 9L 149
Branton Cl. LU2: Lut 7N 47
Brantwood Gdns. EN2: Enf 6K 155
Brantwood Rd. LU1: Lut 1E 66
BRAUGHING 2C 56
BRAUGHING FRIARS 4H 57
Braughing Rd. SG11: Alb, B'ing 1D 56
Braunds All. SG5: Hit 3M 33
Brawlings La. SL9: Chal P 4D 158
Bray Cl. WD6: Bore 3C 152
Bray Dr. SG1: Stev 7N 35
Brayes Mnr. SG5: Stot 6F 10
Bray Lodge EN8: C'hunt 1J 145
Bray Rd. NW7 6K 165
Bray's Ct. LU2: Lut 6K 47
BRAYS GROVE 7C 118
Brays Mead CM18: Harl 8B 118
Brays Rd. LU2: Lut 6K 47
Brayton Gdns. EN2: Enf 6J 155
Brazier Cl. MK45: Bar C 8D 18
Braziers End HP5: Bell 3A 120
Braziers Fld. SG13: H'ford 9D 94
(not continuous)
Braziers Quay CM23: Bis S 2J 79
Breach La. SG13: Lit B 9H 113
Breachwell Pl. LU7: Ched 7M 61
BREACHWOOD GREEN 8F 48
Bread & Cheese La. EN7: C'hunt 7B 132
EN10: Brox 7B 132
Breadcroft La. AL5: Harp 5C 88
Breakmead AL7: Welw G 2A 112
Breakspear SG2: Stev 6B 52
Breakspear Av. AL1: St Alb 3G 127
Breakspear Ct. WD5: Abb L 3H 137
Breakspeare Cl. WD24: Watf 2K 149
Breakspeare Rd. WD5: Abb L 4G 137
Breakspear Pl. WD5: Abb L 3H 137
Breakspear Rd. Nth. UB9: Hare 8M 159
Breakspear Way HP2: Hem H 2E 124
Breaks Rd. AL10: Hat 8H 111
Brearley Cl. HA8: Edg 7C 164
Brecken Cl. AL4: St Alb 7H 109
Brecon Cl. LU1: Lut 2F 66
Brecon Rd. EN3: Pon E 6G 156
Breeze Ter. EN8: C'hunt 1H 145
Bren Ct. *EN3: Enf L 1L 157*
(off Colgate Pl.)
Brendon Av. LU2: Lut 8L 47
Brendon Ct. WD7: Rad 7J 139
Brendon Way EN1: Enf 9C 156
Brent Ct. SG1: Stev 4L 51
Brenthall Towers CM17: Harl 8E 118
BRENT PELHAM 9K 29
Brent Pl. EN5: Barn 7M 153
Brent Way N3 6N 165
Brentwood Cl. LU5: Hou R 3G 44
Brereton Ct. HP3: Hem H 4A 124
Bressay Dr. NW7 7G 165
Bressey Av. EN1: Enf 3E 156
Brett Ho. EN8: C'hunt 1H 145
Brett Pl. WD24: Watf 1J 149
Brett Rd. EN5: Barn 7J 153
Bretts Mead LU1: Lut 3E 66
Bretts Mead Ct. LU1: Lut 2E 66
Brewers Cl. CM23: Bis S 3E 78
Brewers Hill Rd. LU6: Duns 8B 44
Brewery La. CM24: Stans 2N 59
SG7: Bald 2L 23
Brewery Rd. EN11: Hod 8L 115
(not continuous)
Brewery Yd. CM24: Stans 2N 59
Brewhouse Hill AL4: Wheat 7K 89
Brewhouse La. SG14: H'ford 9A 94
Briants Cl. HA5: Pin 9A 162
Briarcliff HP1: Hem H 1H 123
Briar Cl. EN8: C'hunt 2G 144
HP4: Pot E 7D 104
LU2: Lut 5L 47
Briardale HA8: Edg 4D 164
SG1: Stev 5L 51
SG12: Ware 4G 94
Briarley Cl. EN10: Worm 4K 133
Briar Patch La. SG6: L Gar 8D 22
Briar Rd. AL4: St Alb 8L 109
WD25: Watf 7J 137
Briars, The CM18: Harl 9A 118
EN8: C'hunt 4J 145
SG13: H'ford 9E 94
WD3: Sar 9K 135
WD23: B Hea 9F 150
Briars Cl. AL10: Hat 9G 110
Briars La. AL10: Hat 9G 110
Briars Wood AL10: Hat 9F 110
Briarswood EN7: Gof O 1B 144
Briar Wlk. HA8: Edg 7C 164
Briarway HP4: Berk 2N 121
Briarwood Dr. HA6: North 9J 161
Briary Gro. HA8: Edg 9B 164
Briary La. SG8: Roys 8C 8
Briary Wood End AL6: Wel 8M 71
Briary Wood La. AL6: Wel 8M 71
Brickcroft EN10: Turn 8J 133
Brickcroft Hoppit CM17: Harl 5E 118
BRICKENDON 9A 114
Brickendon Ct. EN11: Hod 8L 115
Brickendon Grange Golf Course 1N 131
Brickendon La. SG13: B'don, H'ford 3A 114
(not continuous)
Bricket Rd. AL1: St Alb 3D 166 (2E 126)
BRICKET WOOD 3A 138
Bricket Wood Common 5B 138
Bricket Wood Paintball Cen. 2C 138
Bricket Wood Station (Rail) 3B 138
Brickfield AL10: Hat 3G 129
Brickfield Av. HP3: Hem H 3D 124
Brickfield Ct. AL10: Hat 3H 129
Brickfield La. EN5: Ark 8F 152
Brickfields, The SG12: Ware 5F 94
Brickfields Cotts. WD6: Bore 5N 151
Brickfields Ind. Est. HP2: Hem H 7D 106
Brickhill Farm Pk. Homes LU1: Pep 8E 66
BRICK HOUSE END 5D 42
Brick Kiln Barns LU1: Cad 2N 65
Brick Kiln Cl. WD19: Watf 8N 149
Brick Kiln La. CB11: Rick, Rick G 1L 43
LU2: C'hoe, Tea G 5A 48
SG4: C'ton, Hit 5L 33
Brick Kiln Rd. SG1: Stev 3J 51
Brick Knoll Pk. AL1: St Alb 3K 127
Brick La. EN1: Enf 4F 156
EN3: Enf H 4F 156
HA7: Stanm 7L 163
Brickly Rd. LU4: Lut 4L 45
Brickmakers La. HP3: Hem H 3D 124
Brick Row SG8: Chris 1N 17
Brickwall Cl. AL6: Ayot P 7G 90
Brickyard La. SG8: Reed 7J 15
Bride Hall La. AL6: Ayot L 4A 90
BRIDEN'S CAMP 3K 105
Bridewell Cl. SG9: Bunt 2J 39
Bridewell M. *SG14: H'ford 9B 94*
(off Railway St.)
Bridge, The WD4: Kin L 2D 136
Bridge Cl. EN1: Enf 4F 156
Bridge Ct. AL5: Harp 4A 88
AL7: Welw G 9M 91
HP4: Berk 1A 122
WD7: Rad 8J 139
Bridgedown Golf Course 3K 153
Bridge End SG9: Bunt 2J 39
Bridgefields AL7: Welw G 8M 91
BRIDGEFOOT 3N 9
Bridgefoot SG9: Bunt 3J 39
SG12: Ware 6H 95
Bridgefoot Ho. WD7: Rad 4G 139
Bridgefoot La. EN6: Pot B 6J 141
Bridgeford Ho. *CM23: Bis S 2H 79*
(off South St.)
WD18: Watf 7B 166 (5K 149)
Bridge Ga. N21 9A 156
Bridge Ga. Cen.
AL7: Welw G 9M 91
Bridgeman Dr. LU5: Hou R 4G 45
Bridgend Rd. EN1: Enf 8G 144
Bridgenhall Rd. EN1: Enf 3D 156
Bridge Pde. *N21 9A 156*
(off Ridge Av.)
Bridge Pk. AL7: Welw G 8L 91
Bridge Pl. WD17: Watf 7M 149
Bridgepoint Ct. *AL2: Bri W 3N 137*
(off Old Watford Rd.)
Bridger Cl. WD25: Watf 6M 137
Bridge Rd. AL7: Welw G 8J 91
AL8: Welw G 8J 91
SG1: Stev 2H 51
SG3: Dat 6N 71
SG6: L Gar 5F 22
WD4: Hun C 6E 136
Bridge Rd. E. AL7: Welw G 9L 91
Bridge Rd. W. SG1: Stev 3H 51
Bridges Ct. SG14: H'ford 9A 94
Bridges Rd. HA7: Stanm 5G 162
Bridge St. CM23: Bis S 1H 79
HP1: Hem H 3N 123
HP4: Berk 1A 122
LU1: Lut 1G 66
SG5: Hit 4M 33
Bridgewater Ct. HP4: Lit G 7N 83
Bridgewater Gdns. HA8: Edg 9N 163
Bridgewater Hill HP4: Berk 7K 103
Bridgewater Monument 8H 83
Bridgewater Rd. HP4: Berk 9L 103
Bridgewater Way WD23: Bush 8C 150
Bridgeways EN11: Hod 9M 115
Bridle Cl. AL3: St Alb 9F 108
EN3: Enf L 1K 157
EN11: Hod 4L 115
Bridle La. WD3: Loud 5M 147
Bridle Manor HP22: Halt 5B 100
Bridle M. EN5: Barn 6M 153
Bridle Path WD17: Watf 4K 149
Bridle Way EN11: Hod 5L 115
HP4: Berk 8L 103
HP23: Hast 9K 101
SG12: Gt A 9L 95
Bridleway Nth. EN11: Hod 4L 115
Bridleway Sth. EN11: Hod 5L 115

Bridlington Rd.—Bulls Cross

Bridlington Rd. N9 9F 156
WD19: Watf 3M 161
Brierley Cl. LU2: Lut 7M 47
LU6: Duns 3F 64
Briers, The EN6: Pot B 5A 142
Briery Ct. WD3: Chor 6K 147
Briery Fld. WD3: Chor 6K 147
Briery Way HP2: Hem H 9C 106
Brigadier Av. EN2: Enf 2A 156
Brigadier Hill EN2: Enf 2A 156
Brigadier Ho. *NW9* 9F 164
(off Heritage Av.)
Briggens Park Golf Course 3F 116
Brighton Rd. WD24: Watf 2J 149
Brighton Way SG1: Stev 1G 50
Brightside, The EN3: Enf H 3H 157
Brightview Cl. AL2: Bri W 2N 137
Brightwell Av. LU6: Tot 1N 63
Brightwell Rd. WD18: Watf 7J 149
Brightwen Gro. HA7: Stanm 2H 163
Brill Cl. LU2: Lut 7M 47
Brimfield Cl. LU2: Lut 7M 47
BRIMSDOWN 4K 157
Brimsdown Av. EN3: Enf H 4J 157
Brimsdown Ind. Est. EN3: Brim 3K 157
(Lockfield Av.)
EN3: Brim 4K 157
(Stockingswater La.)
Brimsdown Station (Rail) 5J 157
Brimstone Dr. SG1: Stev 9B 36
Brimstone Wlk. HP4: Berk 8K 103
Brindley Ct. HA7: Stanm 7L 163
Brindley Way HP3: Hem H 7B 124
Brinkburn Cl. HA8: Edg 9B 164
Brinkburn Gdns. HA8: Edg 9A 164
Brinklow Ct. AL3: St Alb 5C 126
Brinley Cl. EN8: C'hunt 4H 145
Brinsley Rd. HA3: Har W 9E 162
Brinsmead AL2: Frog 9F 126
Briscoe Cl. EN11: Hod 6K 115
Briscoe Rd. EN11: Hod 6K 115
Bristol Ho. *WD6: Bore* 4A 152
(off Eldon Av.)
Bristol Rd. LU3: Lut 5C 46
Briston M. NW7 7G 164
Britain St. LU5: Duns 9F 44
Britannia SG11: Puck 7B 56
Britannia Av. LU3: Lut 4D 46
Britannia Bus. Pk. EN8: Wal C 8K 145
Britannia Ct. *EN8: Wal C* 7K 145
(off Eleanor Cross Rd.)
Britannia Est. LU3: Lut 7D 46
Britannia Pl. CM23: Bis S 3G 78
Britannia Rd. EN8: Wal C 7K 145
British Schools Mus. 4N 33
Brittains Ri. SG16: L Ston 1F 20
Brittain Way SG2: Stev 5A 52
Brittany Ct. LU6: Duns 9F 44
Brittany Ho. EN2: Enf 2A 156
Britten Cl. WD6: Elst 8L 151
Britton Av. AL3: St Alb 2E 126
Britwell Dr. HP4: Berk 8B 104
Brive Rd. LU5: Duns 1H 65
Brixham Cl. SG1: Stev 2H 51
Brixton La. CB11: Rick G 6J 43
CM23: Man, Ugl 6J 43
Brixton Rd. WD24: Watf 3K 149
Broad Acre AL2: Bri W 3N 137
Broad Acres AL10: Hat 6F 110
Broadacres LU2: Lut 3F 46
Broad Baulk SG9: Bunt 2H 39
BROAD COLNEY 2L 139
Broad Colney Lakes Nature Reserve 1L 139
Broad Ct. AL7: Welw G 9L 91
Broadcroft HP2: Hem H 9N 105
SG6: L Gar 9F 22
Broadcroft Av. HA7: Stanm 9L 163
Broadfield CM20: Harl 5A 118
CM23: Bis S 7H 59
Broadfield Cl. SG10: M Had 7J 77
Broadfield Ct. *HA2: Harr* 8C 162
(off Broadfields)
WD23: B Hea 2F 162
Broadfield Pde. *HA8: Edg* 3B 164
(off Glengall Rd.)
Broadfield Pl. AL8: Welw G 1H 111
Broadfield Rd. HP2: Hem H 2B 124
SG3: Dat 7A 72
Broadfields AL5: Harp 5A 88
CM21: H Wyc 6D 98
EN7: Gof O 2N 143
HA2: Harr 9C 162
Broadfields Av. HA8: Edg 4B 164
N21 8M 155
Broadfields Hgts. HA8: Edg 4B 164
Broadfields La. WD19: Watf 1K 161
Broadfield Sq. EN1: Enf 4F 156
Broadfield Way SG10: M Had 7J 77
WD25: A'ham 9C 138
Broadgates Av. EN4: Had W 3A 154
BROAD GREEN 1M 17
Broad Grn. SG13: Bay 5L 113
Broadgreen Rd. EN7: C'hunt 8B 132
BROADGREEN WOOD 6L 113
Broad Grn. Wood SG13: Bay 6L 113
Broad Hall *AL10: Hat* 2F 128
(off Bishops Ri.)
Broadhall Way SG1: Stev 7K 51
SG2: Stev 8B 52
Broadhead Strand NW9 8F 164
Broadhurst Av. HA8: Edg 4B 164
Broadlake Cl. AL2: Lon C 9L 127
Broadlands Av. EN3: Enf H 5F 156
Broadlands Cl. EN3: Enf H 5G 156
EN8: Wal C 7G 145
Broadlawns Ct. HA3: Har W 8G 163
Broadleaf Av. CM23: Bis S 4F 78
Broadleaf Gro. AL8: Welw G 6H 91
Broadley Gdns. WD7: Shen 5M 139
Broadley Rd. CM19: Harl 9J 117
Broad Mead LU3: Lut 6C 46
Broadmead SG4: Hit 5A 34
Broadmead Cl. HA5: Hat E 7N 161
Broadmeadow Ride SG4: St Ipo 6A 34
Broadmeads SG12: Ware 6H 95
Broadoak Av. EN3: Enf W 8H 145
Broad Oak Ct. *LU2: Lut* 6M 47
(off Handcross Rd.)
BROADOAK END 7L 93
Broad Oak La. SG14: H'ford 7L 93
Broad Oaks Cl. AL5: Harp 9B 88
Broad Oak Way SG2: Stev 7M 51
Broad Rd. WD24: Watf 9J 137
Broadstone Rd. AL5: Harp 9D 88
Broad St. HP2: Hem H 1N 123
Broadview SG1: Stev 3L 51
Broadview Rd. HP5: C'ham 9F 120
Broad Wlk. CM20: Harl 5N 117
LU5: Duns 8E 44
N21 9M 155
Broadwalk, The HA6: North 9E 160
Broadwalk Shop. Cen. HA8: Edg 6B 164
BROADWATER 9N 51
Broadwater EN6: Pot B 3A 142
HP4: Berk 9N 103
SG2: Stev 8A 52
Broadwater Av. SG6: L Gar 6E 22
Broadwater Cres. AL7: Welw G 1K 111
SG2: Stev 7M 51
Broadwater Dale SG6: L Gar 6E 22
Broadwater La. SG2: A'ton, Stev 8B 52
Broadwater Rd. AL7: Welw G 1L 111
AL8: Welw G 1K 111
Broadway SG6: L Gar 7E 22
Broadway, The AL1: St Alb 2D 166 (2E 126)
AL4: Wheat 2J 89
AL9: Hat 9J 111
EN6: Pot B 5M 141
(not continuous)
HA3: Weal 9F 162
HA6: North 9J 161
HA7: Stanm 5K 163
NW7 5E 164
SL9: Chal P 8A 158
(off Market Pl.)
WD17: Watf 7E 166 (5L 149)
Broadway Av. CM17: Harl 2D 118
Broadway Cinema, The 6F 22
Brocas Way LU7: Hort 5M 61
Brockenhurst Gdns. NW7 5E 164
Brocket Ct. EN11: Hod 8L 115
LU4: Lut 3N 45
Brocket Hall Golf Course 8E 90
Brocket Rd. AL8: Lem, Welw G 2F 110
EN11: Hod 8L 115
Brockett Cl. AL8: Welw G 9H 91
Brocket Vw. AL4: Wheat 6L 89
Brockhurst Cl. HA7: Stanm 6G 162
Brocklesbury Cl. WD24: Watf 6E 166 (5M 149)
Brockles Mead CM19: Harl 9M 117
Brockley Av. HA7: Stanm 3M 163
Brockley Cl. HA7: Stanm 4M 163
Brockley Hill HA7: Stanm 1K 163
Brockleyside HA7: Stanm 4M 163
Brockswood La. AL8: Welw G 8G 91
Brockton Cl. LU1: Lut 1C 66
Brockwell Shott SG2: Walk 9G 37
Brodewater Rd. WD6: Bore 4B 152
Brodie Rd. EN2: Enf 2A 156
Bromborough Grn. WD19: Watf 5L 161
Bromefield HA7: Stanm 8K 163
Bromet Cl. WD17: Watf 2H 149
(not continuous)
Bromleigh Cl. EN8: C'hunt 1J 145
BROMLEY 1F 76
Bromley HP23: Lon M 3F 80
Bromley Cl. CM20: Harl 2D 118
Bromley Gdns. LU5: Hou R 4G 44
(not continuous)
Bromley La. SG10: M Had 9E 56
SG11: Stand 9E 56
Brompton Cl. LU3: Lut 1B 46
Brompton Gdns. LU3: Lut 1B 46
Bronte Av. SG5: Stot 1C 22
Bronte Cres. HP2: Hem H 5D 106
Bronte Paths SG2: Stev 3B 52
Brook Av. HA8: Edg 6B 164
Brook Bank EN1: Enf 1F 156
Brookbridge La. SG3: Dat 6C 72
Brook Cl. HP22: Ast C 1C 100
LU6: Duns 8D 44
NW7 7L 165
WD6: Bore 4B 152
Brook Cotts. CM24: Stans 4N 59
Brook Ct. HA8: Edg 5B 164
LU3: Lut 8F 46
WD7: Rad 6H 139
Brookdene Av. WD19: Watf 9K 149
Brookdene Dr. HA6: North 7H 161
Brook Dr. SG2: Stev 9A 52
WD7: Rad 6G 139
Brooke Cl. WD23: Bush 9D 150
Brooke End AL3: Red 2J 107
Brooke Gdns. CM23: Bis S 1L 79
Brooke Ho. WD23: Bush 9D 150
BROOK END
LU7 3C 82
SG5 7E 10
SG9 3A 38
Brook End CM21: Saw 5F 98
SG8: S Mor 2D 6
SG12: W'side 3B 96
Brookend Dr. MK45: Bar C 8D 18
Brooke Rd. SG8: Roys 5D 8
Brooker Rd. EN9: Wal A 7N 145
Brooke Way WD23: Bush 9D 150
Brook Farm Cl. CM23: Bis S 4E 78
Brookfield SG2: A'ton 7D 52
Brookfield Av. LU5: Hou R 4F 44
NW7 6H 165
Brookfield Cen. EN8: C'hunt 9H 133
Brookfield Cl. HP23: Tring 2N 101
NW7 6H 165
Brookfield Ct. EN8: C'hunt 9H 133
Brookfield Cres. NW7 6H 165
Brookfield Gdns. EN8: C'hunt 9H 133
Brookfield Ho. *HP2: Hem H* 3N 123
(off Selden Hill)
Brookfield La. SG2: A'ton, Ast E 5E 52
Brookfield La. E. EN8: C'hunt 9H 133
Brookfield La. W. EN8: C'hunt 1F 144
(not continuous)
Brookfield Pk. LU5: Hou R 4F 44
Brookfield Retail Pk. EN8: C'hunt 8H 133
Brookfields CM21: Saw 5F 98
EN3: Pon E 6H 157
Brookfield Wlk. LU5: Hou R 5G 44
Brookhill SG2: Stev 9M 51
Brookhill Cl. EN4: E Bar 7D 154
Brookhill Rd. EN4: E Bar 7D 154
Brookhouse Pl. CM23: Bis S 9H 59
Brooklands Cl. LU4: Lut 3M 45
Brooklands Ct. AL1: St Alb 2E 166 (2F 126)
N21 7B 156
Brooklands Gdns. EN6: Pot B 5L 141
Brook La. CM21: Saw 5F 98
HP4: Berk 9M 103
SG10: M Had, All G 8N 77
(not continuous)
Brooklane Fld. CM18: Harl 9D 118
Brooklea Cl. NW9 8E 164
Brookmans Av. AL9: B Pk 8M 129
BROOKMANS PARK 8L 129
Brookmans Park Golf Course 7N 129
Brookmans Park Station (Rail) 9L 129
Brookmill Cl. WD19: Watf 9K 149
Brook Pk. Cl. N21 7N 155
Brook Pl. EN5: Barn 7N 153
Brook Rd. CM21: Saw 6F 98
CM24: Stans 3N 59
EN8: Wal C 7K 145
SG8: Bass 2K 7
WD6: Bore 3A 152
Brooks Ct. SG14: H'ford 8L 93
Brooksfield AL7: Welw G 8A 92
Brookshill HA3: Har W 5E 162
Brookshill Av. HA3: Har W 5E 162
Brookshill Dr. HA3: Har W 5E 162
Brookshill Ga. HA3: Har W 5E 162
Brookside AL10: Hat 9D 110
CM19: Harl 9J 117
EN4: E Bar 8D 154
EN6: S Mim 5G 140
EN11: Hod 8L 115
HP22: Halt 5B 100
N21 8L 155
SG5: Shil 2N 19
SG6: L Gar 6F 22
SG13: H'ford 9C 94
WD24: Watf 1M 149
Brookside Caravans WD19: Watf 9K 149
Brookside Cl. EN5: Barn 8L 153
Brookside Cotts. WD4: Hun C 7E 136
Brookside Cres. EN6: Cuff 9K 131
Brookside Gdns. EN1: Enf 1G 156
Brookside Rd. WD19: Watf 9K 149
Brookside Sth. EN4: E Bar 9F 154
Brookside Wlk. N12 6N 165
Brook St. HP22: Ast C 1C 100
HP23: Tring 2N 101
LU3: Lut 9F 46
LU6: Edle 4K 63
SG5: Stot 6E 10
Brookvale SG16: U Sto 1F 20
Brook Vw. CM24: Stans 4N 59
SG4: Hit 4C 34
Brookview Ct. EN1: Enf 7C 156
Brook Wlk. HA8: Edg 6D 164
Broom Cl. AL10: Hat 3F 128
EN7: C'hunt 9E 132
Broom Cnr. *AL5: Harp* 7D 88
(off Barnfield Rd.)
Broomer Pl. EN8: C'hunt 2G 144
Broomfield AL2: Par S 9D 126
CM20: Harl 3D 118
Broomfield Av. EN10: Turn 8J 133
Broomfield Cl. AL6: Wel 3J 91
Broomfield Ct. AL10: Hat 8G 111
Broomfield Ho. *HA7: Stanm* 3H 163
(off Stanmore Hill)
Broomfield Ri. WD5: Abb L 5F 136
Broomfield Rd. AL6: Wel 3J 91
Broom Gro. SG3: Kneb 3M 71
WD17: Watf 2J 149
Broomgrove Gdns. HA8: Edg 8A 164
Broom Hill AL6: Wel 9N 71
HP1: Hem H 3H 123
Broomhills AL7: Welw G 8N 91
Broomleys AL4: St Alb 8L 109
Brooms Cl. AL8: Welw G 6K 91
Brooms Rd. LU2: Lut 9J 47
Broomstick Ind. Est. *LU6: Edle* 4K 63
(off High St.)
Broom Wlk. SG1: Stev 4L 51
Broughinge Rd. WD6: Bore 4B 152
Broughton Av. LU3: Lut 4E 46
N3 9L 165
Broughton Hill SG6: L Gar 5G 23
Broughton Way WD3: R'orth 9K 147
Brow, The HP8: Chal G 3A 158
WD25: Watf 6K 137
Browneymead La. SG9: Gt Hor 1E 40
Brownfields AL7: Welw G 8M 91
Brownfields Ct. AL7: Welw G 8N 91
Brownfield Way AL4: Wheat 1J 89
Browning Cl. SG8: Roys 4E 8
Browning Dr. SG4: Hit 2B 34
Browning Rd. AL5: Harp 5D 88
EN2: Enf 1B 156
LU4: Lut 7K 45
Brownings, The AL2: Lon C 9J 127
Browningss La. SG4: Bre G 8E 48
Brownlow Av. LU6: Edle 5K 63
Brownlow Cl. EN4: E Bar 7C 154
Brownlow Farm Barns HP1: Hem H 9G 105
Brownlow Ga. HP4: Ring 6M 83
Brownlow La. LU7: Ched 9M 61
Brownlow Rd. HP4: Berk 9N 103
WD6: Bore 6A 152
Brown's Cl. LU4: Lut 6N 45
Brownsea Wlk. NW7 6K 165
Browns Hedge LU7: Pits 4A 82
Brown's La. HP23: Hast 7L 101
Browns Spring HP4: Pot E 7F 104
BROXBOURNE 3K 133
Broxbournebury M. EN10: Brox 2G 132
Broxbourne Bus. Cen. EN8: C'hunt 8H 133
Broxbourne Par 3 Pay & Play Golf Course 4J 133
Broxbourne Station (Rail) 2L 133
Broxbourne Wood National Nature Reserve 2B 132
Broxdell SG1: Stev 3L 51
Broxley Mead LU4: Lut 4M 45
Bruce Gro. WD24: Watf 2L 149
Bruce Rd. EN5: Barn 5L 153
HA3: Weal 9F 162
Bruce Way EN8: Wal C 6H 145
Brummell Pl. CM17: Harl 3E 118
Brunel Ct. AL1: St Alb 1F 166
HA8: Edg 4N 163
HP3: Hem H 4N 123
LU4: Lut 6H 45
Brunel Rd. LU4: Lut 6H 45
SG2: Stev 2N 51
Brunel Wlk. SG5: Stot 1B 22
Brunswick Ct. EN4: E Bar 7C 154
EN11: Hod 9L 115
(off Rawdon Dr.)
Brunswick Ho. N3 8M 165
Brunswick Rd. EN3: Enf L 2L 157
Brunswick St. LU2: Lut 9G 47
Brushrise WD24: Watf 9K 137
Brushwood Dr. WD3: Chor 6F 146
Brussels Way LU3: Lut 9A 30
Bryan Rd. CM23: Bis S 9H 59
Bryanston Ct. HP2: Hem H 3N 123
Bryanstone Rd. EN8: Wal C 7K 145
Bryant Cl. EN5: Barn 7M 153
Bryant Ct. AL5: Harp 4B 88
Bryants Acre HP22: Wen 9A 100
Bryants Cl. SG5: Shil 1A 20
Bryce Cl. SG12: Ware 4H 95
Bryn-y-mawr Rd. EN1: Enf 6D 156
Bryony Rd. SG5: Stot 7F 10
Bryony Way LU6: Duns 8B 44
Buchanan Cl. N21 7L 155
Buchanan Ct. LU2: Lut 9K 47
WD6: Bore 4C 152
Buchanan Dr. LU2: Lut 9K 47
Bucketsland La. WD6: Bore 2D 152
Buckfast Ho. N14 7H 155
Buckingham Av. N20 9B 154
Buckingham Cl. EN1: Enf 4C 156
Buckingham Ct. AL1: St Alb 1G 166
NW4 9G 165
Buckingham Dr. LU2: Lut 7M 47
Buckingham Gdns. HA8: Edg 7M 163
Buckingham Gro. WD6: Bore 6D 152
Buckingham Lodge EN11: Hod 8L 115
Buckingham Pde. HA7: Stanm 5K 163
SL9: Chal P 8B 158
(off Market Pl.)
Buckingham Rd. HA8: Edg 7N 163
HP23: Tring 3K 101
WD6: Bore 6D 152
WD24: Watf 1L 149
BUCKLAND
HP22 9E 80
SG9 3H 27
Buckland WD19: Watf 3M 161
Buckland Cl. NW7 4G 165
Buckland Ri. HA5: Pin 8L 161
Buckland Rd. HP22: Buck 1F 100
SG8: Bark 2L 27
Bucklands, The WD3: R'orth 9K 147
Bucklands Cft. HP23: Wils 7H 81
BUCKLAND WHARF 2F 100
Buckland Wharf Ct. HP22: Ast C 2F 100
Buckle Cl. LU3: Lut 2B 46
Bucklersbury SG5: Hit 4M 33
Bucklers Cl. EN10: Worm 4K 133
Bucknalls Cl. WD25: Watf 5N 137
Bucknalls Dr. AL2: Bri W 4A 138
Bucknalls La. WD25: Watf 5M 137
Buck's All. SG13: Bay, Lit B 9H 113
Buck's Av. WD19: Watf 9N 149
BUCKS HILL 8N 135
Bucks Hill WD4: Buc H 6M 135
Buckthorn Av. SG1: Stev 5L 51
Buckton Rd. WD6: Bore 2N 151
Buckwells Fld. SG14: H'ford 6A 94
Buckwood Av. LU5: Duns 8H 45
Buckwood La. LU6: Stud 8E 64
Buckwood Rd. AL3: Mark, Stud 9J 65
LU6: Stud 9J 65
Buddcroft AL7: Welw G 8A 92
Bude Cres. SG1: Stev 2G 51
BUILDING END 4L 17
Building End Rd. SG8: Chris 5L 17
BULBOURNE 7A 82
Bulbourne Cl. HP1: Hem H 3K 123
HP4: Berk 8K 103
Bulbourne Ct. HP23: Tring 8M 81
Bulbourne Ho. *HP1: Hem H* 4M 123
(off Cotterells)
Bulbourne Rd. HP23: Bulb, Tring 8N 81
Bullace Cl. HP1: Hem H 1K 123
Bullbeggars La. HP4: Berk, Pot E 2C 122
BULLEN'S GREEN 4F 128
Bullens Grn. La. AL4: Col H 4E 128
Bullescroft Rd. HA8: Edg 3A 164
Bullfields CM21: Saw 3G 99
Bullhead Rd. WD6: Bore 5C 152
Bull La. AL4: Wheat 9H 89
CB11: L Lwr, L Upp 1L 29
SG9: Buck 3G 27
SG9: Cot 2A 38
SL9: Chal P, Ger C 9A 158
Bullock's Hill SG4: St Wal 8A 50
Bullock's La. SG13: H'ford 2A 114
Bull Plain SG14: H'ford 9B 94
Bullpond La. LU6: Duns 9E 44
Bull Rd. AL5: Harp 7C 88
Bullrush Cl. AL10: Hat 1H 129
BULLS CROSS 8E 144

Bulls Cross—Cambridge Rd.

Bulls Cross EN2: Enf ... 8E 144
Bulls Cross Ride EN7: Wal C ... 6E 144
BULL'S GREEN ... 9D 72
Bullsland Gdns. WD3: Chor ... 8E 146
Bullsland La. WD3: Chor ... 8E 146
Bulls La. AL9: B Pk, Welh G ... 6K 129
BULLSMILL ... 3N 93
Bullsmill La. SG14: Stap, Water ... 3M 93
BULLSMOOR ... 8G 144
Bullsmoor Cl. EN8: Wal C ... 8G 144
Bullsmoor Gdns. EN8: Wal C ... 8F 144
Bullsmoor La. EN1: Enf ... 8E 144
EN3: Enf W ... 8G 144
EN7: Wal C ... 8E 144
Bullsmoor Ride EN8: Wal C ... 8G 144
Bullsmoor Way EN8: Wal C ... 8G 144
Bull Stag Grn. AL9: Hat ... 7J 111
Bull Theatre, The ... 6M 153
Bullwell Cres. EN8: C'hunt ... 2J 145
BULSTRODE ... 2H 135
Bulstrode Cl. WD4: Chippf ... 2H 135
Bulstrode La. HP3: Hem H ... 7K 123
WD4: Chippf, Kin L ... 2H 135
Bulwer Gdns. EN5: N Bar ... 6B 154
Bulwer Link SG1: Stev ... 6L 51
Bulwer Rd. EN5: N Bar ... 6A 154
Buncefield La. HP2: Hem H ... 8E 106
(not continuous)
Buncefield Terminal HP2: Hem H ... 9F 106
Bungalows, The AL5: Harp ... 4D 88
CM17: M Tye ... 3M 119
HP4: Berk ... 4H 103
HP5: C'dge ... 9A 120
Bunhill Cl. LU6: Duns ... 9C 44
Bunkers La. HP3: Hem H ... 7C 124
Bunnsfield AL7: Welw G ... 8B 92
Bunns La. NW7 ... 6E 164
(not continuous)
Bunstrux HP23: Tring ... 2M 101
Bunting Ct. NW9 ... 9E 164
BUNTINGFORD ... 3J 39
Buntingford Bus. Pk.
SG9: Bunt ... 2G 39
Buntingford Rd. SG11: Puck ... 5A 56
Bunting Rd. LU4: Lut ... 4K 45
Bunyan Cl. HP23: Tring ... 1N 101
SG5: Pirt ... 7E 20
Bunyan Ho. LU3: Lut ... 8F 46
Bunyan Rd. SG5: Hit ... 2M 33
Bunyans Cl. LU3: Lut ... 4C 46
Burbage Cl. EN8: C'hunt ... 4K 145
Burbery Cl. UB9: Hare ... 9N 159
Burchell Ct. WD23: Bush ... 9D 150
Bure Ct. EN5: N Bar ... 7A 154
Burfield Cl. AL10: Hat ... 7G 111
Burfield Ct. LU2: Lut ... 6M 47
Burfield Rd. WD3: Chor ... 7F 146
Burford Cl. LU3: Lut ... 9B 30
Burford Gdns. EN11: Hod ... 7M 115
Burford Ho. EN11: Hod ... 7M 115
Burford M. EN11: Hod ... 7L 115
Burford Pl. EN11: Hod ... 7L 115
Burford St. EN11: Hod ... 8L 115
Burford Wlk. LU5: Hou R ... 4H 45
Burford Way SG5: Hit ... 9K 21
Burgage Ct. *SG12: Ware* ... 6H 95
(off Burgage La.)
Burgage La. SG12: Ware ... 6H 95
BURGE END ... 6D 20
Burge End La. SG5: Pirt ... 6D 20
Burges Cl. LU6: Duns ... 3G 65
Burgess Cl. EN7: C'hunt ... 7A 132
Burgess Ct. *WD6: Bore* ... 2N 151
(off Aycliffe Rd.)
Burgess La. SG9: S'don ... 7C 26
Burghley Av. CM23: Bis S ... 9E 58
WD6: Bore ... 7C 152
Burghley Cl. SG2: Stev ... 9N 51
Burgoyne Hatch CM20: Harl ... 5C 118
Burgundy Cft. AL7: Welw G ... 2M 111
Burgundy Ho. *EN2: Enf* ... 2A 156
(off Bedale Rd.)
Burhill Gro. HA5: Pin ... 9N 161
Burke Rd. HP22: Wen ... 9B 100
Burleigh Gdns. N14 ... 9H 155
Burleigh Mead AL9: Hat ... 7J 111
Burleigh Rd. AL1: St Alb ... 2J 127
EN1: Enf ... 6C 156
EN8: C'hunt ... 5J 145
HP2: Hem H ... 3E 124
SG13: H'ford ... 8E 94
Burleigh Way EN2: Enf ... 5B 156
EN6: Cuff ... 3K 143
Burley SG6: L Gar ... 2F 22
Burley Hill CM17: Harl ... 7F 118
Burley Ho. WD5: Abb L ... 5H 137
Burley Rd. CM23: Bis S ... 4J 79
Burlington Cl. HA5: E'cote ... 9K 161
Burlington Ri. EN4: E Bar ... 9D 154
Burlington Rd. EN2: Enf ... 3B 156
BURLOES ... 7G 9
Burn Cl. WD25: A'ham ... 5E 150
Burncroft Av. EN3: Enf H ... 4G 157
Burnell Gdns. HA7: Stanm ... 9L 163
Burnell Ri. SG6: L Gar ... 6D 22
Burnells Way CM24: Stans ... 2N 59
Burnell Wlk. SG6: L Gar ... 6E 22
Burnet Cl. HP3: Hem H ... 3A 124
Burnett Sq. SG14: H'ford ... 8L 93
Burnham Cl. AL6: Wel ... 1B 92
EN1: Enf ... 2C 156
NW7 ... 7G 164
BURNHAM GREEN ... 1B 92
Burnham Grn. Rd. AL6: Wel ... 1B 92
SG3: Dat ... 1B 92
Burnham Rd. AL1: St Alb ... 2H 127
LU2: Lut ... 7K 47
Burnhams, The HP22: Ast C ... 1B 100
Burnley Cl. WD19: Watf ... 5L 161
Burnsall Pl. AL5: Harp ... 9D 88
Burns Cl. SG2: Stev ... 1B 52
SG4: Hit ... 2B 34
Burns Dr. HP2: Hem H ... 5D 106
BURN'S GREEN ... 7L 53
Burnside AL1: St Alb ... 4J 127
CM21: Saw ... 5F 98
EN11: Hod ... 8K 115
SG14: H'ford ... 1M 113
Burnside Cl. AL10: Hat ... 6H 111
EN5: N Bar ... 5N 153
Burnside Ter. CM17: Harl ... 3H 119
Burns Rd. SG8: Roys ... 5C 8
Burnt Cl. LU3: Lut ... 2B 46
Burntfarm Ride EN2: Crew H ... 7M 143
EN7: Wal C ... 6N 143
Burnthouse La. SG7: Clo ... 8E 24
Burnt Mill CM20: Harl ... 4M 117
(Burnt Mill Ind. Est.)
CM20: Harl ... 3N 117
(Edinburgh Way)
Burnt Mill Cl. CM20: Harl ... 3M 117
Burnt Mill Ind. Est. CM20: Harl ... 3M 117
Burnt Mill La. CM20: Harl ... 3M 117
BURNT OAK ... 8B 164
Burnt Oak B'way. HA8: Edg ... 7A 164
Burnt Oak Flds. HA8: Edg ... 8C 164
Burnt Oak Station (Underground) ... 8C 164
Burr Cl. AL2: Lon C ... 9M 127
MK45: Bar C ... 7E 18
Burrell Cl. HA8: Edg ... 2B 164
Burrow Cl. WD17: Watf ... 9H 137
Burrowfield AL7: Welw G ... 2K 111
Burrows Chase EN9: Wal A ... 8N 145
Burrs La. SG8: Bark ... 9N 15
SG8: Lit ... 3H 7
Burrs Pl. LU1: Lut ... 2G 67
Burr St. LU2: Lut ... 9G 47
LU6: Duns ... 9E 44
Bursland SG6: L Gar ... 5D 22
Bursland Rd. EN3: Pon E ... 6H 157
Burston Dr. AL2: Par S ... 1D 138
Burton Av. WD18: Watf ... 8A 166 (6J 149)
Burton Cl. AL4: Wheat ... 2K 89
SG5: Stot ... 1C 22
Burton Dr. EN3: Enf L ... 1L 157
Burton Grange EN7: C'hunt ... 9C 132
Burtonhole Cl. NW7 ... 4K 165
Burtonhole La. N12 ... 4L 165
NW7 ... 5J 165
Burton La. EN7: Gof O ... 2C 144
Burton's La. HP8: Chal G ... 4A 146
WD3: Chor ... 7C 146
Burtons Mill CM21: Saw ... 4H 99
(not continuous)
Burton's Way HP8: Chal G ... 4A 146
Burvale Ct. WD18: Watf ... 7B 166 (5K 149)
Burwell Rd. SG2: Stev ... 5A 52
Burwood Pl. EN4: Had W ... 3B 154
Bury, The HP1: Hem H ... 1M 123
SG4: Cod ... 6F 70
WD3: R'orth ... 1N 159
Bury Ct. HP1: Hem H ... 2M 123
Burycroft AL8: Welw G ... 6L 91
Burydale SG2: Stev ... 8A 52
Burydell La. AL2: Par S ... 9E 126
BURY END
SG5 ... 1N 19
SG8 ... 1D 28
Bury End SG5: Pirt ... 7E 20
Bury Farm Cl. LU7: Slapt ... 2A 62
Buryfield Maltings *SG12: Ware* ... 5G 95
(off Watton Rd.)
Buryfield Ter. SG12: Ware ... 6G 95
Buryfield Way SG12: Ware ... 6G 94
BURY GREEN
EN7 ... 4E 144
SG11 ... 1A 78
Bury Grn. AL4: Wheat ... 7K 89
HP1: Hem H ... 1M 123
Bury Grn. Rd. EN7: C'hunt ... 4E 144
EN7: Wal C ... 5E 144
Bury Hall Vs. N9 ... 9D 156
Bury Hill HP1: Hem H ... 1L 123
Bury Hill Cl. HP1: Hem H ... 1M 123
Buryholme EN10: Worm ... 5K 133
Bury Lake Young Mariners ... 2M 159
Bury La. LU3: Stre ... 5C 30
SG3: Dat ... 4C 72
SG4: Cod ... 7F 70
SG8: Chris ... 3N 17
SG8: Melb, Meld ... 1G 9 & 1L 9
(not continuous)
SG14: Bram ... 4G 92
WD3: R'orth ... 1N 159
Bury Mead SG15: Arl ... 5A 10
Burymead SG1: Stev ... 9J 35
Burymead La. SG9: Cot ... 3B 38
Bury Mdws. WD3: R'orth ... 1N 159
Bury Mead Rd. SG5: Hit ... 9N 21
Bury M. *WD3: R'orth* ... 1N 159
(off Bury La.)
BURY PARK ... 9E 46
Bury Pk. Ind. Pk. LU1: Lut ... 8E 46
Bury Pk. Rd. LU1: Lut ... 8E 46
Bury Ri. HP3: Hem H ... 7G 123
Bury Rd. AL10: Hat ... 8J 111
CM17: Harl ... 2E 118
HP1: Hem H ... 1M 123
SG5: Shil ... 2N 19
Bury St. N9 ... 9D 156
Bury St. W. N9 ... 9B 156
Burywick AL5: Harp ... 1C 108
Bushbarns EN7: C'hunt ... 2E 144
Bushby Av. EN10: Worm ... 4K 133
Bush Ct. N14 ... 9J 155
Bushell Grn. WD23: B Hea ... 2E 162
Bushells Wharf HP23: Tring ... 9M 81
BUSHEY ... 8B 150
Bushey Cl. AL7: Welw G ... 1A 112
LU6: Whip ... 7C 64
Bushey Cft. CM18: Harl ... 8A 118
Bushey Golf Course ... 8B 150
Bushey Grn. AL7: Welw G ... 1A 112
Bushey Grove Leisure Cen. ... 5A 150
Bushey Gro. Rd. WD23: Bush ... 6M 149
Bushey Hall Dr. WD23: Bush ... 6N 149
Bushey Hall Golf Course ... 6N 149
Bushey Hall Pk. WD23: Bush ... 5N 149
Bushey Hall Rd.
WD23: Bush ... 8G 166 (6M 149)
BUSHEY HEATH ... 1E 162
Bushey Ley AL7: Welw G ... 1A 112
Bushey Mill Cres. WD24: Watf ... 1L 149
Bushey Mill La. WD23: Bush ... 2M 149
WD24: Watf ... 1L 149
Bushey Museum & Art Gallery ... 8B 150
Bushey Pk. WD23: Bush ... 8B 150
Bushey Station (Rail & Overground) ... 8M 149
Bushey Vw. Wlk. WD24: Watf ... 4M 149
Bush Fair CM18: Harl ... 8B 118
Bush Fair Ct. N14 ... 8G 155
Bushfield Cl. HA8: Edg ... 2B 164
Bushfield Cres. HA8: Edg ... 2B 164
Bushfield Rd. HP3: Bov ... 7F 122
Bush Gro. HA7: Stanm ... 8L 163
Bush Hall La. AL9: Hat ... 6K 111
Bush Hill N21 ... 9A 156
Bush Hill Pde. EN1: Enf ... 9B 156
N9 ... 9B 156
BUSH HILL PARK ... 8D 156
Bush Hill Park Golf Course ... 7A 156
Bush Hill Park Station (Rail) ... 8D 156
Bush Hill Rd. N21 ... 8B 156
Bush Ho. *CM18: Harl* ... 8B 118
(off Bush Fair)
Bushmead Ct. LU2: Lut ... 3G 46
Bushmead Rd. LU2: Lut ... 4G 46
Bush Spring SG7: Bald ... 2N 23
Bushwood Cl. AL9: Welh G ... 5H 129
Business & Technology Cen.
SG1: Stev ... 4H 51
Business Centre, The LU2: Lut ... 2K 67
Business Centre East SG6: L Gar ... 5J 23
Business Centre West SG6: L Gar ... 5J 23
Business Innovation Centre, The
EN3: Enf L ... 9K 145
(off Innova Bus. Pk.)
Buslins La. HP5: C'ham ... 9C 120
Butchers Baulk SG8: Roys ... 6D 8
Butchers La. SG4: Hit ... 5N 33
SG4: Pres ... 3L 49
Bute Ct. *LU1: Lut* ... 9G 46
(off Bute St.)
Butely Rd. LU4: Lut ... 3L 45
Bute Sq. LU1: Lut ... 1G 66
Bute St. LU1: Lut ... 1G 66
(not continuous)
Bute St. Mall *LU1: Lut* ... 1G 66
(within The Mall Shop. Cen.)
Butler Cl. HA8: Edg ... 9B 164
Butler Hall *AL10: Hat* ... 2F 128
(off Bishops Ri.)
Butlers Ct. EN8: Wal C ... 5J 145
Butlers Dr. E4 ... 2N 157
Butlers Hall La. CM23: Thorl ... 5D 78
Butlers Yd. SG7: Bald ... 2L 23
Butlin Rd. LU1: Lut ... 1D 66
Butlin's Path LU1: Lut ... 9D 46
Buttercup Cl. AL10: Hat ... 5F 110
LU6: Duns ... 1D 64
Buttercup La. LU6: Duns ... 2D 64
Buttercup Rd. SG5: Stot ... 7F 10
Butterfield LU2: Lut ... 3K 47
Butterfield Ct. SG7: Bald ... 3L 23
Butterfield Grn. Rd. LU2: Lut ... 3J 47
Butterfield La. AL1: St Alb ... 6F 126
Butterfield Rd. AL4: Wheat ... 7K 89
Butterfly Ct. NW9 ... 8E 164
Butterfly Cres. HP3: Hem H ... 7C 124
Butterfly La. WD6: Elst ... 5H 151
Butterfly World
St Albans ... 8A 126
Buttermere Av. LU6: Duns ... 2F 64
Buttermere Cl. AL1: St Alb ... 3J 127
Buttermere Pl. WD25: Watf ... 6J 137
Butterscotch Row WD5: Abb L ... 5F 136
Buttersweet Ri. CM21: Saw ... 6G 98
Butterwick WD25: Watf ... 9N 137
Butterworth Path LU2: Lut ... 9G 46
Butt Fld. Vw. AL1: St Alb ... 6D 126
Butt La. CM23: Man ... 8F 42
Buttlehide WD3: Map C ... 5G 158
Buttondene Cres. EN10: Brox ... 4M 133
Buttons La. SG4: Whit ... 1M 69
Butts, The EN10: Turn ... 6J 133
Butts End HP1: Hem H ... 1K 123
BUTTS GREEN ... 3N 29
Butts Grn. SG4: W'ton ... 1B 36
Buttsmead HA6: North ... 7E 160
Buttway SG7: Ashw ... 8K 5
Buxton Cl. AL4: St Alb ... 8L 109
Buxton Path WD19: Watf ... 3L 161
Buxton Rd. LU1: Lut ... 1F 66
Buxtons La. SG8: G Mor ... 2A 6
Buzzard Rd. LU4: Lut ... 5K 45
Bycullah Av. EN2: Enf ... 5N 155
Bycullah Rd. EN2: Enf ... 4N 155
Byde St. SG14: H'ford ... 8A 94
Byers Cl. EN6: Pot B ... 7B 142
(not continuous)
Byewaters WD18: Watf ... 8E 148
Bye Way, The HA3: Weal ... 8F 162
Byeway, The WD3: R'orth ... 2A 160
Byfield AL8: Welw G ... 6L 91
Byfield Cl. LU4: Lut ... 8L 45
Byfleet Ind. Est. WD18: Watf ... 1E 160
Byford Ho. EN5: Barn ... 6K 153
BYGRAVE ... 7B 12
Bygrave *SG1: Stev* ... 8J 35
(off Lister Cl.)
Bygrave Rd. SG7: Bald ... 2M 23
Byland Cl. N21 ... 9L 155
Bylands Cl. CM23: Bis S ... 2F 78
Bylands Ho. AL3: Red ... 8J 87
Byng Dr. EN6: Pot B ... 4N 141
Bynghams CM19: Harl ... 8J 117
Byng Rd. EN5: Barn ... 4K 153
Byrd Ct. SG1: Stev ... 5K 51
Byrd Wlk. SG7: Bald ... 4M 23
Byre Rd. N14 ... 8G 154
Byron Av. WD6: Bore ... 7A 152
WD24: Watf ... 3M 149
Byron Cl. EN7: C'hunt ... 9D 132
SG2: Stev ... 2B 52
SG4: Hit ... 2B 34
Byron Ct. EN2: Enf ... 4N 155
EN8: C'hunt ... 1F 144
Byron Pl. HP2: Hem H ... 5D 106
Byron Rd. AL5: Harp ... 5B 88
HA3: Weal ... 9G 162
LU4: Lut ... 7L 45
NW7 ... 5G 164
SG8: Roys ... 5E 8
Byron Ter. N9 ... 8G 156
Byslips Rd. LU6: Stud ... 4G 84
By The Mount AL7: Welw G ... 1K 111
By the Wood WD19: Watf ... 2M 161
Byway, The EN6: Pot B ... 6N 141
Byways HP4: Berk ... 9B 104
By-Wood End SL9: Chal P ... 5D 158

C

Cabot Cl. SG2: Stev ... 2N 51
CADDINGTON ... 4A 66
Caddington Cl. EN4: E Bar ... 7D 154
Caddington Comn. AL3: Mark ... 8A 66
Caddington Golf Course ... 2N 65
Caddington Pk. *LU1: Lut* ... 8L 45
(off Skimpot La.)
Caddington Rd. LU1: Lut ... 6G 66
Caddis Cl. HA7: Stanm ... 7G 163
Cade Cl. SG6: L Gar ... 2J 23
Cade Pl. HP22: Halt ... 8D 100
Cades Cl. LU1: Lut ... 2C 66
Cades La. LU1: Lut ... 2C 66
Cadia Cl. LU1: Cad ... 4A 66
Cadmore Ct. EN8: C'hunt ... 1H 145
SG14: H'ford ... 7L 93
Cadmore La. EN8: C'hunt, Turn ... 1H 145
Cadogan Gdns. N3 ... 8N 165
N21 ... 7M 155
CADWELL ... 6N 21
Cadwell Ct. SG4: Hit ... 9A 22
Cadwell Grn. SG4: Hit ... 9A 22
Cadwell La. SG4: Hit ... 9N 21
Caelian Pl. AL3: St Alb ... 5C 126
Caernafon Ho. HA7: Stanm ... 5H 163
Caernarvon Cl. HP2: Hem H ... 2N 123
SG2: Stev ... 1A 72
Caernarvon Ct. HP2: Hem H ... 2N 123
Caesars Ct. AL3: St Alb ... 2C 166
Caesars Rd. AL4: Wheat ... 7L 89
Cage Pond Rd. WD7: Shen ... 6N 139
Cain Cl. AL1: St Alb ... 4G 127
Cain Ct. *EN8: C'hunt* ... 1H 145
(off Wycliffe Cl.)
Cairns Cl. AL4: St Alb ... 3L 127
Cairn Way HA7: Stanm ... 6G 163
Caishowe Rd. WD6: Bore ... 3B 152
Caister Cl. HP2: Hem H ... 3A 124
SG1: Stev ... 9G 35
Cain Ct. SG8: Roys ... 6D 8
Cakebread's La. CB11: Clav ... 7N 29
Calais Cl. EN7: C'hunt ... 8B 132
Calcutt Cl. LU5: Duns ... 7J 45
Caldecot Av. EN7: C'hunt ... 2D 144
CALDECOTE ... 3K 11
Caldecote Gdns. WD23: Bush ... 9F 150
CALDECOTE HILL ... 9G 151
Caldecote La. WD23: Bush ... 8G 150
Caldecote Rd. SG7: New ... 3K 11
Caldecot Way EN10: Worm, Brox ... 4K 133
Calder Av. AL9: B Pk ... 8N 129
Calder Cl. EN1: Enf ... 5C 156
Calder Gdns. HA8: Edg ... 9A 164
Calder Way SG1: Stev ... 7N 35
Calderwood Pl. EN4: Had W ... 3A 154
Caldew Ct. NW7 ... 7G 165
Caldwell Rd. WD19: Watf ... 4M 161
Caleb Cl. LU4: Lut ... 7B 46
Caledonian Ct. WD17: Watf ... 4K 149
Caledon Rd. AL2: Lon C ... 8K 127
CALIFORNIA ... 2C 64
California SG7: Bald ... 2M 23
California La. WD23: B Hea ... 1E 162
California Pl. *WD23: B Hea* ... 1E 162
(off High Rd.)
Callaghan Ct. HP4: Berk ... 1A 122
Callanders, The WD23: B Hea ... 1F 162
Callisto Ct. HP2: Hem H ... 8B 106
Callowland Pl. WD24: Watf ... 2K 149
Callowlands *WD24: Watf* ... 3K 149
(off Leavesden Rd.)
Calnwood Rd. LU4: Lut ... 7L 45
Calshot Way EN2: Enf ... 5N 155
Calthorpe Gdns. HA8: Edg ... 5M 163
(not continuous)
Calton Av. SG14: H'ford ... 8L 93
Calton Ct. SG14: H'ford ... 9L 93
Calton Ho. *SG14: H'ford* ... 9L 93
(off Windsor Dr.)
Calton Rd. EN5: N Bar ... 8B 154
Calverley Cl. CM23: Bis S ... 4G 78
Calverton Rd. LU3: Lut ... 3B 46
Calvert Rd. EN5: Barn ... 4K 153
Camberley Av. EN1: Enf ... 6C 156
Camberley Pl. AL5: Harp ... 9E 88
Camborne Dr. HP2: Hem H ... 7A 106
Cambourne Av. N9 ... 9H 157
Cambrian Way HP2: Hem H ... 8A 106
Cambridge Cl. EN8: C'hunt ... 2G 145
Cambridge Cotts. SG11: H Cro ... 6J 75
Cambridge Ct. SG11: Puck ... 7N 55
Cambridge Dr. EN6: Pot B ... 4K 141
Cambridge Gdns. EN1: Enf ... 4E 156
N21 ... 9B 156
Cambridge Pde. EN1: Enf ... 3E 156
Cambridge Rd. AL1: St Alb ... 3J 127
CB11: Que ... 4N 43
CM20: Harl ... 9E 98
CM21: Saw ... 4G 98
CM22: Ugl ... 4N 43
CM24: Stans ... 2N 59
SG4: Hit ... 2B 34

Cambridge Rd. SG8: Bark, Barl 7A **16**
SG8: Barl 1D **16**
SG8: Melb 1N **9**
SG11: Puck 7N **55**
WD18: Watf 9D **166** (6L **149**)
Cambridge St. LU1: Lut 3G **67**
Cambridge Ter. HP4: Berk 1A **122**
N9 9C **156**
Cam Cen. SG4: Hit 8A **22**
Camden Ho. HP1: Hem H 3N **123**
Camden Row HA5: Pin 9L **161**
Cameron Cl. SG2: Stev 2A **52**
Cameron Ct. SG12: Ware 5H **95**
Cameron Cres. HA8: Edg 8B **164**
Cameron Dr. EN8: Wal C 7H **145**
Camfield AL7: Welw G 4M **111**
Camfield Pl. AL9: Ess 3C **130**
Camford Way LU3: Lut 1K **45**
Camlet Way AL3: St Alb 1C **126**
EN4: Barn, Had W 4N **153**
CAMP, THE 4J **127**
Campania Gro. LU3: Lut 1C **46**
Campbell Cl. CM17: Harl 8D **118**
SG4: Hit 2B **34**
SG9: Bunt 3H **39**
Campbell Cft. HA8: Edg 5A **164**
Campbell La. LU7: Pits 4A **82**
Camp Dr. LU5: Hou R 4E **44**
Campers Av. SG6: L Gar 6E **22**
Campers Rd. SG6: L Gar 6D **22**
Campers Wlk. SG6: L Gar 6E **22**
Campfield Rd. AL1: St Alb 3H **127**
SG14: H'ford 9N **93**
Campfield Way SG6: L Gar 6D **22**
Campian Cl. LU6: Duns 8B **44**
Campine Cl. EN8: C'hunt 1H **145**
Campion Av. SG5: Stot 7F **10**
Campion Cl. WD25: Watf 6J **137**
Campion Ct. SG1: Stev 1J **51**
Campion Rd. AL10: Hat 6F **110**
HP1: Hem H 3H **123**
Campions, The
CM24: Stans 2N **59**
WD6: Bore 2N **151**
Campions Cl. WD6: Bore 1B **152**
Campions Ct. HP4: Berk 1M **121**
Campion Way HA8: Edg 4C **164**
SG8: Roys 8E **8**
Campkin Mead SG2: Stev 6C **52**
Camp Rd. AL1: St Alb 2G **127**
Campshill La. SG2: Stev 3N **51**
CAMPUS, THE 8D **106**
Campus, The AL8: Welw G 8K **91**
HP2: Hem H 9D **106**
Campus E. AL8: Welw G 8K **91**
Campus Five SG6: L Gar 4J **23**
Campus W. AL8: Welw G 8K **91**
Campus West Theatre 8K **91**
Camp Vw. Rd. AL1: St Alb 3J **127**
Camrose Av. HA8: Edg 9N **163**
Cam Sq. SG4: Hit 8A **22**
Canada La. EN10: Turn 8J **133**
(not continuous)
Canadas, The EN10: Turn 8J **133**
Canal Ct. HP4: Berk 1B **122**
Canal Side UB9: Hare 7K **159**
Canalside HP4: Berk 8K **103**
Canal Way UB9: Hare 6K **159**
Canberra Cl. AL3: St Alb 7G **109**
Canberra Gdns. LU3: Lut 3D **46**
Canberra Ho. AL1: St Alb 3D **166**
Candale Cl. LU6: Duns 2F **64**
Candlefield Cl. HP3: Hem H 5C **124**
Candlefield Rd. HP3: Hem H 5C **124**
Candlefield Wlk.
HP3: Hem H 5C **124**
Candlestick La. EN7: C'hunt 8F **132**
Caneswordе Rd. LU6: Duns 1D **64**
Canfield CM23: Bis S 9G **59**
Canford Cl. EN2: Enf 4M **155**
Cangels Cl. HP1: Hem H 4K **123**
Canham Cl. SG4: Kimp 7L **69**
Cannix Cl. SG2: Stev 7N **51**
Cannon Ho. *SG4: Hit* *4N* ***33***
(off Queen St.)
Cannon La. LU2: Lut 4K **47**
Cannon M. EN9: Wal A 6M **145**
Cannon Rd. WD18: Watf 7L **149**
Cannons Brook Golf Course 5K **117**
Cannons Cl. CM23: Bis S 8J **59**
Cannons Ct. SG11: Puck 6A **56**
Cannons Ga. EN8: C'hunt 8K **133**
Cannons Mead CM24: Stans 2M **59**
Cannons Mdw. AL6: Tew 6D **92**
Cannons Mill La. CM23: Bis S 7J **59**
(not continuous)
Cannon St. AL3: St Alb 1C **166** (1E **126**)
Canonbury Cotts. EN1: Enf 3C **156**
Canonbury Rd. EN1: Enf 3C **156**
Canon Mohan Cl. N14 8F **154**
Canons Brook CM19: Harl 6K **117**
Canons Cl. HA8: Edg 6N **163**
WD7: Rad 8J **139**
Canons Cnr. HA8: Edg 4M **163**
Canons Ct. HA8: Edg 6N **163**
Canons Dr. HA8: Edg 6M **163**
Canonsfield AL4: Wheat 6L **89**
AL6: Wel 8L **71**
Canonsfield Ct. AL6: Wel 8L **71**
Canonsfield Rd. AL6: Wel 8L **71**
Canons Ga. CM20: Harl 5K **117**
CANONS PARK 7L **163**
Canons Pk. HA7: Stanm 6L **163**
Canons Pk. Cl. HA8: Edg 7M **163**
Canons Park Station (Underground) 7M **163**
Canons Rd. SG12: Ware 5G **95**
Canons Rdbt. CM19: Harl 6J **117**
Canopus Way HA6: North 4J **161**
Canopy La. CM17: Harl 5E **118**
Canterbury Cl. HA6: North 6H **161**
LU3: Lut 5B **46**
Canterbury Ct. *AL1: St Alb* *9G* ***108***
(off Battlefield Rd.)
NW9 9E **164**
Canterbury Ho. *WD6: Bore* *4A* ***152***
(off Stratfield Rd.)
WD24: Watf *4L* ***149***
(off Anglian Cl.)
Canterbury Rd. WD6: Bore 4A **152**
WD17: Watf 4K **149**
Canterbury Way SG1: Stev 9L **35**
WD3: Crox G 5E **148**
Cantilupe Cl. LU6: Eat B 2H **63**
Capability Grn. LU1: Lut 4H **67**
Capel Ct. SG11: L Had 7A **58**
Capel Cres. HA7: Stanm 2H **163**
Capel Ho. WD19: Watf 4M **161**
Capella Rd. HA6: North 4H **161**
Capell Av. WD3: Chor 7F **146**
Capell Rd. WD3: Chor 7G **146**
Capell Way WD3: Chor 7G **146**
Capel Manor Gdns. 8E **144**
Capel Rd. EN1: Enf 9F **144**
EN4: E Bar 8D **154**
WD19: Watf 8N **149**
Capelvere Wlk. WD17: Watf 3G **149**
Cape Rd. AL1: St Alb 2J **127**
Capital Bus. Cen. WD24: Watf 9M **137**
Capital Bus. Pk. WD6: Bore 5C **152**
Capital Pl. CM19: Harl 7K **117**
Capitol Way NW9 9C **164**
Caponfield AL7: Welw G 2A **112**
Cappell La. SG12: Stan A 9N **95**
Capron Rd. LU4: Lut 5A **46**
LU5: Duns 7D **44**
Capstan Ride EN2: Enf 4M **155**
Captain's Cl. HP5: C'ham 9E **120**
Captains Wlk. HP4: Berk 2A **122**
Capuchin Cl. HA7: Stanm 6J **163**
Caractacus Cott. Vw. WD18: Watf 9J **149**
Caractacus Grn. WD18: Watf 8H **149**
Caravan La. WD3: R'orth 9A **148**
Carbis Cl. E4 9N **157**
Carbone Hill EN6: Cuff, New S, N'haw 9H **131**
SG13: New S 9H **131**
Carde Cl. SG14: H'ford 8L **93**
Cardiff Cl. SG2: Stev 1A **72**
Cardiff Gro. LU1: Lut 1F **66**
Cardiff Rd. EN3: Pon E 6F **156**
LU1: Lut 1F **66**
WD18: Watf 8K **149**
Cardiff Rd. Ind. Est. WD18: Watf 8K **149**
Cardiff Way WD5: Abb L 5J **137**
Cardigan Ct. *LU1: Lut* *1F* ***66***
(off Cardigan St.)
Cardigan Gdns. *LU1: Lut* *9F* ***46***
(off Cardigan St.)
Cardigan M. *LU1: Lut* *9F* ***46***
(off Cardigan St.)
Cardigan Pl. *LU1: Lut* *9F* ***46***
(off Cardigan St.)
Cardigan St. LU1: Lut 1F **66**
Cardinal Av. WD6: Bore 5B **152**
Cardinal Cl. EN7: C'hunt 8D **132**
HA8: Edg 7C **164**
Cardinal Ct. *LU2: Lut* *8F* ***46***
(off Earls Meade)
WD6: Bore 5A **152**
Cardinal Gro. AL3: St Alb 4C **126**
Cardinal Pl. AL2: Par S 7E **126**
Cardinals Ga. SG8: Roys 7C **8**
Cardinal Way HA3: Weal 9F **162**
Cardy Rd. HP1: Hem H 3L **123**
Carew Rd. HA6: North 6G **161**
Carew Way WD19: Watf 3A **162**
Carey Pl. WD17: Watf 8D **166** (6L **149**)
Careys Cft. HP4: Berk 7L **103**
Carfax Cl. LU4: Lut 6H **45**
Cargrey Ho. HA7: Stanm 5K **163**
Carisbrook Cl. EN1: Enf 3D **156**
Carisbrooke Av. WD24: Watf 3M **149**
Carisbrooke Cl. HA7: Stanm 9L **163**
SG2: Stev 9M **51**
Carisbrooke Ho. HA6: North 5H **161**
Carisbrooke Rd. AL5: Harp 5D **88**
LU4: Lut 8A **46**
Carisbrook Rd. AL2: Chis G 8C **126**
Carlbury Cl. AL1: St Alb 3J **127**
Carleton Ri. AL6: Wel 1J **91**
Carleton Rd. EN8: C'hunt 1H **145**
Carling Pl. SG5: Hit 9L **21**
Carlisle Av. AL1: St Alb 1F **166**
AL3: St Alb 9E **108**
Carlisle Cl. LU6: Duns 2E **64**
Carlisle Ho. WD6: Bore 4A **152**
Carlisle Rd. NW9 9C **164**
Carlow Ct. LU6: Duns 9D **44**
Carlton Av. N14 7J **155**
Carlton Bank AL5: Harp 6C **88**
Carlton Cl. HA8: Edg 5A **164**
LU3: Lut 7E **46**
WD6: Bore 6D **152**
Carlton Ct. AL5: Harp 6C **88**
N3 7N **165**
WD19: Watf 8L **149**
Carlton Cres. LU3: Lut 6E **46**
Carlton Pl. HA6: North 5D **160**
Carlton Ri. SG8: Melb 2N **9**
Carlton Rd. AL5: Harp 5B **88**
Carman Ct. HP23: Tring 3L **101**
Carmelite Cl. HA3: Har W 8D **162**
Carmelite Rd. HA3: Har W 8D **162**
LU4: Lut 6K **45**
Carmelite Wlk. HA3: Har W 8D **162**
Carmelite Way HA3: Har W 9D **162**
Carmen Ct. *WD6: Bore* *3N* ***151***
(off Aycliffe Rd.)
Carnaby Rd. EN10: Brox 2J **133**
Carnarvon Av. EN1: Enf 5D **156**
Carnarvon Rd. EN5: Barn 5L **153**
Carnegie Cl. EN3: Enf L 2M **157**
Carnegie Gdns. LU3: Lut 1C **46**
Carnegie Rd. AL3: St Alb 7E **108**
CARNELES GREEN 4F **132**
Caro La. HP3: Hem H 4D **124**
Carol Cl. LU3: Lut 5D **46**
Carole Ct. *LU1: Lut* *3G* ***67***
(off Chase St.)
Caroline Ct. HA7: Stanm 6H **163**
Caroline Pl. WD19: Watf 8N **149**
Caroline Sharpe Ho. AL4: St Alb 7K **109**
Carolyn Ct. LU3: Lut 5D **46**
Caroon Dr. WD3: Sar 9L **135**
Carpenders Av. WD19: Watf 3N **161**
Carpenders Cl. AL5: Harp 3M **87**
CARPENDERS PARK 3M **161**
Carpenders Park Station (Overground) 3M **161**
Carpenders, The CM23: Bis S 4E **78**
Carpenters Cl. EN5: N Bar 8A **154**
Carpenters Rd. EN1: Enf 9G **144**
Carpenters Wood Dr. WD3: Chor 6E **146**
Carpenters Yd. HP23: Tring 3N **101**
Carpenter Way EN6: Pot B 6B **142**
Carr Cl. HA7: Stanm 6H **163**
Carriages, The SG12: Ware 6H **95**
Carriden Ct. SG14: H'ford 7L **93**
Carrigans CM23: Bis S 9G **59**
Carrington Av. WD6: Bore 7B **152**
Carrington Cl. EN5: Ark 7G **153**
WD6: Bore 7C **152**
Carrington Ct. SG8: Roys 7D **8**
Carrington Cres. HP22: Wen 7A **100**
Carrington Pl. HP23: Tring 1N **101**
Carrington Sq. HA3: Har W 6D **162**
Carrs La. N21 7A **156**
Carsdale Cl. LU3: Lut 3C **46**
Carson Rd. EN4: C'ters 6E **154**
Cartel Bus. Est. CM20: Harl 2D **118**
Carteret Rd. LU2: Lut 8L **47**
Carterhatch La. EN1: Enf 2D **156**
Carterhatch Rd. EN3: Enf H 3G **157**
Carters Cl. SG2: Stev 5C **52**
SG15: Arl 5A **10**
Carters Dr. CM24: Stans 4N **59**
Cartersfield Rd. EN9: Wal A 7N **145**
CARTER'S GREEN 4N **119**
Carters Hill CM23: Man 9J **43**
Carters La. SG5: Hit 3H **33**
Carters Leys CM23: Bis S 9F **58**
Carters Mead CM17: Harl 8E **118**
Carters Wlk. SG15: Arl 5A **10**
Carters Way SG15: Arl 5A **10**
Carterweys LU5: Duns 7H **45**
Carthagena Est. EN10: Brox 2N **133**
Cartmel Dr. LU6: Duns 2E **64**
Cart Path WD25: Watf 6L **137**
Cart Track, The HP3: Hem H 7B **124**
Cartwright Rd. SG1: Stev 8B **36**
SG8: Roys 8D **8**
Carve Ley AL7: Welw G 1A **112**
Carvers Cft. SG3: Dat 6A **72**
Cary Wlk. WD7: Rad 7J **139**
Casel Ct. *HA7: Stanm* *2H* ***163***
(off Brightwen Gro.)
Cashio La. SG6: L Gar 2G **23**
Caslon Way SG6: L Gar 2F **22**
Cassander Pl. *HA5: Pin* *8N* ***161***
(off Holly Gro.)
Cassandra Ga. EN8: C'hunt 9K **133**
Cassio Apartments *WD17: Watf* *4K* ***149***
(off Malden Rd.)
Cassiobridge Rd. WD18: Watf 6G **149**
Cassiobridge Ter. WD18: Watf 7F **148**
Cassiobury Ct. WD17: Watf 4G **149**
Cassiobury Dr. WD17: Watf 6A **166** (2G **149**)
Cassiobury Park 7A **166** (5G **149**)
Cassiobury Pk. Av.
WD18: Watf 7A **166** (5G **149**)
Cassio Ho. *WD18: Watf* *6H* ***149***
(off Manhattan Av.)
Cassio Pl. WD18: Watf 6G **149**
Cassio Rd. WD18: Watf 7B **166** (5K **149**)
Cassio Wharf WD18: Watf 7F **148**
Cassius Dr. AL3: St Alb 4C **126**
Castano Ct. WD5: Abb L 4G **137**
Castellane Cl. HA7: Stanm 7G **163**
Castile Ct. EN8: Wal C 7L **145**
Castile Gdns. WD4: Kin L 2B **136**
Castings Ho. SG6: L Gar 4G **23**
Castle Bridges SG14: H'ford 9A **94**
Castle Cl. EN11: Hod 5N **115**
LU7: Pits 4B **82**
WD23: Bush 8C **150**
Castle Ct. SG5: Hit 1L **33**
Castle Cft. Rd. LU1: Lut 1C **66**
Castleford Cl. WD6: Bore 2N **151**
Castle Gate *SG14: H'ford* *1A* ***114***
(off Castle St.)
Castle Gate Way HP4: Berk 8N **103**
Castle Hill HP4: Berk 8N **103**
Castle Hill Av. HP4: Berk 9N **103**
Castle Hill Cl. HP4: Berk 9N **103**
Castle Hill Ct. HP4: Berk 8N **103**
Castle Hill Rd. LU6: Tot 1L **63**
Castleleigh Ct. EN2: Enf 7B **156**
Castle Mead HP1: Hem H 4L **123**
Castle Mead Gdns. SG14: H'ford 9A **94**
Castle M. HP4: Berk 1A **122**
Castle Pk. Rd. HP22: Wen 8A **100**
Castlereagh Ho. HA7: Stanm 6J **163**
Castle Ri. AL4: Wheat 5G **89**
Castle Rd. AL1: St Alb 2J **127**
EN3: Enf H 3J **157**
EN11: Hod 5N **115**
Castle Row *HP23: Tring* *3M* ***101***
(off Albert St.)
Castles Cl. SG5: Stot 4F **10**
Castle St. CM23: Bis S 2H **79**
HP4: Berk 1N **121**
HP22: W'rave 6A **60**
LU1: Lut 2G **66**
(not continuous)
SG14: H'ford 1A **114**
Castle Vw. CM23: Bis S 1J **79**
Castle Village HP4: Berk 8B **104**
Castle Wlk. CM24: Stans 3N **59**
Castlewood Rd. EN4: C'ters 5C **154**
Catalina Ct. AL1: St Alb 2F **166**
Catalonia Apartments *WD18: Watf* *6H* ***149***
(off Metropolitan Sta. App.)
Catchacre LU6: Duns 1D **64**
Catesby Grn. LU3: Lut 9C **30**
Catham Cl. AL1: St Alb 4J **127**
Catharine Ho. WD19: Watf 3K **161**
Cathedral Ct. AL3: St Alb 4C **126**
Cathedral Vw. AL3: St Alb 3C **166**
Catherall Rd. LU3: Lut 3D **46**
Catherine Cl. HP2: Hem H 6D **106**
Catherine Cotts. HP23: Wigg 6C **102**
Catherine Ct. N14 7H **155**
Catherine Rd. EN3: Enf W 1J **157**
Catherine St. AL3: St Alb 1C **166** (1E **126**)
Cat Hill EN4: E Bar 8D **154**
Cathrow M. EN11: Hod 5L **115**
Catisfield Rd. EN3: Enf W 1J **157**
Catkin Cl. HP1: Hem H 1L **123**
Catlin St. HP3: Hem H 5L **123**
Catsbrook Rd. LU3: Lut 3D **46**
Catsdell Bottom HP3: Hem H 5D **124**
Catsey La. WD23: Bush 9D **150**
Catsey Woods WD23: Bush 9D **150**
Catterick Way WD6: Bore 3N **151**
CATTLEGATE 6K **143**
Cattlegate Cotts. EN6: N'haw 4J **143**
Cattlegate Hill EN6: Cuff, N'haw 5J **143**
Cattlegate Rd. EN2: Crew H 7K **143**
EN6: Cuff, N'haw 4J **143**
Cattley Cl. EN5: Barn 6L **153**
Cattlins Cl. EN7: C'hunt 2C **144**
Cattsdell HP2: Hem H 9A **106**
Caudery Pl. HP22: Halt 8C **100**
Caulfield Gdns. HA5: Pin 9L **161**
Causeway, The CB11: L Upp 9M **17**
CM23: Bis S 1H **79**
EN6: Pot B 4B **142**
(not continuous)
SG8: Bass, Knee 1N **7**
SG8: Ther 4D **14**
SG9: B Pel 1L **41**
SG9: Bunt 2J **39**
SG9: Fur P 6K **41**
SG11: Alb 9H **41**
SG11: L Had 7N **57**
Causeway Bus. Centre, The *CM23: Bis S* *1H* ***79***
(off Adderley Rd.)
Causeway Cl. EN6: Pot B 4C **142**
Causeway Ho. WD5: Abb L 4G **137**
Causeyware Rd. N9 9G **156**
Cautherly La. SG12: Gt A 1K **115**
Cavalier *SG1: Stev* *9H* ***35***
(off Ingleside Dr.)
Cavalier Cl. LU3: Lut 3C **46**
Cavalier Ct. HP4: Berk 1N **121**
Cavalli Apartments *WD18: Watf* *6G* ***149***
(off Moderna M.)
Cavan Ct. AL10: Hat 1G **128**
Cavan Dr. AL3: St Alb 6E **108**
Cavan Pl. HA5: Hat E 8A **162**
Cavan Rd. AL3: Red 9J **87**
CAVE GATE 5A **28**
Cavell Ct. CM23: Bis S 2K **79**
Cavell Dr. CM23: Bis S 2K **79**
EN2: Enf 4M **155**
Cavell Rd. EN7: C'hunt 9D **132**
Cavell Wlk. SG2: Stev 4B **52**
(not continuous)
SG5: Stot 1D **22**
Cavendish Av. N3 9N **165**
Cavendish Cl. HP22: Wen 8A **100**
Cavendish Ct. WD3: Crox G 7F **148**
Cavendish Cres. WD6: Elst 6A **152**
Cavendish Dr. HA8: Edg 6N **163**
Cavendish Pl. *AL10: Hat* *1F* ***128***
(off Aldykes)
Cavendish Rd. AL1: St Alb 2G **127**
AL3: Mark 1N **85**
EN5: Barn 5J **153**
LU3: Lut 7D **46**
SG1: Stev 4G **51**
Cavendish Way AL10: Hat 9E **110**
Cawdon Row SG8: Melb 2M **9**
Cawkell Cl. CM24: Stans 2M **59**
Cawley Hatch CM19: Harl 6J **117**
Caxton Cen. AL3: St Alb 6G **108**
Caxton Ct. EN8: Wal C 8J **145**
LU3: Lut *5B* ***46***
(off Roman Rd.)
Caxton Gate SG1: Stev 5H **51**
Caxton Hill SG13: H'ford 9C **94**
Caxton Pl. SG1: Stev 5H **51**
Caxton Rd. EN11: Hod 4M **115**
Caxton Way SG1: Stev 5H **51**
WD18: Watf 9F **148**
Cecil Av. EN1: Enf 6D **156**
Cecil Cl. CM23: Bis S 1M **79**
Cecil Ct. CM18: Harl 9M **117**
EN2: Enf 6B **156**
EN5: Barn 5K **153**
EN8: C'hunt 5J **145**
Cecil Cres. AL10: Hat 7H **111**
Cecil Rd. AL1: St Alb 2G **127**
EN2: Enf 5A **156**
EN6: S Mim 5G **141**
EN8: C'hunt 5J **145**
EN11: Hod 6N **115**
HA3: Weal 9F **162**
N14 9H **155**
SG13: H'ford 3A **114**
Cecil St. WD24: Watf 2K **149**
Cedar Av. EN3: Enf H 4G **157**
EN4: E Bar 9D **154**
EN8: Wal C 6H **145**
SG5: Ick 7M **21**
Cedar Cl. CM21: Saw 6G **99**
EN6: Pot B 3N **141**
LU4: Lut 6H **45**
SG8: Melb 2M **9**
SG12: Ware 7H **95**
SG14: H'ford 9N **93**
Cedar Ct. AL4: St Alb 2L **127**
CM23: Bis S 8H **59**
LU1: Lut *9F* ***46***
(off Collingdon St.)
WD25: Watf *6M* ***137***
(off Lych Ga.)
Cedar Cres. SG8: Roys 7B **8**

Colindale Av.—Cotswold Way

Colindale Av. AL1: St Alb 4G 126
NW9 ....9E 164
Colindale Bus. Pk. NW9 ....9C 164
Colindale Station (Underground) 9E 164
Colin Rd. LU2: Lut 7H 47
Colin Rd. Footpath *LU2: Lut* *8H 47*
(off Colin Rd.)
College Av. HA3: Har W 8F 162
College Bus. Pk. HP22: Ast C 6A 80
College Cl. AL3: Flam 6D 86
AL9: N Mym 1K 141
CM23: Bis S 1F 78
HA3: Har W 7F 162
SG12: Ware 7H 95
College Ct. EN3: Pon E 7G 156
EN8: C'hunt 3G 145
College Gdns. E4 ....9M 157
EN2: Enf 3B 156
College Hill Rd. HA3: Har W 7F 162
College Lake Wildlife Cen. 6A 82
College La. AL10: Hat 2E 128
(not continuous)
College Park Wildlife Cen. 6A 82
College Pl. AL3: St Alb 2B 166 (2D 126)
College Rd. AL1: St Alb 3J 127
EN2: Enf 4B 156
EN8: C'hunt 3G 144
EN11: Hod 6K 115
HA3: Har W 8F 162
SG5: Hit 2N 33
SG13: Hail, Hert H 4G 115
WD5: Abb L 4H 137
College Rd. Nth. HP22: Ast C 6B 80
College Rd. Sth. HP22: Ast C 9C 80
College Sq. CM20: Harl 6N 117
College St. AL3: St Alb 2C 166 (2E 126)
College Ter. N3 ....9M 165
College Way AL8: Welw G 8K 91
HA6: North 6F 160
College Yd. AL3: St Alb 2C 166
WD24: Watf 2K 149
Collens Rd. AL5: Harp 1C 108
Collenswood Rd. SG2: Stev 5A 52
Collet Cl. EN8: C'hunt 1H 145
Collet Gdns. EN8: C'hunt 1H 145
Collett Rd. HP1: Hem H 2M 123
SG12: Ware 5H 95
Colleyland WD3: Chor 6G 146
Collier Dr. HA8: Edg 9A 164
COLLIERS END 2L 75
Collingdon Ct. LU1: Lut 9F 46
Collingdon St. LU1: Lut 9F 46
Collings Wells Cl. LU1: Cad 4A 66
(not continuous)
Collingtree LU2: Lut 5K 47
Collingwood Cl. LU4: Lut 6N 45
Collingwood Ct. EN5: N Bar 7A 154
SG8: Roys 6D 8
Collingwood Dr. AL2: Lon C 7L 127
Collins Av. HA7: Stanm 9M 163
Collins Ct. *WD23: Bush* *7C 150*
(off Lea Cl.)
Collins Cross CM23: Bis S 8K 59
Collins Grn. SG8: Ther 1C 26
Collins Mdw. CM19: Harl 6L 117
Collins Wood Res. Pk. LU1: Cad 4N 65
Collinwood Av. EN3: Enf H 5G 156
Collison Cl. SG4: Hit 9C 22
Collyer Rd. AL2: Lon C 9L 127
Colman Ct. HA7: Stanm 6J 163
Colman Pde. EN1: Enf 5C 156
Colmer Pl. HA3: Har W 7E 162
Colmore Rd. EN3: Pon E 6G 157
Colnbrook Cl. AL2: Lon C 9M 127
Colne Av. WD3: R'orth 2K 159
WD19: Watf 8K 149
Colne Bri. Retail Pk. WD17: Watf 8M 149
Colne Gdns. AL2: Lon C 9M 127
Colne Lodge WD3: R'orth 1K 159
Colne Mead WD3: R'orth 2K 159
Colne Rd. N21 ....9B 156
Colne Valley Retail Pk.
WD17: Watf 9G 166 (7M 149)
Colne Way HP2: Hem H 6B 106
WD24: Watf 9L 137
WD25: Watf 9L 137
Colne Way Ct. WD24: Watf 1M 149
Colne Way Ind. Pk. WD25: Watf 9M 137
Colney Fields Shop. Pk. AL2: Lon C 1N 139
COLNEY HEATH 5D 128
Colney Heath La. AL4: St Alb 2L 127
COLNEY STREET 3F 138
Colnhurst Rd. WD17: Watf 3J 149
Colonel's Wlk. EN2: Enf 5N 155
Colonial Bus. Pk. WD24: Watf 3L 149
Colonial Way WD24: Watf 3L 149
Colonnade, The AL3: St Alb 2C 166
EN8: C'hunt 1H 145
SG6: L Gar *5F 22*
(off Station Pl.)
Colonnades, The *AL10: Hat* *7J 111*
(off Beaconsfield Cl.)
Colonsay HP3: Hem H 4E 124
Colosseum, The 6A 166 (5J 149)
Colston Cres. EN7: Gof O 9N 131
Colt Hatch CM20: Harl 4L 117
Colthurst Gdns. EN11: Hod 6A 116
Colt M. EN3: Enf L 1L 157
Colts, The CM23: Bis S 4G 79
Colts Cnr. SG2: Stev 5A 52
Colts Cft. SG8: Gt Chi 2H 17
Coltsfield CM24: Stans 1N 59
Coltsfoot AL7: Welw G 2A 112
Coltsfoot, The HP1: Hem H 3H 123
Coltsfoot Dr. SG8: Roys 7E 8
Coltsfoot Grn. LU4: Lut 4K 45
Coltsfoot La. SG3: Dat 8B 72
Coltsfoot Rd. SG12: Ware 4J 95
Columbia Av. HA8: Edg 8B 164
Columbia Rd. EN10: Turn 8J 133
Columbia Wharf EN3: Pon E 8J 157
Columbus Cl. SG2: Stev 2N 51
Columbus Gdns. HA6: North 8J 161
Colville Rd. N9 ....9F 156
Colvin Gdns. EN8: Wal C 8H 145
Colwell Ct. LU2: Lut 7N 47
Colwell Ri. LU2: Lut 7N 47
Colwyn Cl. SG1: Stev 2H 51
Colyer Cl. AL6: Wel 4M 91
Combe Ho. WD18: Watf 8G 149
Combe Rd. WD18: Watf 8H 149
Combe St. HP1: Hem H 2M 123
Combewood WD25: Watf 5L 137
Comer Ho. EN5: N Bar 6B 154
Comet Cl. WD25: Watf 7H 137
Comet Rd. AL10: Hat 9F 110
Comet Way AL9: Hat 6G 110
AL10: Hat 1E 128
Comfrey Rd. SG5: Stot 8D 10
Commander Av. NW9 ....9G 164
Commerce Way SG6: L Gar 5F 22
Common, The AL3: Red 1K 107
AL5: Harp 3K 87
AL10: Hat 8G 110
HA7: Stanm 2F 162
HP4: Pot E 8C 104
WD4: Chippf 5K 135
WD4: Kin L 1C 136
WD7: Shen 4J 139
Common Fld. HP23: Wigg 5B 102
Commonfields CM20: Harl 5A 118
Common Gdns. HP4: Pot E 8E 104
Common Ga. Rd. WD3: Chor 7G 147
Common La. AL5: Harp 2E 88
SG5: Hex 8K 19
SG7: Ashw 7K 5
SG8: Chris, L Chis 7K 17
WD4: Kin L 1B 136
WD7: Rad 3F 150
WD25: Let H 3F 150
Commonmeadow La. WD25: A'ham 7C 138
Common Ri. SG4: Hit 1A 34
Common Rd. HA7: Stanm 4E 162
LU6: Kens 7E 64
LU6: Stud 4C 84
SG5: Stot 4F 10
WD3: Chor 6G 146
Commons, The AL7: Welw G 3N 111
Commonside Rd. CM18: Harl 9B 118
Commons La. HP2: Hem H 1A 124
SG4: Kimp 7J 69
Common Vw. SG6: L Gar 3G 23
Common Vw. Sq. SG6: L Gar 3G 23
COMMONWOOD 7L 135
Common Yd. *SG12: Ware* *6J 95*
(off Star St.)
Community Way WD3: Crox G 7C 148
Comp, The LU6: Eat B 2J 63
Compass Cl. HA8: Edg 4N 163
Compass Point HP4: Berk 8J 103
Comp Ga. LU6: Eat B 2J 63
Compton Av. LU4: Lut 5N 45
Compton Cl. HA8: Edg 7C 164
Compton Gdns. AL2: Chis G 8C 126
Compton Pl. SG1: Stev 8B 36
WD19: Watf 3N 161
Compton Rd. HP22: Wen 9B 100
N21 ....9M 155
Compton Ter. N21 ....9M 155
Comreddy Cl. EN2: Enf 3N 155
Comroston *EN11: Hod* *8L 115*
(off Brocket Rd.)
Comyne Rd. WD24: Watf 9H 137
Comyns, The WD23: B Hea 1D 162
Concorde Dr. HP2: Hem H 2N 123
Concorde St. LU2: Lut 9H 47
Concord Rd. EN3: Pon E 7F 156
Concourse, The *NW9* *8F 164*
(off Quakers Course)
Condor Ct. WD24: Watf 2K 149
Conduit La. EN3: Pon E 8J 157
EN11: Hod 8L 115
SG9: Gt Hor 1E 40
Conduit La. E. EN11: Hod 8M 115
CONEY ACRE 1M 43
Coney Cl. AL10: Hat 2H 129
Coneydale AL8: Welw G 7K 91
(not continuous)
Coney Gree CM21: Saw 4F 98
Conical Cnr. EN2: Enf 4A 156
Conifer Cl. EN7: C'hunt 2D 144
SG2: Stev 2C 52
Conifer Ct. CM23: Bis S 9H 59
Conifer Gdns. EN1: Enf 8C 156
Conifers, The HP3: Hem H 5J 123
LU1: Lut 2F 66
WD25: Watf 8L 137
Conifer Wlk. SG2: Stev 2B 52
Coningesby Dr. WD17: Watf 3G 148
Coningsby Av. NW9 ....9E 164
Coningsby Bank AL1: St Alb 6E 126
Coningsby Cl. AL9: Welh G 6K 129
Coningsby Ct. WD7: Rad 9G 139
Coningsby Dr. EN6: Pot B 6C 142
Conisbee Ct. N14 ....7H 155
Coniston Cl. HP3: Hem H 3E 124
Coniston Ct. *NW7* *7L 165*
(off Langstone Way)
Coniston Lodge WD17: Watf 4J 149
Coniston Rd. LU3: Lut 4B 46
WD4: Kin L 1B 136
Connaught Av. E4 ....9N 157
EN1: Enf 4C 156
EN4: E Bar 9E 154
Connaught Cl. EN1: Enf 4C 156
HP2: Hem H 9C 106
Connaught Gdns. HP4: Berk 7K 103
Connaught Ho. *WD23: Bush* *6A 150*
(off Royal Connaught Dr.)
Connaught Rd. AL3: St Alb 9D 108
AL5: Harp 5C 88
EN5: Barn 8K 153
HA3: Weal 8G 163
LU4: Lut 8A 46
Connelly La. SG5: Stot 1C 22
Connemara Cl. WD6: Bore 8D 152
Connop Rd. EN3: Enf W 2H 157
Connors Cl. SG8: G Mor 1A 6
Conquerors Hill AL4: Wheat 7M 89
Conquest Cl. SG4: Hit 5N 33
Conquest Rd. LU5: Hou R 4H 45
Conrad Ct. *NW9* *9E 164*
(off Needleman Cl.)
Constable Cl. LU5: Hou R 4G 45
Constable Ct. LU4: Lut 7C 46
Constable Gdns. HA8: Edg 8A 164
Constance Rd. EN1: Enf 8C 156
Constantine Cl. SG1: Stev 9M 35
Constantine Pl. SG7: Bald 2A 24
Convent Cl. EN5: Barn 4M 153
SG5: Hit 2N 33
Convent Ct. HP23: Tring 3L 101
Convent Gdns. SG7: Bald 4M 23
Conway Cl. HA7: Stanm 6H 163
LU5: Hou R 4H 45
Conway Gdns. EN2: Enf 2C 156
Conway Ho. WD6: Bore 6C 152
Conway Rd. LU4: Lut 8D 46
Conwy Pl. LU7: Pits 4A 82
Cony Cl. EN7: C'hunt 8C 132
Conyers, The CM20: Harl 4M 117
Cookfield Cl. LU6: Duns 9B 44
Cook Rd. SG2: Stev 2A 52
Cooksaldick La. CB11: L Lwr 3N 29
Cooks Cl. SL9: Chal P 6B 158
Cooks Hole Rd. EN2: Enf 2N 155
Cooks Mead WD23: Bush 8C 150
Cook's Mdw. LU6: Edle 4J 63
Cooks Spinney CM20: Harl 4C 118
(not continuous)
Cooks Vennel HP1: Hem H 9K 105
Cooks Way AL10: Hat 2H 129
SG4: Hit 1A 34
COOKS WHARF 2N 81
Cooks Wharf Cotts. LU7: Ched 2N 81
Coombe Av. HP22: Wen 9A 100
Coombe Cl. AL10: Hat 8F 110
HA8: Edg 9N 163
Coombe Dr. LU6: Duns 1B 64
Coombe Gdns. HP4: Berk 9K 103
Coombe Hill Rd. WD3: R'orth 9K 147
Coombehurst Cl. EN4: C'ters 4E 154
Coombelands SG8: Roys 5E 8
Coombe Rd. SG8: Kel, Roys 2M 13
WD23: Bush 9E 150
Coombes Rd. AL2: Lon C 8K 127
Cooms Wlk. HA8: Edg 8C 164
Cooper Cl. SG16: L Ston 1F 20
Coopers All. *SG5: Hit* *3M 33*
(off Tilehouse St.)
Coopers Cl. CM23: Bis S 4D 78
SG2: Stev 5C 52
SG4: Kimp 7J 69
Coopers Ct. SG12: Ware 6J 95
SG14: H'ford *9A 94*
(off The Folly)
Coopers Cres. WD6: Bore 3C 152
Coopers Fld. SG6: L Gar 4D 22
Coopers Ga. AL4: Col H 4B 128
COOPERS GREEN 6B 110
Coopers Grn. La. AL4: St Alb 8M 109
AL8: Welw G 5C 110
AL10: Hat 5C 110
Cooper's Hill SG4: Kimp 8J 69
Cooper's La. EN6: N'haw, Pot B 4C 142
Coopers La. Rd. EN6: N'haw, Pot B 4C 142
Coopers Mdw. AL3: Red 9J 87
Coopers M. AL5: Harp 7B 88
WD25: Watf 4L 137
Coopers Rd. EN6: Pot B 3B 142
Coopers Wlk. EN8: C'hunt 1H 145
Coopers Way LU5: Hou R 5D 44
Coopers Yd. *SG5: Hit* *3M 33*
(off Payne's Pk.)
Cooper Way HP4: Berk 1A 122
Cooters End La. AL5: Harp 3N 87
LU1: Lut 3N 87
LU2: E Hyd 9A 68
Cooters Hill Barns AL5: Harp 2A 88
(not continuous)
Copenhagen Cl. LU3: Lut 1N 45
Copinger Wlk. HA8: Edg 8B 164
Copley Rd. HA7: Stanm 5K 163
Copmans Wick WD3: Chor 7G 146
Coppens, The SG5: Stot 7G 10
Copper Beech Cl. HP3: Hem H 5J 123
Copper Beech Dr. SG6: L Gar 6E 22
Copper Beeches AL5: Harp 6C 88
AL6: Wel 9K 71
Copper Ct. CM21: Saw 5G 98
Copperdale Ct. WD18: Watf 7G 149
Copperfield Cl. SG5: Stot 1C 22
Copperfields AL7: Welw G 1B 112
LU4: Lut 5M 45
SG8: Roys 7C 8
Copperfields Ct. LU5: Hou R 5G 45
Coppermill Ct. WD3: W Hyd 7J 159
Coppermill La. UB9: Hare 7H 159
WD3: Hare, W Hyd 7H 159
Copper Mill Lock UB9: Hare 7K 159
Copper Ridge SL9: Chal P 5C 158
Copperwood SG13: H'ford 9D 94
Coppice, The CM23: Bis S 3F 78
EN2: Enf 6N 155
EN5: N Bar *8A 154*
(off Great Nth. Rd.)
HP2: Hem H 1D 124
HP23: Wigg 5A 102
WD19: Watf 8L 149
Coppice Cl. AL10: Hat 3F 128
HA7: Stanm 6G 162
Coppice Hatch CM18: Harl 8N 117
Coppice Mead SG5: Stot 7E 10
Coppice Wlk. N20 ....3N 165
Coppings, The EN11: Hod 5L 115
Coppins, The AL3: Mark 2N 85
HA3: Har W 6F 162
Coppins Cl. HP4: Berk 1K 121
Copse, The CM23: Bis S 9L 59
HP1: Hem H 9H 105
SG13: H'ford 9E 94
WD23: Bush 5M 149
Copse Cl. HA6: North 9E 160
Copse Hill AL6: Wel 8N 71
CM19: Harl 9L 117
Copse Way HP5: C'ham 9E 120
LU3: Lut 1N 45
Copsewood Rd. WD24: Watf 3K 149
Copse Wood Way HA6: North 8D 160
Copshall Cl. CM18: Harl 9A 118
COPT HALL 4N 67
Copthall Cl. CM22: Gt Hal 4N 79
SL9: Chal P 7C 158
Copthall Cnr. SL9: Chal P 7B 158
Copthall Dr. NW7 ....7G 164
Copthall Gdns. NW7 ....7G 165
Copthall La. SL9: Chal P 7B 158
Copthall Leisure Cen. 7H 165
Copthorn Av. EN10: Brox 2K 133
Copthorne LU2: Lut 6M 47
Copthorne Cl. WD3: Crox G 7B 148
Copthorne Rd. WD3: Crox G 8B 148
Coral Cl. LU6: Eat B 2J 63
Coral Gdns. HP2: Hem H 1B 124
Corals Mead AL7: Welw G 1K 111
Coram Cl. HP4: Berk 2N 121
Coran Cl. N9 ....9H 157
Corbar Cl. EN4: Had W 3C 154
Corbridge Dr. LU2: Lut 7N 47
Corby Cl. AL2: Chis G 7B 126
Corby Cres. EN2: Enf 6K 155
Cordell Cl. EN8: C'hunt 1J 145
Corder Cl. AL3: St Alb 5B 126
Cordons Cl. SL9: Chal P 8A 158
Cordwainer Ct. *CM23: Bis S* *3J 79*
(off London Rd.)
COREY'S MILL 8H 35
Coreys Mill La. SG1: Stev 9H 35
Corfe Cl. HP2: Hem H 3A 124
WD6: Bore 5D 152
Corfe Rd. LU7: Pits 4A 82
Corfield Rd. N21 ....7L 155
Corinium Gdns. LU3: Lut 1C 46
Corinium Ga. AL3: St Alb 4B 126
Cormorant Ho. EN3: Pon E 7H 157
Cornbury Rd. HA8: Edg 7L 163
Corncastle Path LU1: Lut 2F 66
Corncastle Rd. LU1: Lut 2E 66
Corncrake Cl. LU2: Lut 4L 47
Corncroft AL10: Hat 7H 111
Cornel Cl. LU1: Lut 1C 66
Cornel Ct. LU1: Lut 1C 66
Cornelia Ct. AL5: Harp 5B 88
Cornelius Ho. *WD18: Watf* *6H 149*
(off Chiltern Cl.)
Cornell Ct. EN3: Enf H 5J 157
Corner Cl. SG6: L Gar 5E 22
Cornerfield AL10: Hat 6H 111
CORNER HALL 4N 123
Corner Hall HP3: Hem H 4M 123
(not continuous)
Corner Hall Av. HP3: Hem H 4N 123
Corner Ho. *CM18: Harl* *8B 118*
(off Tye Grn. Village)
Corner Mead NW9 ....7F 164
Corners AL7: Welw G 8N 91
Corner Vw. AL9: Welh G 6J 129
Corner Wood AL3: Mark 2N 85
Corn Exchange
Hertford *9B 94*
(off Fore St.)
Cornfield Cres. HP4: Berk 7H 103
Cornfield Rd. WD23: Bush 6C 150
Cornfields SG2: Stev 2B 52
Cornfields, The HP1: Hem H 3L 123
Cornflower Cres. SG5: Stot 7E 10
Cornflower Way AL10: Hat 6E 110
Cornhill Dr. EN3: Enf W 1J 157
Cornish Ct. N9 ....9F 156
Corn Mead AL8: Welw G 6J 91
Cornmill EN9: Wal A 6M 145
Cornwall Av. N3 ....7N 165
Cornwall Cl. EN8: Wal C 6J 145
Cornwall Ct. HA5: Hat E 7A 162
Cornwall Ho. CM23: Bis S 4G 78
Cornwall Pl. E4 ....6M 157
Cornwall Rd. AL1: St Alb 4F 126
AL5: Harp 5C 88
HA5: Hat E 7A 162
Coronation Av. SG8: Roys 8C 8
Coronation Rd. CM23: Bis S 3G 79
SG12: Ware 5H 95
Coronation Row SG8: Reed 7J 15
Coroner's Court
North London 6M 153
Corporate Ho. HA3: Har W 8E 162
Corringham Ct.
AL1: St Alb 1G 166 (1G 126)
Corry's End AL4: Col H 4E 128
Corton Cl. SG1: Stev 1H 51
Corvus Cl. SG8: Roys 5E 8
Cory Wright Way AL4: Wheat 6M 89
Cosford M. HP22: Halt 8D 100
Cosgrove Way LU1: Lut 8N 45
Cosmia Ct. *WD23: Bush* *7N 149*
(off Vale Rd.)
Cosne M. AL5: Harp 8D 88
Costins Wlk. *HP4: Berk* *1A 122*
(off Robertson Rd.)
Cosy Corner HP22: Ast C 1C 100
Cotefield LU4: Lut 6M 45
Cotesmore Rd. HP1: Hem H 3H 123
Cotlandswick AL2: Lon C 7K 127
Cotman Gdns. HA8: Edg 9A 164
Cotney Cft. SG2: Stev 6C 52
Cotsmoor *AL1: St Alb* *2G 126*
(off Granville Rd.)
Cotswold HP2: Hem H 8A 106
Cotswold Av. WD23: Bush 8D 150
Cotswold Bus. Pk. LU1: Cad 6N 65
Cotswold Cl. AL4: St Alb 6K 109
Cotswold Dr. SG1: W'ton 6N 35
Cotswold Gdns. LU3: Lut 2M 45
Cotswold Grn. EN2: Enf 6L 155
Cotswolds AL10: Hat 2G 128
Cotswold Way EN2: Enf 5L 155

184 A-Z Hertfordshire

Cuckoo Hill—Dene Gdns.

Cuckoo Hill HA5: E'cote, Pin . . . 9L 161
Cuckoo's Nest LU2: Lut . . . 1J 67
Cucumber La. AL9: Ess . . . 2D 130
SG13: New S . . . 2D 130
CUFFLEY . . . 2K 143
Cuffley Av. WD25: Watf . . . 7M 137
Cuffley Cl. LU3: Lut . . . 5B 46
Cuffley Ct. HP2: Hem H . . . 6E 106
Cuffley Hill EN7: Cuff, Gof O . . . 2L 143
Cuffley Station (Rail) . . . 2L 143
Culgaith Gdns. EN2: Enf . . . 6K 155
Cullen Cl. LU3: Lut . . . 6E 46
Cullera Cl. HA6: North . . . 6H 161
Culloden Rd. EN2: Enf . . . 4N 155
Culrose Ct. SG2: Stev . . . 9M 51
Culver Ct. SG10: M Had . . . 7J 77
Culverden Rd. WD19: Watf . . . 3K 161
Culver Gro. HA7: Stanm . . . 9K 163
Culverhouse Rd. LU3: Lut . . . 5E 46
Culverlands Cl. HA7: Stanm . . . 4J 163
Culver Rd. AL1: St Alb . . . 1F 126
Culworth Cl. LU1: Cad . . . 5A 66
Cumberland Cl. HP3: Hem H . . . 6G 125
SG14: H'ford . . . 6A 94
Cumberland Ct.
AL3: St Alb . . . 1E 166 (1F 126)
EN11: Hod . . . 7L 115
Cumberland Dr. AL3: Red . . . 9K 87
Cumberland Gdns. NW4 . . . 9L 165
Cumberland Lodge *EN11: Hod* . . . *8L 115*
(off Taverners Way)
Cumberland St. LU1: Lut . . . 2G 67
LU5: Hou R . . . 5E 44
CUMBERLOW GREEN . . . 9K 25
Cumberlow Pl. HP2: Hem H . . . 3E 124
Cumbria Cl. LU5: Hou R . . . 4H 45
Cunard Ct. *HA7: Stanm* . . . *2H 163*
(off Brightwen Gro.)
Cunard Cres. N21 . . . 8B 156
Cundalls Rd. SG12: Ware . . . 5J 95
Cunningham Av. AL1: St Alb . . . 4G 127
AL10: Hat . . . 8D 110
EN3: Enf W . . . 9J 145
Cunningham Ct. EN8: C'hunt . . . 1J 145
Cunningham Hill Rd. AL1: St Alb . . . 4G 127
Cunningham Rd. EN8: C'hunt . . . 9J 133
CUPID GREEN . . . 6C 106
Cupid Grn. La.
HP2: Gad R, Hem H . . . 3A 106
Curie Gdns. NW9 . . . 9E 164
Curlew Cl. HP4: Berk . . . 2N 121
SG6: L Gar . . . 2E 22
Curlew Ct. EN10: Worm . . . 5K 133
Curlew Cres. SG8: Roys . . . 4E 8
Curlew Ho. EN3: Pon E . . . 7H 157
Curlew Rd. LU2: Lut . . . 4L 47
Curo Pk. AL2: Frog . . . 9F 126
Currie St. SG13: H'ford . . . 9C 94
Curry Ri. NW7 . . . 6K 165
Curteys CM17: Harl . . . 1F 118
Curthwaite Gdns. EN2: Enf . . . 6J 155
Curtis Cl. WD3: R'orth . . . 1K 159
Curtis Cotts. HP5: Ash G . . . 6K 121
Curtis Rd. HP3: Hem H . . . 3F 124
Curtiss Dr. WD25: Watf . . . 7H 137
Curtiss Ho. NW9 . . . 9F 164
Curtis Way HP4: Berk . . . 2A 122
Curtlington Ho. *HA8: Edg* . . . *9C 164*
(off Burnt Oak B'way.)
Curzon Av. EN3: Pon E . . . 7H 157
HA7: Stanm . . . 8H 163
Curzon Ga. Ct. WD17: Watf . . . 3J 149
Curzon Rd. LU3: Lut . . . 8E 46
Cussans Ho. WD18: Watf . . . 8G 149
Cussen Pl. LU3: Lut . . . 2N 45
Cussons Cl. EN7: C'hunt . . . 2E 144
Cusworth Wlk. LU6: Duns . . . 8B 44
Cusworth Way LU6: Duns . . . 8B 44
Cutenhoe Rd. LU1: Lut . . . 4G 66
Cutforth Rd. CM21: Saw . . . 4G 99
Cuthberts Cl. EN7: C'hunt . . . 2D 144
Cutlers Cl. CM23: Bis S . . . 4E 78
Cutlers Grn. LU2: Lut . . . 7A 48
Cutmore Dr. AL4: Col H . . . 4B 128
Cut Throat La. SG9: B Pel . . . 9L 29
Cutthroat La. EN11: Hod . . . 6K 115
CUTTING HILL . . . 8L 53
Cuttsfield Ter. HP1: Hem H . . . 3J 123
Cutts La. SG4: Kimp . . . 7L 69
Cuttys La. SG1: Stev . . . 4L 51
Cwmbran Ct. HP2: Hem H . . . 7B 106
Cygnet Cl. HA6: North . . . 6E 160
WD6: Bore . . . 3C 152
Cygnet Ct. CM23: Bis S . . . 2J 79
Cygnet Way *CM19: Royd* . . . *5D 116*
(off Roydon Mill Leisure Pk.)
Cylers Thicket AL6: Wel . . . 1J 91
Cymbeline Ct. AL3: St Alb . . . 1A 166
Cypress Av. AL7: Welw G . . . 1B 112
EN2: Crew H . . . 8M 143
Cypress Rd. HA3: Har W . . . 9E 162
Cypress Wlk. WD25: Watf . . . 8K 137
Cyprus Av. N3 . . . 9L 165
Cyprus Gdns. N3 . . . 9L 165
Cyprus Rd. N3 . . . 9M 165
Cyril Dumpleton Ho. AL2: Lon C . . . 8L 127
Cyrils Way AL1: St Alb . . . 5E 126

D

Dacorum District Sports Cen. . . . 4M 123
Dacorum Way HP1: Hem H . . . 2M 123
(not continuous)
Dacre Cres. SG4: Kimp . . . 7K 69
Dacre Gdns. WD6: Bore . . . 7D 152
Dacre Grn. SG8: Roys . . . 7F 8
Dacre Ind. Est. EN8: C'hunt . . . 2K 145
Dacre Rd. HP22: Halt . . . 7D 100
SG5: Hit . . . 2A 34
Dad's Wood CM20: Harl . . . 6M 117
Daffodil Cl. AL10: Hat . . . 5F 110
Dagger La. WD6: Elst . . . 8H 151
Daggsdell Rd. HP1: Hem H . . . 9H 105
DAGNALL . . . 2N 83
Dagnall Rd. HP1: Gt Gad . . . 8D 84
HP4: Lit G . . . 6B 84
LU6: Duns, Whip . . . 6N 63
Dagnalls SG6: L Gar . . . 9F 22
Dagnall Way LU6: Edle . . . 8K 63
Dahlia Cl. EN7: C'hunt . . . 7A 132
LU2: Lut . . . 6K 47
Daimler Dr. LU6: Duns . . . 7C 44
Daintrees SG12: Widf . . . 3H 97
Daintry Lodge HA6: North . . . 6H 161
Dairy Cl. EN3: Enf W . . . 1G 157
Dairy Farm La. UB9: Hare . . . 9M 159
Dairyglen Av. EN8: C'hunt . . . 4J 145
Dairy M. SG12: Huns . . . 8G 96
WD18: Watf . . . 7J 149
Dairy Way WD5: Abb L . . . 2H 137
Daisy Ct. SG6: L Gar . . . 3G 23
Daisy Dr. AL10: Hat . . . 6F 110
Daisy La. SG5: Stot . . . 7E 10
Daisy Pl. LU3: Lut . . . 2M 45
Dalby Cl. LU4: Lut . . . 6L 45
Dale, The SG6: L Gar . . . 6E 22
Dale Av. AL4: Wheat . . . 2J 89
HA8: Edg . . . 8N 163
Dale Cl. EN5: N Bar . . . 8A 154
HA5: Pin . . . 8K 161
LU5: Duns . . . 8J 45
SG4: Hit . . . 6N 33
Dale Ct. CM21: Saw . . . 6F 98
EN2: Enf . . . 3A 156
WD25: Watf . . . 6J 137
Dale Rd. LU1: Lut . . . 1E 66
LU5: Duns . . . 8J 45
Daleside Dr. EN6: Pot B . . . 6M 141
Dales Path WD6: Bore . . . 7D 152
Dales Rd. WD6: Bore . . . 7D 152
Dalewood AL5: Harp . . . 6E 88
AL7: Welw G . . . 1C 112
Dalkeith Gro. HA7: Stanm . . . 5L 163
Dalkeith Rd. AL5: Harp . . . 5D 88
Dalling Dr. LU5: Hou R . . . 4F 44
Dallow Rd. LU1: Lut . . . 9A 46
Dalmeny Rd. EN5: N Bar . . . 8B 154
Dalroad Ind. Est. LU1: Lut . . . 9D 46
Dalrymple Cl. N14 . . . 9J 155
Dalston Gdns. HA7: Stanm . . . 8M 163
Dalton Cl. LU3: Lut . . . 9D 30
Dalton Gdns. CM23: Bis S . . . 4G 79
Dalton Ho. HA7: Stanm . . . 5H 163
Dalton Pl. *LU7: Pits* . . . *4A 82*
(off Lancaster Way)
Dalton Rd. HA3: Weal . . . 9E 162
Dalton St. AL3: St Alb . . . 1C 166 (1E 126)
Daltons Wharf HP4: Berk . . . 1A 122
Dalton Way SG4: Whit . . . 1M 69
WD17: Watf . . . 7M 149
Daltry Cl. SG1: Stev . . . 8J 35
Daltry Rd. SG1: Stev . . . 8J 35
(not continuous)
Damask Cl. HP23: Tring . . . 2A 102
SG4: W'ton . . . 2A 36
DAMASK GREEN . . . 2A 36
Damask Grn. HP1: Hem H . . . 3H 123
Damask Grn. Rd. SG4: W'ton . . . 2A 36
Dammersey Cl. AL3: Mark . . . 3B 86
Damson Cl. WD24: Watf . . . 1J 149
Damson Wlk. *SG7: Ashw* . . . *1F 12*
(off Sunnymead Orchard)
Damson Way AL4: St Alb . . . 9K 109
Danby Ct. EN2: Enf . . . 5A 156
DANCERSEND . . . 5H 101
Dancers End La.
HP23: Chiv, Tring . . . 3G 101
Dancersend Nature Reserve . . . 7F 100
DANCERS HILL . . . 9K 141
Dancers Hill Rd. EN5: Barn . . . 9J 141
Dancers La. EN5: Barn . . . 8J 141
Dancote SG3: Kneb . . . 3M 71
Dane Acres CM23: Bis S . . . 9F 58
Danebridge La. SG10: M Had . . . 6L 77
Danebridge Rd. SG10: M Had . . . 6K 77
Dane Cl. AL5: Harp . . . 3D 88
SG5: Stot . . . 4F 10
Dane Ct. SG13: H'ford . . . 9C 94
DANE END
SG8 . . . 8F 14
SG12 . . . 1C 74
Dane End Ho. *SG1: Stev* . . . *9J 35*
(off North Rd.)
Dane End La. SG4: W'ton . . . 6D 36
Danefield Rd. SG5: Pirt . . . 7D 20
Dane Ho. CM23: Bis S . . . 9F 58
Daneland EN4: E Bar . . . 8E 154
Danemead EN11: Hod . . . 5L 115
Dane O'Coys Rd. CM23: Bis S . . . 8F 58
Dane Pk. CM23: Bis S . . . 9F 58
Dane Rd. LU3: Lut . . . 7D 46
MK45: Bar C . . . 8F 18
Danes, The AL2: Par S . . . 1D 138
DANESBURY . . . 1J 91
Danesbury La. AL6: Wel . . . 8K 71
Danesbury Pk. AL6: Wel . . . 9J 71
SG14: H'ford . . . 8B 94
Danesbury Park Golf Course . . . 9J 71
Danesbury Pk. Rd. AL6: Wel . . . 9H 71
Danescroft SG6: L Gar . . . 2F 22
Danesgate SG1: Stev . . . 5K 51
Daneshill Ho. *SG1: Stev* . . . *4K 51*
(off Danestrete)
DANE STREET . . . 2B 68
Dane St. CM23: Bis S . . . 1J 79
Danestrete SG1: Stev . . . 4K 51
Daniel Ct. NW9 . . . 8E 164
Daniells AL7: Welw G . . . 8N 91
Danleigh Ct. N14 . . . 9J 155
Danvers Cft. HP23: Tring . . . 1A 102
Danvers Dr. LU3: Lut . . . 9E 30
Danziger Way WD6: Bore . . . 3C 152
Darblay Cl. AL4: San . . . 1N 109
Darby Dr. AL6: Wel . . . 5L 71
EN9: Wal A . . . 6N 145
Darcy Cl. EN8: C'hunt . . . 4J 145
Darkes La. EN6: Pot B . . . 5N 141
Dark La. AL5: Harp . . . 8E 88
EN7: C'hunt . . . 3E 144
HP22: W'rave . . . 5A 60
SG4: Cod . . . 8E 70
SG9: S'don . . . 2N 25
SG11: Gt Mun, Hau . . . 4C 54
SG12: Ware . . . *5J 95*
(off Musley La.)
SG12: Ware . . . 4K 95
(Elder Rd.)
Darlands Dr. EN5: Barn . . . 7K 153
Darley Cft. AL2: Par S . . . 1C 138
DARLEYHALL . . . 8D 48
Darley Rd. LU2: Wan E . . . 8C 48
N9 . . . 9D 156
SG4: Bre G . . . 8C 48
Darlington Ct. CM17: Harl . . . 2E 118
Darnhills WD7: Rad . . . 8G 139
Darnicle Hill EN7: New S, Gof O, C'hunt . . . 7L 131
Darrington Rd. WD6: Bore . . . 3M 151
Darr's La. HP4: Berk . . . 9H 103
Dart, The HP2: Hem H . . . 6B 106
Dartford Av. N9 . . . 8G 157
Dartmouth M. LU4: Lut . . . 6N 45
Darvells Yd. WD3: Chor . . . 6G 147
Darwin Cl. AL3: St Alb . . . 7F 108
HP2: Hem H . . . 5D 106
Darwin Gdns. WD19: Watf . . . 5L 161
Darwin Rd. SG2: Stev . . . 3A 52
Dashes, The CM20: Harl . . . 5A 118
(not continuous)
DASSELS . . . 7B 40
Datchet Cl. HP2: Hem H . . . 6D 106
DATCHWORTH . . . 5C 72
Datchworth Ct. EN1: Enf . . . 7C 156
DATCHWORTH GREEN . . . 7C 72
Datchworth Mus. . . . 7C 72
Datchworth Turn HP2: Hem H . . . 2E 124
Dauphin Ct. *LU2: Lut* . . . *8F 46*
(off Earls Meade)
Davenham Av. HA6: North . . . 5H 161
Davenham Pl. HA6: North . . . 5H 161
Davenport CM17: Harl . . . 7G 118
Daventer Dr. HA7: Stanm . . . 7G 163
David Evans Ct. SG6: L Gar . . . 4D 22
David Harrowell Ho. SG15: Arl . . . 8A 10
David Lloyd Leisure
Bushey . . . 4B 150
Enfield . . . 4E 156
Hatfield . . . 8E 110
Luton . . . 3H 67
Stevenage . . . 5J 51
Davidson Ho. HP2: Hem H . . . 1N 123
Davies St. SG13: H'ford . . . 9C 94
Da Vinci Ct. WD25: Watf . . . 9M 137
Davis Ct. AL1: St Alb . . . 3E 166 (2F 126)
Davis Cres. SG5: Pirt . . . 6E 20
Davison Cl. EN8: C'hunt . . . 1H 145
Davison Ct. *SG6: L Gar* . . . *5H 23*
(off Bidwell Cl.)
Davison Dr. EN8: C'hunt . . . 1H 145
Davis Row SG15: Arl . . . 8A 10
Davy Ho. AL1: St Alb . . . 3G 126
Davys Cl. AL4: Wheat . . . 8M 89
Dawes La. AL4: Wheat . . . 6L 89
WD3: Sar . . . 1H 147
Dawley AL7: Welw G . . . 6M 91
Dawley Ct. HP2: Hem H . . . 7C 106
Dawlish Cl. SG2: Stev . . . 1B 72
Dawlish Rd. LU4: Lut . . . 6B 46
Dawn Ct. AL1: St Alb . . . 3H 127
DAW'S END . . . 6D 28
Daws Hill E4 . . . 4N 157
Daws La. NW7 . . . 5F 164
SG9: Buck . . . 3J 27
Dawson Ter. N9 . . . 9G 156
Dayemead AL7: Welw G . . . 3A 112
Days Cl. AL10: Hat . . . 9F 110
SG8: Roys . . . 8C 8
Days Mead AL10: Hat . . . 9F 110
Deacon Cl. AL1: St Alb . . . 6E 126
Deacons Cl. HA5: Pin . . . 9K 161
WD6: Elst . . . 6A 152
Deacons Ct. *LU2: Lut* . . . *9F 46*
(off Villa Rd.)
Deaconsfield Rd. HP3: Hem H . . . 5N 123
Deacons Hgts. WD6: Elst . . . 8A 152
Deacons Hill WD6: Elst . . . 8N 151
WD19: Watf . . . 8L 149
Deacon's Hill Rd. WD6: Elst . . . 6N 151
Deacons Way SG5: Hit . . . 1L 33
Deadfield La. SG14: Let G . . . 4E 112
Deadhearn La. HP8: Chal G . . . 1B 158
Deadman's Ash La. WD3: Sar . . . 9L 135
Dead Woman's La. SG4: Pres . . . 3F 48
Deakin Cl. WD18: Watf . . . 9G 149
Deal Ct. *NW9* . . . *9F 164*
(off Hazel Cl.)
Dean, The HP22: W'rave . . . 5A 60
Deanacre Cl. SL9: Chal P . . . 6B 158
Dean Ct. HA8: Edg . . . 6B 164
WD25: Watf . . . 6M 137
Deancroft Rd. SL9: Chal P . . . 6B 158
Dean Dr. HA7: Stanm . . . 9M 163
Deane Ct. HA6: North . . . 8G 161
Deanes Cl. LU1: Lut . . . 2F 66
Dean Fld. HP3: Bov . . . 9D 122
Dean La. AL3: Mark . . . 6J 85
HP2: Gad R . . . 6J 85
Dean Moore Cl. AL1: St Alb . . . 4C 166 (3D 126)
Deansbrook Cl. HA8: Edg . . . 7C 164
Deansbrook Rd. HA8: Edg . . . 7B 164
Deans Cl. HA8: Edg . . . 6C 164
HP23: Tring . . . 2M 101
WD5: Abb L . . . 5F 136
Deanscroft SG3: Kneb . . . 3M 71
Deans Dr. HA8: Edg . . . 5D 164
Deans Furlong HP23: Tring . . . 2M 101
Dean's Gdns. AL4: St Alb . . . 7H 109
Deans La. HA8: Edg . . . 6C 164
Deans Lawn HP4: Berk . . . 1N 121
Deans Mdw. HP4: Dag . . . 2N 83
Deans Way HA8: Edg . . . 5C 164
Deansway HP3: Hem H . . . 5B 124
Dean Wlk. HA8: Edg . . . 6C 164
Dean Way HP22: Ast C . . . 2E 100
Deard's End La. SG3: Kneb . . . 2M 71
Deards Wood SG3: Kneb . . . 3M 71
Dearlove Pl. *CM23: Bis S* . . . *1J 79*
(off Hockerill St.)
Dearmer Ho. *SL9: Chal P* . . . *5B 158*
(off Micholls Av.)
Dearne Cl. HA7: Stanm . . . 5H 163
Dearsley Rd. EN1: Enf . . . 5E 156
Debden Cl. NW9 . . . 8E 164
Debenham Ct. EN5: Barn . . . 7J 153
Debenham Rd. EN7: C'hunt . . . 9F 132
De Bohun Av. N14 . . . 8G 154
Deborah Lodge HA8: Edg . . . 8B 164
Deburgh Cl. EN10: Worm . . . 4K 133
Debussy NW9 . . . 9F 164
Dee, The HP2: Hem H . . . 6B 106
Deepdene EN6: Pot B . . . 4K 141
Deepdene Ct. N21 . . . 8N 155
Deep Denes LU2: Lut . . . 7J 47
Deeping Cl. SG3: Kneb . . . 4M 71
Deer Cl. SG13: H'ford . . . 9D 94
Deercote Ct. EN8: C'hunt . . . 3H 145
Deerfield Cl. SG12: Ware . . . 5H 95
Deerings, The AL5: Harp . . . 1B 108
Deerleap Gro. E4 . . . 7M 157
Deer Pk. CM19: Harl . . . 9K 117
Deer Pk. Wlk. HP5: C'ham . . . 9J 121
Deer Pk. Way EN9: Wal A . . . 9M 145
Deerswood Av. AL10: Hat . . . 2H 129
Deeves Hall La. EN6: Rid . . . 6E 140
Defiant *NW9* . . . *9F 164*
(off Further Acre)
De Havilland Aircraft Heritage Cen. . . . 2B 140
De Havilland Cl. AL10: Hat . . . 8F 110
De Havilland Ct. WD7: Shen . . . 5M 139
De Havilland Ho. *AL10: Hat* . . . *8J 111*
(off Endymion M.)
De Havilland Rd. HA8: Edg . . . 9A 164
De Havilland Way WD5: Abb L . . . 5H 137
Deimos Dr. HP2: Hem H . . . 8C 106
Delahay Ri. HP4: Berk . . . 8M 103
Delamare Rd. EN8: C'hunt . . . 3J 145
Delamere Gdns. NW7 . . . 6D 164
Delamere Rd. WD6: Bore . . . 3B 152
Delco Way LU6: Duns . . . 7C 44
Delfcroft SG12: Ware . . . 4G 94
Delfield Gdns. LU1: Cad . . . 4A 66
Delhi Rd. EN1: Enf . . . 9D 156
Delius Cl. WD6: Elst . . . 8K 151
Dell, The AL1: St Alb . . . 9H 109
AL3: Mark . . . 2N 85
AL6: Wel . . . 3N 91
EN9: Wal A . . . 9N 145
HA5: Pin . . . 9M 161
HA6: North . . . 2G 160
LU1: Cad . . . 5A 66
LU2: Lut . . . 8A 48
SG1: Stev . . . 4L 51
SG7: Bald . . . 5L 23
SG8: Roys . . . 8C 8
SG13: H'ford . . . 3A 114
SL9: Chal P . . . 6B 158
WD7: Rad . . . 9H 139
Dell Cl. AL5: Harp . . . 4C 88
Dellcot Cl. LU2: Lut . . . 4K 47
Dellcott Cl. AL8: Welw G . . . 8J 91
Dell Ct. HA6: North . . . 7F 160
Dellcroft Way AL5: Harp . . . 9B 88
Dellcut Rd. HP2: Hem H . . . 9C 106
Dell Farm Outdoor Education Cen. . . . 7C 64
Dellfield AL1: St Alb . . . 3G 127
SG12: Wad . . . 8H 75
Dell Fld. Av. HP4: Berk . . . 8M 103
Dell Fld. Cl. HP4: Berk . . . 8L 103
WD7: Rad . . . 8G 138
WD17: Watf . . . 4J 149
Dellfield Ct. CM17: Harl . . . 2E 118
LU2: Lut . . . 7M 47
WD17: Watf . . . 4J 149
Dellfield Rd. AL10: Hat . . . 9G 111
Dell La. CM22: L Hal, Spel . . . 8H 79
CM23: Bis S . . . 1J 79
Dell Mdw. HP3: Hem H . . . 6A 124
Dellmeadow WD5: Abb L . . . 3G 136
Dellmont Rd. LU5: Hou R . . . 4E 44
Dell Nature Reserve . . . 4J 147
Dellors Cl. EN5: Barn . . . 7K 153
Dell Ri. AL2: Par S . . . 8C 126
Dell Rd. EN3: Enf W . . . 2G 157
HP4: Berk . . . 7H 103
LU5: Hou R . . . 4E 44
WD24: Watf . . . 1J 149
Dells, The *CM23: Bis S* . . . *1H 79*
(off South St.)
HP3: Hem H . . . 3D 124
Dells Cl. E4 . . . 9M 157
Dell Side WD24: Watf . . . 1J 149
Dellsome La. AL4: Col H . . . 5E 128
AL9: Welh G . . . 5F 128
Dell Spring SG9: Bunt . . . 2J 39
Dellswood Cl. EN11: Hod . . . 5K 115
SG13: H'ford . . . 1C 114
Dellwood WD3: R'orth . . . 1L 159
Delmar Av. HP2: Hem H . . . 3F 124
Delmer Ct. *WD6: Bore* . . . *2N 151*
(off Aycliffe Rd.)
Delmer End La. AL3: Flam . . . 5E 86
Delphine Cl. LU1: Lut . . . 2C 66
DELROW . . . 3D 150
Delroy Ct. N20 . . . 9B 154
Delta Gain WD19: Watf . . . 2M 161
Delta Pk. Ind. Est. EN3: Brim . . . 5K 157
Demontfort Ri. SG12: Ware . . . 4G 94
Denbigh Cl. HP2: Hem H . . . 3A 124
Denbigh Rd. LU3: Lut . . . 7D 46
Denby SG6: L Gar . . . 7H 23
Denby Grange CM17: Harl . . . 6G 118
Dencora Centre, The AL1: St Alb . . . 2H 127
EN3: Brim . . . 5J 157
Dencora Way LU3: Lut . . . 1L 45
Dendridge Cl. EN1: Enf . . . 1F 156
Dene Gdns. HA7: Stanm . . . 5K 163

Dene Ho.—Duncombe Dr.

Dene Ho. N14 9J 155
Dene La. SG2: A'ton 7C 52
Dene Rd. HA6: North 6E 160
Denes, The HP3: Hem H 6B 124
Denewood EN5: N Bar 7B 154
Denewood Cl. WD17: Watf 1H 149
Denewood M. WD17: Watf 1H 149
Denham Cl. HP2: Hem H 6C 106
LU3: Lut 1A 46
(not continuous)
Denham La. SL9: Chal P 6C 158
Denham Wlk. SL9: Chal P 6C 158
Denham Way WD3: Map C, W Hyd 6H 159
WD6: Bore 3C 152
Denleigh Gdns. N21 9M 155
Denmark Cl. LU3: Lut 9A 30
Denmark St. WD17: Watf 4K 149
Dennis Cl. HP22: Ast C 2F 100
Dennis Ct. AL3: St Alb 1D 166 (1E 126)
Dennis Gdns. HA7: Stanm 5K 163
Dennis La. HA7: Stanm 3J 163
Dennis Pde. N14 9J 155
Denny Av. EN9: Wal A 7N 145
Denny Ct. CM23: Bis S 7K 59
Denny Ga. EN8: C'hunt 9K 133
Denny Rd. N9 9F 156
Denny's La. HP4: Berk 3K 121
De Novo Pl. *AL1: St Alb* *2G 126*
(off Stanhope Rd.)
Densley Cl. AL8: Welw G 7K 91
Denton Cl. EN5: Barn 7J 153
LU4: Lut 5L 45
Denton Ho. WD19: Watf 3L 161
Denton Rd. SG1: Stev 5L 51
Dents Cl. SG6: L Gar 8J 23
Denvers Yd. SG11: Barw 5A 76
Derby Av. HA3: Har W 8E 162
Derby Ho. HA5: Pin 9M 161
Derby Lodge N3 9M 165
Derby Rd. EN3: Pon E 7F 156
EN11: Hod 9A 116
LU4: Lut 7M 45
WD17: Watf 8D 166 (5L 149)
(not continuous)
Derby Way SG1: Stev 1A 52
Derry Leys AL10: Hat 7E 110
Derwent Av. EN4: E Bar 9E 154
HA5: Hat E 6N 161
LU3: Lut 2D 46
NW7 6D 164
Derwent Cl. WD25: Watf 7L 137
Derwent Cres. HA7: Stanm 9K 163
Derwent Dr. LU6: Duns 3F 64
Derwent Rd. AL5: Harp 3L 87
HP3: Hem H 3E 124
LU2: Lut 9J 47
Desborough Cl. AL7: Welw G 3A 112
SG14: H'ford 6A 94
Desborough Dr. AL6: Tew 2B 92
Desborough Rd. SG4: Hit 2C 34
Des Fuller Ct. *LU1: Lut* *2H 67*
(off Chequer St.)
Desmond Ho. EN4: E Bar 8D 154
Desmond Rd. WD24: Watf 9H 137
De Soissons Cl. AL8: Welw G 2H 111
De Tany Ct. AL1: St Alb 5C 166 (3E 126)
Deva Cl. AL3: St Alb 4B 126
De Vere Leisure Club 9H 159
Devereux Dr. WD17: Watf 2G 149
De Vere Wlk. WD17: Watf 4G 149
Devey Cl. SG3: Kneb 3M 71
Devey Way SG14: H'ford 6M 93
Devil's La. SG13: B'don 3N 131
Devoils La. CM23: Bis S 1H 79
Devon Ct. AL1: St Alb 3F 126
Devon Mead AL10: Hat 7E 110
Devon Rd. LU2: Lut 9K 47
WD24: Watf 3M 149
Devonshire Bus. Cen. EN6: Pot B 3L 141
SG6: L Gar 4H 23
Devonshire Bus. Pk. WD6: Bore 5D 152
Devonshire Cl. SG2: Stev 9N 51
Devonshire Ct. *HA5: Hat E* *8A 162*
(off Devonshire Rd.)
Devonshire Cres. NW7 7K 165
Devonshire Gdns. N21 9A 156
Devonshire Ho. WD23: Bush 6A 150
Devonshire Rd. AL5: Harp 5C 88
HA5: Hat E 8A 162
NW7 7K 165
Dewars Cl. AL6: Wel 1J 91
DEWES GREEN 1B 42
Dewes Grn. Rd. CM23: Ber 1B 42
Dewgrass Gro. EN8: Wal C 8H 145
Dewhurst Rd. EN8: C'hunt 2F 144
Dewpond Cl. SG1: Stev 1J 51
Dewsbury Rd. LU3: Lut 3D 46
Dexter Cl. AL1: St Alb 3H 127
LU3: Lut 9D 30
Dexter Rd. EN5: Barn 8K 153
UB9: Hare 9M 159
Dharam Marg WD25: A'ham, Let H 4D 150
Dialmead EN6: Rid 7F 140
DIAMOND END 2D 68
Diamond Ind. Cen. SG6: L Gar 4J 23
Diamond Rd. WD24: Watf 2J 149
Dianne Way EN4: E Bar 6D 154
Dickasons SG8: Melb 1N 9
Dickens Blvd. SG5: Stot 1C 22
Dickens Cl. AL3: St Alb 1E 126
EN7: C'hunt 8E 132
Dickens Ct. AL10: Hat 7H 111
HP2: Hem H 5D 106
Dickenson Way SG12: Ware 5H 95
Dicker Mill SG13: H'ford 8B 94
Dicket Mead AL6: Wel 2J 91
Dickinson Av. WD3: Crox G 8C 148
Dickinson Quay HP3: Hem H 7A 124
Dickinsons Fld. AL5: Harp 8D 88
Dickinson Sq. WD3: Crox G 8D 148
Dick Smiths Wlk. SG7: Ashw 8L 5
Dickson EN7: C'hunt 9D 132
Digby Cl. LU4: Lut 8A 46
Dig Dag Hill EN7: C'hunt 9D 132
DIGSWELL 4L 91
Digswell Cl. WD6: Bore 2A 152
Digswell Ct. AL8: Welw G 7L 91
Digswell Hill AL6: Wel 6G 91
Digswell Ho. AL8: Welw G 5K 91
Digswell Ho. M. AL8: Welw G 5K 91
Digswell La. AL6: Wel 5M 91
Digswell Lodge AL8: Welw G 7K 91
DIGSWELL PARK 5K 91
Digswell Pk. Rd. AL6: Wel 4L 91
AL8: Welw G 4K 91
Digswell Pl. AL8: Welw G 6H 91
Digswell Ri. AL8: Welw G 7K 91
Digswell Rd. AL8: Welw G 8K 91
DIGSWELL WATER 5M 91
Dimmocks La. WD3: Sar 9L 135
Dimsdale Cres. CM23: Bis S 3K 79
Dimsdale Dr. EN1: Enf 9E 156
Dimsdale St. SG14: H'ford 9A 94
Dinant Link Rd. EN11: Hod 7L 115
Dingle Cl. EN5: Ark 8F 152
Dingles Ct. HA5: Pin 8M 161
Dinmore HP3: Bov 1C 134
Dinsdale Gdns. EN5: N Bar 7A 154
Dione Rd. HP2: Hem H 8B 106
Dishforth La. NW9 7E 164
Dison Cl. EN3: Enf H 3H 157
Disraeli Pl. SG5: Stot 1C 22
Ditchfield Rd. EN11: Hod 5L 115
Ditchling Cl. LU2: Lut 6L 47
Ditchling Ct. AL1: St Alb 2E 166
Ditchmore La. SG1: Stev 3K 51
Ditton Grn. LU2: Lut 6N 47
Divot Pl. SG13: H'ford 8F 94
Dixies Cl. SG7: Ashw 1C 12
Dixon Pl. SG9: Bunt 3J 39
Dixons Ct. SG12: Ware 7J 95
Dixons Hill Cl. AL9: N Mym 7H 129
Dixons Hill Rd. AL9: N Mym, Welh G 7H 129
DJ's Jungle Adventure
St Albans 7G 109
Dobbin Cl. HA3: Ken 9H 163
Dobbins La. HP22: Wen 9A 100
DOBB'S WEIR 9A 116
Dobb's Weir Rd. CM19: Hod, Royd 9N 115
EN11: Hod 9N 115
Dockerell Rd. CM24: Stans 4N 59
Docklands SG5: Pirt 7E 20
Dockyard SG12: Ware 6J 95
Doctor's Commons Rd. HP4: Berk 1M 121
Dodd Rd. WD24: Watf 9J 137
Dodds La. HP2: Hem H 7M 105
Dodgen La. CM23: Man 8G 43
Dodwood AL7: Welw G 1A 112
Doggetts Cl. EN4: E Bar 7D 154
Doggetts Way AL1: St Alb 4D 126
Dog Kennel La. AL10: Hat 8G 111
SG8: Roys 7D 8
WD3: Chor 6J 147
Dognell Grn. AL8: Welw G 8H 91
Dolesbury Dr. AL6: Wel 8L 71
Dollimore Cl. SG4: Cod 7F 70
Dollis Av. N3 8M 165
Dollis Brook Wlk. EN5: Barn 8L 153
Dolliscroft NW7 7L 165
Dollis M. N3 8N 165
Dollis Pk. N3 8M 165
Dollis Rd. N3 7L 165
NW7 7L 165
Dollis Valley Dr. EN5: Barn 8M 153
Dollis Valley Way EN5: Barn 8M 153
Dolmans Pl. LU6: Duns 9E 44
Dolphin Dr. LU5: Hou R 4H 45
Dolphin La. SG8: Melb 1L 9
Dolphin Sq. *HP23: Tring* *3M 101*
(off Frogmore St.)
Dolphin Way CM23: Bis S 9J 59
Dolphin Yd. AL1: St Alb 3C 166
SG12: Ware 6H 95
SG14: H'ford 9B 94
DOME, THE 9L 137
Dominic Ct. EN9: Wal A 6M 145
Doncaster Cl. SG1: Stev 1B 52
Doncaster Grn. WD19: Watf 5L 161
Doncaster Rd. N9 9F 156
Donkey La. EN1: Enf 4E 156
HP23: Tring 3K 101
(not continuous)
Donne Cl. SG8: Roys 5C 8
Donnefield Av. HA8: Edg 7M 163
Donovan Pl. N21 7L 155
Doolittle La. LU6: Tot 3M 63
Doolittle Mdws. HP3: Hem H 7B 124
Dorant Ho. AL3: St Alb 7E 108
Dorchester Av. EN11: Hod 6L 115
Dorchester Cl. LU5: Duns 8E 44
Dorchester Ct. *AL1: St Alb* *3H 127*
(off Dexter Cl.)
N14 9G 155
WD3: Crox G 7E 148
WD19: Watf *8N 149*
(off Chalk Hill)
Dorchester Ho. *SG6: L Gar* *5F 22*
(off Station Pl.)
Dordans Rd. LU4: Lut 5A 46
Dorel Cl. LU2: Lut 7H 47
Dorian Cl. HP23: Tring 2B 102
Dormans Cl. HA6: North 7F 160
Dormer Cl. EN5: Barn 7K 153
Dormers HP3: Bov 9H 123
Dormie Cl. AL3: St Alb 9D 108
Dornan Ct. LU1: Lut 3G 66
Dorriens Cft. HP4: Berk 7K 103
Dorrington Cl. LU3: Lut 8E 46
Dorrofield Cl. WD3: Crox G 7E 148
Dorset Cl. HP4: Berk 9K 103
Dorset Ct. HA6: North 8H 161
LU1: Lut *2H 67*
(off Kingsland Rd.)
Dorset Dr. HA8: Edg 6N 163
Dorset Ho. *CM23: Bis S* *1H 79*
(off Portland Rd.)
Dorset M. N3 8N 165
Douglas Av. WD24: Watf 1M 149
Douglas Cl. AL6: Wel 4L 91
EN4: Had W 2C 154
HA7: Stanm 5H 163
Douglas Cres. LU5: Hou R 6D 44
Douglas Dr. SG1: Stev 1N 51
Douglas Gdns. HP4: Berk 9K 103
Douglas Ho. *EN8: C'hunt* *1H 145*
(off Davison Dr.)
Douglas Pl. LU5: Hou R 7D 44
Douglas Rd. AL5: Harp 5A 88
LU4: Lut 7C 46
Douglas Way AL7: Welw G 9B 92
Doulton Cl. CM17: Harl 7G 119
Dove Cl. CM23: Bis S 5G 78
CM24: Stans 2N 59
NW7 7F 164
Dovecotes SG7: Ashw 9M 5
Dovecott, The SG5: Pirt 7D 20
Dove Ct. AL10: Hat 1G 129
Dovedale CM21: H Wyc 6C 98
LU2: Lut 3G 46
SG2: Stev 5A 52
SG12: Ware 4G 94
Dovedale Cl. UB9: Hare 9M 159
Dovehouse Cl. LU6: Edle 4K 63
Dovehouse Cft. CM20: Harl 4C 118
Dovehouse Hill LU2: Lut 7K 47
Dovehouse La. LU6: Kens 9F 64
SG2: Walk 8F 36
Dove La. EN6: Pot B 7B 142
Dove Pk. HA5: Hat E 7B 162
WD3: Chor 8E 146
Dover Cl. LU3: Lut 6C 46
LU7: Pits 5B 82
Dovercourt Gdns. HA7: Stanm 5M 163
Doverfield EN7: Gof O 2A 144
Dove Rd. SG1: Stev 7M 35
Dover Way WD3: Crox G 6E 148
Dowding Pl. HA7: Stanm 6H 163
Dowding Way WD25: Watf 7H 137
Dower Ct. *SG4: Hit* *5N 33*
(off London Rd.)
Dower M. HP4: Berk 1N 121
Dowley Wood AL7: Welw G 1A 112
Dowling Ct. HP3: Hem H 5N 123
Downage NW4 9J 165
(not continuous)
Downalong WD23: B Hea 1E 162
Down Edge AL3: Red 1H 107
Downedge AL3: St Alb 1C 126
Downer Dr. WD3: Sar 9K 135
Downes Ct. N21 9M 155
Downes Rd. AL4: St Alb 7J 109
Downfield Cl. SG13: Hert H 2G 114
Downfield Ct. SG12: Thun 2F 94
Downfield Rd. EN8: C'hunt 4J 145
SG13: Hert H, R Grn 2G 114
Downfields AL8: Welw G 2H 111
Down Grn. La. AL4: Wheat 7J 89
Downhall Ley SG9: Bunt 3J 39
Downhurst Av. NW7 5D 164
Downing Ct. *WD6: Bore* *3N 151*
(off Bennington Dr.)
Downings Wood WD3: Map C 5G 159
Downland Ct. N20 9B 154
Downlands LU3: Lut 2M 45
SG2: Stev 2C 52
SG7: Bald 2N 23
SG8: Roys 7C 8
Downlands Ct. LU4: Lut 7K 45
Downlands Pk. Homes LU1: Pep 8E 66
DOWNS, THE 8J 43
Downs, The AL10: Hat 2G 128
CM20: Harl 6A 118
Downs Ct. LU1: Lut 1E 66
Downsfield AL10: Hat 3H 129
DOWNSIDE 1G 65
Downside HP2: Hem H 1A 124
Downs La. AL10: Hat 2G 128
Downs Rd. EN1: Enf 6C 156
LU1: Lut 1E 66
LU5: Duns 9G 44
Downs Vw. LU4: Lut 5N 45
LU5: Duns 1G 65
Downswat Ct. SG8: Roys 7C 8
Downton Ct. LU3: Lut 9F 46
Downview LU4: Lut 7L 45
Dowry Wlk. WD17: Watf 2H 149
Doyle Pl. SG5: Stot 1C 22
Dragonfly Ct. *NW9* *8E 164*
(off Heybourne Cres.)
Dragon Rd. AL10: Hat 8D 110
(not continuous)
Drakes Cl. EN8: C'hunt 1H 145
Drakes Dr. AL1: St Alb 5J 127
HA6: North 8D 160
SG2: Stev 2A 52
Drakes Mdw. CM17: Harl 2G 118
Drake St. EN2: Enf 3B 156
Drakes Way AL10: Hat 2H 129
Draper Ct. AL3: Red 1K 107
Drapers Cott. Homes NW7 4F 164
(not continuous)
Drapers M. LU3: Lut 8E 46
Drapers Rd. EN2: Enf 4N 155
Drapers Way SG1: Stev 2J 51
Drayman's Cl. CM23: Bis S 3D 78
Drayton Av. EN6: Pot B 5L 141
DRAYTON BEAUCHAMP 1H 101
Drayton Ford WD3: R'orth 2K 159
Drayton Gdns. N21 9N 155
Drayton Hollow HP23: Hast, Tring 6K 101
Drayton Rd. LU4: Lut 6J 45
WD6: Bore 6A 152
Drew Av. NW7 6L 165
Drey, The SL9: Chal P 5B 158
Driffield Ct. *NW9* *8E 164*
(off Pageant Av.)
Drift Way SG9: S'don 9M 13
Driftway SG8: Reed 8J 15
Driftway, The HP2: Hem H 2B 124
Driftwood Av. AL2: Chis G 8B 126
Drinnan Ct. *LU2: Lut* *8F 46*
(off Clarendon Rd.)
Drive, The AL2: Lon C 7H 127
AL4: Wheat 9J 69
AL5: Harp 6B 88
AL6: Wel 7N 71
AL9: B Pk 7N 129
CM20: Harl 5A 118
CM21: Saw 5G 98
EN2: Enf 3B 156
(Farr Rd.)
EN2: Enf 8F 142
(St Nicholas Ho's.)
EN5: Barn 5L 153
EN5: N Bar 8B 154
EN6: Pot B 6M 141
EN7: C'hunt 9F 132
EN7: Gof O 1N 143
EN11: Hod 6L 115
HA6: North 9G 161
HA8: Edg 5A 164
LU7: I Ast 7E 62
N3 7N 165
SG13: New S 6K 131
SG14: H'ford 7A 94
SL9: Chal P 7B 158
WD3: R'orth 7L 147
WD7: Rad 7H 139
WD17: Watf 1F 148
Drive Ct. HA8: Edg 5A 164
DRIVER'S END 4G 70
Driver's End La. SG4: Cod 4F 70
Driveway, The EN6: Cuff 1K 143
HP1: Hem H 3L 123
Dromey Gdns. HA3: Har W 7G 162
Drop La. AL2: Bri W 3C 138
Drover La. CB11: Rick 2G 42
CM23: Ber 2G 42
Drovers La. AL4: Wheat 1L 109
Drovers Way AL3: St Alb 2C 166 (2E 126)
AL10: Hat 6H 111
CM23: Bis S 3E 78
LU6: Duns 9C 44
Drummond Dr. HA7: Stanm 7G 163
Drummond Ride HP23: Tring 1M 101
Drummonds, The LU4: Lut 7M 45
Drury Cl. LU5: Hou R 4F 44
Drury La. LU5: Hou R 4F 44
SG8: Melb 1N 9
SG12: Huns 6G 97
Drycroft AL7: Welw G 4L 111
Dryden Cres. SG2: Stev 1A 52
Dryden Rd. EN1: Enf 8C 156
HA3: Weal 8G 163
Dryfield Rd. HA8: Edg 6C 164
Drysdale Av. E4 9M 157
Drysdale Cl. HA6: North 7G 160
Dubrae Cl. AL3: St Alb 4B 126
Duchess Cl. CM23: Bis S 1D 78
Duchess Ct. *LU5: Duns* *8F 44*
(off The Mall)
Duchess Cres. HA7: Stanm 3G 162
Duchie's Piece Nature Reserve 6D 82
Duchy Rd. EN4: Had W 2C 154
DUCK END 8N 59
Ducketts La. SG10: M Had 7N 77
Ducketts Mead CM19: Royd 5E 116
Ducketts Wharf CM23: Bis S 2H 79
Ducketts Wood SG12: Thun 9H 75
Duck La. SG2: B'ton 5J 53
Duck Lees La. EN3: Pon E 6J 157
Duckling La. CM21: Saw 5G 99
Duckmore La. HP23: Tring 5K 101
Ducksbury Ind. Est. EN11: Hod 9A 116
Ducks' Grn. SG8: Ther 7D 14
Duck's Hill Rd. HA6: North 8D 160
DUCKS ISLAND 8K 153
Duck St. SG9: Fur P 5H 41
Du Cros Dr. HA7: Stanm 6L 163
Dudley Av. EN8: Wal C 5H 145
Dudley Cl. HP3: Bov 9D 122
Dudley Hill Cl. AL6: Wel 8L 71
Dudley Ho. HP3: Bov 9D 122
Dudley St. LU2: Lut 9G 46
Dudrich M. EN2: Enf 3M 155
DUDSWELL 6H 103
Dudswell Cnr. HP4: Berk 6G 103
Dudswell La. HP4: Berk 6H 103
Dudswell Mill HP4: Berk 6G 103
Dugdale Ct. SG5: Hit 1K 33
DUGDALE HILL 6L 141
Dugdale Hill La. EN6: Pot B 6L 141
Dugdales WD3: Crox G 6C 148
Dukeminster Est. LU5: Duns 8F 44
Dukes Av. HA8: Edg 6N 163
N3 8N 165
Dukes Ct. *LU5: Duns* *8F 44*
(off The Mall)
Duke's La. SG5: Hit 2N 33
Dukes Pk. CM20: Harl 3B 118
Dukes Ride CM23: Bis S 9E 58
LU2: Lut 8F 46
Duke St. EN11: Hod 7L 115
LU2: Lut 9G 47
(not continuous)
WD17: Watf 7D 166 (5L 149)
Dukes Way HP4: Berk 8L 103
Dukes Yd. WD24: Watf 2J 149
Dulwich Way WD3: Crox G 7C 148
Dumas Way WD18: Watf 6G 149
Dumbarton Av. EN8: Wal C 7H 145
Dumbletons, The WD3: Map C 4H 159
Dumfries Cl. WD19: Watf 3H 161
Dumfries Ct. *LU1: Lut* *2F 66*
(off Dumfries St.)
Dumfries St. LU1: Lut 2F 66
(not continuous)
Dunblane Cl. HA8: Edg 2B 164
Duncan Cl. AL7: Welw G 1L 111
EN5: N Bar 6B 154
Duncan Ct. AL1: St Alb 4G 127
Duncan Way WD23: Bush 4A 150
Duncombe Cl. LU3: Lut 3E 46
SG14: H'ford 7A 94
Duncombe Ct. LU5: Duns 7H 45
Duncombe Dr. LU5: Duns 7H 45

Duncombe Rd.—Elmcroft Av.

Duncombe Rd. HP4: Berk 8J 103
SG14: H'ford 8A 94
Duncots Cl. SG5: Ick 8M 21
Dundale Rd. HP23: Tring 1L 101
Dundas M. EN3: Enf L 1L 157
Dundee Way EN3: Brim 5J 157
Dunedin Ho. SG8: Roys 7C 8
(off Briary La.)
Dunfermline Ho. WD19: Watf 3L 161
Dunford Ct. HA5: Hat E 7A 162
Dunham M. AL9: Hat 8J 111
Dunhams Ct. SG6: L Gar 4H 23
Dunham's La. SG6: L Gar 4H 23
Dunkerley Ct. SG6: L Gar 4G 23
Dunkirks M. SG13: H'ford 2B 114
Dunlin SG6: L Gar 2E 22
Dunlin Rd. HP2: Hem H 6A 106
Dunmow Ct. LU3: Lut 7F 46
Dunmow Rd. CM23: Bis S 1J 79
Dunn Cl. SG1: Stev 6L 51
Dunn Mead NW9 7F 164
Dunnock Cl. WD6: Bore 6A 152
Dunny La. WD4: Chippf 6H 135
Dunraven Av. LU1: Lut 9C 46
Dunraven Dr. EN2: Enf 4M 155
Dunsby Rd. LU3: Lut 3C 46
Dunsley Pl. HP23: Tring 3N 101
Dunsmore WD19: Watf 1M 161
Dunsmore Cl. WD23: Bush 8E 150
Dunsmore Rd. LU1: Lut 2D 66
Dunsmore Way WD23: Bush 8E 150
DUNSTABLE 9E 44
Dunstable Cl. LU4: Lut 8C 46
Dunstable Ct. LU4: Lut 8B 46
Dunstable Downs 5B 64
Dunstable Downs Golf Course 3C 64
Dunstable Leisure Centre & Harpers Fitness 8E 44
Dunstable Pl. LU1: Lut 1F 66
Dunstable Rd. AL3: Flam, Red 5G 87
HP4: Dag 2N 83
LU1: Cad 3J 65
LU1: Lut 9E 46
LU4: Lut 7K 45
LU5: Chalg 1C 44
LU5: Hou R 5E 44
LU6: Duns, Tot 1N 63
LU6: Eat B, Tot 3L 63
LU6: Kens, Stud 4C 64
LU6: Whip 2N 83
Dunstable St. AL3: Mark 8M 65
Dunstall Rd. MK45: Bar C 9E 18
Dunstalls CM19: Harl 9J 117
Dunster Cl. EN5: Barn 6K 153
UB9: Hare 8L 159
Dunster Ct. WD6: Bore 5D 152
Dunster Rd. HP2: Hem H 5D 106
Dunsters Mead AL7: Welw G 2N 111
Dunston Hill HP23: Tring 2M 101
DUNTON 1F 4
Dunton La. SG18: Big 1A 4
(not continuous)
Dunwich Farm SG1: Stev 3G 50
Durants Pk. Av. EN3: Pon E 6H 157
Durants Rd. EN3: Pon E 6G 157
Durban Rd. E. WD18: Watf 8A 166 (6J 149)
Durban Rd. W. WD18: Watf 8A 166 (6J 149)
Durbar Rd. LU4: Lut 8C 46
Durham Cl. CM21: Saw 6E 98
SG12: Stan A 1M 115
Durham Ho. WD6: Bore 4A 152
(off Canterbury Rd.)
Durham Rd. LU2: Lut 9J 47
LU7: Pits 4A 82
SG1: Stev 9N 35
WD6: Bore 5C 152
Durler Gdns. LU1: Lut 3F 66
Durnsford Ct. EN3: Enf H 5J 157
(off Enstone Rd.)
Durrant Ct. HA3: Har W 9F 162
Durrants Dr. WD3: Crox G 5E 148
Durrants Hill Rd. HP3: Hem H 5N 123
Durrants Ho. WD3: Crox G 5D 148
Durrants La. HP4: Berk 1J 121
Durrants Path HP5: C'ham 9E 120
Durrants Rd. HP4: Berk 9K 103
Dury Rd. EN5: Barn 3M 153
Duxford Cl. LU3: Lut 2D 46
Duxons Turn HP2: Hem H 1D 124
Dwight Rd. WD18: Watf 9F 148
Dyers Ct. CM23: Bis S 3E 78
Dyers Rd. LU6: Eat B 1J 63
Dyes La. SG1: Stev 6F 50
SG4: Lang 5E 50
Dyke La. AL4: Wheat 9L 89
Dylan Cl. WD6: Elst 9L 151
Dylan Ct. LU5: Hou R 4F 44
Dymoke Grn. AL4: St Alb 7H 109
Dymoke M. SG1: Stev 1J 51
Dymokes Way EN11: Hod 5L 115
Dyrham La. EN5: Barn 9G 141
Dyrham Park 2G 153
Dyrham Park Country Club & Golf Course 1H 153
Dyson Ct. WD17: Watf 9E 166 (6L 149)
Dysons Cl. EN8: Wal C 6H 145

E

Eagle Cen. Way LU4: Lut 2L 45
Eagle Cl. EN3: Pon E 6G 157
LU4: Lut 5K 45
Eagle Ct. SG7: Bald 2L 23
SG13: H'ford 8F 94
Eagle Dr. NW9 9E 164
Eagle Way AL10: Hat 2G 128
Ealing Cl. WD6: Bore 3D 152
Earhart Ho. NW9 9G 164
(off East Dr.)
Earleswood Ct. HP3: Hem H 6N 123
Earlsbury Gdns. HA8: Edg 4A 164
Earls Cl. CM23: Bis S 2F 78
Earls Cnr. EN6: S Mim 6G 140
Earls Ct. LU5: Duns 8F 44
Earls Hill Gdns. SG8: Roys 7C 8
Earls La. EN6: Rid, S Mim 5E 140
Earlsmead SG6: L Gar 8F 22
Earls Meade LU2: Lut 8F 46
Earl St. WD17: Watf 7D 166 (5L 149)
Earnshaw Dr. SG5: Stot 1C 22
Easedale Cl. LU6: Duns 2F 64
Easington Rd. SG12: Dan E 1C 74
Easingwold Gdns. LU1: Lut 9B 46
EASNEYE 8N 95
EAST BARNET 8D 154
East Barnet Golf Course 5A 154
E. Barnet Rd. EN4: E Bar 6C 154
Eastbourne Av. SG1: Stev 3G 50
Eastbrook Av. N9 9G 157
Eastbrook Way HP2: Hem H 2A 124
East Burrowfield AL7: Welw G 2K 111
EASTBURY 4H 161
Eastbury Av. EN1: Enf 3D 156
HA6: North 5G 161
Eastbury Ct. AL1: St Alb 1G 126
EN5: N Bar 7B 154
(off Lyonsdown Rd.)
WD19: Watf 9L 149
Eastbury Farm Cl. HA6: North 4G 161
Eastbury Pl. HA6: North 5H 161
Eastbury Rd. HA6: North 6G 160
WD19: Watf 9K 149
Eastcheap SG6: L Gar 5F 22
East Cl. AL2: Chis G 7C 126
EN4: C'ters 6F 154
SG1: Stev 4M 51
SG4: Hit 1B 34
EAST COMMON 8D 88
East Comn. AL3: Red 2J 107
AL5: Harp 9D 88
Eastcote Dr. AL5: Harp 9E 88
Eastcott Cl. LU2: Lut 8M 47
East Cres. EN1: Enf 7D 156
East Dr. AL4: St Alb 1M 127
CM21: Saw 6G 98
HA6: North 2G 161
NW9 9G 164
WD25: Watf 9K 137
E. Duck Lees La. EN3: Pon E 6J 157
EASTEND 5H 117
East End LU5: Hou R 4F 44
East End Farm HA5: Pin 9A 162
EAST END GREEN 3J 113
East End Rd. N3 9N 165
East End Way HA5: Pin 9N 161
Eastern Av. EN8: Wal C 6K 145
LU5: Duns 9G 44
SG16: Henl 1K 21
Eastern Av. Ind. Est. LU5: Duns 9G 45
Eastern Way SG6: L Gar 3G 22
Eastfield Av. WD24: Watf 3M 149
Eastfield Cl. LU2: Lut 5L 47
Eastfield Ct. AL4: St Alb 8L 109
Eastfield Rd. EN3: Enf W 2H 157
EN8: Wal C 4K 145
SG8: Roys 7E 8
East Flint HP1: Hem H 1J 123
(not continuous)
East Ga. CM20: Harl 5N 117
Eastgate SG1: Stev 5K 51
Eastglade HA6: North 5H 161
East Grn. HP3: Hem H 7B 124
EASTHALL 7B 50
Easthall Ho. SG1: Stev 8J 35
(off North Rd.)
Eastham Cl. EN5: Barn 7L 153
East Herts Golf Course 4M 55
East Hill LU3: Lut 3D 46
Easthill Rd. LU5: Hou R 4F 44
Eastholm SG6: L Gar 3G 22
Eastholm Grn. SG6: L Gar 3G 22
EAST HYDE 9A 68
East La. AL4: Wheat 6L 89
WD5: Abb L, Bed 1H 137
WD25: Watf 2J 137
Eastlea Av. WD25: Watf 1N 149
E. Lodge La. EN2: Crew H, Enf 9J 143
Eastman Way HP2: Hem H 8C 106
SG1: Stev 8B 36
East Mead AL7: Welw G 3A 112
East Mimms HP2: Hem H 1A 124
Eastmoor Ct. AL5: Harp 9D 88
Eastmoor Pk. AL5: Harp 8D 88
East Mt. AL4: Wheat 6L 89
Eastnor HP3: Bov 1D 134
Easton Gdns. WD6: Bore 6E 152
Eastor AL7: Welw G 6N 91
East Pk. CM17: Harl 3E 118
CM21: Saw 6G 98
East Point CM19: Harl 6H 117
E. Pole Cotts. N14 6J 155
East Reach SG2: Stev 7N 51
East Ridgeway EN6: Cuff 1K 143
East Riding AL6: Tew 2C 92
East Rd. CM20: Harl 2D 118
CM23: Bis S 1K 79
EN3: Enf W 2G 157
EN4: E Bar 9F 154
HA8: Edg 8B 164
East St. HP2: Hem H 2N 123
LU2: Lill 8M 31
SG12: Ware 6H 95
East Vw. AL9: Ess 8E 112
EN5: Barn 4M 153
SG4: St Ipo 8C 34
East Wlk. CM20: Harl 5N 117
EN4: E Bar 9F 154
EASTWICK 2K 117
Eastwick Cres. WD3: R'orth 2J 159
Eastwick Hall La. CM20: East, Gil 9K 97
Eastwick Rd. CM20: East, Harl 2L 117
CM20: Gil, Harl 1A 118
Eastwick Row HP2: Hem H 3C 124
East Wing HP4: Berk 7H 103
East Wood WD25: A'ham 9C 138
Eastwood Ct. HP2: Hem H 1C 124
Easy Way LU2: Lut 2M 67
EATON BRAY 2J 63
Eaton Bray Rd. LU6: N'all 4G 62
Eaton Cl. HA7: Stanm 4J 163
Eaton Ct. HA8: Edg 4A 164
Eaton Gdns.
EN10: Brox, Worm 4K 133
Eaton Gate HA6: North 6E 160
Eatongate Cl. LU6: Eat B 4J 63
Eaton Grn. Ct. LU2: Lut 9L 47
Eaton Grn. Rd. LU2: Lut 9L 47
Eaton Grn. Rdbt. LU2: Lut 9L 47
Eaton Ho. CM23: Bis S 9K 59
(off Stortford Hall Rd.)
Eaton Pk. LU6: Eat B 2K 63
Eaton Pl. LU2: Lut 8M 47
Eaton Rd. AL1: St Alb 2J 127
EN1: Enf 6C 156
HP2: Hem H 8D 106
Eaton Valley Rd. LU2: Lut 8K 47
Eaton Way WD6: Bore 3N 151
Ebberns Rd. HP3: Hem H 5N 123
Ebeneezer Ct. SG14: H'ford 9A 94
(off North Rd.)
Ebenezer St. LU1: Lut 2F 66
Ebury App. WD3: R'orth 1N 159
Ebury Cl. HA6: North 5E 160
Ebury Rd. WD3: R'orth 1N 159
WD17: Watf 6E 166 (5L 149)
Ebury Rdbt. WD3: R'orth 1N 159
Eccleston Cl. EN4: C'ters 6E 154
Echo Hill SG8: Roys 8C 8
Eddington Cres. AL7: Welw G 3K 111
Eddiwick Av. LU5: Hou R 2G 44
Eddy St. HP4: Berk 9L 103
Edenbridge Rd. EN1: Enf 8C 156
Eden Cl. EN3: Enf L 2L 157
Edenhall Cl. HP2: Hem H 3F 124
Edens Cl. CM23: Bis S 1K 79
Edens Mt. CM21: Saw 3H 99
Edenvale EN7: Gof O 2F 144
Edgars Ct. AL7: Welw G 1L 111
Edgbaston Dr. WD7: Shen 5M 139
Edgbaston Rd. WD19: Watf 3K 161
Edgcott Cl. LU3: Lut 9D 30
Edge, The HP3: Hem H 5N 123
Edge Centre Sports Complex 2B 34
Edgecote Cl. LU1: Cad 5A 66
Edgehill Gdns. LU3: Lut 1M 45
Edgewood Dr. LU2: Lut 3L 47
Edgeworth Cl. SG2: Stev 8B 52
Edgeworth Ct. EN4: C'ters 6D 154
(off Fordham Rd.)
Edgeworth Rd. EN4: C'ters 6D 154
EDGWARE 6A 164
EDGWARE BURY 1N 163
Edgwarebury Gdns. HA8: Edg 5A 164
Edgwarebury La. HA8: Edg 1N 163
(not continuous)
WD6: Elst 9M 151
Edgware Ct. HA8: Edg 6A 164
Edgware Rd. NW9 9C 164
Edgware Station (Underground) 6B 164
Edgware Way HA8: Edg 1L 163
NW7 1L 163
WD6: Elst 1L 163
Edinburgh Av. WD3: R'orth 8K 147
Edinburgh Cres. EN8: Wal C 6J 145
Edinburgh Dr. WD5: Abb L 5J 137
Edinburgh Gdns. CM23: Bis S 2F 78
Edinburgh Ga. CM20: Harl 3N 117
Edinburgh Pl. CM20: Harl 2C 118
Edinburgh Way CM20: Harl 3N 117
Edington Rd. EN3: Enf H 4G 157
Edison Cl. AL4: St Alb 3K 127
Edison Ct. WD18: Watf 8J 149
Edison Rd. EN3: Brim 4K 157
SG2: Stev 3A 52
Edison Way SG5: Stot 1B 22
Edith Bell Ho. SL9: Chal P 6B 158
Edith Ho. EN9: Wal A 6M 145
Edkins Cl. LU2: Lut 4G 46
EDLESBOROUGH 4J 63
Edlyn Cl. HP4: Berk 9K 103
Edmond Beaufort Dr. AL3: St Alb 9E 108
Edmonds Dr. SG2: Stev 5C 52
Edmund M. WD4: Kin L 2C 136
Edmunds Rd. SG14: H'ford 8L 93
Edmund's Twr. CM19: Harl 6M 117
Edrick Rd. HA8: Edg 6C 164
Edrick Wlk. HA8: Edg 6C 164
Edridge Cl. WD23: Bush 7D 150
Edson Cl. WD25: Watf 6H 137
Edulf Rd. WD6: Bore 3B 152
Edward Amey Cl. WD25: Watf 9L 137
Edward Cl. AL1: St Alb 3G 127
N9 9D 156
WD5: Abb L 5H 137
Edward Cotts. SG11: Gt Mun 6G 54
Edward Ct. HP3: Hem H 6N 123
Edward Gro. EN4: E Bar 7C 154
Edward Rd. EN4: E Bar 7C 154
Edwards Ct. EN8: C'hunt 3J 145
EDWARDS GREEN 7B 114
Edward St. LU2: Lut 8H 47
LU6: Duns 8D 44
Edwick Ct. EN8: C'hunt 2H 145
Edwin Rd. HA8: Edg 6D 164
Edwin Ware Ct. HA5: Pin 9L 161
EDWORTH 7C 4
Edworth Rd. SG18: L'ford 8A 4
Edwyn Cl. EN5: Barn 8J 153
Egdon Dr. LU2: Lut 3F 46
Egerton Rd. HP4: Berk 8L 103
Egg Farm La. WD4: Kin L 3D 136
WD5: Abb L 3D 136
Egglesfield Cl. HP4: Berk 8J 103
Eggleton Dr. HP23: Tring 1M 101
Eider Ct. CM23: Bis S 2H 79
Eight Acres HP23: Tring 2M 101
(not continuous)
Eighth Av. LU3: Lut 2N 45
Eisenberg Cl. SG7: Bald 2A 24
Elaine Gdns. LU1: Wood 7C 66
Elbourn Way SG8: Bass 1M 7
Elbow La. SG2: Stev 9A 52
SG13: Hert H, Hod, H'ford 8F 114
Elbrook La. SG7: Ashw 8M 5
Eldefield SG6: L Gar 4C 22
Elderbek Cl. EN7: C'hunt 1E 144
Elderberry Cl. AL2: Bri W 4A 138
LU2: Lut 5K 47
Elderberry Dr. SG4: St Ipo 6A 34
Elderberry Way WD25: Watf 8K 137
Elder Ct. SG13: H'ford 8C 94
WD23: B Hea 2F 162
Elderfield AL7: Welw G 9A 92
CM17: Harl 2F 118
Elderflower Ho. SG5: Hit 3N 33
(off Whinbush Rd.)
Elder Rd. SG12: Ware 4K 95
Elder Way SG1: Stev 6K 51
Eldon Av. WD6: Bore 4A 152
Eldon Ho. NW9 9G 164
(off East Dr.)
Eldon Rd. EN11: Hod 9A 116
LU4: Lut 7M 45
Eleanor Av. AL3: St Alb 9E 108
Eleanor Cres. NW7 5K 165
Eleanor Cross Rd. EN8: Wal C 7J 145
Eleanore Pl. AL3: St Alb 1E 126
Eleanor Gdns. EN5: Barn 7K 153
Eleanor Ho. SL9: Chal P 5B 158
(off Micholls Av.)
Eleanor Rd. EN8: Wal C 6J 145
SG14: H'ford 8A 94
SL9: Chal P 8A 158
Eleanor's Cl. SG12: Thun 9H 75
Eleanors Ct. LU6: Duns 9E 44
Eleanors Cross LU6: Duns 9E 44
Eleanor Way EN8: Wal C 7K 145
Electric Av. EN3: Enf L 9K 145
Eley Pl. WD19: Watf 9M 149
Elfrida Rd. WD18: Watf 7L 149
Elgar Cl. WD6: Elst 9L 151
Elgar Path LU2: Lut 8G 46
Elgin Av. HA3: Ken 9J 163
Elgin Dr. HA6: North 7G 160
Elgin Ho. SG4: Hit 4A 34
Elgin Rd. EN8: C'hunt 3G 145
EN10: Worm 6K 133
Elgood Av. HA6: North 6H 161
Eliot Rd. SG2: Stev 3B 52
SG8: Roys 5D 8
Eliot Way SG5: Stot 9C 10
Elizabeth Av. EN2: Enf 5N 155
HP6: L Chal 3A 146
Elizabeth Cl. AL7: Welw G 9B 92
EN5: Barn 5K 153
SG14: H'ford 9L 93
Elizabeth Ct. AL4: St Alb 8L 109
(not continuous)
LU1: Lut 2F 66
(off Chapel St.)
LU5: Duns 9F 44
(off Englands La.)
WD17: Watf 2H 149
Elizabeth Dr. HP23: Tring 9N 81
Elizabeth Gdns. HA7: Stanm 6K 163
Elizabeth Ho. AL7: Welw G 9B 92
HP2: Hem H 1N 123
(off Chapel St.)
WD24: Watf 4L 149
Elizabeth Ride N9 9F 156
Elizabeth Rd. CM23: Bis S 3G 79
Elizabeth St. LU1: Lut 2F 66
Elizabeth Way CM19: Harl 7J 117
CM20: Harl 7J 117
Ella Ct. LU2: Lut 8H 47
Elland Cl. EN5: N Bar 7C 154
Ellenborough Cl. CM23: Bis S 3F 78
ELLENBROOK 9D 110
Ellenbrook Cl. WD24: Watf 3L 149
Ellenbrook Cres. AL10: Hat 9D 110
Ellenbrook La. AL10: Hat 9D 110
Ellen Cl. HP2: Hem H 1B 124
Ellenhall Cl. LU3: Lut 8E 46
Ellen M. HP2: Hem H 1B 124
Ellerdine Cl. LU3: Lut 5D 46
Ellerton Lodge N3 9N 165
Ellesborough Cl. WD19: Watf 5L 161
Ellesfield AL6: Wel 2H 91
Ellesmere Av. NW7 3D 164
Ellesmere Cl. LU6: Tot 2N 63
Ellesmere Gro. EN5: Barn 7M 153
Ellesmere Rd. HP4: Berk 1A 122
Ellice SG6: L Gar 7H 23
Elliman Ct. HP23: Tring 3L 101
Ellingham Cl. HP2: Hem H 9C 106
Ellingham Rd.
HP2: Hem H 1B 124
Elliot Rd. WD17: Watf 2J 149
Elliott Cl. AL7: Welw G 3K 111
Elliott Ct. CM23: Bis S 9J 59
Elliott Rd. HA7: Stanm 6H 163
Ellis Av. SG1: Stev 1L 51
SL9: Chal P 8C 158
Ellis Cl. EN11: Hod 4K 115
HA8: Edg 6E 164
Ellis Flds. AL3: St Alb 8F 108
Ellis Ho. AL1: St Alb 4G 166 (3G 126)
Elliswick Rd. AL5: Harp 5C 88
Ellwood Ct. WD25: Watf 7K 137
Ellwood Gdns. WD25: Watf 7L 137
Ellwood Ho. SL9: Chal P 8B 158
Ellwood Ri. HP8: Chal G 2A 158
Elm Av. LU1: Cad 5A 66
WD19: Watf 9N 149
Elmbank N14 9K 155
Elmbank Av. EN5: Barn 6J 153
Elmbridge CM17: Harl 3H 119
Elmbrook Cl. CM23: Bis S 4G 78
Elmbrook Dr. CM23: Bis S 5G 78
Elmcote HA5: Pin 9M 161
Elmcote Way WD3: Crox G 8B 148
Elm Ct. EN4: E Bar 9D 154
HP4: Berk 1M 121
WD17: Watf 6B 166 (5K 149)
Elmcroft Av. N9 8F 156

Games Rd.—Goldfield Rd.

Games Rd. EN4: C'ters 5D **154**
Gammon Cl. HP3: Hem H 3C **124**
Gammons Farm Cl. WD24: Watf 9H **137**
Gammons La. EN7: C'hunt 7C **132**
WD24: Watf 9G **137**
(not continuous)
Gamnel HP23: Tring 8M **81**
Gamnel Ter. HP23: Tring 8N **81**
Ganders Ash WD25: Watf 6J **137**
Gandhi Ct. WD24: Watf 4M **149**
Gangies Hill CM21: H Wyc 4C **98**
GANNOCK GREEN 9N **13**
Ganton Wlk. WD19: Watf 4M **161**
GANWICK 9N **141**
GANWICK CORNER 8N **141**
Ganymede Pl. HP2: Hem H 8B **106**
Gaping La. SG5: Hit 3L **33**
Garden Av. AL10: Hat 4G **128**
Garden Bus. Cen.
AL7: Welw G 8L **91**
Garden City HA8: Edg 6A **164**
Garden Cl. AL1: St Alb 1J **127**
AL5: Harp 1B **108**
EN5: Ark 6J **153**
HP22: Halt 6B **100**
SG3: Dat 6N **71**
SG8: Roys 6E **8**
WD17: Watf 4H **149**
Garden Cotts. AL2: Frog 9E **126**
Garden Ct. AL4: Wheat 6L **89**
AL7: Welw G 8L **91**
HA7: Stanm 5K **163**
LU3: Lut 5C **46**
N12 5N **165**
Garden End SG8: Melb 2M **9**
Gardeners Cott. SG13: Lit B 1G **131**
Garden Fld. SG2: A'ton 7D **52**
Garden Fld. La. HP4: Berk 3C **122**
Garden Flds. LU2: C'hoe 6N **47**
SG4: Kimp 7L **69**
Garden Ho. SG13: H'ford 1A **114**
Garden Houses, The CM21: Saw 4K **99**
Gardenia Av. LU3: Lut 5B **46**
Gardenia Av. Pas. LU3: Lut 5C **46**
Gardenia Rd. EN1: Enf 8C **156**
Garden La. SG8: Roys 8D **8**
Garden Pl. SG8: Bass 1M **7**
Garden Reach HP8: Chal G 5A **146**
Garden Rd. LU6: Duns 1F **64**
SG3: Dat 6A **72**
SG9: Bunt 2J **39**
WD5: Abb L 4G **137**
Garden Row SG5: Hit 2N **33**
Gardens, The AL9: B Pk 9L **129**
SG5: Stot 6E **10**
SG6: L Gar 7F **22**
SG7: Bald 3L **23**
WD17: Watf 4H **149**
Gardens End LU5: Hou R 4F **44**
Gardens of the Rose 8A **126**
Garden Ter. SG12: C End 3C **94**
Garden Ter. Rd. CM17: Harl 2E **118**
Garden Wlk. SG1: Stev 4L **51**
SG8: Roys 6E **8**
Gardiner Cl. EN3: Pon E 8H **157**
Gardiners, The CM17: Harl 7D **118**
Gardiners La. SG7: Ashw 9M **5**
Gardner Ct. LU1: Lut 4G **66**
WD25: Watf 8L **137**
Gardners Cl. LU6: Duns 1B **64**
GARDNERS END 7N **37**
Gareth Ct. *WD6: Bore 2N 151*
(off Aycliffe Rd.)
Garfield *EN2: Enf 7B 156*
(off London Rd.)
Garfield Ct. LU2: Lut 6M **47**
Garfield Rd. EN3: Pon E 6G **157**
Garfield St. WD24: Watf 2K **149**
Garland Cl. EN8: C'hunt 4J **145**
HP2: Hem H 1N **123**
Garland Ct. AL1: St Alb 3F **166**
Garland Rd. HA7: Stanm 8M **163**
SG12: Ware 6J **95**
Garland Way HP22: Ast C 1D **100**
Garnault Rd. EN1: Enf 2D **156**
Garner Dr. EN10: Turn 8J **133**
Garners Cl. SL9: Chal P 6C **158**
Garners End SL9: Chal P 6B **158**
Garners Rd. SL9: Chal P 6B **158**
Garnett Cl. WD24: Watf 1M **149**
Garnett Dr. AL2: Bri W 2A **138**
Garrard Way AL4: Wheat 7L **89**
Garratt Rd. HA8: Edg 7A **164**
Garratts Cl. SG14: H'ford 9A **94**
Garratts Rd. WD23: Bush 9D **150**
Garrett Cl. LU6: Duns 3G **65**
Garretts Mead LU2: Lut 6K **47**
Garrick Ct. HA8: Edg 4N **163**
Garrick Dr. NW4 9J **165**
Garrick Pk. NW4 9K **165**
Garrison Ct. SG4: Hit 3N **33**
Garrowsfield EN5: Barn 8M **153**
Garsmouth Way WD25: Watf 9M **137**
GARSTON 8L **137**
Garston Cres. WD25: Watf 7L **137**
Garston Dr. WD25: Watf 7L **137**
Garston La. WD25: Watf 7M **137**
Garston Pk. Pde. WD25: Watf 7M **137**
Garston Station (Rail) 8M **137**
Garter Ct. *LU2: Lut 8F 46*
(off Knights Fld.)
Garth, The WD5: Abb L 6F **136**
Garthland Dr. EN5: Barn 7H **153**
Garth Rd. SG6: L Gar 8E **22**
Gartlet Rd. WD17: Watf 6D **166** (5L **149**)
Gartons Cl. EN3: Pon E 6G **157**
Gascoyne Cl. EN6: S Mim 5G **140**
Gascoyne Way SG13: H'ford 9A **94**
SG14: H'ford 9A **94**
Gaskarth Rd. HA8: Edg 8C **164**
Gaskell Pl. SG5: Stot 1C **22**
Gas La. SG8: Bark 9N **15**
GASTON GREEN 9K **79**
Gaston Hill CM22: L Hal 9K **79**
Gatcombe Ct. *AL1: St Alb 3H 127*
(off Dexter Cl.)
Gatcombe Way EN4: C'ters 5E **154**
Gate Cl. WD6: Bore 3C **152**
Gate Cotts. WD3: Chor 6G **146**
Gatecroft HP3: Hem H 4B **124**
(not continuous)
Gate End HA6: North 7J **161**
Gatehill Gdns. LU3: Lut 9D **30**
Gatehill Rd. HA6: North 7H **161**
Gatehouse M. SG9: Bunt 3J **39**
Gate Ho. Pl. WD18: Watf 7A **166** (5J **149**)
Gatekeeper Way SG14: Watt S 5J **73**
Gater Dr. EN2: Enf 3B **156**
Gates NW9 9F **164**
Gatesbury Way SG11: Puck 6A **56**
Gatesdene Cl. HP4: Lit G 7N **83**
Gateshead Rd. WD6: Bore 3N **151**
Gates Orchard HP22: Ast C 1C **100**
Gates Way SG1: Stev 3J **51**
Gateway, The WD18: Watf 7G **148**
Gateway 1000 SG1: Stev 7K **51**
Gateway Cl. HA6: North 6E **160**
Gateway Ct. *AL2: Bri W 3N 137*
(off The Uplands)
Gateways, The EN7: Gof O 1B **144**
GATLEY END 7E **6**
Gatley End Farm SG8: S Mor 6H **6**
Gatting Cl. HA8: Edg 7C **164**
Gatward Cl. N21 8N **155**
Gatwick Cl. CM23: Bis S 8K **59**
Gauldie Way SG11: Stand 7A **56**
Gaumont App. WD17: Watf 6C **166** (5K **149**)
Gauntlet *NW9 9F 164*
(off Five Acre)
Gaunts Way SG6: L Gar 1F **22**
Gavel Cen. AL3: St Alb 7G **108**
Gaveston Dr. HP4: Berk 8M **103**
Gawlers CM23: Ber 2C **42**
Gaydon La. NW9 8E **164**
Gayland Av. LU2: Lut 9K **47**
Gaylor Way SG1: Stev 1K **51**
Gayton Cl. LU3: Lut 5D **46**
Gaywood Av. EN8: C'hunt 3H **145**
Gazelda Ind. Est. WD17: Watf 7L **149**
Gean Wlk. AL10: Hat 3G **129**
Geddes Rd. WD23: Bush 6D **150**
Geddings Rd. EN11: Hod 8M **115**
Geddington Ct. EN8: Wal C 7L **145**
Geescroft Wlk. AL5: Harp 9B **88**
Gelding Cl. LU4: Lut 4J **45**
General's Walk, The EN3: Enf W 1J **157**
Genotin Rd. EN1: Enf 5B **156**
Genotin Ter. EN1: Enf 5B **156**
Gentian Gdns. SG5: Stot 7E **10**
Gentle Ct. SG7: Bald 3L **23**
Gentlemans Row EN2: Enf 5A **156**
Gentlemens Fld. SG12: Ware 4F **94**
George V Av. HA5: Pin 9A **162**
George V Cl. WD18: Watf 6H **149**
George V Way WD3: Sar 9L **135**
George Fld. Ho. *WD3: R'orth 9N 147*
(off Northway)
George Gange Way HA3: Weal 9F **162**
George Grn. *CM22: L Hal 7K 79*
(off Lower Rd.)
George Grn. Bungs. CM22: L Hal 8K **79**
George Grn. Vs. CM22: L Hal 8K **79**
George La. SG8: Roys 7D **8**
George Lighton Ct. SG2: Stev 4A **52**
George Lovell Dr. EN3: Enf L 1L **157**
George M. EN2: Enf 5B **156**
Georges Mead WD6: Elst 8M **151**
George St. AL3: Mark 2A **86**
AL3: St Alb 3C **166** (2E **126**)
HP2: Hem H 1N **123**
HP4: Berk 1A **122**
LU1: Lut 1G **66**
LU6: Duns 8E **44**
SG14: H'ford 9A **94**
WD18: Watf 9D **166** (6L **149**)
George St. West LU1: Lut 1G **66**
Georges Wood Rd. AL9: B Pk 8N **129**
George Wlk. *SG12: Ware 6H 95*
(off High St.)
Georgewood Rd. HP3: Hem H 7B **124**
Georgian Cl. HA7: Stanm 7H **163**
Georgian Ct. EN5: N Bar 6B **154**
N3 8M **165**
Georgina Ct. SG15: Arl 9A **10**
Gerard Av. CM23: Bis S 4G **78**
Gernon Rd. SG6: L Gar 6F **22**
Gernon Wlk. SG6: L Gar 6F **22**
(not continuous)
Gerrards Cl. N14 7H **155**
Gerrards Cross Golf Course 9C **158**
Gertrude Peake Pl. *AL3: Red 1K 107*
(off High St.)
Gervase Rd. HA8: Edg 8C **164**
Gews Cnr. EN8: C'hunt 2H **145**
Ghyll Gdns. *HP4: Berk 7H 103*
(off Cornfield Cres.)
Giant Tree Hill WD23: B Hea 1E **162**
Gibberd Gallery *6N 117*
(within Harlow Civic Cen.)
Gibberd Garden, The 9G **99**
Gibbons Cl. AL4: San 5K **109**
WD6: Bore 3M **151**
Gibbons Way SG3: Kneb 3M **71**
Gibbs Cl. EN8: C'hunt 2H **145**
Gibbs Couch WD19: Watf 3M **161**
Gibbs Fld. CM23: Bis S 3F **78**
Gibbs Grn. HA8: Edg 4C **164**
Gibraltar Lodge AL5: Harp 4E **88**
Gibson Cl. N21 8M **155**
SG4: Hit 3B **34**
Gibson Ct. CM18: Harl 9N **117**
Gidian Ct. AL2: Par S 9E **126**
Gifford's La. SG11: Hau 6D **54**
Gilbert Burnet Ho. HP3: Hem H 4B **124**
Gilbert Ct. AL5: Harp 3C **88**
Gilbert Gro. HA8: Edg 8D **164**
Gilbert Rd. UB9: Hare 9N **159**
Gilbert St. EN3: Enf W 1G **157**
Gilbert Way HP4: Berk 1L **121**
Gilbey Av. CM23: Bis S 2K **79**
Gilbey Cres. CM24: Stans 1N **59**
Gilda Av. EN3: Pon E 7J **157**
Gilda Ct. NW7 8G **164**
Gildea Cl. HA5: Hat E 7B **162**
Gilded Acre LU6: Duns 3F **64**
Gilden Cl. CM17: Harl 2G **118**
Gilden Way CM17: Harl 3E **118**
Gilder Cl. LU3: Lut 1C **46**
Gilderdale LU4: Lut 3L **45**
Gilders CM21: Saw 5F **98**
Giles Cl. AL4: San 5K **109**
Giles Rd. HP22: Halt 8C **100**
Gilhams Ct. HP4: Berk 9L **103**
Gillam St. LU2: Lut 9G **47**
Gillan Grn. WD23: B Hea 2D **162**
Gillan Way *LU5: Hou R 4H 45*
(off Houghton Pk. Rd.)
Gill Cl. WD18: Watf 8E **148**
Gill Edge CM24: Stans 4N **59**
Gillian Av. AL1: St Alb 6D **126**
Gillian Ho. HA3: Har W 6F **162**
Gilliats Grn. WD3: Chor 6G **146**
Gilliflower Ho. EN11: Hod 9L **115**
Gillings Ct. *EN5: Barn 6L 153*
(off Wood St.)
Gillison Cl. SG6: L Gar 6H **23**
Gills Hill AL3: Mark 6M **85**
WD7: Rad 8G **139**
Gills Hill La. WD7: Rad 9G **138**
Gills Hollow WD7: Rad 9G **139**
Gillsted Ct. AL3: St Alb 7E **108**
Gillum Cl. EN4: E Bar 9E **154**
Gilmour Cl. EN2: Enf, Wal C 8E **144**
Gilmour Ho. NW9 9G **164**
Gilpin Cl. LU5: Hou R 4G **45**
Gilpin Grn. AL5: Harp 6D **88**
Gilpin Rd. SG12: Ware 7J **95**
Gilpin's Gallop SG12: Stan A 1M **115**
Gilpin's Ride HP4: Berk 9B **104**
Gilpin St. LU6: Duns 7D **44**
Gilroy Rd. HP2: Hem H 1N **123**
GILSTON 1N **117**
Gilston La. CM20: Gil 8M **97**
Gilston Pk. CM20: Gil 8M **97**
Gilwell Cl. E4 6M **157**
Gilwell La. E4 6N **157**
GILWELL PARK 6N **157**
Gilwell Pk. E4 5N **157**
Gingers Cl. HP22: Ast C 1D **100**
Ginns Rd. SG9: Fur P, S Pel 5N **41**
Gippeswyck Cl. HA5: Pin 8M **161**
Gipsy La. CM23: Bis S, Farn, Stans 5K **59**
CM24: Stans 5K **59**
LU1: Lut 2J **67**
SG3: Kneb 3L **71**
Girdle Rd. SG4: Hit 9A **22**
Girons Cl. SG4: Hit 4B **34**
Girton Ct. EN8: C'hunt 3J **145**
Girton Way WD3: Crox G 7E **148**
Gisburne Way WD24: Watf 1J **149**
Gladbeck Way EN2: Enf 6N **155**
Gladden Ct. CM18: Harl 9A **118**
Gladding Rd. EN7: C'hunt 7N **131**
Glade, The AL8: Welw G 7J **91**
EN2: Enf 5M **155**
N21 8L **155**
SG6: L Gar 8F **22**
SG7: Bald 4L **23**
Glades, The HP1: Hem H 1H **123**
Gladeside AL4: St Alb 8L **109**
N21 8L **155**
Gladesmere Ct. WD24: Watf 9K **137**
Gladsmuir Rd. EN5: Barn 4L **153**
Gladstone Av. LU1: Lut 1E **66**
Gladstone Ct. SG2: Stev 9N **51**
Gladstone Dr. SG5: Stot 1D **22**
Gladstone Pl. EN5: Barn 6K **153**
Gladstone Rd. EN11: Hod 7M **115**
SG12: Dan E 9D **54**
SG12: Ware 5G **95**
WD17: Watf 7E **166** (5L **149**)
Gladwin Way CM20: Harl 4N **117**
Glaisdale LU4: Lut 4M **45**
Glamis Cl. EN7: C'hunt 2E **144**
HP2: Hem H 5D **106**
Glamis Pl. HP2: Hem H 1A **124**
Glan Avon M. CM17: Harl 7E **118**
Glanfield HP2: Hem H 8A **106**
Glanleam Rd. HA7: Stanm 4L **163**
Glanville Cres. SG1: Stev 9B **36**
Glanville M. HA7: Stanm 5H **163**
Glassmill Ho. *HP4: Berk 1A 122*
(off Robertson Rd.)
Gleave Cl. AL1: St Alb 1J **127**
Glebe, The CM5: M Lav 9M **119**
CM20: Harl 4A **118**
SG2: Stev 3B **52**
SG4: St Ipo 8C **34**
WD4: Kin L 2C **136**
WD25: Watf 6M **137**
Glebe Av. EN2: Enf 5N **155**
SG15: Arl 5A **10**
Glebe Cl. AL9: Ess 8E **112**
HP3: Hem H 5A **124**
LU7: Pits 2B **82**
SG14: H'ford 7B **94**
SG14: Watt S 5J **73**
SL9: Chal P 7A **158**
Glebe Cotts. AL9: Ess 8E **112**
Glebe Ct. AL10: Hat 8J **111**
CM23: Bis S 9K **59**
EN8: C'hunt 2H **145**
HA7: Stanm 5K **163**
SG14: Watt S 5K **73**
WD25: Watf 6M **137**
Glebe Ho. *SL9: Chal P 7A 158*
(off Windmill Rd.)
Glebe Ho's. AL9: Ess 8E **112**
Glebeland AL10: Hat 9J **111**
Glebelands CM20: Harl 3B **118**
Glebe La. EN5: Ark 7G **152**
Glebe Meadows Nature Reserve 5A **10**
Glebe Rd. AL6: Wel 2H **91**
HA7: Stanm 5K **163**
SG6: L Gar 4G **23**
SG14: H'ford 7B **94**
SL9: Chal P 8A **158**
Glebe Rd. Ind. Est. SG6: L Gar 4G **22**
Glebe Vw. SG2: Walk 8H **37**
(not continuous)
Gleed Av. WD23: B Hea 2E **162**
Glemsford Cl. LU4: Lut 3L **45**
Glemsford Dr. AL5: Harp 5E **88**
Glen, The EN2: Enf 6N **155**
HA6: North 7F **160**
HP2: Hem H 6B **106**
LU1: Cad 5A **66**
Glenbower Ct. AL4: St Alb 2L **127**
Glenbrook Nth. EN2: Enf 6L **155**
Glenbrook Sth. EN2: Enf 6L **155**
Glen Chess WD3: Loud 6M **147**
Glencoe Rd. WD23: Bush 8B **150**
Glencorse Grn. WD19: Watf 4M **161**
Glendale HP1: Hem H 2L **123**
Glendale Av. HA8: Edg 4N **163**
Glendale Wlk. EN8: C'hunt 3J **145**
Glendean Ct. EN3: Enf L 9J **145**
Glendevon Cl. HA8: Edg 3B **164**
Glendor Gdns. NW7 4D **164**
Gleneagles HA7: Stanm 7J **163**
Gleneagles Cl. WD19: Watf 4M **161**
Gleneagles Dr. LU2: Lut 3G **47**
Glenester Cl. EN11: Hod 5L **115**
(not continuous)
GLEN FABA 7B **116**
Glen Faba Rd. CM19: Royd 8B **116**
Glenferrie Rd. AL1: St Alb 2H **127**
Glenfield Ct. SG14: H'ford 8L **93**
Glenfield Rd. LU3: Lut 3E **46**
Glengall Pl. AL1: St Alb 5F **126**
Glengall Rd. HA8: Edg 3B **164**
Glenhaven Av. WD6: Bore 5A **152**
Glenhill Cl. N3 9N **165**
Glenloch Rd. EN3: Enf H 4G **157**
Glen Luce EN8: C'hunt 4H **145**
Glenlyn Av. AL1: St Alb 3J **127**
Glenmere Av. NW7 7G **164**
Glenmire Ter. SG12: Stan A 2A **116**
Glenmore Gdns. WD5: Abb L 5J **137**
Glenshee Cl. HA6: North 6E **160**
Glenthorpe Gdns. HA7: Stanm 3G **162**
Glenview Gdns. HP1: Hem H 2L **123**
Glenview Rd. HP1: Hem H 2L **123**
Glenville Av. EN2: Enf 2A **156**
Glen Way WD17: Watf 2G **149**
Glenwood AL7: Welw G 1C **112**
EN10: Brox 1K **133**
Glenwood Cl. SG2: Stev 7B **52**
Glenwood Rd. NW7 3E **164**
Glevum Cl. AL3: St Alb 4A **126**
Globe Cl. AL5: Harp 6C **88**
Globe Ct. EN10: Worm 5K **133**
SG14: H'ford 7A **94**
Globe Cres. CM23: Farn 3F **58**
Globe Ho. WD3: Chor 6F **146**
Glossop Way SG15: Arl 5B **10**
Gloucester Av. EN8: Wal C 6J **145**
Gloucester Cl. SG1: Stev 8L **35**
Gloucester Ct. AL10: Hat 8F **110**
WD3: Crox G 5D **148**
WD18: Watf 6H **149**
Gloucester Gdns. EN4: C'ters 6F **154**
Gloucester Gro. HA8: Edg 8D **164**
Gloucester Ho. WD6: Bore 4A **152**
Gloucester Rd. EN2: Enf 2A **156**
EN5: N Bar 7A **154**
LU1: Lut 2H **67**
Gloucester Ter. *LU1: Lut 9F 46*
(off Liverpool Rd.)
Glover Centre, The SG5: Hit 1N **33**
Glover Cl. EN7: C'hunt 9D **132**
Glovers Cl. SG13: H'ford 2A **114**
Glovers Ct. SG5: Hit 1N **33**
Glovers La. HP23: Tring 3M **101**
Glyn Av. EN4: E Bar 6C **154**
Glyn Ct. HA7: Stanm 6J **163**
Glynde, The SG2: Stev 9A **52**
Glyn Rd. EN3: Pon E 6G **156**
Glynswood SL9: Chal P 7C **158**
Glynswood Pl. HA6: North 7D **160**
Go Ape
Trent Park 5F **154**
Wendover Woods 8E **100**
Goat La. EN1: Enf 2D **156**
Gobions La. SG14: Bram, Stap 9J **73**
Gobions Way EN6: Pot B 1A **142**
Goblins Grn. AL7: Welw G 1K **111**
Go Bowling 8E **44**
Goddard Ct. HA3: Ken 9H **163**
Goddard Dr. WD23: Bush 7D **150**
Goddard End SG2: Stev 8B **52**
Goddards Cl. SG13: Lit B 1H **131**
Godfrey Cl. SG2: Stev 6A **52**
Godfreys Cl. LU1: Lut 2D **66**
Godfreys Ct. LU1: Lut 2D **66**
Godfries Cl. AL6: Tew 4D **92**
Godsafe CM17: Harl 3G **119**
Godwin Cl. E4 2N **157**
Goffs Cres. EN7: Gof O 2A **144**
Goff's La. EN7: Gof O 2A **144**
GOFF'S OAK 1A **144**
Goffs Oak Av. EN7: Gof O 1N **143**
Goff's Sports & Arts Cen. 2E **144**
Golda Cl. EN5: Barn 8K **153**
Golda Ct. N3 9M **165**
Goldbeaters Gro. HA8: Edg 6E **164**
Gold Cl. EN10: Brox 2J **133**
Goldcrest Cl. LU4: Lut 4K **45**
Goldcrest Way WD23: Bush 1D **162**
Goldcroft HP3: Hem H 4C **124**
Golden Ct. EN4: E Bar 6D **154**
Golden Dell AL7: Welw G 4M **111**
Goldens Way SG14: H'ford 6M **93**
Golden Willows Pk. Homes SG5: Ick 5M **21**
Golders Cl. HA8: Edg 5B **164**
Goldfield Rd. HP23: Tring 3L **101**

H

Hale La.—Harvey Ho.

Hale La. HA8: Edg 5B 164
NW7 5D 164
Hale Rd. HP22: Wen 9B 100
SG13: H'ford 1B 114
Hales Ct. WD25: Watf 9L 137
Hales Mdw. AL5: Harp 5B 88
Hales Pk. HP2: Hem H 1E 124
Hales Pk. Cl. HP2: Hem H 1E 124
Haleswood Rd. HP2: Hem H 1D 124
Half Acre HA7: Stanm 5K 163
SG5: Hit 4L 33
SG8: Roys 6E 8
Halfacre Hill SL9: Chal P 8C 158
Half Acre La. SG9: Gt Hor 1D 40
Half Acres CM23: Bis S 9H 59
Halfhide La. EN8: C'hunt, Turn 9H 133
EN10: C'hunt 8J 133
Half Moon La. AL3: Mark, Pep 1B 86
LU1: Pep 8E 66
LU5: Duns 1G 64
Half Moon Mdw. HP2: Hem H 6E 106
Half Moon M. AL1: St Alb 3D 166 (2E 126)
Half Moon Pl. LU6: Duns 1G 64
Halford Cl. HA8: Edg 9B 164
Halford Ct. AL10: Hat 8E 110
Halfway Av. LU4: Lut 8N 45
Halifax NW9 9F 164
Halifax Cl. AL2: Bri W 4A 138
WD25: Watf 7H 137
Halifax Rd. EN2: Enf 4A 156
WD3: Hero 9F 146
Halifax Way AL7: Welw G 9D 92
Hallam Cl. WD24: Watf 4L 149
Hallam Gdns. HA5: Hat E 7N 161
Halland Way HA6: North 6F 160
Hall Barns AL7: Welw G 9A 92
Hall Barns, The SG9: Fur P 6J 41
Hall Cl. WD3: R'orth 1K 159
Hall Dr. UB9: Hare 8M 159
Halley Rd. EN9: Wal A 9M 145
Halleys Ridge SG14: H'ford 1M 113
Halley's Way LU5: Hou R 5G 44
Hall Farm Cl. HA7: Stanm 4J 163
Hallfield CB11: Que 1N 43
Hall Gdns. AL4: Col H 5D 128
Hall Grn. CM22: L Hal 2M 99
HALL GROVE 2A 112
Hall Gro. AL7: Welw G 2A 112
Hall Heath Cl. AL1: St Alb 9J 109
Halliday Cl. WD7: Shen 5M 139
Hallingbury Cl. CM22: L Hal 7K 79
HALLINGBURY PLACE 6N 79
Hallingbury Rd. CM21: Saw 3J 99
CM22: Bis S 2J 79
CM23: Bis S 2J 79
Halling Hill CM20: Harl 4B 118
Hall La. NW4 8G 165
SG3: Dat 6N 71
SG4: Kimp 8K 69
SG8: Gt Chi 2H 17
SG9: Gt Hor 1D 40
Hall Mead SG6: L Gar 5C 22
Hallmores EN10: Brox 1L 133
Hallowell Rd. HA6: North 7G 161
Hallowes Cres. WD19: Watf 3J 161
Hall Pk. HP4: Berk 2B 122
Hall Park Ga. HP4: Berk 3B 122
Hall Park Hill HP4: Berk 3B 122
Hall Pl. AL1: St Alb 1E 166
Hall Pl. Cl. AL1: St Alb 1E 166 (1F 126)
Hall Pl. Gdns. AL1: St Alb 1E 166 (1F 126)
Hall Rd. HP2: Hem H 9D 106
Halls Cl. AL6: Wel 3J 91
HALLS GREEN
CM19 9F 116
SG4 4D 36
Hallsgreen La. SG4: W'ton 5C 36
Hallside SG18: Dunt 1E 4
Hallside Rd. EN1: Enf 2D 156
Hall Walk, The HP4: Berk 1A 122
(off Lit. Bridge Rd.)
Hallwicks Rd. LU2: Lut 6K 47
Hallworth Dr. SG5: Stot 6E 10
Hallworth Ho. SG5: Stot 6E 10
(off Hallworth Dr.)
Halsbury Cl. HA7: Stanm 4J 163
Halsbury Ct. HA7: Stanm 5J 163
Halsey Dr. HP1: Hem H 9J 105
SG4: Hit 3B 34
Halsey Pk. AL2: Lon C 1N 139
Halsey Pl. WD24: Watf 2K 149
Halsey Rd. WD18: Watf 7B 166 (5K 149)
Halstead Gdns. N21 9B 156
Halstead Hill EN7: Gof O 2C 144
Halstead Rd. EN1: Enf 6C 156
N21 9B 156
Halter Cl. WD6: Bore 7D 152
HALTON 6B 100
HALTON CAMP 7C 100
Halton Camp 6C 100
Halton Cl. AL2: Par S 1D 138
Halton La. HP22: Halt, Wen 7A 100
HP22: West T 3A 100
Halton Stadium (Sports Arena) 6A 100
Halton Tennis Cen. 5B 100
Halton Wood Rd. HP22: Halt 9D 100
Haltside AL10: Hat 1E 128
Halwick Cl. HP1: Hem H 4L 123
Halyard Cl. LU3: Lut 3D 46
Halyard Ind. Est. SG6: L Gar 4H 23
Hamberlins La. HP4: Berk 8F 102
Hamble Ct. WD18: Watf 8A 166 (6J 149)
Hambleden Pl. WD7: Rad 8G 139
Hambling Pl. LU6: Duns 9C 44
Hamblings Cl. WD7: Shen 6L 139
Hambridge Way SG5: Ick, Pirt 7E 20
Hambro Cl. LU2: E Hyd 9A 68
Hamburgh Ct. EN8: C'hunt 1H 145
Ham Ct. NW9 9E 164
Hamels Dr. SG13: H'ford 8F 94
Hamels La. SG9: W'mill 1K 55
Hamels Park 4L 55
Hamer Cl. HP3: Bov 1D 134
Hamer Ct. LU2: Lut 1F 46
Hamilton Av. EN11: Hod 6L 115
N9 9E 156
Hamilton Cl. AL2: Bri W 4B 138
EN4: C'ters 6D 154
EN6: S Mim 6G 140
HA7: Stanm 2F 162
HP4: Dag 2N 83
Hamilton Ct. AL10: Hat 2H 129
Hamilton Mead HP3: Bov 9D 122
Hamilton Rd. AL1: St Alb 1H 127
EN4: C'ters 6D 154
HP4: Berk 1M 121
N9 9E 156
WD4: Hun C 6E 136
WD19: Watf 3K 161
Hamilton St. WD18: Watf 7L 149
Hamilton Way N3 6N 165
Hamlet, The HP4: Pot E 7D 104
Hamlet Cl. AL2: Bri W 3A 138
Hamlet Ct. EN1: Enf 7C 156
Hamlet Hill CM19: Royd 9D 116
Hamlyn Cl. HA8: Edg 3M 163
Hammarsfield Cl. SG11: Stand 7A 56
Hammarskjold Rd. CM20: Harl 4M 117
Hammerdell SG6: L Gar 4D 22
HAMMERFIELD 2L 123
Hammer La. HP2: Hem H 1B 124
Hammer Pde. WD25: Watf 6J 137
Hammers Ga. AL2: Chis G 8B 126
Hammers La. NW7 5G 164
Hammersmith Cl. LU5: Hou R 4F 44
Hammersmith Gdns. LU5: Hou R 3F 44
Hammond Cl. AL6: Wel 3J 91
EN5: Barn 7L 153
EN7: C'hunt 8D 132
SG1: Stev 3K 51
Hammond Ct. LU1: S End 7E 66
Hammond Rd. EN1: Enf 4F 156
Hammonds End La. AL5: Harp 1N 107
Hammonds Hill AL5: Harp 2A 108
Hammond's La. AL4: San 3L 109
HAMMOND STREET 8C 132
Hammondstreet Rd. EN7: C'hunt 7N 131
Hammondswick AL5: Harp 2A 108
Hamonde Cl. HA8: Edg 2B 164
Hamonte SG6: L Gar 7J 23
Hampden SG4: Kimp 7K 69
Hampden Cl. SG6: L Gar 3H 23
Hampden Cres. EN7: C'hunt 4F 144
Hampden Hill SG12: Ware 5K 95
Hampden Hill Cl. SG12: Ware 5J 95
Hampden Pl. AL2: Frog 2F 138
Hampden Ri. SG8: Roys 9D 8
Hampden Rd. HA3: Har W 8D 162
HP22: Wen 9B 100
SG4: Hit 1C 34
SG6: L Gar 3H 23
SL9: Chal P 8A 158
Hampden Way WD17: Watf 9G 136
Hampermill La. WD19: Watf 2H 161
Hampshire Ho. SL9: Chal P 5B 158
Hampshire Way LU3: Lut 9A 30
Hampstead Cl. AL2: Bri W 4A 138
Hampton Cl. SG2: Stev 1B 72
WD6: Bore 7C 152
Hampton Gdns. CM21: Saw 8D 98
Hampton M. EN3: Enf H 5G 156
Hampton Rd. CM24: Stans 4N 59
LU4: Lut 8D 46
Hamstel Rd. CM20: Harl 5L 117
Hamsworth Ct. SG14: H'ford 8L 93
Hanaper Dr. SG8: Barl 2C 16
Hanbury Cl. EN8: C'hunt 2J 145
SG12: Ware 6J 95
Hanbury Cotts. AL9: Ess 8D 112
Hanbury Dr. N21 7L 155
SG12: Thun 2G 94
Hanbury La. AL9: Ess 8D 112
Hanbury Manor Golf Course 2G 94
Hanbury M. SG12: Thun 1G 94
Hancock Ct. WD6: Bore 3C 152
Hancock Dr. LU2: Lut 3G 46
Hancroft Rd. HP3: Hem H 4B 124
Hancross Cl. AL2: Bri W 3N 137
Handa Cl. HP3: Hem H 5D 124
Handcross Rd. LU2: Lut 6M 47
Handel Cl. HA8: Edg 6N 163
Handel Pde. HA8: Edg 7A 164
(off Whitchurch La.)
Handel Way HA8: Edg 7A 164
Handford Ct. WD25: Watf 7M 137
Hand La. CM21: Saw 6E 98
Handley Ga. AL2: Bri W 2A 138
Handley Page Way AL2: Col S 3G 138
Handpost Hill EN6: N'haw 1G 143
Handpost Lodge Gdns. HP2: Hem H 3F 124
HANDSIDE 1J 111
Handside Cl. AL8: Welw G 9J 91
Handside Grn. AL8: Welw G 8J 91
Handside La. AL8: Welw G 2H 111
Handsworth Way WD19: Watf 3J 161
Hangar Ruding WD19: Watf 3A 162
Hanger Cl. HP1: Hem H 3L 123
HANGHILL 6J 101
Hangmans La. AL6: Wel 8M 71
Hankins La. NW7 2E 164
Hanover Cl. SG2: Stev 8M 51
Hanover Ct. CM21: Saw 6H 99
EN9: Wal A 6N 145
(off Quakers La.)
EN11: Hod 8L 115
LU4: Lut 4N 45
WD3: Crox G 7C 148
Hanover Gdns. WD5: Abb L 3H 137
Hanover Grange AL5: Harp 4N 87
Hanover Grn. HP1: Hem H 4K 123
Hanover Ho. AL7: Welw G 2M 111
Hanover Pl. MK45: Bar C 7E 18
Hanover Wlk. AL10: Hat 3F 128
Hansart Way EN2: Enf 3M 155
HANSCOMBE END 3M 19
Hanscombe End Rd. SG5: Shil 3M 19
Hanselin Cl. HA7: Stanm 5G 163
Hansells Mead CM19: Royd 6E 116
Hansen Dr. N21 7L 155
Hanshaw Dr. HA8: Edg 8D 164
Hanswick Cl. LU2: Lut 7K 47
Hanworth Cl. LU2: Lut 2F 46
Hanyards End EN6: Cuff 1K 143
Hanyards La. EN6: Cuff 1J 143
Happy Valley Ind. Est. WD4: Kin L 1D 136
Harbert Gdns. AL2: Par S 2C 138
Harberts Rd. CM19: Harl 6L 117
Harborne Cl. WD19: Watf 5L 161
Harbour Ct. WD23: Bush 7C 150
Harbury Dell LU3: Lut 2D 46
Harcourt Av. HA8: Edg 3C 164
Harcourt Rd. HP23: Tring 2A 102
WD23: Bush 7C 150
Harcourt St. LU1: Lut 3G 66
Hardenwick Ct. AL5: Harp 5B 88
(off Townsend Rd.)
Harding Cl. AL3: Red 1K 107
LU3: Lut 2A 46
WD25: Watf 6L 137
Harding Ct. AL5: Harp 3C 88
Harding Pde. AL5: Harp 6C 88
(off Station Rd.)
Hardings AL7: Welw G 8B 92
Hardings Cl. HP3: Hem H 5L 123
Hardingstone Ct. EN8: Wal C 7K 145
Hardwick Cl. HA7: Stanm 5K 163
SG2: Stev 1B 72
Hardwicke Pl. AL2: Lon C 9L 127
Hardwick Grn. LU3: Lut 2C 46
Hardy Cl. EN5: Barn 8L 153
SG4: Hit 3C 34
Hardy Dr. SG8: Roys 5D 8
Hardy Rd. HP2: Hem H 1B 124
Hardy Way EN2: Enf 3M 155
SG5: Stot 1C 22
Harebell AL7: Welw G 3L 111
Harebell Cl. SG13: H'ford 9F 94
Harebreaks, The WD24: Watf 9J 137
Harebridge La. HP22: Halt 4D 100
Hare Cres. WD25: Watf 5J 137
HAREFIELD 8M 159
Harefield CM20: Harl 5C 118
SG2: Stev 6B 52
Harefield Cl. EN2: Enf 3M 155
Harefield Ct. LU1: Lut 9B 46
Harefield Grn. NW7 6J 165
Harefield Pl. AL4: St Alb 8L 109
Harefield Rd. LU1: Lut 9B 46
WD3: R'orth 2N 159
Hare La. AL10: Hat 2H 129
Harepark Cl. HP1: Hem H 1J 123
Hare Pk. Ter. SG16: U Sto 1F 20
HARESFOOT PARK 4M 121
HARE STREET
CM19 6L 117
SG9, Buntingford 2B 40
SG9, Cottered 4M 37
Hare St. CM19: Harl 6L 117
Hare St. Rd. SG9: Bunt, H St 3K 39
Hare St. Springs CM19: Harl 6M 117
Harewood WD3: R'orth 6L 147
(not continuous)
Harewood Rd. WD19: Watf 3K 161
Harford Cl. E4 9M 157
Harford Dr. WD17: Watf 2G 149
Harforde Ct. SG13: H'ford 9E 94
Harford Rd. E4 9M 157
Hargrave Cl. CM24: Stans 1N 59
Hargreaves Av. EN7: C'hunt 4F 144
Hargreaves Cl. EN7: C'hunt 4F 144
Hargreaves Rd. SG8: Roys 8D 8
Harkett Cl. HA3: Weal 9G 162
Harkett Ct. HA3: Weal 9G 162
Harkness EN7: C'hunt 2F 144
Harkness Ct. SG4: Hit 1B 34
(off Franklin Gdns.)
Harkness Rd. HP2: Hem H 1N 123
Harkness Way SG4: Hit 9C 22
Harlech Rd. LU7: Pits 4A 82
WD5: Abb L 4J 137
Harlequin, The WD17: Watf 8D 166 (6L 149)
(not continuous)
Harlesden Rd. AL1: St Alb 2H 127
Harlestone Cl. LU3: Lut 9C 30
Harley Ct. AL4: St Alb 7L 109
Harley Ho. WD6: Bore 4B 152
(off Brook Cl.)
Harling Rd. LU6: Eat B 4L 63
Harlings SG13: Hert H 4G 115
Harlington Rd. MK45: Shar 9A 18
HARLOW 6N 117
Harlow Bowl 5N 117
Harlow Bus. Cen. CM19: Harl 7K 117
Harlow Bus. Pk. CM19: Harl 6H 117
Harlow Comn. CM17: Harl 9E 118
Harlow Ct. HP2: Hem H 7C 106
Harlow Leisurezone 6N 117
Harlow Mill Station (Rail) 1E 118
Harlow Outdoors (Centre for Outdoor Learning) 3M 117
Harlow Rd. CM17: Harl, M Tye 3L 119
CM19: Royd 6F 116
CM21: Harl, Saw 8E 98
CM22: Harl, She 8K 99
Harlow Stadium (Greyhound) 5H 117
Harlow Town FC 5J 117
Harlow Town Station (Rail) 3N 117
HARLOW TYE 3K 119
Harlyn Dr. HA5: E'cote 9K 161
Harman Rd. EN1: Enf 7D 156
Harmer Dell AL6: Wel 3M 91
HARMER GREEN 2N 91
Harmer Grn. La. AL6: Wel 4M 91
Harmonds Wood Cl. EN10: Brox 1J 133
Harmonia Ct. WD17: Watf 2J 149
Harmony Cl. AL10: Hat 7G 111
Harmsworth Way N20 1M 165
Harness Way AL4: St Alb 8L 109
Harold Cl. CM19: Harl 7J 117
Harold Ct. EN8: Wal C 7K 145
(off Holdbrook Sth.)
Harold Cres. EN9: Wal A 5N 145
Harold Rd. MK45: Bar C 8E 18
Harold's Bridge 6N 145
Harolds Rd. CM19: Harl 7J 117
HARPENDEN 6B 88
Harpenden & District Indoor Bowls Club 6E 88
HARPENDENBURY 7J 87
Harpenden Common Golf Course 9C 88
Harpenden Golf Course 1A 108
Harpenden La. AL3: Red 9K 87
Harpenden Leisure Cen. 7B 88
Harpenden Ri. AL5: Harp 4N 87
Harpenden Rd. AL3: St Alb 2C 108
AL4: Wheat 7H 89
Harpenden Station (Rail) 6C 88
Harper Cl. N14 7H 155
Harper Ct. SG1: Stev 4M 51
Harper La. WD7: Rad, Shen 5G 139
Harpers Gym 8L 127
Harpsfield B'way. AL10: Hat 8F 110
Harps Hill AL3: Mark 2A 86
Harptree Way AL1: St Alb 9H 109
Harrier Rd. NW9 9E 164
Harriet Ho. HP3: Hem H 7A 124
Harriet Walker Way WD3: R'orth 9J 147
Harriet Way WD23: Bush 9E 150
Harrington Cl. CM23: Bis S 1J 79
Harrington Ct. SG13: Hert H 3G 115
Harrington Hgts. LU5: Hou R 4D 44
Harris Cl. EN2: Enf 3N 155
Harris Ct. MK45: Bar C 7D 18
Harris La. LU2: Lut 5J 47
SG5: Gt Off 8E 32
WD7: Shen 7A 140
Harrison Cl. HA6: North 6E 160
SG4: Hit 3N 33
Harrison La. SG13: H'ford 1D 114
Harrison Rd. EN9: Wal A 8N 145
Harrisons CM23: Birc 7M 59
Harrison Wlk. EN8: C'hunt 3H 145
Harris Rd. WD25: Watf 8J 137
Harris's La. SG12: Ware 5G 94
Harrogate Rd. WD19: Watf 3L 161
Harrow Arts Cen. 7B 162
Harrow Av. EN1: Enf 8D 156
Harrowbond Rd. CM17: Harl 5E 118
Harrow Ct. SG1: Stev 4L 51
Harrowden Ct. LU2: Lut 9K 47
Harrowdene SG2: Stev 5B 52
Harrowden Rd. LU2: Lut 9K 47
Harrow Dr. N9 9D 156
Harrowes Meade HA8: Edg 3A 164
Harrow Vw. HA2: Harr 9D 162
Harrow Way WD19: Watf 3N 161
HARROW WEALD 8F 162
Harrow Weald Pk. HA3: Har W 6E 162
Harrow Yd. HP23: Tring 3M 101
Harry Scott Ct. LU4: Lut 3M 45
Harston Dr. EN3: Enf L 2L 157
Hartcroft Cl. HP3: Hem H 3D 124
Hartfield Av. WD6: Elst 6A 152
Hartfield Cl. WD6: Elst 7A 152
Hartfield Ct. SG12: Ware 5H 95
Hartford Av. HA3: Ken 9J 163
Hartforde Rd. WD6: Bore 4A 152
Harthall La. HP3: Hem H 9F 124
WD4: Kin L 1D 136
HARTHAM 8B 94
Hartham La. SG14: H'ford 9A 94
Hartham Leisure Cen. 8B 94
HART HILL 8H 47
Hart Hill Dr. LU2: Lut 9H 47
Hart Hill La. LU2: Lut 9H 47
Hart Hill Path LU2: Lut 9H 47
Hartington Pl. SG6: L Gar 2H 23
Hartland Cl. HA8: Edg 2A 164
N21 8A 156
Hartland Ct. SG5: Hit 3L 33
Hartland Dr. HA8: Edg 2A 164
Hartland Rd. EN8: C'hunt 3H 145
Hart La. LU2: Lut 8J 47
Hartley Av. NW7 5F 164
Hartley Cl. NW7 5F 164
Hartley Rd. LU2: Lut 9H 47
Hart Lodge EN5: Barn 5L 153
Hartmoor M. EN3: Enf W 1H 157
Hartop Cl. LU7: I Ast 6D 62
LU7: Pits 4C 82
Hartop Ct. LU2: Lut 9M 47
Hart Rd. AL1: St Alb 4D 166 (3E 126)
CM17: Harl 1E 118
Hartsbourne Av. WD23: B Hea 2D 162
Hartsbourne Cl. WD23: B Hea 2E 162
Hartsbourne Country Club & Golf Course 2D 162
Hartsbourne Pk. WD23: B Hea 2F 162
Hartsbourne Rd. WD23: B Hea 2E 162
Hartsbourne Way HP2: Hem H 3E 124
Harts Cl. WD23: Bush 4B 150
Hartsfield Rd. LU2: Lut 7J 47
Hartspring La. WD23: Bush 4B 150
WD25: A'ham 4B 150
Hartsway EN3: Pon E 6G 156
Hartswood Cl. WD23: Bush 4B 150
Hartswood Grn. WD23: B Hea 2E 162
Hart Wlk. LU2: Lut 8J 47
Hartwell Gdns. AL5: Harp 6N 87
Hartwood LU2: Lut 9H 47
(off Hart Hill Dr.)
Harvest Cl. LU4: Lut 6K 45
Harvest Ct. AL4: St Alb 7L 109
AL6: Wel 9L 71
SG6: Will 9G 23
Harvest End WD25: Watf 9M 137
Harvesters AL4: St Alb 7K 109
(off Harvest Ct.)
Harvest La. SG2: Stev 2C 52
Harvest Mead AL10: Hat 8H 111
Harvest Rd. WD23: Bush 6C 150
Harvey Cen. App. CM20: Harl 6N 117
Harvey Cen. (Shop. Cen.)
CM20: Harl 6M 117
Harvey Cl. NW9 9E 164
Harveyfields EN9: Wal A 7N 145
Harvey Ho. EN3: Enf L 1K 157

A-Z Hertfordshire 195

Harvey Rd.—Hermitage, The

Harvey Rd. AL2: Lon C 8K 127
LU6: Duns 1A 64
SG2: Stev 3A 52
WD3: Crox G 8C 148
Harveys Cotts. SG11: L Had 9B 58
Harvey's Hill LU2: Lut 4H 47
Harvington Pk. LU7: Pits 4B 82
Harvingwell Pl. HP2: Hem H 9D 106
Harwood Cl. AL6: Tew 5D 92
AL8: Welw G 5L 91
Harwood Hill AL8: Welw G 5L 91
Harwood Pk. Crematorium SG3: Kneb 2B 72
Harwoods, The SG12: Ware 5F 94
Harwoods Rd. WD18: Watf 9A 166 (6J 149)
Harwoods Yd. N21 9M 155
Hasedines Rd. HP1: Hem H 1K 123
Haseldine Mdws. AL10: Hat 1F 128
Haseldine Rd. AL2: Lon C 8L 127
Haselfoot SG6: L Gar 5E 22
Haselwood Dr. EN2: Enf 6N 155
Hasketon Dr. LU4: Lut 3L 45
Haslemere CM23: Bis S 4J 79
Haslemere Bus. Cen. EN1: Enf 6F 156
Haslemere Estate, The EN11: Hod 8A 116
Haslemere Ind. Est. AL7: Welw G 8M 91
CM23: Bis S 4J 79
Haslewood Av. EN11: Hod 8L 115
Haslingden Cl. AL5: Harp 4M 87
Hasluck Gdns. EN5: N Bar 8A 154
HASSOBURY 2G 59
Haste Hill Golf Course 9G 161
Hastings Cl. EN5: N Bar 6B 154
SG1: Stev 1G 50
Hastings Ho. EN3: Enf H 4G 156
Hastings Rd. MK45: Bar C 8E 18
Hastings St. LU1: Lut 2F 66
Hastings Way WD3: Crox G 6E 148
WD23: Bush 6N 149
HASTINGWOOD 9H 119
Hastingwood Bus. Cen. CM17: H'wood 9J 119
Hastingwood Rd. CM5: M Lav 9H 119
CM17: Harl, H'wood, M Lav 9H 119
HASTOE 7L 101
Hastoe Hill HP23: Hast 6L 101
Hastoe La. HP23: Hast, Tring 4M 101
Hastoe Row HP23: Hast 7M 101
Hatch, The EN3: Enf H 3H 157
HATCH END 7A 162
Hatch End Station (Overground) 7B 162
Hatch End Swimming Pool 7B 162
Hatch Grn. CM22: L Hal 8K 79
HATCHING GREEN 9B 88
Hatching Grn. Cl. AL5: Harp 9B 88
Hatch La. SG4: W'ton 6M 23
Hat Factory, The *1G 66*
(off Bute St.)
HATFIELD 8H 111
Hatfield Av. AL10: Hat 5D 110
Hatfield Bus. Pk. AL10: Hat 6E 110
(not continuous)
Hatfield Cres. HP2: Hem H 7B 106
HATFIELD GARDEN VILLAGE 6F 110
Hatfield Heath Rd. CM21: Saw 4J 99
Hatfield House 9K 111
HATFIELD HYDE 3M 111
Hatfield Leisure Cen. 2H 129
Hatfield Pk. 9L 111
Hatfield Rd. AL1: St Alb 2E 166 (2F 126)
AL4: Smal, St Alb 2L 127
AL9: Ess 5D 112
EN6: Pot B 3B 142
WD24: Watf 3K 149
Hatfield Station (Rail) 8J 111
Hatfield Swimming Pool 8G 110
Hathaway Cl. HA7: Stanm 5H 163
LU4: Lut 7L 45
Hathaway Ct. AL4: St Alb 2M 127
Hatherleigh Cl. NW7 6K 165
Hatherleigh Gdns. EN6: Pot B 5C 142
Hatherley Chase LU2: Lut 7G 47
Hatters La. WD18: Watf 8F 148
Hatters Way LU1: Lut 8L 45
Hatton Ho. *EN8: C'hunt* *2H 145*
(off Church La.)
Hatton Pl. *LU2: Lut* *9G 46*
(off Midland Rd.)
Hatton Rd. EN8: C'hunt 2H 145
Hatton Wlk. *EN2: Enf* *6B 156*
(off London Rd.)
HAULTWICK 6D 54
Havelock Ri. LU2: Lut 8G 47
Havelock Rd. HA3: Weal 9F 162
LU2: Lut 8G 46
WD4: Kin L 1B 136
Haven, The AL3: Flam 7D 86
SG5: Stot 6F 10
Haven Cl. AL10: Hat 8F 110
Havenhurst Ri. EN2: Enf 4M 155
Haven Lodge *EN1: Enf* *8C 156*
(off Village Rd.)
Havensfield WD4: Chippf 4L 135
Havercroft Cl. AL3: St Alb 4C 126
Haverdale LU4: Lut 5M 45
Haverford Way HA8: Edg 8N 163
Havers La. CM23: Bis S 3H 79
Havers Pde. *CM23: Bis S* *3H 79*
(off Havers La.)
Havilland Ct. HA8: Edg 4N 163
Haward Rd. EN11: Hod 6N 115
Hawbush Cl. AL6: Wel 3H 91
Hawbush Ri. AL6: Wel 2G 91
Hawes Cl. HA6: North 7H 161
Hawes La. E4 2N 157
Haweswater Dr. WD25: Watf 7L 137
Hawfield Gdns. AL2: Par S 8C 126
Hawkdene E4 8M 157
Hawkenbury CM19: Harl 8L 117
Hawker *NW9* *8F 164*
(off Everglade Strand)
Hawkes Dr. AL3: Red 1K 107
Hawkes La. SG1: Stev 2L 51
Hawkesley Ct. WD7: Rad 8G 139
Hawkesworth Cl. HA6: North 7G 160
Hawkfield SG6: L Gar 3E 22
Hawkfields LU2: Lut 3G 47
Hawkins Cl. NW7 5D 164
WD6: Bore 4C 152
Hawkins Hall La. SG3: Dat 6D 72
Hawkins Way HP3: Bov 8D 122
Hawkshead Ct. *EN8: Wal C* *7K 145*
(off Eleanor Way)
Hawkshead La.
AL9: B Pk, N Mym 1J 141
Hawkshead Rd. EN6: Pot B 1M 141
Hawkshill AL1: St Alb 3H 127
Hawkshill Dr. HP3: Hem H 5J 123
Hawksmead Cl. EN3: Enf W 9H 145
Hawksmoor WD7: Shen 6A 140
Hawksmouth E4 9N 157
Hawkwell Dr. HP23: Tring 2A 102
Hawkwood Cres. E4 8M 157
HAWRIDGE 4D 120
HAWRIDGE COMMON 3C 120
Hawridge La. HP5: Bell, Haw 5C 120
Hawridge Va. HP5: Haw 4D 120
Hawsley Rd. AL5: Harp 2B 108
Hawthorn Av. LU2: Lut 5K 47
Hawthorn Cl. AL5: Harp 8E 88
LU6: Duns 1F 64
SG5: Hit 4L 33
SG8: Roys 6F 8
SG14: H'ford 8M 93
WD5: Abb L 5J 137
WD17: Watf 2H 149
Hawthorn Ct. *HA5: Pin* *9L 161*
(off Rickmansworth Rd.)
Hawthorn Cres. LU1: Cad 5A 66
Hawthorne Av. EN7: C'hunt 4F 144
Hawthorne Cl. EN7: C'hunt 4F 144
Hawthorne Ct. HA6: North 9J 161
Hawthorne La. HP1: Hem H 1J 123
Hawthorne Rd. WD7: Rad 7H 139
Hawthornes AL10: Hat 2F 128
Hawthorn Gro. EN2: Enf 2B 156
EN5: Ark 8F 152
Hawthorn Hill SG6: L Gar 4E 22
Hawthorn M. NW7 8L 165
Hawthorn Ri. CM23: Thorl 5H 79
Hawthorn Rd. EN11: Hod 6M 115
Hawthorns AL8: Welw G 7K 91
Hawthorns, The EN6: Rid 6E 140
HP3: Hem H 6J 123
HP4: Berk 9L 103
SG1: Stev 5M 51
SG12: Ware 4G 94
WD3: Map C 5G 158
Hawthorn Way AL2: Chis G 6B 126
SG8: Roys 6F 8
SG16: L Ston 1F 20
Hawtrees WD7: Rad 8G 138
Haybluff Dr. SG1: W'ton 6N 35
Haybourn Mead HP1: Hem H 3L 123
Hay Cl. WD6: Bore 4C 152
Haycock Round SG1: W'ton 7N 35
Haycroft CM23: Bis S 1L 79
LU2: Lut 3G 46
Haycroft Rd. SG1: Stev 2K 51
Hayden Rd. EN9: Wal A 8N 145
Haydens Rd. CM20: Harl 6M 117
Haydock Rd. SG8: Roys 7F 8
Haydon Cl. EN1: Enf 8C 156
Haydon Dell WD23: Bush 8A 150
Haydon Dell Farm WD23: Bush 9A 150
Haydon Rd. WD19: Watf 8N 149
Hayes Cl. LU2: Lut 4K 47
Hayes Wlk. EN6: Pot B 6A 142
EN10: Turn 7K 133
Hayfield SG2: Stev 2C 52
Hayfield Cl. WD23: Bush 6C 150
Haygarth SG3: Kneb 4N 71
HAY GREEN 6D 14
Hayhurst Rd. LU4: Lut 7L 45
Hay La. AL5: Harp 6B 88
Hayley Bell Gdns. CM23: Bis S 5H 79
Hayley Comn. SG2: Stev 6B 52
Hayley Ct. LU5: Hou R 3F 44
Hayling Dr. LU2: Lut 6M 47
Hayling Rd. WD19: Watf 3J 161
Hayllar Ct. EN11: Hod 8L 115
Haymarket Rd. LU4: Lut 5H 45
Haymeads AL8: Welw G 6L 91
Haymeads La. CM23: Bis S 1L 79
Haymoor SG6: L Gar 4E 22
Haynes Cl. AL7: Welw G 1N 111
Haynes Mead HP4: Berk 8L 103
Haysman Cl. SG6: L Gar 4H 23
HAY STREET 9B 40
Hay St. SG8: S Mor 3C 6
Hayton Cl. LU3: Lut 8D 30
Hay Wains SG3: Dat 6A 72
Hayward Cl. SG1: Stev 3M 51
Hayward Copse WD3: Loud 6N 147
Haywood Cl. HA5: Pin 9M 161
Haywood Cres. WD17: Watf 2J 149
Haywood Dr. HP3: Hem H 5J 123
WD3: Chor 7J 147
Haywood La. SG8: Ther 6E 14
Haywood Pk. WD3: Chor 7J 147
Haywoods La. SG8: Roys 6E 8
Hazelbank WD3: Crox G 8E 148
Hazelbury Av. WD5: Abb L 5E 136
Hazelbury Ct. *LU1: Lut* *9E 46*
(off Hazelbury Cres.)
Hazelbury Cres. LU1: Lut 9E 46
Hazel Cl. AL6: Wel 4L 91
EN7: C'hunt 8C 132
NW9 9E 164
Hazel Ct. SG4: Hit 3A 34
WD7: Shen 6N 139
Hazelcroft HA5: Hat E 6C 162
Hazeldell SG14: Watt S 5J 73
Hazeldell Link HP1: Hem H 3H 123
Hazeldell Rd. HP1: Hem H 3H 123
Hazeldene EN8: Wal C 5J 145
LU6: N'all 3F 62
Hazeldene Dr. HA5: Pin 9L 161
HAZEL END 4K 59
Hazelend Rd. CM23: Bis S, Farn 4K 59
Hazel Gdns. CM21: Saw 6H 99
HA8: Edg 4B 164
Hazelgreen Cl. N21 9N 155
Hazel Gro. AL7: Welw G 8A 92
AL10: Hat 3F 128
EN1: Enf 8E 156
SG5: Stot 7E 10
WD25: Watf 8K 137
Hazel Gro. Ho. AL10: Hat 2F 128
Hazel Mead EN5: Ark 7H 153
Hazelmere Rd. AL4: St Alb 8K 109
SG2: Stev 9N 51
Hazel Rd. AL2: Par S 1C 138
HP4: Berk 2A 122
Hazels, The AL6: Tew 5D 92
Hazel Tree Rd. WD24: Watf 1K 149
Hazelwood Cl. LU2: Lut 5K 47
SG5: Hit 2N 33
Hazelwood Dr. AL4: St Alb 9K 109
HA5: Pin 9K 161
Hazelwood La. WD5: Abb L 5E 136
Hazelwood Rd. EN1: Enf 8D 156
WD3: Crox G 8E 148
Hazelwood Sports Club 9A 156
Hazely HP23: Tring 2A 102
HBS Sports Cen. 3M 33
Heacham Cl. LU4: Lut 5L 45
Headingley Cl. EN7: C'hunt 8D 132
SG1: Stev 1L 51
WD7: Shen 5M 139
Headlands Dr. HP4: Berk 9B 104
Headstone La. HA2: Harr 9C 162
HA3: Har W 7C 162
Headstone Lane Station (Overground) 8C 162
Healey Rd. WD18: Watf 8H 149
Healy Ct. EN5: Barn 8K 153
Hearle Way AL10: Hat 7E 110
Heartwood Forest 2G 109
HEATH, THE 7E 48
Heath, The SG4: Bre G 7E 48
WD7: Rad 6H 139
Heath Av. AL3: St Alb 9E 108
SG8: Roys 7C 8
Heathbourne Rd. HA7: Stanm 2F 162
WD23: B Hea 1F 162
Heath Brow HP1: Hem H 4M 123
Heathbrow Rd. AL6: Wel 8L 71
Heathcliff Av. SG5: Stot 1B 22
Heath Cl. AL5: Harp 8D 88
EN6: Pot B 3A 142
HP1: Hem H 3M 123
LU1: Lut 2D 66
Heathcote Av. AL10: Hat 7G 111
Heathcote Gdns. CM17: Harl 6G 118
Heath Ct. *SG1: Stev* *8B 36*
(off Admiral Dr.)
SG14: H'ford *8L 93*
(off The Ridgeway)
Heathcroft AL7: Welw G 9B 92
Heathdene Mnr. WD17: Watf 3H 149
Heath Dr. EN6: Pot B 3N 141
SG12: Ware 4H 95
HEATH END 2D 120
Heath End HP4: Berk 4D 120
HP5: Haw 4D 120
Heather Cl. CM23: Bis S 2F 78
WD5: Abb L 5J 137
Heather Ct. AL2: Lon C 9L 127
Heather Dr. EN2: Enf 4N 155
Heather Gdns. EN9: Wal A 9N 145
Heather La. WD24: Watf 8H 137
Heather Mead LU6: Eat B 3J 63
Heathermere SG6: L Gar 2F 22
Heather Ri. WD23: Bush 4A 150
Heather Rd. AL8: Welw G 2J 111
Heathers, The SG13: H'ford 9C 94
Heather Wlk. HA8: Edg 5B 164
Heather Way EN6: Pot B 5M 141
HA7: Stanm 6G 163
HP2: Hem H 1N 123
Heath Farm Ct. WD17: Watf 1F 148
Heath Farm La. AL3: St Alb 9F 108
Heathfield SG8: Roys 7B 8
Heathfield Cl. EN6: Pot B 3A 142
LU1: Cad 4B 66
WD19: Watf 9L 149
Heathfield Ct. *AL1: St Alb* *1F 126*
(off Avenue Rd.)
Heathfield Path LU1: Cad 4B 66
Heathfield Rd. LU3: Lut 5E 46
SG5: Hit 1M 33
WD23: Bush 6N 149
Heathgate SG13: Hert H 4F 114
Heath Hall SG7: Bald 4F 24
Heath Hill SG4: Cod 7D 70
Heathlands AL6: Wel 7M 71
Heathlands Dr. AL3: St Alb 9F 108
Heath La. HP1: Hem H 4M 123
SG4: Cod 7E 70
SG13: Hert H 4G 114
Heath Lodge WD23: B Hea 1F 162
Heath Pk. Ho.
HP1: Hem H 4M 123
Heath Rd. AL1: St Alb 1F 126
AL6: Wel 7L 71
EN6: Pot B 3N 141
SG4: Bre G 8E 48
WD19: Watf 9M 149
Heath Row CM23: Bis S 8K 59
Heaths Cl. EN1: Enf 4C 156
Heathside AL1: St Alb 9F 108
AL4: Col H 5B 128
Heathside Cl. HA6: North 5F 160
Heathside Rd. HA6: North 5F 160
Heathview *AL5: Harp* *6C 88*
(off Milton Rd.)
Heath Way WD7: Shen 3K 139
Heaton Ct. EN8: C'hunt 2H 145
WD17: Watf 2J 149
Heaton Dell LU2: Lut 8N 47
Heay Flds. AL7: Welw G 8B 92
Hebden Cl. LU4: Lut 5L 45
HEBING END 7L 53
Heckford Cl. WD18: Watf 8E 148
Hector *NW9* *8F 164*
(off Five Acre)
Heddon Ct. Av. EN4: C'ters 7E 154
Heddon Ct. Pde. EN4: C'ters 7F 154
Heddon Rd. EN4: C'ters 7E 154
Hedgebrooms AL7: Welw G 8B 92
Hedge Hill EN2: Enf 3N 155
Hedge Row HP1: Hem H 9K 105
Hedgerow SL9: Chal P 6B 158
Hedgerow, The LU4: Lut 4M 45
Hedgerow Cl. SG2: Stev 1B 52
Hedgerow La. EN5: Ark 7H 153
Hedgerows CM21: Saw 5H 99
Hedgerows, The CM23: Bis S 2K 79
SG2: Stev 1C 52
Hedgerow Wlk. EN8: C'hunt 3H 145
Hedges, The AL3: St Alb 7D 108
Hedges Cl. AL10: Hat 8H 111
Hedgeside HP4: Pot E 7D 104
Hedgeside Rd. HA6: North 5E 160
Hedges Way WD3: Crox G 9B 148
Hedley Cl. HP22: Ast C 2F 100
Hedley Ri. LU2: Lut 7N 47
Hedley Rd. AL1: St Alb 2J 127
Hedley Vs. AL1: St Alb 2J 127
Hedworth Av. EN8: Wal C 6H 145
Heene Rd. EN2: Enf 3B 156
Heighams CM19: Harl 9J 117
Heights, The *HP2: Hem H* *8B 106*
(off Jupiter Dr.)
LU3: Lut *4A 46*
(off Marsh Rd.)
Helena Cl. EN4: Had W 2C 154
Helena Pl. HP2: Hem H 9N 105
Helens Ga. EN8: C'hunt 8K 133
HELHAM GREEN 3C 96
Helions Rd. CM19: Harl 6L 117
Helios Ct. AL10: Hat 9E 110
Hellards Rd. SG1: Stev 2K 51
Hellebore Ct. SG1: Stev 1A 52
Hellen Way WD19: Watf 4M 161
Helmsley Cl. LU4: Lut 4M 45
Helston Cl. HA5: Hat E 7A 162
Helston Gro. HP2: Hem H 6N 105
Helston Pl. WD5: Abb L 5H 137
HEMEL HEMPSTEAD 1N 123
Hemel Hempstead Ind. Est.
HP2: Hem H 7D 106
(Brickfields Ind. Est., not continuous)
HP2: Hem H 1D 124
(Maylands Ct.)
Hemel Hempstead Rd. AL3: Red 6E 106
AL3: St Alb 3N 125
HP3: Hem H 4F 124
HP4: Dag, Lit G 4A 84
Hemel Hempstead Station (Rail) 5K 123
Hemel Hempstead Town FC 2C 124
Hemingford Dr. LU2: Lut 3F 46
Hemingford Rd. WD17: Watf 9G 136
Heming Rd. HA8: Edg 7B 164
Hemmings, The HP4: Berk 2K 121
Hemming Way WD25: Watf 8J 137
Hemp La. HP23: N Gnd, Wigg 5C 102
Hempstall AL7: Welw G 2A 112
Hempstalls Cl. SG12: Huns 7G 97
Hempstead La. HP4: Pot E 8E 104
Hempstead Rd. HP3: Bov 9D 122
WD4: Kin L 8B 124
WD17: Watf 5A 166 (9F 136)
(not continuous)
Hemsley Rd. WD4: Kin L 2D 136
Hemswell Dr. NW9 8E 164
Henbury Way WD19: Watf 3M 161
Henderson Cl. AL3: St Alb 7D 108
Henderson Pl. SG13: Epp G 3H 131
WD5: Bed 9H 125
Henderson Rd. N9 9F 156
Hendon Av. N3 8L 165
Hendon Crematorium NW7 8K 165
Hendon Golf Course 7J 165
Hendon Hall Ct. NW4 9K 165
Hendon La. N3 9L 165
Hendon Wood La. NW7 8F 152
Hendren Ct. SG1: Stev 9N 35
Henge Way LU3: Lut 2N 45
Henley Cl. LU5: Hou R 4H 45
Henley Ct. N14 9H 155
Henley Ho. AL1: St Alb 4E 166
Henmarsh Ct. SG13: H'ford 2C 114
Henry Cl. EN2: Enf 2C 156
Henry Ct. HA7: Stanm 7L 163
LU6: Duns 9D 44
Henry Darlot Dr. NW7 5K 165
Henry Moore Foundation, The 9K 77
Henry Rd. EN4: E Bar 7C 154
Henrys Grant AL1: St Alb 5E 166 (3F 126)
Henry St. HP3: Hem H 6N 123
HP23: Tring 3M 101
Henry Wells Sq. HP2: Hem H 7B 106
Hensby M. WD19: Watf 8N 149
Hensley Cl. AL6: Wel 1J 91
SG4: Hit 4B 34
Henstead Pl. LU2: Lut 8M 47
Hepburn Ct. EN6: S Mim 5G 141
WD6: Bore *6A 152*
(off Whitehall Cl.)
Hepworth Ct. SG2: Stev 3B 52
Heracles *NW9* *8F 164*
(off Five Acre)
Heracles Cl. AL2: Par S 1D 138
Herald Cl. CM23: Bis S 2F 78
Herbert St. HP2: Hem H 1N 123
Hercules Way WD25: Watf 7H 137
Hereford Rd. LU4: Lut 6K 45
Hereward Cl. EN9: Wal A 5N 145
Herga Ct. WD17: Watf 4J 149
Heriots Cl. HA7: Stanm 4H 163
Heritage Av. NW9 9F 164
Heritage Cl. AL3: St Alb 3C 166 (2E 126)
Heritage Wlk. WD3: Chor 5H 147
Herkomer Cl. WD23: Bush 8C 150
Herkomer Rd. WD23: Bush 7B 150
Herm Ho. EN3: Enf W 2H 157
Hermitage, The SG15: Arl 4B 10

Hermitage Cl.—Hillpath

Hermitage Cl. EN2: Enf 4N 155
Hermitage Ct. EN6: Pot B 6B 142
Hermitage Ho. *CM24: Stans* *2M 59*
(off Bentfield Rd.)
Hermitage Rd. SG5: Hit 3N 33
Hermitage Way HA7: Stanm 8H 163
Herne Ct. WD23: Bush 9D 150
Herne Rd. SG1: Stev 9H 35
WD23: Bush 8C 150
Herneshaw AL10: Hat 2F 128
Herns La. AL7: Welw G 8A 92
Herns Way AL7: Welw G 7N 91
Heron Cl. CM21: Saw 6F 98
HP3: Hem H 7B 124
WD3: R'orth 2N 159
Heron Ct. CM23: Bis S 1J 79
NW9 ....9E 164
Heron Dr. LU2: Lut 3G 47
SG12: Stan A 3N 115
Heronfield EN6: Pot B 3B 142
Herongate Cl. EN1: Enf 4D 156
Herongate Rd. EN8: C'hunt 9J 133
Heron Mead EN3: Enf L 2L 157
Heron Path HP22: Wen 9A 100
Heron Pl. UB9: Hare 6K 159
Herons Elm HP4: Berk 7J 103
HERONSGATE 9F 146
Heronsgate HA8: Edg 5A 164
Heronsgate Rd. WD3: Chor 8E 146
Heronslea WD25: Watf 9L 137
Heronslea Dr. HA7: Stanm 5M 163
Herons Ri. EN4: E Bar 6D 154
Herons Way AL1: St Alb 6H 127
(not continuous)
Herons Wood CM20: Harl 4L 117
Heronswood Pl. AL7: Welw G 1N 111
Heronswood Rd. AL7: Welw G 9N 91
Heron Wlk. HA6: North 4G 161
Heron Way AL10: Hat 2G 128
CM19: Royd 5D 116
SG5: Stot 6E 10
SG8: Roys 5E 8
Herrington Av. CM24: Stans 4N 59
HERRINGWORTH HALL 6G 55
HERTFORD 9B 94
Hertford Cl. EN4: C'ters 5C 154
Hertford County Yacht Club 3A 116
Hertford Ct. WD3: Crox G 6D 148
Hertford East Station (Rail) 9C 94
HERTFORD HEATH 2G 114
Hertford Heath Nature Reserve 4F 114
Hertford Ho. SG1: Stev 3H 51
Hertford M. EN6: Pot B 4B 142
Hertford Mus. 9B 94
Hertford North Station (Rail) 9N 93
Hertford Pl. WD3: Map C 4J 159
Hertford Rd. AL6: Ess, Hat, Wel, Tew 2J 91
AL6: Tew 5D 92
AL9: Ess, Hat 5J 111
AL9: Hat 7J 111
EN3: Enf H, Enf W 5G 156
EN4: C'ters 5B 154
EN8: Wal C 5G 156
EN11: Hert H, Hod 5H 115
N9 ....9F 156
SG2: Stev 8M 51
SG12: Gt A 2K 115
SG12: Ware 7G 95
SG14: Bram, Pans 5D 92
Hertfordshire Golf Course, The 2G 133
Hertfordshire Showground 6H 87
Hertfordshire Sports Village 9D 110
HERTINGFORDBURY 1L 113
Hertingfordbury Hill SG14: H'bury 2J 113
Hertingfordbury Rd.
SG14: H'bury, H'ford 1L 113
Herts Bus. Cen. AL2: Lon C 8L 127
Hertsmere Ind. Pk. WD6: Bore 5D 152
Hertswood Cen. 3C 152
Hertswood Ct. EN5: Barn 6L 153
Herts Young Mariners Base 3K 145
Hervey Cl. N3 ....8N 165
Hervey Way N3 ....8N 165
Hester Ho. CM20: Harl 4M 117
Heswall Ct. *LU1: Lut* *2H 67*
(off Bailey St.)
Heswell Grn. WD19: Watf 3J 161
Hetchleys HP1: Hem H 8K 105
Hever Cl. LU7: Pits 5B 82
Hewett Cl. HA7: Stanm 4J 163
Hewitt Cl. AL4: Wheat 8L 89
Hewlett Path LU3: Lut 5A 46
Hewlett Rd. LU3: Lut 4A 46
Hexham Rd. EN5: N Bar 6A 154
HEXTON 9K 19
Hexton Chalk Pit Nature Reserve 2K 31
Hexton Rd. LU2: Lill 6K 31
MK45: Bar C 9E 18
SG5: Hit 2E 32
Heybourne Cres. NW9 ....8E 164
Heybridge Ct. SG14: H'ford 8L 93
Heybrigge Cl. AL3: Red 1J 107
Heydon Rd. SG8: Gt Chi 2H 17
Heydons Cl. AL3: St Alb 9E 108
Heyford End AL2: Par S 1D 138
Heyford Rd. WD7: Rad 1G 150
Heyford Way AL10: Hat 8G 111
(Broomfield Ct.)
AL10: Hat 7J 111
(Whitefield Ho.)
Heysham Dr. WD19: Watf 5L 161
Heywood Av. NW9 ....8E 164
Heywood Ct. HA7: Stanm 5K 163
Heywood Dr. LU2: Lut 7H 47
Hibbert Av. WD24: Watf 2M 149
Hibbert Lodge SL9: Chal P 9A 158
Hibbert Rd. HA3: Weal 9G 163
Hibberts Ct. SG6: L Gar 4E 22
Hibbert St. LU1: Lut 2G 66
Hibbert St. Almshouses *LU1: Lut* *2G 66*
(off Hibbert St.)
Hibbert St. Pas. *LU1: Lut* *2G 66*
(off Castle St.)
Hibiscus Cl. HA8: Edg 4C 164
Hickling Cl. LU2: Lut 8M 47
Hickling Way AL5: Harp 4D 88
Hickman Cl. EN10: Brox 2H 133
Hickman Ct. LU3: Lut 1N 45
HICKMAN'S HILL 8C 24
Hickory Cl. N9 ....9E 156
Hicks Rd. AL3: Mark 2A 86
Hidalgo Ct. HP2: Hem H 9B 106
Hideaway, The WD5: Abb L 4H 137
Hide Ct. *CM23: Bis S* *3J 79*
(off Tanners Wharf)
Hides, The CM20: Harl 5N 117
Higgins Rd. EN7: C'hunt 8B 132
Higgins Wlk. SG1: Stev 9J 35
HIGH, THE 6N 117
High Acres EN2: Enf 5N 155
WD5: Abb L 5F 136
Higham Dr. LU2: Lut 8M 47
HIGHAM GOBION 5J 19
Higham Gobion Rd. MK45: Bar C 7E 18
SG5: H Gob 7E 18
Higham Rd. SG5: H Gob, Shil 5J 19
High Ash Rd. AL4: Wheat 8K 89
High Av. SG6: L Gar 6D 22
Highbanks Rd. HA5: Hat E 6C 162
HIGH BARNET 4K 153
High Barnet Station (Underground) 6N 153
Highbarns HP3: Hem H 7C 124
High Beech N21 ....8L 155
High Beech Rd. LU3: Lut 2N 45
High Birch Ct. *EN4: E Bar* *6D 154*
(off Park Rd.)
Highbridge Cl. WD7: Rad 6H 139
Highbridge Retail Pk. EN9: Wal A 7M 145
Highbridge St. EN9: Wal A 6M 145
(not continuous)
Highbury Av. EN11: Hod 6L 115
Highbury Rd. LU3: Lut 8E 46
SG4: Hit 4A 34
Highbush Rd. SG5: Stot 7E 10
High Canons WD6: Bore 1C 152
Highclere Ct. *AL1: St Alb* *1F 126*
(off Avenue Rd.)
Highclere Dr. HP3: Hem H 6C 124
High Cl. WD3: R'orth 7M 147
Highcroft SG2: Stev 8M 51
Highcroft Rd. HP3: Hem H 6K 123
Highcroft Trailer Gdns. HP3: Bov 8E 122
HIGH CROSS
SG11 ....6J 75
WD25 ....1E 150
High Cross WD25: A'ham 1E 150
High Dane SG4: Hit 1A 34
High Dells AL10: Hat 1F 128
High Elms AL5: Harp 9B 88
CM18: Harl 8B 118
High Elms Cl. HA6: North 6E 160
High Elms La. SG2: B'ton 2H 73
SG12: Watt S 2H 73
SG14: Watt S 2H 73
WD25: Watf 4K 137
HIGHFIELD 9B 106
Highfield CM18: Harl 7C 118
CM21: Saw 4G 98
HP8: Chal G 2A 158
SG6: L Gar 7D 22
WD4: Kin L 1A 136
WD19: Watf 3A 162
WD23: B Hea 2F 162
WD25: Watf 7H 137
Highfield Av. AL5: Harp 7D 88
CM23: Bis S 2L 79
Highfield Cl. HA6: North 8G 161
Highfield Ct. N14 ....8H 155
SG1: Stev 2L 51
SL9: Chal P 5C 158
Highfield Cres. HA6: North 8G 160
Highfield Dr. EN10: Brox 3J 133
Highfield Farm SG13: H'ford 8E 114
Highfield Hall AL4: St Alb 6M 127
Highfield Ho. HP2: Hem H 9B 106
Highfield La. AL4: St Alb 4K 127
HP2: Hem H 9B 106
Highfield Mnr. AL4: St Alb 6M 127
Highfield Oval AL5: Harp 4B 88
Highfield Pk. Cen. 3K 127
Highfield Pk. Dr. AL4: St Alb 5J 127
Highfield Rd. AL4: San 5J 109
EN7: C'hunt 8C 132
HA6: North 8G 161
HP4: Berk 2A 122
HP23: Tring 3K 101
HP23: Wigg 5B 102
LU4: Lut 8D 46
SG13: H'ford 2B 114
WD23: Bush 7N 149
Highfields CB11: L Upp 2N 29
EN6: Cuff 1K 143
WD7: Rad 8G 139
Highfields Cl. LU5: Duns 7K 45
Highfield Way EN6: Pot B 5A 142
WD3: R'orth 8K 147
High Firs WD7: Rad 8H 139
High Firs Cres. AL5: Harp 7E 88
Highgate Gro. CM21: Saw 5F 98
High Gro. AL3: St Alb 9E 108
AL8: Welw G 8J 91
Highgrove Ct. EN8: Wal C 7G 145
High Ho. Est. CM17: Harl 2H 119
Highland Dr. HP3: Hem H 2D 124
WD23: Bush 9C 150
Highland Rd. CM23: Thorl 5H 79
HA6: North 9H 161
Highlands AL9: Hat 6J 111
SG8: Roys 7E 8
WD19: Watf 1L 161
Highlands, The EN5: N Bar 6N 153
EN6: Pot B 3B 142
HA8: Edg 9B 164
WD3: R'orth 9L 147
Highlands Av. N21 ....7L 155
Highlands Cl. SL9: Chal P 7C 158
Highlands End SL9: Chal P 7C 158
Highlands La. SL9: Chal P 7C 158
Highlands Rd. EN5: N Bar 7N 153
HIGHLANDS VILLAGE 7L 155
High La. CM17: She 9N 99
CM22: M Tye, She 9N 99
CM24: Stans 9N 43
Highlea Cl. NW9 ....7E 164
High Mead LU3: Lut 6C 46
Highmead CM24: Stans 1N 59
High Meads AL4: Wheat 7K 89
Highmill SG12: Ware 4H 95
High Molewood SG14: H'ford 7N 93
Highmoor AL5: Harp 3B 88
High Moors HP22: Halt 6A 100
High Oak Rd. SG12: Ware 5H 95
High Oaks AL3: St Alb 6D 108
EN2: Enf 2L 155
HA6: North 5H 161
High Oaks Rd. AL8: Welw G 8H 91
Highover Cl. LU2: Lut 8K 47
Highover Rd. SG6: L Gar 6D 22
Highover Way SG4: Hit 1B 34
High Pastures CM22: She 6M 99
High Plash SG1: Stev 4L 51
High Point *LU1: Lut* *2F 66*
(off Ruthin Cl.)
High Ridge AL5: Harp 4N 87
EN6: Cuff 9K 131
LU2: Lut 8L 47
High Ridge Cl. HP3: Hem H 7N 123
Highridge Pl. *EN2: Enf* *2L 155*
(off Oak Av.)
High Ridge Rd. HP3: Hem H 7N 123
High Rd. AL9: Ess 3D 130
EN10: Turn, Worm, Brox 7J 133
HA3: Har W 7F 162
SG5: Shil 4N 19
SG11: H Cro 7J 75
SG14: Stap, Water 1L 93
WD23: B Hea 1E 162
WD25: Watf 8H 137
High Rd. Turnford EN10: Turn 8J 133
High Rd. Whetstone N20 ....9B 154
High St. AL2: Lon C 7K 127
AL3: Flam 5D 86
AL3: Mark 1N 85
AL3: Red 1K 107
AL3: St Alb 3C 166 (2E 126)
AL4: Col H 4B 128
AL4: San 5J 109
AL4: Wheat 7L 89
AL5: Harp 5B 88
AL6: Wel 2J 91
CM17: Harl 2E 118
CM19: Royd 5E 116
CM23: Bis S 1H 79
EN3: Pon E 8G 156
EN5: Barn 5L 153
EN6: Pot B 6A 142
EN8: C'hunt 2H 145
EN8: Wal C 6J 145
(not continuous)
EN11: Hod 1L 133
HA3: Har W, Weal 9F 162
HA6: North 8H 161
HA8: Edg 6A 164
HP1: Hem H 1M 123
HP3: Bov 9D 122
HP4: Berk 7J 103
HP22: Wen 9A 100
HP23: Tring 3M 101
LU4: Lut 6M 45
LU5: Hou R 5E 44
LU6: Eat B 2H 63
LU6: Edle 5J 63
LU7: Ched 9M 61
LU7: I'hoe 2C 82
MK45: Pull 3A 18
NW7 ....5H 165
SG1: Stev 2J 51
SG2: Walk 2G 52
SG4: Cod 6E 70
SG4: G'ley 5J 35
SG4: Gos 7N 33
SG4: Kimp 7J 69
SG4: Whit 1M 69
SG5: Gt Off 7D 32
SG5: Hit 3M 33
SG5: Pirt 7E 20
SG5: Stot 6E 10
SG7: Ashw 9M 5
SG7: Bald 3M 23
SG7: Hinx 7E 4
SG8: Bark 9N 15
SG8: Barl 3C 16
SG8: Bass 1M 7
SG8: Chris 1N 17
SG8: G Mor 1A 6
SG8: Melb 2L 9
SG8: Reed 7J 15
SG8: Roys 7D 8
SG9: Bunt 2J 39
SG10: M Had 5J 77
SG11: Puck 6N 55
SG11: Stand 8C 56
SG12: Huns 7G 96
SG12: Stan A 2N 115
SG12: Ware 6H 95
SG12: Widf 3H 97
SG14: Watt S 4J 73
SG15: Arl 5A 10
SG18: Dunt 1F 4
SL9: Chal P 8B 158
UB9: Hare 9M 159
WD3: R'orth 1N 159
WD4: Kin L 2C 136
WD5: Abb L 4G 137
WD5: Bed 9H 125
WD6: Elst 8L 151
WD17: Watf 6B 166 (5K 149)
WD23: Bush 8B 150
High St. Grn. HP2: Hem H 9C 106
High St. Nth. LU6: Duns 7C 44
High St. Sth. HP4: Berk 7J 103
LU6: Duns 9E 44
HIGH TOWN 9G 47
Hightown Community Sports & Arts Cen. 9H 47
High Town Ent. Cen. *LU2: Lut* *9H 47*
(off York St.)
High Town Rd. LU2: Lut 9G 47
High Tree Cl. CM21: Saw 6F 98
High Trees EN4: E Bar 7D 154
HP2: Hem H 2N 123
High Vw. AL3: Mark 3A 86
AL10: Hat 2F 128
CM23: Birc 6L 59
HP8: Chal G 2A 158
SG5: Hit 4L 33
WD3: Chor 6K 147
WD18: Watf 8H 149
Highview NW7 ....3D 164
Highview Av. HA8: Edg 4C 164
Highview Cl. EN6: Pot B 6B 142
High Vw. Ct. HA3: Har W 7F 162
Highview Gdns. AL4: St Alb 6K 109
EN6: Pot B 6B 142
HA8: Edg 4C 164
Highview Lodge *EN2: Enf* *5N 155*
(off The Ridgeway)
High Vw. Pk. WD4: Kin L 1F 136
Highway, The HA7: Stanm 8G 163
High Wickfield AL7: Welw G 1B 112
Highwood Av. WD23: Bush 3A 150
High Wood Cl. LU1: Lut 1B 66
Highwood Ct. EN5: N Bar 7N 153
Highwood Gro. NW7 ....5D 164
Highwoodhall La. HP3: Hem H 7C 124
HIGHWOOD HILL 3F 164
Highwood Hill NW7 ....2F 164
High Wood Rd. EN11: Hod 5K 115
HIGH WYCH 6C 98
High Wych La. CM21: H Wyc, Saw 6C 98
High Wych Rd. CM21: H Wyc, Saw 9A 98
High Wych Way HP2: Hem H 5C 106
Hilberry Ct. WD23: Bush 9C 150
Hilbury AL10: Hat 1F 128
Hilfield La. WD25: A'ham 3C 150
Hilfield La. Sth. WD23: Bush 8G 150
Hiliary Gdns. HA7: Stanm 9K 163
Hiljon Cres. SL9: Chal P 8B 158
Hill, The AL4: Wheat 7L 89
CM17: Harl 2E 118
Hillary Cl. LU3: Lut 2N 45
Hillary Cres. LU1: Lut 2E 66
Hillary Ho. *WD6: Bore* *5B 152*
(off Eldon Av.)
Hillary Ri. EN5: N Bar 6N 153
SG15: Arl 7B 10
Hillary Rd. HP2: Hem H 1C 124
Hillborough Cres. LU5: Hou R 2F 44
Hillborough Rd. LU1: Lut 2F 66
Hillbrow SG6: L Gar 6D 22
Hill Cl. AL5: Harp 3D 88
EN5: Barn 7J 153
HA7: Stanm 4J 163
LU3: Lut 2E 46
LU7: W'field 1B 44
Hill Comn. HP3: Hem H 6C 124
Hill Ct. EN4: E Bar 6D 154
EN6: Pot B 7B 142
Hill Cres. N20 ....2N 165
Hill Crest EN6: Pot B 7B 142
SG4: Whit 2M 69
Hillcrest AL3: St Alb 4C 126
AL10: Hat 9G 110
N21 ....9M 155
SG1: Stev 4L 51
SG7: Bald 4M 23
Hillcrest Av. HA8: Edg 4B 164
LU2: Lut 1E 46
Hillcrest Caravan Site LU1: Wood 6B 66
Hillcrest Cl. EN7: Gof O 2A 144
Hillcrest Pk. SG6: L Gar 5B 22
Hillcrest Rd. WD7: Shen 6A 140
Hill Cft. WD7: Rad 6H 139
Hillcroft LU6: Duns 8B 44
Hillcroft Cl. LU4: Lut 3M 45
Hillcroft Cres. WD19: Watf 1K 161
Hilldown Rd. HP1: Hem H 9K 105
Hilldyke Rd. AL4: Wheat 8L 89
Hille Bus. Cen. WD24: Watf 3K 149
HILL END
AL9 ....7N 111
UB9 ....6L 159
Hill End La. AL4: St Alb 5J 127
Hill End Pit Nature Reserve 4B 50
Hill End Rd. UB9: Hare 7M 159
Hillersdon Av. HA8: Edg 5N 163
Hill Farm Av. WD25: Watf 6J 137
(not continuous)
Hill Farm Cl. WD25: Watf 6J 137
Hill Farm Ind. Est. WD25: Watf 6J 137
Hill Farm La. AL3: St Alb 6K 107
AL6: Ayot L 1B 90
Hill Farm Rd. SL9: Chal P 7B 158
Hillfield AL10: Hat 6H 111
Hillfield Av. SG4: Hit 9A 22
Hillfield Ct. HP2: Hem H 2A 124
Hillfield Rd. HP2: Hem H 2N 123
SL9: Chal P 7B 158
Hillfield Sq. SL9: Chal P 7B 158
HILLFOOT END 2N 19
Hillfoot Rd. SG5: Shil 2N 19
Hillgate SG4: Hit 8A 22
Hill Grn. La. HP23: Wigg 5D 102
Hillgrove SL9: Chal P 8B 158
Hillgrove Bus. Pk. EN9: Naz 4N 133
Hill Ho. SG13: H'ford 1A 114
Hill Ho. Av. HA7: Stanm 7G 163
Hill Ho. Cl. N21 ....9M 155
SL9: Chal P 7B 158
Hilliard Rd. HA6: North 8H 161
Hillier Cl. EN5: N Bar 8A 154
Hillingdon Rd. WD25: Watf 7J 137
Hill Ley AL10: Hat 9F 110
Hill Leys EN6: Cuff 1K 143
Hillmead HP4: Berk 2L 121
SG1: Stev 3N 51
Hillpath SG6: L Gar 5H 23

A-Z Hertfordshire 197

Honey Way—James Way

Honey Way SG8: Roys 6E 8
HONEYWICK 1J 63
Honeywick La. LU6: Eat B 1J 63
Honeywood Cl. EN6: Pot B 6C 142
Honeywood Light Ind. Est.
SG9: Cot 2B 38
Honister Cl. HA7: Stanm 8J 163
Honister Gdns. HA7: Stanm 7J 163
Honister Pl. HA7: Stanm 8J 163
Honiton Gdns. NW7 7K 165
Honiton Ho. EN3: Pon E 5H 157
Honiton M. LU3: Lut 3A 46
Honor St. CM17: Harl 5E 118
Honors Yd. HP23: Tring 3M 101
Honours Mead HP3: Bov 9D 122
Hoo, The CM17: Harl 1E 118
Hoo Bit Nature Reserve 3M 31
Hoo Cotts. SG5: Gt Off 9E 32
Hood Av. N14 8G 155
Hoodcote Gdns. N21 9N 155
HOO END 4L 69
Hoo Farm Cotts. SG5: Gt Off 9E 32
Hook, The EN5: N Bar 8C 154
Hookfield CM18: Harl 8A 118
Hook Ga. EN1: Enf 9F 144
Hook La. EN6: N'haw 5E 142
HOOK'S CROSS 2E 72
Hook Wlk. HA8: Edg 6C 164
Hoo La. SG5: Gt Off 9E 32
Hoopers M. WD23: Bush 1C 162
Hoops La. SG8: Ther 6D 14
Hoo St. LU1: Lut 3G 66
Hope Grn. WD25: Watf 6J 137
Hope Pl. HP22: Halt 8D 100
Hopewell Rd. SG7: Bald 3K 23
Hop Garden Way WD25: Watf 4L 137
Hopground Cl. AL1: St Alb 4H 127
Hopkins Cres. AL4: San 5J 109
Hopkins Yd. AL1: St Alb 4E 166 (3F 126)
Hopleys Garden 5J 77
Hoppers Rd. N21 9M 155
Hopton Rd. SG1: Stev 2G 51
Hopwood Cl. WD17: Watf 9G 136
Horace Brightman Cl. LU3: Lut 2C 46
Horace Gay Gdns. SG6: L Gar 6E 22
Hordle Gdns. AL1: St Alb 4G 127
Horn & Horseshoe La. CM17: Harl 8G 119
Hornbeam Cl. NW7 3F 164
SG14: H'ford 8N 93
WD6: Bore 3A 152
Hornbeam Ct. SG4: Gt Wym 5E 34
Hornbeam La. AL9: Ess 3D 130
Hornbeams AL2: Bri W 3A 138
AL7: Welw G 1A 112
Hornbeams, The CM20: Harl 4L 117
SG2: Stev 5A 52
Hornbeams Av. EN1: Enf 8G 144
Hornbeam Spring SG3: Kneb 4M 71
Hornbeam Way EN7: C'hunt 2D 144
Hornets, The WD18: Watf 9C 166 (6K 149)
Horneywood La. SG9: Throck 1N 37
HORN HILL 4E 158
Horn Hill SG4: Whit 2L 69
Horn Hill La. SL9: Chal P 5C 158
Hornhill Rd. WD3: Map C 5E 158
Hornsby Cl. LU2: Lut 8L 47
Horns Cl. SG13: H'ford 2A 114
Hornsfield AL7: Welw G 8B 92
Horns Mill Rd. SG13: H'ford 3N 113
Horns Rd. SG13: H'ford 1A 114
Horrocks Cl. SG12: Ware 4H 95
Horsa Gdns. AL10: Hat 8D 110
Horsecroft Pl. CM19: Harl 7H 117
Horsecroft Rd. CM19: Harl 6H 117
HA8: Edg 7D 164
HP1: Hem H 4K 123
Horse Hill HP5: Ley H 5A 134
Horselers HP3: Hem H 5C 124
Horsemans Ride AL2: Chis G 8B 126
Horseshoe, The HP3: Hem H 4E 124
Horseshoe Bus. Pk. AL2: Bri W 3C 138
Horseshoe Cl. LU7: Ched 9L 61
SG8: Barl 3C 16
Horseshoe Cotts. *SG4: Hit* 4N 33
(off Park St.)
Horseshoe Ct. *SG12: Stan A* 2A 116
(off Thele Av.)
Horseshoe Hill SG9: Gt Hor 2D 40
Horseshoe La. EN2: Enf 5A 156
N20 1K 165
SG9: Gt Hor 3C 40
WD25: Watf 5K 137
Horsham Cl. LU2: Lut 7M 47
Horshams CM19: Harl 6M 117
Horsler Cl. MK45: Bar C 9E 18
Horsleys WD3: Map C 5G 158
HORTON 5M 61
Horton Gdns. HP2: Hem H 5C 106
Horton Rd. LU7: Hort, I'hoe 5M 61
LU7: Slapt 4A 62
Horton Wharf Rd. LU7: Slapt 4A 62
Horwood Cl. WD3: R'orth 9K 147
Horwood Ct. WD24: Watf 1M 149
Hospital Rd. SG15: Arl 8A 10
Hotshots Tenpin Bowl 4B 124
Hotspur Way EN2: Enf 8D 144
Houghton Ct. LU5: Hou R 5F 44
Houghton Hall Pk. LU5: Hou R 6F 44
Houghton M. *LU1: Lut* 2F 66
(off Windsor St.)
Houghton Pde. LU6: Duns 7D 44
HOUGHTON PARK 3H 45
Houghton Pk. Rd. LU5: Hou R 3H 45
HOUGHTON REGIS 5E 44
Houghton Regis Leisure Centre & Harpers Fitness 2H 45
Houghton Regis Trad. Est. LU5: Hou R 5E 44
Houghton Rd. LU4: Chalt 1J 45
LU5: Duns, Hou R 7D 44
LU6: Duns 7D 44
Houndsden Rd. N21 8L 155
Houndsfield Rd. N9 9F 156
Housden Cl. AL4: Wheat 8M 89
Housefield Way AL4: St Alb 5K 127
House La. AL4: San, St Alb 5K 109
SG15: Arl 5A 10
House on the Hill Toy Mus. 2N 59
Housewood End HP1: Hem H 8L 105
HOUSHAM TYE 4M 119
Housham Tye Rd. CM17: Harl, M Tye 3L 119
Housman Av. SG8: Roys 4C 8
Howard Agne Cl. HP3: Bov 9D 122
Howard Centre, The AL8: Welw G 9K 91
Howard Cl. AL1: St Alb 4K 127
LU3: Lut 5C 46
SG5: Stot 7E 10
WD23: B Hea 9F 150
WD24: Watf 1J 149
Howard Ct. *AL1: St Alb* 4E 126
(off Cottonmill La.)
SG6: L Gar 7H 23
Howard Dr. SG6: L Gar 8G 23
WD6: Bore 6D 152
Howarde Ct. SG1: Stev 3J 51
Howard Ga. SG6: L Gar 7H 23
Howard Ho. AL8: Welw G 9K 91
Howard Pk. Cnr. SG6: L Gar 5G 22
Howard Pl. LU5: Duns 1G 64
Howard Rd. HA7: Stanm 8L 163
Howards Cl. HA5: Pin 9K 161
Howards Dr. HP1: Hem H 8J 105
Howardsgate AL8: Welw G 8K 91
(not continuous)
Howards Wood SG6: L Gar 8H 23
Howard Way CM20: Harl 3B 118
EN5: Barn 7K 153
Howberry Cl. HA8: Edg 6L 163
Howberry Grn. SG15: Arl 9A 10
Howberry Rd. HA7: Stanm 6L 163
HA8: Edg 6L 163
Howcroft Cres. N3 7N 165
Howe Cl. WD7: Shen 5M 139
Howe Dell AL10: Hat 9H 111
HOWE GREEN
CM22 6N 79
SG13 7F 112
Howell Hill Cl. LU7: Ment 3J 61
Howe Rd. HP3: Hem H 4C 124
Howes Cl. N3 9N 165
How Fld. AL5: Harp 4N 87
Howfield Grn. EN11: Hod 5L 115
Howicks Grn. AL7: Welw G 3N 111
Howland Ct. HA5: Hat E 6B 162
Howland Gth. AL1: St Alb 6D 126
Howlands AL7: Welw G 3L 111
Howlands Ho. AL7: Welw G 3N 111
Howse Rd. EN9: Wal A 8M 145
Howton Pl. WD23: B Hea 1E 162
HOW WOOD 9D 126
How Wood AL2: Par S 1C 138
How Wood Station (Rail) 1D 138
Hoylake Ct. LU1: Lut 3H 67
Hoylake Gdns. WD19: Watf 4M 161
Hubbard's Hall Est. CM17: Harl 5G 119
Hubbards Rd. WD3: Chor 7G 146
Huckleberry Cl. LU3: Lut 1C 46
Hudgell Rd. CM24: Stans 4N 59
HUDNALL 8C 84
Hudnall Cnr. HP4: Lit G 8D 84
Hudnall La. HP4: Lit G 9A 84
Hudson *NW9* 8F 164
(off Five Acre)
Hudson Cl. AL1: St Alb 5E 126
WD24: Watf 9H 137
Hudson Ct. LU6: Duns 8D 44
Hudson Rd. SG2: Stev 2A 52
Hudsons Ct. EN6: Pot B 4N 141
Huggins La. AL9: Welh G 5J 129
Hughenden Rd. AL4: St Alb 8J 109
Hughendon EN5: N Bar 6A 154
Hughes Ct. LU3: Lut 1D 46
Hugh's Twr. CM20: Harl 5N 117
Hugh Vs. CM23: Bis S 3J 79
Hugo Cl. WD18: Watf 6G 149
Hugo Gryn Way WD7: Shen 4M 139
Hull Cl. EN7: C'hunt 8B 132
Hull La. SG11: B'ing 2B 56
Humber Ct. SG1: Stev 7M 35
Humberstone Cl. LU4: Lut 7A 46
Humberstone Rd. LU4: Lut 7A 46
Humphrys Rd. LU5: Duns 6G 45
Hundred Acre NW9 9F 164
Hundred Acres EN8: Wal C 7L 145
Hungerdown E4 9N 157
HUNSDON 6G 96
Hunsdon AL7: Welw G 9C 92
HUNSDONBURY 8G 96
Hunsdon Rd. SG12: Huns, Stan A 2B 116
SG12: Widf 4G 97
Hunsdon Rd. Cotts. SG12: Stan A 1B 116
Hunston Cl. LU4: Lut 4L 45
Hunt Cl. AL4: St Alb 8L 109
Hunt Ct. N14 9G 155
Hunter Cl. EN6: Pot B 6A 142
WD6: Bore 7C 152
Huntercrombe Gdns. WD19: Watf 4L 161
Hunters Cl. HP3: Bov 2D 134
HP23: Tring 1N 101
SG2: Stev 2C 52
SG5: Stot 6E 10
Hunters Ga. WD25: Watf 6J 137
Hunter's La. WD25: Watf 6H 137
Hunters Oak HP2: Hem H 7D 106
Hunters Pk. HP4: Berk 9B 104
Hunters Reach EN7: C'hunt 2D 144
Hunters Ride AL2: Bri W 4B 138
Hunters Way AL7: Welw G 3M 111
EN2: Enf 3M 155
SG8: Roys 7E 8
Hunter Wlk. WD6: Bore 7D 152
Hunt Hill Cl. SG1: Stev 7A 36
Huntingdon Cl. EN10: Worm 6J 133
Huntingdon Rd. SG1: Stev 1H 51
Hunting Ga. HP2: Hem H 7A 106
SG4: Hit 8A 22
Hunting Ga. Cl. EN2: Enf 5M 155
Huntly Dr. N3 6N 165
HUNTON BRIDGE 6E 136
HUNTON BRIDGE 8F 136
Hunton Bri. Hill WD4: Hun C 6E 136
Hunton Cl. WD4: Hun C 6E 136
Hunts Cl. LU1: Lut 2E 66
Huntsman Cl. SG11: Puck 6A 56
Huntsmans Cl. HP4: Dag 2N 83
Hunts Mead EN3: Enf H 5H 157
Huntsmill Rd. HP1: Hem H 3H 123
Hurlock Cl. LU6: Duns 2D 64
Hurlock Way LU4: Lut 4M 45
Hurn Gro. CM23: Bis S 8L 59
Huron Rd. EN10: Turn 8J 133
Hurricane Trad. Cen. NW9 8G 164
Hurricane Way WD5: Abb L 5J 137
Hurst Cl. AL7: Welw G 1B 112
CM23: Bis S 1G 79
SG7: Bald 2N 23
Hurst Ct. WD17: Watf 2J 149
Hurst Dr. EN8: Wal C 7H 145
Hurstleigh WD3: Chor 7F 146
Hurstlings AL7: Welw G 1A 112
Hurstmead Ct. HA8: Edg 4B 164
Hurst Path *LU7: Pits* 4B 82
(off Stirling Pl.)
Hurst Pl. HA6: North 8D 160
Hurst Ri. EN5: N Bar 5N 153
Hurst Way LU3: Lut 4A 46
Hutchings Lodge WD3: R'orth 1A 160
Hutton Cl. LU4: Lut 6A 46
SG14: H'ford 9M 93
Hutton Ct. *N9* 9G 156
(off Tramway Av.)
Hutton Gdns. HA3: Har W 7D 162
Hutton La. HA3: Har W 7D 162
Hutton Row HA8: Edg 7C 164
Hutton Wlk. HA3: Har W 7D 162
Hyatt Trad. Est. SG1: Stev 4G 51
Hyburn Cl. AL2: Bri W 3A 138
HP3: Hem H 3D 124
Hyde, The SG2: Stev 6B 52
SG12: Ware 5F 94
Hydean Way SG2: Stev 6N 51
Hyde Av. EN6: Pot B 6A 142
SG5: Stot 7E 10
Hyde Cl. AL5: Harp 3C 88
EN5: Barn 5M 153
Hyde Ct. AL2: Lon C 9J 127
EN8: Wal C 7J 145
Hyde Grn. E. SG2: Stev 6A 52
Hyde Grn. Nth. SG2: Stev 6A 52
Hyde Grn. Sth. SG2: Stev 6A 52
Hyde Ho. *LU2: Lut* 9H 47
(off Crescent Ri.)
Hyde La. AL2: Frog, Par S 1D 138
(not continuous)
HP3: Bov 9C 122
HP3: Hem H 9C 124
LU2: P Grn 6C 68
Hyde Mdws. HP3: Bov 1D 134
Hyde Rd. LU1: Cad 4A 66
WD17: Watf 5A 166 (4J 149)
Hyde Ter. HP3: Hem H 6G 125
Hyde Valley AL7: Welw G 2M 111
Hyde Vw. Rd. AL5: Harp 3C 88
Hyde Way AL7: Welw G 9L 91
Hyperion Ct. HP2: Hem H 8B 106
Hyver Hill NW7 8D 152

I

Ian Sq. EN3: Enf H 3H 157
Ibberson Way SG4: Hit 3A 34
Ibsley Way EN4: C'ters 7D 154
Iceni Ct. SG6: L Gar 4H 23
ICKLEFORD 7M 21
Ickleford *SG1: Stev* 8J 35
(off Lister Cl.)
Ickleford Bury SG5: Ick 8M 21
Ickleford Rd. SG5: Hit 1N 33
Ickley Cl. LU4: Lut 4L 45
Icknield Cl. AL3: St Alb 4A 126
HP22: Wen 9B 100
SG5: Ick 7M 21
Icknield Grn. HP23: Tring 9M 81
(not continuous)
SG6: L Gar 5E 22
Icknield Rd. LU3: Lut 5B 46
Icknield St. LU6: Duns 9E 44
Icknield Vs. *LU6: Duns* 9E 44
(off Icknield St.)
Icknield Wlk. SG8: Roys 6E 8
Icknield Way HP23: Tring 3J 101
LU3: Lut 3C 46
LU7: I Ast 1E 82
SG6: L Gar 5C 22
SG7: Bald 2L 23
Icknield Way E. SG7: Bald 2M 23
Icknield Way Ind. Est. HP23: Tring 3K 101
Icon, The SG1: Stev 4J 51
Idenbury Ct. LU1: Lut 1E 66
Ilex Ct. HP4: Berk 1M 121
Ilford Cl. LU2: Lut 6L 47
Ilkley Rd. WD19: Watf 5M 161
Illingworth Way EN1: Enf 7C 156
Imber Cl. N14 9H 155
Imberfield LU4: Lut 6M 45
Imperial Cancer Research Cen. 7F 140
Imperial Pk. WD24: Watf 3L 149
Imperial Pl. WD6: Bore 5B 152
Imperial Way HP3: Hem H 6A 124
WD3: Crox G 9D 148
WD24: Watf 3L 149
Impresa Pk. EN11: Hod 7N 115
Indells AL10: Hat 1F 128
Index Ct. LU6: Duns 1G 64
Index Dr. LU6: Duns 1G 64
Ingelheim Ct. SG1: Stev 2K 51
Ingersoll Rd. EN3: Enf W 2G 157
Inglefield EN6: Pot B 3N 141
Ingles AL8: Welw G 6K 91
Ingleside Dr. SG1: Stev 8G 35
Inglewood Gdns. AL2: St Alb 7F 126
Ingram Cl. HA7: Stanm 5K 163
Ingram Gdns. LU2: Lut 2F 46
Inkerman Rd. AL1: St Alb 4E 166 (3F 126)
Inkerman St. LU1: Lut 1F 66
Innes Ct. HP3: Hem H 5N 123
Innova Bus. Pk. EN3: Enf L 9K 145
Innova Way EN3: Enf L 9K 145
Inn's Cl. SG1: Stev 3K 51
Inskip Cres. SG1: Stev 4L 51
Interchange, The AL10: Hat 6D 110
Inverness Av. EN1: Enf 3C 156
IO Centre EN9: Wal A 8L 145
IO Centre, The AL10: Hat 7E 110
Iona Cl. SG1: Stev 8M 35
Ionian Way HP2: Hem H 8B 106
Iredale Vw. SG7: Bald 2N 23
Irene Stebbings Ho. AL4: St Alb 1K 127
Ireton Ct. SG1: Stev 3J 51
Iris Wlk. HA8: Edg 4C 164
Irkdale Av. EN1: Enf 3D 156
Iron Dr. SG13: H'ford 8F 94
Irvine Av. HA3: Ken 9J 163
Irving Cl. CM23: Bis S 4F 78
Irving Cres. LU7: Ched 8M 61
Isabel Ct. EN11: Hod 6M 115
Isabel Ga. EN8: C'hunt 8K 133
Isabella Cl. N14 9H 155
Isabelle Cl. EN7: Gof O 2A 144
Isenburg Way HP2: Hem H 6N 105
Isherwood Cl. SG8: Roys 5C 8
Island Cen. Way EN3: Enf L 1L 157
Island Ct. CM23: Bis S 3J 79
Islay Ho. WD18: Watf 8H 149
Isle of Wight La. LU6: Kens 4C 64
Islip Gdns. HA8: Edg 7D 164
Isopad Ho. *WD6: Bore* 5B 152
(off Shenley Rd.)
Italstyle Building, The CM21: Saw 9E 98
Itaska Cotts. WD23: B Hea 1F 162
Itch La. SG11: Alb 2M 57
Ivanhoe Dr. HA3: Ken 9H 163
Ivatt Ct. SG4: Hit 3C 34
Iveagh Cl. HA6: North 8D 160
Iveagh Ct. HP2: Hem H 1N 123
Iveagh Ho. AL7: Welw G 9B 92
Ivel Cl. MK45: Bar C 8F 18
Ivel Ct. SG6: L Gar 7J 23
Ivel Rd. SG1: Stev 2J 51
Ivel Way SG5: Stot 4F 10
SG7: Bald 5N 23
Ivere Dr. EN5: N Bar 8A 154
Ives Rd. SG14: H'ford 8N 93
IVINGHOE 2C 82
IVINGHOE ASTON 7E 62
Ivinghoe Bus. Cen. LU5: Hou R 6E 44
Ivinghoe Cl. AL4: St Alb 6K 109
EN1: Enf 3C 156
WD25: Watf 8M 137
Ivinghoe Golf Course 1D 82
Ivinghoe Rd. WD3: R'orth 9K 147
WD23: Bush 9E 150
Ivinghoe Way LU6: Edle 7J 63
Ivory Cl. AL4: St Alb 4K 127
Ivory Ct. HP3: Hem H 5A 124
Ivybridge EN10: Brox 1L 133
Ivy Cl. LU6: Duns 8B 44
Ivy Ct. LU1: Lut 9D 46
Ivy Ho. WD19: Watf 8M 149
Ivy Ho. La. HP4: Berk 1B 122
Ivy La. SG8: Roys 7A 8
Ivy Lea WD3: R'orth 1K 159
Ivy Rd. LU1: Lut 9E 46
N14 9H 155
Ivy Ter. EN11: Hod 6N 115
Ivy Wlk. AL10: Hat 6E 110
HA6: North 8G 160

J

Jackdaw Cl. SG2: Stev 5C 52
Jackdaws AL7: Welw G 9B 92
Jackets La. HA6: North 8D 160
UB9: Hare, North 7C 160
Jacketts Fld. WD5: Abb L 4H 137
Jackman's Pl. SG6: L Gar 5H 23
Jacks Hill SG4: G'ley 3J 35
SG6: Will 3J 35
Jacks Hill Pk. SG4: G'ley 3J 35
Jacks La. UB9: Hare 8K 159
Jackson Pl. HP22: Halt 8C 100
Jackson Rd. EN4: E Bar 8D 154
Jacksons Cl. LU6: Edle 4J 63
Jacksons Ct. *SG9: Bunt* 3J 39
(off High St.)
Jacksons Dr. EN7: C'hunt 1E 144
Jacksons Hill CM20: Harl 4A 118
Jackson's La. SG8: Reed 7J 15
Jackson Sq. CM23: Bis S 1H 79
Jackson St. SG7: Bald 2L 23
Jackson Wharf *CM23: Bis S* 1H 79
(off Adderley Rd.)
Jack Stevens Cl. CM17: Harl 8E 118
Jacob Ct. AL4: St Alb 4K 127
Jacob M. HA7: Stanm 2H 163
Jacob's Ladder *AL9: Hat* 9J 111
(off The Broadway)
Jakes Vw. AL2: Par S 9D 126
James Bedford Cl. HA5: Pin 9L 161
James Cl. WD23: Bush 7N 149
James Ct. AL2: Lon C 9J 127
HA6: North 8H 161
LU1: Lut 2G 66
LU4: Lut 7L 45
NW9 9E 164
James Foster Ho. SG5: Hit 1M 33
James Lee Sq. EN3: Enf L 2L 157
James Marshall Commercial Cen.
AL5: Harp 6B 88
Jameson Ct. *AL1: St Alb* 1G 126
(off Avenue Rd.)
Jameson Rd. AL5: Harp 4C 88
James St. EN1: Enf 7D 156
James Way SG1: Stev 2J 51
WD19: Watf 4M 161

Kingsbridge Dr.—Langley Way

Kingsbridge Dr. NW7 .7K **165**
Kingsbridge Rd. CM23: Bis S .9J **59**
Kingsbury Av.
AL3: St Alb .1A **166** (1D **126**)
LU5: Duns .8H **45**
Kingsbury Ct. LU5: Duns .8F **44**
Kingsbury Gdns. LU5: Duns .8J **45**
Kingsbury M. AL3: St Alb .1C **126**
Kingsbury Watermill Mus. .1C **126**
Kings Chase Vw. EN2: Enf .4M **155**
Kingsclere Pl. EN2: Enf .4A **156**
Kings Cl. HA6: North .6H **161**
HP8: Chal G .2A **158**
WD4: Chippf .4L **135**
WD18: Watf .9D **166** (6K **149**)
King's Cotts. *CM23: Bis S* .*2H* ***79***
(off South St.)
Kings Ct. AL5: Harp .7C **88**
CM23: Bis S .9J **59**
HP4: Berk .9N **103**
LU5: Duns .*8F* ***44***
(off The Mall)
SG1: Stev .5K **51**
Kingscroft AL7: Welw G .8A **92**
Kingscroft Av. LU5: Duns .8E **44**
Kingsdale Ho. AL6: Wel .4H **91**
Kingsdale Rd. HP4: Berk .2L **121**
Kingsdon La. CM17: Harl .7E **118**
Kingsdown SG4: Hit .4B **34**
Kingsdown Av. LU2: Lut .5F **46**
King's Dr. HA8: Edg .4N **163**
Kings Farm Rd. WD3: Chor .8G **146**
Kingsfield EN11: Hod .6L **115**
Kingsfield Ct. WD19: Watf .9M **149**
Kingsfield Dr. EN3: Enf W .8H **145**
Kingsfield Rd. SG12: Dan E .1C **74**
WD19: Watf .9M **149**
Kingsfield Way EN3: Enf W .8H **145**
Kingsgate AL3: St Alb .4C **126**
Kings Head Ct. CM21: Saw .5G **98**
Kings Head Hill E4 .9M **157**
Kingshead Ho. NW7 .4H **165**
Kings Heath Pk. AL5: Harp .1D **88**
Kings Hedges SG5: Hit .1K **33**
(not continuous)
Kingshill HP4: Berk .2M **121**
Kingshill Av. AL4: St Alb .8J **109**
Kingshill Ct. EN5: Barn .6L **153**
Kingshill Dr. HA3: Ken .9J **163**
Kingshill La. LU2: Lill .7L **31**
Kingshill Way HP4: Berk .3L **121**
Kings Ho. SG8: Roys .8C **8**
Kingsland CM18: Harl .8M **117**
EN6: Pot B .6M **141**
Kingsland Cl. LU5: Hou R .5H **45**
Kingsland Ct. *LU1: Lut* .*2H* ***67***
(off Kingsland Rd.)
Kingsland Rd. HP1: Hem H .4K **123**
LU1: Lut .2H **67**
Kingsland Way SG7: Ashw .9M **5**
King's La. WD4: Chippf .4K **135**
KINGS LANGLEY .2C **136**
Kings Langley By-Pass
HP1: Hem H .4G **123**
HP3: Hem H .4G **123**
WD4: Kin L .4G **123**
Kings Langley Station (Rail) .3E **136**
Kingsley Av. EN8: C'hunt .2F **144**
SG5: Stot .9C **10**
WD6: Bore .4N **151**
Kingsley Ct. AL7: Welw G .4M **111**
HA8: Edg .3B **164**
Kingsley Rd. LU3: Lut .4C **46**
Kingsley Wlk. HP23: Tring .2M **101**
Kings Mead LU6: Edle .5K **63**
Kingsmead AL4: St Alb .8L **109**
CM21: Saw .6G **98**
EN5: N Bar .6N **153**
EN6: Cuff .1K **143**
EN8: C'hunt .1H **145**
Kingsmead Cl. CM19: Royd .7E **116**
Kingsmead Ct. *LU6: Duns* .*8D* ***44***
(off High St. Nth.)
KINGSMEAD HILL .7E **116**
Kings Mdw. WD4: Kin L .1C **136**
Kingsmead Rd. CM23: Bis S .9J **59**
Kings M. *HP2: Hem H* .*1N* ***123***
(off George St.)
Kingsmill Ct. AL10: Hat .2H **129**
Kingsmoor Rd. CM19: Harl .8L **117**
Kings Mt. SG7: Bald .2M **23**
King's Oak WD3: Crox G .6C **148**
Kings Pde. *HA8: Edg* .*5A* ***164***
(off Edgwarebury La.)
WD18: Watf .9B **166**
Kings Pk. Ind. Est. WD4: Kin L .2D **136**
Kings Pl. AL10: Hat .7J **111**
Kings Rd. AL2: Lon C .8K **127**
AL3: St Alb .1A **166** (2C **126**)
EN5: Barn .5J **153**
EN8: Wal C .6J **145**
HP4: Berk .2L **121**
HP8: Chal G .2A **158**
SG5: Hit .2N **33**
SG13: H'ford .8E **94**
Kingston Ct. LU2: Lut .8H **47**
Kingston Pl. HA3: Har W .7G **162**
Kingston Rd. EN4: E Bar .7C **154**
LU2: Lut .8H **47**
Kingston Va. SG8: Roys .8E **8**
King St. AL3: Mark .2A **86**
CM23: Bis S .1H **79**
HP23: Tring .3M **101**
LU1: Lut .1G **66**
LU5: Duns .1F **64**
LU5: Hou R .5E **44**
SG8: Roys .7D **8**
WD18: Watf .9D **166** (6L **149**)
King St. M. CM23: Bis S .1H **79**
KING'S WALDEN .5H **49**
Kings Walden Ri. SG2: Stev .2B **52**
King's Walden Rd. SG5: Gt Off .8D **32**
Kings Wlk. SG8: Roys .7D **8**
Kings Way SG1: Stev .4J **51**
Kingsway EN3: Pon E .7F **156**
EN6: Cuff .3K **143**
LU1: Lut .8C **46**
LU4: Lut .8C **46**
LU5: Duns .8F **44**
SG5: Stot .5F **10**
SG8: Roys .5C **8**
SG12: Ware .4H **95**
SL9: Chal P .9B **158**
Kingsway Gdns. SG5: Stot .5E **10**
Kingsway Ind. Est. LU1: Lut .9C **46**
Kingsway Nth. Orbital Rd. WD25: Watf .8H **137**
KINGSWELL END .3F **48**
Kingswell Ride EN6: Cuff .3K **143**
KINGSWOOD .7K **137**
Kingswood Av. SG4: Hit .1D **34**
Kingswood Cl. EN1: Enf .7C **156**
N20 .9B **154**
Kingswood Pk. N3 .9M **165**
Kingswood Rd. WD25: Watf .7K **137**
Kingwell Rd. EN4: Had W .2C **154**
King William Cl. MK45: Bar C .7F **18**
King William Ct. *EN9: Wal A* .*8N* ***145***
(off Kendal Rd.)
Kinloch Ct. AL5: Harp .5C **88**
Kinmoor Cl. LU3: Lut .1N **45**
Kinross Cl. HA8: Edg .2B **164**
Kinross Cres. LU3: Lut .1M **45**
Kinsbourne Cl. AL5: Harp .3L **87**
Kinsbourne Ct. *AL5: Harp* .*4A* ***88***
(off Luton Rd.)
Kinsbourne Cres. AL5: Harp .3M **87**
KINSBOURNE GREEN .3K **87**
Kinsbourne Grn. La. AL5: Harp, Red .2K **87**
Kintyre Pl. *WD18: Watf* .*8H* ***149***
(off Explorer Dr.)
Kipling Cl. SG4: Hit .3C **34**
Kipling Cres. SG5: Stot .1C **22**
Kipling Gro. HP2: Hem H .5D **106**
Kipling Pl. HA7: Stanm .6G **162**
Kipling Rd. SG8: Roys .4E **8**
Kipling Way AL5: Harp .6C **88**
Kirby Cl. HA6: North .6H **161**
Kirby Dr. LU3: Lut .9B **30**
Kirby Rd. LU6: Duns .9D **44**
Kircutt Farm Cl. LU6: N'all .3D **62**
Kirkcaldy Grn. WD19: Watf .3L **161**
Kirkdale Ct. *LU1: Lut* .*2G* ***67***
(off Albert Rd.)
Kirkdale Rd. AL5: Harp .5B **88**
Kirkland Dr. EN2: Enf .3A **156**
Kirklands AL8: Welw G .5K **91**
Kirkstone Dr. LU6: Duns .2E **64**
Kirkwick Av. AL5: Harp .2E **88**
Kirkwood Rd. LU4: Lut .6H **45**
Kirton Wlk. HA8: Edg .7C **164**
Kirton Way LU5: Hou R .3H **45**
Kitchener Cl. AL1: St Alb .3J **127**
Kitchener Ho. SL9: Chal P .4B **158**
Kitcheners La. SG2: Walk .9G **37**
Kitchen Garden Ct. SG5: Hit .4M **33**
Kitching La. SG1: Stev .4F **50**
Kite Fld. HP4: Berk .7J **103**
Kite Way SG6: L Gar .3E **22**
Kitsbury Ct. HP4: Berk .1M **121**
Kitsbury Rd. HP4: Berk .1M **121**
Kitsbury Ter. HP4: Berk .1M **121**
Kit's La. SG7: Wall .3H **25**
Kitson Way CM20: Harl .5M **117**
Kitswell Way WD7: Rad .6G **139**
Kitten La. SG12: Stan A .2B **116**
Kitters Grn. WD5: Abb L .4G **137**
KITT'S END .1L **153**
Kitts End Rd. EN5: Barn .9K **141**
Kiwi Ct. SG5: Hit .1N **33**
Knap Cl. SG6: L Gar .3J **23**
KNEBWORTH .3N **71**
Knebworth Cl. EN5: N Bar .6A **154**
Knebworth Country Pk. .1H **71**
Knebworth Ct. CM23: Bis S .2F **78**
Knebworth Ga. SG2: Stev .9M **51**
Knebworth Golf Course .2M **71**
Knebworth House .2J **71**
Knebworth Path WD6: Bore .6D **152**
Knebworth Station (Rail) .3M **71**
KNEESWORTH .1B **8**
Kneesworth St. SG8: Roys .6C **8**
Knella Grn. AL7: Welw G .9N **91**
Knella Rd. AL7: Welw G .1L **111**
Knella Rd. Workshops AL7: Welw G .9N **91**
Knight Ct. *E4* .*9N* ***157***
(off The Ridgeway)
Knightsbridge Ct. WD18: Watf .6G **149**
Knightsbridge Way HP2: Hem H .1A **124**
Knights Cl. CM23: Bis S .9D **58**
LU6: Eat B .3J **63**
SG9: Bunt .4J **39**
Knightscote Cl. UB9: Hare .9N **159**
Knights Ct. CM21: Saw .5G **99**
LU6: Eat B .3J **63**
SG7: Bald .5L **23**
SG11: Stand .8C **56**
WD23: B Hea .1E **162**
Knights Fld. LU2: Lut .8F **46**
Knightsfield AL7: Welw G .6L **91**
AL8: Welw G .5J **91**
Knights Grn. WD3: Chor .5H **147**
Knights Orchard AL3: St Alb .2B **166** (2D **126**)
HP1: Hem H .9J **105**
Knights Rd. HA7: Stanm .4K **163**
Knights Row CM23: Bis S .2G **79**
Knights Templars Grn. SG1: Stev .1B **52**
SG2: Stev .1B **52**
Knights Templar Sports Cen. .3L **23**
Knight St. CM21: Saw .5G **99**
Knightswood Cl. HA8: Edg .2C **164**
Knoll, The SG13: H'ford .8F **94**
Knoll Cres. HA6: North .9G **161**
(not continuous)
Knoll Dr. N14 .9F **154**
Knolles Cres. AL9: Welh G .5H **129**
Knoll Grn. HP2: Hem H .9A **106**
Knoll Ri. LU2: Lut .5G **47**
Knolls Cl. HP22: W'rave .5A **60**
Knolls Vw. LU6: N'all .3F **62**
Knoll Vw. SG11: H Cro .4K **75**
Knott Cl. SG1: Stev .7A **36**
Knotts Cl. LU6: Duns .3D **64**
Knowle SG1: Stev .9H **35**
Knowle, The EN11: Hod .9L **115**
Knowle Dr. AL5: Harp .8E **88**
Knowl Pk. WD6: Elst .7M **151**
Knowl Piece SG4: Hit .8A **22**
Knowl Way WD6: Elst .7N **151**
Knox-Johnston Sports Cen. .2M **121**
Knutsford Av. WD24: Watf .2M **149**
Knutsford Rd. SG8: Bass .1M **7**
Koh-I-Noor Av. WD23: Bush .8B **150**
Korda Cl. WD6: Bore .4C **152**
Kristiansand Way SG6: L Gar .3J **23**
Kymswell Rd. SG2: Stev .5B **52**
Kynance Cl. LU2: Lut .6J **47**
Kynance Gdns. HA7: Stanm .8K **163**
Kynaston Cl. HA3: Har W .7E **162**
Kynaston Rd. EN2: Enf .3B **156**
Kynaston Wood HA3: Har W .7E **162**
Kyrkeby SG6: L Gar .7J **23**
Kytes Dr. WD25: Watf .6M **137**
Kytes Est. WD25: Watf .6M **137**

L

Laburnham Cl. EN5: Barn .5M **153**
Laburnum Cl. CM22: She .7L **99**
EN8: C'hunt .4H **145**
LU3: Lut .2E **46**
Laburnum Ct. HA7: Stanm .4K **163**
Laburnum Gro. AL2: Chis G .7C **126**
LU3: Lut .2D **46**
Laburnum Lodge N3 .9M **165**
Laburnum Rd. EN11: Hod .6M **115**
Laburnum Way EN7: Gof O .1N **143**
Lacerta Ct. SG6: L Gar .3K **23**
Lacey Dr. HA8: Edg .4N **163**
Lachbury Cl. LU1: Lut .2C **66**
Lackmore Rd. EN1: Enf .8G **144**
Lacre Way SG6: L Gar .4J **23**
Ladbroke Rd. EN1: Enf .8D **156**
Ladbrooke Cl. EN6: Pot B .5N **141**
Ladbrooke Dr. EN6: Pot B .5N **141**
Ladies Gro. AL3: St Alb .1C **126**
(not continuous)
Lady Aylesford Av. HA7: Stanm .5H **163**
Lady Cooper Ct. HP4: Berk .8B **104**
Ladycroft Wlk. HA7: Stanm .8L **163**
Lady Gro. AL7: Welw G .4L **111**
Ladygrove Ct. SG4: Pres .4N **49**
Ladyhill LU4: Lut .3L **45**
Lady Margaret Gdns. SG12: Ware .4J **95**
Lady Mdw. WD4: Kin L .9N **123**
Lady St John Sq. SG14: H'ford .6M **93**
Lady's Cl. WD18: Watf .9C **166** (6L **149**)
Ladyshot CM20: Harl .5D **118**
Ladysmith Cl. NW7 .7G **165**
Ladysmith Rd. AL3: St Alb .1E **126**
EN1: Enf .5C **156**
(not continuous)
HA3: Weal .9F **162**
LU7: I'hoe .2C **82**
Lady Spencer's Gro.
AL1: St Alb .4B **166** (3D **126**)
AL3: St Alb .4B **166** (3D **126**)
Ladywalk WD3: Map C .5H **159**
Ladywell Prospect CM21: Saw .6J **99**
Ladywood Cl. WD3: Loud .5L **147**
Ladywood Rd. SG14: H'ford .9L **93**
Laelia Ho's. AL1: St Alb .3H **127**
LA Fitness
Edgware .6A **164**
New Barnet .6C **154**
Northwood .9H **161**
Southgate .9J **155**
Lagley Ho. HP4: Berk .9L **103**
Lagley Mdw. HP4: Berk .9L **103**
Laguna Ct. AL1: St Alb .2F **166**
Laharna Trad. Est. WD24: Watf .2L **149**
Laidlaw Dr. N21 .7L **155**
Laidon Sq. HP2: Hem H .7N **105**
Lake, The WD23: B Hea .1E **162**
Lake Dr. WD23: B Hea .2E **162**
Lakeland Cl. HA3: Har W .6E **162**
Lakeman Ho. SL9: Chal P .5C **158**
Lakenheath N14 .7H **155**
Lakes Ct. SG12: Stan A .2M **115**
Lakeside EN2: Enf .6J **155**
HP23: Tring .1M **101**
Lakeside Ct. WD6: Elst .7A **152**
Lakeside Cres. EN4: E Bar .7E **154**
Lakeside Pl. AL2: Lon C .9L **127**
Lakeside Rd. EN8: C'hunt .1G **144**
Lake Vw. CM23: Bis S, Thorl .4E **78**
EN6: Pot B .6B **142**
(not continuous)
HA8: Edg .5N **163**
LU5: Hou R .6D **44**
WD4: Kin L .1D **136**
Lakeview LU3: Lut .7F **46**
Laleham Av. NW7 .3D **164**
Lalleford Rd. LU2: Lut .8L **47**
Lalsham Ho. WD19: Watf .3L **161**
Lamb Cl. AL10: Hat .1H **129**
WD25: Watf .7L **137**
Lamb Ct. AL4: Wheat .8M **89**
Lambe Rd. HP22: Halt .8D **100**
Lambert Cl. LU2: Lut .3L **47**
Lambert Ct. WD23: Bush .6M **149**
Lamberton Ct. *WD6: Bore* .*3A* ***152***
(off Gateshead Rd.)
Lamb La. AL3: Red .1K **107**
Lamb Mdw. SG15: Arl .9A **10**
Lambourn Chase WD7: Rad .9G **138**
Lambourn Dr. LU2: Lut .3G **46**
Lambourne Gdns. EN1: Enf .4D **156**
Lambourn Gdns. AL5: Harp .4A **88**
Lambs Cl. EN6: Cuff .2L **143**
LU5: Duns .8J **45**
Lambscroft Way SL9: Chal P .9B **158**
Lambs Gdns. SG12: Widf .3G **97**
Lamb's Wlk. EN2: Enf .4A **156**
Lambton Av. EN8: Wal C .6H **145**
Lamer La. AL4: Wheat .2K **89**
Lamers Rd. LU2: Lut .7K **47**
Lamex Stadium, The .7L **51**
Lammas Mead SG5: Hit .9M **21**
Lammasmead EN10: Worm .5K **133**
Lammas Path SG2: Stev .5A **52**
Lammas Rd. LU7: Ched .9M **61**
SG14: Watt S .4J **73**
WD18: Watf .7L **149**
Lammas Way SG6: L Gar .3F **22**
Lamorna Cl. LU3: Lut .3B **46**
WD7: Rad .7J **139**
Lamorna Gro. HA7: Stanm .8L **163**
Lampits EN11: Hod .8M **115**
Lamsey Rd. HP3: Hem H .4N **123**
Lanacre Av. NW9 .8D **164**
Lancaster Av. EN4: Had W .2B **154**
LU2: Lut .1E **46**
SG5: Hit .2M **33**
Lancaster Cl. MK45: Bar C .7F **18**
NW9 .7F **164**
SG1: Stev .8L **35**
Lancaster Dr. HP3: Bov .9C **122**
Lancaster Ga. CM21: Saw .7E **98**
Lancaster Ho. EN2: Enf .3B **156**
Lancaster Rd. AL1: St Alb .9G **109**
EN2: Enf .3B **156**
EN4: E Bar .7C **154**
SG5: Hit .2M **33**
Lancaster Rd. Ind. Est. EN4: E Bar .7C **154**
Lancaster Way AL6: Wel .4J **91**
CM23: Bis S .9E **58**
LU7: Pits .4A **82**
WD5: Abb L .4H **137**
Lancelot Gdns. EN4: E Bar .9F **154**
Lancing Ho. *WD24: Watf* .*4L* ***149***
(off Hallam Cl.)
Lancing Rd. LU2: Lut .6M **47**
Lancing Way WD3: Crox G .7D **148**
Lancot Av. LU6: Duns .1B **64**
Lancotbury Cl. LU6: Tot .1M **63**
Lancot Dr. LU6: Duns .9B **44**
Lancot Meadow .9B **44**
Lancot Pl. LU6: Duns .9B **44**
LU6: Tot .1M **63**
Lancrets Path LU1: Lut .1F **66**
Landau Way EN10: Turn .7K **133**
Landford Cl. WD3: R'orth .2A **160**
Landmead Rd. EN8: C'hunt .2J **145**
Land Pk. LU6: Kens .6E **64**
Landrace Rd. LU4: Lut .5H **45**
Landra Gdns. N21 .8N **155**
Landridge Dr. EN1: Enf .2F **156**
Landsdown Cl. EN5: N Bar .6B **154**
Landseer Cl. HA8: Edg .9A **164**
Landseer Rd. EN1: Enf .7E **156**
Lands End WD6: Elst .8L **151**
Lane End AL10: Hat .3F **128**
CM17: Harl .7G **118**
HP4: Berk .1K **121**
Lanefield Wlk. AL8: Welw G .9J **91**
Lane Gdns. WD23: B Hea .9F **150**
Lanercost Cl. AL6: Wel .9N **71**
Lanercost Gdns. N14 .9K **155**
Laneside HA8: Edg .5C **164**
Langbridge Cl. SG4: Hit .5A **34**
Langdale Av. AL5: Harp .5E **88**
Langdale Cl. LU6: Duns .1F **64**
Langdale Ct. HP2: Hem H .8A **106**
Langdale Gdns. EN8: Wal C .8H **145**
Langdale Lodge *WD3: R'orth* .*9N* ***147***
(off Parsonage Rd.)
Langdale Rd. LU6: Duns .1D **64**
Langdale St. CM17: Harl .5E **118**
Langdale Ter. WD6: Bore .5C **152**
Langdon St. HP23: Tring .3M **101**
Langford Cl. AL4: St Alb .9K **109**
Langford Cres. EN4: C'ters .6E **154**
Langford Dr. LU2: Lut .6J **47**
Langford Rd. EN4: C'ters .6E **154**
Langham Cl. AL4: St Alb .6L **109**
LU2: Lut .2F **46**
Langham Gdns. HA8: Edg .7C **164**
N21 .7M **155**
Langham Ho. LU1: Lut .9F **46**
Langham Rd. HA8: Edg .6C **164**
Langholme WD23: Bush .1D **162**
Langland Cl. HA6: North .7E **160**
Langland Ct. HA7: Stanm .9L **163**
Langland Dr. HA5: Pin .7N **161**
Langleigh SG6: L Gar .2F **22**
LANGLEY
CB11 .9M **17**
SG4 .8F **50**
Langley Av. HP3: Hem H .5A **124**
LANGLEYBURY .7D **136**
Langleybury Flds. WD4: L'bury .7B **136**
Langleybury La. WD4: L'bury .1D **148**
WD17: Watf .1D **148**
Langley Ct. EN7: Gof O .1A **144**
Langley Cres. AL3: St Alb .9D **108**
HA8: Edg .3C **164**
WD4: Kin L .3C **136**
Langley Gro. AL4: San .4K **109**
Langley Hill WD4: Kin L .2B **136**
Langley Hill Cl. WD4: Kin L .2C **136**
Langley La. SG4: Lang .7D **50**
WD5: Abb L .4H **137**
WD25: Watf .4H **137**
Langley Lodge La. WD4: Kin L .4A **136**
Langley Pk. NW7 .6E **164**
Langley Rd. WD4: Chippf .3L **135**
WD5: Abb L .4G **137**
WD17: Watf .3H **149**
Langley Row EN5: Barn .3M **153**
Langley Sidings SG1: Stev .7K **51**
Langley St. LU1: Lut .2G **67**
Langley Tennis Club .7D **124**
Langley Ter. Ind. Pk. *LU1: Lut* .*2G* ***67***
(off Latimer Rd.)
Langley Way WD17: Watf .4G **149**

Langley Wharf—Ley Wlk.

Langley Wharf WD4: Kin L . . . 9C 124
Langmead Dr. WD23: B Hea . . . 1F 162
LANGRIDGE . . . 7N 133
Langridge Ct. LU6: Duns . . . 8C 44
Langstone Ley AL7: Welw G . . . 9A 92
Langstone Way NW7 . . . 7K 165
Langthorne Av. SG1: Stev . . . 3L 51
Langton Av. N20 . . . 9B 154
Langton Gro. HA6: North . . . 5E 160
Langton Ho. EN11: Hod . . . 8K 115
Langton Rd. EN11: Hod . . . 7K 115
HA3: Har W . . . 7D 162
Langton's La. SG11: Old G . . . 1F 74
SG12: Dan E . . . 1F 74
Langwood WD17: Watf . . . 3J 149
Langwood Gdns. WD17: Watf . . . 3J 149
Langworthy HA5: Hat E . . . 6B 162
Lankester Rd. SG8: Roys . . . 8C 8
Lannock SG6: L Gar . . . 7K 23
Lannock Hill SG4: W'ton . . . 9K 23
SG6: Will . . . 9K 23
Lanrick Copse HP4: Berk . . . 9B 104
Lansbury Rd. EN3: Enf H . . . 3H 157
Lansdowne Cl. WD25: Watf . . . 8M 137
Lansdowne Ct. EN10: Brox . . . 1L 133
Lansdowne Rd. HA7: Stanm . . . 6K 163
LU3: Lut . . . 8E 46
N3 . . . 7N 165
Lansdown Rd. SL9: Chal P . . . 8A 158
Lanterns SG2: Stev . . . 2B 52
Lanterns, The *SG8: Roys* . . . *7D 8*
(off Melbourn St.)
Lanterns La. SG2: Ast E . . . 3C 52
Lantern Vw. SG8: Melb . . . 2M 9
Lanthony Ct. SG15: Arl . . . 8A 10
Lanthorn Cl. EN10: Brox . . . 1J 133
Laporte Way LU4: Lut . . . 8B 46
Lapwing Cl. HP2: Hem H . . . 7A 106
Lapwing Dell SG6: L Gar . . . 9H 23
Lapwing Pl. WD25: Watf . . . 5L 137
Lapwing Ri. SG2: Stev . . . 6C 52
Lapwing Rd. LU4: Lut . . . 5K 45
Lapwing Way WD5: Abb L . . . 4J 137
Larch Av. AL2: Bri W . . . 3N 137
SG4: St Ipo . . . 6A 34
Larch Cl. EN7: C'hunt . . . 9C 132
Larches, The AL4: St Alb . . . 7L 109
HA6: North . . . 6E 160
HP4: Berk . . . 9H 103
LU2: Lut . . . 8F 46
SG12: Ware . . . 3G 94
WD23: Bush . . . 7M 149
Larches Av. EN1: Enf . . . 8G 144
Larch Grn. NW9 . . . 8E 164
Larch La. AL6: Wel . . . 8M 71
Larch Ri. HP4: Berk . . . 9L 103
Larch Vw. HP1: Hem H . . . 3L 123
Larchwood CM23: Bis S . . . 3F 78
Larchwood Rd. HP2: Hem H . . . 9B 106
Lark Ct. *NW9* . . . *8E 164*
(off Lanacre Av.)
Larken Cl. WD23: Bush . . . 1D 162
Larken Dr. WD23: Bush . . . 1D 162
Larkens Cl. SG11: Puck . . . 6A 56
Larkin Pl. SG8: Roys . . . 4D 8
Larkins Cl. SG7: Bald . . . 2M 23
Larkins La. SG10: M Had . . . 7J 77
Larkinson SG1: Stev . . . 2J 51
Lark Ri. AL10: Hat . . . 2G 128
Larksfield SG12: Ware . . . 4J 95
Larksfield Gro. EN1: Enf . . . 3F 156
Larkspur Cl. CM23: Bis S . . . 2F 78
HP1: Hem H . . . 1H 123
Larkspur Gdns. LU4: Lut . . . 7B 46
Larkspur Gro. HA8: Edg . . . 4C 164
Larks Ridge AL2: Chis G . . . 9B 126
Larksway CM23: Bis S . . . 2E 78
Larkswood CM17: Harl . . . 8E 118
Larkswood Ri. AL4: St Alb . . . 6K 109
Larmans Rd. EN3: Enf W . . . 9G 145
Larwood Gro. SG1: Stev . . . 1N 51
LATCHFORD . . . 3B 76
Latchford M. AL4: Wheat . . . 6L 89
Latchford Pl. HP1: Hem H . . . 3K 123
LATCHMORE BANK . . . 6K 79
Latchmore Bank CM22: L Hal . . . 7K 79
Latchmore Bank Cotts. CM22: Gt Hal . . . 6K 79
Latchmore Cl. SG4: Hit . . . 5N 33
LATCHMORE COMMON . . . 7K 79
Lathkill Cl. EN1: Enf . . . 9E 156
Lathwell Ct. LU2: Lut . . . 8F 46
LATIMER . . . 1B 146
Latimer Chase WD3: Chen . . . 4F 146
Latimer Cl. HA5: Pin . . . 8L 161
HP2: Hem H . . . 6C 106
WD18: Watf . . . 9G 148
Latimer Ct. EN8: Wal C . . . 7K 145
Latimer Gdns. AL7: Welw G . . . 9A 92
HA5: Pin . . . 8L 161
Latimer Rd. EN5: N Bar . . . 5A 154
HP5: C'ham, Lati . . . 1A 146
LU1: Lut . . . 2G 67
WD3: Chen . . . 1D 146
Latium Cl. AL1: St Alb . . . 3E 126
Lattimore Ho. AL1: St Alb . . . 4E 166
Lattimore Rd. AL1: St Alb . . . 4E 166 (3F 126)
AL4: Wheat . . . 7K 89
LATTON BUSH . . . 9C 118
Latton Bush Cen. CM18: Harl . . . 9A 118
Latton Comn. Rd. CM18: Harl . . . 9C 118
Latton Grn. CM18: Harl . . . 9B 118
Latton Hall Cl. CM20: Harl . . . 5C 118
Latton Ho. CM18: Harl . . . 9D 118
Latton St. CM17: Harl . . . 7D 118
(not continuous)
CM20: Harl . . . 5C 118
(not continuous)
Latymer Gdns. N3 . . . 9L 165
Latymer Rd. N9 . . . 9D 156
Lauder Ct. N14 . . . 9K 155
Lauderdale Rd. WD4: Hun C . . . 6E 136
Laughton Ct. WD6: Bore . . . 4C 152
Launceston WD3: Chor . . . 8E 146
Launton Cl. LU3: Lut . . . 9D 30
Laura Cl. EN1: Enf . . . 7C 156
Laureate Way HP1: Hem H . . . 9L 105
Laurel Av. EN6: Pot B . . . 5M 141
Laurel Bank HP3: Hem H . . . 5J 123
Laurel Bank Rd. EN2: Enf . . . 3A 156
Laurel Cl. HP2: Hem H . . . 1B 124
WD19: Watf . . . 9M 149
Laurel Ct. EN6: Cuff . . . 2L 143
Laureldene SG10: M Had . . . 7J 77
Laurel Dr. N21 . . . 9M 155
Laurel Edge *AL1: St Alb* . . . *1G 126*
(off Avenue Rd.)
Laurel Flds. EN6: Pot B . . . 4M 141
Laurel Gdns. E4 . . . 9M 157
NW7 . . . 3D 164
Laurel Lodge La. EN5: Barn . . . 9J 141
Laurel M. SG7: Bald . . . 2M 23
Laurel Pk. HA3: Har W . . . 7G 162
Laurel Rd. AL1: St Alb . . . 2G 127
SL9: Chal P . . . 8A 158
Laurels, The AL2: Bri W . . . 1B 138
EN7: C'hunt . . . 9C 132
HP4: Pot E . . . 8E 104
LU4: Lut . . . 5N 45
WD6: Bore . . . 3A 152
WD23: B Hea . . . 2F 162
Laurelsfield AL3: St Alb . . . 5C 126
Laurelside Wlk. LU5: Duns . . . 7K 45
Laurel Way N20 . . . 3N 165
SG5: Ick . . . 8M 21
Lauries Cl. HP1: Hem H . . . 4F 122
Laurimel Cl. HA7: Stanm . . . 6J 163
Laurino Pl. WD23: B Hea . . . 2D 162
Lavender Cl. AL10: Hat . . . 6E 110
CM20: Harl . . . 5A 118
CM23: Bis S . . . 2F 78
EN7: C'hunt . . . 9D 132
LU2: Lut . . . 2G 46
Lavender Ct. SG7: Bald . . . 2L 23
Lavender Cres. AL3: St Alb . . . 9D 108
Lavender Cft. *SG4: Hit* . . . *4B 34*
(off Wymondley Rd.)
Lavender Flds. SG5: Hit . . . 3K 33
Lavender Gdns. EN2: Enf . . . 3N 155
HA3: Har W . . . 6F 162
Lavender Hill EN2: Enf . . . 3M 155
Lavender Rd. EN2: Enf . . . 3B 156
Lavender Wlk. HP2: Hem H . . . 9N 105
Lavender Way SG5: Hit . . . 3L 33
Lavinia Av. WD25: Watf . . . 7M 137
Lavrock La. WD3: Crox G . . . 9B 148
Lawford Av. WD3: Chor . . . 8F 146
Lawford Cl. LU1: Lut . . . 1E 66
WD3: Chor . . . 8F 146
Law Hall La. SG4: Ben . . . 9H 49
Law Hall La. Cotts. SG4: Ben . . . 9H 49
Lawley Rd. N14 . . . 9G 154
Lawn, The CM20: Harl . . . 3D 118
Lawn Av. SG4: Kimp . . . 7K 69
Lawn Cl. N9 . . . 9D 156
Lawn Gdns. LU1: Lut . . . 3F 66
Lawn La. HP3: Hem H . . . 4N 123
Lawn Path LU1: Lut . . . 5E 66
(not continuous)
Lawns, The AL3: St Alb . . . 1A 166 (1D 126)
AL8: Welw G . . . 6K 91
HA5: Hat E . . . 7C 162
HP1: Hem H . . . 1H 123
LU5: Duns . . . 8E 44
SG2: Stev . . . 5C 52
SG8: Melb . . . 2M 9
WD7: Shen . . . 6M 139
Lawns Cl. SG5: Gt Off . . . 8D 32
Lawns Close, The SG8: Melb . . . 2L 9
Lawns Ct. SG8: Roys . . . 8D 8
Lawns Drive, The EN10: Brox . . . 3K 133
Lawnswood EN5: Barn . . . 7L 153
Lawn Va. HA5: Pin . . . 9N 161
Lawrance Gdns. EN8: C'hunt . . . 1H 145
Lawrance Rd. AL3: St Alb . . . 7D 108
Lawrence Av. CM21: Saw . . . 3G 99
NW7 . . . 4E 164
SG1: Stev . . . 2L 51
SG6: L Gar . . . 7G 23
SG12: Stan A . . . 2N 115
Lawrence Cl. SG4: Hit . . . 1B 34
SG14: H'ford . . . 8K 93
Lawrence Ct. NW7 . . . 5E 164
WD19: Watf . . . 3M 161
Lawrence Cres. HA8: Edg . . . 9A 164
LAWRENCE END PARK . . . 4D 68
Lawrence End Rd.
LU2: P Grn, Wan G . . . 5D 68
Lawrence Gdns. NW7 . . . 3F 164
Lawrence Hall *LU1: Lut* . . . *1G 67*
(off John St.)
Lawrence Hall End AL7: Welw G . . . 3L 111
Lawrence Ho. CM21: Saw . . . 8G 98
Lawrence Ind. Est. LU6: Duns . . . 7C 44
Lawrence Mead SG4: L Wym . . . 6F 34
Lawrence Moorings CM21: Saw . . . 6H 99
Lawrence St. NW7 . . . 5F 164
Lawrence Way LU6: Duns . . . 7C 44
Lawson Rd. EN3: Enf H . . . 3G 156
Lawton Rd. EN4: C'ters . . . 5C 154
Laxton Cl. LU2: Lut . . . 8N 47
Laxton Gdns. SG7: Bald . . . 4N 23
WD7: Shen . . . 5M 139
Layard Rd. EN1: Enf . . . 3D 156
Laybrook AL4: St Alb . . . 7H 109
Layham Dr. LU2: Lut . . . 8M 47
Layhill HP2: Hem H . . . 9N 105
Layston Mdw. SG9: Bunt . . . 4K 39
Layston Pk. SG8: Roys . . . 8D 8
Layton St. AL7: Welw G . . . 3L 111
Leabank *LU3: Lut* . . . *3A 46*
(off Penhill)
Lea Bank Ct. LU3: Lut . . . 3A 46
LEA BRIDGE CORNER . . . 9B 68
Lea Bushes WD25: Watf . . . 8N 137
Lea Cl. CM23: Bis S . . . 8K 59
WD23: Bush . . . 7C 150
Leacroft AL5: Harp . . . 4E 88
Leaders Cl. HP22: W'rave . . . 5A 60
Leaf Cl. HA6: North . . . 7F 160
Leafield LU3: Lut . . . 3A 46
(Five Springs)
LU3: Lut . . . 5B 46
(Thorneycroft Cl.)
Leafields LU5: Hou R . . . 3F 44
Leaford Ct. WD24: Watf . . . 9H 137
Leaford Cres. WD24: Watf . . . 1H 149
Leaforis Rd. EN7: C'hunt . . . 1E 144
Leaf Rd. LU5: Hou R . . . 3E 44
Leaf Way AL1: St Alb . . . 5E 126
Leafwing Ct. *SG1: Stev* . . . *8B 36*
(off Admiral Dr.)
Leafy La. HP23: Tring . . . 5K 101
LEAGRAVE . . . 4M 45
Leagrave High St. LU4: Lut . . . 6J 45
Leagrave Rd. LU3: Lut . . . 6C 46
LU4: Lut . . . 7D 46
Leagrave Station (Rail) . . . 4A 46
LEA GREEN . . . 5L 111
Lea Gro. CM23: Bis S . . . 8K 59
Leahoe Gdns. SG13: H'ford . . . 1A 114
Lea Ind. Est. AL5: Harp . . . 3D 88
Lea Manor Recreation Cen. . . . 1B 46
Leamington Ho. HA8: Edg . . . 5N 163
Leamington Rd. LU3: Lut . . . 2C 46
Lea Mt. EN7: Gof O . . . 1C 144
Leander Ct. NW9 . . . 8E 164
Leander Gdns. WD25: Watf . . . 1N 149
Lea Rd. AL5: Harp . . . 4C 88
EN2: Enf . . . 3B 156
EN9: Wal A . . . 7L 145
EN11: Hod . . . 6N 115
WD24: Watf . . . 2K 149
Lea Rd. Ind. Pk. EN9: Wal A . . . 7L 145
Lea Rd. Trad. Est. EN9: Wal A . . . 7L 145
Leas, The HP3: Hem H . . . 6C 124
SG7: Bald . . . 4L 23
WD23: Bush . . . 3A 150
Leasey Bri. La. AL4: Wheat . . . 6G 89
Leasey Dell Dr. AL4: Wheat . . . 5H 89
Leaside HP2: Hem H . . . 3E 124
LU5: Hou R . . . 3H 45
Leaside Bus. Cen. EN3: Brim . . . 4K 157
Leaside Ct. AL5: Harp . . . 4D 88
Leaside Wlk. *SG12: Ware* . . . *6H 95*
(off East St.)
Leat Cl. CM21: Saw . . . 4H 99
Leathersellers Cl. *EN5: Barn* . . . *5L 153*
(off The Avenue)
Leathwaite Cl. LU3: Lut . . . 3B 46
LEA VALLEY . . . 5G 88
Lea Valley Rd. E4 . . . 7J 157
EN3: Pon E . . . 7J 157
Lea Valley Sports Cen. . . . 8G 145
LEAVESDEN . . . 5H 137
Leavesden Country Pk. . . . 5J 137
Leavesden Ct. WD5: Abb L . . . 4J 137
LEAVESDEN GREEN . . . 6J 137
LEAVESDEN GREEN . . . 8G 137
Leavesden Pk. WD25: Watf . . . 6H 137
Leavesden Rd. HA7: Stanm . . . 6H 163
WD24: Watf . . . 2K 149
Leavesden Studios
WD4: Hun C . . . 6G 137
Leaves Spring SG2: Stev . . . 7M 51
Lea Vw. EN9: Wal A . . . 6M 145
Lea Wlk. AL5: Harp . . . 3D 88
Lebanon Cl. WD17: Watf . . . 9F 136
Le Corte Cl. WD4: Kin L . . . 2B 136
Lectern La. AL1: St Alb . . . 6F 126
Leda Av. EN3: Enf W . . . 2H 157
Leda M. HP2: Hem H . . . 9B 106
Ledgemore La.
HP2: Gad R, Gt Gad . . . 3H 105
Ledwell Rd. LU1: Cad . . . 5B 66
Lee, The HA6: North . . . 5H 161
Leeches Way LU7: Ched . . . 9M 61
Lee Cl. EN5: N Bar . . . 6B 154
SG12: Stan A . . . 2N 115
SG13: H'ford . . . 2A 114
Leecroft Rd. EN5: Barn . . . 7L 153
Leefe Way EN6: Cuff . . . 1J 143
Leeming Rd. WD6: Bore . . . 3N 151
Lee Rd. EN1: Enf . . . 8E 156
NW7 . . . 7K 165
Lees Av. HA6: North . . . 8H 161
Leeside EN5: Barn . . . 7L 153
EN6: Pot B . . . 5C 142
Leeside Works SG12: Stan A . . . 2N 115
Leeswood Ct. SG14: H'ford . . . 8L 93
Leete Pl. SG8: Roys . . . 6C 8
Lee Valley Athletics Cen. . . . 9J 157
Lee Valley Boat Cen. . . . 3L 133
Lee Valley Golf Course . . . 9J 157
Lee Valley Park Farms . . . 1N 145
Lee Valley Park Info. Cen. . . . 9E 144
Lee Valley Regional Pk. . . . 4L 145
Lee Valley White Water Cen. . . . 6L 145
Lee Vw. EN2: Enf . . . 3N 155
Leeway Cl. HA5: Hat E . . . 7A 162
Leggatts Cl. WD24: Watf . . . 9H 137
Leggatts Ri. WD25: Watf . . . 8J 137
Leggatts Way WD24: Watf . . . 9H 137
Leggatts Wood Av. WD24: Watf . . . 9K 137
Leggett Gro. SG1: Stev . . . 1L 51
Leggfield Ter. HP1: Hem H . . . 2J 123
Leghorn Cres. LU4: Lut . . . 6K 45
Legions Way CM23: Bis S . . . 9J 59
Legra Av. EN11: Hod . . . 8L 115
Leicester Cl. LU4: Lut . . . 8A 46
Leicester Rd. EN5: N Bar . . . 7A 154
LU4: Lut . . . 8A 46
Leigh Comn. AL7: Welw G . . . 2L 111
Leigh Ct. WD6: Bore . . . 4D 152
Leigh Rodd WD19: Watf . . . 3A 162
Leighton Av. HA5: Pin . . . 9N 161
Leighton Buzzard Rd.
HP1: Gt Gad, Hem H . . . 3H 105
Leighton Cl. HA8: Edg . . . 9A 164
Leighton Ct. EN8: C'hunt . . . 2H 145
LU6: Duns . . . 9D 44
Leighton Linslade Southern By-Pass
LU6: Sew, Tot . . . 5A 44
Leighton Rd. EN1: Enf . . . 7D 156
HA3: Har W . . . 9E 162
HP22: W'rave . . . 5A 60
LU6: Edle, N'all . . . 1C 62
LU7: Bill . . . 1C 62
LU7: Ment, Slapt . . . 1L 61
Leinster M. EN5: Barn . . . 5L 153
Leisure World
Hemel Hempstead . . . 3B 124
Lemark Cl. HA7: Stanm . . . 6K 163
Lemonfield Dr. WD25: Watf . . . 5N 137
LEMSFORD . . . 1F 110
Lemsford Ct. WD6: Bore . . . 6C 152
Lemsford Hall *AL10: Hat* . . . *8D 110*
(off Mosquito Way)
Lemsford La. AL8: Welw G . . . 1H 111
Lemsford Rd. AL1: St Alb . . . 2G 166 (2G 126)
AL10: Hat . . . 8F 110
Lemsford Village AL8: Lem . . . 1F 110
(not continuous)
Lennon Ct. LU1: Lut . . . 1E 66
Lennox Grn. LU2: Lut . . . 7A 48
Lensbury Cl. EN8: C'hunt . . . 1J 145
Leonard Ct. HA3: Har W . . . 8F 162
Leonard Pulham Ho. HP22: Halt . . . 7C 100
Leonard's Cl. AL6: Wel . . . 8L 71
Lerwick Ct. EN1: Enf . . . 7C 156
Lesbury Cl. LU2: Lut . . . 8N 47
Leslie Cl. SG2: Stev . . . 7B 52
Lester Ct. WD24: Watf . . . 1L 149
Lester Hall *LU1: Lut* . . . *1G 67*
(off John St.)
Lester M. *LU2: Lut* . . . *8G 46*
(off Frederick St.)
Leston Cl. LU6: Duns . . . 3G 64
Letchford Ter. HA3: Har W . . . 8C 162
Letchmore Cl. SG1: Stev . . . 3K 51
LETCHMORE HEATH . . . 3F 150
Letchmore Rd. SG1: Stev . . . 3K 51
(not continuous)
WD7: Rad . . . 9H 139
Letchworth Arts Cen. . . . *5F 22*
(off The Arcade)
Letchworth Business & Retail Pk.
SG6: L Gar . . . 4J 23
Letchworth Cl. WD19: Watf . . . 5M 161
LETCHWORTH GARDEN CITY . . . 5F 22
Letchworth Garden City Station (Rail) . . . 5F 22
Letchworth Ga. SG6: L Gar . . . 6H 23
Letchworth Golf Course . . . 9F 22
Letchworth La. SG6: L Gar . . . 8F 22
Letchworth Museum & Art Gallery . . . 6F 22
Letchworth Point SG6: L Gar . . . 5H 23
Letchworth Rd. HA7: Stanm . . . 7M 163
LU3: Lut . . . 5C 46
SG6: L Gar . . . 4K 23
SG7: Bald, L Gar . . . 4K 23
Letchworth Shop. Cen. SG6: L Gar . . . 5F 22
Letchworth Swimming Pool . . . 4F 22
Letchworth Tennis Club . . . 8F 22
Letter Box Row SG4: Gos . . . 7N 33
LETTY GREEN . . . 4G 112
LEVEL'S GREEN . . . 4F 58
Levenage La. SG12: Huns, M Had, Widf . . . 4H 97
Leven Cl. EN8: Wal C . . . 6H 145
WD19: Watf . . . 5M 161
Levendale LU4: Lut . . . 4M 45
Leven Dr. EN8: Wal C . . . 6H 145
LEVENS GREEN . . . 8H 55
Leventhorpe Pool & Gym . . . 3G 98
Leven Way HP2: Hem H . . . 7N 105
Leveret Cl. WD25: Watf . . . 7J 137
LEVERSTOCK GREEN . . . 3E 124
Leverstock Grn. Rd. HP2: Hem H . . . 1C 124
HP3: Hem H . . . 2D 124
(not continuous)
Leverstock Grn. Way HP3: Hem H . . . 2E 124
Leverton Way EN9: Wal A . . . 6N 145
Lewes Way WD3: Crox G . . . 6E 148
Lewington Ct. EN3: Enf W . . . 1H 157
Lewins Rd. SL9: Chal P . . . 9A 158
Lewis Cl. N14 . . . 9H 155
UB9: Hare . . . 9M 159
Lewis Ho. WD18: Watf . . . 8H 149
Lewis La. SG15: Arl . . . 6A 10
SL9: Chal P . . . 8B 158
LEWSEY FARM . . . 5J 45
Lewsey Pk. Ct. LU4: Lut . . . 5K 45
Lewsey Park Pool . . . 5K 45
Lewsey Rd. LU4: Lut . . . 6L 45
Lexden Ter. *EN9: Wal A* . . . *7N 145*
(off Sewardstone Rd.)
Lexington Cl. WD6: Bore . . . 5N 151
Lexington Ct. *EN6: Pot B* . . . *4K 141*
(off Mimms Hall Rd.)
Lexington Way EN5: Barn . . . 6K 153
Leyburne Rd. LU3: Lut . . . 3D 46
Leycroft Way AL5: Harp . . . 8F 88
Leyden Rd. SG1: Stev . . . 6K 51
Ley Farm Cl. WD25: Watf . . . 9L 137
LEY GREEN . . . 3G 49
Leygreen Cl. LU2: Lut . . . 9J 47
Leyhill Dr. LU1: Lut . . . 4D 66
Ley Hill Rd. HP3: Bov . . . 2B 134
Ley Ho. AL7: Welw G . . . 9B 92
Leyland Av. AL1: St Alb . . . 4E 126
EN3: Enf H . . . 4J 157
Leyland Cl. EN8: C'hunt . . . 1G 145
Leyland Rd. LU6: Duns . . . 7C 44
Leys, The AL4: St Alb . . . 8L 109
HP22: Halt . . . 5B 100
HP23: Tring . . . 2N 101
WD7: Rad . . . 1H 151
Leys Av. SG6: L Gar . . . 5F 22
Leys Cl. UB9: Hare . . . 8N 159
Leysdown AL7: Welw G . . . 9C 92
Leys Gdns. EN4: C'ters . . . 7F 154
Leys Rd. HP3: Hem H . . . 4A 124
Leys Rd. E. EN3: Enf H . . . 3J 157
Leys Rd. W. EN3: Enf H . . . 3J 157
Leys Sq. N3 . . . 8N 165
Leyton Grn. AL5: Harp . . . 6B 88
Leyton Rd. AL5: Harp . . . 6B 88
Ley Wlk. AL7: Welw G . . . 9B 92

Moor, The—New Common

MOOR, THE . . . 1N 9
Moor, The SG8: Melb . . . 1M 9
Moorcroft HA8: Edg . . . 8B 164
Moore Ct. HA7: Stanm . . . 8L 163
Moore Cres. LU5: Hou R . . . 5F 44
Moore Ho. AL3: St Alb . . . 4B 126
MOOR END . . . 3K 63
Moor End LU6: Eat B . . . 4K 63
Moorend AL7: Welw G . . . 3N 111
Moor End Cl. LU6: Eat B . . . 4K 63
Moor End La. LU6: Eat B . . . 3K 63
Moor End Rd. HP1: Hem H . . . 3M 123
Moore Rd. HP4: Berk . . . 8K 103
Moorfield Rd. EN3: Enf H . . . 3G 156
MOOR GREEN . . . 8A 38
Moor Hall La. CM23: Bis S, Thorl . . . 6D 78
Moor Hall Rd. CM17: Harl . . . 2H 119
Moorhen Way *CM19: Royd* . . . *5D 116*
(off Roydon Mill Leisure Pk.)
Moorhouse NW9 . . . 8F 164
Moorhouse Rd. HA3: Ken . . . 9M 163
Moorhurst Av. EN7: Gof O . . . 2M 143
Mooring Ri. LU1: Cad . . . 5N 65
Moorings, The AL1: St Alb . . . 1G 166
CM23: Bis S . . . 3J 79
WD23: Bush . . . 6N 149
Moorland Gdns. LU2: Lut . . . 9F 46
Moorland Rd. AL5: Harp . . . 3C 88
HP1: Hem H . . . 4K 123
Moorlands AL2: Frog . . . 1F 138
AL7: Welw G . . . 3N 111
Moorlands Av. NW7 . . . 6H 165
Moorlands Ct. SG8: Melb . . . 1M 9
Moorlands Reach CM21: Saw . . . 6H 99
Moor La. WD3: R'orth . . . 1B 160
WD3: Sar . . . 9H 135
Moor La. Crossing WD18: Watf . . . 9E 148
Moormead Cl. SG5: Hit . . . 4L 33
Moormead Hill SG5: Hit . . . 4K 33
Moor Mill La. AL2: Col S . . . 2F 138
(not continuous)
MOOR PARK . . . 3E 160
Moor Park . . . 3C 160
Moor Pk. HP22: Wen . . . 7A 100
Moor Pk. Golf Course . . . 3C 160
Moor Pk. Ind. Cen. WD18: Watf . . . 9E 148
Moor Pk. Rd. HA6: North . . . 5F 160
Moor Park Station (Underground) . . . 3F 160
Moor Path LU3: Lut . . . 9F 46
Moors, The AL7: Welw G . . . 8N 91
Moorside AL7: Welw G . . . 3N 111
HP3: Hem H . . . 5L 123
Moors La. HP5: Orch L . . . 9M 121
Moors Ley SG2: Walk . . . 9F 36
Moor St. LU1: Lut . . . 9E 46
Moors Wlk. AL7: Welw G . . . 8A 92
Moortown Rd. WD19: Watf . . . 4L 161
Moor Vw. WD18: Watf . . . 9J 149
Moorview Ho. *HP2: Hem H* . . . *3N 123*
(off The Spires)
Moorymead Cl. SG14: Watt S . . . 5J 73
Moran Cl. AL2: Bri W . . . 4A 138
Moray Cl. HA8: Edg . . . 2B 164
Morcom Rd. LU5: Duns . . . 2H 65
MORDEN GREEN . . . 4D 6
Morecambe Cl. LU4: Lut . . . 6L 45
SG1: Stev . . . 2H 51
Morecambe Gdns. HA7: Stanm . . . 4L 163
Morefields HP23: Tring . . . 9M 81
Morell Cl. EN5: N Bar . . . 5B 154
Morello Gdns. SG4: Hit . . . 5A 34
Moremead EN9: Wal A . . . 6N 145
Moreton Av. AL5: Harp . . . 5A 88
Moreton Cl. EN7: C'hunt . . . 2N 132
NW7 . . . 6J 165
Moreton End Cl. AL5: Harp . . . 5A 88
Moreton End La. AL5: Harp . . . 5N 87
Moreton Pk. Ind. Est. LU2: Lut . . . 7J 47
Moreton Pl. AL5: Harp . . . 4A 88
Moreton Rd. Nth. LU2: Lut . . . 7J 47
Moreton Rd. Sth. LU2: Lut . . . 7J 47
Morgan Cl. HA6: North . . . 6H 161
LU4: Lut . . . 6A 46
SG1: Stev . . . 9K 35
Morgan Gdns. WD25: A'ham . . . 2C 150
Morgan's Cl. SG13: H'ford . . . 2B 114
Morgan's Rd. SG13: H'ford . . . 2B 114
Morgan's Wlk. SG13: B'don, H'ford . . . 3B 114
Morice Rd. EN11: Hod . . . 6K 115
Morland Cl. LU6: Duns . . . 2D 64
Morland Way EN8: C'hunt . . . 1J 145
Morley Cres. HA8: Edg . . . 2C 164
Morley Cres. E. HA7: Stanm . . . 9K 163
Morley Cres. W. HA7: Stanm . . . 9K 163
Morley Gro. CM20: Harl . . . 4M 117
Morley Hill EN2: Enf . . . 2B 156
Morley La. SG11: Latch . . . 3C 76
Morningside WD3: R'orth . . . 1M 159
Mornington AL6: Wel . . . 3N 91
Mornington Rd. E4 . . . 9N 157
WD7: Rad . . . 7H 139
Morpeth Av. WD6: Bore . . . 2N 151
Morpeth Cl. HP2: Hem H . . . 3A 124
Morphou Rd. NW7 . . . 6L 165
Morrell Cl. LU3: Lut . . . 2C 46
Morrell Ct. AL7: Welw G . . . 8M 91
Morris Cl. LU3: Lut . . . 1A 46
(not continuous)
SL9: Chal P . . . 8C 158
Morris Ho. CM18: Harl . . . 9M 117
Morrison Ct. *EN5: Barn* . . . *6L 153*
(off Manor Way)
Morris Rd. LU6: Duns . . . 7C 44
Morriston Cl. WD19: Watf . . . 5L 161
Morris Way AL2: Lon C . . . 8L 127
Morse Cl. UB9: Hare . . . 9M 159
Morson Rd. EN3: Pon E . . . 8J 157
Mortain Dr. HP4: Berk . . . 8K 103
Mortimer Cl. LU1: Lut . . . 1B 66
WD23: Bush . . . 8C 150
Mortimer Cres. AL3: St Alb . . . 4B 126
Mortimer Dr. EN1: Enf . . . 7C 156
Mortimer Ga. EN8: C'hunt . . . 9K 133
Mortimer Hill HP23: Tring . . . 2N 101
Mortimer Ri. HP23: Tring . . . 2N 101
Mortimer Rd. SG8: Roys . . . 6E 8
Mortlock Cl. SG8: Melb . . . 1M 9
Mortlock St. SG8: Melb . . . 1M 9
Morton Cl. LU7: Pits . . . 3A 82
Morton Dr. CM24: Stans . . . 4N 59
Morton St. SG8: Roys . . . 6D 8
Morven Cl. EN6: Pot B . . . 4B 142
Mosaic Ho. HP2: Hem H . . . 2N 123
Mosquito Way AL10: Hat . . . 8E 110
Mossbank Av. LU2: Lut . . . 9L 47
Moss Cl. HA5: Pin . . . 9A 162
WD3: R'orth . . . 2N 159
Mossdale Ct. *LU4: Lut* . . . *4M 45*
(off Glaisdale)
Mossendew Cl. UB9: Hare . . . 8N 159
Moss Grn. AL7: Welw G . . . 2L 111
Moss La. CM17: Harl . . . 5E 118
HA5: Pin . . . 8N 161
Mossman Dr. LU1: Cad . . . 4A 66
Moss Rd. WD25: Watf . . . 7K 137
Moss Side AL2: Bri W . . . 3A 138
Moss Way SG5: Hit . . . 1K 33
Mostyn Rd. HA8: Edg . . . 7E 164
LU3: Lut . . . 5A 46
WD23: Bush . . . 7D 150
Mottingham Rd. N9 . . . 8H 157
Motts Cl. SG14: Watt S . . . 4J 73
MOTT'S GREEN . . . 1M 99
Mott St. E4 . . . 2N 157
Moules Yd. SG7: Ashw . . . 1C 12
Moulton Ri. LU2: Lut . . . 9H 47
Mount, The EN6: Pot B . . . 3A 142
EN7: C'hunt . . . 8B 132
LU3: Lut . . . 9F 46
SG8: Barl . . . 3C 16
SG8: Lit . . . 3H 7
WD3: R'orth . . . 8M 147
Mountbatten Cl. AL1: St Alb . . . 5J 127
Mountbel Rd. HA7: Stanm . . . 8H 163
Mount Cl. EN4: C'ters . . . 6F 154
HP1: Hem H . . . 2J 123
HP22: Ast C . . . 2E 100
Mount Dr. AL2: Par S . . . 7E 126
CM24: Stans . . . 4N 59
Mounteagle SG8: Roys . . . 8D 8
Mt. Echo Dr. E4 . . . 9M 157
Mountfield Path LU2: Lut . . . 7G 47
Mountfield Rd. HP2: Hem H . . . 2A 124
LU2: Lut . . . 7G 47
N3 . . . 9M 165
Mountfitchet Castle . . . 3N 59
Mountfitchet Rd. CM24: Stans . . . 4N 59
Mt. Garrison SG4: Hit . . . 3N 33
Mt. Grace Rd. EN6: Pot B . . . 4N 141
Mountgrace Rd. LU2: Lut . . . 3L 47
Mount Gro. HA8: Edg . . . 3C 164
Mountjoy SG4: Hit . . . 1C 34
Mount Keen SG1: W'ton . . . 7B 36
Mount Nugent HP5: C'ham . . . 9E 120
Mount Pde. EN4: C'ters . . . 6D 154
MOUNT PLEASANT
CM23 . . . 7F 42
UB9 . . . 8K 159
Mt. Pleasant AL3: St Alb . . . 1A 166 (1C 126)
EN4: C'ters . . . 6D 154
SG5: Hit . . . 4L 33
SG13: Hert H . . . 2G 114
SL9: Chal P . . . 5B 158
UB9: Hare . . . 8K 159
Mt. Pleasant Cl. AL9: Hat . . . 6J 111
Mt. Pleasant Cotts. *N14* . . . *9J 155*
(off The Wells)
Mount Pleasant Golf Course . . . 1G 20
Mt. Pleasant La. AL2: Bri W . . . 3N 137
AL9: Hat . . . 5J 111
Mt. Pleasant Rd. LU3: Lut . . . 4A 46
Mount Rd. AL4: Wheat . . . 6L 89
EN4: E Bar . . . 7D 154
SG14: H'ford . . . 1M 113
Mountside HA7: Stanm . . . 8H 163
Mt. Sorrell SG13: H'ford . . . 9D 94
Mount Vw. AL2: Lon C . . . 9M 127
EN2: Enf . . . 2L 155
HA6: North . . . 6H 161
NW7 . . . 3D 164
WD3: R'orth . . . 1L 159
Mountview Av. LU5: Duns . . . 2G 65
Mount Vw. Rd. E4 . . . 9N 157
Mountview Rd. EN7: C'hunt . . . 8C 132
Mount Way AL7: Welw G . . . 3M 111
Mountway EN6: Pot B . . . 3N 141
Mountway Cl. AL7: Welw G . . . 3M 111
Mowat Ind. Est. WD24: Watf . . . 2L 149
Mowbray Cres. SG5: Stot . . . 6F 10
Mowbray Gdns. SG4: Hit . . . 5A 34
Mowbray Pde. HA8: Edg . . . 4A 164
Mowbray Rd. CM20: Harl . . . 4B 118
EN5: N Bar . . . 7B 154
HA8: Edg . . . 4A 164
Mowbrays, The SG5: Stot . . . 5F 10
Moxes Wood LU3: Lut . . . 2A 46
Moxom Av. EN8: C'hunt . . . 3J 145
Moxon St. EN5: Barn . . . 5M 153
Moyne Ho. AL7: Welw G . . . 9B 92
Moynihan Dr. N21 . . . 7K 155
Mozart Ct. SG1: Stev . . . 4J 51
MUCH HADHAM . . . 5J 77
Much Hadham La. SG10: M Had . . . 2J 77
Muddy La. SG6: L Gar . . . 8F 22
Mud La. AL1: St Alb . . . 3D 126
AL5: Harp . . . 1E 108
Muirfield LU2: Lut . . . 3G 47
Muirfield Cl. WD19: Watf . . . 5L 161
Muirfield Grn. WD19: Watf . . . 4K 161
Muirfield Rd. WD19: Watf . . . 4K 161
Muirhead Way SG3: Kneb . . . 3M 71
Mulberry Cl. AL2: Par S . . . 1C 138
EN4: E Bar . . . 6C 154
EN10: Turn . . . 6K 133
HP23: Tring . . . 1M 101
LU1: Lut . . . 1D 66
SG5: Stot . . . 7F 10
WD17: Watf . . . 9G 136
Mulberry Ct. CM23: Bis S . . . 3J 79
HP1: Hem H . . . 1N 123
SG8: Roys . . . *7D 8*
(off Up. King St.)
Mulberry Gdns. CM17: Harl . . . 2F 118
WD7: Shen . . . 6M 139
Mulberry Grn. CM17: Harl . . . 2F 118
Mulberry Lodge *WD19: Watf* . . . *8M 149*
(off Eastbury Rd.)
Mulberry Mead AL10: Hat . . . 5F 110
Mulberry Pl. AL3: Red . . . 2K 107
HA2: Harr . . . 9D 162
Mulberry Ter. *CM17: Harl* . . . *2D 118*
(off Broadway Av.)
Mulberry Way SG5: Hit . . . 9L 21
Mull Ho. WD18: Watf . . . 7H 149
Mullion Cl. HA3: Har W . . . 8C 162
LU2: Lut . . . 4K 47
Mullion Wlk. WD19: Watf . . . 4M 161
Mullway SG6: L Gar . . . 5C 22
Mulready Wlk. HP3: Hem H . . . 6A 124
Mundells AL7: Welw G . . . 7M 91
EN7: C'hunt . . . 9E 132
Mundells Ct. AL7: Welw G . . . 7M 91
MUNDEN . . . 7C 138
Munden Dr. WD25: Watf . . . 1N 149
Munden Gro. WD24: Watf . . . 2L 149
Munden Rd. SG12: Dan E . . . 1C 74
Munden Vw. WD25: Watf . . . 9M 137
Mundesley Cl. SG1: Stev . . . 9H 35
WD19: Watf . . . 4L 161
Mungo Pk. Cl. WD23: B Hea . . . 2D 162
Muntings, The SG2: Stev . . . 6N 51
Munts Mdw. SG4: W'ton . . . 1B 36
Murchison Rd. EN11: Hod . . . 5M 115
Muriel Av. WD18: Watf . . . 7L 149
Murray Cres. HA5: Pin . . . 8M 161
Murray Rd. HA6: North . . . 8G 160
HP4: Berk . . . 8N 103
Murrell La. SG5: Stot . . . 7G 10
Murton Ct. AL1: St Alb . . . 1F 166 (1F 126)
Museum Ct. HP23: Tring . . . 3M 101
Museum of Domestic Design & Architecture
MODA . . . 9F 164
Museum of Harlow . . . 3D 118
Museum of St Albans . . . 1E 166 (1F 126)
Musgrave Cl. EN4: Had W . . . 3B 154
EN7: C'hunt . . . 9D 132
Muskalls Cl. EN7: C'hunt . . . 9E 132
Musket Cl. EN4: E Bar . . . 8C 154
Muskham Rd. CM20: Harl . . . 3C 118
Musk Hill HP1: Hem H . . . 3H 123
Musleigh Mnr. SG12: Ware . . . 6K 95
Musley Hill SG12: Ware . . . 5J 95
Musley La. SG12: Ware . . . 5J 95
(not continuous)
Mussons Path LU2: Lut . . . 9G 46
Muswell Cl. LU3: Lut . . . 3D 46
Mutchetts Cl. WD25: Watf . . . 6N 137
Mutford Cft. LU2: Lut . . . 8M 47
Mutton La. EN6: Pot B, S Mim . . . 4J 141
Myddelton Av. EN1: Enf . . . 2C 156
Myddelton Cl. EN1: Enf . . . 3D 156
Myddelton Gdns. N21 . . . 9A 156
Myddelton House Gdns. . . . 9D 144
Myddleton Cl. HA7: Stanm . . . 2H 163
Myddleton Path EN7: C'hunt . . . 4F 144
Myddleton Rd. SG12: Ware . . . 7H 95
Myers Cl. WD7: Shen . . . 5M 139
Myles Ct. EN7: Gof O . . . 2A 144
Mylne Cl. EN8: C'hunt . . . 9G 133
Mylne Ct. EN11: Hod . . . 5L 115
Mymms Dr. AL9: B Pk . . . 8N 129
Mymms Ho. AL9: Welh G . . . 5J 129
Myrtle Gdns. SG16: L Ston . . . 1H 21
Myrtle Grn. HP1: Hem H . . . 1H 123
Myrtle Gro. EN2: Enf . . . 2B 156
Myrtleside Cl. HA6: North . . . 7F 160
Myson Way CM23: Bis S . . . 1L 79

N

Nags Head Cl. SG13: H'ford . . . 8F 94
Nags Head Rd. EN3: Pon E . . . 6G 157
Nails La. CM23: Bis S . . . 1H 79
Nairn Cl. AL5: Harp . . . 9E 88
Nairn Grn. WD19: Watf . . . 3J 161
Namco Entertainment . . . *9F 46*
(within The Galaxy Cen.)
Nan Aires HP22: W'rave . . . 5A 60
Nan Clark's La. NW7 . . . 2E 164
Nancy Downs WD19: Watf . . . 9L 149
Nancy's La. CB11: L Lwr . . . 3M 29
Nanscott Ho. WD19: Watf . . . 3M 161
Nanterre Ct. WD17: Watf . . . 5A 166 (4J 149)
Nap, The WD4: Kin L . . . 2C 136
Napier NW9 . . . 8F 164
Napier Cl. AL2: Lon C . . . 7L 127
Napier Ct. EN8: C'hunt . . . 1F 144
LU1: Lut . . . 1F 66
Napier Dr. WD23: Bush . . . 6N 149
Napier Rd. EN3: Pon E . . . 7H 157
LU1: Lut . . . 1F 66
Nappsbury Rd. LU4: Lut . . . 4N 45
NAPSBURY . . . 9K 127
Napsbury Av. AL2: Lon C . . . 8K 127
Napsbury La. AL1: St Alb . . . 5N 127
Nardini *NW9* . . . *8F 164*
(off Long Mead)
Naresby Fold HA7: Stanm . . . 6K 163
Narrowbox La. SG2: Stev . . . 2B 52
Nascot Pl. WD17: Watf . . . 4K 149
Nascot Rd. WD17: Watf . . . 4K 149
Nascot St. WD17: Watf . . . 4K 149
Nascot Wood Rd. WD17: Watf . . . 1H 149
Naseby Rd. LU1: Lut . . . 1D 66
Nash Cl. AL9: Welh G . . . 5K 129
HP4: Berk . . . 9L 103
LU5: Hou R . . . 4G 45
SG2: Stev . . . 3A 52
SG3: Dat . . . 6D 72
WD6: Elst . . . 6N 151
Nashes Farm La. AL4: San . . . 7L 109
Nash Grn. HP3: Hem H . . . 7B 124
Nash Lee Rd. HP22: Wen . . . 9A 100
Nashleigh Ho. HP5: C'ham . . . 9J 121
NASH MILLS . . . 8B 124
Nash Mills La. HP3: Hem H . . . 8B 124
Nash Mills Recreation Cen. . . . 8B 124
Nash Rd. SG8: Roys . . . 8D 8
NAST HYDE . . . 1E 128
NASTY . . . 4H 55
Nathan Ct. *N9* . . . *9G 156*
(off Causeyware Rd.)
Nathaniel Wlk. HP23: Tring . . . 1M 101
Nathans Cl. AL6: Wel . . . 1J 91
Nation Way E4 . . . 9N 157
Natural History Museum at Tring . . . 3N 101
Navarre Ct. WD4: Kin L . . . 1D 136
Navigation Dr. EN3: Enf L . . . 2L 157
Navigation Ho. *CM23: Bis S* . . . *1H 79*
(off Adderley Rd.)
Nayland Cl. LU2: Lut . . . 8N 47
Naylor Gro. EN3: Pon E . . . 7H 157
Nazeing Glass Mus. . . . 3M 133
NAZEING MARSH . . . 5M 133
NAZEING MEAD . . . 1N 133
Nazeing New Rd. EN10: Brox . . . 3L 133
Nazeing Rd. EN9: Brox, Naz . . . 4N 133
Neagh Cl. SG1: Stev . . . 7B 36
Neagle Cl. WD6: Bore . . . 3C 152
Neal Cl. HA6: North . . . 8J 161
Neal Ct. SG14: H'ford . . . 9A 94
Neal St. WD18: Watf . . . 7L 149
Near Acre NW9 . . . 8F 164
Neatby Ct. EN8: C'hunt . . . 1H 145
Necton Rd. AL4: Wheat . . . 7M 89
Needham Rd. LU4: Lut . . . 3L 45
Needleman Cl. NW9 . . . 9E 164
Neighbours Cotts.
HP23: Wigg . . . 5B 102
Neild Way WD3: R'orth . . . 9J 147
Nell Gwynn Cl. WD7: Shen . . . 5M 139
Nelson Av. AL1: St Alb . . . 5J 127
Nelson Rd. CM23: Bis S . . . 3J 79
EN3: Pon E . . . 8H 157
HA7: Stanm . . . 6K 163
HP4: Dag . . . 2N 83
Nelson St. SG14: H'ford . . . 8N 93
Neptune Ct. *LU5: Hou R* . . . *3H 45*
(off Trident Dr.)
Neptune Ct. WD6: Bore . . . 5A 152
Neptune Dr. HP2: Hem H . . . 9A 106
Neptune Ga. SG2: Stev . . . 9C 36
Neptune Sq. LU5: Hou R . . . 3H 45
Nero Ho. AL1: St Alb . . . 3G 126
Nesbitts All. EN5: Barn . . . 5M 153
Neston Rd. WD24: Watf . . . 1L 149
Nestor Av. N21 . . . 8N 155
Netherby Cl. HP23: Tring . . . 9A 82
Netherby Gdns. EN2: Enf . . . 6K 155
Nether Cl. N3 . . . 7N 165
Nethercott Cl. LU2: Lut . . . 8L 47
Nethercourt Av. N3 . . . 6N 165
Netherfield Ct. SG12: Stan A . . . 3A 116
Netherfield La. SG12: Stan A . . . 3A 116
Netherfield Rd. AL5: Harp . . . 2C 108
Netherhall Rd. CM19: Royd . . . 8C 116
Netherlands Rd. EN5: N Bar . . . 8C 154
Netherstones SG5: Stot . . . 5F 10
NETHER STREET . . . 2H 97
Nether St. N3 . . . 7N 165
SG12: Widf . . . 2H 97
Netherway AL3: St Alb . . . 5B 126
Netley Dell SG6: L Gar . . . 8H 23
NETTESWELL . . . 5A 118
Netteswell Dr. CM20: Harl . . . 5N 117
Netteswell Orchard CM20: Harl . . . 5N 117
Netteswell Rd. CM20: Harl . . . 3A 118
Netteswell Twr. CM20: Harl . . . 4N 117
Nettle Cl. LU4: Lut . . . 5H 45
Nettlecroft AL7: Welw G . . . 8A 92
HP1: Hem H . . . 3L 123
NETTLEDEN . . . 5F 104
Nettleden Rd. HP1: Hem H, Net . . . 4D 104
HP4: Hem H, Net, Pot E . . . 8C 104
HP4: Lit G . . . 9A 84
Nevell's Grn. SG6: L Gar . . . 4F 22
Nevells Rd. SG6: L Gar . . . 5F 22
Nevil Cl. HA6: North . . . 5F 160
Neville Cl. EN6: Pot B . . . 4M 141
Neville Rd. LU3: Lut . . . 4C 46
Neville Rd. Pas. LU3: Lut . . . 4C 46
Nevilles Ct. SG6: L Gar . . . 3J 23
Nevill Gro. WD24: Watf . . . 3K 149
Nevis Rd. SG1: W'ton . . . 6N 35
Newark Cl. SG8: Roys . . . 5C 8
Newark Grn. WD6: Bore . . . 5D 152
Newark Rd. LU4: Lut . . . 7C 46
Newark Rd. Path LU4: Lut . . . 7C 46
New Barnes Av. AL1: St Alb . . . 5H 127
NEW BARNET . . . 6C 154
New Barnet Station (Rail) . . . 7C 154
New Barn La. CM22: Gt Hal, L Hal . . . 7K 79
New Barns La. SG10: M Had . . . 4G 77
New Bedford Rd. LU1: Lut . . . 9F 46
LU2: Lut . . . 6F 46
LU3: Lut . . . 3E 46
Newberries Av. WD7: Rad . . . 8J 139
Newbiggin Path WD19: Watf . . . 4L 161
Newbold Rd. LU3: Lut . . . 2D 46
Newbolt SG8: Roys . . . 5D 8
Newbolt Rd. HA7: Stanm . . . 5G 163
Newbury Av. EN3: Enf L . . . 2K 157
Newbury Cl. CM23: Bis S . . . 9G 59
LU4: Lut . . . 7A 46
SG1: Stev . . . 9K 35
Newbury Rd. LU5: Hou R . . . 3H 45
Newby Cl. EN1: Enf . . . 4C 156
Newcastle Cl. SG1: Stev . . . 7M 35
New Cl. SG3: Kneb . . . 2M 71
SG8: Lit . . . 3J 7
Newcombe Pk. NW7 . . . 5E 164
Newcombe Rd. LU1: Lut . . . 1E 66
Newcome Path WD7: Shen . . . 7A 140
Newcome Rd. WD7: Shen . . . 7A 140
New Common CM22: L Hal . . . 3N 99

New Cotts.—Norton Bury La.

New Cotts. AL3: Mark 1A 86
SG4: Ben 1H 69
SG4: K Wal 4G 49
New Ct. SG3: Dat 6N 71
Newcourt Bus. Pk. CM18: Harl 9M 117
Newdigate Grn. UB9: Hare 8N 159
Newdigate Rd. UB9: Hare 8M 159
Newdigate Rd. E. UB9: Hare 8N 159
Newell La. SG2: Crom, Luff 3H 37
Newell Ri. HP3: Hem H 5A 124
Newell Rd. CM24: Stans 5N 59
HP3: Hem H 5A 124
Newells SG6: L Gar 7J 23
Newells Hedge LU7: Pits 2B 82
Newells Way SG6: L Gar 6K 23
New England Cl. SG4: St Ipo 6N 33
New England St. AL3: St Alb 2B 166 (2D 126)
New Farm La. HA6: North 8G 161
Newfield La. HP2: Hem H 2A 124
Newfields AL8: Welw G 1H 111
Newfield Way AL4: St Alb 4K 127
Newford Cl. HP2: Hem H 1D 124
New Ford Rd. EN8: Wal C 7K 145
New Forge Pl. *AL3: Red* *1K 107*
(off High St.)
New Frontiers Science Pk. CM19: Harl 8K 117
New Frontiers Science Pk. Nth.
CM19: Harl 6J 117
Newgale Gdns. HA8: Edg 8N 163
Newgate SG2: Stev 5N 51
Newgate Cl. AL4: St Alb 8L 109
NEWGATE STREET 6J 131
Newgate St. SG13: New S 4J 131
Newgatestreet Rd. EN7: Gof O 7N 131
Newgate St. Village SG13: New S 6K 131
NEW GREENS 7E 108
New Greens Av. AL3: St Alb 6E 108
NEW GROUND 4E 102
Newground Rd. HP23: Aldb, N Gnd 4E 102
NEWHALL 5E 118
New Hall Cl. HP3: Bov 9D 122
Newhaven SG2: Stev 2A 52
New Horizon Bus. Cen. CM19: Harl 6J 117
Newhouse Cres. WD25: Watf 5K 137
New Ho. Pk. AL1: St Alb 5H 127
Newhouse Rd. HP3: Bov 8D 122
New Inn Rd. SG7: Hinx 9E 4
New Kent Rd. AL1: St Alb 3D 166 (2E 126)
Newland Cl. AL1: St Alb 5H 127
HA5: Hat E 6N 161
Newland Dr. EN1: Enf 3F 156
Newland Gdns. SG13: H'ford 9C 94
NEWLANDS 3M 163
Newlands *AL9: Hat* *7J 111*
(off Old Hertford Rd.)
SG6: L Gar 8G 22
Newlands Av. WD7: Rad 7G 138
Newlands Cl. HA8: Edg 3M 163
Newlands Cl. E. SG4: Hit 6N 33
Newlands Cl. W. SG4: Hit 6N 33
Newlands La. SG4: Hit 6N 33
Newlands Pk. Caravan Site WD5: Bed 8H 125
Newlands Pl. EN5: Barn 7K 153
Newlands Rd. HP1: Hem H 1H 123
LU1: Lut 4D 66
Newlands Wlk. WD25: Watf 6M 137
Newlands Way EN6: Pot B 3A 142
Newlyn Cl. AL2: Bri W 3N 137
SG1: Stev 3G 50
Newlyn Ho. HA5: Hat E 7A 162
Newlyn Rd. EN5: Barn 6M 153
Newman Av. SG8: Roys 7F 8
New Mnr. Cft. HP4: Berk 1N 121
Newmans Ct. SG14: Watt S 5J 73
Newmans Dr. AL5: Harp 5A 88
NEWMAN'S END 9N 99
Newman's Way EN4: Had W 3B 154
Newmarket Ct. AL3: St Alb 1D 126
Newmarket Rd. SG8: Roys 7E 8
(not continuous)
NEW MILL 1N 101
NEW MILL END 7N 67
New Mill Ter. HP23: Tring 9N 81
NEWNHAM 5M 11
Newnham Cl. LU2: Lut 8M 47
Newnham Hall 4M 11
Newnham Pde. EN8: C'hunt 3H 145
Newnham Rd. SG7: New, R'well 5M 11
Newnham Way SG7: Ashw 3N 11
New Pde. WD3: Chor 6F 146
New Pde. Flats WD3: Chor 6F 146
New Pk. Dr. HP2: Hem H 1D 124
New Park La. SG2: A'ton 7E 52
New Pk. Rd. SG13: New S 6H 131
UB9: Hare 8M 159
New Path CM23: Bis S 2H 79
New Pl. AL6: Wel 3H 91
New Pond St. CM17: Harl 5F 118
Newport Cl. EN3: Enf W 1J 157
Newport Lodge *EN1: Enf* *7C 156*
(off Village Rd.)
Newport Mead WD19: Watf 4M 161
Newports CM21: Saw 6E 98
New Provident Pl. HP4: Berk 1A 122
Newquay Gdns. WD19: Watf 2K 161
New River Arms EN10: Turn 7J 133
New River Av. SG12: Stan A 2M 115
New River Cl. EN11: Hod 7M 115
New River Ct. EN7: C'hunt 4F 144
SG12: Ware 7J 95
New River Trad. Est.
EN8: C'hunt 8H 133
New Rd. AL6: Wel 4M 91
AL8: Welw G 3G 111
CM17: Harl 2F 118
EN6: S Mim 6G 141
EN10: Brox 1L 133
HP4: Berk 8J 103
(High St.)
HP4: Berk 9A 104
(White Hill)
HP8: Chal G 5B 146
HP22: Ast C, Buck 1D 100
HP23: Tring 9M 81
New Rd. HP23: Wils 7J 81
(not continuous)
NW7 7L 165
(Bittacy Ct.)
NW7 9F 152
(Hendon Wood La.)
SG3: Dat 6N 71
SG8: Gt Chi 1H 17
SG8: Melb, Hey 1M 9 & 3M 9
SG11: L Had 1K 77
SG12: Ware 6H 95
SG14: H'ford 7A 94
WD3: Crox G 7C 148
WD3: Sar 3J 147
WD4: Chippf 3J 135
WD6: Elst 8L 151
WD7: Rad 9F 138
WD7: Shen 7A 140
WD17: Watf 9E 166 (6L 149)
WD25: Let H 3F 150
New Row CM22: She 7L 99
NEWSELLS 5A 16
Newsholme Dr. N21 7L 155
Newsom Pl. AL1: St Alb 1F 166 (1F 126)
New Station Cotts. EN10: Brox 2L 133
Newstead AL10: Hat 3F 128
Newstead Way CM20: Harl 4M 117
New St. CM21: Saw 4G 99
HP4: Berk 1A 122
LU1: Lut 2F 66
LU1: S End 7E 66
LU7: Ched 9L 61
WD18: Watf 8D 166 (6L 149)
NEWTON 1D 4
Newton Cl. AL5: Harp 9E 88
EN11: Hod 4M 115
Newton Cres. WD6: Bore 6C 152
Newtondale LU4: Lut 4M 45
Newton Dr. CM21: Saw 6F 98
Newton Ho. EN3: Enf H 5H 157
Newton Rd. HA3: Har W 9F 162
SG2: Stev 3A 52
Newtons Way SG4: Hit 4N 33
Newton Wlk. HA8: Edg 8B 164
NEW TOWN
CM23 2H 79
LU1 3H 67
NEWTOWN 2J 39
New Town SG4: Cod 7F 70
New Town Rd. CM23: Bis S 2H 79
LU1: Lut 2G 67
New Town St. LU1: Lut 2G 67
New Villas HP23: Tring 1D 102
New Wlk. SG5: Shil 2A 20
NEW WAY 6L 119
New Way La. CM17: Harl, M Tye 7K 119
New Wood AL7: Welw G 8B 92
New Woodfield Grn. LU5: Duns 2H 65
Nexus Ct. AL1: St Alb 3E 126
Niagara Cl. EN8: C'hunt 2H 145
Nicholas Cl. AL3: St Alb 8E 108
WD24: Watf 1K 149
Nicholas Ho. AL4: St Alb 3L 127
Nicholas La. SG14: H'ford 9A 94
Nicholas Pl. SG1: Stev 9K 35
Nicholas Rd. WD6: Elst 8N 151
Nicholas Way HA6: North 8E 160
HP2: Hem H 9B 106
LU6: Duns 9E 44
Nichol Cl. N14 9J 155
Nicholls Cl. AL3: Red 1H 107
MK45: Bar C 8E 18
Nicholls Fld. CM18: Harl 7C 118
Nichols Cl. LU2: Lut 7L 47
Nicholson Ct. EN11: Hod 8M 115
Nickleby Way SG5: Stot 1C 22
Nickmar Ct. LU3: Lut 7F 46
Nicky La. HP2: Hem H 9A 106
Nicola Cl. HA3: Har W 9E 162
Nicol Cl. SL9: Chal P 8A 158
Nicoll Way WD6: Bore 7D 152
Nicol Rd. SL9: Chal P 8A 158
Nicolson NW9 8E 164
Nicolson Dr. WD23: B Hea 1D 162
Nidderdale HP2: Hem H 8B 106
Nighthawk NW9 8F 164
Nightingale Cl. LU2: Lut 3L 47
WD5: Abb L 4J 137
WD7: Rad 9G 138
Nightingale Ct. *LU3: Lut* *9E 46*
(off Waldeck Rd.)
SG5: Hit 2A 34
SG14: H'ford 9A 94
WD3: R'orth 9M 147
WD7: Rad 8H 139
Nightingale La. AL1: St Alb 5K 127
AL4: St Alb 6K 127
Nightingale Lodge HP4: Berk 1M 121
Nightingale Pl. WD3: R'orth 9N 147
Nightingale Rd. EN7: C'hunt 7A 132
HP22: Wen 9A 100
N9 8G 157
SG5: Hit 2N 33
WD3: R'orth 9M 147
WD23: Bush 7B 150
Nightingales CM17: Harl 8E 118
CM23: Bis S 2K 79
Nightingales La. HP8: Chal G 6A 146
Nightingale Ter. SG15: Arl 9A 10
Nightingale Wlk.
HP2: Hem H 5E 106
SG2: Stev 4B 52
Nightingale Way SG5: Stot 1C 22
SG7: Bald 5L 23
SG8: Roys 5E 8
Nimbus Pk. LU5: Hou R 6F 44
Nimbus Way SG4: Hit 3C 34
Nimmo Dr. WD23: B Hea 9E 150
Nimrod NW9 8E 164
Nimrod Cl. AL4: St Alb 9K 109
Nimrod Dr. AL10: Hat 8D 110
Nine Acre La. AL10: Hat 1F 128
Nine Ashes SG12: Huns 8G 96
Ninesprings Way SG4: Hit 4B 34
Ninfield Ct. *LU2: Lut* *6L 47*
(off Telscombe Way)
Ninian Rd. HP2: Hem H 6A 106
Ninnings Cotts. AL5: Harp 7B 88
Ninning's La. AL6: Wel 6L 71
Ninnings Rd. SL9: Chal P 7C 158
Ninnings Way SL9: Chal P 7C 158
Ninth Av. LU3: Lut 2N 45
Niton Cl. EN5: Barn 8K 153
Niven Cl. WD6: Bore 3C 152
Noahs Cl. EN3: Enf W 2G 156
Noahs Ct. Gdns. SG13: H'ford 1C 114
Noake Mill La. HP1: Hem H 6K 105
Nobel Vs. EN9: Wal A 7N 145
NOBLAND GREEN 8D 76
Nobles, The CM23: Bis S 2F 78
Nocton Hall Dr. HP22: Halt 8D 100
Nodes Dr. SG2: Stev 8N 51
Node Way Gdns. AL6: Wel 4J 91
Noel NW9 8E 164
Noke, The SG2: Stev 9A 52
Noke La. AL2: Chis G 8N 125
Noke La. Bus. Cen. AL2: Chis G 9A 126
Nokes, The HP1: Hem H 9K 105
Noke Shot AL5: Harp 3D 88
Noke Side AL2: Chis G 9B 126
Nokeside SG2: Stev 9A 52
Nolan Path *WD6: Bore* *3N 151*
(off Bennington Dr.)
Nolton Pl. HA8: Edg 8N 163
NOMANSLAND 9L 89
Nook, The SG12: Stan A 2M 115
Norbury Av. WD24: Watf 3L 149
Norbury Gro. NW7 3E 164
Norcott Cl. LU5: Duns 1G 65
Norcott Ct. HP4: Berk 5H 103
NORCOTT HILL 4H 103
Norfolk Av. WD24: Watf 2L 149
Norfolk Cl. EN4: C'ters 6F 154
Norfolk Ct. EN5: Barn 6L 153
Norfolk Gdns. WD6: Bore 6D 152
Norfolk Rd. EN3: Pon E 8F 156
EN5: N Bar 5N 153
LU2: Lut 1J 67
LU5: Duns 2H 65
SG9: Bunt 2J 39
WD3: R'orth 1A 160
Norfolk Way CM23: Bis S 4G 79
Norgetts La. SG8: Melb 1N 9
Norman Av. CM23: Bis S 2F 78
Norman Booth Recreation Cen. 3F 118
Norman Cl. AL1: St Alb 5F 126
EN9: Wal A 6N 145
Norman Ct. CM24: Stans 2N 59
EN6: Pot B 3B 142
N3 *8N 165*
(off Nether St.)
Norman Cres. HA5: Pin 8L 161
Normandy Av. EN5: Barn 7M 153
Normandy Ct. HP2: Hem H 1N 123
Normandy Dr. HP4: Berk 8M 103
Normandy Ho. EN2: Enf 2A 156
Normandy Rd. AL3: St Alb 1C 166 (9E 108)
Normandy Way EN11: Hod 7N 115
Norman Rd. AL6: Wel 4H 91
LU3: Lut 7D 46
MK45: Bar C 7E 18
Normans Cl. SG6: L Gar 2F 22
Normansfield Cl. WD23: Bush 9C 150
Normans La. AL6: Wel 6L 71
SG8: Roys 8D 8
Norman's Way CM24: Stans 2N 59
Norman Way LU6: Duns 9B 44
Normill Ter. HP22: Ast C 9A 80
Norrington End AL3: Red 6G 86
Norris *NW9* *8F 164*
(off Withers Mead)
Norris Cl. AL2: Lon C 8J 127
CM23: Bis S 1L 79
Norris Gro. EN10: Brox 2J 133
Norris La. EN11: Hod 7L 115
Norris Ri. EN11: Hod 7K 115
Norris Rd. EN11: Hod 8L 115
Norry's Cl. EN4: C'ters 6E 154
Norry's Rd. EN4: C'ters 6E 154
North Acre NW9 8E 164
NORTHALL 3E 62
Northall Cl. LU6: Eat B 2H 63
Northall Rd. LU6: Eat B 3H 63
Northampton Rd. EN3: Pon E 6J 157
North App. HA6: North 2E 160
WD25: Watf 8H 137
North Av. SG6: L Gar 3H 23
WD7: Shen 5M 139
NORTHAW 3E 142
Northaw Cl. HP2: Hem H 6D 106
NORTHAW PARK 5E 142
Northaw Pl. EN6: N'haw 3C 142
Northaw Rd. E. EN6: Cuff 4J 143
Northaw Rd. W. EN6: N'haw 3E 142
North Barn EN10: Brox 3M 133
Northbridge Rd. HP4: Berk 8K 103
Northbrook Dr. HA6: North 8G 160
Nth. Brook End SG8: S Mor 2C 6
Northbrook Rd. EN5: Barn 8L 153
Northbrooks CM19: Harl 7M 117
NORTHCHURCH 8J 103
NORTHCHURCH COMMON 5K 103
Northchurch Comn. HP4: Berk 7K 103
Northchurch La. HP5: Ash G 3G 121
Northcliffe LU6: Eat B 2J 63
Northcliffe Dr. N20 1M 165
North Cl. AL2: Chis G 7C 126
EN5: Barn 7J 153
SG8: Roys 6C 8
North Comn. AL3: Red 2J 107
(not continuous)
Northcote HA5: Pin 9L 161
North Cotts. AL2: Lon C 7H 127
Northcotts AL9: Hat 8J 111
Northcotts Long Elms Cl. *WD5: Abb L* *6F 136*
(off Long Elms Cl.)
North Ct. AL3: Mark 2A 86
Northcourt WD3: R'orth 1K 159
North Cres. N3 9M 165
North Dene NW7 3D 164
Northdown Rd. AL10: Hat 3G 128
SL9: Chal P 6B 158
Northdrift Way LU1: Lut 2D 66
North Dr. AL4: St Alb 9M 109
AL9: Hat 7J 111
SG11: H Cro 6J 75
NORTH END 5B 14
North End SG8: Bass 1M 7
Northend HP3: Hem H 4D 124
Northfield AL10: Hat 6H 111
SG11: B'ing 2C 56
SG11: Puck 7A 56
Northfield Gdns. WD24: Watf 1L 149
Northfield Rd. AL5: Harp 3D 88
CM21: Saw 3G 99
EN3: Pon E 7F 156
EN4: C'ters 5D 154
EN8: Wal C 5J 145
HP23: Tring 9B 82
SG7: Ashw 1K 5
WD6: Bore 3B 152
Northfields LU5: Duns 6D 44
SG6: L Gar 2F 22
North Gate CM20: Harl 5M 117
Northgate HA6: North 7E 160
SG1: Stev 4K 51
Northgate Bus. Cen. EN1: Enf 5F 156
Northgate End CM23: Bis S 9H 59
Northgate Ho. *EN8: C'hunt* *2J 145*
(off Turners Hill)
Northgate Path WD6: Bore 2N 151
Northgate Pl. *CM23: Bis S* *9H 59*
(off Northgate End)
North Grn. NW9 7E 164
SG14: H'ford 6L 93
North Gro. CM18: Harl 7C 118
North Herts Leisure Cen. 5J 23
North Hill WD3: Chor 4H 147
North Ho. *CM18: Harl* *8B 118*
(off Bush Fair)
Northiam N12 4N 165
(not continuous)
Northlands EN6: Pot B 4C 142
North Lodge EN5: N Bar 7B 154
Nth. Luton Ind. Est. LU4: Lut 2L 45
NORTH MYMMS 7G 129
Northolm HA8: Edg 4D 164
Northolme Gdns. HA8: Edg 8A 164
Northolt Av. CM23: Bis S 8K 59
Nth. Orbital Commercial Pk. AL1: St Alb 6H 127
Nth. Orbital Rd. AL1: St Alb 6E 126
AL2: Chis G 3M 137
AL2: St Alb 6E 126
AL4: Smal, St Alb 6L 127
WD3: Map C 5H 159
WD3: W Hyd 8H 159
North Pde. HA8: Edg 9A 164
North Pl. CM20: Harl 1C 118
EN9: Wal A 6M 145
SG5: Hit 1L 33
North Ride AL6: Wel 1J 91
Northridge Way HP1: Hem H 3J 123
North Riding AL2: Bri W 3B 138
North Rd. EN8: Wal C 6J 145
EN11: Hod 7L 115
HA8: Edg 8B 164
HP4: Berk 1M 121
N9 9F 156
SG1: Stev 7J 35
SG14: H'ford 6M 93
WD3: Chor 7G 146
North Rd. Av. SG14: H'ford 8M 93
North Rd. Gdns. SG14: H'ford 9N 93
Northside AL4: San 5J 109
Nth. Station Way LU6: Duns 8C 44
North St. CM23: Bis S 9H 59
LU2: Lut 9G 46
(not continuous)
North Ter. CM23: Bis S 9H 59
Northumberland Av. EN1: Enf 3F 156
Northumberland Hall
AL9: N Mym 1K 141
Northumberland Rd. EN5: N Bar 8B 154
Northview HP1: Hem H 4G 122
North Vw. Cotts. SG12: Widf 3G 97
Northview Rd. LU2: Lut 7H 47
LU5: Hou R 7D 44
NORTH WATFORD 1K 149
North Way NW9 9B 164
Northway AL7: Welw G 5M 91
WD3: R'orth 9N 147
Northway Cir. NW7 4D 164
Northway Ct. NW7 4E 164
Northway Cres. NW7 4D 164
Northwell Dr. LU3: Lut 9A 30
Nth. Western Av. WD24: Watf 8H 137
WD25: A'ham 4C 150
(Elton Way)
WD25: A'ham 7F 150
(Tylers Way)
WD25: A'ham, Watf 1N 149
WD25: Watf 8F 136
(not continuous)
Northwick Rd. WD19: Watf 4L 161
Northwold Dr. HA5: Pin 9L 161
NORTHWOOD 6G 160
Northwood AL7: Welw G 9C 92
Northwood Cl. EN7: C'hunt 9D 132
Northwood Golf Course 7F 160
NORTHWOOD HILLS 9J 161
Northwood Hills Cir. HA6: North 8J 161
Northwood Hills Station (Underground) 9J 161
Northwood Rd. UB9: Hare 8M 159
Northwood Sports Cen. 8K 161
Northwood Station (Underground) 7G 160
Northwood Way HA6: North 7H 161
UB9: Hare 8N 159
Norfolk Rd. SL9: Chal P 6C 158
NORTON 2H 23
Norton Almshouses *EN8: C'hunt* *3H 145*
(off Turner's Hill)
Norton Bury La. SG6: Nort 1J 23

A-Z Hertfordshire 209

O

Queens Rd.—Richmond Ct.

Queens Rd. SG14: H'ford 1B 114
WD17: Watf 8D 166 (6L 149)
(Carey Pl., not continuous)
WD17: Watf 5D 166 (4L 149)
(Orphanage Rd.)
Queens Rd. Est. EN5: Barn 5K 153
Queen's Square, The HP2: Hem H 2B 124
Queen St. AL3: St Alb 2B 166 (2D 126)
HP23: Tring 3M 101
LU5: Hou R 5E 44
LU7: Pits 3B 82
SG4: Hit 4N 33
SG5: Stot 7G 10
WD4: Chippf 5K 135
Queens Wlk. E4 9N 157
Queens Way EN8: Wal C 7K 145
WD7: Shen 5M 139
Queensway AL10: Hat 8G 111
EN3: Pon E 6F 156
HP1: Hem H 1M 123
HP2: Hem H 1A 124
LU5: Duns 8E 44
SG1: Stev 4K 51
SG8: Roys 6D 8
Queensway Bus. Cen. EN3: Pon E 6F 156
Queensway Ho's. *AL10: Hat* *8G 111*
(off Queensway)
Queensway Ind. Est. EN3: Pon E 6G 156
Queensway Pde. LU5: Duns 8E 44
Queenswood Cres. WD25: Watf 6J 137
Queenswood Dr. SG4: Hit 1C 34
Queenswood Pk. N3 9L 165
Quendell Wlk. HP2: Hem H 2A 124
QUENDON 1N 43
Quickbeams AL7: Welw G 6N 91
Quickley Brow WD3: Chor 8E 146
Quickley La. WD3: Chor 8E 146
Quickley Ri. WD3: Chor 8F 146
Quickmoor La. WD4: Buc H 6L 135
Quickswood LU3: Lut 2C 46
Quickwood Cl. WD3: R'orth 8K 147
Quills SG6: L Gar 7K 23
Quilter Cl. LU3: Lut 5B 46
Quinbury La. SG8: Bark 9A 16
Quinces Cft. HP1: Hem H 9K 105
Quincey Rd. SG12: Ware 4G 94
Quin Ct. SG11: B'ing 2C 56
Quinn Way SG6: L Gar 6J 23
Quinta Dr. EN5: Barn 7H 153

R

Raban Cl. SG2: Stev 8B 52
Raban Ct. SG7: Bald 2M 23
RABLEY 5D 140
RABLEY HEATH 5K 71
Rabley Heath Rd. AL6: Rab H, Wel 8G 70
Rackham Dr. LU3: Lut 4E 46
Radburn Cl. CM18: Harl 9C 118
Radburn Cnr. SG6: L Gar 6J 23
Radburn Ct. LU6: Duns 8D 44
Radburn Way SG6: L Gar 7H 23
Radcliffe Av. EN2: Enf 3A 156
Radcliffe Rd. HA3: Weal 9H 163
N21 9N 155
SG5: Hit 2A 34
RADLETT 8H 139
Radlett Golf Cen. 5H 139
Radlett La. WD7: Rad, Shen 7L 139
Radlett Park Golf Course 5L 151
Radlett Pk. Rd. WD7: Rad 7H 139
Radlett Rd. AL2: Col S, Frog 2F 138
WD17: Watf 6E 166 (5L 149)
WD24: Watf 6E 166 (5L 149)
WD25: A'ham 2C 150
Radlett Station (Rail) 8H 139
Radley Ct. *AL1: St Alb* *2F 166*
(off Newsome Pl.)
Radnor Ct. HA3: Har W 8G 163
Radnor Gdns. EN1: Enf 3C 156
Radnor Rd. LU4: Lut 5J 45
Radstone Pl. LU2: Lut 8A 48
RADWELL 8J 11
Radwell Cotts. SG7: R'well 8J 11
Radwell La. SG7: R'well 8J 11
Raebarn Gdns. EN5: Barn 7H 153
Raeburn Rd. HA8: Edg 8A 164
Raffin Cl. SG3: Dat 5C 72
Raffin Grn. La. SG3: Dat 5C 72
SG14: Watt S 5C 72
Raffin Pk. SG3: Dat 5D 72
Raffles Ct. HA8: Edg 4N 163
RAF Museum London 9G 164
Ragged Hall La. AL2: Chis G, Pot C 6M 125
Raglan Av. EN8: Wal C 7H 145
Raglan Cl. LU4: Lut 6J 45
Raglan Gdns. WD19: Watf 1K 161
Raglan Ho. HP4: Berk 1L 121
Raglan Rd. EN1: Enf 9D 156
Rags La. EN7: C'hunt 1C 144
(not continuous)
Railway, The SG16: Henl 1J 21
Railway Cotts. HP23: Tring 1E 102
WD4: Kin L 3D 136
WD7: Rad 8J 139
WD24: Watf 3K 149
Railway Pl. SG13: H'ford 9C 94
Railway Rd. EN8: Wal C 6K 145
Railway St. SG13: H'ford 9B 94
SG14: H'ford 9B 94
Railway Ter. WD4: Kin L 9C 124
WD24: Watf 3K 149
Rainbow Cl. AL3: Red 9H 87
Rainbow Ct. WD19: Watf 8L 149
Rainbow Rd. CM17: M Tye 3N 119
Rainer Cl. EN8: C'hunt 2H 145
Rainsborough Ct. SG13: H'ford 9E 94
Rainsford Cl. HA7: Stanm 5K 163
Rainsford Rd. CM24: Stans 1M 59
Raleigh Cres. SG2: Stev 1N 51
Raleigh Gro. LU4: Lut 8N 45
Raleigh Rd. EN2: Enf 6B 156
Raleigh Way N14 9J 155
Rally, The SG15: Arl 5A 10
(not continuous)
Ralph Swingler Pl. SG6: L Gar 7F 22
Ralston Way WD19: Watf 2M 161
Ramblers La. CM17: Harl 5F 118
Ramblers Way AL7: Welw G 1A 112
Rambling Way HP4: Pot E 8E 104
Ramerick Gdns. SG15: Arl 1N 21
Ram Gorse CM20: Harl 4L 117
Ramillies Rd. NW7 2E 164
Ramney Dr. EN3: Enf L 9J 145
Ramparts, The AL3: St Alb 3C 126
Ramridge Rd. LU2: Lut 7J 47
Ramryge Ct. AL1: St Alb 4E 126
Ramsay Cl. EN10: Brox 3J 133
Ramsbury Rd. AL1: St Alb 3F 126
Ramscote La. HP5: Bell, C'ham 6D 120
Ramscroft Cl. N9 9C 156
Ramsdell SG1: Stev 4M 51
Ramsey Cl. AL1: St Alb 4H 127
AL9: B Pk 9C 130
LU4: Lut 6J 45
Ramsey Ct. LU4: Lut 6J 45
Ramsey Lodge Ct.
AL1: St Alb 1F 166 (1F 126)
Ramsey Rd. MK45: Bar C 8E 18
Ramsey Way N14 9H 155
Ramson Ri. HP1: Hem H 3H 123
Ram Yd. SG15: Arl 8A 10
Ranch House, The EN7: C'hunt 7N 131
Randall Ct. NW7 7G 165
Randalls Hill SG2: Stev 6A 52
Randalls Ride HP2: Hem H 9N 105
Randalls Wlk. AL2: Bri W 3A 138
Randolph Ct. *HA5: Hat E* *7B 162*
(off The Avenue)
Randon Cl. HA2: Harr 9C 162
Rand's Cl. SG5: Hol 4J 21
Rand's Mdw. SG5: Hol 4J 21
Ranelagh Cl. HA8: Edg 4A 164
Ranelagh Dr. HA8: Edg 4A 164
Ranelagh Rd. HP2: Hem H 2D 124
Ranleigh Wlk. AL5: Harp 9E 88
Rannoch Cl. HA8: Edg 2B 164
Rannoch Wlk. HP2: Hem H 7N 105
Ranock Cl. LU3: Lut 1N 45
Ranskill Ct. WD6: Bore 3A 152
Ranskill Rd. WD6: Bore 3A 152
Ransom Cl. SG4: Hit 6N 33
WD19: Watf 9L 149
Ransom's Yd. SG5: Hit 3N 33
Rant Mdw. HP3: Hem H 4C 124
(not continuous)
Ranulf Cl. CM17: Harl 9E 98
Ranworth Av. EN11: Hod 4M 115
SG2: Stev 1B 72
Ranworth Cl. HP3: Hem H 4N 123
Ranworth Gdns. EN6: Pot B 4K 141
Raphael Cl. WD7: Shen 5M 139
Raphael Dr. WD24: Watf 4M 149
Rapper Ct. LU3: Lut 9E 46
Rasehill Cl. WD3: R'orth 7M 147
Rathgar Cl. N3 9M 165
Rathlin HP3: Hem H 5D 124
Ratty's La. EN11: Hod 8A 116
Ravenbank Rd. LU2: Lut 4L 47
Raven Cl. NW9 9E 164
WD3: R'orth 9M 147
WD18: Watf 7G 148
Raven Ct. AL10: Hat 1G 129
Ravenfield Rd. AL7: Welw G 9M 91
(not continuous)
Ravenhill Way LU4: Lut 4K 45
Ravensburgh Cl. MK45: Bar C 8D 18
Ravens Cl. EN1: Enf 4C 156
Ravens Ct. HP4: Berk 8B 104
HP23: Lon M 3G 81
Ravenscourt LU6: Duns 6C 44
Ravenscourt Pk. EN5: Barn 6K 153
Ravenscroft AL5: Harp 9E 88
EN10: Brox *2K 133*
(off High Rd.)
WD25: Watf 8N 137
Ravenscroft Cotts. EN5: N Bar 6N 153
Ravenscroft Pk. EN5: Barn 5K 153
Ravensdell HP1: Hem H 1J 123
Ravens La. HP4: Berk 1A 122
Ravensmead SL9: Chal P 5C 158
Ravensthorpe LU2: Lut 5K 47
Ravens Wharf HP4: Berk 1A 122
Ravenswood Pk. HA6: North 6J 161
Rawdon Dr. EN11: Hod 9L 115
Rawlins Cl. N3 9L 165
Raybarn Rd. HP1: Hem H 9K 105
Raydean Rd. EN5: N Bar 7A 154
Raydon Rd. EN8: C'hunt 5H 145
Rayfield AL8: Welw G 6K 91
Ray Gdns. HA7: Stanm 5J 163
Rayleigh Ho. WD5: Abb L 5H 137
Raymer Cl. AL1: St Alb 1F 166 (1F 126)
Raymond Cl. WD5: Abb L 5F 136
Raymond Ct. EN6: Pot B 7B 142
Raymonds Cl. AL7: Welw G 2L 111
Raymonds Plain AL7: Welw G 2L 111
Raynham Cl. CM23: Bis S 9L 59
Raynham Rd. CM23: Bis S 9K 59
Raynham St. SG13: H'ford 8C 94
Raynham Way LU2: Lut 8M 47
Raynsford Rd. SG12: Ware 6J 95
Raynton Rd. EN3: Enf W 1H 157
Ray's Hill HP5: Bell 3A 120
Readers Cl. LU6: Duns 7D 44
Readings, The CM18: Harl 9B 118
WD3: Chor 5J 147
Reading Way NW7 5K 165
Reaper Cl. LU4: Lut 5H 45
Recreation Ground
CM24: Stans 3N 59
HP22: W'rave 6A 60
Recreation Rd. LU5: Hou R 3F 44
Rectory Cl. AL9: Ess 8E 112
CM23: Thorl 5F 78
HA7: Stanm 5J 163
LU7: Slapt 2B 62
Rectory Cl. N3 8M 165
SG9: Buck 3H 27
SG12: Huns 7G 96
Rectory Cft. SG1: Stev 9K 35
Rectory Dr. CM23: Farn 3F 58
Rectory Farm Rd. EN2: Enf 2L 155
(not continuous)
Rectory Fld. CM19: Harl 8L 117
Rectory Gdns. AL10: Hat 9H 111
Rectory La. CM19: Harl 8L 117
CM23: Farn 3E 58
HA7: Stanm 5J 163
HA8: Edg 6A 164
HP4: Berk 1N 121
LU2: Lill 8M 31
SG1: Stev 9J 35
SG3: Dat 5B 72
SG14: Watt S 5J 73
WD3: R'orth 1N 159
WD4: Kin L 1C 136
WD7: Shen 6N 139
Rectory Rd. AL8: Welw G 6H 91
WD3: R'orth 1N 159
Rectory Wood CM20: Harl 5M 117
Redan Rd. SG12: Ware 4J 95
REDBOURN 1K 107
Redbournbury La. AL3: St Alb 4M 107
Redbournbury Watermill 4M 107
Redbourne Av. N3 8N 165
Redbourn Golf Course 7K 87
Redbourn Hall *AL10: Hat* *8D 110*
(off Mosquito Way)
Redbourn Ind. Est. AL3: Red 1K 107
Redbourn La. AL5: Harp 9L 87
Redbourn Mus. 2J 107
Redbourn Recreation Cen. 8J 87
Redbourn Rd. AL3: Hem H 7C 106
AL3: St Alb 4M 107
HP2: Hem H 7C 106
Red Brick Row CM22: L Hal 8K 79
Redburn Ind. Est. EN3: Pon E 8H 157
Redcar Dr. SG1: Stev 3G 51
Redcote End AL5: Harp 8B 88
REDCOTES GREEN 8D 34
Redding Ho. WD18: Watf 8G 149
Redding La. AL3: Red 6G 86
Reddings AL8: Welw G 7J 91
HP3: Hem H 4C 124
Reddings, The NW7 3F 164
WD6: Bore 5N 151
Reddings Av. WD23: Bush 7C 150
Reddings Cl. HP22: Wen 8A 100
NW7 4F 164
Redditch Ct. HP2: Hem H 7B 106
Redfern Ct. *WD18: Watf* *7G 148*
(off Whippendell Rd.)
Redferns Cl. LU1: Lut 2C 66
Redferns Ct. LU1: Lut 2C 66
Redfield Cl. AL3: Red 1J 107
LU6: Duns 9B 44
Redgrave Gdns. LU3: Lut 1B 46
Redhall Cl. AL10: Hat 3F 128
Redhall Dr. AL10: Hat 4F 128
Redhall End AL4: Col H 4E 128
Redhall La. AL4: Col H 4E 128
WD3: Chan C 3A 148
Redheath Cl. WD25: Watf 8H 137
REDHILL 5J 25
Redhill Dr. HA8: Edg 9B 164
Redhill Rd. SG5: Hit 2K 33
Red Hills EN11: Hod 1F 132
Redhoods Way E. SG6: L Gar 4E 22
Redhoods Way W. SG6: L Gar 5E 22
Red Ho. Cl. SG12: Ware 7J 95
Red Ho. Ct. LU5: Hou R 5E 44
Redlands Rd. EN3: Enf H 3J 157
Red Lion Cl. WD25: A'ham 1D 150
Red Lion Cotts. SG5: Gt Off 8E 32
Red Lion Ct. AL9: Hat 7J 111
CM23: Bis S 1J 79
Red Lion Cres. CM17: Harl 8E 118
Red Lion La. CM17: Harl 8E 118
HP1: Hem H 4K 105
HP2: Gad R, Hem H 4K 105
HP3: Hem H 8C 124
WD3: Sar 8K 135
Red Lion Yd. SG12: W'side 3C 96
WD17: Watf 8D 166 (5L 149)
Red Lodge WD6: Bore 5N 151
Red Lodge Gdns. HP4: Berk 2L 121
Redmire Cl. LU4: Lut 3L 45
Redoubt Cl. SG4: Hit 1A 34
Red Rails LU1: Lut 3E 66
Red Rails Ct. LU1: Lut 3E 66
Redricks La. CM21: Saw 9A 98
Red Rd. WD6: Bore 5N 151
Redrose Trad. Cen. EN4: E Bar 7C 154
Redvers Cl. CM23: Bis S 7J 59
Redwell Ct. EN8: Wal C 7K 145
Red Willow CM19: Harl 9J 117
Redwing Cl. SG2: Stev 5B 52
Redwing Gro. WD5: Abb L 4J 137
Redwing Ri. SG8: Roys 5E 8
Redwood Cl. AL1: St Alb 2K 127
N14 9J 155
WD19: Watf 4L 161
Redwood Dr. HP3: Hem H 4A 124
LU3: Lut 1M 45
Redwood Gdns. E4 8M 157
Redwood Ri. WD6: Bore 1B 152
Redwoods AL6: Wel 8L 71
AL8: Welw G 4K 91
SG14: H'ford 8A 94
Redwood Way EN5: Barn 7K 153
REED 7J 15
Reed Cl. AL2: Lon C 9M 127
REED END 6G 14
Reedham Cl. AL2: Bri W 2B 138
Reedings Way CM21: Saw 3H 99
Reed Pl. AL5: Harp 4A 88
Reeds, The AL7: Welw G 1K 111
Reeds Chapel *WD24: Watf* *4L 149*
(off Keele Cl.)
Reeds Cres. WD24: Watf 4L 149
Reeds Dale LU2: Lut 7A 48
Reeds Wlk. WD24: Watf 6E 166 (4L 149)
(not continuous)
Reel Cinema, The
Borehamwood *5A 152*
(within The Point)
Reenglass Rd. HA7: Stanm 4L 163
Rees Dr. HA7: Stanm 4M 163
Reeve Rd. CM24: Stans 4N 59
Reeves Av. LU3: Lut 5D 46
Reeves La. CM19: Royd 9F 116
Reeves Pightle SG8: Gt Chi 1J 17
Regal Cl. SG11: Stand 7B 56
Regal Ct. HP23: Tring 3M 101
SG5: Hit 2N 33
Regal Way WD24: Watf 2L 149
Regency Ct. *HA7: Stanm* *7L 163*
(off Unwin Way)
Regency Cl. CM23: Bis S 1G 79
Regency Ct. AL1: St Alb 2J 127
CM18: Harl 9C 118
EN1: Enf 7B 156
EN10: Worm 5K 133
HP2: Hem H 2N 123
LU6: Duns 1F 64
WD17: Watf *3J 149*
(off Langley Rd.)
Regency Ct. Pk. Homes SG16: L Ston 1F 20
Regency Cres. NW4 9K 165
Regency Ho. N3 9M 165
Regent Cl. AL4: St Alb 7K 109
AL7: Welw G 1L 111
WD4: Kin L 2C 136
Regent Ct. AL7: Welw G 9L 91
SG5: Stot 5F 10
Regent Gdns. SG5: Stot 6E 10
Regent Gate EN8: Wal C 7H 145
Regent Link *LU1: Lut* *2G 66*
(off Regent St.)
Regents Cl. HA8: Edg 4M 163
WD7: Rad 7H 139
Regents Ct. HA5: Pin 9M 161
Regents Pk. Rd. N3 9M 165
Regent St. LU1: Lut 1F 66
LU6: Duns 8E 44
SG5: Stot 6E 10
WD24: Watf 2K 149
Regina Cl. EN5: Barn 5K 153
Reginald M. CM17: Harl 5E 118
Reginald Rd. HA6: North 8H 161
Reginald St. LU2: Lut 8F 46
Regis Rd. LU4: Lut 5H 45
Rembrandt Rd. HA8: Edg 9A 164
Remus Cl. AL1: St Alb 6E 126
Rendlesham Av. WD7: Rad 1G 150
Rendlesham Cl. SG12: Ware 5F 94
Rendlesham Rd. EN2: Enf 3N 155
Rendlesham Way WD3: Chor 8F 146
Rennie Ct. EN3: Enf L 2L 157
Rennison Cl. EN7: C'hunt 9D 132
Renshaw Cl. LU2: Lut 7N 47
Repton Cl. LU3: Lut 3A 46
Repton Grn. AL3: St Alb 7E 108
Repton Way WD3: Crox G 7C 148
Reservoir Rd. N14 7H 155
Reson Way HP1: Hem H 3L 123
Reston Cl. WD6: Bore 2A 152
Reston Path LU2: Lut 7N 47
WD6: Bore 2A 152
Retford Cl. WD6: Bore 2A 152
Retreat, The HP6: L Chal 3B 146
LU5: Duns 8J 45
WD4: Kin L 4E 136
Reveley Cotts. WD23: Bush 8B 150
Revels Cl. SG14: H'ford 7B 94
Revels Rd. SG14: H'ford 7B 94
Rex Cinema
Berkhamsted 1N 121
Reynard Copse CM23: Bis S 8H 59
Reynards Rd. AL6: Wel 9H 71
Reynards Way AL2: Bri W 2A 138
Reynard Way SG13: H'ford 9F 94
Reynolds SG6: L Gar 2F 22
Reynolds Cl. HP1: Hem H 1K 123
Reynolds Cres. AL4: San 6J 109
Reynolds Dr. HA8: Edg 9N 163
Reynolds Wlk. HP5: C'ham 9E 120
Rhee Spring SG7: Bald 2A 24
Rhodes Av. CM23: Bis S 3H 79
Rhodes Gallery & Bishop's Stortford Mus.
2J 79
Rhodes Way WD24: Watf 4M 149
Rhubarb M. *CM17: Harl* *5E 118*
(off The Chase)
Rhymes, The HP1: Hem H 9L 105
Ribbledale AL2: Lon C 9N 127
Ribblesdale HP2: Hem H 8A 106
Rib Cl. SG11: Stand 7B 56
Ribocon Way LU4: Lut 2L 45
Ribston Cl. WD7: Shen 6L 139
Rib Va. SG14: H'ford 6B 94
Rib Way SG9: Bunt 3J 39
Riccall Ct. *NW9* *8E 164*
(off Pageant Av.)
Riccat La. SG1: Stev 7M 35
Rice Cl. HP2: Hem H 1B 124
Richards Cl. LU1: Lut 2D 66
WD23: Bush 9E 150
Richards Ct. LU1: Lut 2D 66
Richardson Cl. AL2: Lon C 9M 127
(not continuous)
Richardson Cres. EN7: C'hunt 7N 131
Richardson Pl. AL4: Col H 4B 128
Richards St. AL10: Hat 7D 110
Richard Stagg Cl. AL1: St Alb 4K 127
Richard St. LU5: Duns 9F 44
Richfield Rd. WD23: Bush 9D 150
Richmond Cl. CM23: Bis S 9E 58
EN8: C'hunt 2G 144
SG12: Ware 4F 94
WD6: Bore 7D 152
Richmond Ct. AL1: St Alb 2H 127
AL10: Hat 2H 129
EN6: Pot B 4B 142

Rosemoor Cl.—St Andrews Cl.

Rosemoor Cl. AL7: Welw G 1M 111
Rosemount CM19: Harl 8L 117
Roseneath Av. N21 . . . . . 9N 155
Roseneath Wlk. EN1: Enf 6C 156
Rosen's Wlk. HA8: Edg 3B 164
Rosetti Lodge SG8: Roys 5D 8
Rose Va. EN11: Hod 8L 115
Roseville N21 . . . . . 9M 155
(off The Green)
Rose Wlk. AL4: St Alb 9K 109
LU5: Hou R 3H 45
SG8: Roys 6C 8
Rose Walk, The WD7: Rad 9J 139
Rose Way HA8: Edg 4C 164
Rose Wood Cl. LU2: Lut 7H 47
Rosewood Ct. HP1: Hem H 1H 123
Rosewood Dr. EN2: Crew H 8M 143
Roslyn Cl. EN10: Brox 3J 133
Roslyn Way LU5: Hou R 4D 44
Ross Cl. AL10: Hat 6H 111
HA3: Har W 7D 162
LU1: Lut 2D 66
Ross Ct. SG2: Stev 2A 52
Ross Cres. WD25: Watf 8J 137
Rossdale Dr. N9 . . . . . 8G 156
Rossendale Cl. EN2: Enf 9N 143
Rossfold Rd. LU3: Lut 1N 45
Rossgate HP1: Hem H 9K 105
Ross Haven Pl. HA6: North 8H 161
Rossington Av. WD6: Bore 2M 151
Rossington Cl. EN1: Enf 2F 156
Rossiter Flds. EN5: Barn 8L 153
Rosslyn Av. EN4: E Bar 8D 154
Rosslyn Cres. LU3: Lut 4E 46
Rosslyn Rd.
WD18: Watf 7B 166 (5K 149)
Rossmore Cl. EN3: Pon E 6H 157
ROSSWAY 2G 120
Ross Way HA6: North 4H 161
Rossway LU1: S End 7D 66
Rossway Dr. WD23: Bush 7D 150
Rossway La. HP23: Wigg 6E 102
Rossway St. LU1: S End 7E 66
Roswell Cl. EN8: C'hunt 3J 145
Rothamsted Av. AL5: Harp 6A 88
Rothamsted Ct. AL5: Harp 6B 88
ROTHAMSTED ESTATE 8M 87
Rotheram Av. LU1: Lut 3D 66
Rother Cl. WD25: Watf 7L 137
Rotherfield LU2: Lut 6M 47
Rotherfield Rd. EN3: Enf W 1H 157
Rotherwood Cl. LU6: Duns 8B 44
Rothesay Ct. HP4: Berk 1L 121
Rothesay Rd. LU1: Lut 1F 66
Rothschild Av. HP22: Ast C 1D 100
Rothschild Ct. HP4: Berk 7G 103
Roughdown Av. HP3: Hem H 5K 123
Roughdown Rd. HP3: Hem H 5L 123
Roughdown Vs. Rd. HP3: Hem H 5K 123
Roughs, The HA6: North 3G 161
Roughwood Cl. WD17: Watf 2G 148
Roughwood Cft. HP8: Chal G 7A 146
Roughwood La. HP8: Chal G 9B 146
Roundabout Ho. HA6: North 8J 161
Roundabout La. AL6: Wel 8M 71
ROUND BUSH 2E 150
Roundbush La. WD25: A'ham 2D 150
Roundcroft EN7: C'hunt 8D 132
Roundfield Av. AL5: Harp 3E 88
ROUND GREEN 7J 47
Roundhaye SG11: Puck 6A 56
Roundhedge Way EN2: Enf 2L 155
Roundhill Dr. EN2: Enf 6L 155
Round Ho. Ct. EN8: C'hunt 2H 145
Roundings, The SG13: Hert H 5F 114
Round Mead SG2: Stev 6C 52
Roundmoor Dr. EN8: C'hunt 2J 145
Roundway, The WD18: Watf 8H 149
Round Wood WD4: Kin L 9A 124
Roundwood AL5: Harp 4N 87
Roundwood Cl. AL6: Wel 8K 71
SG4: Hit 9C 22
Roundwood Ct. AL5: Harp 4N 87
Roundwood Dr. AL8: Welw G 8J 91
Roundwood Gdns. AL5: Harp 5N 87
Roundwood La. AL5: Harp 4K 87
Roundwood Pk. AL5: Harp 4N 87
Rounton Dr. WD17: Watf 2H 149
Rousebarn La. WD3: Chan C, Crox G 2B 148
Row, The HP5: Haw 3B 120
Rowan Cl. AL2: Bri W 4B 138
AL4: St Alb 2M 127
HA7: Stanm 6G 162
LU1: Lut 1D 66
SG4: W'ton 2A 36
WD7: Shen 6M 139
Rowan Ct. WD6: Bore 6A 152
Rowan Cres. SG1: Stev 2K 51
SG6: L Gar 4E 22
Rowan Dr. EN10: Turn 7K 133
Rowan Gro. SG4: St Ipo 6A 34
Rowans AL7: Welw G 6N 91
Rowans, The EN10: Brox 1J 133
HP1: Hem H 2K 123
SG7: Bald 4L 23
SL9: Chal P 9A 158
Rowantree Cl. N21 . . . . . 9B 156
Rowantree Rd. EN2: Enf 4N 155
N21 . . . . . 9B 156
Rowan Wlk. AL10: Hat 3G 129
CM21: Saw 5G 99
EN5: N Bar 7A 154
Rowan Way AL5: Harp 7D 88
Rowanwood M. EN2: Enf 4N 155
Rowborough Rd. HP22: Halt 7C 100
Rowbourne Pl. EN6: Cuff 1J 143
Rowcroft HP1: Hem H 3H 123
Rowden Farm Barns LU7: Led 1K 61
Rowelfield LU2: Lut 8L 47
Rowington Ct. LU2: Lut 7N 47
Rowland Cl. LU7: Pits 4B 82
Rowland Pl. HA6: North 7G 161
Rowland Rd. SG1: Stev 5M 51
Rowlands Av. HA5: Hat E 5B 162
Rowlands Cl. EN8: C'hunt 3H 145
NW7 . . . . . 7G 164
Rowlands Ct. EN8: C'hunt 3H 145
(off Turner's Hill)
Rowland Way SG6: L Gar 5F 22
Rowlatt Ct. AL1: St Alb 1F 166
Rowlatt Dr. AL3: St Alb 4B 126
Rowley Cl. WD19: Watf 8N 149
Rowley Ct. EN1: Enf 7C 156
(off Wellington Rd.)
Rowley Gdns. EN8: C'hunt 1H 145
ROWLEY GREEN 6F 152
Rowley Green Common Nature Reserve . . . 6F 152
Rowley Grn. Rd. EN5: Ark 7F 152
Rowley La. EN5: Ark 6E 152
WD6: Bore 3D 152
Rowley Lane Golf Course 6E 152
Rowley Lane Sports Ground 6E 152
Rowley's Rd. SG13: H'ford 8D 94
Rowley Wlk. HP2: Hem H 6E 106
Row Mdw. Cotts. HP2: Gad R 7K 85
Rowney Gdns. CM21: Saw 7E 98
Rowney La. SG12: Dan E, Sac 4F 74
Rowney Wood CM21: Saw 6E 98
Rows, The CM20: Harl 5N 117
(off North Ga.)
Rowsley Av. NW4 . . . . . 9J 165
Roxley Ct. SG6: Will 2H 35
Roxley Mnr. SG6: Will 2H 35
Royal Av. EN8: Wal C 6J 145
Royal Connaught Dr. WD23: Bush 6A 150
Royal Connaught Pk. WD23: Bush 6A 150
Royal Ct. EN1: Enf 8C 156
HP3: Hem H 5A 124
HP23: Tring 1E 102
WD18: Watf 6G 148
Royal Epping Forest & Chingford Golf Course 8N 157
Royale Wlk. LU6: Duns 1F 64
Royal Gunpowder Mills 5M 145
Royal Ho's. MK45: Bar C 7E 18
Royal London Mall LU1: Lut 1G 66
Royal Oak Cl. SG9: Chippg 6H 27
Royal Oak Cotts. HP1: Hem H 9N 105
(off High St.)
Royal Oak Gdns. CM23: Bis S 2G 79
Royal Oak La. SG5: Pirt 7E 20
Royal Rd. AL1: St Alb 2J 127
Royal Veterinary College, The
Hawkshead Campus, Boltons Park Site 2N 141
Hawkshead Campus, Hawkshead La. 1K 141
Royce Cl. EN10: Brox 3K 133
LU6: Duns 1C 64
Royce Gro. WD25: Watf 7H 137
ROYDON 5E 116
Roydonbury Ind. Est. CM19: Harl 6H 117
Roydon Cl. LU4: Lut 5K 45
Roydon Ct. HP2: Hem H 5C 106
Roydon Lodge Chalet Est. CM19: Royd 5F 116
Roydon Mill Leisure Pk. (Caravan & Camping Pk.)
CM19: Royd 5D 116
Roydon Rd. CM19: Harl 5H 117
SG12: Stan A 2A 116
Roydon Station (Rail) 5E 116
Royle Cl. SL9: Chal P 7C 158
Roy Rd. HA6: North 7H 161
Royse Gro. SG8: Roys 9D 8
ROYSTON 7D 8
Royston & District Mus. 7D 8
Royston Cave 7D 8
Royston Cl. SG14: H'ford 9N 93
Royston Golf Course 7C 8
Royston Gro. HA5: Hat E 6B 162
Royston Leisure Cen. 5F 8
Royston Pk. Rd. HA5: Hat E 6A 162
Royston Rd. AL1: St Alb 3J 127
SG7: Bald, Byg, S End 2M 23
(not continuous)
SG8: Bark 7N 15
SG8: Barl 1C 16
SG8: Lit, Roys 4J 7
SG8: Melb 1G 8
SG9: Chippg, Bunt 8H 27
Royston Station (Rail) 6C 8
Rubens Ct. WD25: Watf 9M 137
Rubin Pl. EN3: Enf L 1L 157
Ruby Way NW9 . . . . . 8F 164
RUCKLERS LANE 9N 123
Rucklers La. WD4: Kin L 1K 135
Ruckles Cl. SG1: Stev 4L 51
Rudd Cl. SG2: Stev 6A 52
Ruddock Cl. HA8: Edg 7C 164
Ruddy Way NW7 . . . . . 6F 164
Rudham Gro. SG6: L Gar 8J 23
Rudolph Rd. WD23: Bush 8B 150
Rudyard Cl. LU4: Lut 6N 45
Rudyard Gro. NW7 . . . . . 6C 164
Rue de St Lawrence EN9: Wal A 7N 145
Rueley Dell Rd. LU2: Lill 8M 31
Rufford Cl. WD17: Watf 1H 149
Rufforth Ct. NW9 . . . . . 8E 164
(off Pageant Av.)
Rugby Av. N9 . . . . . 9D 156
Rugby Lodge WD24: Watf 8G 137
Rugby Way WD3: Crox G 7D 148
Ruislip Lido Railway 9F 160
Ruislip Woods (National Nature Reserve) 9E 160
Rumballs Cl. HP3: Hem H 5C 124
Rumballs Ct. CM23: Bis S 4E 78
Rumballs Rd. HP3: Hem H 5C 124
Rumbold Rd. EN11: Hod 6N 115
Rumsley EN7: C'hunt 9E 132
Runcie Cl. AL4: St Alb 7H 109
Runcorn Cres. HP2: Hem H 7B 106
Rundells CM18: Harl 9C 118
SG6: L Gar 7K 23
Runfold Av. LU3: Lut 4C 46
Runham Cl. LU4: Lut 5L 45
Runham Rd. HP3: Hem H 4A 124
Runley Rd. LU1: Lut 9A 46
Runnalow SG6: L Gar 4D 22
Runnymede Ct. LU3: Lut 3B 46
Runsley AL7: Welw G 6M 91
Runswick Ct. SG1: Stev 2G 51
Runway, The AL10: Hat 7D 110
Runway Cl. NW9 . . . . . 9F 164
Rupert Ho. AL7: Welw G 8B 92
Rupert Neve Cl. SG8: Melb 2L 9
Rusbridge Ct. SG7: Bald 2L 23
(off Football Cl.)
Ruscombe Dr. AL2: Par S 8D 126
Rushall Grn. LU2: Lut 7M 47
Rushby Mead SG6: L Gar 5G 22
Rushby Pl. SG6: L Gar 6G 23
Rushby Wlk. SG6: L Gar 5G 22
Rush Cl. SG12: Stan A 2N 115
RUSHDEN 7L 25
Rushdene Av. EN4: E Bar 9D 154
Rushden Gdns. NW7 . . . . . 6J 165
Rushden Rd. SG9: S'don 5M 25
Rush Dr. EN9: Wal A 9N 145
Rushendon Furlong LU7: Pits 2C 82
Rushen Dr. SG13: Hert H 3G 114
Rushes Ct. CM23: Bis S 3J 79
Rushes Mead CM18: Harl 8A 118
Rushey Hill EN2: Enf 6L 155
Rushfield CM21: Saw 5G 99
EN6: Pot B 5K 141
Rushfield Rd. SG12: Ware 4K 95
RUSH GREEN
SG4 . . . . . 5D 50
SG13 . . . . . 9G 94
Rushleigh Av. EN8: C'hunt 4H 145
Rushleigh Grn. CM23: Bis S 5F 78
Rush Leys Ct. AL2: Lon C 9H 127
Rushmead Cl. HA8: Edg 2B 164
Rushmere Ct. HP3: Hem H 6C 124
Rushmere La. HP5: Orch L . . . . . 9L 121 & 1A 134
Rushmoor Cl. WD3: R'orth 2N 159
Rushmoor Ct. WD18: Watf 8E 148
Rushmore Cl. LU1: Cad 3A 66
Rushton Av. WD25: Watf 8J 137
Rushton Ct. EN8: C'hunt 2H 145
Rushton Gro. CM17: Harl 6F 118
Ruskin Cl. EN7: C'hunt 8C 132
Ruskin Ct. N21 . . . . . 9L 155
Ruskin La. SG4: Hit 3C 34
Rusling Ct. WD17: Watf 6C 166 (4K 149)
Rusper Cl. HA7: Stanm 4K 163
Rusper Grn. LU2: Lut 6M 47
Russell Av. AL3: St Alb 2C 166 (2E 126)
Russell Cl. HA6: North 5E 160
HP6: L Chal 3A 146
LU6: Kens 8H 65
SG2: Stev 7A 52
SG8: S Mor 3C 6
Russell Ct. AL2: Bri W 3B 138
EN5: N Bar 6B 154
N14 . . . . . 8J 155
Russell Cres. WD25: Watf 8H 137
Russellcroft Rd. AL8: Welw G 8J 91
Russell End SG8: S Mor 3C 6
Russell Gro. NW7 . . . . . 5E 164
Russell La. WD17: Watf 9F 136
Russell Mead HA3: Har W 8G 163
Russell Pl. HP3: Hem H 5L 123
Russell Ri. LU1: Lut 2F 66
Russell Rd. EN1: Enf 2D 156
HA6: North 5E 160
Russell's Ride EN8: C'hunt 4J 145
Russell's Slip SG5: Hit 4L 33
Russell St. LU1: Lut 2F 66
SG14: H'ford 9A 94
Russell Wlk. SG5: Stot 9D 10
Russell Way WD19: Watf 9K 149
Russet Cl. EN7: C'hunt 8C 132
Russet Dr. AL4: St Alb 3K 127
WD7: Shen 5M 139
Russets, The SL9: Chal P 9A 158
Russett Ho. AL7: Welw G 9C 92
Russettings HA5: Hat E 7A 162
(off Westfield Pk.)
Russett Way LU5: Duns 8G 45
Russettwood AL7: Welw G 1C 112
Russet Way SG8: Melb 1N 9
Rustle Ct. CM17: Harl 7E 118
RUSTLING END 9D 50
Ruston Gdns. N14 . . . . . 8F 154
Rutherford Cl. SG1: Stev 3G 51
WD6: Bore 4C 152
Rutherford Way WD23: B Hea 1E 162
Ruthin Cl. LU1: Lut 3F 66
Ruthven Av. EN8: Wal C 6H 145
Rutland Ct. EN3: Pon E 7F 156
LU2: Lut 1J 67
Rutland Cres. LU2: Lut 1J 67
Rutland Gdns. HP2: Hem H 1B 124
Rutland Hall LU2: Lut 1J 67
(off Crawley Grn. Rd.)
Rutland Path LU2: Lut 1J 67
Rutland Pl. WD23: B Hea 1E 162
Rutts, The WD23: B Hea 1E 162
Ryall Cl. AL2: Bri W 2N 137
Ryan Ct. WD19: Watf 9N 149
Ryans Ct. LU2: Lut 8H 47
Ryan Way WD24: Watf 3L 149
Rydal Cl. NW4 . . . . . 8L 165
Rydal Ct. HA8: Edg 5N 163
WD25: Watf 5K 137
Rydal Mt. EN6: Pot B 6L 141
Rydal Way EN3: Pon E 8G 157
LU3: Lut 4B 46
RYDE, THE 6J 111
Ryde, The AL9: Hat 7J 111
Ryder Av. SG5: Ick 8L 21
Ryder Cl. HP3: Bov 1D 134
SG13: H'ford 8F 94
WD23: Bush 8C 150
Ryders Av. AL4: Col H, Smal 2E 128
Ryder Seed M. AL1: St Alb 4C 166 (3E 126)
Ryders Hill SG1: Stev 7B 36
Ryder Way SG5: Ick 8L 21
Rydinghurst Rd. SL9: Chal P 5B 158
Rye, The LU6: Eat B 1G 63
N14 . . . . . 9J 155
Rye Cl. AL5: Harp 3C 88
SG1: Stev 7M 35
WD6: Bore 6D 152
Ryecroft AL10: Hat 2F 128
CM19: Harl 6L 117
SG1: Stev 2L 51
Ryecroft Cl. HP2: Hem H 3E 124
Ryecroft Ct. AL4: St Alb 2N 127
Ryecroft Cres. EN5: Barn 7H 153
Ryecroft Way LU2: Lut 6J 47
Ryefeld Cl. EN11: Hod 4N 115
Ryefield LU3: Lut 9C 30
Ryefield Ct. HA6: North 9J 161
Ryefield Cres. HA6: North 9J 161
Ryefield Pde. HA6: North 9J 161
(off Joel St.)
Rye Gdns. SG7: Bald 2A 24
Rye Hill AL5: Harp 3C 88
LU2: Lut 8F 46
(off Cromwell Hill)
Rye House Gatehouse 6N 115
Rye House Kart Raceway 6A 116
Rye House Laser Combat 6A 116
Rye House Stadium 6A 116
Rye House Station (Rail) 6N 115
Ryelands AL7: Welw G 3M 111
Rye Mead Cotts. EN11: Hod 6N 115
RYE MEADS 5A 116
Rye Meads Nature Reserve 5A 116
Rye Meads Nature Reserve Vis. Cen. 5A 116
RYE PARK 6M 115
Rye Park Ind. Est. EN11: Hod 7N 115
Rye Rd. EN11: Hod 6M 115
Rye St. CM23: Bis S 9H 59
Rye Way HA8: Edg 6N 163
Rylands Heath LU2: Lut 7A 48
Ryman Ct. WD3: Chor 8F 146
Rymill Cl. HP3: Bov 1D 134
Ryton Cl. LU1: Lut 1D 66

S

Saberton Cl. AL3: Red 2H 107
SACOMBE 4C 74
SACOMBE GREEN 4E 74
Sacombe Grn. LU3: Lut 9D 30
Sacombe Grn. Rd. SG12: Sac 4C 74
Sacombe M. SG2: Stev 1C 72
Sacombe Pound SG12: Sac 5C 74
Sacombe Rd. HP1: Hem H 9J 105
SG14: H'ford, Stap, Water 4N 93
Sacombs Ash La. CM21: All G 9A 78
Saddleback La. SG8: Bass 1M 7
Saddlers Cl. CM23: Bis S 4E 78
EN5: Ark 7H 153
HA5: Hat E 6B 162
SG7: Bald 3L 23
WD6: Bore 7D 152
Saddlers M. AL3: Mark 2A 86
Saddlers Path WD6: Bore 7D 152
(off Farriers Way)
Saddlers Pl. SG8: Roys 6C 8
Saddlers Wlk. WD4: Kin L 2C 136
Saddlescombe Way N12 . . . . . 5N 165
Sadleir Rd. AL1: St Alb 4F 126
Sadler Cl. EN7: C'hunt 7A 132
Sadlers Mead CM18: Harl 7C 118
Sadlers Way SG14: H'ford 9M 93
Sadlier Rd. SG11: Stand 7A 56
Saffron Cl. EN11: Hod 7K 115
LU2: Lut 3F 46
SG15: Arl 5A 10
Saffron Cres. CM21: Saw 4H 99
SAFFRON GREEN 3F 152
Saffron Hill SG6: L Gar 5E 22
Saffron La. HP1: Hem H 1K 123
Saffron Mdw. SG11: Stand 7B 56
Saffron Ri. LU6: Eat B 2J 63
Saffron St. SG8: Roys 8F 8
Saimet NW9 . . . . . 7F 164
(off Wiggins Mead)
Sainfoin End HP2: Hem H 9C 106
St Agnells Ct. HP2: Hem H 7C 106
St Agnells La. HP2: Hem H 6B 106
ST ALBANS 3C 166 (2E 126)
St Albans Abbey Station (Rail) 4E 126
St Albans Cathedral 3B 166 (2D 126)
St Albans City FC 1G 126
St Albans Clocktower 3C 166
St Albans Dr. SG1: Stev 9L 35
St Albans Ent. Cen. AL3: St Alb 7F 108
St Albans Highway SG4: Gos, Pres 9N 33
St Albans Hill HP3: Hem H 5A 124
St Albans La. WD5: Bed 8H 125
St Albans Link SG1: Stev 9L 35
St Albans Organ Mus. 3J 127
St Albans Retail Pk. AL1: St Alb 4E 126
St Albans Rd. AL3: Red 2L 107
AL4: San, St Alb 8G 109
AL5: Harp 6C 88
EN5: Barn 8H 141
EN6: S Mim 4E 140
HP2: Hem H 4N 123
HP3: Hem H 4N 123
SG4: Cod 1E 90
WD17: Watf 5B 166 (4K 149)
WD24: Watf 4K 149
WD25: Watf 4K 149
St Albans Rd. E. AL10: Hat 8H 111
St Albans Rd. W. AL10: Hat 8F 110
(Gloucester Ct.)
AL10: Hat 9C 110
(Poplar Av., not continuous)
St Albans South Signal Box 4G 166
St Albans Station (Rail) 3G 166 (2G 126)
St Albans Sub Aqua Club 3E 126
St Aldates Ct. LU3: Lut 6D 46
St Alphage Wlk. HA8: Edg 9C 164
St Alphege Rd. N9 . . . . . 9G 156
St Andrew M. SG14: H'ford 9A 94
St Andrew's Av. AL5: Harp 6A 88
St Andrews Cl. HA7: Stanm 9K 163
LU1: S End 7D 66

Sheridan Rd.—Southwark Cl.

Sheridan Rd. LU3: Lut 7E 46
WD19: Watf 9M 149
Sheridan Wlk. EN10: Brox 2J 133
Sheriden Cl. LU6: Duns 8E 44
Sheriff Way WD25: Watf 6J 137
Sheringham Av. N14 7J 155
SG1: Stev 9H 35
Sheringham Cl. LU2: Lut 2E 46
Sherington Av. HA5: Hat E 7B 162
Sherland Ct. *WD7: Rad* 9H 139
(off The Dell)
Sherrards Mans. AL8: Welw G 6H 91
SHERRARDSPARK 7J 91
Sherrardspark Rd. AL8: Welw G 7J 91
Sherrards Way EN5: Barn 7N 153
Shervington Gro. LU3: Lut 6D 46
Sherwood SG6: L Gar 3F 22
Sherwood Av. AL4: St Alb 8J 109
EN6: Pot B 5L 141
Sherwood Ct. CM23: Bis S 1H 79
WD25: Watf 7H 137
Sherwood Ho. CM18: Harl 8B 118
WD5: Abb L 4H 137
(off College Rd.)
Sherwood Pl. HP2: Hem H 7B 106
Sherwood Rd. LU4: Lut 7C 46
NW4 9J 165
Sherwoods Ri. AL5: Harp 7E 88
Sherwoods Rd. WD19: Watf 9N 149
Shetland Cl. WD6: Bore 8D 152
Shetland Ho. *WD18: Watf* 8H 149
(off Pioneer Way)
Shillingford Cl. NW7 7K 165
SHILLINGTON 2A 20
Shillington Gro. WD17: Watf 3J 149
Shillington Rd. SG5: Pirt, Shil 4N 19
SG5: Shil 2B 20
SG16: L Ston 2B 20
Shillitoe Av. EN6: Pot B 5K 141
Shingle Cl. LU3: Lut 1C 46
Ship La. HP23: Mars 5L 81
LU7: Pits 4B 82
Shire Balk SG7: Ashw 8B 6
Shire Cl. EN10: Turn 8K 133
Shire Ct. HP2: Hem H 1C 124
SG1: Stev 2J 51
Shire Hall
Hertford 9B 94
(off Fore St.)
Shire La. HP8: Chal G 2D 158
HP23: Chol, Hast 8K 101 & 1A 120
SL9: Chal P 3E 158
(not continuous)
WD3: Chor 1D 158
(Bullsland La.)
WD3: Chor 7E 146
(Chalfont La.)
Shiremeade WD6: Elst 7N 151
SHIRE PARK 7L 91
Shires, The LU2: Lut 8F 46
SG8: Roys 7E 8
WD25: Watf 4K 137
Shirley Cl. EN8: C'hunt 2G 144
EN10: Worm 6K 133
SG2: Stev 1A 52
Shirley Gro. N9 9G 157
Shirley Rd. AL1: St Alb 3G 126
EN2: Enf 5A 156
LU1: Lut 9E 46
WD5: Abb L 5H 137
WD17: Watf 3J 149
Shirwell Cl. NW7 7K 165
Shoelands Ct. NW9 9D 164
Shoe La. CM17: Harl 7H 119
Shooters Rd. EN2: Enf 3N 155
SHOOTERSWAY 1K 121
Shootersway HP4: Berk 8F 102
HP23: Wigg 8F 102
Shootersway La. HP4: Berk 2K 121
Shootersway Pk. HP4: Berk 2K 121
Shoplands AL8: Welw G 5K 91
Shopwick Pl. WD6: Elst 8L 151
Shoreham Cl. SG1: Stev 1G 50
Shortcroft CM23: Bis S 9M 59
Shortcroft Ct. MK45: Bar C 9D 18
Shortgate N12 4M 165
Shortgreen La. SG9: Mee 6J 29
Short Hale LU7: Pits 4B 82
Shortlands Grn. AL7: Welw G 1M 111
Shortlands Pl. CM23: Bis S 9H 59
Short La. AL2: Bri W 2N 137
SG2: Ast E 5D 52
Shortmead Dr. EN8: C'hunt 4J 145
Short Path LU5: Hou R 3F 44
Shothanger Way HP3: Bov 7G 123
Shottfield Cl. AL4: San 4K 109
Shott La. SG6: L Gar 5G 23
Shrubberies, The AL1: St Alb 3E 126
Shrubbery, The HP1: Hem H 1H 123
Shrubbery Gdns. N21 9N 155
Shrubbery Gro. SG8: Roys 9D 8
Shrubhill Rd. HP1: Hem H 3J 123
Shrublands AL9: B Pk 8A 130
Shrublands, The EN6: Pot B 6L 141
Shrublands Av. HP4: Berk 1L 121
Shrublands Rd. HP4: Berk 9L 103
Shrubs Rd. UB9: R'orth 6B 160
Shugars Grn. HP23: Tring 2N 101
Shurland Av. EN4: E Bar 8C 154
Siamese M. N3 8N 165
Sibley Av. AL5: Harp 8E 88
Sibley Cl. LU2: Lut 6K 47
Sibthorpe Rd. AL9: Welh G 6K 129
Siccut Rd. SG4: L Wym 6E 34
Sicklefield Cl. EN7: C'hunt 8D 132
Siddons Rd. SG2: Stev 3B 52
Sidford Cl. HP1: Hem H 2J 123
Sidings, The AL10: Hat 1E 128
EN10: Worm 4K 133
HP2: Hem H 2N 123
Sidings Ct. *SG14: H'ford* 9A 94
(off Port Hill)
Siding Way AL2: Lon C 8H 127
Sidmouth Cl. WD19: Watf 2K 161
Sidney Ter. CM23: Bis S 2H 79
HP22: Wen 9A 100
Silam Rd. SG1: Stev 4L 51
Silas Ct. *WD17: Watf* 3J 149
(off Lockhart Rd.)
Silecroft Rd. LU2: Lut 9J 47
Silk Ho. NW9 9D 164
Silkin Ct. SG2: Stev 6C 52
Silkin Way SG1: Stev 4K 51
Silkmead Farm Ind. Est. SG9: H St 8B 28
Silk Mill Ct. WD19: Watf 8K 149
Silk Mill Rd. AL3: Red 2K 107
WD19: Watf 9K 149
Silk Mill Way HP23: Tring 1M 101
Silkstream Pde. HA8: Edg 8C 164
Silkstream Rd. HA8: Edg 8C 164
Sillence Ct. *SG8: Roys* 7D 8
(off Up. King St.)
Silsden Cres. HP8: Chal G 3A 158
SILSOE 1E 18
Silver Birch Av. SG5: Stot 4F 10
Silver Birch Ct. EN8: C'hunt 4H 145
Silvercliffe Gdns. EN4: E Bar 6D 154
Silver Cl. HA3: Har W 7E 162
Silver Ct. AL7: Welw G 8N 91
SG5: Hit 2M 33
Silverdale EN2: Enf 6K 155
Silverdale Rd. WD23: Bush 7N 149
Silver Dell WD24: Watf 8H 137
Silverfield EN10: Worm 4K 133
Silver Hill WD6: Bore 9C 140
Silver Pl. WD18: Watf 6G 149
Silverston Way HA7: Stanm 6K 163
Silver St. CM24: Stans 3M 59
EN1: Enf 5B 156
EN7: Wal C, Gof O 3N 143
EN9: Wal A 7N 145
LU1: Lut 1G 66
SG7: Ashw 9M 5
SG8: G Mor 1A 6
SG8: Lit 3H 7
SG9: Ans 6D 28
Silverthorn Dr. HP3: Hem H 6D 124
Silver Trees AL2: Bri W 3A 138
Silverwood Cl. HA6: North 8E 160
Silvesters CM19: Harl 8J 117
Simmonds Ri. HP3: Hem H 4N 123
Simon Ct. WD23: Bush 8B 150
Simon Dean HP3: Bov 9D 122
Simon Peter Ct. EN2: Enf 4N 155
Simpkins Dr. MK45: Bar C 7E 18
Simplicity La. CM17: Harl 5F 118
Simpson Cl. LU4: Lut 7N 45
N21 7K 155
Simpson Dr. SG7: Bald 3M 23
Simpsons Ct. SG7: Bald 3M 23
Sinclare Cl. EN1: Enf 3D 156
Sinderby Cl. WD6: Bore 3N 151
Sinfield Cl. SG1: Stev 4N 51
Singleton Scarp N12 5N 165
Singlets La. AL3: Flam 5D 86
Sirdane Ho. AL4: San 6J 109
Sir Herbert Janes Village LU4: Lut 5N 45
Sirius Rd. HA6: North 5H 161
Sir James Altham Pool 5M 161
Sir John Newsom Way AL7: Welw G 3L 111
Sir Joseph's Wlk. AL5: Harp 7B 88
Sir Theodore's Way *AL8: Welw G* 8K 91
(off Wigmores Nth.)
Sish Cl. SG1: Stev 3K 51
(not continuous)
Sish La. SG1: Stev 3K 51
Siskin Cl. SG8: Roys 5E 8
WD6: Bore 6A 152
WD23: Bush 6N 149
Siskin Ho. WD18: Watf 8F 148
Sisson Cl. SG2: Stev 7B 52
Sittingbourne Av. EN1: Enf 8B 156
Sitwell Gro. HA7: Stanm 5G 162
Six Acres HP3: Hem H 5C 124
Six Hills Way SG1: Stev 6J 51
SG2: Stev 5L 51
Sixth Av. SG6: L Gar 5J 23
WD25: Watf 8M 137
Skegness Rd. SG1: Stev 1G 51
Skegsbury La. SG4: Kimp 7G 68
Skelton Cl. LU3: Lut 9D 30
Sketty Rd. EN1: Enf 5D 156
Skidmore Way WD3: R'orth 1A 160
Skillen Lodge HA5: Pin 5D 160
Skimpans Cl. AL9: Welh G 6K 129
Skimpot La. LU1: Lut 8L 45
Skimpot Rd. LU4: Lut 8K 45
LU5: Duns 8K 45
Skinners St. CM23: Bis S 4E 78
Skipton Cl. SG2: Stev 9M 51
Skua Cl. LU4: Lut 4K 45
Skye Ho. WD18: Watf 8H 149
Skylark Cnr. SG2: Stev 6C 52
Skylark Pl. SG8: Roys 5E 8
Skys Wood Rd. AL4: St Alb 7J 109
Slacksbury Hatch CM19: Harl 6L 117
Slade Ct. EN5: N Bar 5A 154
WD7: Rad 8H 139
Slade Oak La. SL9: Ger C 9E 158
Slades Cl. EN2: Enf 5M 155
Slades Gdns. EN2: Enf 4M 155
Slades Hill EN2: Enf 5M 155
Slades Ri. EN2: Enf 5M 155
SLAPTON 2A 62
Slapton La. LU6: N'all 3C 62
LU7: Slapt 3C 62
Slapton Rd. LU7: Bill, L Bill 1A 62
Slatter NW9 7F 164
Sleaford Grn. WD19: Watf 3M 161
Sleapcross Gdns. AL4: Smal 3B 128
SLEAPSHYDE 3B 128
Sleaps Hyde SG2: Stev 8B 52
Sleapshyde La. AL4: Smal 3B 128
Sleddale HP2: Hem H 8A 106
Sleets End HP1: Hem H 9L 105
Slickett's La. LU6: Edle 5K 63
Slimmons Dr. AL4: St Alb 7H 109
Slipe, The LU7: Ched 9M 61
Slipe La. EN10: Worm 6K 133
SLIP END
LU1 7D 66
SG7 6F 12
Slip La. SG3: Old K 3H 71
Slippers Hill HP2: Hem H 1N 123
Sloan Ct. SG1: Stev 3M 51
Sloansway AL7: Welw G 6M 91
Slough Rd. CM21: All G 1B 98
Slowmans Cl. AL2: Par S 1D 138
Slype, The AL4: Wheat 1G 89
AL5: Harp 1G 89
Small Acre HP1: Hem H 2J 123
Smallcroft AL7: Welw G 8A 92
SMALLFORD 2B 128
Smallford La. AL4: Smal 3B 128
Smallford Works AL4: Smal 3B 128
Smallwood Cl. AL4: Wheat 8M 89
Smarts Grn. EN7: C'hunt 8D 132
Smeathman Ct. HP1: Hem H 3M 123
Smeaton Rd. EN3: Enf L 1L 157
Smithcombe Cl. MK45: Bar C 8E 18
Smithfield HP2: Hem H 9N 105
Smiths Cotts. CM22: Ugl 6N 43
Smiths Cres. AL4: Smal 3B 128
SMITH'S END 4C 16
Smith's End La. SG8: Barl 3C 16
Smiths La. EN7: C'hunt 8B 132
Smiths La. Mall *LU1: Lut* 1G 67
(within The Mall Shop. Cen.)
Smiths Sq. *LU1: Lut* 1G 67
(within The Mall Shop. Cen.)
Smith St. WD18: Watf 9D 166 (6L 149)
Smithy, The SG11: L Had 7L 57
SMUG OAK 3C 138
Smug Oak Grn. Bus. Cen. AL2: Bri W 2C 138
Smug Oak La. AL2: Bri W, Col S 3C 138
SNAILSWELL 6M 21
Snailswell La. SG5: Ick 6M 21
Snakes and Ladders 6E 44
Snakes La. N14 5G 155
Snaresbrook Dr. HA7: Stanm 4L 163
Snatchup AL3: Red 1J 107
Snells Mead SG9: Bunt 3K 39
Snipe, The SG4: W'ton 1A 36
Snowberry Cl. EN5: Barn 5M 153
Snow Centre, The 4B 124
Snowdonia Way SG1: W'ton 6N 35
Snowdrop Cl. CM23: Bis S 2E 78
SNOW END 6D 28
Snowford Cl. LU3: Lut 2C 46
Snowhill Cotts. HP5: Ash G 6K 121
Snow La. CM24: Stans 5N 59
Snowley Pde. *CM23: Bis S* 8K 59
(off Manston Dr.)
Soames Pl. EN4: Had W 4A 154
Soane Sq. HA7: Stanm 3F 162
Soham Rd. EN3: Enf L 1K 157
Solar Ct. WD18: Watf 7H 149
Solar Way EN3: Enf L 9K 145
Solesbridge Cl. WD3: Chor 5J 147
Solesbridge La. WD3: Chor, Sar 5J 147
Sollershott E. SG6: L Gar 7F 22
Sollershott Hall SG6: L Gar 7F 22
Sollershott W. SG6: L Gar 7E 22
Solna Rd. N21 9B 156
Solomon's Hill WD3: R'orth 9N 147
Solway HP2: Hem H 9B 106
Solway Rd. Nth. LU3: Lut 5C 46
Solway Rd. Sth. LU3: Lut 6C 46
Somaford Gro. EN4: E Bar 8C 154
Somerby Cl. EN10: Brox 1J 133
Somercoates Cl. EN4: C'ters 5D 154
SOMERIES 3M 67
Someries Arch LU1: Lut 3L 67
Someries Castle 3M 67
Someries Hill LU2: Lut 7L 47
Someries Rd. AL5: Harp 3D 88
HP1: Hem H 9J 105
Somersby Cl. LU1: Lut 3G 66
Somerset Av. LU2: Lut 7J 47
Somerset Ho. *LU3: Lut* 5B 46
(off Leafield)
Somerset Rd. EN3: Enf L 2L 157
EN5: N Bar 7A 154
Somersham AL7: Welw G 9C 92
Somers Rd. AL9: Welh G 6J 129
Somers Sq. AL9: Welh G 5J 129
Somers Way WD23: Bush 9D 150
Somerton Ct. SG1: Stev 2L 51
Somery Wlk. WD25: A'ham 9C 138
Sommer's Ct. SG12: Ware 6J 95
Sommerville Ct. *WD6: Bore* 3N 151
(off Alconbury Cl.)
Sonia Cl. WD19: Watf 9L 149
Sonia Ct. HA8: Edg 7N 163
Sonnets, The HP1: Hem H 1L 123
SOOTFIELD GREEN 1K 49
Soothouse Spring AL3: St Alb 7G 108
Soper M. EN3: Enf L 2L 157
Soper Sq. CM17: Harl 5E 118
Sopers Rd. EN6: Cuff 2L 143
SOPWELL 5F 126
Sopwell La. AL1: St Alb 4C 166 (3E 126)
Sopwell Nunnery (remains) 4F 126
Sopwith NW9 7F 164
Sorbus Ct. EN2: Enf 4N 155
Sorbus Rd. EN10: Turn 7K 133
Sorrel Cl. LU3: Lut 1C 46
SG8: Roys 8F 8
Sorrel Dr. SG5: Stot 7E 10
Sorrel Gth. SG4: Hit 4A 34
Sotheron Rd. WD17: Watf 5D 166 (5L 149)
Souberie Av. SG6: L Gar 6F 22
Souldern St. WD18: Watf 9B 166 (7K 149)
Southacre Way HA5: Pin 8L 161
Southall Cl. SG12: Ware 5H 95
Southam M. WD3: Crox G 8D 148
Southampton Gdns. LU3: Lut 9A 30
South App. HA6: North 3F 160
South Av. E4 9M 157
Sth. Bank Rd. HP4: Berk 8K 103
SOUTH BARNET 9F 154
South Beds Golf Course 8F 30
Southbourne Av. NW9 9C 164
Southbourne Ct. NW9 9C 164
Southbrook CM21: Saw 6G 99
Southbrook Dr. EN8: C'hunt 1H 145
Southbury Av. EN1: Enf 6E 156
Southbury Ho. *EN8: Wal C* 5H 145
(off High St.)
Southbury Leisure Cen. 5E 156
Southbury Rd. EN1: Enf 5C 156
EN3: Pon E 5C 156
Southbury Station (Rail) 6F 156
Sth. Charlton Mead La. EN11: Hod 9N 115
Southcliffe Dr. SL9: Chal P 5B 158
South Cl. AL2: Chis G 7C 126
EN5: Barn 5M 153
SG7: Bald 4M 23
SG8: Roys 6B 8
South Comn. AL3: Red 1K 107
Sth. Cottage Dr. WD3: Chor 7J 147
Sth. Cottage Gdns. WD3: Chor 7J 147
South Dene HP2: Gad R 7K 85
NW7 3D 164
Southdown Ct. AL10: Hat 3G 129
Southdown Ho. AL5: Harp 7D 88
Southdown Ind. Est. AL5: Harp 8D 88
Southdown Rd. AL5: Harp 6C 88
AL10: Hat 3G 129
Sth. Drift Way LU1: Lut 2D 66
South Dr. AL4: St Alb 2L 127
EN6: Cuff 3K 143
SOUTH-END 1L 97
South End SG8: Bass 1M 7
Southend Cl. SG1: Stev 2K 51
South End La. LU6: N'all 4E 62
Southern Av. SG16: Henl 1J 21
SOUTHERN GREEN 7M 25
Southern Lodge CM19: Harl 9M 117
Southern Ri. LU2: E Hyd 8A 68
(not continuous)
Southern Ter. EN11: Hod 5M 115
Southern Way CM17: Harl 8E 118
CM18: Harl 9N 117
CM19: Harl 9K 117
LU6: Stud 3F 84
SG6: L Gar 2E 22
Southernwood Cl. HP2: Hem H 1C 124
Southerton Way WD7: Shen 6M 139
Southfield AL7: Welw G 2K 111
EN5: Barn 8K 153
SG11: B'ing 2C 56
Southfield Av. WD24: Watf 2L 149
Southfield Rd. EN3: Pon E 8F 156
EN8: Wal C 5J 145
EN11: Hod 7L 115
Southfields NW4 9H 165
SG6: L Gar 2F 22
SG11: Stand 7B 56
Southfields Rd. LU6: Duns 2G 64
Southfield Way AL4: St Alb 8L 109
SOUTHGATE 9J 155
South Gate CM20: Harl 6N 117
Southgate SG1: Stev 5K 51
(not continuous)
Southgate Cir. N14 9J 155
Southgate Cotts. WD3: R'orth 9N 147
Southgate Hockey Cen. 5G 155
Southgate Ho. *EN8: C'hunt* 3J 145
(off Turner's Hill)
Southgate Leisure Cen. 9J 155
Southgate Rd. EN6: Pot B 6B 142
SOUTH HATFIELD 2F 128
South Herts Golf Course 1N 165
South Hill HA6: North 8G 160
South Hill Cl. SG4: Hit 4A 34
South Hill Rd. HP1: Hem H 2M 123
South Ley AL7: Welw G 3L 111
South Ley Ct. AL7: Welw G 3L 111
Sth. Lodge Cres. EN2: Enf 6J 155
(not continuous)
Sth. Lodge Dr. N14 6J 155
Sth. Lodge M. SG7: Bald 4M 23
Southlynne Ho. *LU2: Lut* 9H 47
(off Crescent Ri.)
South Mead NW9 8F 164
Southmead Cres. EN8: C'hunt 3J 145
South Mill Ct. CM23: Bis S 2J 79
Southmill Rd. CM23: Bis S 2J 79
Southmill Trad. Cen. CM23: Bis S 2J 79
SOUTH MIMMS 5G 140
SOUTH MIMMS SERVICE AREA 7H 141
South Mundells AL7: Welw G 8M 91
Sth. Ordnance Rd. EN3: Enf L 2L 157
Southover N12 3N 165
SOUTH OXHEY 4L 161
South Pde. HA8: Edg 9A 164
South Pk. Av. WD3: Chor 7J 147
South Pk. Gdns. HP4: Berk 9M 103
South Pl. CM20: Harl 2C 118
EN3: Pon E 7G 157
EN9: Wal A 6N 145
SG5: Hit 2L 33
South Riding AL2: Bri W 3A 138
South Rd. CM20: Harl 3C 118
CM23: Bis S 2J 79
HA8: Edg 8B 164
LU1: Lut 2F 66
SG7: Bald 4M 23
SG11: Puck, Stand 7A 56
WD3: Chor 7F 146
Southsea Av. WD18: Watf 8A 166 (6J 149)
Southsea Rd. SG1: Stev 1H 51
South St. CM23: Bis S 1H 79
EN3: Pon E 7G 157
SG8: Lit 3H 7
SG12: Stan A 2N 115
SG14: H'ford 9B 94
South St. Commercial Cen. *CM23: Bis S* 2H 79
(off South St.)
South Vw. SG6: L Gar 6F 22
Southview Cl. EN7: C'hunt 2C 132
South Vw. Rd. HA5: Pin 6K 161
Southview Rd. AL5: Harp 4D 88
South Vw. Vs. HP4: Berk 2B 122
Southwark Cl. SG1: Stev 9A 36

220 A-Z Hertfordshire

Southwark Ho.—Stephenson Cl.

Southwark Ho. *WD6: Bore* ... *4A* **152**
(off Stratfield Rd.)
South Way AL9: Hat ... 3H **129**
AL10: Hat ... 4F **128**
EN9: Wal A ... 9N **145**
WD5: Abb L ... 6F **136**
Southway N20 ... 2N **165**
Sth. Weald Dr. EN9: Wal A ... 6N **145**
Southwell Ct. SG8: Melb ... 1N **9**
Southwold Cl. SG1: Stev ... 3G **50**
Southwold Rd. WD24: Watf ... 1L **149**
Southwood Rd. LU5: Duns ... 2H **65**
Soval Ct. HA6: North ... 7F **160**
Sovereign Bus. Cen. EN3: Brim ... 5K **157**
Sovereign Ct. CM19: Harl ... 9L **117**
HA6: North ... 8J **161**
HA7: Stanm ... 7L **163**
WD18: Watf ... 6J **149**
Sovereign M. EN4: C'ters ... 5E **154**
Sovereign Pk. AL4: St Alb ... 3L **127**
HP2: Hem H ... 9D **106**
LU4: Lut ... 8B **46**
Sowerby Av. LU2: Lut ... 6L **47**
Space2Play ... 8A **22**
Spalding Cl. HA8: Edg ... 7E **164**
Spandow Ct. *LU1: Lut* ... *2F* **66**
(off Elizabeth St.)
Sparhawke SG6: L Gar ... 2G **22**
Sparrow Cl. LU4: Lut ... 5K **45**
Sparrow Dr. SG2: Stev ... 5C **52**
Sparrow Hall Bus. Pk.
LU6: Edle ... 5H **63**
Sparrows CB11: L Upp ... 9N **17**
Sparrows Herne WD23: Bush ... 9C **150**
Sparrows Way WD23: Bush ... 9D **150**
Sparrowswick Ride AL3: St Alb ... 6D **108**
Sparrow Wlk. WD25: Watf ... 8J **137**
Spayne Cl. LU3: Lut ... 1D **46**
Spear Cl. LU3: Lut ... 3A **46**
Spectre Ct. AL10: Hat ... 8E **110**
Speedwell Cl. HP1: Hem H ... 3H **123**
LU3: Lut ... 1C **46**
Speedwell Way SG5: Stot ... 7E **10**
Speke Cl. SG2: Stev ... 4C **52**
SPELLBROOK ... 8H **79**
Spellbrooke SG5: Hit ... 2L **33**
Spellbrook La. CM21: Saw ... 9F **78**
Spellbrook La. E. CM22: Spel ... 8H **79**
Spellbrook La. W. CM23: Spel ... 9G **78**
Spencer Av. EN7: C'hunt ... 8C **132**
Spencer Cl. CM24: Stans ... 3M **59**
N3 ... 9N **165**
Spencer Courtyard *N3* ... *9M* **165**
(off Regents Pk. Rd.)
Spencer Dr. SG8: Melb ... 1N **9**
Spencer Ga. AL1: St Alb ... 9F **108**
Spencer Pl. AL4: San ... 4K **109**
Spencer Rd. HA3: Weal ... 9F **162**
LU3: Lut ... 8E **46**
Spencers Cft. CM18: Harl ... 8D **118**
SPENCERSGREEN ... 7H **101**
Spencer St. AL3: St Alb ... 2C **166** (2E **126**)
SG13: H'ford ... 8C **94**
Spencer Wlk. WD3: R'orth ... 7M **147**
Spencer Way HP1: Hem H ... 8K **105**
SG2: Stev ... 1N **71**
SG6: L Gar ... 3F **22**
Spenser Cl. SG8: Roys ... 4D **8**
Spenser Rd. AL5: Harp ... 6D **88**
Sperberry Hill SG4: St Ipo ... 8B **34**
Speyhawk Pl. EN6: Pot B ... 2B **142**
Speyside N14 ... 8H **155**
Sphere Ind. Estate, The
AL1: St Alb ... 2H **127**
Sphinx Pl. LU6: Duns ... 7C **44**
Spicer Ct. EN1: Enf ... 5C **156**
Spicersfield EN7: C'hunt ... 9E **132**
Spicers La. CM17: Harl ... 2E **118**
Spicer St. AL3: St Alb ... 3B **166** (2D **126**)
Spindleberry Cl. AL6: Wel ... 9N **71**
Spindles La. CM24: Stans ... 3M **59**
Spinney, The AL5: Harp ... 4N **87**
AL7: Welw G ... 1L **111**
CM20: Harl ... 5C **118**
CM24: Stans ... 4N **59**
EN5: N Bar ... 4A **154**
EN6: Pot B ... 4C **142**
EN7: C'hunt ... 3F **144**
EN10: Brox ... 1K **133**
HA6: North ... 6J **161**
HA7: Stanm ... 4M **163**
HP4: Berk ... 2K **121**
N21 ... 9M **155**
SG2: Stev ... 2C **52**
SG7: Bald ... 4L **23**
SG13: H'ford ... 9D **94**
WD17: Watf ... 3J **149**
WD25: A'ham ... 2E **150**
Spinney Bungalows LU7: Slapt ... 2A **62**
Spinney Cl. SG4: Hit ... 4B **34**
Spinney Ct. CM21: Saw ... 4G **98**
Spinney Cres. LU6: Duns ... 9C **44**
Spinney La. AL6: Wel ... 6K **71**
Spinney Rd. LU3: Lut ... 2N **45**
Spinney Row AL2: Lon C ... 8J **127**
Spinneys Dr. AL3: St Alb ... 4C **126**
Spinney St. SG13: H'ford ... 9E **94**
Spinning Wheel Mead
CM18: Harl ... 9C **118**
Spire Grn. Cen. CM19: Harl ... 7H **117**
Spires, The CM23: Bis S ... 1F **78**
HP2: Hem H ... 3N **123**
Spires Shop. Centre, The
EN5: Barn ... 5L **153**
SPITALBROOK ... 1L **133**
Spittlesea Rd. LU2: Lut ... 1L **67**
Spoondell LU6: Duns ... 1C **64**
Spooners Dr. AL2: Par S ... 9D **126**
Sportspace
Longdean ... 5D **124**
Tring ... 2N **101**
Spratts La. LU6: Kens ... 6H **65**
Springbank N21 ... 8L **155**
Spring Brook HP22: Ast C ... 2E **100**
Spring Cl. CM19: Harl ... 6L **117**
EN5: Barn ... 7K **153**
HP5: Lati ... 9A **134**
UB9: Hare ... 8N **159**
WD6: Bore ... 3A **152**
Spring Cotts. EN10: Turn ... 6J **133**
Spring Ct. Rd. EN2: Enf ... 2M **155**
Spring Crofts WD23: Bush ... 7B **150**
Spring Dr. SG2: Stev ... 9N **51**
Springfield SG18: Dunt ... 1E **4**
WD23: B Hea ... 1E **162**
Springfield Cl. EN6: Pot B ... 4D **142**
HA7: Stanm ... 3H **163**
N12 ... 5N **165**
WD3: Crox G ... 7D **148**
Springfield Ct. CM23: Bis S ... 9G **58**
WD3: R'orth ... 1L **159**
Springfield Cres. AL5: Harp ... 3B **88**
Springfield Ho. AL8: Welw G ... 2J **111**
Springfield Rd. AL1: St Alb ... 3H **127**
AL4: Smal ... 2B **128**
EN8: C'hunt ... 5J **145**
HP2: Hem H ... 1B **124**
HP4: Berk ... 7K **103**
LU3: Lut ... 3E **46**
LU6: Eat B ... 3A **64**
WD25: Watf ... 6K **137**
Springfields AL8: Welw G ... 2H **111**
EN5: N Bar ... *7A* **154**
(off Somerset Rd.)
EN10: Brox ... 1K **133**
Spring Gdn. La. HP4: Berk ... 9H **103**
Spring Gdns. WD25: Watf ... 8L **137**
Spring Glen AL10: Hat ... 1F **128**
Springhall Ct. *CM21: Saw* ... *5G* **98**
(off Spring M.)
Springhall La. CM21: Saw ... 6G **99**
Springhall Rd. CM21: Saw ... 5G **98**
Springhead SG7: Ashw ... 9M **5**
Spring Hills CM20: Harl ... 5K **117**
Spring Lake HA7: Stanm ... 4J **163**
Spring La. HP1: Hem H ... 9J **105**
SG8: Bass ... 1N **7**
SG9: Cot ... 5A **38**
Springle La. SG13: Hail ... 3K **115**
Spring M. CM21: Saw ... 5G **98**
Spring Pl. LU1: Lut ... 2F **66**
N3 ... 9N **165**
Spring Rd. AL5: Harp ... 3J **87**
SG6: L Gar ... 5E **22**
(not continuous)
Springs, The EN10: Turn ... 7J **133**
SG13: H'ford ... 8D **94**
Springshott SG6: L Gar ... 6E **22**
Spring Valley Bus. Cen. AL3: St Alb ... 7F **108**
Spring Vw. Rd. SG12: Ware ... 7G **95**
Spring Villa Pk. HA8: Edg ... 7A **164**
Spring Villa Rd. HA8: Edg ... 7A **164**
Spring Wlk. EN10: Brox ... 4G **133**
Spring Way HP2: Hem H ... 9D **106**
Springwell Av. WD3: R'orth ... 2K **159**
Springwell Ct. SG12: Stan A ... 2N **115**
WD3: R'orth ... 2K **159**
Springwell La. UB9: Hare ... 3K **159**
WD3: R'orth ... 3K **159**
Springwood EN7: C'hunt ... 8E **132**
Springwood Cl. UB9: Hare ... 8N **159**
Springwood Cres. HA8: Edg ... 2B **164**
Springwood Wlk. AL4: St Alb ... 8L **109**
Spruce Way AL2: Par S ... 9C **126**
Spur, The EN8: C'hunt ... 1H **145**
SG1: Stev ... 5L **51**
Spur Cl. WD5: Abb L ... 6F **136**
Spurcroft LU3: Lut ... 9E **30**
Spur Rd. HA8: Edg ... 4M **163**
Spurrs Cl. SG4: Hit ... 3B **34**
Square, The AL3: Red ... 9H **87**
CM21: Saw ... 5G **99**
CM22: Ugl ... 7N **43**
EN10: Worm ... 5K **133**
HP1: Hem H ... 2N **123**
HP4: Pot E ... *7E* **104**
(off The Front)
LU6: Duns ... 9E **44**
SG9: Chipp ... 6H **27**
SG10: M Had ... 5J **77**
SG11: B'ing ... 2C **56**
WD24: Watf ... 1K **149**
Square St. CM17: Harl ... 5E **118**
Squires Cl. CM23: Bis S ... 9E **58**
Squires Ct. EN11: Hod ... 9L **115**
Squires Ride HP2: Hem H ... 5B **106**
Squirrel Chase HP1: Hem H ... 1H **123**
Squirrels, The AL7: Welw G ... 1B **112**
SG13: H'ford ... 9F **94**
WD23: Bush ... 8E **150**
Squirrels Cl. CM23: Bis S ... 9H **59**
Stablebridge Rd. HP22: Ast C ... 2E **100**
Stable Cotts. SG11: L Had ... 7A **58**
Stable Ct. AL1: St Alb ... 9F **108**
Stable End Cotts. HP23: Wigg ... 5C **102**
Stable M. AL1: St Alb ... 1F **166**
Stable Rd. HP22: Halt ... 7C **100**
Stables, The CM20: Gil ... 9M **97**
CM21: Saw ... 3K **99**
SG13: H'ford ... 1C **114**
WD25: A'ham ... 9C **138**
Stables M. AL9: B Pk ... 1C **142**
Staburn Ct. HA8: Edg ... 9C **164**
Stacey Ct. *CM23: Bis S* ... *2H* **79**
(off Apton Rd.)
Stackfield CM20: Harl ... 3C **118**
Stacklands AL8: Welw G ... 2H **111**
Staddles CM22: L Hal ... 8K **79**
Stadium Ind. Est. LU4: Lut ... 8L **45**
Stadium Way CM19: Harl ... 5J **117**
WD18: Watf ... 7K **149**
Stafford Cl. EN8: C'hunt ... 2F **144**
N14 ... 7H **155**
Stafford Ct. EN10: Brox ... 2L **133**
Stafford Dr. EN10: Brox ... 2L **133**
Stafford Ho. *CM23: Bis S* ... *3H* **79**
(off Havers La.)
EN10: Brox ... 2L **133**
Stafford Rd. HA3: Har W ... 7D **162**
Staffords CM17: Harl ... 2G **118**
Stag Cl. HA8: Edg ... 9B **164**
Stagg Hill EN4: Had W ... 8C **142**
EN6: Pot B ... 8C **142**
Stag Grn. Av. AL9: Hat ... 7J **111**
Stag La. HA8: Edg ... 9B **164**
HP4: Berk ... 9M **103**
NW9 ... 9B **164**
WD3: Chor ... 8F **146**
Stainer Rd. WD6: Bore ... 3L **151**
Stainers CM23: Bis S ... 3E **78**
STAINES GREEN ... 2J **113**
Staines Sq. LU6: Duns ... 1F **64**
Stains Cl. EN8: C'hunt ... 1J **145**
Stainton Ct. *WD23: Bush* ... *7C* **150**
(off Farrington Av.)
Stainton Rd. EN3: Enf H ... 3G **157**
Stake Piece Rd. SG8: Roys ... 8C **8**
Stakers Ct. AL5: Harp ... 6C **88**
Stamford Av. SG8: Roys ... 6D **8**
Stamford Cl. EN6: Pot B ... 5C **142**
HA3: Har W ... 7F **162**
Stamford Ct. HA8: Edg ... 4N **163**
SG8: Roys ... 6D **8**
Stamford Rd. WD17: Watf ... 4K **149**
Stamford Yd. SG8: Roys ... 7C **8**
STANBOROUGH ... 3F **110**
Stanborough Av. WD6: Bore ... 1A **152**
Stanborough Cl. AL8: Welw G ... 1J **111**
WD6: Bore ... 2A **152**
Stanborough Grn. AL8: Welw G ... 2J **111**
Stanborough La. AL8: Welw G ... 3H **111**
Stanborough M. AL8: Welw G ... 2K **111**
Stanborough Pk. WD25: Watf ... 8L **137**
Stanborough Park Watersports Activity Cen.
... 3H **111**
Stanborough Rd. AL8: Welw G ... 3H **111**
Stanbridge Vw. MK45: Bar C ... 9E **18**
Stanbury Av. WD17: Watf ... 1G **148**
Standalone Farm ... 3D **22**
Standard Rd. EN3: Enf W ... 2J **157**
Standfield WD5: Abb L ... 4G **136**
Standhill Cl. SG4: Hit ... 4N **33**
Standhill Rd. SG4: Hit ... 4N **33**
STANDON ... 8C **56**
Standon Bus. Pk. SG11: Stand ... 8B **56**
Standon Ct. SG11: Stand ... 8C **56**
STANDON GREEN END ... 4H **75**
Standon Hill SG11: Puck, Stand ... 7N **55**
Standon Mill *SG11: Stand* ... *7C* **56**
(off Kent's La.)
Standon Rd. SG11: L Had, Alb ... 6H **57**
Standring Ri. HP3: Hem H ... 5L **123**
Stane Cl. CM23: Bis S ... 8H **59**
Stane Fld. SG6: L Gar ... 8H **23**
Stanelow Cres. SG11: Stand ... 7A **56**
Stane St. SG7: Bald ... 2N **23**
Stanfields Ct. CM20: Harl ... 5A **118**
Stanford Rd. LU2: Lut ... 7J **47**
Stangate Cres. WD6: Bore ... 7D **152**
Stangate Gdns. HA7: Stanm ... 4J **163**
Stangate Lodge N21 ... 8L **155**
Stanhope Av. HA3: Har W ... 8E **162**
N3 ... 9M **165**
Stanhope Cl. HP22: Wen ... 7A **100**
Stanhope Gdns. NW7 ... 5F **164**
Stanhope Rd. AL1: St Alb ... 2G **126**
EN5: Barn ... 8J **153**
EN8: Wal C ... 6J **145**
Stanier Ri. HP4: Berk ... 7K **103**
Stanley Av. AL2: Chis G ... 7B **126**
Stanley Cl. MK45: Pull ... 3A **18**
Stanley Dr. AL10: Hat ... 2H **129**
Stanley Gdns. HP23: Tring ... 3L **101**
WD6: Bore ... 3M **151**
Stanley Livingstone Ct. *LU1: Lut* ... *2F* **66**
(off Stanley St.)
Stanley Maude Ho. *SL9: Chal P* ... *4B* **158**
(off Micholls Av.)
Stanley Rd. EN1: Enf ... 5C **156**
HA6: North ... 8J **161**
LU3: Stre ... 5C **30**
SG2: Stev ... 1A **52**
SG13: H'ford ... 1C **114**
WD17: Watf ... 7E **166** (6L **149**)
Stanley St. LU1: Lut ... 2F **66**
Stanley Wlk. *LU1: Lut* ... *2F* **66**
(off Stanley St., not continuous)
STANMORE ... 5J **163**
Stanmore & Edgware Golf Cen. ... 3L **163**
Stanmore Chase AL4: St Alb ... 3L **127**
Stanmore Common Local Nature Reserve
... 2G **163**
Stanmore Country Park (Local Nature Reserve)
... 3K **163**
Stanmore Cres. LU3: Lut ... 5B **46**
Stanmore Golf Course ... 7J **163**
Stanmore Hill HA7: Stanm ... 3H **163**
Stanmore Lodge HA7: Stanm ... 4J **163**
Stanmore Rd. SG1: Stev ... 2K **51**
WD24: Watf ... 3K **149**
Stanmore Station (Underground) ... 4L **163**
Stanmount Rd. AL2: Chis G ... 7B **126**
Stannington Path WD6: Bore ... 3A **152**
STANSTEAD ABBOTTS ... 2N **115**
Stanstead Dr. EN11: Hod ... 6M **115**
Stanstead Innings ... 3A **116**
Stanstead Rd. EN11: Hod ... 7M **115**
SG12: Gt A, R Grn, Ware ... 9G **94**
SG13: H'ford, Hert H, R Grn ... 8E **94**
Stansted Hill SG10: M Had ... 7K **77**
STANSTED MOUNTFITCHET ... 3N **59**
Stansted Mountfitchet Station (Rail) ... 3N **59**
Stansted Mountfitchet Windmill ... 3N **59**
Stansted Rd. CM23: Birc, Bis S ... 1J **79**
Stanta Bus. Cen. AL3: St Alb ... 7G **108**
Stanton Cl. AL4: St Alb ... 7L **109**
Stanton Rd. LU4: Lut ... 8M **45**
Stantons CM20: Harl ... 5L **117**
Stants Vw. SG13: H'ford ... 8D **94**
Stanway Gdns. HA8: Edg ... 5C **164**
Staplefield Cl. HA5: Pin ... 7N **161**
STAPLEFORD ... 1M **93**
Stapleford AL7: Welw G ... 9C **92**
Stapleford Rd. LU2: Lut ... 5K **47**
Stapleton Cl. EN6: Pot B ... 4C **142**
Stapleton Rd. WD6: Bore ... 2A **152**
Staple Tye CM18: Harl ... 9N **117**
Staple Tye Shop. Cen. CM18: Harl ... 9M **117**
Stapley Rd. AL3: St Alb ... 1C **166** (1E **126**)
Stapylton Rd. EN5: Barn ... 5L **153**
Star Cl. EN3: Pon E ... 8G **156**
Star Holme Ct. SG12: Ware ... 6J **95**
Starkey Cl. EN7: C'hunt ... 7A **132**
Starlight Way AL4: St Alb ... 4K **127**
Starling Ct. CM23: Bis S ... 2H **79**
Starling La. EN6: Cuff ... 1L **143**
Starling Pl. WD25: Watf ... 5L **137**
Starlings Bri. SG5: Hit ... 2N **33**
Star St. SG12: Ware ... 6J **95**
STARTOP'S END ... 6L **81**
Startop's End Reservoir (Nature Reserve) ... 7L **81**
Startpoint LU1: Lut ... 1E **66**
Stately Ct. LU3: Lut ... 8F **46**
Statham Cl. LU3: Lut ... 9D **30**
Stathams Ct. AL3: Red ... 2J **107**
Station App. AL5: Harp ... 6C **88**
CM20: Harl ... 1E **118**
EN5: N Bar ... 6B **154**
EN8: Wal C ... 7J **145**
HA6: North ... 7G **161**
HP3: Hem H ... 5K **123**
HP7: L Chal ... 3A **146**
N12 ... 4N **165**
SG3: Kneb ... 3M **71**
SG4: Hit ... 2A **34**
WD3: Chor ... 6G **146**
WD4: Kin L ... 3D **136**
WD7: Rad ... 8H **139**
WD19: Watf ... 3M **161**
Station Cl. AL9: B Pk ... 8L **129**
EN6: Pot B ... 4M **141**
N3 ... 8N **165**
SG16: Henl ... 1J **21**
Station Ct. LU5: Duns ... 9G **44**
SG12: Ware ... *6H* **95**
(off Station Rd.)
Stationers Pl. HP3: Hem H ... 7A **124**
Station Footpath WD4: Kin L ... 3D **136**
(not continuous)
Station Forecourt *WD3: R'orth* ... *9N* **147**
(off Homestead Rd.)
Station Hill SG9: W'mill ... 7L **39**
Station M. EN6: Pot B ... 4N **141**
Station Pde. EN4: C'ters ... 6F **154**
HA3: Ken ... 9H **163**
HA8: Edg ... 7M **163**
SG6: L Gar ... *5F* **22**
(off Station Pl.)
Station Pl. SG6: L Gar ... 5F **22**
Station Rd. AL2: Bri W ... 4B **138**
AL4: Smal ... 1B **128**
AL4: Wheat ... 6L **89**
AL5: Harp ... 6C **88**
AL6: Wel ... 4L **91**
AL9: B Pk, N Mym, Welh G ... 6J **129**
CM17: Harl ... 2E **118**
CM21: Saw ... 4G **99**
CM23: Bis S ... 1H **79**
CM24: Stans ... 3N **59**
E4 ... 9N **157**
EN5: N Bar ... 7A **154**
EN6: Cuff ... 2L **143**
EN9: Wal C, Wal A ... 7L **145**
EN10: Brox ... 2K **133**
HA8: Edg ... 6A **164**
HP1: Hem H ... 4L **123**
HP4: Berk ... 9A **104**
HP23: Lon M ... 3F **80**
HP23: Tring, Aldb ... 2N **101**
LU1: Lut ... 9G **46**
LU4: Lut ... 4A **46**
LU5: Duns ... 9G **44**
LU7: Ched ... 8L **61**
LU7: I'hoe ... 2C **82**
N3 ... 8N **165**
N21 ... 9N **155**
NW7 ... 6E **164**
SG3: Kneb ... 3M **71**
SG6: L Gar ... 5F **22**
SG7: Ashw ... 9N **5**
SG7: Ashw, Ods ... 5C **6**
SG7: Bald ... 2M **23**
SG8: Melb, Meld ... 1L **9**
SG8: S Mor ... 5C **6**
SG9: Bunt ... 3J **39**
SG10: M Had ... 7H **77**
SG11: B'ing, Puck ... 5A **56**
SG11: Puck, Stand ... 6A **56**
SG12: Stan A ... 2N **115**
SG12: Ware ... 6H **95**
SG14: Let G ... 3G **112**
SG14: Watt S ... 5J **73**
SG15: Arl ... 8A **10**
SG16: L Ston ... 1F **20**
WD3: R'orth ... 9N **147**
WD4: Kin L ... 2D **136**
WD6: Bore ... 6A **152**
WD7: Rad ... 8H **139**
WD17: Watf ... 4K **149**
Station Ter. AL2: Par S ... 8E **126**
SG4: Hit ... 2A **34**
Station Way AL1: St Alb ... 3G **166** (2G **126**)
SG6: L Gar ... 5E **22**
Station Yd. AL4: Smal ... 2B **128**
SG9: Bunt ... 4J **39**
Staveley Rd. LU4: Lut ... 8M **45**
LU6: Duns ... 2E **64**
Steeplands WD23: Bush ... 9C **150**
STEEPLE MORDEN ... 3C **6**
Steeple Vw. CM23: Bis S ... 9G **59**
Sten Cl. EN3: Enf L ... 1L **157**
Stephens Cl. LU2: Lut ... 6J **47**
Stephens Ct. AL5: Harp ... 4D **88**
Stephens Gdns. LU2: Lut ... 7J **47**
Stephenson Cl. EN11: Hod ... 8A **116**
SG8: Roys ... 6B **8**

Stephenson Ct.—Swanhill

Stephenson Ct. SG12: Ware 7J 95
Stephenson M. SG2: Stev 5A 52
Stephenson Wlk. SG5: Stot 1C 22
Stephenson Way WD23: Bush 8F 166 (6M 149)
Stephenson Wharf HP3: Hem H 7B 124
Stephens Way AL3: Red 1J 107
Stephyns Chambers HP1: Hem H 3N 123
Stepnells HP23: Mars 6M 81
Stepped Gable M. CM21: H Wyc 6C 98
Stepping Stones, The *LU3: Lut* 4A 46
(off Mt. Pleasant Rd.)
Steppingstones LU6: Duns 9C 44
Sterling Av. EN8: Wal C 7H 145
HA8: Edg 4N 163
Sterling Ct. AL7: Welw G 7N 91
SG1: Stev 5K 51
Sterling Rd. EN2: Enf 3B 156
Sternberg Centre, The 9N 165
STEVENAGE 4K 51
Stevenage Arts & Leisure Cen. 4K 51
Stevenage Arts Society (Springfield House) 2J 51
Stevenage Borough Football Academy 7N 51
Stevenage Business & Industrial Pk.
SG1: Stev 8A 36
Stevenage Community Arts Cen. 6L 51
Stevenage Cres. WD6: Bore 3M 151
Stevenage Ent. Cen. SG1: Stev 2H 51
Stevenage FC 7L 51
Stevenage Golf Course 8C 52
Stevenage Leisure Pk. SG1: Stev 5J 51
Stevenage Mus. 4L 51
Stevenage Ri. HP2: Hem H 7B 106
Stevenage Rd. SG1: Stev 6C 34
SG2: Stev, Walk 1D 52
SG3: Kneb 9M 51
SG4: Hit, L Wym 5N 33
SG4: L Wym, St Ipo 7B 34
(not continuous)
Stevenage Station (Rail) 4J 51
Stevenage Swimming Cen. 4L 51
Stevens Cl. EN6: Pot B 6K 141
Stevens Grn. WD23: B Hea 1D 162
Stevenson Cl. EN5: N Bar 9C 154
Steward Cl. EN8: C'hunt 3J 145
STEWARDS 9N 117
Stewards Pool 9M 117
Stewart Clark Ct. LU6: Duns 8D 44
Stewart Cl. WD5: Abb L 5H 137
Stewart Pl. SG12: Ware 6J 95
Stewart Rd. AL5: Harp 5C 88
Stewarts, The CM23: Bis S 1G 79
Stewarts Lodge WD5: Abb L 4H 137
Stewarts Way CM23: Man 8H 43
Steynings Way N12 5N 165
Stile Cft. CM18: Harl 8C 118
Stile Plantation SG8: Roys 8E 8
Stilton Path WD6: Bore 2A 152
Stipers Cl. LU6: Duns 3H 65
STIPERS HILL 3G 65
Stirling Bus. Pk. EN8: Wal C 7K 145
Stirling Cl. SG2: Stev 1C 72
SG4: Hit 3C 34
STIRLING CORNER 8D 152
Stirling Cnr. EN5: Ark 8D 152
Stirling Ho. WD6: Bore 6C 152
Stirling Pl. LU7: Pits 4A 82
Stirling Retail Pk. WD6: Bore 8D 152
Stirling Rd. HA3: Weal 9G 162
Stirling Way AL7: Welw G 9D 92
WD5: Abb L 5J 137
WD6: Bore 8D 152
Stoat Cl. SG13: H'ford 9E 94
Stobarts Cl. SG3: Kneb 2M 71
Stock Bank SG8: Bark 3N 15
Stockbreach Cl. AL10: Hat 8G 110
Stockbreach Rd. AL10: Hat 8G 110
Stockbridge Cl. EN7: C'hunt 8C 132
Stockbridge Mdws. SG8: Melb 1L 9
Stockens Dell SG3: Kneb 4M 71
Stockens Grn. SG3: Kneb 4M 71
Stockers Farm Rd. WD3: R'orth 3N 159
Stocker's Lake (Nature Reserve) 3L 159
Stockfield Av. EN11: Hod 6L 115
Stockford Av. NW7 7K 165
Stockholm Way LU3: Lut 1A 46
Stocking Hill SG9: Cot 2N 37
Stocking La. SG5: Gt Off 6D 32
SG8: Nuth 1F 28
SG13: Bay 9M 113
STOCKING PELHAM 3A 42
Stockings La. SG13: How G, Lit B 7J 113
SG13: Lit B 9J 113
Stocking Springs Wood Nature Reserve 3C 90
Stockingstone Rd. LU2: Lut 6F 46
Stockingswater La. EN3: Brim 4K 157
Stockmen Fld. CM23: Bis S 3E 78
Stockport Rd. WD3: Hero 9F 146
Stocks Mdw. HP2: Hem H 1C 124
Stocks Rd. HP23: Aldb 6G 82
LU7: I'hoe 4E 82
Stockton Cl. EN5: N Bar 6B 154
Stockton Gdns. NW7 3E 164
Stockwell Cl. EN7: C'hunt 1E 144
HA8: Edg 9C 164
Stockwell La. EN7: C'hunt 1F 144
(not continuous)
Stockwell Lodge Medical Village
EN7: C'hunt 1E 144
Stockwood Country Pk. 4E 66
Stockwood Ct. *LU1: Lut* 2F 66
(off Stockwood Cres.)
Stockwood Cres. LU1: Lut 2F 66
Stockwood Discovery Cen. 4F 66
Stockwood Park Athletics Cen. 5E 66
Stockwood Park Golf Course 4F 66
Stokers Cl. LU5: Duns 9G 44
Stondon Rd. SG5: Shil 1D 20
Stonebank AL8: Welw G 9K 91
Stonecroft SG3: Kneb 3M 71
Stonecroft Cl. EN5: Ark 6H 153
Stone Cross CM20: Harl 5N 117
Stonecross AL1: St Alb 1F 126
Stonecross Cl. AL1: St Alb 1F 126
Stonecross La. SG9: H St 3A 40
Stonecross Rd. AL10: Hat 7H 111
STONEGROVE 4N 163
Stonegrove HA8: Edg 4M 163
Stone Gro. Ct. HA8: Edg 5N 163
Stonegrove Gdns. HA8: Edg 5M 163
Stone Hall Cotts. CM22: L Hal 2N 99
Stone Hall Rd. N21 9L 155
Stonehill Ct. E4 9M 157
Stonehills AL8: Welw G 8K 91
Stonehorse Rd. EN3: Pon E 7G 157
Stonelea Rd. HP3: Hem H 4B 124
Stoneleigh CM21: Saw 4F 98
Stoneleigh Av. EN1: Enf 2F 156
Stoneleigh Cl. EN8: Wal C 6H 145
LU3: Lut 2D 46
Stoneleigh Dr. EN11: Hod 5M 115
Stoneley SG6: L Gar 2F 22
Stonemason Cl. AL5: Harp 4C 88
Stonemead AL8: Welw G 4K 91
Stones All. WD18: Watf 8B 166 (6K 149)
Stonesdale LU4: Lut 5M 45
Stoneways Cl. LU4: Lut 3N 45
Stoney Cl. HP4: Berk 8K 103
Stoney Comn. CM24: Stans 4N 59
Stoney Comn. Rd. CM24: Stans 4M 59
Stoneycroft AL7: Welw G 8N 91
HP1: Hem H 2K 123
HP23: Aldb 1G 103
Stoneyfield Dr. CM24: Stans 3N 59
Stoney Flds. SG14: Watt S 5J 73
Stoneyfields Gdns. HA8: Edg 4D 164
Stoneyfields La. HA8: Edg 5C 164
Stoneygate Rd. LU4: Lut 7N 45
Stoney La. HP1: Hem H 5D 122
HP3: Bov 9E 122
HP5: Haw 4D 120
WD4: Chippf 3H 135
Stoney Pl. CM24: Stans 4N 59
Stonnells Cl. SG6: L Gar 3F 22
Stony Cft. SG1: Stev 3L 51
Stonycroft Cl. EN3: Enf H 4J 157
Stony Hills SG12: C End 1A 94
Stony La. HP6: L Chal 2B 146
LU2: Tea G, Wan E 8B 48
SG4: K Wal 8B 48
Stony Wood CM18: Harl 7N 117
Stookslade HP22: W'rave 5A 60
STOPSLEY 5J 47
STOPSLEY COMMON 3G 47
Stopsley Mobile Home Pk.
LU2: Lut 5H 47
Stopsley Way LU2: Lut 6J 47
(not continuous)
Storehouse La. SG4: Hit 4N 33
Storey Ct. WD23: Bush 7C 150
Storey St. HP3: Hem H 6N 123
Storksmead Rd. HA8: Edg 7E 164
Stormont Rd. SG5: Hit 1N 33
Stornoway HP3: Hem H 4D 124
Stortford Hall Ind. Pk.
CM23: Bis S 1K 79
Stortford Hall Pk. CM23: Bis S 9K 59
Stortford Hall Rd. CM23: Bis S 9K 59
Stortford Pk. Cotts. CM23: Bis S 1E 78
Stortford Rd. CM22: Hat H 3N 99
EN11: Hod 7M 115
SG11: L Had 7M 57
SG11: Stand 7C 56
Stort Lodge CM23: Bis S 9F 58
Stort Mill CM20: Harl 9D 98
Stort Rd. CM23: Bis S 2H 79
Stort Twr. CM20: Harl 4B 118
Stort Valley Ind. Est. CM23: Bis S 7J 59
STOTFOLD 6F 10
STOTFOLD GREEN 4F 10
Stotfold Rd. SG4: Hit 6C 22
SG6: L Gar 6C 22
(Icknield Way)
SG6: L Gar 4C 22
(Wilbury Rd.)
SG7: Cald 4H 11
SG15: Arl 4A 10
Stotfold Watermill 6G 11
Stow, The CM20: Harl 4B 118
Stox Mead HA3: Har W 8E 162
Strafford Cl. EN6: Pot B 5N 141
Strafford Ct. SG3: Kneb 3N 71
Strafford Ga. EN6: Pot B 5N 141
Strafford Rd. EN5: Barn 5L 153
Strandburgh Pl. HP3: Hem H 4D 124
Strangers Way LU4: Lut 5M 45
Strangeways WD17: Watf 9G 136
Stratfield Dr. EN10: Brox 1J 133
Stratfield Pk. Cl. N21 9N 155
Stratfield Rd. WD6: Bore 5N 151
Stratford Cl. HP22: Ast C 1B 100
Stratford Ct. WD17: Watf 3K 149
Stratford Rd. LU4: Lut 8D 46
WD17: Watf 4J 149
Stratford Way AL2: Bri W 2A 138
HP3: Hem H 5L 123
WD17: Watf 4H 149
Strathmore Av. LU1: Lut 3G 67
SG5: Hit 1M 33
Strathmore Ct. SG5: Hit 1N 33
Strathmore Gdns. HA8: Edg 9B 164
Strathmore Rd. SG4: Whit 2M 69
Strathmore Wlk. LU1: Lut 2H 67
Stratton Av. EN2: Enf 1B 156
Stratton Bus. Pk. SG18: Big 2A 4
Stratton Cl. HA8: Edg 6N 163
Stratton Ct. *HA5: Hat E* 7A 162
(off Devonshire Rd.)
Stratton Gdns. LU2: Lut 5F 46
Stratton Ho. *HA8: Edg* 4N 163
(off Lacey Dr.)
Stratton Pk. SG18: Big 1A 4
(not continuous)
Stratton Pl. HP23: Tring 2M 101
Strawberry Cres. AL2: Lon C 8J 127
Strawberry Fld. AL10: Hat 3G 129
LU3: Lut 2A 46
Strawberry Flds. SG12: Ware 5F 94
Strawfields AL7: Welw G 8A 92
Strawmead AL10: Hat 7H 111
Strawplaiters Cl. SG3: Dat 6N 71
Straw Plait Way SG15: Arl 8A 10
Straws Hadley Ct. HP22: W'rave 6A 60
Strayfield Rd. EN2: Enf 9M 143
Stream La. HA8: Edg 5B 164
Streamside Ct. *HP23: Tring* 9N 81
(off Morefields)
Streatfield Rd. HA3: Ken 9L 163
STREATLEY 4C 30
Streatley Rd. LU3: U Sun 6A 30
Street, The CM22: She 7K 99
CM23: Ber 3D 42
CM23: Man 7H 43
SG7: Wall 3H 25
SG8: Kel 7C 14
SG9: Fur P 5J 41
SG11: B'ing 2C 56
SG11: Hau 6D 54
WD4: Chippf 4K 135
Stretton Way WD6: Bore 2M 151
Stringers Cotts. *SL9: Chal P* 8A 158
(off The Vale)
Stringers La. SG2: A'ton 8D 52
Stripling Way WD18: Watf 8J 149
Stroma Cl. HP3: Hem H 4E 124
Stronnell Cl. LU2: Lut 6J 47
Stronsay Cl. HP3: Hem H 4E 124
Stroud Wood Bus. Cen.
AL2: Frog 9F 126
Stuart Ct. WD6: Elst 8L 151
Stuart Dr. SG4: Hit 3B 34
SG8: Roys 5D 8
Stuart Pl. LU1: Lut 1F 66
Stuart Rd. AL6: Wel 4H 91
EN4: E Bar 9D 154
HA3: Weal 9G 163
MK45: Bar C 7E 18
Stuarts Cl. HP3: Hem H 4N 123
Stuart St. LU1: Lut 1F 66
LU6: Duns 8D 44
Stuart St. Pas. LU1: Lut 1F 66
Stuart Way EN7: C'hunt 4F 144
Stubbings Hall La. EN9: Wal A 1N 145
Stubbs Cl. LU5: Hou R 4G 45
Stud Grn. WD25: Watf 5J 137
STUDHAM 3F 84
Studham La. HP4: Dag 1N 83
LU6: Whip 8D 64
Studios, The WD23: Bush 8B 150
Studio Tour Dr. WD25: Watf 7G 137
Studio Way WD6: Bore 4C 152
Studlands Ri. SG8: Roys 7E 8
Stud La. AL3: St Alb 3C 108
Studley Rd. LU3: Lut 8F 46
Sturgeon Rd. SG4: Hit 9B 22
Sturgeon's Way SG4: Hit 9B 22
Sturla Cl. SG14: H'ford 8N 93
Sturlas Way EN8: Wal C 6H 145
Sturmer Cl. AL4: St Alb 3K 127
Sturrock Way SG4: Hit 4C 34
Stylecroft Rd. HP8: Chal G 2A 158
Stylemans La. CM22: Bis S 3K 79
Styles Cl. LU2: Lut 7L 47
Such Cl. SG6: L Gar 4H 23
Sudbury Ct. AL1: St Alb 3F 126
Sudbury Rd. LU4: Lut 3L 45
Suez Rd. EN3: Brim 6J 157
Suffolk Cl. AL2: Lon C 7K 127
LU4: Lut 6K 45
WD6: Bore 7D 152
Suffolk Rd. EN3: Pon E 7F 156
EN6: Pot B 5L 141
LU5: Duns 2J 65
SG8: Roys 7E 8
Sugar La. HP1: Hem H 4E 122
Sugden Ct. LU6: Duns 9D 44
Sulgrave Cres. HP23: Tring 1A 102
Sullivan Cres. UB9: Hare 9N 159
Sullivan Way WD6: Elst 8K 151
Summer Ct. HP2: Hem H 9N 105
Summer Dale AL8: Welw G 5K 91
Summerfield AL10: Hat 3G 129
Summerfield Cl. AL2: Lon C 8K 127
Summerfield Ct. *SG5: Stot* 6E 10
(off Regent St.)
Summerfield Rd. LU1: Lut 9B 46
WD25: Watf 8J 137
Summer Gro. WD6: Elst 8L 151
Summer Hill WD6: Elst 7A 152
Summerhill Ct. *AL1: St Alb* 1G 126
(off Avenue Rd)
Summerhill Gro. EN1: Enf 8C 156
Summerhouse La. UB9: Hare 7K 159
WD25: A'ham 4D 150
Summerhouse Way WD5: Abb L 3H 137
Summerlands Rd. AL4: St Alb 7K 109
Summerleas Cl. HP2: Hem H 2A 124
Summerleys LU6: Eat B 4J 63
Summer Pl. WD18: Watf 8H 149
Summers Rd. LU2: Lut 8L 47
Summer St. LU1: S End 6E 66
Summers Way AL2: Lon C 9M 127
Summerswood La. WD6: Bore 7E 140
Summer Vw. Ct. *LU1: Lut* 9F 46
(off Mill St.)
Summer Wlk. AL3: Mark 2A 86
Summit Cen. EN6: Pot B 3L 141
Summit Cl. HA8: Edg 7A 164
Summit Rd. EN6: Pot B 3L 141
SUMNERS 9K 117
Sumpter Yd. AL1: St Alb 3C 166 (3E 126)
Sunbower Av. LU6: Duns 6B 44
Sunbury Av. NW7 5D 164
Sunbury Ct. EN5: Barn 6L 153
Sunbury Gdns. NW7 5D 164
Suncote Av. LU6: Duns 6B 44
Suncote Cl. LU6: Duns 7B 44
Sundale AL1: St Alb 1F 166
Sunderland Av. AL1: St Alb 1H 127
Sunderland Est. WD4: Kin L 2D 136
Sunderland Gro. WD25: Watf 7H 137
Sundew Rd. HP1: Hem H 3H 123
Sundon La. LU5: Hou R 4F 44
SUNDON PARK 2M 45
Sundon Pk. Pde. LU3: Lut 2M 45
Sundon Pk. Rd. LU3: Lut 1L 45
Sundon Rd. LU3: Stre 5B 30
LU4: Chalt, L Sun 1J 45
LU5: Hou R 4F 44
Sundown Av. LU5: Duns 1G 65
Sun Hill SG8: Roys 8C 8
Sun La. AL5: Harp 4B 88
Sunmead Rd. HP2: Hem H 9N 105
Sunningdale CM23: Bis S 2G 78
LU2: Lut 6H 47
Sunningdale Cl. HA7: Stanm 6H 163
Sunningdale Ct. LU2: Lut 6H 47
Sunningdale Lodge *HA8: Edg* 5N 163
(off Stonegrove)
Sunningdale M. AL7: Welw G 5L 91
Sunningfields Cres. NW4 9H 165
Sunningfields Rd. NW4 9H 165
Sunnybank LU7: Ched 9L 61
Sunnybank Rd. EN6: Pot B 6N 141
Sunnybrook Cl. HP22: Ast C 9C 80
Sunny Cft. CM18: Harl 9B 118
Sunnydale Gdns. NW7 6D 164
Sunnydell AL2: Chis G 8C 126
Sunnyfield AL9: Hat 6K 111
NW7 4F 164
Sunny Gdns. Pde. NW4 9H 165
Sunny Gdns. Rd. NW4 9H 165
Sunny Hill SG9: Bunt 3K 39
(not continuous)
Sunnyhill Rd. HP1: Hem H 2L 123
WD3: W Hyd 6G 159
Sunnymead Orchard SG7: Ashw 1F 12
Sunnymede Av. HP5: C'ham 9J 121
Sunny Road, The EN3: Enf H 3H 157
SUNNYSIDE 5A 34
Sunnyside CM24: Stans 3N 59
Sunnyside Cotts. HP5: Ash G 8L 121
Sunnyside Dr. E4 9N 157
Sunnyside Rd. SG4: Hit 5A 34
Sunridge Av. LU2: Lut 7G 47
Sunrise Cres. HP3: Hem H 2A 124
Sunrise Ind. Est. LU2: Lut 7J 47
Sunrise Vw. NW7 6F 164
Sunset Av. E4 9M 157
Sunset Dr. LU2: Lut 6H 47
Sunset Vw. EN5: Barn 4L 153
Sun Sq. *HP1: Hem H* 9N 105
(off Chapel St.)
Sun St. CM21: Saw 6H 99
EN9: Wal A 6N 145
SG5: Hit 4M 33
SG7: Bald 3L 23
Surrey Cl. N3 9L 165
Surrey Pl. HP23: Tring 3M 101
Surrey St. LU1: Lut 2G 67
Sursham Ct. AL3: Mark 2A 86
Susan Edwards Ho. *SL9: Chal P* 4B 158
(off Micholls Av.)
Sussex Cl. EN11: Hod 7L 115
LU4: Lut 5J 45
Sussex Pl. LU2: Lut 7M 47
Sussex Ring N12 5N 165
Sussex Rd. WD24: Watf 1J 149
Sussex Way EN4: C'ters 7G 154
Sutcliffe Cl. SG1: Stev 1N 51
WD23: Bush 6D 150
Sutherland Av. EN6: Cuff 1J 143
Sutherland Cl. EN5: Barn 6L 153
Sutherland Ct. AL7: Welw G 8M 91
WD18: Watf 8E 148
Sutherland Pl. LU1: Lut 3F 66
Sutherland Rd. EN3: Pon E 8H 157
N9 9F 156
Sutherland Way EN6: Cuff 1J 143
Sutton Acres CM22: L Hal 9M 79
Sutton Cl. EN10: Brox 1J 133
HP23: Tring 9N 81
Sutton Ct. SG12: Ware 7J 95
Sutton Cres. EN5: Barn 7K 153
Sutton Gdns. LU1: Cad 5A 66
LU3: Lut 3N 45
Sutton Path WD6: Bore 5A 152
Sutton Rd. AL1: St Alb 3J 127
WD17: Watf 7D 166 (5L 149)
(not continuous)
Swale Cl. SG1: Stev 7N 35
Swallow Cl. LU4: Lut 5K 45
WD3: R'orth 9M 147
WD23: Bush 1D 162
Swallow Ct. AL7: Welw G 9M 91
CM23: Bis S 2J 79
EN3: Enf W 1G 157
SG14: H'ford 9A 94
Swallowdale La. HP2: Hem H 8C 106
Swallow End AL7: Welw G 9M 91
Swallowfields AL7: Welw G 9M 91
(not continuous)
Swallow Gdns. AL10: Hat 2G 129
Swallow La. AL1: St Alb 5J 127
Swallow Pk. HP2: Hem H 7D 106
Swallows CM17: Harl 2E 118
Swallows, The AL7: Welw G 5M 91
Swallows Oak WD5: Abb L 4H 137
Swallowtail Ct. *SG1: Stev* 9B 36
(off Birdwing Wlk.)
Swallowtail Wlk. HP4: Berk 7K 103
Swan & Pike Rd. EN3: Enf L 2L 157
Swan Cl. HP5: C'ham 9F 120
LU7: I Ast 7E 62
WD3: R'orth 9N 147
Swan Ct. *CM23: Bis S* 2H 79
(off South St.)
HP1: Hem H 3M 123
LU6: Duns 9E 44
Swan Dr. NW9 9E 164
Swan Fld. Ct. AL6: Wel 3G 91
Swan Fld. Ho. WD3: R'orth 9N 147
Swanfield Rd. EN8: Wal C 6J 145
Swan Gdns. LU5: Duns 9F 44
Swangley's La. SG3: Kneb 3N 71
Swanhill AL7: Welw G 6N 91

222 A-Z Hertfordshire

Three Stiles—Turkey Street

Three Stiles SG2: B'ton .5K 53
Three Tuns Cl. SG15: Arl .8A 10
Three Valleys Way WD23: Bush .7M 149
Thresher Cl. CM23: Bis S .3E 78
LU4: Lut .5J 45
THRESHERS BUSH .7K 119
Thricknells Cl. LU3: Lut .2A 46
Thrift Farm La. WD6: Bore .4C 152
Thriftfield HP2: Hem H .9N 105
Thrifts La. SG12: Ware .8K 95
Thrimley La. CM23: Farn .3D 58
Thristers Cl. SG6: L Gar .8H 23
THROCKING .1D 38
Throcking La. SG9: Bunt, Throck .9F 26
(not continuous)
Throcking Rd. SG9: Cot .2B 38
Throstle Pl. WD25: Watf .5L 137
Thrums, The WD24: Watf .1K 149
Thrush Av. AL10: Hat .2G 128
Thrush Grn. WD3: R'orth .9M 147
Thrush La. EN6: Cuff .1K 143
Thumbswood AL7: Welw G .3N 111
Thumpers HP2: Hem H .9A 106
Thundercourt SG12: Ware .5H 95
Thunderfield Cl. EN10: Brox .1J 133
Thunderfield Grove Nature Reserve .6D 132
Thunder Hall *SG12: Ware* .*5H 95*
(off Thundercourt)
THUNDRIDGE .9H 75
Thundridge Bus. Pk. SG12: Thun .9H 75
Thundridge Cl. AL7: Welw G .1A 112
Thundridge Hill SG12: Thun .1K 95
Thurgood Rd. EN11: Hod .6L 115
Thurlow Cl. LU4: Lut .5J 45
SG1: Stev .8K 35
Thurnall Av. SG8: Roys .8D 8
Thurnall Cl. SG7: Bald .3M 23
Thyme Cl. LU2: Lut .2G 46
Thyme Ct. NW7 .8L 165
Tibbett Cl. LU6: Duns .2G 64
Tibbles Cl. WD25: Watf .8N 137
Tibbs Hill Rd. WD5: Abb L .3H 137
Tiberius Rd. LU3: Lut .3B 46
Tiberius Sq. AL3: St Alb .4B 126
Tichborne WD3: Map C .5G 159
Tickenhall Dr. CM17: Harl .7F 118
Tiger Moth Way AL10: Hat .8D 110
Tilbury Cl. HA5: Hat E .7A 162
Tilbury Mead CM18: Harl .8C 118
Tilecroft AL8: Welw G .5K 91
TILEGATE GREEN .8N 119
Tilegate Ho. *CM18: Harl* .*8B 118*
(off Tilegate Rd.)
Tilegate Rd. CM5: H Lav, M Lav .9M 119
CM18: Harl .8B 118
Tilehouse Cl. WD6: Bore .5N 151
Tilehouse La. UB9: Den .8H 159
WD3: W Hyd .8H 159
Tilehouse St. SG5: Hit .4M 33
Tile Kiln Cl. HP3: Hem H .3D 124
Tilekiln Cl. EN7: C'hunt .2D 144
Tile Kiln Cres. HP3: Hem H .3D 124
Tile Kiln La. HP3: Hem H .3C 124
Tilgate LU2: Lut .6M 47
Tillage Cl. AL4: St Alb .4L 127
Tillers Link SG2: Stev .7N 51
Tillingham Way N12 .4N 165
Tillotson Rd. HA3: Har W .7C 162
Tillwicks Rd. CM18: Harl .7B 118
Tillsworth Wlk. AL4: St Alb .6K 109
Timber Cl. SG12: Stan A .1M 115
Timbercroft AL7: Welw G .6M 91
Timberdene NW4 .9K 165
Timberidge WD3: Loud .6N 147
Timberland Fishery .7G 117
Timberlands Caravan Site
LU1: Pep .8E 66
Timber Orchard SG14: Water .5M 93
Timbers Ct. AL5: Harp .5A 88
Times Cl. SG5: Hit .9L 21
Timplings Row HP1: Hem H .9L 105
Timworth Cl. LU2: Lut .8M 47
Tingeys Cl. AL3: Red .1J 107
Tingeys Top La. EN2: Crew H .9M 143
Tinkers La. HP23: Wigg .8E 102
Tinsley Cl. LU1: Lut .3D 66
Tintagel Cl. HP2: Hem H .6N 105
LU3: Lut .5D 46
Tintagel Dr. HA7: Stanm .4L 163
Tintern Cl. AL5: Harp .3L 87
SG2: Stev .1N 71
Tintern Gdns. N14 .9K 155
Tinwell M. WD6: Bore .7D 152
Tippendell La. AL2: Chis G, Par S .7B 126
Tippett Ct. SG1: Stev .6K 51
Tippetts Cl. EN2: Enf .3A 156
Tipple Hill Rd. LU1: Aley G, Wood .6B 66
Tiptree Dr. EN2: Enf .6B 156
Tiree Cl. HP3: Hem H .4D 124
Titan Ct. AL10: Hat .9E 110
LU4: Lut .8B 46
Titan Rd. HP2: Hem H .8B 106
Titchfield Rd. EN3: Enf W .1J 157
Titchmarsh Cl. SG8: Roys .6D 8
Tithe Barn Cl. AL1: St Alb .5D 126
Tithe Barn Ct. *WD5: Abb L* .*2H 137*
(off Dairy Way)
Tithe Cl. NW7 .8G 164
SG4: Cod .7F 70
TITHE FARM .3G 44
Tithe Farm Rd. LU5: Hou R .3E 44
Tithelands CM19: Harl .9J 117
Tithe Mdw. WD18: Watf .9F 148
Tithe Wlk. NW7 .8G 164
Titian Av. WD23: B Hea .9F 150
Titmore Ct. SG4: L Wym .8E 34
TITMORE GREEN .8E 34
Titmus Cl. SG1: Stev .3L 51
Titmus Rd. HP22: Halt .7D 100
Tiverton Ct. AL5: Harp .9F 88
Tiverton Ho. EN3: Enf H .5H 157
Tiverton Rd. EN6: Pot B .4C 142
HA8: Edg .9N 163
Tiverton Way NW7 .7K 165
Toby Ct. *N9* .*9G 156*
(off Tramway Av.)
Toddbrook CM19: Harl .7L 117
Todd Cl. WD6: Bore .4C 152
Toddington Rd. LU4: Lut .3L 45
TODD'S GREEN .9G 34
Todhunter Ter. EN5: N Bar .6N 153
Toland Cl. LU4: Lut .8M 45
Tolcarne Dr. HA5: E'cote .9J 161
Tolgate Ct. LU6: Duns .1G 65
Tollgate Cl. WD3: Chor .6J 147
Tollgate Rd. AL4: Col H .5D 128
AL9: N Mym .7G 129
EN8: Wal C .8H 145
Tollpit End HP1: Hem H .8K 105
Tollsworth Way SG11: Puck .6A 56
Tolmers Av. EN6: Cuff .1K 143
Tolmers Gdns. EN6: Cuff .2K 143
Tolmers M. SG13: New S .7K 131
Tolmers Pk. SG13: New S .7K 131
Tolmers Rd. EN6: Cuff, N'haw .8J 131
Tolpits Cl. WD18: Watf .7H 149
Tolpits La. WD18: Watf .1E 160
Tolpits La. Caravan Site WD18: Watf .9G 149
Tomkins Cl. WD6: Bore .3M 151
Tomlins Cl. SG8: Barl .3C 16
Tomlinson Av. LU4: Lut .5H 45
Tompkins Cl. HP22: Ast C .2E 100
Toms Cft. HP2: Hem H .3A 124
Tomsfield AL10: Hat .1E 128
Toms Hill HP23: Aldb .2H 103
WD3: Chan C .9A 136
Toms Hill Cl. HP23: Aldb .1H 103
Toms Hill Rd. HP23: Aldb .1H 103
Toms La. WD4: Kin L .2D 136
WD5: Bed .1F 136
Tonman Ho. AL1: St Alb .3E 166 (2F 126)
TONWELL .9C 74
Tooke Cl. HA5: Pin .8N 161
Toorack Rd. HA3: Har W .9E 162
Tooveys Mill Cl. WD4: Kin L .2C 136
TopGolf
Watford .2N 149
Top Ho. Ri. E4 .9N 157
Topland Rd. SL9: Chal P .7A 158
Topstreet Way AL5: Harp .7D 88
Torbridge Cl. HA8: Edg .7M 163
Torkildsen Way CM20: Harl .4N 117
Tornay Ct. LU7: Slapt .2B 62
Torquay Cres. SG1: Stev .2H 51
Torquay Dr. LU4: Lut .5N 45
Torridge Wlk. HP2: Hem H .6B 106
Torrington Dr. EN6: Pot B .4C 142
Torrington Rd. HP4: Berk .1M 121
Tortoiseshell Way HP4: Berk .8K 103
Torwood Cl. HP4: Berk .1K 121
Torworth Rd. WD6: Bore .3N 151
Tot La. CM23: Birc, Stans .6M 59
TOTTERIDGE .1M 165
Totteridge Comn. N20 .2G 165
Totteridge Fields Local Nature Reserve .1G 165
Totteridge Grn. N20 .2N 165
Totteridge La. N20 .2N 165
Totteridge Rd. EN3: Enf W .1H 157
Totteridge Village N20 .1L 165
TOTTERNHOE .1M 63
Totternhoe Quarry Nature Reserve .1M 63
Totternhoe Rd. LU6: Duns .1B 64
LU6: Eat B .2H 63
Totton M. AL3: Red .1K 107
Totts La. SG2: Walk .9G 37
Toulmin Dr. AL3: St Alb .7D 108
Tourist Info. Cen.
Bishop's Stortford .1H 79
Borehamwood .4B 152
Dunstable .9F 44
Enfield .6B 156
Harpenden .7B 88
Hertford .9B 94
Letchworth Garden City .5F 22
Luton .1G 66
St Albans .2D 166 (2E 126)
Tring, Akeman St. .3M 101
Waltham Abbey .6N 145
Wendover .9B 100
Tovey Av. EN11: Hod .6L 115
Tovey Cl. AL2: Lon C .8L 127
Tower Cen. EN11: Hod .7L 115
Tower Cl. HP4: Berk .2L 121
SG4: L Wym .7F 34
SG13: Hert H .*4G 114*
(off London Rd.)
Tower Ct. LU2: Lut .8J 47
Tower Hgts. EN11: Hod .7L 115
TOWER HILL .3J 135
Tower Hill SG10: M Had .6J 77
WD4: Chippf .2H 135
Tower Hill La. AL4: San .1N 109
Tower Point EN2: Enf .6B 156
Tower Rd. LU2: Lut .9J 47
SG4: Cod .6E 70
SG12: Ware .5J 95
Towers, The SG1: Stev .5K 51
Towers Rd. HA5: Pin .8N 161
HP2: Hem H .1A 124
SG1: Stev .5K 51
Tower St. SG14: H'ford .7A 94
Tower Vw. SG4: Whit .2L 69
WD23: B Hea .9F 150
Tower Way LU2: Lut .9J 47
Town, The EN2: Enf .5B 156
Town Cen. AL10: Hat .8G 111
Towne Rd. SG8: Roys .8D 8
Town Farm AL4: Wheat .7L 89
LU7: Ched .9M 61
Town Farm Cl. SG8: G Mor .1A 6
Town Farm Cres. SG11: Stand .7C 56
Townfield WD3: R'orth .9M 147
Townfields AL10: Hat .8G 111
Town Hall Arc. *HP4: Berk* .*1N 121*
(off High St.)
Town La. SG2: B'ton .5J 53
Townley SG6: L Gar .7K 23
Townmead Rd. EN9: Wal A .7N 145
Town Mill M. *SG14: H'ford* .*9A 94*
(off Mill Bri.)
TOWNSEND .9E 108
Townsend HP2: Hem H .9N 105
Townsend Av. AL1: St Alb .1E 166 (1F 126)
Townsend Centre, The LU5: Hou R .6E 44
Townsend Cl. AL5: Harp .6A 88
SG8: Bark .9N 15
Townsend Dr. AL3: St Alb .8E 108
Townsend Farm Rd. LU5: Hou R .6E 44
Townsend Ind. Est. LU5: Hou R .6E 44
Townsend La. AL5: Harp .6N 87
Townsend M. SG1: Stev .3J 51
Townsend Pl. SG4: St Ipo .8A 34
Townsend Rd. AL5: Harp .5B 88
Townsend School Swimming Pool .6D 108
Townsend Ter. *LU5: Hou R* .*5D 44*
(off Houghton Rd.)
Townsend Way HA6: North .7H 161
Townshend St. SG13: H'ford .9C 94
Townside LU6: Edle .5K 63
Townsley Cl. LU1: Lut .2G 66
Town Sq. SG1: Stev .4K 51
Tracey Ct. LU1: Lut .2G 66
Tracy Ct. HA7: Stanm .7K 163
Tracyes Rd. CM18: Harl .8D 118
Trafalgar Av. EN10: Brox .3K 133
Trafalgar Trad. Est. EN3: Brim .6J 157
Trafford Cl. SG1: Stev .9L 35
WD7: Shen .5M 139
Traherne Cl. SG4: Hit .5N 33
Trajan Ga. SG2: Stev .9C 36
Tramway Av. N9 .9G 156
Tranmere Rd. N9 .9D 156
Tranters Yd. *SG7: Bald* .*2M 23*
(off Whitehorse St.)
Trap Rd. SG8: G Mor, S Mor .1B 6
Trapstyle Rd. SG12: Ware .5E 94
Travellers Cl. AL9: Welh G .5J 129
Travellers La. AL9: Welh G .4J 129
AL10: Hat .1G 129
Travertine Cl. LU5: Hou R .6D 44
Trayles SG8: Melb .1N 9
Treacle La. SG9: Rush .8L 25
Treacy Cl. WD23: B Hea .2D 162
Trebellan Dr. HP2: Hem H .1B 124
Treehanger Cl. HP23: Tring .2N 101
Treetop Cl. LU2: Lut .8H 47
Tree Tops SL9: Chal P .5B 158
Treetops AL6: Wel .9L 71
Treetops Cl. HA6: North .5F 160
Trefoil Cl. LU4: Lut .5J 45
Trefusis Wlk. WD17: Watf .3G 149
Tregelles Rd. EN11: Hod .5L 115
Tregenna Cl. N14 .7H 155
Tremaine Gro. HP2: Hem H .7A 106
Trenchard Av. HP22: Halt .8C 100
(not continuous)
Trenchard Cl. HA7: Stanm .6H 163
NW9 .8E 164
Trent Cl. SG1: Stev .1L 51
WD7: Shen .5M 139
Trent Gdns. N14 .8G 154
TRENT PARK .4G 154
Trent Park (Country Park) .3G 154
Trent Park Golf Course .6H 155
Trent Rd. LU3: Lut .6C 46
Trentwood Side EN2: Enf .5L 155
Tresco Rd. HP4: Berk .9K 103
Trescott Cl. LU2: Lut .7N 47
Tresilian Av. N21 .7L 155
Tresilian Sq. HP2: Hem H .6C 106
Trestle Theatre .3K 127
Tretawn Gdns. NW7 .4E 164
Tretawn Pk. NW7 .4E 164
Trevalga Way HP2: Hem H .7A 106
Trevellance Way WD25: Watf .6M 137
Trevelyan Pl. AL1: St Alb .4D 126
Trevelyan Way HP4: Berk .8M 103
Trevena Gdns. AL6: Wel .2H 91
Trevera Ct. EN3: Pon E .6J 157
EN8: Wal C .*6J 145*
(off Eleanor Rd.)
EN11: Hod .7L 115
Treves Cl. N21 .7L 155
Trevor Cl. EN4: E Bar .8C 154
HA3: Har W .7G 163
Trevor Gdns. HA8: Edg .8D 164
Trevor Rd. HA8: Edg .8D 164
SG4: Hit .2A 34
Trevose Way WD19: Watf .3L 161
Trewenna Dr. EN6: Pot B .5C 142
Triangle, The SG4: Hit .4N 33
Triangle Pas. EN4: E Bar .6B 154
Trident Centre, The WD24: Watf .3L 149
Trident Dr. LU5: Hou R .3G 45
Trident Ind. Est. EN11: Hod .8N 115
Trident Rd. WD25: Watf .7H 137
Triggs Way LU2: C'hoe .6N 47
Trigg Ter. SG1: Stev .3L 51
Trigg Way SG8: Melb .1N 9
Trimley Cl. LU4: Lut .4L 45
TRIMS GREEN .9E 78
Trinder Rd. EN5: Barn .7J 153
TRING .3M 101
Tring By-Pass HP23: Hast, Tring, Wigg .3J 101
TRINGFORD .7L 81
Tringford Reservoir (Nature Reserve) .8L 81
Tringford Rd. HP23: Tring, T'ford .7L 81
Tring Hill HP22: Buck .3G 100
HP23: Tring .3G 101
Tring Ho. WD18: Watf .9G 149
Tring Rd. HP4: Berk .7H 103
HP22: Halt, Wen .9B 100
HP22: W'rave .6B 60
HP23: Gub, Lon M .3G 81
HP23: Wils .6H 81
LU6: Edle, Duns .8L 63
LU7: I'hoe, I Ast .2E 82
Tring Station (Rail) .1E 102
TRING WHARF .9N 81
Trinity Av. EN1: Enf .8D 156
Trinity Cl. CM23: Bis S .2H 79
HA6: North .6G 160
Trinity Ct. AL1: St Alb .1F 166
EN2: Enf .4A 156
SG14: H'ford .7A 94
WD17: Watf .3H 149
Trinity Gro. SG14: H'ford .8A 94
Trinity Hall Cl. WD24: Watf .6E 166 (5L 149)
Trinity Ho. EN8: Wal C .5J 145
WD6: Bore .4A 152
Trinity La. EN8: Wal C .5J 145
Trinity M. HP2: Hem H .3F 124
Trinity Pl. SG1: Stev .3K 51
Trinity Rd. LU3: Lut .4C 46
SG1: Stev .3J 51
SG5: Stot .5F 10
SG12: Ware .5J 95
SG13: Hert H .3G 114
Trinity St. CM23: Bis S .2H 79
EN2: Enf .4A 156
Trinity Wlk. HP2: Hem H .3F 124
SG13: Hert H .3G 114
Trinity Way CM23: Bis S .2H 79
Tripton Rd. CM18: Harl .7A 118
Tristan Lodge WD23: Bush .6M 149
Tristram Rd. SG4: Hit .9A 22
Triton Way HP2: Hem H .9B 106
Triumph Ct. LU1: Lut .2G 66
Trojan Ct. LU4: Lut .8B 46
Trojan Ter. CM21: Saw .4G 99
Troon Gdns. LU2: Lut .3G 46
Trooper Rd. HP23: Aldb .1G 103
Trotters Bottom EN5: Barn .1G 152
Trotter's Gap SG12: Stan A .2B 116
Trotters Rd. CM18: Harl .9C 118
Trout Ri. WD3: Loud .5L 147
Troutstream Way WD3: Loud .6K 147
Trouvere Pk. HP1: Hem H .9L 105
Trowbridge Gdns. LU2: Lut .7G 47
Trowley AL3: Flam .6D 86
TROWLEY BOTTOM .7D 86
Trowley Bottom AL3: Flam .7D 86
Trowley Hgts. AL3: Flam .5D 86
Trowley Hill Rd. AL3: Flam .7D 86
Trowley Ri. WD5: Abb L .4G 137
True Lovers Ct. HA6: North .7F 160
Trueman Cl. HA8: Edg .7B 164
Truemans Rd. SG5: Hit .9L 21
truGym
Luton .1G 67
Stevenage .6K 51
Trumper Rd. SG1: Stev .9L 35
Trumpington Dr. AL1: St Alb .5E 126
Truncalls *LU1: Lut* .*3F 66*
(off Sutherland Pl.)
Trundlers Way WD23: B Hea .1F 162
Truro Ct. SG1: Stev .8M 35
Truro Gdns. LU3: Lut .4D 46
Truro Ho. HA5: Hat E .7A 162
Trust Ind. Est. SG4: Hit .8A 22
Trust Rd. EN8: Wal C .7J 145
Tubbs Cft. AL7: Welw G .1A 112
Tucker's Row CM23: Bis S .2H 79
Tucker St. WD18: Watf .7L 149
Tudor Av. EN7: C'hunt .4E 144
WD24: Watf .2M 149
Tudor Cl. AL10: Hat .3F 128
EN7: C'hunt .4F 144
MK45: Bar C .7E 18
NW7 .6G 165
SG1: Stev .9J 35
SG12: Huns .7G 96
Tudor Ct. AL2: Lon C .8L 127
CM21: Saw .4G 98
LU6: Duns .7D 44
SG5: Hit .4L 33
SG8: Knee .1B 8
WD3: R'orth .1K 159
WD6: Bore .4M 151
Tudor Cres. EN2: Enf .3A 156
Tudor Dr. LU5: Hou R .5H 45
WD24: Watf .2M 149
Tudor Ent. Pk. HA3: Weal .9E 162
Tudor Gdns. HA3: Har W .9E 162
Tudor Hgts. SG14: H'ford .7N 93
Tudor Ho. *HA5: Pin* .*9L 161*
(off Pinner Hill Rd.)
Tudor Mnr. Gdns. WD25: Watf .5M 137
Tudor Orchard HP4: Berk .8J 103
Tudor Pde. WD3: R'orth .9K 147
Tudor Ri. EN10: Brox .3J 133
Tudor Rd. AL3: St Alb .7F 108
AL4: Wheat .7M 89
AL6: Wel .4H 91
EN5: N Bar .5N 153
HA3: Har W, Weal .9E 162
HA5: Pin .9L 161
LU3: Lut .7D 46
N9 .9F 156
Tudor Sq. *SG12: Ware* .*6H 95*
(off West St.)
Tudor Vs. EN7: Gof O .2C 144
(not continuous)
Tudor Wlk. *SG12: Ware* .*6H 95*
(off Church St.)
WD24: Watf .1M 149
Tudor Way EN9: Wal A .6N 145
N14 .9J 155
SG14: H'ford .9M 93
WD3: R'orth .1K 159
Tudor Well Cl. HA7: Stanm .5J 163
Tuffnell Ct. *EN8: C'hunt* .*1H 145*
(off Coopers Wlk.)
Tuffnells Way AL5: Harp .3M 87
Tulip Cl. LU3: Lut .2M 45
Tumbler Rd. CM18: Harl .7C 118
Tunbridge Ct. AL1: St Alb .1G 166
Tunfield Rd. EN11: Hod .5M 115
Tunnel Way LU7: Pits .5A 82
Tunnel Wood Cl. WD17: Watf .1H 149
Tunnel Wood Rd. WD17: Watf .1H 149
Tunnmeade CM20: Harl .5C 118
Turf La. SG4: G'ley .6H 35
Turin Ho. WD18: Watf .6G 149
Turin Rd. N9 .9G 156
TURKEY STREET .1F 156

224 A-Z Hertfordshire

Watford Indoor Bowls Club—West Sq.

Watford Indoor Bowls Club 6L 137
Watford Interchange WD24: Watf 3L 149
Watford Junction Station (Rail & Overground) 4L 149
Watford Leisure Cen.
Central 6A 166 (5J 149)
Woodside 6L 137
Watford Metro Cen. WD18: Watf 9E 148
Watford Mus. 9E 166 (6L 149)
Watford North Station (Rail) 1L 149
Watford Palace Theatre 7C 166 (5K 149)
Watford Rd. AL1: St Alb 9B 126
AL2: Chis G 9B 126
HA6: North 7H 161
WD3: Crox G 8C 148
WD4: Hun C, Kin L 3C 136
WD6: Elst 8J 151
WD7: Rad 9F 138
Watford Station (Underground) 5H 149
Watford Way NW4 9G 165
NW7 4E 164
Watkin M. EN3: Enf L 1L 157
Watkins Cl. HA6: North 8H 161
Watkins Ri. EN6: Pot B 5A 142
WATLING 7D 164
Watling Av. HA8: Edg 8C 164
Watling Cl. HP2: Hem H 7A 106
Watling Ct. LU5: Hou R 5E 44
LU6: Duns 7D 44
WD6: Elst 8L 151
Watling Farm Cl. HA7: Stanm 1K 163
Watling Gdns. LU6: Duns 2G 64
Watling Ho. *AL3: St Alb* *4C 126*
(off King Harry La.)
Watling Knoll WD7: Rad 6G 139
Watling Mans. WD7: Rad 8J 139
Watling Pl. LU5: Hou R 5E 44
Watling St. AL1: St Alb 4D 126
AL2: Par S 7E 126
AL3: Flam, Mark 1N 85
LU6: Duns, Sew 3A 44
LU6: Kens 4K 65
WD6: Elst 2J 151
WD7: Rad 4G 138
Watling St. Caravan Pk.
AL2: Par S 7D 126
Watlington Rd. CM17: Harl 2F 118
Watling Vw. AL1: St Alb 5D 126
Watson Av. AL3: St Alb 8G 108
Watson Ct. WD18: Watf 7K 149
Watson Rd. SG1: Stev 3J 51
Watson's Wlk. AL1: St Alb 4E 166 (3F 126)
Watsons Yd. *CM23: Bis S* *9H 59*
(off Hadham Rd.)
Watson Way CM24: Stans 4N 59
WATTON AT STONE 5J 73
Watton-at-Stone Station (Rail) 5J 73
Watton Hall *AL10: Hat* *9D 110*
(off Mosquito Way)
Watton Rd. SG2: Stev 3N 71
SG3: Dat 7D 72
SG3: Kneb 3N 71
SG12: Ware 5G 94
SG14: Watt S 7D 72
Watts Cl. SG11: L Had 7M 57
Watts Yd. CM23: Man 8J 43
Wauluds Bank 3A 46
Wauluds Bank Dr. LU3: Lut 1N 45
Wavell Cl. EN8: C'hunt 9J 133
Wavell Ho. AL1: St Alb 4J 127
Waveney HP2: Hem H 6B 106
Waveney Rd. AL5: Harp 4D 88
Waverley Cl. SG2: Stev 9N 51
Waverley Ct. EN2: Enf 5N 155
Waverley Gdns. HA6: North 8J 161
Waverley Gro. N3 9K 165
Waverley Ind. Est. HA1: Harr 9E 162
Waverley Lodge *AL3: St Alb* *9E 108*
(off Falmouth Ct.)
Waverley Rd. AL3: St Alb 9D 108
EN2: Enf 5N 155
Waxhouse Ga. AL3: St Alb 3C 166 (2E 126)
Waxwell Cl. HA5: Pin 9M 161
Waxwell Farm Ho. HA5: Pin 9M 161
Waxwell La. HA5: Pin 9M 161
Wayfarers Pk. HP4: Berk 1K 121
Wayletts Dr. CM23: Bis S 1K 79
Waynes Ct. LU1: Lut 1G 67
Wayre, The CM17: Harl 2E 118
Wayre St. CM17: Harl 2E 118
Waysbrook SG6: L Gar 7H 23
Wayside EN6: Pot B 6C 142
LU6: Duns 3G 64
WD4: Chippf 3L 135
WD7: Shen 6L 139
Wayside, The HP3: Hem H 3E 124
Wayside Av. WD23: Bush 8E 150
Wayside Cl. N14 8H 155
Wayside Ct. AL2: Bri W 3A 138
Waysmeet SG6: L Gar 7H 23
Waytemore Castle 1J 79
Waytemore Rd. CM23: Bis S 2G 78
Weald La. HA3: Har W 9E 162
Weald Ri. HA3: Har W 7G 162
WEALDSTONE 9D 162
Wealdwood Gdns. HA5: Hat E 6C 162
Weall Grn. WD25: Watf 5K 137
Weardale Gdns. EN2: Enf 3B 156
Weatherby LU6: Duns 9B 44
Weatherby Rd. LU4: Lut 7N 45
Weavers Orchard SG15: Arl 8A 10
Weavers Rd. HP23: Tring 2K 101
Weaver St. CM23: Bis S 4E 78
Weavers Way SG7: Bald 3N 23
Webb Cl. SG6: L Gar 6J 23
Webber Cl. WD6: Elst 8L 151
Webb Ri. SG1: Stev 2M 51
Webley Ct. *EN3: Enf L* *1L 157*
(off Sten Cl.)
Webster Ct. WD3: R'orth 1A 160
Wedgewood Cl. HA6: North 7E 160
Wedgewood Dr. CM17: Harl 7G 118
Wedgewood Ga. SG1: Stev 8A 36
Wedgewood Ga. Ind. Est. SG1: Stev 8A 36
Wedgewood Rd. LU4: Lut 5J 45
SG4: Hit 3B 34
Wedgwood Ct. SG1: Stev 8B 36
Wedgwood Pk. SG1: Stev 8B 36
Wedgwood Way SG1: Stev 9A 36
Wedhey CM19: Harl 6M 117
Wedmore Rd. SG4: Hit 4A 34
Wedon Way SG7: Byg 8B 12
Weighton Rd. HA3: Har W 8E 162
Welbeck Cl. WD6: Bore 5A 152
Welbeck Ri. AL5: Harp 9E 88
Welbeck Rd. EN4: E Bar 8D 154
LU2: Lut 9G 47
Welbury Av. LU3: Lut 2E 46
Welch Pl. HA5: Pin 8L 161
Welclose St. AL3: St Alb 3B 166 (2D 126)
Welcote Dr. HA6: North 6F 160
Weldon Cl. LU2: Lut 8N 47
Weldon Ct. N21 7L 155
Welham Cl. AL9: Welh G 6J 129
WD6: Bore 3A 152
Welham Ct. *AL9: Welh G* *6J 129*
(off Dixons Hill Rd.)
WELHAM GREEN 6J 129
Welham Green Station (Rail) 5K 129
Welham Mnr. AL9: Welh G 6J 129
Welkin Grn. HP2: Hem H 1E 124
Wellands AL10: Hat 7G 111
Well App. EN5: Barn 7J 153
Wellbrook M. HP23: Tring 2N 101
Wellbury Ter. HP2: Hem H 2E 124
Wellcroft HP1: Hem H 1L 123
LU7: I'hoe 2D 82
Wellcroft Cl. AL7: Welw G 2N 111
Wellcroft Rd. AL7: Welw G 1N 111
WELL END 2D 152
Well End Rd. WD6: Bore 1C 152
Wellen Ri. HP3: Hem H 5A 124
Weller M. EN2: Enf 3M 155
Wellers Gro. EN7: C'hunt 1E 144
Wellesley Av. HA6: North 5H 161
Wellesley Cres. EN6: Pot B 6L 141
Wellesley Pk. M. EN2: Enf 4N 155
Wellfield Av. LU3: Lut 1M 45
Wellfield Cl. AL10: Hat 8G 111
Wellfield Ct. SG1: Stev 9A 36
Wellfield Rd. AL10: Hat 7G 110
Well Gth. AL7: Welw G 1L 111
Wellgate Rd. LU4: Lut 7N 45
Well Grn. SG14: Bram 3H 93
Well Gro. N20 9B 154
WELL HEAD 3A 64
Wellhead Rd. LU6: Tot 1N 63
Wellhouse Cl. LU1: Lut 1C 66
Wellhouse La. EN5: Barn 6J 153
Wellingham Av. SG5: Hit 1L 33
Wellington Av. HA5: Hat E 8A 162
Wellington Cl. WD19: Watf 3A 162
Wellington Cotts. SG11: Col E 1L 75
Wellington Ct. *LU1: Lut* *2F 66*
(off Wellington St.)
Wellington Dr. AL7: Welw G 9B 92
Wellington Ho. *WD24: Watf* *4L 149*
(off Exeter Cl.)
Wellington Mnr. *LU1: Lut* *1F 66*
(off Wellington St.)
Wellington Pl. EN10: Worm 5G 133
Wellington Rd. AL1: St Alb 3J 127
AL2: Lon C 8L 127
EN1: Enf 7C 156
HA3: Weal 9F 162
HA5: Hat E 8A 162
SG2: Stev 4B 52
WD17: Watf 4K 149
Wellington St. LU1: Lut 2F 66
SG14: H'ford 8N 93
Wellington Ter. LU5: Duns 9F 44
Well La. CM19: Harl 5K 117
LU7: Led, Wing 1G 60
WELLPOND GREEN 8G 56
Well Rd. EN5: Barn 7J 153
EN6: N'haw 1D 142
Well Row SG13: Bay 8L 113
Wells, The N14 9J 155
Wells Cl. AL3: St Alb 1A 166 (1D 126)
AL5: Harp 3N 87
EN7: C'hunt 7A 132
Wells Ct. WD17: Watf 9E 166 (7L 149)
Wellsfield WD23: Bush 7M 149
Wellside Cl. EN5: Barn 6J 153
Wellspring Way WD17: Watf 9E 166 (7L 149)
Wellstead Av. N9 9H 157
Wellstones WD17: Watf 7C 166 (6K 149)
Wellswood Cl. HP2: Hem H 1D 124
Wells Yd. *SG12: Ware* *6H 95*
(off High St.)
WD17: Watf 7C 166 (5K 149)
Welsummer Way EN8: C'hunt 1H 145
Weltech Cen. AL7: Welw G 9N 91
Weltmore Rd. LU3: Lut 3B 46
WELWYN 2J 91
Welwyn By-Pass Rd. AL6: Wel 4J 91
Welwyn Ct. HP2: Hem H 7B 106
WELWYN GARDEN CITY 8K 91
Welwyn Garden City Golf Course 9H 91
Welwyn Garden City Station (Rail) 9K 91
Welwyn Hall *AL10: Hat* *8E 110*
(off Mosquito Way)
Welwyn Hall Gdns. AL6: Wel 2J 91
WELWYN HEATH 8L 71
Welwyn North Station (Rail) 4M 91
Welwyn Rd. SG14: H'ford 8K 93
Welwyn Roman Baths 2J 91
Wemborough Rd. HA7: Stanm 8J 163
WENDOVER 9A 100
Wendover Cl. AL4: St Alb 6K 109
AL5: Harp 6E 88
Wendover Ct. AL6: Wel 2J 91
Wendover Dr. AL6: Wel 2J 91
Wendover Hgts. HP22: Halt 8C 100
Wendover Ho. *WD18: Watf* *9G 149*
(off Chenies Way)
Wendover Lodge *AL6: Wel* *2J 91*
(off Church St.)
Wendover Way LU2: Lut 6H 47
WD23: Bush 8D 150
Wendover Woods 9E 100
Wendy Cl. EN1: Enf 8D 156
Wengeo La. SG12: Ware 5F 94
(not continuous)
Wenham Ct. SG2: Walk 1G 52
Wenham Pl. AL10: Hat 8G 111
Wenlock Rd. HA8: Edg 7B 164
Wenlock St. LU2: Lut 9G 46
Wensley Cl. AL5: Harp 9E 88
Wensleydale HP2: Hem H 8B 106
LU2: Lut 8G 46
Wensum Ct. WD3: R'orth 1N 159
Wensum Rd. SG1: Stev 7M 35
Wensum Way WD3: R'orth 1N 159
Wenta Bus. Centre, The
WD24: Watf 1M 149
Wentbridge Path WD6: Bore 2A 152
Wentworth Av. LU4: Lut 3M 45
N3 7N 165
WD6: Elst 7N 151
Wentworth Cl. EN6: Pot B 4N 141
N3 7N 165
WD17: Watf 2H 149
Wentworth Cotts. EN10: Brox 4J 133
SG11: Hau 7D 54
Wentworth Ct. CM23: Bis S 2F 78
WD19: Pin, Watf 5M 161
Wentworth Pk. N3 7N 165
Wentworth Pl. HA7: Stanm 6J 163
Wentworth Rd. EN5: Barn 5K 153
SG13: H'ford 3A 114
Wenwell Cl. HP22: Ast C 2F 100
Wesley Av. SG13: H'ford 1B 114
Wesley Cl. EN7: Gof O 1A 144
SG15: Arl 8A 10
Wesley Ho. AL1: St Alb 3D 166
Wesley Pl. *AL3: Mark* *2A 86*
(off Albert St.)
Wesley Rd. AL3: Mark 2A 86
Wessex Ct. EN5: Barn 6K 153
Wessex Dr. HA5: Hat E 7N 161
Wessex Ho. WD23: Bush 6A 150
Westall Cl. SG13: H'ford 1A 114
West All. SG5: Hit 3M 33
Westall M. SG13: H'ford 1A 114
West Av. AL2: Chis G 7C 126
N3 6N 165
SG7: Bald 3L 23
West Bank EN2: Enf 4A 156
Westbere Dr. HA7: Stanm 5L 163
Westbourne M. AL1: St Alb 3D 166 (2E 126)
Westbourne Mobile Home Pk.
LU3: Lut 4B 46
Westbourne Rd. LU4: Lut 8D 46
Westbrook CM19: Harl 9J 117
Westbrook Cl. EN4: C'ters 5C 154
SG8: S Mor 5C 6
Westbrook Ct. SG4: Hit 5N 33
Westbrook Cres. EN4: C'ters 5C 154
Westbrook Sq. EN4: C'ters 5C 154
West Burrowfield AL7: Welw G 2K 111
Westbury EN8: C'hunt 3H 145
Westbury Cl. LU5: Hou R 6E 44
SG5: Hit 2L 33
Westbury Farm Cl. SG5: Gt Off 7D 32
Westbury Gdns. LU2: Lut 6F 46
Westbury Gro. N12 6N 165
Westbury Pl. SG6: L Gar 6E 22
Westbury Ri. CM17: Harl 7F 118
Westbury Rd. HA6: North 4G 160
N12 6N 165
WD18: Watf 7K 149
Westbush Cl. EN11: Hod 5K 115
West Chantry HA3: Har W 8C 162
Westchester Dr. NW4 9K 165
West Cl. EN4: C'ters 6F 154
EN5: Barn 7H 153
EN11: Hod 6L 115
SG1: Stev 4M 51
SG4: Hit 1B 34
Westcombe Dr. EN5: Barn 7N 153
West Comn. AL3: Red 2J 107
AL5: Harp 7C 88
(not continuous)
West Comn. Cl. AL5: Harp 1C 108
West Comn. Gro. AL5: Harp 9C 88
West Comn. Way AL5: Harp 1B 108
Westcott AL7: Welw G 8C 92
West Ct. CM21: Saw 4G 98
SG8: Roys 7C 8
Westcroft HP23: Tring 3M 101
Westcroft Cl. EN3: Enf W 2G 157
Westcroft Ct. EN10: Brox 1L 133
Westdean La. HP5: C'dge 9A 120
West Dene HP2: Gad R 7K 85
Westdown Gdns. LU6: Duns 1C 64
West Dr. HA3: Har W 6E 162
SG15: Arl 8A 10
WD25: Watf 9K 137
West Dr. Gdns. HA3: Har W 6E 162
Westell Cl. SG7: Bald 3N 23
WEST END 9B 112
West End SG7: Ashw 1B 12
West End La. AL9: Ess, Hat 9B 112
EN5: Barn 6K 153
HA5: Pin 9M 161
West End Rd. EN10: Brox 4C 132
LU7: Ched 9L 61
Westerdale HP2: Hem H 8A 106
LU4: Lut 5L 45
Western Av. SG16: Henl 1J 21
Western Cl. SG6: L Gar 2E 22
Western Ct. N3 6N 165
Western Mans. *EN5: N Bar* *7A 154*
(off Great Nth. Rd.)
Western Pde. EN5: N Bar 7N 153
Western Rd. HP23: Tring 3L 101
LU1: Lut 2F 66
Western Ter. EN11: Hod 5M 115
Western Way EN5: Barn 8N 153
LU5: Duns 8H 45
SG6: L Gar 3E 22
Westfield AL7: Welw G 8N 91
AL9: Hat 5M 129
CM18: Harl 7A 118
Westfield Av. AL5: Harp 4B 88
WD24: Watf 1L 149
Westfield Cl. CM23: Bis S 9G 58
EN3: Enf H 5J 157
EN8: Wal C 4K 145
SG5: Hit 3L 33
Westfield Community Sports Cen. 7H 149
Westfield Ct. AL4: St Alb 8L 109
Westfield Dr. AL5: Harp 3C 88
Westfield La. SG5: Hit 3L 33
Westfield Pk. HA5: Hat E 7A 162
Westfield Pl. AL5: Harp 3C 88
Westfield Rd. AL5: Harp 4B 88
CM23: Bis S 9G 58
EN11: Hod 7K 115
HP4: Berk 8J 103
LU6: Duns 9C 44
LU7: Pits 4A 82
NW7 3D 164
SG14: H'ford 7A 94
Westfields AL3: St Alb 4B 126
Westfield Wlk. EN8: Wal C 4K 145
West Finchley Station (Underground) 6N 165
West Gate CM20: Harl 6M 117
(not continuous)
Westgate Ct. EN8: Wal C 8H 145
LU6: Duns 9D 44
West Gate M. WD18: Watf 7G 149
Westgate Shop. Cen. SG1: Stev 4K 51
W. Hertfordshire Crematorium
WD25: Watf 4M 137
W. Herts Bus. Cen. *WD6: Bore* *5B 152*
(off Eldon Av.)
West Herts Golf Course 5F 148
West Hill EN11: Hod 6K 115
LU6: Duns 3E 64
SG5: Hit 3L 33
West Hill Rd. EN11: Hod 7K 115
LU1: Lut 3G 66
West Hill Way N20 1N 165
Westholm SG6: L Gar 3F 22
WEST HYDE
LU1 9L 67
WD3 7H 159
W. Hyde La. SL9: Chal P 7C 158
Westland Cl. WD25: Watf 7H 137
Westland Dr. AL9: B Pk 9L 129
WESTLAND GREEN 9H 57
Westland Rd. SG3: Kneb 3M 71
WD17: Watf 5C 166 (4K 149)
West La. SG5: Gt Off 8D 32
SG5: Pirt 6E 20
West Lawn WD25: A'ham 9C 138
Westlea LU4: Lut 5M 45
Westlea Av. WD25: Watf 9N 137
Westlea Cl. EN10: Worm 5K 133
Westlea Rd. EN10: Worm 5K 133
Westlecote Gdns. LU2: Lut 5F 46
Westleigh Gdns. HA8: Edg 8A 164
WEST LEITH 5K 101
West Leith HP23: Tring 4K 101
Westlinton Cl. NW7 6L 165
Westly Wood AL7: Welw G 8N 91
West Mead AL7: Welw G 3A 112
Westmeade Cl. EN7: C'hunt 2F 144
Westmere Dr. NW7 3D 164
WESTMILL
SG5 1L 33
SG9 7K 39
Westmill La. SG5: Hit, Ick 9K 21
West Mill Lawns SG5: Hit 1L 33
Westmill Rd. SG5: Hit 9K 21
SG12: Ware, W'mill 3E 94
Westminster Ct. AL1: St Alb 4D 126
AL5: Harp 8D 88
EN8: Wal C 6L 145
Westminster Gdns. LU5: Hou R 3F 44
Westminster Ho. HA3: Har W 7G 162
WD24: Watf *4L 149*
(off Hallam Cl.)
Westminster Lodge Leisure Cen. 3D 126
Westmoor Gdns. EN3: Enf H 4H 157
Westmoor Rd. EN3: Enf H 4H 157
Westmorland Av. LU3: Lut 4B 46
Westmount Apartments *WD18: Watf* *6H 149*
(off Metropolitan Sta. App.)
WESTON 1A 36
Weston Av. SG8: Roys 6C 8
Weston Cl. EN6: Pot B 5M 141
Weston Ct. HP22: Ast C 1B 100
N20 *9B 154*
(off Farnham Cl.)
Weston Dr. HA7: Stanm 8J 163
Westonia Ct. EN3: Enf W 9H 145
Weston Rd. EN2: Enf 4B 156
HP22: Ast C, West T 3A 100
SG1: Stev 1L 51
(not continuous)
Weston Way SG7: Bald 3L 23
West Pde. LU6: Duns 9D 44
West Pas. *HP23: Tring* *3M 101*
(off Albert St.)
West Pl. CM20: Harl 3C 118
Westpole Av. EN4: C'ters 6F 154
Westray HP3: Hem H 4E 124
West Reach SG2: Stev 7M 51
Westridge Cl. HP1: Hem H 2J 123
West Riding AL2: Bri W 3A 138
AL6: Tew 2C 92
West Rd. CM20: Harl 2C 118
CM21: Saw 4D 98
CM23: Bis S 2G 79
CM24: Stans 4N 59
EN4: E Bar 9F 154
HP4: Berk 9L 103
Westron Gdns. HP23: Tring 2N 101
West Side EN10: Turn 7J 133
HP3: Hem H 7B 124
Westside NW4 9H 165
West Side Bus. Cen. CM19: Harl 7H 117
West Sq. CM20: Harl 5M 117

A-Z Hertfordshire 227

Willow Wlk.—Woodside Park

Willow Wlk. AL6: Wel 8J 71
N21 8L 155
Willow Way AL2: Chis G 9B 126
AL5: Harp 3D 88
AL10: Hat 3F 128
EN6: Pot B 6A 142
HP1: Hem H 9L 105
LU3: Lut 4A 46
LU5: Hou R 3G 44
(off Kent Rd.)
WD7: Rad 9F 138
Wills Gro. NW7 5G 165
Wilmington Cl. WD18: Watf 7B 166 (5K 149)
Wilsden Av. LU1: Lut 2E 66
Wilshaw Cl. NW4 9G 165
Wilshere Av. AL1: St Alb 4D 126
Wilshere Ct. *SG4: Hit 4N 33*
(off Queen St.)
Wilshere Cres. SG4: Hit 2C 34
Wilshere Rd. AL6: Wel 2G 91
Wilsmere Dr. HA3: Har W 7F 162
Wilson Cl. CM23: Bis S 3J 79
SG1: Stev 9K 35
Wilson Ct. NW9 9D 164
Wilsons La. SG7: Ashw 9L 5
Wilson St. N21 9M 155
WILSTONE 6J 81
WILSTONE BRIDGE 6J 81
Wilstone Dr. AL4: St Alb 6K 109
WILSTONE GREEN 7J 81
Wilstone Reservoir (Nature Reserve) 8H 81
Wilton Cl. CM23: Bis S 1K 79
Wilton Ct. WD17: Watf 6D 166 (5L 149)
Wilton Cres. SG13: H'ford 3A 114
Wilton Rd. EN4: C'ters 6E 154
SG5: Hit 1M 33
Wilton Way SG13: H'ford 3A 114
Wiltron Ho. SG1: Stev 3H 51
Wiltshire Cl. NW7 5F 164
Wiltshire Rd. SG2: Stev 5N 51
Wimborne Cl. CM21: Saw 5F 98
Wimborne Gro. WD17: Watf 1G 149
Wimborne Rd. LU1: Lut 9D 46
Wimple Rd. LU4: Lut 7K 45
Winch Cl. SG4: Cod 8F 70
Winchdells HP3: Hem H 5C 124
Winchester Cl. CM23: Bis S 4F 78
EN1: Enf 7C 156
EN9: Wal A 6M 145
SG1: Stev 8N 35
Winchester Ct. AL1: St Alb 2F 166
Winchester Gdns. LU3: Lut 9A 30
Winchester Ho. AL3: St Alb 4A 166 (3D 126)
Winchester Rd. HA6: North 9H 161
N9 9D 156
Winchester Way WD3: Crox G 7D 148
Winchfield LU1: Cad 4A 66
Winchfield Way WD3: R'orth 9M 147
WINCH HILL 1C 68
WINCHMORE HILL 9M 155
Winchmore Hill Rd. N14 9J 155
N21 9J 155
Winchmore Hill Station (Rail) 9N 155
Winchmore Vs. *N21 9L 155*
(off Winchmore Hill Rd.)
Winch St. LU2: Lut 8H 47
Windermere Av. AL1: St Alb 4J 127
(not continuous)
N3 9N 165
Windermere Cl. HP3: Hem H 3E 124
LU6: Duns 1E 64
SG1: Stev 8C 36
WD3: Chor 7G 146
Windermere Ct. WD17: Watf 4J 149
Windermere Cres. LU3: Lut 4B 46
Windermere Hall HA8: Edg 5N 163
Windermere Ho. EN5: N Bar 6A 154
Windhill AL7: Welw G 8N 91
CM23: Bis S 2G 78
(The Firs)
CM23: Bis S 1G 79
(Windhill Old Rd.)
Windhill Flds. CM23: Bis S 1G 78
Windhill Gdns. CM23: Bis S 2G 79
Windhill Old Rd. CM23: Bis S 1G 79
Winding Hill SG10: M Had 4K 77
Winding Shot HP1: Hem H 1K 123
Winding Shott SG14: Bram 3H 93
Windmill Av. AL4: St Alb 7K 109
Windmill Cl. CM24: Stans 3M 59
LU7: I'hoe 2D 82
SG8: Bark 7N 15
SG8: Bass 1N 7
Windmill Cotts. SG12: Thun 1H 95
Windmill Dr. WD3: Crox G 8B 148
Windmill Fld. SG12: Ware 7H 95
Windmill Flds. CM17: Harl 2H 119
Windmill Gdns. EN2: Enf 5M 155
Windmill Hill CM23: Man 6G 43
EN2: Enf 5N 155
SG4: Hit 3N 33
SG9: Bunt 4K 39
WD4: Chippf 5J 135
(not continuous)
Windmill La. EN5: Ark 8F 152
EN8: C'hunt 3J 145
SG5: C'ton 5J 33
WD23: B Hea 1F 162
Windmill Rd. AL3: Mark 1B 86
HP2: Hem H 2A 124
LU1: Lut 1H 67
LU1: Pep 1B 86
SG4: Bre G 6E 48
SL9: Chal P 7A 158
Windmills SG12: Dan E 9C 54
Windmill St. WD23: B Hea 1F 162
Windmill Trad. Est. LU1: Lut 1J 67
Windmill Vw. SG8: S Mor 5B 6
Windmill Way HP23: Tring 2L 101
SG10: M Had 7H 77
Windmore Av. EN6: Pot B 4J 141
Windridge Cl. AL3: St Alb 4B 126
Windrush Cl. SG1: Stev 7N 35
Winds End Cl. HP2: Hem H 9C 106
Windsor Av. HA8: Edg 4B 164
Windsor Cl. AL6: Wel 4H 91
EN7: C'hunt 3E 144
HA6: North 9J 161
HP2: Hem H 4A 124
HP3: Bov 1D 134
N3 9L 165
SG2: Stev 1A 72
WD6: Bore 3A 152
Windsor Ct. AL1: St Alb 3H 127
LU1: Lut 2F 66
N14 9H 155
WD4: Kin L 2C 136
WD6: Bore 4C 152
WD23: Bush 9D 150
(off Catsey La.)
Windsor Dr. EN4: E Bar 8E 154
LU5: Hou R 4G 44
SG14: H'ford 9L 93
Windsor Gdns. CM23: Bis S 1E 78
Windsor Ho. WD23: Bush 6A 150
Windsor Ind. Est. SG13: H'ford 8F 94
Windsor Pde. MK45: Bar C 7E 18
Windsor Pl. CM20: Harl 2C 118
LU5: Hou R 4G 44
Windsor Rd. AL6: Wel 4H 91
EN3: Enf W 9H 145
EN5: Barn 8K 153
HA3: Har W 8D 162
LU7: Pits 4B 82
(Castle Cl.)
LU7: Pits 4A 82
(Long Hale)
MK45: Bar C 7E 18
N3 9L 165
SG8: Roys 7F 8
WD24: Watf 2L 149
Windsor St. LU1: Lut 2F 66
Windsor Wlk. LU1: Lut 2F 66
Windsor Way WD3: R'orth 1K 159
Windward Cl. EN3: Enf W 8H 145
Windy Ri. SG12: Dan E 1D 74
Winfield Mobile Home Pk.
WD25: A'ham 3C 150
Winfield St. LU6: Duns 8E 44
Winford Dr. EN10: Brox, Worm 4K 133
Wingate Bus. Cen. AL9: Welh G 5J 129
Wingate Ct. LU4: Lut 7B 46
Wingate Gdns. AL6: Wel 2H 91
Wingate Ho. LU4: Lut 7B 46
Wingate Rd. LU4: Lut 7B 46
LU5: Duns 8H 45
Wingate Way AL1: St Alb 3H 127
Wingbury Courtyard Bus. Village
HP22: W'rave 3C 60
WINGFIELD 1A 44
Wingfield Ct. WD18: Watf 8E 148
WINGRAVE 5A 60
Wingrave Rd. HP23: Gub, T'ford, Wils 4J 81
HP23: Tring 1N 101
Wingrove E4 9L 157
Winifred Cl. EN5: Ark 8F 152
Winifred Rd. HP3: Hem H 6N 123
Winifred Ter. EN1: Enf 9D 156
Winkers Cl. SL9: Chal P 8C 158
Winkers La. SL9: Chal P 8C 158
Winkfield Cl. LU4: Lut 8L 45
WINKWELL 4G 122
Winkwell HP1: Hem H 4G 122
Winnington Rd. EN3: Enf W 2G 156
Winnipeg Way EN10: Turn 7J 133
Winscombe Way HA7: Stanm 5H 163
Winsdon Ct. *LU1: Lut 2F 66*
(off Winsdon Rd.)
WINSDON HILL 1E 66
Winsdon Path *LU1: Lut 2F 66*
(off Russell St.)
Winsdon Rd. LU1: Lut 2F 66
Winslow Cl. LU3: Lut 5E 46
Winslow Rd. HP22: W'rave 5A 60
Winsmoor Ct. EN2: Enf 5N 155
Winston Churchill Way
EN8: Wal C 6G 145
Winston Cl. HA3: Har W 6G 162
SG5: Hit 3L 33
Winston Ct. HA3: Har W 7C 162
Winston Gdns. HP4: Berk 1K 121
Winston Way EN6: Pot B 6N 141
Winstre Rd. WD6: Bore 3A 152
Winterscroft Rd. EN11: Hod 7K 115
Winters La. SG2: Walk 9H 37
Winterstoke Gdns. NW7 5G 164
Winthorpe Gdns. WD6: Bore 3N 151
Winton App. WD3: Crox G 7E 148
Winton Cl. LU2: Lut 3F 46
N9 9H 157
SG6: L Gar 3K 23
Winton Cres. WD3: Crox G 7D 148
Winton Dr. EN8: C'hunt 2J 145
WD3: Crox G 8D 148
Winton Gdns. HA8: Edg 7N 163
Winton Rd. SG12: Ware 6K 95
Winton Ter. AL1: St Alb 5F 166
Wisden Ct. SG1: Stev 9M 35
Wisden Rd. SG1: Stev 9M 35
Wisdom Dr. SG13: H'ford 9C 94
Wise Ct. *WD18: Watf 6G 148*
(off Raven Cl.)
Wise La. NW7 5G 164
Wiseman Cl. LU2: Lut 2G 46
Wisemans Gdns. CM21: Saw 6E 98
Wise's La. AL9: N Mym 9J 129
Wissen Dr. SG6: L Gar 5H 23
Wistaria Dr. AL2: Lon C 8J 127
Wisteria Cl. NW7 6F 164
Wistlea Cres. AL4: Col H 4B 128
Wistow Rd. LU3: Lut 3C 46
Witchford AL7: Welw G 9C 92
Withers Mead NW9 8F 164
Withey Beds Local Nature Reserve, The 2D 160
Withy Cl. LU4: Lut 4L 45
Withy Pl. AL2: Par S 1D 138
Witley Grn. *LU2: Lut 7M 47*
(off Rushall Grn.)
Witney Cl. HA5: Hat E 6A 162
Witneys, The CM22: L Hal 8K 79
Witter Av. SG5: Ick 7M 21
Wivelsfield LU6: Eat B 2J 63
Wiveton Cl. LU2: Lut 2F 46
Woburn Av. CM23: Bis S 1E 78
Woburn Cl. SG2: Stev 1B 72
WD23: Bush 8D 150
Woburn Ct. *LU4: Lut 4N 45*
(off Vincent Rd.)
Wodecroft Rd. LU3: Lut 3D 46
Wodson Park Leisure Cen. 3H 95
Wolfsburg Ct. LU4: Lut 4M 45
Wolmer Cl. HA8: Edg 4A 164
Wolmer Gdns. HA8: Edg 3A 164
Wolseley Rd. HA3: Weal 9F 162
Wolsey Av. EN7: C'hunt 2D 144
Wolsey Bus. Pk.
WD18: Watf 9F 148
Wolsey Gro. HA8: Edg 7D 164
Wolsey Rd. EN1: Enf 4F 156
HA6: North 2E 160
HP2: Hem H 3N 123
Wolstenholme HA7: Stanm 5J 163
Wolstonbury N12 5N 165
Wolston Cl. LU1: Lut 1E 66
Wolverley Ho. SG7: Ashw 9M 5
Wolverton Rd. HA7: Stanm 6J 163
Wolverton Way N14 7H 155
Wolvescroft SG3: Dat 6N 71
Wolvesmere SG3: Dat 6N 71
Wonnacott Pl. EN3: Enf W 9H 145
Wood, The WD19: Watf 2N 161
Woodacre Dr. AL6: Wel 8N 71
Woodall Av. EN3: Pon E 8H 157
Woodall Rd. EN3: Pon E 8H 157
Woodbank WD3: R'orth 8M 147
Woodbank Dr. HP8: Chal G 3A 158
Woodberry Cl. NW7 7K 165
Woodberry Way E4 9N 157
Woodbine Cl. CM19: Harl 8M 117
Woodbine Gro. EN2: Enf 2B 156
Woodbridge Cl. LU4: Lut 5A 46
Woodbury Hill LU2: Lut 7G 47
Woodbury Hill Path LU2: Lut 7G 46
Wood Cl. AL10: Hat 9H 111
LU6: Kens 7H 65
WOODCOCK HILL 5A 160
Woodcock Hill AL4: San, St Alb 5L 109
HP4: Berk 9J 103
WD3: R'orth 5A 160
WD6: Elst 8B 152
Woodcock Hill Est. WD3: R'orth 4A 160
Woodcock Rd. LU1: Lut 1C 66
SG2: Stev 7C 52
SG8: Roys 5E 8
Wood Comn. AL10: Hat 6H 111
Woodcote Av. NW7 6J 165
Woodcote Cl. EN3: Pon E 8G 157
EN8: C'hunt 3G 145
Woodcote Ho. *SG4: Hit 3N 33*
(off Queen St.)
Woodcote Lawns HP5: C'ham 9E 120
Wood Cres. HP3: Hem H 3N 123
Woodcroft CM18: Harl 8M 117
SG5: Hit 4M 33
(off Wratten Rd. E.)
Woodcroft Av. HA7: Stanm 8H 163
NW7 6E 164
SG12: Stan A 2A 116
Woodcutter Pl. AL2: Par S 9D 126
Wood Dr. SG2: Stev 7A 52
WOOD END 2B 54
Wood End AL2: Par S 1D 138
Wood End Cl. HP2: Hem H 1E 124
Woodend Gdns. EN2: Enf 6K 155
Wood End Hill AL5: Harp 4M 87
Wood End La.
AL3: Flam, Mark 8N 85
Wood End Rd. AL5: Harp 4M 87
Woodfall Av. EN5: Barn 7M 153
Woodfarm Rd. HP2: Hem H 2A 124
Woodfield Av. HA6: North 4G 161
Woodfield Cl. CM24: Stans 3N 59
EN1: Enf 6C 156
Woodfield Dr. EN4: E Bar 9F 154
HP3: Hem H 4F 124
Woodfield Gdns. HP3: Hem H 4F 124
Woodfield Ga. LU5: Duns 2H 65
Woodfield La. AL9: Hat 5C 130
SG13: New S 5C 130
Woodfield Ri. WD23: Bush 9E 150
Woodfield Rd. AL7: Welw G 9M 91
SG1: Stev 9J 35
WD7: Rad 9H 139
Woodfields CM24: Stans 3N 59
WD18: Watf 9D 166
Woodfield Ter. CM24: Stans 3N 59
UB9: Hare 9L 159
Woodfield Way AL4: St Alb 8K 109
Woodford Cres. HA5: Pin 9K 161
Woodforde Cl. SG7: Ashw 9N 5
Woodford Rd. LU5: Duns 8H 45
WD17: Watf 5D 166 (4L 149)
Woodgate WD25: Watf 6K 137
Woodgate Av. EN6: N'haw 6G 142
Woodgate Cres. HA6: North 6J 161
Woodgate M. WD17: Watf 3J 149
Woodgrange Av. EN1: Enf 8E 156
Woodgrange Ct. EN11: Hod 9L 115
Woodgrange Gdns. EN1: Enf 8E 156
Woodgrange Ter. EN1: Enf 8E 156
Wood Grn. Cl. LU2: Lut 4K 47
SG2: Stev 1A 72
Wood Grn. Rd. LU2: Lut 4K 47
Wood Grn. Way EN8: C'hunt 4J 145
WOODHALL 2L 111
Woodhall Av. HA5: Pin 8N 161
Woodhall Cl. SG14: H'ford 7A 94
Woodhall Ct. AL7: Welw G 1L 111
Woodhall Dr. HA5: Pin 8M 161
Woodhall Ga. HA5: Pin 7M 161
Woodhall Gro. CM23: Bis S 2F 78
Woodhall Ho. AL7: Welw G 2M 111
Woodhall La. AL7: Welw G 1L 111
HP2: Hem H 1A 124
WD7: Shen 8M 139
WD19: Watf 3M 161
Woodhall Rd. HA5: Pin 7M 161
Woodham Way SG12: Stan A 2N 115
WOODHILL 5C 130
Woodhill CM18: Harl 9A 118
Woodhouse Eaves HA6: North 5J 161
Woodhouse La. EN10: Brox 3D 132
Woodhurst SG6: L Gar 3F 22
Woodhurst Av. WD25: Watf 7M 137
Wooding Gro. CM19: Harl 6L 117
Woodland Av. HP1: Hem H 3L 123
LU3: Lut 7D 46
Woodland Cen. (YMCA) 4J 137
Woodland Chase WD3: Crox G 9D 148
Woodland Cl. HP1: Hem H 3L 123
HP23: Tring 4L 101
Woodland Ct. AL3: St Alb 7G 108
Woodland Dr. AL4: St Alb 1K 127
WD17: Watf 3H 149
(not continuous)
Woodland La. WD3: Chor 5G 147
Woodland Mt. SG13: H'ford 9D 94
Woodland Pl. HP1: Hem H 3L 123
WD3: Chor 6J 147
Woodland Ri. AL8: Welw G 7J 91
LU6: Stud 9E 64
Woodland Rd. E4 9N 157
SG13: Hert H 3G 114
WD3: Map C 5G 159
Woodlands AL2: Par S 9D 126
AL5: Harp 4N 87
AL9: B Pk 8A 130
CM23: Bis S 9L 59
LU1: Cad 5A 66
SG8: Roys 7E 8
WD7: Rad 7H 139
Woodlands, The HA7: Stanm 5J 163
Woodlands Av. HP4: Berk 2A 122
LU5: Hou R 5F 44
Woodlands Cl. EN11: Hod 9L 115
WD6: Bore 6B 152
Woodlands Dr. EN11: Hod 1L 133
HA7: Stanm 6G 162
WD4: Kin L 1E 136
Woodlands Mead SG4: W'ton 2A 36
Woodlands Pk. Homes AL6: Wel 8K 71
Woodlands Rd. EN2: Enf 2B 156
HP3: Hem H 9C 124
N9 9G 156
SG12: Thun 1H 95
SG13: H'ford 9D 94
WD23: Bush 7N 149
Woodland Way AL6: Wel 9M 71
EN7: Gof O 1N 143
NW7 6F 164
SG2: Stev 8M 51
SG7: Bald 5M 23
WD5: Bed 9H 125
Wood La. CM23: Birc 7N 59
HA7: Stanm 3H 163
HP2: Hem H 3N 123
HP22: Halt 8C 100
SG5: Pirt 9B 20
SG9: Mee 5K 29
SG12: Ware 5L 95
Wood La. End HP2: Hem H 1C 124
Woodlea AL2: Chis G 7B 126
Woodlea Gro. HA6: North 6F 160
Woodley Rd. SG12: Ware 5K 95
Woodleys CM20: Harl 5C 118
Woodman Rd. HP3: Hem H 4A 124
Woodmans Ho. WD17: Watf 9E 166 (6L 149)
Woodmer Cl. SG5: Shil 1N 19
Woodmere LU3: Lut 9C 30
Woodmere Av. WD24: Watf 2M 149
Woodmere Ct. N14 9G 155
WOODMER END 1N 19
Woodmill M. EN11: Hod 6M 115
Woodpecker Cl. AL10: Hat 3F 128
CM23: Bis S 2E 78
HA3: Har W 8G 163
N9 8F 156
WD23: Bush 1D 162
Woodredon Cl. CM19: Royd 7E 116
Wood Ride EN4: Had W 3C 154
Woodridge Cl. EN2: Enf 3M 155
Woodridge Way HA6: North 6G 160
Woodridings Av. HA5: Hat E 8A 162
Woodridings Cl. HA5: Hat E 7N 161
Woods, The HA6: North 5J 161
WD7: Rad 7J 139
Woods Av. AL10: Hat 9G 111
Woods Cl. LU6: Kens 7H 65
Woodshots Mdw. WD18: Watf 7F 148
WOODSIDE
AL9 3N 129
LU1 5D 66
WD25 5K 137
Woodside CM23: Birc 9M 59
EN7: C'hunt 4E 144
LU6: Eat B 2J 63
SG13: Hert H 4G 114
WD6: Elst 6M 151
WD24: Watf 9J 137
Woodside Animal Farm & Leisure Park 8B 66
Woodside Cl. HA7: Stanm 5J 163
SL9: Chal P 9B 158
Woodside Ct. WD25: Watf 6L 137
Woodside Gdns. SG4: Hit 3N 33
WOODSIDE GREEN
AL9 3A 130
CM22 7N 79
Woodside Hill SL9: Chal P 9B 158
Woodside Ho. AL8: Welw G 8K 91
Woodside Ind. Est. LU5: Duns 6G 45
Woodside Ind. Pk. SG6: L Gar 4H 23
Woodside La. AL9: Hat 3M 129
Woodside Leisure Pk. WD25: Watf 6K 137
Woodside Open Air Theatre 3N 33
WOODSIDE PARK 4N 165
Woodside Park 9M 59

A-Z Hertfordshire 229

HOSPITALS, HOSPICES and selected HEALTHCARE FACILITIES covered by this atlas.

N.B. Where it is not possible to name these facilities on the map,
the reference given is for the road in which they are situated.

BARNET HOSPITAL 6K **153**
    Wellhouse Lane
    BARNET
    EN5 3DJ
    Tel: 0845 111 4000

BISHOPS WOOD BMI HOSPITAL 6D **160**
    Rickmansworth Road
    NORTHWOOD
    HA6 2JW
    Tel: 01923 835814

BUSHEY SPIRE HOSPITAL 9G **150**
    Heathbourne Road
    Bushey Heath
    BUSHEY
    WD23 1RD
    Tel: 0845 603 9090

CAVELL BMI HOSPITAL 4M **155**
    Cavell Drive
    ENFIELD
    EN2 7PR
    Tel: 020 8366 2122

CHALFONTS & GERRARDS CROSS HOSPITAL 8A **158**
    Hampden Road,
    Chalfont St Peter
    GERRARDS CROSS
    SL9 9DR
    Tel: 01753 883821

CHASE FARM HOSPITAL 2M **155**
    127 The Ridgeway
    ENFIELD
    EN2 8JL
    Tel: 0845 111 4000

CHESHUNT COMMUNITY HOSPITAL 4J **145**
    King Arthur Court
    Cheshunt
    WALTHAM CROSS
    EN8 8XN
    Tel: 01992 622157

CHESHUNT MINOR INJURIES UNIT 4J **145**
    Within Cheshunt Community Hospital
    King Arthur Court
    WALTHAM CROSS
    EN8 8XN

DANESBURY NEUROLOGICAL CENTRE 3H **91**
    School Lane
    WELWYN
    AL6 9SB
    Tel: 01438 841841

EDGWARE COMMUNITY HOSPITAL 7B **164**
    Burnt Oak Broadway
    EDGWARE
    HA8 0AD
    Tel: 020 8952 2381

ERNEST GARDINER DAY HOSPITAL 6H **23**
    Pearsall Close
    LETCHWORTH GARDEN CITY
    SG6 1QZ
    Tel: 01462 670955

GARDEN HOUSE HOSPICE 6H **23**
    Gillison Close
    LETCHWORTH GARDEN CITY
    SG6 1QU
    Tel: 01462 679540

GROVE HOUSE (HOSPICE) 9D **108**
    Waverley Road
    ST. ALBANS
    AL3 5QX
    Tel: 01727 731000

HAREFIELD HOSPITAL 8M **159**
    Hill End Road
    Harefield
    UXBRIDGE
    UB9 6JH
    Tel: 01895 823737

HARPENDEN MEMORIAL HOSPITAL 5C **88**
    Carlton Road
    HARPENDEN
    AL5 4TA
    Tel: 01582 760196

HARPENDEN SPIRE HOSPITAL 3B **88**
    Ambrose Lane
    HARPENDEN
    AL5 4BP
    Tel: 01582 763191

HEMEL HEMPSTEAD GENERAL HOSPITAL 3N **123**
    Hillfield Road
    HEMEL HEMPSTEAD
    HP2 4AD
    Tel: 01442 213141

HEMEL HEMPSTEAD PRIORY GRANGE 7J **123**
    Longcroft Lane
    Felden
    HEMEL HEMPSTEAD
    HP3 0BN
    Tel: 01442 255371

HERTFORD COUNTY HOSPITAL 9N **93**
    North Road
    HERTFORD
    SG14 1LP
    Tel: 01707 328111

HERTS & ESSEX HOSPITAL 2K **79**
    Cavell Drive
    BISHOP'S STORTFORD
    CM23 5JH
    Tel: 01279 655191

HOSPICE OF ST FRANCIS 8H **103**
    Spring Garden Lane
    off Shootersway
    BERKHAMSTED
    HP4 3GW
    Tel: 01442 869550

ISABEL HOSPICE (DAY CARE) 2A **112**
    Hall Grove
    WELWYN GARDEN CITY
    AL7 4PH
    Tel: 01707 382550

ISABEL HOSPICE (IN-PATIENT CARE) 4N **111**
    Howlands
    WELWYN GARDEN CITY
    AL7 4HQ
    Tel: 01707 382560

KEECH HOSPICE CARE 8C **30**
    Great Bramingham Lane
    LUTON
    LU3 3NT
    Tel: 01582 492339

KINGSLEY GREEN 4K **139**
    Harper Lane
    Shenley
    RADLETT
    WD7 9HQ
    Tel: 01923 854861

KING'S OAK BMI HOSPITAL 2M **155**
    The Ridgeway
    ENFIELD
    EN2 8SD
    Tel: 020 8370 9500

LISTER HOSPITAL 8H **35**
    Coreys Mill Lane
    STEVENAGE
    SG1 4AB
    Tel: 01438 314333

LUTON & DUNSTABLE HOSPITAL 7M **45**
    Lewsey Road
    LUTON
    LU4 0DZ
    Tel: 0845 1270127

MICHAEL SOBELL HOUSE (HOSPICE) 6D **160**
Mount Vernon Hospital
Rickmansworth Road
NORTHWOOD
HA6 2RN
Tel: 01923 844531

MOUNT VERNON HOSPITAL 6D **160**
Rickmansworth Road
NORTHWOOD
HA6 2RN
Tel: 01923 826111

NATIONAL SOCIETY FOR EPILEPSY 4C **158**
Chesham Lane
Chalfont St Peter
GERRARDS CROSS
SL9 0RJ
Tel: 01494 601300

NHS URGENT CARE CENTRE 5M **117**
Princess Alexandra Hospital
Hamstel Row
HARLOW
CM20 1QX
Tel: 01279 694775

NHS WALK-IN CENTRE (EDGWARE) 7B **164**
Edgware Community Hospital
Burnt Oak Broadway
EDGWARE
HA8 0AD
Tel: 020 8732 6459

NHS WALK-IN CENTRE (LUTON) 1G **66**
14-16 Chapel Street
LUTON
LU1 2SE
Tel: 01582 709290

NORTH LONDON PRIORY HOSPITAL 9K **155**
The Bourne
ENFIELD
N14 6RA
Tel: 020 8882 8191

PEACE HOSPICE 6A **166** (5J **149**)
Peace Drive
WATFORD
WD17 3PH
Tel: 01923 330330

PINEHILL PRIVATE HOSPITAL 3A **34**
Benslow Lane
HITCHIN
SG4 9QZ
Tel: 01462 422822

POTTERS BAR COMMUNITY HOSPITAL 7B **142**
Barnet Road
POTTERS BAR
EN6 2RY
Tel: 01707 653286

PRINCESS ALEXANDRA HOSPITAL 5L **117**
Hamstel Road
HARLOW
CM20 1QX
Tel: 01279 444455

PROSPECT HOUSE 6A **166** (5J **149**)
Peace Drive
WATFORD
WD17 3XE
Tel: 01923 693900

QUEEN ELIZABETH II HOSPITAL 4N **111**
Howlands
WELWYN GARDEN CITY
AL7 4HQ
Tel: 01707 3289111

QUEEN VICTORIA MEMORIAL HOSPITAL 3G **91**
73 School Lane
WELWYN
AL6 9PW
Tel: 01438 841815

RIVERS PRIVATE HOSPITAL 6E **98**
High Wych Road
SAWBRIDGEWORTH
CM21 0HH
Tel: 01279 600282

ROYAL NATIONAL ORTHOPAEDIC HOSPITAL 2J **163**
Brockley Hill
STANMORE
HA7 4LP
Tel: 020 8954 2300

ROYSTON HOSPITAL 9D **8**
London Road
ROYSTON
SG8 9EN
Tel: 01763 242134

ST ALBANS CITY HOSPITAL 9D **108**
Waverley Road
ST. ALBANS
AL3 5PN
Tel: 01727 866122

STEVENAGE CYGNET HOSPITAL 8H **35**
Graveley Road
STEVENAGE
SG1 4YS
Tel: 01438 342942

URGENT CARE CENTRE (HEMEL HEMPSTEAD) 2N **123**
Hemel Hempstead Hospital
Hillfield Road
HEMEL HEMPSTEAD
HP2 4AD
Tel: 01442 213141

WATFORD GENERAL HOSPITAL 7K **149**
Vicarage Road
WATFORD
WD18 0HB
Tel: 01923 244366

MIX
Paper from
responsible sources
FSC
www.fsc.org
FSC® C005461

SAFETY CAMERA INFORMATION

PocketGPSWorld.com's CamerAlert is a self-contained speed and red light camera warning system for SatNavs and Android or Apple iOS smartphones/tablets. Visit www.cameralert.co.uk to download.

Safety camera locations are publicised by the Safer Roads Partnership which operates them in order to encourage drivers to comply with speed limits at these sites. It is the driver's absolute responsibility to be aware of and to adhere to speed limits at all times.

By showing this safety camera information it is the intention of Geographers' A-Z Map Company Ltd., to encourage safe driving and greater awareness of speed limits and vehicle speed. Data accurate at time of printing.

Printed and bound in the United Kingdom by Polestar Wheatons Ltd., Exeter.